Ecuador

An Economic and Social

Editors
Vicente Fretes-Cibils
Marcelo M. Giugale
José Roberto López-Cálix

Agenda in the New Millennium

THE WORLD BANK

WASHINGTON, DC

Cover design: Carol Levie
Photograph: Ronald Jones
Art: *Dueños de la Noche* (1987) by Gonzalo Endara Crow

ISBN 0-8213-5545-7

Library of Congress Cataloging-in-Publication Data has been applied for.

Contents

Part I
Preserving Stability with Fiscal Discipline and Accelerating Growth with Competitiveness

Part II
Boosting Sustainable and Equitable Social Development

Part III
Building a Quality Government That Serves All Ecuadorans and Fights against Corruption

Preface

Ecuador is at a crossroads as it enters the new millennium. Political, economic, and social instability have long affected this country's path of development. Though it is rich in cultural traditions and natural endowments, the stop-go cycles of past public policies have prevented the country from fully utilizing its potential for economic prosperity and social equity. The newly inaugurated administration has the opportunity to break with the past by defining a development agenda that is based on a shared vision. In this agenda, stability, growth, competitiveness, social development, decentralization, and anticorruption efforts would constitute the mileposts along a road benefiting all Ecuadorans. We at the World Bank feel honored by the authorities' invitation to publish this compendium of policy notes for Ecuador that we have prepared and which, from an independent point of view, provides an account of Ecuador's current development challenges, many of the reasons behind those challenges, and some options to overcome them. The analysis here does not claim to provide definitive solutions to all of Ecuador's challenges. Rather, we hope that this volume can enrich the national debate among Ecuadorans as they search for their own solutions to these challenges.

The work presented here is organized around three overarching themes: Fiscal Consolidation and Growth, Social Development, and Quality of Government. The main messages within each of these themes are captured in their respective Thematic Chapters, and summarized and brought together in an opening Synthesis. The importance of these three broad themes has become increasingly evident all around the world during the last decade, and has been accentuated by globalization (financial and commercial) and by the information technology revolution. Understanding those forces is critically important because, in the end, their value will be measured by one simple yardstick—their impact on people's quality of life, especially among the poor.

Any government operating under these conditions would confront the need for difficult reforms. For Ecuador, the twin—banking and currency—crises that led to dollarization make reform even harder. Current regional and international conditions do not facilitate matters, and are unlikely to do so in the near future. The financial crisis in the Southern Cone restricts access to external funding, and sagging global growth is dampening Ecuador's exports. The country is also beginning to feel the impact of the illegal drug trade. Finally, the reforms necessary to consolidate dollarization are still only half completed. Yet, inaction brings higher costs than action.

Without strengthened reform, the Ecuadoran economy risks spiraling into a cycle of recession and increasing poverty.

The new government has expressed its determination to address, head on, the challenge of reforms. In the few months since taking office, the administration has rallied early support for some major changes in policy direction in the fiscal, structural, and social areas. We at the World Bank stand ready to support those efforts. We view this as central to our institution's mission of poverty reduction and to our commitment to see Ecuador succeed.

This book is the product of the analytical work of a large number of World Bank staff members. It documents Ecuador's main development trends, policies, and options, and places the country in the context of relevant international comparisons. Extensive dialogue, reflection, and direct operational work with our counterparts in the Ecuadoran government and elsewhere are detailed in this volume, which spells out critical lessons and challenges that are relevant for Ecuador and for Latin America as a whole. Finally, the book proposes policy matrices for each sector and topic, including a proposed sequencing of policy steps.

I am extremely grateful for the cooperation and contributions of our many friends in Ecuador to this very important endeavor, both directly and through several years of working side by side with us. I would like to thank the staff members who have compiled this book—editors, authors, and producers. Their work reveals not only their professional talents, but also, and more importantly, their passion for poverty reduction.

Finally, I wish to express our gratitude to the Ecuadoran authorities for giving us the privilege of being partners in their country's quest for development.

David De Ferranti
Vice President
Latin America and the
Caribbean Regional Office
Washington, D.C.
March 7, 2003

Editor Biographies

VICENTE FRETES-CIBILS, a native of Argentina, completed his undergraduate work at the *Universidad Nacional del Nordeste*, in Argentina, and subsequently pursued postgraduate studies at the University of Pennsylvania and North Carolina State University, where he received, respectively, a master's degree in Business Administration and a Ph.D. in Economics. Following his university studies, he joined the World Bank in 1987 through the latter's Young Professionals Program. Following stints in the Bank's Office of the Vice-President for Europe and the Middle East and its Treasury Department, he served from 1988 to 1992 as Economist in the Office of the Vice-President for West Africa Operations. Subsequently, from 1992 to 1996, he served as Chief Economist in the Department of Operations for Andean Countries, supervising adjustment programs and heading up economic and analytical missions to Bolivia. From 1996 to 2002, Mr. Fretes-Cibils served as Senior Economist for Venezuela, and subsequently for Colombia and Mexico. He is currently Lead Economist in the Poverty Reduction and Economic Management Sector for the subregion of countries that includes Bolivia, Ecuador, Peru, and Venezuela. Additionally, he has taught at Argentina's *Universidad Nacional del Nordeste* and at North Carolina State University, and has published numerous works addressing topics in the areas of finance, applied econometrics, public finance, international economics, and economic development.

MARCELO M. GIUGALE, of Argentine/Italian nationality, obtained his Ph.D. and M.Sc. in Economics from the London School of Economics and his bachelor's degree in Economics from Argentina's *Universidad Católica*. Upon completion of his university studies, Mr. Giugale joined the Word Bank in 1989 as an Economist in the Department of Financial Research. From 1990 to 1994, he served as Chief Economist in the Office of the Vice-President for Middle Eastern Operations, supervising structural adjustment programs in Egypt and directing the Bank's post-war reconstruction effort in Lebanon. From 1994 to 1998, Mr. Giugale served as Chief Economist for the Eastern Europe and Central Asia regions, where he was responsible for the Bank's loan portfolio as well as for economic analysis work involving Lithuania and Kazakhstan. From September 1998 to October 2002, he occupied the post of Lead Economist for the Colombia, Mexico, and Venezuela Department. He is currently Subregional Director for the Andean countries of Bolivia, Ecuador, Peru, and Venezuela. In addition, he has lectured at the London

School of Economics and at the American University in Cairo, and has also published widely on applied econometrics, finance, business economics, and economic development.

JOSÉ ROBERTO LÓPEZ-CÁLIX, a native of El Salvador, is Senior Economist in the Economic Policy Group for the World Bank's Latin America and the Caribbean Region. Mr. López-Cálix obtained his Ph.D., M.Sc., and bachelor's degrees from the Catholic University in Louvain, Belgium, and an M.Sc. degree with a major in International Finance from the University of Pittsburgh. He began his professional career by working in a number of international organizations, including the United Status Agency for International Development, the Canadian International Development Agency, the United States Congress, and the Inter-American Development Bank, specializing in macroeconomic policy, econometric analysis, public finance, international migration, and foreign debt management. From 1989 to 1991, Mr. López-Cálix served as General Director for the Ministry of Planning's Economic and Social Advisory Group with responsibility for El Salvador's special budget, and in this capacity was a member of the team that designed and implemented structural adjustment policies to govern the transition between the pre- and postwar periods. In 1994, he joined the World Bank in Washington, D.C., where he worked in the Department of Central American Operations. Two years later, he was named Manager of the Bank's Office in Guatemala. In 1999, together with Guatemala's Integrated Financial Management Project Team, he was awarded the prestigious "President James D. Wolfensohn Award." In 2000, he returned to Washington, D.C., and since that time has worked primarily with the Department for Ecuador, Bolivia, Peru, and Venezuela. Mr. López-Calix has been a Visiting Professor at Florida International University in Miami and has published numerous books and articles on specialized subjects, including parallel exchange markets, international coordination in macroeconomic policy, public finance, public expenditure monitoring surveys, trade policy and free trade agreements, and family remittances.

Acknowledgments

This volume is the result of a team effort and, as such, it has benefited from an array of invaluable contributions. Our thanks are therefore due to a large number of people. First, the chapters' authors, for not only providing material of outstanding technical quality, but also for their remarkable effort, even working in record time during New Year's and Christmas holidays, and thus enriching the Ecuador debate at a crucial time. We consider ourselves fortunate to share this book with these principal authors—Gabriela Arcos, Marcelo Bortman, Robert Buergenthal, Maria Dakolias, María Donoso-Clark, Franz Drees, Daniel Dulitzky, Philippe Durand, Jonas Frank, Mario Guadamillas, Dominique Hachette, Anthony James, Emmanuel James, Giovanni Majnoni, Yira Mascaró, Eleodoro Mayorga, Alexandra Ortiz, Juan Quintero, Francesca Recanatini, Jeffrey Rinne, Rafael Rofman, Carlos Rojas, Carolina Sánchez-Páramo, Ernesto Sánchez-Triana, Osvaldo Schenone, Mitchell A. Seligson, Ilias Skamnelos, Elaine Tinsley, Eloy Vidal, and Pierre Werbrouck. All authors are affiliated with the World Bank Group unless otherwise indicated in the respective chapter. Other authors of individual chapters are recognized in the credits of each specific chapter.

While this book reflects the authors' views (and not necessarily the views of the World Bank, its Board of Directors, or its member countries), its production was institutionally housed at the World Bank. We thus benefited greatly from the general guidance of Guillermo Perry (Chief Economist for the Latin America and the Caribbean Region) and from the auspices of the office of David de Ferranti (Vice President for Latin American and the Caribbean Region). We also thank McDonald Benjamin, Daniel Cotlear, Andrea Silverman, and Fernando Montes-Negret for their support and comments.

We also recognize the importance of and thank the participants of the workshop held on January 11th, 2003 in Quito, Ecuador. This workshop not only brought together a majority of the authors under one roof for a day of candid discussions but also, and more important, included officials and consultants from both past and current government administrations. Of the consultants and government officials present at the workshop, we would especially like to thank the following: Sr. Presidente Lucio Gutierrez, Patricio Ortiz, Luis Felipe Mantilla, Nina Pacari, Nelson Herrera, Luis Macas, Doris Solís, Carmen Tene, Marcelo Cevallos, Marco Paez, Nelson Alvarez, Alberto Andino, Saúl Velasco, Ing. Patricio Pugarín, Estuardo Peñaherrera, Patricio Acosta, Mauricio Calderón, Antonio Tramontana, Edgar Isch, Augusto Barrera, Hernan Plaza, Víctor Acosta, María Fuentes, Manuel Chiriboga, Alberto Wray, Gabriel Montalvo, Frederic Pinel, Rosa María Torres, Diego Mancheno, María Belen Freire, Oswaldo Aguirre, Mauricio Yépez, Victor Hugo Jijón, Mauro Terán, Juan Granja, Patricio Ruiz, Rocío Bohórquez, Ramiro Galarza, John Arroyo, Javier Game, Pedro Páez, Francisco Hidalgo, Fernando Suárez, A. Polibio Córdova C., Patricia Carrera, Carlos Arboleda, Bayardo Granjas, Juan Escalante, Mauricio Pareja Cevallos, Fernando Buendía, Mauricio Pozo, Virgilio Hernández, Jose Vallejo, Horacio Yépez, Lenin Parreño, Aase Smedler, Fernando Uzcategui, Antonio Albiñana, Juan Villacís, Mario Acosta, Roberto Salazar, Fernando Alban Bonilla, Romelio Gualan, Benito Suarez, Luis Tapia, David Yuravlivker, and Francisco Andino. Their comments, suggestions, and inputs along with those from the many others who attended this workshop added greatly to this volume.

We are especially thankful for the work of Esperanza Berrocal and her entire team from Comunicación Global, Mellen Candage, Robert A. Croese, Richard Crum, Jan D. Gibboney, Andrea Harold, and Carol Levie for their exceptional work in preparing the Spanish version of this publication as well as piecing together the English version. We are especially grateful for the work of Michael Geller who gave key support to the editorial process of this work; as well as to Chris Humphrey for having collaborated on the English version's technical editing for various chapters. The World Bank team in Ecuador should also receive a well-deserved thank-you for their outstanding support and help in coordinating the January 11th workshop in Quito: Gabriela Beltrán, Alexandra Del Castillo, Edmundo Espinoza, Ana Lucia Jimenez, Pilar Larreamendy, Raul Subia, Vinicio Valdivieso, Ana Maria Vicuña, and Ana Maria Villaquiran. Without them, achieving the right environment for these important discussions would not have been possible. The World Bank team in Washington was also a strong component during this whole process: Oscar Avalle, Sara Calvo, Ivonne Escobedo, María Antonieta González, Christopher Hale, Patricia Holt, Francisco Irías, Crummella Myers, Marianella Rivadeneira, Judy Rivers, Rosalía Rushton, Esther Samuel, Margaret Stroude, and Eduardo Wallentin.

Finally, we would like to thank the World Bank publication team. Santiago Pombo-Bejarano and Stephenie DeKouadio supervised the entire process and provided key information and assistance at all stages of publication. The team from Alfaguara, Colombia turned out a wonderful product in Spanish under a high level of stress and a strict deadline. Patricia Endara and Ronald Jones led us to the wonderful artwork of Gonzalo Endara Crow that graces the cover of this volume. Our sincere thanks to all of them.

Vicente Fretes-Cibils, Marcelo M. Giugale, and *José R. López-Cálix*
Washington, D.C.
April 2003

Acronyms and Abbreviations

AADT	Annual average daily traffic
ADV	Added distribution value
AFTA	American Free Trade Agreement
AGD	Deposit Guarantee Agency (*Agencia de Garantía de Depósitos*)
ALADI	Latin American Integration Association
ALCA	Free Trade Zone of the Americas (*Área Libre de Comercio de las Americas*)
AME	Association of Municipalities of Ecuador
API	American Petroleum Institute
APRENDO	Academic achievement testing
BCE	Central Bank of Ecuador (*Banco Central de Ecuador*)
BEDE	Ecuadoran Development Bank
BIRF	The International Bank of Reconstruction and Promotions (*Banco Internacional de Reconstrucción y Fomento*)
BNF	National Development Bank (*Banco Nacional de Fomento*)
BPD	Barrels per day
CAE	Ecuadoran Customs Corporation (*Corporación Aduanero de Ecuador*)
CAF	Andean Corporation of Promotion (*Corporación Andina de Fomento*)
CAN	Andean Community of Nations (*Comunidad Andina de Naciones*)
CEDEGE	Center for Development of the Guayas Basin
CEL	Special Bidding Committee
CELADE	Latin American Demography Center *Centro (Latinoamericano de Demografía)*
CEMs	Educational Matrix Centers (*Centros Educativos Matrices*)
CENACE	National Center for Energy Control
CEPE	Centre for Energy Policy and Economics
CET	Common External Tariff

CETUR	Ecuadoran Tourism Corporation
CFN	National Finance Corporation
CGC	Comptroller General Office (*Controloría General de Cuentas*)
CID	Center for International Development Harvard University
CIF	Cost and Freight
CNJ	National Council on the Judiciary
CNRH	National Council on Hydraulic Resources
CNT	National Transport Council (*Consejo Nacional de Transporte*)
CNTTT	National Land Transit and Transport Council
CODENPE	Council for the Development of the Indigenous Nations and Peoples of Ecuador
COMEXI	Trade and Investment Council (*Consejo de Comercio Exterior e Inversiones*)
CONADES	National Wages Council (*Consejo Nacional de Salarios*)
CONAM	National Modernization Council
CONAREM	National Council for Public Sector Remuneration
CONATEL	National Telecommunications Council
CONCOPE	Consortium of Provincial Councils of Ecuador
CONELEC	Ecuador National Electricity Council (*Consejo Eléctrico de Ecuador*)
CONSEP	National Council for the Control of Substances
COPEFEN	Coordinator of the Emergency Program to Cope with the El Niño Phenomenon
CORPECUADOR	Ecuador Corporation (*Corporación del Ecuador*)
CORPEI	Exportation and Investment Promotion Corporation (*Corporación de Promoción de Exportaciones e Inversiones)*
COSUDE	*Consejo Superior de Educación*
CPC	Code of Civil Procedure
CREA	Center for the Economic Reconversion of Azuay
CRM	Center for the Reconversion of Manabí
CTI	Technical Commission on Investments of the IESS (*Comisión Técnica de Inversiones*)
DAC	Civil Aviation Office
DECEVALE S.A.	Depository of Stocks (*Depositaria de Valores*)
DIGMER	Maritime Transport Administration
DINEPP	National Directorate of Continuing Popular Education (*Dirección Nacional de Educación Popular Permanente*)

DNP   National Personnel Directorate
DVP   Delivery versus Payment
EAP   Population, Environment, and Energy Program
ECAPAG   Guayaquil Potable Water and Sewage Company
           (*Empresa cantonal de Agua Potable y de alcantarillado de Guayaquil*)
ECOPETROL Colombian Petroleum Company *(Empresa Colombiana de Petróleo)*
ECORAE   Amazon Development Fund (*Fondo para desarrollo de la region Amazonizo*)
EDAP   Pension Savings Deposit Institutions (*Entidades Depositarias del Ahorro Previsional*)
EEQ   Quito Electric Company (*Empresa Eléctrica Quito*)
EMAAP   Water and Sanitation Municipal Enterprise (*Empresa Municipal de Alcantarillado y Agua Potable*)
EMAAP-Q   Water and Sanitation Municipal Enterprise of Quito (*Empresa Municipal de Alcantarillado y Agua Potable de Quito*)
EMELEC   Electricity Municipal Enterprise (*Empresa Municipal de Electricidad*)
EMETEL   Telecom Municipal Enterprise (*Empresa Estatal de Telecommunicaciones*)
ENAP   National Petroleum Enterprise (*Empresa Nacional del Petróleo*), Chile
ENDEMAIN III Survey on Demographics and Maternal and Infant Health (*Encuesta Demográfica y de Salud Materna e Infantil*)
ENFE   Ecuadoran National Railway Company
ENTEL   Telecom State Enterprise
EPHF   Essential Public Health Functions
EPR   Effective protection rate
ESMAP   Energy Sector Management Assistance Programme
FASBASE   Strengthening and Expanding the Scope of Basic Health Services in Ecuador (*Fortalecimiento y Ampliación de los Servicios Básicos de Salud en el Ecuador*)
FEIREP   Fund for Stabilization, Social and Productive Investment, and Reduction of Public Debt *(Fondo de Estabilización, Inversión Social y Productiva, y Reducción del Endeudamiento Público)*
FENAJE   National Federation of Judicial Officials
FERUM   Rural and Marginal Urban Electrification Fund
FISE   Emergency Social Investment Fund

FLAR	Latin American Reserve Fund
FODESEC	Municipal Development Fund (*Fondo de desarrollo seccional*)
FONDEPRO	Credit Fund for the Development of Production (*Fondo de credito para el desarrollo de la producción*)
FONDIFA	National Children's Fund
FONDVIAL	Transportation Fund (*Fondo vial*)
FOPEDEUPO	Permanent Fund for University and Polytechnic Development
FTAA	Free Trade Agreement of the Americas
FTA	Free trade agreement
GDP	Gross domestic product
GEF	Global Environmental Facility
GSP	General System of Preferences
GSRT	Gross Settlement in Real Time
GUO	Global Urban Observatory of the United Nations
HDI	Human Development Index
HRM	Human resources management
ICE	Special Consumption Tax (*Impuesto a los Consumos Especiales*)
ICT	Information and communications technology
IDB	Inter-American Development Bank
IEOS	Ecuadoran Institute for Water and Sanitation Works
IESS	Ecuadoran Social Security Institute (*Instituto Ecuatoriano de Seguridad Social*)
IMCI	Integrated Management of Childhood Illness
IMF	International Monetary Fund
INEC	Survey on Employment, Unemployment, and Underemployment
INECEL	Ecuadoran Electricity Institute (*Instituto Ecuatoriano de electrificación*)
INEN	Ecuadoran Standardization Institute
INERHI	Ecuadoran Institute of Hydrological Resources (*Instituto Ecuatoriano de los recursos hidrizos*)
INGALA	National Galapagos Institute (*Instituto nacional galapagos*)
INIAP	National Institute for Agriculture and Livestock Research (*Instituto Nacional de Investigaciones*) *Agropecuarias*
INNFA	National Child and Family Institute
INTERAGUA	International Water Services Guayaquil
IPP	Independent Power Providers

ISP	Internet service provider
ISR	Income Tax (*Impuesto Sobre la Renta*)
ISSFA	Social Security Institute of the Armed Forces
ISSPOL	Social Security Institute of the Police
ITT	*Ishpingo-Tambococha-Tiputini*
ITU	International Telecommunications Union
IVA	Value-Added Tax (*Impuesto al Valor Agregado*)
JASS	Water and sanitation councils
LEXI	Law on Foreign Trade and Investment
LIBOR	London Interbank Offered Rate
LMG	Law on Free Maternity Care
LPG	Liquid petroleum gas
LRFP	Law on Reform of Public Finances
LSCCA	Civil Service and Administrative Career Law
MDMQ	Municipality of the Metropolitan District of Quito
MDOGs	Government ministries, departments, and agencies
MEC	Ministry of Education and Culture
MEF	Ministry of Economy and Finance
MEM	Wholesale Electricity Market
MIDUVI	Ministry of Urban Development and Housing (*Ministerio de Desarrollo Urbano y Vivienda*)
MIVI	Ministry of Housing
MODERSA	Modernization and Development of Comprehensive Health Services Networks (*Modernización y Desarrollo de Redes Integrales de Servicios de Salud*)
MOP	Ministry of Public Works
MSP	Ministry of Public Health
NAP	Network access point
NFPS	Nonfinancial Public Sector
NTB	Nontariff barrier
NTE	Technical Norms of Ecuador
OCP	Heavy crude oil pipeline
ODEPLAN	Planning Office
OLADE	Latin American Energy Organization (*Organización Latinoamericana de Energía*)
ONN	National Standardization Agency
ORI	Children's Rescue Operation (*Operación Rescate Infantil*)
OSCIDI	Civil Service and Institutional Development Office
OTA	Trans Andean Pipelines (*Oleoducto Transandino*)
PACMI	Supplementary Food Program for Mothers and Infants (*Programa de Alimentación Complementaria Materna-Infantil*)

PAHO	Pan-American Health Organization
PANN	National Food and Nutrition Program (*Programa Nacional de Alimentación y Nutrición*)
PDI	Children's Development Program *(Programa de Desarrollo Infantíl)*
PDM	Municipal Development Program
PHO	Panamerican Health Organization
PRAGUAS	Water and Sanitation Program for Rural Communities and Small Municipalities—financed by the World Bank
PROBONA	Native Andean Forests Program
PRODEPINE	Indigenous and Afro-Ecuadoran Peoples Development Project (*Proyecto para el desarrollo de los Pueblos y nacionalidades del Ecuador*)
PROLOCAL	Poverty Reduction and Local Rural Development
PROMEC	Power and Communcations Sectors Modernization and Rural Services Project
PROMECEB	Program for Better Quality Basic Education (*Programa de Mejoramiento de la Calidad de la Educación Básica*)
PROMSA	Program for the Modernization of Agricultural Services (*Programa de Modernización de los Servicios Agropecuarios*)
PRONEPE	National Preschool Education Program *(Programa Nacional de Educación Preescolar)*
PROST	Pension Reform Options Simulation Toolkit
PSP	private sector participation
RER	Real exchange rate
RISE	Ecuadoran Simplified Tax System (*Régimen Impositivo Simplificado Ecuatoriano)*
ROAA	Return on average assets
ROAE	Return on average equity
ROSC	Report on the Observance of Standard and Codes
RUC	Centralized taxpayers registry (*Registro Único de Contribuyentes)*
SAPYSB	Sub-secretariat of Potable Water and Basic Sanitation
SBS	Superintendency of Banks and Insurance (*Superintendencia de Bancos y Seguros*)
SCT	Secretary of Communications and Transportation (*Secretaría de comunicaciones y transportes*)
SELBEN	Ecuadoran Beneficiary Identification and Selection System (*Sistema de Identificación y Selección de Beneficiarios*)

SENATEL	National Secretariat of Telecommunications
SENDA	Secretariat for National Administrative Development
SENDOSEP	National Secretariat for Organizational Development of the Public Sector
SESA	Ecuadoran Animal and Plant Inspection Service
SGO	General Obligatory Insurance (*Seguro General Obligatorio*)
SG	sectional government
SICA	Agricultural Census
SIGEF	Integrated Governmental System of Financial Statistics
SIISE	Integrated System of Social Indicators of Ecuador Social Indicators System of Ecuador (*Sistema Integrado de Indicadores Sociales de Ecuador*)
SIV	Housing Incentives System
SME	Small and medium-sized enterprise
SOTE	TransEcuadoran Pipeline System *(Sistema de Oleoducto Transecuatoriano)*
SPC	Service-providing company
SPNF	*Sector Público No Financiero* (see NFPS)
SP	Service provider
SRI	Internal Revenue Service *(Servicio de Rentas Internas)*
SSC	Rural People's Social Security Program *(Seguro Social Campesino)*
SSO	Obligatory Social Security (*Seguro Social Obligatorio*)
SUMA	Single Environmental Management System
SUPTEL	Telecommunications Authority
SWIFT	Wiring Financial Service
TROLE I	Economic Transformation Law
UCV	Local Road Works Unit
UDENOR	Development Unit of the North
UOST	Trolleybus System Operating Unit
URC	Credit Restructuring Unit (*Unidad de Reestructuración de Créditos*)
USAID	United States Agency for International Development
VAT	Value-Added Tax
WLL	Wireless Local Loop
WTI	West Texas Intermediate
WTO	World Trade Organization

Synthesis

Vicente Fretes-Cibils and José R. López-Cálix

A. Purpose and Organization

In recent years, the World Bank has had the honor and privilege of welcoming incoming administrations of member countries with a series of integrated diagnostic studies and policy recommendations in priority areas of social and economic development, with the goal of reducing poverty. This practice is particularly relevant for Ecuador today, where President Lucio Gutiérrez has taken office to govern a country that is rich in natural resources and has enormous potential to combat poverty and improve the well-being of all citizens. However, these tasks will be hampered by structural economic and social problems, low competitiveness, corruption, and inefficient use of petroleum resources. Ecuador is still suffering the consequences of recent banking and exchange rate crises, which led to the dollarization of the economy. While dollarization helped reverse some of the macroeconomic imbalances, it caused greater economic vulnerability to changes in relative prices in the midst of a global and regional slowdown in economic growth.

The fundamental challenges facing the country are identified within this book, and the solutions represent a break with the past. This is a proposal for an agenda with a broad and integrated vision of economic and social development in Ecuador. The chapters are grouped into the three thematic categories of the new administration's program: (a) Stability and Growth with Competitiveness, (b) Socially Sustainable and Equitable Development, and (c) Quality Government and the War on Corruption. Each category includes selected subjects. Within *Stability and Growth with Competitiveness*, the following subjects are included: fiscal sustainability, tax reform, management of public debt, consolidation of the banking system, expansion of petroleum-related and commercial activities, development of basic infrastructure—electricity, telephone systems, water, and transport—and urban development. *Socially Sustainable and Equitable Development contains* an analysis of the following sectors: education, health, social safety networks, social security and pensions, rural development, and the environment. Within *Quality Government and the War on Corruption,* the following themes are examined: improved governance, civil service reform, judicial reform, and decentralization of public services.

These chapters are meant to be informative rather than exhaustive. They strive to initiate a frank and cordial dialogue, and to gather valuable insights from authorities on all these subjects. The chapters show that the views of the World Bank and the new Gutiérrez administration converge in making poverty reduction the central strategic goal of both the new government's agenda and future Bank assistance to Ecuador. This document was written based on the Bank's rich experience in the country, complemented by recent interviews and data gathered during a Bank mission in November 2002, and presented to the incoming authorities in a workshop held in Quito on January 11, 2003. The World Bank appreciates the efforts of both outgoing and incoming officials in helping facilitate the preparation of this document.

B. Central Message

Since 1979, when it returned to democracy, Ecuador has suffered from high external vulnerability, poor macroeconomic performance, and poor governance. A succession of external adversities—linked to the volatility of oil prices and violent variations in capital flows—and natural calamities, all in combination with poor economic management, resulted in macroeconomic imbalances, with negative impact on growth and social development. During this period, the country went through four severe recessions (1982–83, 1987, 1989, and 1998–99) and three periods of hyperinflation (1983, 1988–93, and 1999–2000). It incurred a high and unsustainable external debt, reflected in various moratoriums on payments and the recent exchange rate depreciation and banking crises, which destroyed 20 banks that accounted for over 50 percent of banking deposits. These bad economic policies were partly caused by weak and too-often-changing public management, and the governance problems that traditionally characterize oil-producing countries. In the last 23 years Ecuador has had 29 finance ministers, meaning each spent an average of 10 months in the post. In addition, Ecuador has been the Latin American country perceived as having the least control over corruption.

Even more important, the last crisis (1998–99) had a devastating effect on employment levels, poverty, and income distribution. While the rate of formal unemployment grew from 10 to nearly 15 percent, poverty incidence increased from 34 to 56 percent between 1995 and 1999, and the Gini coefficient increased from 0.52 to 0.54 during the same period. These indicators imply that the number of poor Ecuadorans grew by over 2 million during the crisis. This crisis severely affected the rural poor, the indigenous population, and particularly those living in the mountains, where the poverty rate increased by 7 percent just between 1998 and 1999. More than a quarter of a million people emigrated and another half million moved into marginal urban areas within the country. Other human and social development indicators, such as infant mortality, malnutrition, and the school desertion rate, also worsened. The level of deterioration of these indicators reveals the depth of the crisis, and the greater vulnerability of the poor, both urban and rural, in confronting the loss of income.

The Ecuadoran economy has begun to recuperate, but it remains fragile. The adoption of the dollar as the local currency, favorable oil prices, rapidly increasing family remittances, and macroeconomic management with mixed results, have all helped gradually to stabilize expectations. These factors have also helped to gradually eliminate hyperinflation, to begin to restore and reestablish the banking system, reach moderate growth levels, and partially reverse the increase in unemployment and poverty levels. Although economic growth is a necessary condition to combat poverty, it will be insufficient unless it is sustainable and participatory, and includes broad sectors of the most vulnerable population (such as the marginalized indigenous population). With this challenge in mind, the central question posed in the book is as follows:

What should the new government's agenda be in order to ensure abandoning the failures of the past, bringing about Ecuador's economic and social recovery and reducing poverty? The answer to this question is based on three lines of action:

- Preserving stability with fiscal discipline and accelerating growth with competitiveness;
- Boosting sustainable and equitable social development; and
- Building a quality government that serves all Ecuadorans and fights against corruption.

PRESERVING STABILITY WITH FISCAL DISCIPLINE AND ACCELERATING GROWTH WITH COMPETITIVENESS. The number one priority for Ecuador continues to be sustained economic growth. Both international experience and the experience of Ecuador itself show that the best tool to combat poverty and protect the most vulnerable citizens is to accelerate economic growth. It is estimated that on average, with each 1 percent increase of the gross domestic product (GDP) per capita, poverty is reduced by approximately .7 percent. It will not be easy to keep the economy on a track of rapid growth in the medium term, but it is feasible and can be achieved through the following key actions:

- First, guarantee a balanced macroeconomic framework, particularly with reference to public accounts, that fosters stability and private investment, and that allows debt reduction to continue. This means fiscal adjustment through collecting more and spending less, addressing liquidity problems in the short term and solvency problems in the medium term, and lowering interest rates to stimulate greater private investment in the economy.
- Second, promote economic expansion and competitiveness by making input markets—particularly the labor market—more flexible, by opening the economy to foreign trade, and by eliminating trade policies that punish exporters.

These actions should be complemented by finishing the reorganization and reform of the financial system, and by promoting the expansion of financial intermediation, access to credit, and economic growth.

- Third, accelerate expansion of the petroleum sector through a legal and regulatory change to bring about legal and fiscal stability, and promote private investment in the oil fields with the greatest reserves. This expansion should be accompanied by programs and projects that fosters transparency in resource management, and also promote the local population's right to be consulted. The legal framework should include provisions to guarantee better management of the environmental and social impact of the oil industry. At the same time, the regulatory framework should eliminate distortions in the prices of and taxes on combustible fuels.

- Fourth, develop physical infrastructure in four main services: water and sanitation, electricity, telecommunications, and transport (highways and roads, railways, ports, and airports). Owing to fiscal restrictions, the government should facilitate private sector expansion in the provision of these services. This will require legal and regulatory changes with the corresponding adjustments in prices and tariffs, the elimination of subsidies (for propane, gasoline, and electricity), and the correction of distortions (such as the lack of incentives to increase investment in road maintenance).

- Fifth, the government needs to direct its attention to the rapid urbanization process in Ecuador, and the resulting growth of poverty in urban areas. To combat this problem, integral urban development programs should be considered in order to raise the standard of living in marginal urban zones and lower the physical, economic, and social vulnerability of residents. In this context, the detection of restrictions on the functioning of real estate markets is a priority, because these restrictions affect accessibility for the poor—and identifying them will permit proposing changes to correct the obstacles confronting the poor.

BOOSTING SUSTAINABLE AND EQUITABLE SOCIAL DEVELOPMENT. Economic growth will be meaningless if Ecuadorans living in poverty (over 7 million) cannot participate in the progress. The government can ensure this participation through the following actions:

- First, facilitate growth, accumulation of human capital, and the strengthening of the social fabric through dedicating more resources and improving the quality of education and health services, particularly for the poor and indigenous in marginal urban and rural areas. On top of the recent reduction in general levels of spending, the public sector is currently not receiving the corresponding returns on resources directed toward education and health. This should be reversed if the intention is to expand coverage and improve the quality of these services.

- Second, the accumulation of human capital should be complemented by eliminating rigidities in markets, particularly the labor market, so that the exchange of goods and services can be achieved with minimal transaction costs, and by promoting an improvement in the income of the poor who have made efforts to improve their education and health (human capital).
- Third, the social safety network should improve efficacy and efficiency in protecting these groups. The accumulation of human capital and elimination of labor market rigidities will not satisfy the needs of all Ecuadorans, particularly the marginalized rural and indigenous poor. In the formal sector, the social security system needs to be reformed, with a better separation of different services such as pensions and health, modernizing their institutional framework and financial management, and broadening coverage. The coverage of noncontributive regimes needs to be extended to the informal sector (such as Small Farmer Social Security) with better targeting and maximizing of the scarce resources allocated to these programs.
- Fourth, despite the prominence of problems brought on by rapid urbanization, the government also needs to diversify its focus to include poverty in general, especially extreme rural poverty. The preparation of a strategy for the development of multisectoral rural development is needed that is diversified and has a territorial approach. This strategy should have three main goals: (a) social and economic cohesion through development of local space; (b) adjustment of agriculture and rural economic diversification; and (c) environmental protection. Ecuador's geographic, economic, and sociocultural diversity means that this strategy must be differentiated and supported by policies that in turn facilitate the following:
  - development by jurisdiction or rural space, in a participatory form, to create economic and social cohesion;
  - the diversification of the rural economy;
  - the creation of nonagrarian employment through investment in rural and social infrastructure;
  - competitiveness of the agrarian sector through transference of technology and research; and
  - environmental conservation through improved territorial organization, reviving methods of soil conservation and appropriate use of natural resources.

BUILDING A QUALITY GOVERNMENT THAT SERVES ALL ECUADORANS AND FIGHTS AGAINST CORRUPTION. The new government begins from a weak institutional standpoint, with an image of being highly corrupt and having problems governing. This image negatively affects the new administration's credibility as it designs and tries to implement public policies, and also influences the ability to provide public services. The government should reestablish governability and prevent corruption through the following actions:

- First, the government should carry out reforms in functions such as supervision, regulation, provision of direct services, acquisition of goods, and contracting of services, among others, and promote total transparency. The government needs to change incentives and separate economic and political links, promoting public oversight and avoiding, wherever possible, state capture by certain economic interest groups. This will not be an easy task and will require an integral plan, because both governance and corruption have an impact on all aspects of public activity and affect the majority of economic and social sectors. This difficult task could begin with a governance pact between the state and civil society, and with the development of an anti-corruption strategy.
- Second, this pact and strategy should be complemented with the strengthening of the civil service and the deepening of judicial reform. These measures will allow all Ecuadorans, particularly those who are excluded today, to have access to justice.
- Third, those who initiate the process of public reform must keep in mind the general context of decentralization and work within this framework. This process faces three challenges to improving public services: (a) improvement of functional decentralization; (b) the transfer of resources and spending competencies to subnational governments; and (c) the delineation of fiscal responsibility of subnational governments, including limits on public debt.

C. The Development Agenda—Diagnostic Study and Policies

Ecuador is committed to the Development Goals of the Millennium. These goals were adopted by the international community within the framework of the United Nations for compliance between 1990 and 2015. They cover the areas of poverty, malnutrition, mother–infant health, education, gender equity, and environmental sustainability. Although data are incomplete for projecting the level of compliance with all goals for Ecuador, our calculations are based on an average annual GDP growth rate in the medium term of 2.7 percent. According to World Bank estimates, it is "probable" that Ecuador will reach goals for primary education (100 percent coverage) and malnutrition (50 percent reduction); it is "possible" that Ecuador will meet goals for lowering infant mortality and mortality of children under age five (66 percent reduction), and also goals for sanitation (a 50 percent drop in the number of people without access to potable water). The Bank believes it is "highly improbable" that Ecuador will meet poverty reduction goals of 50 percent (rates for poverty and extreme poverty). The high sensitivity of these goals—particularly for poverty—to the rate of economic growth demonstrates why Ecuador needs to grow in an accelerated and sustained manner, with rates higher than historical levels, in order to reduce poverty during the next decade. This will be possible only with an integrated development agenda.

Preserving Stability with Fiscal Discipline and Accelerating Growth with Competitiveness

Sustained growth acceleration can take place only within a context of macroeconomic stability and based on a multidimensional agenda of competitiveness. Unfortunately, for several decades, instability has been the rule and not the exception in Ecuadoran macroeconomic policy, and as regards competitiveness, the country is a latecomer to reform.

Dollarization was especially necessary for Ecuador because it needs to build a new reputation and change its image as a country that historically has been politically unstable. By "lifting the veil" of money, dollarization made it evident that problems were not only fiscal in nature, but also social and financial to an even greater degree. The suppression of monetary policy not only remedied a previous fiscal illusion, but also resolved the financial imbalances introduced by hyperinflation and the depreciation of the exchange rate. At the same time, it established new rules for competitiveness, and made it clear that only solid structural reforms will consolidate stability, reactivate the economy, strengthen the financial system, and combat poverty efficiently in the medium term.

It is no secret that in 1999 Ecuador's economy was in such a bad state that a successful dollarization process seemed unlikely. The country had a high fiscal deficit, an unsustainable external debt on which the country had defaulted, exports that depended excessively on oil and were highly vulnerable to unfavorable terms-of-trade shocks, and a banking system in crisis affected by high regional capital flight, which had brought international reserves down to their lowest level. Obviously, this dark landscape was inhospitable for attracting investment. The combination of poor competitiveness and rigid factors markets for the production of services and non-tradable goods (labor and property), made price adjustments that were required to preserve external competitiveness after losing the exchange rate instrument more difficult. Despite all this, and within a short time, Ecuador met two goals through dollarization: the elimination of hyperinflation and the reestablishment of confidence in the banking system. At the same time the Law of Economic Transformation established minimum conditions and the structural reforms needed to ensure that dollarization was sustainable in the medium term.

Ecuador has begun an economic recovery with stability. Economic growth has reached moderate levels (3.6 percent average during 2000–02) and inflation slowly came down to single-digit levels by the end of 2002, after remaining high since 1998. Both of these results are due to a favorable external environment, the recovery of the financial system, the reactivation of domestic demand, and the dynamics of relative prices. The favorable external environment has been characterized by high oil prices, low international interest rates, and significant remittance flows from Ecuadorans living abroad. The financial system has seen a marked recovery of banking deposits and a slight drop in nominal interest rates. The increase in domestic demand is due to the sharp drop in inflation, high oil prices, growing remittances, and the decision by authorities to approve the construction of a new Heavy Crude Oil Pipeline (OCP), which has attracted new foreign investment flows. The adjustment of prices has been determined by international inflation, the later adjustment of prices that comes with the postdollarization dynamic, the maintenance of government prices for products in the basic food basket, and the expansion of domestic demand resulting from the increase in the nominal minimum and average wages in dollars, which practically doubled between April 2000 and October 2002. The economic recovery, combined with emigration and the ensuing remittances, has contributed to the drop in levels of open unemployment and poverty, although these have not returned to precrisis levels.

Despite this progress, significant internal and external imbalances still exist. Internally, while current public sector revenue has improved, primary spending remains expansive. Consequently the primary surplus achieved during the year of dollarization has been cut in half. Externally, an appreciated real exchange rate and the temporary rise of imports related to construction of the new oil pipeline have provoked a strong deficit in the current account of the balance of payments. However, this deficit has been partly mitigated by family remittances from abroad and has been partly compensated for by positive foreign investment flows in capital accounts. As a result, the level of freely available international reserves is still very low (to prevent contingencies), with a tendency to decline, which should be reversed.

The structural reforms that should accompany the dollarization process are either absent or inconclusive. Fiscal adjustment is among the inconclusive reforms, as is the strengthening of the financial system, while the promotion of private investment in the petroleum sector is glaringly absent. Other reforms that have not been carried out include trade reform, the promotion of competitiveness, and private participation in basic infrastructure. For their part, the structural reforms that should have accompanied dollarization remain incomplete or nonexistent. Notable among the incomplete reforms are fiscal adjustment and reforms relating to the strengthening of the financial system. Notable among the nonexistent reforms are reforms to promote private investments in the petroleum section, trade reform, reforms to promote competitiveness and private participation in basic infrastructure.

The likelihood of the collapse of dollarization in the medium term should not be underestimated. To avoid it, Ecuador must move ahead quickly not only on the fiscal front but also with the structural reforms needed to counteract the rigidity involved in the unilateral decision to adopt the dollar as legal currency for circulation, savings, and payments for domestic goods and services transactions. In view of the loss of control over monetary and exchange-rate policy, and of the inability to "inflate" fiscal imbalances and alter relative prices by depreciating the domestic currency, in order to sustain dollarization Ecuador must simultaneously ensure macroeconomic stability through solvency and fiscal stability and introduce flexibility in goods and services markets—particularly for inputs. This course of action would maintain the competitiveness of the country's products on domestic and foreign markets, while at the same time increasing the individual (and total) productivity of the factors of production.

From a macroeconomic perspective, given the initial situation of high public debt (60 percent of GDP in 2002), Ecuador must achieve and maintain significant primary fiscal surpluses that will allow it to lead its stock of debt along a sustainable path—that is, by ensuring short-term liquidity and guaranteeing the country's solvency for promptly meeting its public debt service obligations in the medium term. This means making adjustments in order to obtain primary surpluses in the fiscal accounts estimated at an average of 4 to 5 percent of GDP over the next five years, which would bring the stock of debt below 40 percent of GDP at the middle of the decade. The fiscal adjustment must take into account the volatility of tax revenues as a result of the variability in petroleum prices. To offset it, particularly during a foreseeable scenario of future price reductions, it will be necessary to apply automatic stabilizers and make more efficient use of the extraordinary resources obtained during the current petroleum boom period.

From a microeconomic perspective, and in the absence of control over exchange-rate policy, there is a limited range of instruments available to respond to adverse external shocks or to correct public policy errors in the economy's real sector. Should high rigidity continue in the operations of markets and prices in Ecuador, with high costs not only for production but for goods and services transactions as well, there will be negative effects on competitiveness, economic growth, and job creation, which could also make dollarization unsustainable. The risk lies in the fact that, given the existence of inflexible markets—such as the formal labor market—adjustments to shocks will occur primarily through reductions in amounts produced (and sold), with the corresponding contraction in demand based on inputs, particularly in labor (an abundant factor in Ecuador). This potential situation would not only create pressure to "abandon" the model, in view of increased unemployment, but would also contribute to an increase in commercial banks arrears, as a result of the decline in general economic activity. This would in turn make achieving both fiscal adjustment goals and recovery of the banking system less feasible—creating a vicious circle that would be difficult to break. Two external shocks require particular attention: first, devaluations or depreciations (discrete or continuous) of the currencies of Ecuador's trade partners; and second, appreciation of the dollar against other "strong" currencies in the world. In both cases, the "appreciation" of the dollar will have to be offset by increases in productivity and/or by deflationary adjustments in production and transaction costs so as to be able to maintain competitiveness and avoid the loss of markets. In summary, the *sine qua non* conditions for sustaining dollarization are to achieve and deepen fiscal solvency, expand and introduce flexibility in goods and services markets, and increase the productivity of the factors of production.

The Need for Adjustment and Fiscal Discipline

Postdollarization fiscal performance has not resolved the main obstacles to sustainability in the medium term. On the one hand, the average primary surplus of the

Non-Financial Public Sector (NFPS) has been significant but decreasing—it is projected to fall by more than half, from 7.7 percent in 2000 to 4.0 percent in 2002. On the other hand, it has had to cover high interest payments on public debt, leaving the authorities with a meager fiscal surplus (close to zero in 2002). The primary surpluses could have been higher if not for the expansive spending on salaries and investment. The lesson is clear: there is no point to saving on debt service through successful renegotiations if these savings are consumed by increases in public spending.

Fiscal fragility is rooted in the inherent weaknesses of fiscal revenue and tax policy—rigidity, low quality, and the lack of transparency in spending—and in the persistent threat of loss of liquidity and insolvency of public debt. These problems were identified during the approval process of a fiscal law at the end of 2002—the Law of Responsibility, Stabilization, and Fiscal Transparency. An analysis of each of these fiscal problems follows, taking into account the law's content and possible solutions that go beyond mere legal compliance.

Tax Reform

Fiscal revenue is characterized by the low level of tax collection on non-petroleum-related tax income, which is a consequence of the low Value-Added Tax (IVA) and the excessive number of exemptions, particularly on the Income Tax (ISR), and the high volatility of oil income, which gives fiscal income a procyclical nature. Each dollar drop in the price of a barrel of oil means an income reduction of .4 percent of GDP. Tax policy is highly subject to the different demands of special interest groups, and this is reflected in the excessive use of tax distortions such as the proliferation of taxes, exemptions, and earmarking.

The proliferation of taxes (more than 80) has a negative impact on tax efficiency because it makes it impossible for officials in power to focus on the taxes that are a priority. The multiple exemptions are part of the inefficient goal of trying to "fine-tune" tax policy. Because of this policy, authorities meticulously choose the sector that should pay benefits to be received by other chosen beneficiaries, robbing the process of transparency, as well as equity and efficiency when assigning resources. Failure is particularly acute in terms of meeting redistributive goals in the case of the IVA, and authorities are also inefficient in promoting socially profitable processes in the case of income tax exemptions or exemptions on customs tariffs. Finally, the excessive preallocations or earmarking (over 50) impedes more efficient use of fiscal resources (1.7 percent of the GDP) and also discourages tax collection efforts on the part of sectional governments (provincial or municipal), as they become accustomed to the bad habit of receiving transferences from the central government.

Strengthening of the fiscal position requires various types of tax policy actions. First, we propose increasing non-petroleum-related tax collection by a minimum of 2.5 percent of GDP. This is the amount stipulated in the fiscal law to guarantee a primary surplus that will lower the debt to sustainable levels in the medium term.

To meet this goal it will be necessary to first approve a series of tax policy measures that will generate approximately 1.4 percent of GDP. One of the most important is to limit sales tax exemptions solely to basic unprocessed foodstuffs. This will allow the cancellation of all other exemptions, particularly on income tax and customs tariffs, with a collections effect estimated at 1.1 percent of the GDP.

Second, given that the proposed increase in collection is still not enough to ensure a minimal primary surplus, particularly when faced with the perspective of a highly probable drop in oil prices to "normal" historic levels of below $US18 a barrel, we also recommend increasing the sales tax. It is estimated that collections would increase by .7 percent of GDP for each additional point that the tax is raised.

Third, we propose the repeal of minor taxes. Even if this does not have a significant impact on collections efforts, it will allow tax authorities and contributors to reduce administrative costs and focus on better compliance with sales and income taxes.

Fourth, we recommend eliminating all preallocations of sales and income tax for reasons that extend beyond tax collection, with the exception of the payroll tax earmarked for the Ecuadoran Institute of Social Security. This could be carried out in accordance with Article 22 of the original draft of the fiscal law.

Fifth, it would be very beneficial to reverse or prevent the approval of measures of "relaxed tax collection" proposed at the end of 2002, including the donation of 25 percent of income tax to municipalities, the reduction of the percentage of retention in the sales tax source from 1 percent to .1 percent, and the reduction to zero of the tariff on 158 products.

The internal tax administration has shown a positive change in orientation in recent years, with tangible results. After reforms in the Service of Internal Income (Ecuador's Internal Revenue Service, SRI, which stands for *Servicio de Rentas Internas* in Spanish) and the Ecuadoran Customs Corporation (CAE), there has been a notable improvement in the control of evasion in the SRI, although there has not been evidence of significant improvement in the CAE. The SRI's institutional design and the CAE's low performance are both priority matters for tax administration. Any strengthening of the fiscal position will also require tax administration measures such as the following:

- Reinforcing the independence of the SRI's directorate, thus preventing the use of its resolutions to introduce new discriminatory tax treatments and generators of distortions, and concentrating its efforts solely on the rigorous collection of taxes created by the laws.
- Considering merging the SRI with the CAE, to take advantage of economies of scales and oversee the collection of customs tariffs within the same universe of contributors.
- Reforming the Customs Law, incorporating modifications on the customs labor code that will permit a restructuring similar to the one that had positive results in the SRI.

- Promoting strict compliance with Law 41 of 1999, with official backing at the highest possible level to apply this control mechanism on contraband and the evasion of sales tax, without exceptions or discretion.

Spending Cuts, Reorientation, and Transparency

There are three fundamental problems with public spending: it is inflexible (particularly spending on salaries), it is fragmented, and it is not transparent. Inflexibility is an obstacle to containing spending. Fragmentation means spending cannot be efficiently allocated to meet government priorities. And lack of transparency prevents adequate control and public auditing, and converts it into an involuntary stimulus for tax evasion.

These three problems have reached alarming levels in Ecuador. The rigidity of spending, particularly current accounts, is very severe. For over a decade, primary spending has increased up to around 21.4 percent of GDP. This inflexibility is mainly due to the inertia of the public payroll, and excessive income earmarking—oil-related and non-oil-related—written into over 50 current legal regulations. Fragmentation is due to preallocated revenues in 217 sectional (subnational) governments and multiple objectives mandated by special laws. In 2001, budgetary preallocations corresponded to approximately 30 percent of the total of current income, or about 6 percent of GDP.

This fragmentation and rigidity of spending leaves meager freely-available resources. If the public payroll is deducted from the total current accounts income (30 percent), from service on the net debt (35 percent), and from preallocations (30 percent), the amount left over is barely 5 percent of the total current accounts income, or the equivalent of 1.2 percent of GDP as of 2001. This tiny percentage of domestic resources reflects serious cash flow problems and means the government cannot formulate a minimum budget for poverty reduction without affecting other programs. Finally, this spending is not transparent because (a) there is no centralized public payroll; (b) controls on preallocated spending are absent; (c) central budgetary standards are weak, which also fosters decentralized execution without adequate control mechanisms; and (d) there is no integrated system of financial administration that allows control of consolidated spending, not only of the central government, but also of decentralized entities and sectional governments.

There are various elements to spending reform. First, the 2003 budget should be declared a "national emergency" budget, with concrete measures to limit spending and confront the causes of rigidity. To do this the following is proposed: (a) the limiting of spending growth to zero in real terms in 2003, implying the establishment of limits on the salary mass, on goods and services, and on investments; (b) the immediate suspension of the salary-indexing mechanism based on projected inflation (and not yet carried out) by the National Council for Public Sector Remuneration (CONAREM); (c) the approval of a Salary Unification Law with a neutral fiscal cost; and (d) the repurchase of the most expensive debt in Global Bonds.

Second, fragmented spending should be consolidated and reoriented toward priorities. For this reason it is necessary to explicitly prohibit any new preallocations of income or spending and eliminate nearly all existing preallocations (with the exception of the Ecuadoran Social Security Institute [IESS]). Within the framework of a new decentralization policy, and during the period covering the emergency budget, additional transferences of over 10 to 11 percent assigned to sectional governments should be frozen, with the preparations of a future simultaneous transference of resources and additional competencies, auditing of the subnational debt and the Reprogramming Plan, and new regulations for subnational debt of large cities.

Third, budgetary transparency should be institutionalized at all levels of government by using modern instruments. Once the law is approved, the design and implementation of a modern and consolidated version of the Integrated Governmental System of Financial Statistics (SIGEF) is urgently needed. This entity covers sectional governments.

Sustainability of Public Debt

Ecuador's public debt has been poorly managed for several decades and as a result, the current level of public debt is very high. As a percentage of GDP, it is the second highest in the region. At the same time it carries a heavy debt load: net service consumes 35 percent of the budget. About 80 percent of Ecuador's total debt is external. The debt has three characteristics that somewhat alleviate the situation: 60 percent of the debt is multilateral and bilateral; only 1.4 percent is short-term debt; and after the restructuring of the onerous external debt in 2000 Brady bonds, 75 percent of the debt was set at a fixed rate, reducing the volatility of debt service.

The liquidity situation of Ecuador's public external debt is delicate. The country has immediate problems to resolve over arrears with the Paris Club, estimated at approximately $US181 million in 2002, and a programmed debt service amount of 8.1 percent of GDP (4.7 percent in amortizations and 3.4 percent of GDP in interest) for 2003 and 2004. To bring the debt to sustainable levels in the medium term, Ecuador will need primary surpluses of 5 percent of GDP. To close the financial gap in the next two years, Ecuador will require additional resources of about 4 percent of GDP. In addition, compared to other deeply indebted Latin American countries, Ecuador has limited administrative institutional capacity to manage their debt: it is strictly operative and not analytical, lacks transparency, and is fragmented and suffers from a lack of coordination between the Finance Ministry and the Central Bank.

Ecuador should develop a debt reduction strategy at the same time as it strengthens its institutional capacity. This will entail, first, ensuring a financing plan for 2003 and 2004, based on the following: a solid macroeconomic plan with credibility that permits capture of additional resources from multilateral agencies that can be quickly disbursed, a reprogramming of payments with bilateral creditors, and a repurchase of onerous debt held with private creditors. This reprogramming should include the goal of eliminating all arrears in 2003. Second, this program should require that the fiscal efforts mentioned above achieve a primary surplus of at least 5 percent of GDP. Third, debt management should be transparent, with regular publication of commitments and payments on debt service, including floating debt as stipulated in the fiscal law. Fourth, Ecuador should strengthen institutional support for debt management with the designation of a highly specialized team with adequate technical assistance.

The Competitiveness Agenda

Despite dollarization, both competitiveness abroad and the investment climate at home still do not look very promising. Nearly all global indicators show indisputable and consistent evidence that the competitiveness gaps are significant and growing. Ecuador ranked 54th out of 62 countries evaluated in terms of global competitiveness during the World Economic Forum in 2001. In 2002, Ecuador's ranking deteriorated even further when it was classified as 73rd among 80 countries, with the highest relative percentage for innovation and the lowest in terms of business climate, and respect for countries and for laws.

The implementation of a competitiveness agenda is critical to the sustainability of the dollarization process in the medium term. In consultation with the private sector, the Central Bank and Ministry of Foreign Trade have proposed Agendas for Competitiveness. However, these agendas lack priorities and a consensus on sequencing, which calls into question the realism of the measures proposed and the difficulties of implementing them. This is why one of the first steps of the new administration should be to design a simplified agenda of policies and laws that are critical to strengthening competitiveness. This agenda should begin with the revision of the Law of Competitiveness. The agenda should also include support measures to strengthen both the financial system and the petroleum industry, reform commercial policy, develop basic infrastructure, promote internal competition among firms, and eliminate both market entry-level barriers for new enterprises and rigidity of labor markets.

Strengthening the Financial System

The Ecuadoran financial system has been gradually recovering from the grave twin banking and exchange rate crises of 1998–99, and has been adapting to changes caused by the dollarization of the economy at the onset of 2000. The banking crisis drastically reduced the number of active financial institutions. Meanwhile, dollarization and related institutional changes—particularly those caused by the formal absence of an emergency lender—encouraged surviving institutions to favor holding assets and liabilities with the most liquidity in their balances, and promoting a greater concentration of banking. We are just beginning to see the end of the most dramatic part of the restructuring postcrisis process, thanks to the adoption of a new regulatory framework and more efficient supervision.

The structure and responsibilities of the supervising authorities have also changed. The banking restructuring process has been a test by fire for the entity charged with guaranteeing deposits (the Agency to Guarantee Deposits, AGD, also known as the Deposit Guarantee Agency—*Agencia de Garantía de Depósitos* in Spanish), and for the Superintendency of Banks and Insurance (SBS). On top of that, dollarization has modified the role of the Central Bank of Ecuador (BCE). In effect, because of the lack of monetary policy within a dollarization scheme, the BCE today focuses on liquidity management of the financial system, both to ensure proper functioning of payment mechanisms and to provide liquidity under similar conditions as an emergency lender.

In summary, there are important institutional and operational challenges that are blocking a definitive resolution to the crisis in the financial system. Some of the most pressing problems within the credit portfolio are that there is a high concentration of large loans in the unproductive portfolio and these are frequently awarded to related parties; the insurance coverage on deposits for many banks in the process of dissolution is too high and distorts the incentives of borrowers, increasing the "nonpayment culture"; portfolio quality has greatly deteriorated and credit continues to contract (the credit portfolio as a percentage of GDP is still half of what it was at precrisis levels); and the cost of credit is higher and small borrowers have access to lower amounts of credit. Another problem is that bank levels of liquid assets are high, which is justified in large part by the contraction of credit mentioned above. The impossibility of cushioning against external shocks through exchange policies, together with the lack of a lender of last resort, means that these assets are needed so that banks can absorb the terms-of-trade or international interest-rate shocks. This means a considerable additional financial cost. Finally, other relevant problems include the following: the interbanking payment system is still ineffective, the SBS's supervision of the quality of banking assets is also deficient, the role of the SBS and the AGD in the process of resolution and banking liquidation is too weak, and the balance established by public banks in their dual commercial and social function is inappropriate and works against their financial profitability.

In response to these challenges, banking credit activities need to be improved. First, we propose more efficient management of banking liquidity through centralized management. The BCE is a natural candidate for this central role given its current responsibility in the payment system. Second, the payment system needs to be reformed. The sequence of steps required for this reform should be codified in a public document, and a single net compensation system for checking transactions should be defined.

Third, it is vital for the SBS to continue to improve its procedures, particularly those related to the evaluation of credit risk and portfolio supply rules. In addition, it is important to consider the possibility of formulating procyclical provisions as Spain has done, since the Ecuadoran economy is extremely exposed to oil price cycles. It is also very important that SBS authorities be protected legally as they carry out their duties, and to make the legal changes that will allow them to improve procedures for bank resolution and liquidation. At the same time, the SBS accounting system should be strengthened. Finally, there must be total compliance with international laws governing money laundering (that is, coordinated efforts with related authorities) to increase confidence in the system, ensuring that the SBS can take legal action within a fully integrated legal system.

Fourth, we propose a normalization of exit mechanisms for banks. The formalization of the roles of the SBS and the AGD in the bank resolution and liquidation process should be strengthened, and the AGD functions revised. The alternative of converting them into a "pay box" should be considered. And fifth, we propose a reform of existing public banks (particularly first-tier banks), limiting their activity to targeted areas where subsidies, if needed, are transparent and minimal.

The Oil Sector

The strength of the oil sector is the main factor that determines the growth of the Ecuadoran economy, but it suffers from very serious distortions. The solution requires important actions that in turn depend on a large dose of political will. Some of the main problems in this sector are as follows:

- *Lack of judicial and fiscal stability.* Perhaps the most recent example is the elimination in August 2001 of the right to reimbursement of the IVA, which oil companies have been receiving for their exports. The previous administration was not sufficiently diligent in finding a solution to this problem, which seriously affects investments in the short and medium term. Without a quick solution, the IVA problem will reduce the fiscal impact hoped for when the new heavy crude oil pipeline (OCP) becomes operative.
- *Low production of fields with the greatest reserves and a low level of exploratory activity.* The level of investment in the exploration and development of this sector does not match its potential. Important oil reserves have been found, particularly in fields operated by PetroEcuador, and with new transport capabilities these could be put into production. The new investments should help resolve significant environmental liabilities, and work within programs and projects that respect the consultation rights of local populations. Their benefits should also be subject to a new framework of income distribution.
- *Numerous distortions in the prices and taxes of combustible fuels.* This is reflected in the prices and subsidies for natural gas (GLP). The management of oil income is totally incompetent, and this provokes distortions and promotes a fragmented and unproductive use lacking in transparency. The legal and institutional framework of the sector is outdated. PetroEcuador's monopoly does not allow nondiscriminatory treatment that would provide access to markets—treatment necessary to attract foreign investment and modernize refineries, improve product quality, and reduce the current elevated costs of commercialization and marketing.

The following measures are proposed. First, there should be an immediate solution to the IVA problem, adopting international arbitration or another procedure to resolve this conflict as quickly as possible.

Second, PetroEcuador's oil fields should increase production. The Law of Hydrocarbons contains several legal provisions that could be applied so that private enterprise can participate with PetroEcuador in oil activities. One possible framework is the formation of mixed-ownership corporations. A private investing partner for the *Petroproducción* enterprise could be found through an international bidding process.

Third, oil reserves should be increased. This will require the adoption of a new contract model; the recommendation here is to use the participation model.

Fourth, prior legislation should be complemented by a new legal and institutional framework that suppresses PetroEcuador's monopoly, favors competition, and provides incentives to invest in refineries and new distribution and marketing installations. A new legal framework should include provisions to rationalize responsibilities and ensure better management of the environmental and social impact of oil operations.

Fifth, the elimination of distortions in pricing policies is proposed to provide greater fiscal income, eliminate contraband, and eliminate the government's need to perform the onerous task of managing the price of combustible fuels. At the same time a targeted GLP subsidy should be established to compensate the poorest in the country. The proposed *bono gas*—cash payments to be given to families that currently receive the *Bono Solidario* (cash transfer)—is a good option, and can be improved upon.

Sixth, the system of preallocations of oil income should be revised and made more transparent, with the final identification of funds and accounting done as needed. In the amendment to the fiscal regulations proposed above, the government should establish new rules for oil income, promoting the gradual elimination of earmarking and promoting the optimal use of oil income. The government should create a permanent virtual database for income management that is universally accessible, in order to guarantee complete transparency.

And seventh, legal dispositions should be established to eliminate extrabudgetary spending in the oil sector and prohibit public indebtedness based on projected crude oil sales.

Commercial Reform

Commercial reform is fundamental to promoting nontraditional exports. While it is true that oil exports will continue to be the main engine of growth in Ecuador for the present decade, with the extension of extraction and oil export through the coming OCP, the diminishing role of oil and its replacement by nontraditional exports can be foreseen to occur in less than two decades. Unfortunately, a strong anti-export bias is blocking the development of nontraditional exports. This bias is not new and should not be erroneously attributed to dollarization, but rather has been generated by the discriminatory support given to certain nonproductive sectors that have been favored by an import substitution policy based on high tariffs and other nontariff barriers. This situation is preventing these sectors from modernizing and competing based on profitability. The combination of Ecuadoran tariff levels and tariff dispersion comprises such a wide and diverse range of effective protection rates that they escape government control. Tariff structure totally lacks rationality, desirable in an efficient import substitution policy.

The generalized Ecuadoran custom of protecting "final goods" with a higher tariff than that established for inputs, raw materials, and capital goods used in direct and indirect production, generates effective protection rates (the true protection of the aggregated value of final goods) that are unjustifiably high and vary among products. These rates benefit the sectors with the most efficient lobbies in terms of gaining the desired protection, but are not necessarily the most beneficial to the country's consumers. In addition, the tariff protection provided to many agricultural, agroindustrial products and derivatives, through a "Price Band System" that favors 138 different products, does not function efficiently. Very few bands comply with the goal of reducing price volatility, and if they comply with it, they cannot do it simultaneously with two other objectives of the bands—defending producers and consumers against the price distortions prevailing in international markets, and linking domestic prices with international prices. The Bands System used constitutes an ad valorem variable rate that lacks transparency, and has an upward bias that severely punishes Ecuadoran consumers, particularly the poorest. It has not slowed the tendency of prices to increase in the medium term.

The anti-export bias is reinforced by the discriminatory application of nontariff barriers such as prohibitions, licenses, technical norms, customs procedures, customs evaluations, norms on origin, safeguard measures, and public purchases. The import licenses are one of the most notable nontariff barriers. They are distributed in a nontransparent manner through a tortuous and fraudulent process. They are still applied to more than 20 percent of Ecuadoran imports, and are concentrated in the health and agricultural sectors. The majority of these licenses contradict the norms of the World Trade Organization (WTO). The lack of a national procedure for the application of technical norms is particularly insidious because an additional protectionist measure is added by not applying these norms to domestic products similar to the imported products.

Several measures are recommended to solve these problems. First, the customs tariff should be simplified to two rates of 5 and 10 percent. To the extent to which these efforts are successful and the 0 percent rate is eliminated, the fiscal impact would be neutral. The recent Latin American tendency is toward this type of structure and level. The measure would also have the advantage of homogenizing the effective protection rates, and would signify a huge step toward compliance with the future demands of the Free Trade Agreement of the Americas (FTAA).

Second, prior authorizations that did not register commercial activity from 1991 through 2000 (or 919 tariffs) and prior authorizations with a specific prerequisite (health and phytosanitary, among others) should be immediately eliminated. A single license is sufficient. Those remaining that require prior authorization should be submitted for technical analysis to justify remaining on the list of applicable licenses. If they do not pass this test, they should be eliminated from the legally mandated list.

Third, the number of bands should be drastically reduced, and they should be submitted to markers for an eligibility test applied to imports, and sensitive to the volatility of external prices. In the medium term, given that these bands are incompatible with WTO and FTAA norms, they should be eliminated.

Fourth, an increase in the productivity of the agricultural sector, especially the sector with export potential, should become a focus of permanent public effort, through technology development and transfer, particularly for small and medium producers.

Fifth, 759 existing obligatory technical standards should be evaluated to decide on their future. At the same time, the "deregulation or dismantling" process of obligatory norms should be carried out in a parallel manner with the "regulation or setting up" of the "WTO Regulation" system, information on which is found in the pertinent WTO legal documents. At the same time, laboratories should approve the test for ISO norm 17025.

Sixth, the draft of the Law of Competitiveness should be approved with minor modifications to accelerate the process, and supported with reinforced efficiency of customs controls and reduced corruption.

Development of Basic Infrastructure

The development of physical infrastructure represents another fundamental challenge for Ecuador because of its direct impact on growth, poverty levels, and the quality of life for the most vulnerable population. Four sectors require urgent attention: water and sanitation, electricity, telecommunications, and transport (highways and roads, railways, ports, and airports).

The sectors of water and sanitation, electricity, telecommunications, and transport confront problems such as low coverage (particularly in rural areas), efficiency and quality of services, an uncertain mobilization of resources for new investments and, with the exception of the electricity sector, incomplete institutional and regulatory frameworks. In general terms, the national government should address these challenges by seeking greater local, national, and international private sector participation, by consolidating institutional and legal arrangements. Above all, in the water and sanitation sectors and transport, the government should use central transferences of resources to encourage service providers to improve service and increase coverage.

In addition to these problems, the *water and sanitation* sector is characterized by low recovery of costs through charges, a high dependency on transferences from the central government to cover the deficit, and the lack of an integral national system of water resources. Given that all water and sanitation services comes from decentralized providers that depend on municipal governments, the central government has two main instruments for improving the quality and efficiency of services and ensuring their extension to rural and urban populations that do not yet have coverage: reforming the use of central transferences to provide incentives for profitability among service providers, and perfecting the legal and institutional framework.

The most urgent problems of the *electricity* sector also include inefficiency that is attributable to an incomplete reform process, institutional vulnerability, the uncertain sustainability of the wholesale electricity market, the rate readjustments needed to ensure the financial sustainability of this sector, and incomplete implementation of sectoral environmental policy. To confront these challenges it is imperative to reactivate the participation of the private sector in distribution and generation; moderate or eliminate state interference in the regulatory entity *Compañía Eléctrica del Ecuador* (CONELEC); normalize the wholesale electricity market's financial situation; reinitiate the adjustment of rates with the appropriate "lifeline"-type protection for poorer households; confront the problem of the *Empresa Eléctrica del Ecuador* (EMELEC) enterprise; develop a strategy for rural energy; and consolidate planning and sectoral environmental management systems, particularly in the Ministry of Energy and Mining and in CONELEC.

In addition to the general problems of national infrastructure, the *telecommunications* sector faces specific challenges including artificially low, unsustainable local rates for fixed telephone service; lack of competition in the cellular telephone market, leading to user costs that are among the highest in the region; and very limited Internet access. It is essential for the government to consolidate the institutional and legal framework and encourage greater private sector participation, attracting private capital to Andinatel and Pacifitel in order for them to make the investments the sector requires and to break up the duopoly in the cellular market.

The challenges in the *transport* sector include the poor condition of the highway network, the poor condition of local roads and the lack of transit services to rural areas, environmental problems, incoherent and insufficient sectoral and modal planning, and insufficient capacity and resources available to sectional governments to maintain provincial and local highways in the context of the decentralization process. The national government must contract maintenance services on the basis of results and promote private sector participation through microenterprises to maintain and pave rural roads, foster the creation of mixed ownership cooperatives for rural transport, award prizes for the best performance by sectional governments, improve environmental management in each sector, and transform the Ministry of Public Works into a new Ministry of Transport with regulatory and planning functions.

Urban Development

The "urbanization" of poverty has brought with it the "marginalization" of the cities, especially the large and medium-size ones. The percentages of population living in slums in Quito (30 percent) and Guayaquil (60 percent) are significantly higher than those found in other Latin American cities of a similar size. The situation in certain medium-size cities in the Sierra is also of concern. This has obvious implications for the proliferation of social problems, crime, and violence.

Living conditions in marginal areas are extremely precarious: houses are made of impermanent materials and sometimes even of items scavenged from trash; families live in overcrowded conditions with several persons sleeping in a single room and several families living in each dwelling, in many cases with no sewage hookup or running water. Statistics show that these conditions are most severe in the Sierra. The great number of recent natural disasters in both Quito and in Guayaquil makes living conditions even more precarious for the poor.

The formal housing market has problems of both supply and demand. On the one hand, the poorest population does not have sufficient income to live in acceptable housing, while on the other hand, the prices of developed land are inflated because of urban planning regulations and deficient market conditions. While land partially prepared for development may cost between $50 and $60 per square meter, completely undeveloped land in marginal areas costs $4 per square meter, the only price accessible to the poorest population. The Housing Incentives System (SIV), created in 2000 to improve this situation, provides direct subsidies on demand, but has managed to benefit only the richest 40 percent of the population.

An urban development policy should consider several factors. First, a comprehensive urban improvement program should be designed and implemented based on current and foreseeable quantitative and qualitative deficiencies in housing. This program should be national in scope, and have the fundamental goal of improving living conditions in marginal areas and reducing the physical, economic, and social vulnerability of the people living in these areas. It should be implemented by the municipalities, thus promoting a high degree of community participation. Second, the workings of urban land markets in the big cities must be reviewed to determine the obstacles hampering the availability of serviced land to the poorest population. Third, a system for preventing disasters must be designed and implemented at the national, municipal, and neighborhood levels. Such a system must be based on geo-referenced information systems, risk maps, technical training, public education, and institutional mechanisms that enable the integration of the different agencies that make up "the system." Fourth, it is advisable to examine the distribution of responsibilities for providing urban services, in order to locate and remove bottlenecks, redefine responsibilities among the different state agencies, and boost the capacity of municipal governments to understand, analyze, and reduce urban poverty.

Boosting Sustained and Equitable Social Development

High rural-to-urban migration, natural urban growth, and the country's deteriorating macroeconomic situation in the 1990s have led to increased urban poverty in Ecuador. Whereas in 1995, 19 percent of urban dwellers were poor, in 1999 this figure had jumped to 42 percent—more than double. It is clear that poverty is no longer only rural, and in fact is becoming increasingly urban in Ecuador: 33 percent of the country's poor lived in cities in 1995, while the 1999 figure was 48 percent, which means that almost half the poverty in the country was in urban areas.

At the same time, social spending has declined. During the 1990s, there was a significant reduction in spending on education and health. Education spending dropped from 6 percent of GDP in the 1980s to 2.7 percent in 2000, and health expenditures dropped to 1.7 percent, far below the 2.8 percent spent in 1990. Meanwhile, spending on social protection has risen to 1.5 percent of GDP in recent years (not including the hydrocarbons subsidy).

The health and education sectors share similar problems in terms of poor coverage and low-quality services, especially for poor and indigenous people in the urban periphery and rural areas. There are no anticyclical social programs in Ecuador, despite the country's having an oil-based economy subject to great fluctuations in international prices. The main social protection program is the *Bono Solidario* and various food assistance programs.

The social security system is the traditional "pay-as-you-go" type, combining pensions and health care. It maintains a financial surplus thanks to a young, formal labor force, payment of low benefits, poor coverage, and low-quality health services. This surplus has attracted the interest of several actors, especially the national government, which has deposited a large part of its reserves here, and private groups that have demanded the creation of social programs that have not been very well focused, such as the *Seguro Social Campesino* (Rural People's Social Security Program, SSC), a noncontributory fund for pensions and health services to benefit rural groups in selected areas of the country.

Education

Despite the great advances in primary coverage at the national level, major challenges remain in the area of education: 11 percent of the population over age 15 is illiterate, and the net rate of primary school attendance is close to 90 percent. This drops to 51 percent in secondary school and 14 percent in higher education. There are great differences in coverage between rural and urban areas and between indigenous and nonindigenous populations. The system is unbalanced at all levels: the poor and indigenous school-age population is at a great disadvantage compared to the rest of the population, and basic, diversified, and university education are aimed mainly at the urban population with above-average income.

The quality of basic education is quite low. Results of academic achievement testing (APRENDO) show deficiencies in the quality of teaching at the basic level. This involves factors related to the educational establishment, teachers, and the socioeconomic conditions in which students live. Limited access of students and teachers to scholastic materials affects student results. Nearly a third of primary schools have only one teacher, who in most cases has not been trained in multigrade methodology.

As a result of the severe reductions in public spending, the necessary investments have not been made in the education sector, the maintenance of infrastructure is minimal, teaching supplies provided are insufficient, and teacher salaries have been reduced. Spending on education is very poorly balanced: the fifth quintile of the population with the lowest income receives 12 percent of public spending, while the fifth quintile with the highest income receives 25 percent.

The sector has serious problems of governance and administration. The system is characterized by high turnover of top-level authorities; the Ministry of Education and Culture (MEC) has administrative units with identical functions; the administration is excessively centralized; there is little communication among the MEC, its provincial offices, and schools; the selection, hiring, and promotion of teachers is an opaque process; the distribution of teachers is not adequate (there are too many teachers in some areas and not enough in others); and the salary structure for teachers has no relation to the objectives of improving the quality and balance of the system.

Solving these problems requires comprehensive educational reform. First, all Ecuadoran children should have access to and should complete basic education, and should have access to better-quality schooling. Programs aimed at increasing coverage must be focused on groups that are now underserved, such as those with the lowest income levels and those living in rural and indigenous areas. The MEC must consider innovative choices of methodology, such as "tele-high school," to reach the most underprivileged groups.

Second, to improve quality, the MEC must evaluate different options or strategies to attract new teachers on an ongoing basis, design a plan to provide the educational system with at least the minimum teaching materials that are necessary, and institutionalize the APRENDO system for measuring results, while giving special attention to strengthening bilingual education in the country.

Third, public spending on education must be gradually increased to 1980s levels—that is, 6 percent of GDP.

Fourth, it is essential that the sector be better managed in order to properly allocate economic resources and achieve the desired results. At the same time, pilot decentralization projects must be initiated, offering greater autonomy to the educational system and greater parent participation in school management.

Health

As in education, there are numerous coverage problems in the health sector. About 30 percent of the population still does not have access to basic health services. More than two-thirds of the population does not have formal health insurance and the Ministry of Public Health (MSP) and other public institutions are unable to provide service to almost half of these individuals—precisely those with the worst health indicators. Insufficiently attended births and lack of access to basic health care are the main factors responsible for an unbalanced epidemiological profile.

A direct result of poor coverage is reflected in high infant and maternal mortality rates and premature births. It is estimated that for every 100,000 births, 160 mothers die as a result of complications related to pregnancy, birth, or postnatal problems, and 4,300 children die before their first birthday. Deaths due to infections and violence that particularly affect the young population are as common as mortality due to cancer, and interregional differences in these indicators are so great that life expectancy in the province of Pichincha is 15 times as high as in the Amazon provinces.

Public health spending is insufficient and private spending is unfairly distributed. Private spending represents 80 percent of all health spending, and it is the poorest people whose income is most proportionally affected by this expense (up to 40 percent of their income).

Reform of the health sector requires a number of actions. First, we propose that the Law on Free Maternity Care (LMG) be strengthened and broadened. A model must be established that avoids duplication of coverage and promotes the broadening of coverage, while considering the social and cultural factors that limit the demand for basic services.

Second, coverage by the SSC must be increased along with that of the LMG. The SSC's financial limitations are too great for it to be broadened to cover the remaining 3 million people, but the mother–child population not covered currently may benefit from the services provided under the LMG.

Third, we propose that basic health services be included through the *Bono Solidario* for the retired and disabled: preventive and informational services, outpatient treatment, and hospitalization for prevailing acute illnesses, and a basic package for chronic illnesses and surgery. This would provide coverage to approximately 230,000 pensioners and 8,000 disabled persons who have no other resources for medical attention.

Fourth, the essential functions of the MSP must be redefined, shifting from its role as a supplier of services to a new role as an organism accrediting establishments, monitoring the quality of services, creating a health monitoring system, and providing training in order to intervene in situations of epidemiological risk, among other tasks. As part of the redefinition of the MSP's functions, service provision arrangements could be established with the Ecuadoran Social Security Institute (IESS).

Fifth, we propose creating a regulatory framework for developing a system of regional health services networks with levels scaled according to their complexity. The MSP installations, decentralized establishments, and the SSC would all participate, and at the local level would focus their efforts on primary care and programs for providing basic services.

Sixth, we propose broadening SSC coverage, possibly creating a new insurance program for the poor population, which would consolidate and progressively replace the benefits of the LMG and the provisions of the *Bono Solidario*.

Protecting the Most Vulnerable

The banking and exchange rate crises have generated new demands for social assistance. The most vulnerable groups facing chronic poverty have been joined by groups requiring temporary social assistance. In 2001, Ecuador planned to spend close to $264 million on 22 Priority Social Programs (PSPs), which represents about 1.5 percent of GDP, similar to the average in the countries of the region. About 60 percent of this amount was allocated to two programs for transferring cash: the *Bono Solidario* and the *Beca Escolar* (Educational Scholarships). The two most important programs immediately became the School Breakfast and Lunch program—$US24 million—and the *Bono Solidario*—$US154.5 million, in 2001. Though the subsidies for the consumption of natural gas and gasoline are not included among the 22 PSPs, they came to about $US500 million for 2000.

This social assistance network has its problems. Its functions (and budget) are not countercyclical—that is, they do not have the ability to expand in times of crisis and contract in normal circumstances. This manifests itself in the absence of PSPs with established minimum spending levels, and in the lack of a mechanism for automatically updating the list of beneficiaries. The network also contains several programs with regressive spending, and lacks consistent criteria for maintaining a steady focus. This is not an exception in the area of social spending; in fact, a high percentage of spending on universal social programs ends up benefiting the population with higher-than-average income (for example, energy subsidies or school meals). Also, targeted programs vary in their effectiveness in reaching the lowest-income groups, and do not use consistent targeting criteria (for example, the *Bono Solidario* and National Child and Family Institute [INNFA] programs). Several programs cover vulnerable groups inadequately, despite their multiple interventions. Finally, the *Bono Solidario* has several flaws: it does not have a mechanism that enables it to include new beneficiaries; there were errors in its original focus on the target population; there is a lack of clarity in the program's objectives and benefits are insufficient; and it does not generate mechanisms for ending dependence on the *Bono*. The lack of an evaluation of the impact of the *Bono* prevents a more complete overview of its performance.

To improve the social assistance network, we propose the following. First, its flexibility must be increased. For example, the establishment of minimum budgets for certain PSPs would enable it to set up a "virtual" social assistance fund with protected amounts within the budget to resist cyclical fluctuations.

Second, the creation of a clearly counter-cyclical program, for example, in public works, is feasible. This should offer a sufficiently low salary to attract only very poor persons in crisis.

Third, it is crucial to improve the coordination and targeting of existing programs. To do so, we suggest adopting a single criterion for targeting social assistance programs.

Fourth, it is necessary not only to increase, but also to redirect the *Bono Solidario* toward a conditioned subsidies program. The *Bono* should be oriented toward protecting the health of children and pregnant women in poverty.

Social Security

The Ecuadoran social security system has problems with coverage, management, and institutional status. The coverage of the active and elderly population protected by the formal system (the Obligatory Social Insurance of the IESS) is one of the lowest in the region. An overview of other noncontributory programs, such as the SSC and the *Bono Solidario*, reveals broader coverage, but their benefits are too small to constitute effective protection for the elderly. Another problem is the IESS's uncertain financial balance. The IESS counts as active a state debt corresponding to contributions that have not been deposited for more than a decade. The amount of this debt differs significantly depending on whether it is calculated by the IESS or by the Ministry of Economy and Finances. Furthermore, IESS reserves are not clearly separated or earmarked for health, old age, disability, and death, making it possible that there are invisible cross-subsidies. Another issue is that the state is legally obligated to contribute 40 percent of pensioner benefits each year, even when the IESS pension program has a surplus, thus generating unnecessary fiscal pressure. The legal status of system reform presents another problem. In November 2001, a new Social Security law sanctioned a new institutional design that was to be immediately implemented. However, its full application was blocked by a decision of the Constitutional Court, which in turn was overruled by the judicial system. As a result, the new law is only partially applicable, and the IESS has opted to apply certain aspects of it while ignoring others at its own discretion.

We propose several measures to correct these deficiencies. First, the amount paid out by the SSC (and the *Bono Solidario*) must be corrected to levels close to 50 percent of the poverty line. This would mean redefining a strategy for broadening SSC coverage and noncontributory payments. Second, there must be a quick resolution of the differences between the IESS and the government regarding the government's debt to the IESS, based on clearly presented documentation. Third, we propose effectively separating the accounts and reserves of the IESS according to type of insurance. Fourth, an amendment should be made to correct the Law Reforming the Social Security to eliminate its current confusions and errors and to completely separate pension and health policies. Consideration could also be given in this amendment to reducing the percentage contributed by the state, thus reducing fiscal pressure on it. This could become effective once the state has paid its pending debt with the IESS. Fifth, in the medium term, an integrated coverage model should be applied, extending coverage to segments of society now excluded, especially the poor and the elderly.

Rural Development

Three essential factors highlight the importance of rural development for Ecuador: (a) the economy's high dependence on natural resources, including agricultural products, hydrocarbons, and forest and mining products; (b) the concentration of poverty in predominantly rural areas; and (c) the great natural, social, and cultural wealth and diversity in the rural areas of the country. The contribution made by natural resources from four sectors (agriculture, mining, forestry, and hydrocarbons) comes to about 40 percent of GDP. However, not enough environmental care is taken in the exploitation of these resources, nor are the resulting benefits fairly shared. The result is the accelerating degradation of soils, rivers, and coasts, and a great economic gap between rural and urban areas. Despite the severity of this situation, public policies dealing with rural development in Ecuador have suffered from a lack of coordination, excessive fragmentation by sector and centralization, resulting in inefficient public and private investment. Many rural policies have concentrated on the agricultural sector, while little attention has been given to other areas.

Therefore, a new set of policies must be established to guarantee the sustainability of natural resources, reduce rural poverty, and recognize the value of the cultural and natural wealth of the rural sector. The emphasis on agricultural production as the engine for rural development is shifting in favor of diversified production, links between the rural environment and the cities, access to markets as an engine for growth, and the development of local capacity. At the same time, centralized administrative approaches are being replaced by demand-driven processes and local decisionmaking, in which the aim is to try to discover and incorporate antipoverty strategies proposed by the beneficiaries themselves in their own surroundings.

In this context, with a view toward diversified economic growth and reduced rural poverty, a strategy of diversified, multisectoral rural development with a territorial approach must be designed. This strategy would have three main goals: (a) economic and social cohesion through the development of local spaces, (b) changes in agriculture and rural economic diversification, and (c) environmental protection. Ecuador's geographic, economic, and sociocultural diversity requires that this strategy take a variety of forms and be backed by development policies focusing on participatory action in local or rural spaces to foster economic and social cohesion; diversification of the rural economy; nonagricultural job creation through investment in rural and social infrastructure and fostering a competitive agricultural sector through up-to-date technology and research; and promoting environmental protection through better regulation of land use, recovery of land conservation methods, and other uses of natural resources.

This strategy will also require an institutional structure that facilitates the coordination of the different institutions involved. The institutional regulations that can guide this effort must be based on cooperation among the national public sector, the private sector, the rest of civil society, municipalities and provincial governments, and local governments; coherence among the regulations and activities of the different institutions; programming based on the strategic plans of each jurisdiction; and financial allocations based on the concept of "additionality" as incentives for guaranteeing the implementation of strategic plans.

Environment

The problem of poverty in Ecuador is exacerbated by two key variables: environmental pollution and natural disasters. Any strategy for the country's economic growth and social development will depend on controlling the degradation of the biophysical environment and on the sustainable management of natural resources. Controlling pollution and preventing the effects of natural disasters on the population both demand the highest priority and greatest attention on the part of environmental authorities.

There are two basic ways the state can intervene to develop environmental policy: environmental regulations, and environmental administration and investment. Environmental regulation includes different tools such as economic instruments, direct regulation, and administrative procedures. Environmental administration and investment include the management of state-owned assets and environmental investment in sectors that face the environmental conditions associated with poverty in Ecuador.

Among the choices of tools for environmental regulation, the development and strengthening of command-and-control regulations merits special attention, particularly regulations on zoning ordinances and land use, monitoring of water and air quality, management of dangerous wastes, and final disposal of solid wastes. At the international level, instruments for strategic environmental evaluation are also used to define environmental investment priorities in the various sectors. To reduce rural vulnerability to natural disasters, investment in structural and nonstructural damage prevention resources is urgently needed. Structural measures include resettlement of populations living on flood plains, public works for flood control, use of wetlands as buffers against flooding, and public works to control erosion and stabilize embankments. Nonstructural measures include regulating land use, designing programs for responding and attending to emergencies, and equipping and preparing the population for such events.

Building a Quality Government That Serves All Ecuadorans and Fights against Corruption

The problems of poor government and high levels of corruption in Ecuador are legendary and contribute to poor public services. Moreover, it is worrisome that compared to recent developments in Latin America as a whole, almost all indicators of governance and control of corruption in the country have shown significant and constant deterioration since 1998. The most dramatic changes can be seen in the quality of the country's regulations, civil society control and participation, effective government, respect for the law, and control of corruption (for which Ecuador has the lowest rating of any country in the region). While Ecuadorans are proud of themselves, they express a generalized lack of confidence in national government institutions and a slightly higher level of confidence in subnational governments. On a scale of 0 to 100, the confidence of Ecuadorans in their political system was 37, among the lowest ratings in Latin America.

The results of recent surveys, one by the University of Pittsburgh/Cedatos/Gallup and another by the World Bank, confirm that corruption is a very serious problem, especially in the awarding of contracts and when receiving public services. The frequency of bribery varies according to the service provided, and it is less common among local government services. Nonetheless, if decentralization continues and efforts are not made to establish appropriate controls, people believe that the level of municipal corruption could increase. Evidence shows that corruption worsens poverty and inequality, since the income of the poorest users is proportionally more affected by bribery, which does not necessarily translate into better-quality services. Also, this phenomenon is a disincentive to the population, and limits access to public services. As a result, it is estimated that corruption reduces the state's potential tax income by about a third, rerouting it inappropriately to private hands.

A reform program must focus on both the public sector and the civil service. International experience suggests that public institutions with merit-motivated staff, transparent management, efficient anticorruption mechanisms, high morale, and the will to carry out reforms, both perform better and are capable of significantly reducing corruption. In general, a multidimensional reform plan focusing on three areas is necessary: (a) strengthening existing regulations and institutions in the fight against corruption, which covers not only the public sector, but also the private sector and civil society in general; (b) educating the population regarding the people's right to supervise public functions, which implies the development of mechanisms for monitoring public spending, guaranteeing the population—especially Congress, the media, and civil society organizations—easy, permanent access to fiscal accounts; and (c) improving governance to prevent corruption in its various forms, whether administrative or linked to specific areas such as purchasing from and contracts with public agencies. Each form of corruption is associated with a specific institutional weakness and thus requires an equally specific solution.

In accordance with this general approach, we propose several short-term measures, including a Governance Pact between the state and civil society. The participation of political parties and civil society in the Pact must be actively encouraged by forming an executive committee with broad powers and a clear mandate to design and implement an anticorruption strategy. The Pact must be complemented by similar efforts on the part of the government, aimed at reforming the public administration, such as developing new procedures for providing updated budget information, hiring staff, establishing public service quality standards subject to sanctions if not met, and quickly and reliably reporting corruption. Given their special importance, offers and contracts for public purchasing must be published regularly and immediately on the government's Web site, including all information relating to its decisions in this area.

In the medium term, complementary measures would include modernizing budget management to make it accessible to citizens in electronic form, and regulating finances and contributions to political campaigns to make them transparent and to prevent "state capture" by specific economic interests. Similarly, it is important to ban or strictly limit the use of state resources for political campaigns. It is also essential to strengthen mechanisms for administration, control, and public monitoring of sectional governments, taking advantage of citizens' more moderate perception of corruption at these levels of government. Finally, a National Transparency Campaign would have to be part of the ongoing task of reeducating the populace.

Labor Markets and the Civil Service

Ecuador's dollarization led to a complete transformation of the role of the labor markets, since it meant that their external and internal competitiveness no longer depended on devaluations. This has made a flexible and productive labor market a central feature of sustained economic growth. Also, as mentioned, an efficient civil service is essential in the fight against corruption and to achieve significant improvements in the provision of public services.

Labor indicators show there has been some recovery from the impact of the end-of-century crises. Formal employment declined until 2000, then gradually rose to around the 1998 level. This recovery is partial, however, and hides deeper effects such as that of half a million Ecuadorans (the most economically active population) emigrating to other countries; the continuous migration from the countryside to the cities; and the fact that the underemployment rate remains three times as high as in 1998, which reflects that a growing number of workers work fewer than 40 hours a week (visible underemployment), or are paid less than their stipulated wages (invisible underemployment). The growth of income and real wages shows a similar trend: a steep drop in 1999, followed by a slight recovery to above 1998 levels (both in nominal and real 1998 dollars), with a relatively greater increase in the informal sector than in the formal sector.

Although the Economic Transformation Law simplified wage policy in the private sector and introduced new and more flexible forms of hiring through hourly and temporary contracts, the system continues to be excessively rigid. On one hand, the Sectoral Tables, based on the minimum wage established by the National Wages Council (*Consejo Nacional de Salarios*, CONADES), involve automatic indexing which, in case the parties do not reach an agreement, grants a minimum annual increase similar to the inflation rate projected for the following year. These increases not only have nothing to do with productivity, but also act as just the starting point for additional increases negotiated within each sector or as part of collective agreements. This indexing mechanism, while desirable as a means of quickly lowering inflation, becomes a serious obstacle to competitiveness when inflation stabilizes near international levels. On the other hand, the proliferation of temporary work agencies (about 200 created in recent years, covering about 10 percent of formal employment)—a phenomenon known as "outsourcing"—does not allow for adequate monitoring, worsens labor relations, and makes it difficult to ensure that the minimum labor requirements are being met by the companies doing the hiring.

The civil service also presents serious problems. First, the proliferation of salary perks and contracting under inappropriate categories (services) makes it practically impossible to determine the exact number of workers and the size of the payroll, while raising the cost of "base" salary increases granted by the government. Also, the regulations promulgated by the new CONAREM are virtually irrelevant (more than 150 regulations in less than three years). No agency controls the public payroll, thus leading to ad hoc bilateral labor negotiations between each public institution and the Ministry of the Economy and Finances. The situation is chaotic.

Special attention must be paid to wage levels and the degree of labor flexibility. We propose two measures for the private sector. First, future wage increases must be brought in line with increases in work productivity, simplifying the wage negotiation process by no longer revising wages according to predicted inflation, minimizing the role of the "sectoral tables" and establishing a single minimum wage. Second, sufficient labor flexibility must be guaranteed in the formal sector without imposing excessive costs on workers and reducing the nonwage costs of formal employment through better regulation of the use of temporary work agencies by companies carrying out permanent activities, promoting the use of temporary and by-the-hour contracts when this is necessary, and eliminating the rule on redistributing 15 percent of profits to workers.

Regarding the civil service, the fundamental goal of the new government must be to begin to rationalize the public sector. The draft of the proposed Wage Unification Law (*Ley de Unificación Salarial*) is a good start, though it could be improved. In the context of wage unification, it is advisable to maintain wage supplements based on geographic location for doctors and teachers to guarantee minimum health and education services in remote areas. Wage unification must also be combined with a process for restructuring public employment—reducing personnel if necessary—and reinforcing the system for controlling public hiring by means of a centralized register, as proposed in the draft of the Wage Unification Law, in the SIGEF.

Judicial Reform

Despite the progress made in specific areas of judicial reform, people do not have confidence in the formal Ecuadoran justice system because it is not easily accessible, is slow and inefficient, and is perceived as vulnerable to corruption. These problems, in turn, are associated with the low level of professional training received by those who operate the system, limited resources, and the use of inadequate administration and control models. The initial stage of the Comprehensive Reform Plan, approved in 1996 and revised in 2001, has been completed, and is aimed at laying the groundwork for bigger future changes. But it has not yet managed to improve the administration of justice to a degree perceptible to the public.

In this context, the private sector and the rest of civil society are convinced that a coherent and comprehensive process is essential to achieve medium-term results. This involves actions aimed at recovering public confidence in the administration of justice, improving the professional quality of judges, increasing efficiency in the management of justice, and broadening access to justice. Such a process must enhance what has already been achieved, using it as starting point. This will necessitate a reconsideration of regulations, operators, costs, infrastructure, and administration and management systems. It will also necessitate a reconsideration of the structure of the judicial system and of institutions such as the Constitutional Court and the Justice Ministry, each formally independent but which have an impact on the judicial system.

Decentralization

The main problem of the Ecuadoran public administration system is that centralized decisionmaking has negatively affected the quality of services. Decentralization can—subject to certain rules and principles—contribute to solving this problem. Since the provincial and municipal councils are closer to users of services, these councils could provide more creative and efficient solutions than the central government.

Ecuador faces three main challenges on the road to decentralization: (a) clearly defining areas of responsibility for a second tier of public administration (functional decentralization)—comprising regional development agencies, executive units, social funds, and attached bodies—in relation to the provincial and municipal councils; (b) modifying the transfer of resources to include transfers of authority; and (c) managing local government debt with fiscal responsibility, sustainability, and transparency. Without rules and a framework of clear incentives, decentralization cannot be maintained.

The four most important recommendations for reinforcing decentralization are as follows: First, at the intermediate (provincial) level of government, we propose that a transition strategy be implemented in which dependent, decentralized bodies must report to elected authorities—that is, the Prefect and the Provincial Council. At the ministerial level, this means appointing provincial sectoral managers (decentralized ministerial area) with a list of three candidates proposed by the Prefect; and at the level of regional development bodies, establishing the Directorate according to the provincial prefects that correspond to each jurisdiction, with a representative of the central government. The budget must be approved by this new Directorate.

Second, regarding the special law transferring 15 percent of the central government's current income, we propose that the exact amount transferred be determined and that this transfer process be carried out transparently. If the central government has the fiscal room to raise transfers beyond the current 10 to 11 percent, and once the budget emergency is over, transfers should be made based on the additional income effectively received, and these resources should be pegged to the simultaneous transfer of powers and the delivery of results.

Third, regarding subnational debt, we propose regulating this in a transparent process to promote fiscal responsibility, which means rescheduling debt with municipalities and provincial councils with excessive debt and reporting this in the government's annual budget document. We also suggest publishing the debt write-offs made in the past five years; researching and publishing different ways that local governments can acquire debt (contingencies, floating debt); and requiring that outside agencies give an independent credit rating for new loan applications from the three biggest cities.

Fourth, we propose introducing safeguards to the system for contracting transfers of powers in order to clarify responsibilities and rights at each level of government. This means limiting access to the program for transferring powers by requiring that subnational governments meet minimum standards of accounting, budget management, and regular financial reporting—and completing the transfer agreements with clauses stipulating financial calculations (debt, investments), sanctions for noncompliance, the reversibility of the transfers, and dispute settlement procedures.

D. The Vision of a New Ecuador

This book highlights the difficult fiscal and debt situation faced by the new Ecuadoran officials, and the limitations they themselves see in terms of being able to implement ambitious development while maintaining fiscal discipline. For that reason, the extensive agenda described above requires correct prioritization and sequencing, possibly beginning with measures to consolidate fiscal sustainability and deal with urgent foreign debt commitments. This could be accompanied by a prioritization of spending and the preparation of institutional reforms—especially ones such as the Governance Pact, aimed at eradicating corruption and strengthening governance on the basis of consensus, participation, and active social monitoring—giving the new government an image that suggests change and transparency. The officials should, to the extent possible, avoid giving in to pressures of a populist nature, which usually have a high fiscal cost with only a brief impact on demand. Not only the design but also the implementation of the agenda must be consistent. We believe that a solid start on the part of the government will enable it to earn the political capital to make further medium-term advances in the reform agenda. To facilitate this work, we have attached a set of suggestions for priority action. The intention is not for all of these to be adopted; rather, they represent an independent opinion of the work involved in developing a government agenda. The World Bank recognizes the complexity of creating this vision of a new Ecuador, and will continue to offer its support to officials in the design and implementation of its strategy for economic and social development aimed at reducing poverty.

Table 1. Ecuador: A Possible Order of Priorities in the Design and Implementation of Policies for Boosting Economic and Social Development

FIRST STAGE

Protecting the Macroeconomic Framework	*Send Early Confidence-Building Signals*	*Make Poverty Reduction an Explicit Priority*
• Pass an austere 2003 budget • Announce tax reform (with compensatory social measures) • Reverse "relaxed tax collection" policies • Announce the amalgamation of SRI with Customs within one year • At least freeze overall salary mass (zero growth) in real terms	• Review and widely publicize the state of fiscal accounts • Approve a solid and credible macroeconomic program • Announce a 2003 plan for financing foreign debt • Settle disputes with the oil companies • Make privatization and deregulation priorities on the agenda • Pass the Labor Unification Act (*Ley de Unificación Laboral*) with neutral fiscal cost and give up automatic wage indexing and mandatory application of the Sectorial Tables	• Approve greater spending on education and health in 2003 • Replace the gas subsidy with a more specifically focused subsidy • Increase and apply conditions to *Bono Solidario* benefits • Approve spending on priority social programs at least similar to 2002 levels

The First Steps toward Accelerated Growth	*Design and Initiate the Strategy against Poverty*	*Put Governance at the Top of the Agenda*
• Approve new forms of contracts with oil companies to allow mixed investment • Restart electric rates adjustment • Allow Andinatel and Pacifictel to take part in private ventures • Approve an amended Competition Act and simplify the business registration process • Eliminate preallocations, marginal taxes, and	• Combine the coverage of the Rural People's Social Security program (SSC) and the Free Maternity Care program • Institutionalize the APRENDO program to monitor advances in the quality of education • Complete the participatory evaluation and focus of the Priority Social Programs (and the *Bono*)	• Sign a Governance Pact • Present a Plan for Fighting Corruption and a National Transparency Campaign • Approve a Law on Oil Income Transparency • Post acquisitions and quarterly reports on the fiscal situation on the government website

• pre-import licenses that have specific prerequisites • Evaluate state-owned banks and stiffen regulations on precautionary monitoring	• Evaluate the feasibility of insurance for the elderly, of health care for the retired and disabled through the *Bono Solidario*, and of a cycle-resistant social employment program • During the fiscal emergency, freeze contributions by sectional governments above the 10-to-11-percent level, increasing them afterward, based on new responsibilities • Clear up the state's debt to the IESS and clarify the Law Reforming the Social Security System	• Turn the Ministry of Public Works into a regulatory body and create a Concessions Office • Unify payrolls in an SIGEF module • Approve unified municipal financial system regulations • Complete design of reformed judicial system

SECOND STAGE

Consolidate Stability and Growth	*Implement Poverty-Reduction Strategy*	*Develop Measures for Rural and Urban Development*
• Simplify customs tariffs, reduce the number of bands, and eliminate pre-importation authorizations • Eliminate most of the 759 technical regulations and use WTO regulations • Complete the reform of the hydrocarbons sector • Centralize BCE liquidity management and reform banking payment system • Improve banking systems for resolution and liquidation • Complete sectoral reforms and crossed subsidies in infrastructure • Pass Water and Sewage Act	• Refocus spending on longer-term social objectives • Reevaluate the state's contribution to the IESS and its links with the Ministry of Health • Begin transferring budget resources on the basis of results • Expand virtual SIGEF to other public bodies • Regulate subnational debt, modify system for taking on powers, and develop transition strategy at mid-ministerial level	• Design Urban Improvements Plan • Prepare a Disaster Prevention System • Create technological and financial programs with export potential for the agricultural sector

Part I

Preserving Stability with Fiscal Discipline and Accelerating Growth with Competitiveness

1

Maintaining Stability with Fiscal Discipline and Competitiveness[1]

José R. López-Cálix

Ecuador finds itself at a crossroads. Dollarization has allowed the country to overcome hyperinflation, restore confidence in the banking system, and lift the veil of money that prevented it from seeing clearly the serious imbalances in the fiscal, financial and real sectors that plagued its economy. Based on that achievement, and on their country's temporary boom in petroleum revenues and remittances, the new authorities face a dilemma. They must either take the path of austerity and competitiveness, achieving fiscal discipline as a prerequisite for the structural changes needed to raise Ecuador's productivity and eliminate serious distortions in domestic markets, or once again squander the country's petroleum riches with expansive, anachronistic, and corrupt spending policies that protect private incomes. The known effects on demand of the latter course might be positive in the short term but are undoubtedly disastrous in the medium term, as demonstrated by the crisis of 1999. Although this dilemma is independent of dollarization, there is no doubt that such an exchange system is unsustainable if the latter course is followed.

1. José R. López-Cálix is a principal economist at the World Bank. The chapter was prepared with the valuable research assistance of Elaine Tinsley and Branko Maric. The author appreciates the contributions made by Norbert Schady (Poverty), Carolina Sánchez-Páramo (Labor Markets), and James Hanna (Competitiveness) as well as the valuable suggestions of Vicente Fretes-Cibils, Sara Calvo, and McDonald Benjamin. He is also indebted to the authorities at the Central Bank of Ecuador, Mauricio Yépez, Leopoldo Báez and Francisco Hidalgo; as well as the Ministry of Economy and Finance, Mauricio Pozo, Gilberto Pazmiño, Daniel Badillo; Roberto Salazar, Diego Mancheno, and Mauricio Pareja for their support in the preparation of this chapter and for their comments at the seminar held in Quito on January 11, 2003. At the request of the authorities, this chapter was updated with the new statistical information in the national accounts available as of January 22, 2003.

A. Background

Since its return to democracy in 1979, Ecuador has been characterized by high external vulnerability, weak macroeconomic performance, and ungovernability. Successive external shocks—tied to reductions in petroleum prices or violent fluctuations in the country's capital flows as in 1998—and natural disasters have combined with poor macroeconomic management reflected in high fiscal deficits. These developments often preceded very high rates of inflation (Figure 1) and foreign exchange instability. This led the country to four severe recessions (1982–83, 1987, 1989, and 1998–99); three hyperinflationary periods (1983, 1988–93, and 1999–2000); high and unsustainable external debt reflected in various payment moratoria; and a recent twin crisis—in foreign exchange and banking—that destroyed 20 banks holding 40 percent of bank deposits. Misguided policies were the result of unstable government administration and the traditional ungovernability that is characteristic of the petroleum countries. In 23 years, Ecuador had 29 finance ministers who remained in office an average of 10 months, and was the country with the least perceived control over corruption in Latin America (see chapter 15 on Governance and Corruption). The twin crisis led to formal dollarization of the country in 2000 (Box 1). This chapter analyzes recent macroeconomic performance, challenges on the horizon, and possible solutions.

Ecuador dollarized not by choice but as the inevitable way out for dealing with its twin crises in 1999. The country was very far from having met all the preconditions for successful dollarization, including a solid fiscal position; sustainable public debt; a diversified export structure to accommodate unfavorable shocks to its terms of trade; a sufficiently high level of international reserves (at least to cover the monetary base) as a mechanism for absorbing capital outflows; a sound and competitive banking system under strong supervision to prevent the formation of contingent liabilities; flexible markets for nontradable production factors—particularly labor and real estate—to accommodate the price adjustments required to preserve the competitiveness of the nontradable goods sector or adjust them in case of recession; and a suitable climate for attracting investment that would provide access to technology and respect for the law. Despite these disadvantages, dollarization allowed the country to achieve two short-term objectives. It brought down hyperinflation and restored confidence in the banking system. The law also explicitly indicated the minimum conditions under which Ecuador should gradually achieve sustainable dollarization in the medium term.

The crisis of 1998–99 had a devastating effect on poverty levels. The incidence of poverty (the headcount) increased dramatically from 34 to 56 percent of the population between 1995 and 1999 (Parandekar, Vos, and Winkler 2002). This means that the number of poor people grew by more than two million during the crisis. Similarly, the number of people living in extreme poverty (that is, people whose income is insufficient to cover basic needs) increased from 12 to 21 percent in a similar period. The crisis hit rural areas most severely, especially in the highlands

Figure 1. Relationship between Fiscal Deficits (% GDP) and Inflation, 1980–2002

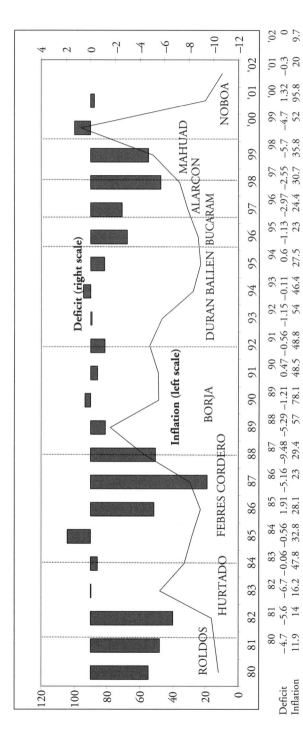

	'80	81	82	83	84	85	86	87	88	89	90	91	92	93	94	95	96	97	98	99	'00	'01	'02
Deficit	−4.7	−5.6	−6.7	−0.06	−0.56	1.91	−5.16	−9.48	−5.29	−1.21	0.47	−0.56	−1.15	−0.11	0.6	−1.13	−2.97	−2.55	−5.7	−4.7	1.32	−0.3	0
Inflation	11.9	14	16.2	47.8	32.8	28.1	23	29.4	57	78.1	48.5	48.8	54	46.4	27.5	23	24.4	30.7	35.8	52	95.8	20	9.7

Source: Gallardo (2001); World Bank.

Box 1. The Economic Transformation Law

Approved by Congress in March 2000, the Law contains measures for transitioning to dollarization and a program of structural reforms, most of which are still incomplete. These measures are as follows:

- *Dollarization*: prohibits the issuance of new sucres, except coins; obligates the Central Bank to a fixed exchange rate (25,000 sucres per $US1) and to withdraw all sucres in circulation; and requires all companies to convert their accounting to dollars.
- *Interest rates*: approves a debt conversion mechanism called *desagio* to transfer all dollar loans and deposits to lower interest rates, which is also applicable to prior debt issued in dollars for a short period; and approves a procedure for establishing maximum legal interest rates in the banking system equal to the London interbank offered rate (LIBOR) plus country risk (as determined by the Central Bank), plus four percentage points.
- *Financial reforms*: strengthens and introduces flexibility in financial supervision, placing legal limits on the immunity of senior officials, and giving greater autonomy to the Superintendency to intervene in troubled banks and dispose of the assets of closed banks; it establishes a limit of $US8,000 on the previously unlimited guarantee on deposits; and establishes provisions for restructuring private sector debt to the banking system.
- *Public spending and deficits*: the fiscal deficit cannot exceed 2.5 percent of GDP, and the three-year moving average must be limited to zero; the measure establishes a limit on increases in current spending; and establishes provisions to make government contracting more transparent.
- *Privatization*: allows the construction of a new heavy crude oil pipeline (OCP) by a private consortium; and authorizes the privatization of telephone companies and the sale of 51 percent of the shares in state electricity companies.
- *Labor market*: approves a reform making it possible to hire hourly workers at a minimum salary of $US0.50 per hour, as well as provisions making it possible to unify extra benefits based on base salary.

---

where the rate increased by 7 percentage points between 1998 and 1999 alone. The degree of deterioration in these indicators reveals the depth of the crisis and the greater vulnerability of the rural poor in dealing with their income losses. The subsequent emigration of more than 300,000 people—3 percent of the labor force—since 1997 made the country a significant recipient of family remittances. These remittances improved national income; had a positive effect on the balance of payments, financing the current account and contributing to the accumulation of reserves; and in particular allowed for improvements in private consumption that partially offset the decline in real salaries. In addition, emigration artificially reduced unemployment, although at the price of eroding the country's human capital (and its social capital in rural communities) in the medium term.

B. Recent Macroeconomic Performance

The Ecuadoran economy is recovering from the crisis but continues to be fragile. The adoption of the dollar, combined with favorable prices for petroleum, strong family remittances, and macroeconomic management with mixed results, has helped to gradually stabilize expectations, eliminate hyperinflation, begin the reorganization and reestablishment of the banking system, start up a fragile economic recovery, and reverse the increases in unemployment and poverty levels. This section summarizes recent trends in the economy (see also Figure 2 and the annex).

In the year 2000, the first year in the transition, economic growth was slight and hyperinflation reached its highest point. The rate of growth was 2.8 percent and inflation was more than 90 percent. This latter figure was the result of the adjustments in the exchange rate and in relative prices that accompanied dollarization and of excessive monetary expansion in sucres in the preceding year. However, the macroeconomic balances improved noticeably: the fiscal accounts showed a strong primary surplus of 7.7 percent of GDP, thanks to higher petroleum revenues and salary compression in dollars (derived primarily from the depreciation in the exchange rate). For its part, the current account showed an exceptional surplus equal to 6.3 percent of gross domestic product (GDP) as a result of good petroleum prices, low growth, the lack of bank credit, and exchange rate depreciation. Bank deposits were unfrozen in the first half of the year but bank credit remained stagnant (Beckerman and Cortés 2002). The relief of the external position led to successful negotiation in March 2002 of the Contingency Agreement with the International Monetary Fund for $US304 million. This agreement was key to ensuring multilateral financing that same month, in order to substitute new 12- and 30-year Global Bonds for the old Brady bonds and Eurobonds at a discounted value of 60 centavos to the dollar (above their value on the secondary markets) in August, and to rescheduling the debt with the Paris Club in September of the same year. By late December 2002, Ecuador's external position, measured in terms of "excess freely disposable reserves," had gone from a deficit of $US254 million in 1999 to a surplus of $US776 million.

Economic recovery began and hyperinflation ended in 2001. Benefiting from a positive external environment characterized by high petroleum prices, low international interest rates, and significant flows of remittances, GDP grew 5.1 percent in 2001 and an estimated 3.0 percent in 2002. Average annual inflation fell to 38 percent in 2001, and was down to single digits by late 2002. The recovery is

Figure 2. Macroeconomic Indicators

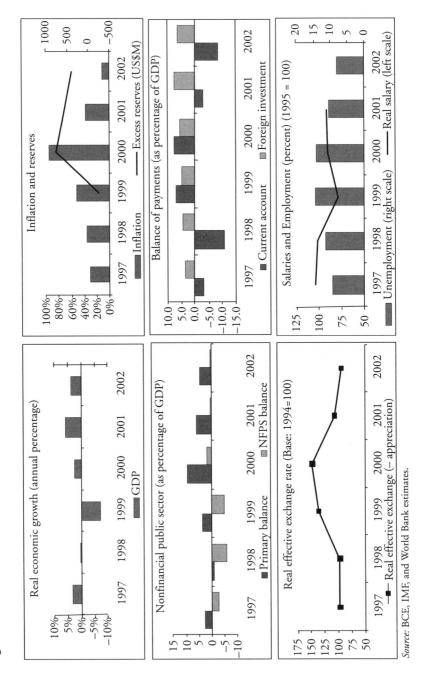

Source: BCE, IMF, and World Bank estimates.

explained by the increase in domestic demand (particularly private demand), stimulated in turn by high petroleum prices; growing remittances; the increase in nominal minimum and average salaries in dollars, which practically doubled between April 2000 and October 2002; and the slow reactivation of private credit (Figure 3) consistent with recovery of the banking system. Construction of the OCP has also attracted new flows of foreign investment. The slow deceleration of inflation corresponds to the behavior expected of a recently dollarized economy, in which the rate of prices tends to be determined by international inflation, the lag in relative price adjustments,[2] control of certain managed prices that belong to the basic basket, and expansion of domestic demand. Economic recovery and migration have helped to bring employment/unemployment rates practically back to their January 1998 levels, but underemployment continues to be three times as high as its pre-crisis level, reflecting more profound changes in labor markets (See chapter 16 on the Labor Market and Civil Service in Ecuador).

Figure 3. Credit to the Private Sector (growth rate, percent)

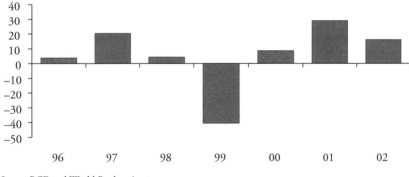

Source: BCE and World Bank estimates.

2. The initial and significant increase in prices—and the slow and gradual decline after dollarization—is not an experience unique to Ecuador. Many Soviet republics experienced the same phenomenon when establishing their Currency Boards. This is explained by the difficulty of determining the "correct" exchange rate. On the one hand, there may be significant undervaluation of the domestic currency at the rate selected, especially if the currency has depreciated significantly during the months preceding dollarization (Beckerman and Cortes 2002). On the other hand, there is the risk of overvaluation of the domestic currency to the point that it is not credible to economic agents. Ecuador chose the risk of undervaluation.

Postdollarization fiscal performance has been mixed, expansive in terms of spending and positive in terms of revenues, which has made it impossible to achieve medium-term fiscal sustainability. The primary surpluses of the Nonfinancial Public Sector (NFPS) have been declining. From 7.7 percent of GDP in 2000, they are projected to fall by more than half, to 4.0 percent of GDP, in 2002. These surpluses have been almost exclusively the result of an increase in current revenues—from petroleum and taxes—which have fluctuated irregularly between 2 and nearly 5 percentage points of GDP as compared to 1999. Unfortunately, these revenues have had to cover a heavy burden of interest on public debt, which left decreasing and meager positive global balances during these three years—close to zero in 2002 (see the annex).[3] In addition, the primary surpluses would probably have been higher if not for the expansive behavior of current primary spending. Spending on salaries and on goods and services almost doubled compared to predollarization levels—from $US1.181 billion and $US511 million in 1999 to $US2.083 billion and $US923 million in 2002—and investment spending regained its high crisis level of more than 6.5 percent of GDP in 2002.

External balances have also shown mixed results. After the strong capital outflow of 1999, and capital recovery in 2000, "excess freely disposable international reserves" have declined two years in a row, and are projected to be about $US400 million in 2002. However, this result conceals very important changes in the components of the balance of payments. On the one hand, the balance in the current account went from a surplus of 6.3 percent in 2000 to a high deficit of a projected 6.6 percent for 2002. More than 80 percent of this imbalance corresponds to the deficit in the trade balance. Short-term factors that explain this are the "boom" in demand that accompanies extraordinary petroleum earnings and import consumption financed by remittances; diseases and difficulties in accessing European markets that have affected the exportable supply of Ecuadoran shrimp and bananas, respectively; the appreciation in the real rate of exchange; and the temporary increase in imports that typifies the construction of the OCP. On the other hand, positive factors in the current account have been the decline in the net interest payments on external debt (nearly $US500 million) and rapid growth in family remittances—the second most important source of foreign currency, about 5.4 percent of GDP in 2002, which financed a large part of the accelerated growth in demand for imports during the postdollarization period. For its part, the capital account shows temporary foreign investment inflows for construction of the OCP; these are estimated by the authorities to be about 3 percentage points of GDP for 2002.

---

3. It should be noted that fiscal surpluses in the NFPS do not include extraordinary outlays to support the recapitalization of the banks, equal to an estimated 1.5 percent of GDP in 2001 and 1.0 percent in 2002, with which they would become a deficit. The 2002 surplus includes the floating debt estimated to be $US722 million in late 2002 ($US181 million in arrears to the Paris Club and $US541 million in accounts payable, the breakdown of which is unknown) according to top officials.

The beginning of economic recovery made possible a decline in urban poverty levels between 2000 and 2001. The employment survey shows a clear 20 percent decline in poverty levels between 1990 and 1997, followed by a sharp increase of nearly 17 points in 1998 and 1999 as the result of the crisis, and subsequently a partial recovery of about 12 points starting in 2000 (still not reaching the rates seen in 1997) (Figure 4). The same survey estimates that the decline in poverty between 2000 and 2001, measured on the basis of incomes, affected both rural areas and cities to an almost identical degree (León 2002)[4].

Figure 4. Ecuador's Urban Poverty, 1988–2001

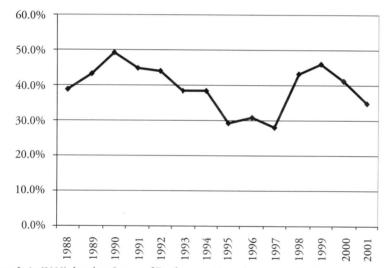

Source: León (2002), based on Surveys of Employment, Unemployment, and Underemployment.

---

4. With respect to measuring poverty according to income, the calculations can be done on the basis of two sources. First, the Urban Survey on Employment, Unemployment, and Underemployment has been conducted each year since 1987. Up to 1999, it covered only urban areas, while as of 2000 it covers both urban and rural areas. Second, since March 1998, the Central Bank of Ecuador has been conducting an employment survey each month in the country's three major cities (Quito, Guayaquil, and Cuenca). To calculate poverty according to income, the poverty line has been set at $US2 per person per day. This has the advantage of facilitating comparison with other countries. Poverty measured according to income has serious disadvantages in comparison with poverty measured according to consumption. Income generally fluctuates cyclically (particularly in rural areas) and is more subject to measurement errors. However, in Ecuador measurements of poverty according to income are indispensable in that they make it possible to track the evolution of poverty since 1999.

C. The Challenges of Maintaining Stability

The transition to dollarization has allowed Ecuador to achieve its immediate objectives of eliminating hyperinflation, with rates slowly approaching international levels, restoring some degree of confidence in the banking system, and beginning the economic recovery. However, its more medium-term objectives are still to be attained: achieving fiscal and external sustainability as preconditions for its program of key structural reforms for consolidating the recovery, strengthening financial systems, and improving competitiveness within a context of changes in relative prices. This section summarizes the most serious macroeconomic challenges to be faced in the next four years.

Ecuador's fiscal position is weak. It is weak for three principal reasons: the high volatility and procyclical character of revenues, particularly petroleum revenues; extreme rigidity, low quality, and lack of transparency in spending; and the high degree of illiquidity and insolvency of public debt.

- **The volatility and procyclical character of tax revenues remain excessive.** Although general economic volatility has declined under dollarization, the behavior of inflation, tax revenues, and the terms of trade continues to be an exception (Table 1). The volatility of Ecuador's terms of trade was not only more than five times as high as the regional average in the second half of the 1990s (19.2 versus a regional average of 3.4 percent) but has also increased by 20 percent in the period after dollarization. It is thus obvious that the Ecuadoran economy's high degree of dependence on international petroleum prices

Table 1. Volatility in Ecuador, 1990–2002

	1990s	*2000–02*	*Change*
Real GDP	3.2%	1.3%	−61%
NFPS Balance [a]	1.7%	0.6%	−65%
Current revenues/GDP [a]	1.0%	1.3%	29%
Petroleum	1.4%	0.9%	−35%
Nonpetroleum	1.3%	1.8%	38%
Primary spending/GDP [a]	0.6%	1.1%	86%
Inflation	12.1%	43.1%	256%
Monetary base	23.4%	5.5%	−77%
Terms of trade	19.2%	23.1%	20%
Real salary growth [b]	10.8%	6.9%	−37%
Growth in private consumption	3.5%	0.9%	−74%

Notes: Volatility defined as standard deviation, in percentage terms, of the above-mentioned variables.
a. Data since 1995.
b. Data since 1997.
Source: World Bank estimates.

makes it very sensitive to external shocks. After Venezuela and Trinidad and Tobago (also petroleum countries), Ecuador has the third-highest concentration of (in excess of 60 percent) exports in a few traditional products in Latin America (Figure 5). This high degree of dependence on petroleum prices is shown in various ways (Figure 6). For example, (i) the correlation between petroleum prices and economic growth is obvious; (ii) the correlation between petroleum prices and tax revenues is even higher (a coefficient of 0.66 in the period 1990–2002); and (iii) for each dollar reduction in the international price per barrel of oil, exports fall by 0.6 percent of GDP and tax revenues fall by 0.4 percent of GDP (Artana 2002), which also reflects their procyclical behavior. It is not surprising that petroleum tax revenues would show strong swings: in terms of GDP, they grew from 3.9 percent in 1998 to 9.2 percent in 2000, falling later to a projected 5.7 percent of GDP in 2002 (see the annex).

- **Spending remains expansive, to a large extent because of budgetary inertia.** Contrasting with the highly variable behavior of revenues, primary spending shows close to zero volatility since the mid-1990s, which reflects its rigidity and explains its expansion (Table 1). Between 1997 and 2002, despite the crisis and subsequent dollarization, primary spending in the NFPS continued its upward trend. In GDP terms, it grew from 19.4 percent in 1997 to 19.9 percent in 2000, and since that time has increased by 1.5 percentage points up to 2002, reaching 21.4 percent of GDP (see the annex). Obviously, this reflects the absence of any adjustments.[5] There are three principal reasons for budgetary inertia: the generous mechanism for indexing salaries based on pro-

Figure 5. Percentage of Four Principal Goods as a Share of Total Exports

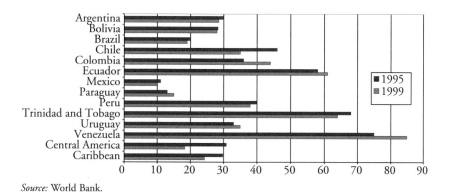

Source: World Bank.

---

5. Alternatively, this figure could include the late recognition of floating debt that has been carried over for years, at about 0.3–0.4 percent of GDP.

Figure 6. The Effect of Petroleum on the Economy

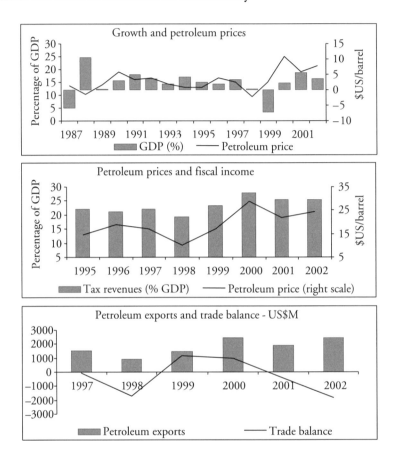

Source: World Bank estimates.

jected inflation that was adopted after dollarization; the many benefits associated with increases in the base salaries of public employees, which act as a multiplier (see chapter 16 on the Labor Market and Civil Service in Ecuador); and the *ex ante* preallocation of "projected" tax revenues in the pro forma budgets contained in more than 50 applicable legal provisions, which make readjustments difficult once they are approved (see chapter 2 on Tax Administration and Policy).

- **The rigidity of spending becomes extreme when debt service payments are added to it.** If we subtract from total current revenues spending on payroll (30 percent), preallocated revenue (30 percent), and debt service payments (35 percent including net amortization), the remaining freely disposable balance for nonsalary primary spending is barely 5 percent of the budget, which was equal to about 1.0 percent of GDP in 2001 (Figure 7). In practice, this percentage amounts to a small budgetary contingency reserve. This flexible amount of internal resources that the authorities have to finance investment or purchases of goods and services (particularly social spending) by the central government is negligible. Given the seasonal nature of tax revenues and the unpredictability of external disbursements, this situation contributes to continuous cash problems. Thus, the inflexibility of spending makes it impossible to adequately plan cash outlays and to redirect spending effectively and efficiently to the priority objectives of a new poverty reduction strategy.[6]

- **Government spending is highly fragmented and thus uncoordinated, subject to weak controls, and lacking in transparency.** The preallocation of some 30 percent of income to more than 50 different agencies and 242 sectional governments (provinces and cantons) that are not subject to any regular coordination, monitoring, or evaluation mechanism leads to fragmented execution of spending,[7] a lack of control over spending, and creates serious obstacles for transparency in spending. The limited number of studies done on the quality of spending in Ecuador is precisely a reflection of its lack of transparency. Financial management is decentralized by law to executing

Figure 7. Distribution of Government Revenues (2001)

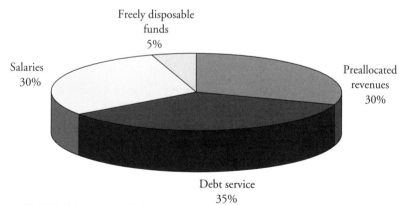

Source: World Bank based on Gallardo (2001).

---

6. For example, note that the Solidarity Bond alone used resources equal to 0.7 percent of GDP in 2001, which would be equal to more than half of freely disposable funds.
7. The fragmentation of spending is understood in the broad sense, that is, based on the preallocation of revenues.

agencies, but is carried out under an integrated financial information system (known as SIGEF in Spanish) that covers a nonconsolidated budget, encompasses only a portion of spending by the central administration, excluding the decentralized and sectional agencies,[8] and reveals spending actions late and not in a virtual format. The absence of control and transparency is deeply rooted. For example, the Social Security Institute did not publish its financial balance sheets for five years and was operating without any external oversight (it now operates under the Superintendency of Insurance). The municipalities, for their part, did not publish their financial statements, either. In turn, while the pro forma budget is not approved before the start of the year, budgets are closed out more than a year after the end of the year, with subsequent verification by the Office of the Comptroller even later.

- **Public debt is illiquid and very high**. The stock of total external debt was estimated at 65.7 percent of GDP in 2002, more than twice the level of exports of goods and services and the highest in Latin America after Argentina, before that country's crisis (Figure 8). Public debt represented 60 percent of GDP that year. The burden of external public debt service is excessive, which creates continuous problems of illiquidity and increases the risk of default. Approximately one out of every three dollars entering the Treasury is used to pay external debt. As of the end of 2002, the spread of Ecuadoran bonds is the second highest in the region with an upward trend: above 1,850 basis points—above Brazil and the average for Latin American bonds—and has been increasing since April 2002, when the government failed to reach an agreement with the IMF (Figure 9).[9] Ecuador also has immediate liquidity problems with arrears to the Paris Club estimated at $US181 million at the end of 2002, and a scheduled amount of debt service of about 8.1 percent of GDP (4.7 percent in amortizations and 3.4 percent in interest for 2003–04). About four-fifths of total debt is external debt. Of this, some 65 percent is official debt—40 percent multilateral and 25 percent bilateral—making it somewhat less vulnerable to changes in emerging markets and offsetting the country's lack of access to international markets. Finally, nearly two-thirds of domestic debt consists of bonds issued by the Deposit Guarantee Agency (AGD) and the National Finance Corporation (CFN) to cover the costs of bank interventions during the banking crisis. The outlook of the three major risk-rating agencies is that the country's ability and desire to pay have improved with dollarization, but with a CCC+ (Standard & Poor's) or Caa 2 (Moody's) rating, Ecuador is still not eligible for a level of investment that

---

8. SIGEF covers about 84 percent of central government spending.
9. Note that the spread did reduce significantly after dollarization, but it remains very sensitive to internal and external events.

Figure 8. Total External Debt (% GDP)

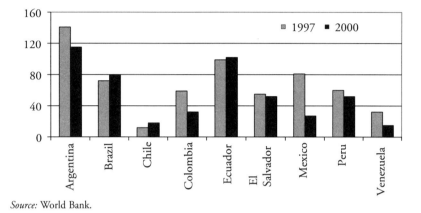

Source: World Bank.

would allow it to issue new sovereign bonds on international capital markets in the near future.[10]

Family remittances have led to a positive transformation in the Ecuadoran economy but have had some adverse effects that should be corrected. Ecuador has become one of the principal recipients of remittances in Latin America (Central Bank of Ecuador [BCE] 2000). It receives about $US1.4 billion in remittances each year, equal to 5.4 percent of GDP in 2002. This inflow of capital has relaxed the restriction on foreign exchange, improving private consumption, which had been affected by the decline in real salaries during the crisis, and helping to alleviate the decline in incomes. Ecuadoran remittances have five distinct characteristics in comparison with the trend in Latin America (Figure 10): (i) remittances intensify with a rather delayed migration toward the end of the 1990s; (ii) they are concentrated in three regions of the country—Azuay (Cuenca), Guayas, and Pichincha, with a clear predominance of the first—that receive about two-thirds of the remittances; (iii) nearly half (45 percent) of the remittances do **not** come from the United States; (iv) a relatively higher percentage is invested in housing; and (v) in per capita terms they are the third highest in Latin America, with a positive effect on the rapid recovery of precrisis income and poverty levels. Despite these positive aspects, remittances

---

10. A risk rating of C means that the issuing institution has obvious deficiencies, probably related to the quality of its assets or the poor structuring of its accounts (fiscal in this case). This leads to a considerable degree of uncertainty and reasonable doubts regarding the institution's ability to confront additional problems in the future.

Figure 9. Ecuador's Financial Risk

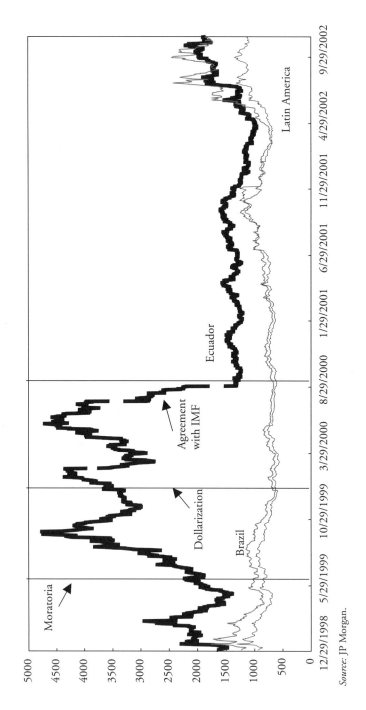

Source: JP Morgan.

also have some macroeconomic effects that are quite similar to those of the country's petroleum boom periods and that contribute to (i) a **change in relative prices**, given that the inflow of foreign currency increases the demand for and prices of tradable goods; (ii) an **increase in the real exchange rate**, as measured by the decline in the ratio of prices for tradable and nontradable goods; and (iii) a **deterioration in the trade account of the balance of payments**, owing to the decline in exports (particularly nontraditional exports) and the increase in imports that result from exchange appreciation. However, there are two important differences between the remittances and the petroleum booms: their **duration,** in that remittances tend to provide a more permanent positive external shock—usually 7–10 years—than booms; and the **productive use of resources**, given that in comparison with petroleum earnings, higher percentages of remittances tend to be consumed in investments in nontradable goods, rather than in imports. Both differences make remittances a welcome phenomenon, the use of which can be maximized.

Of the adverse effects of increased remittances, the change in relative prices to the detriment of tradable goods is the principal problem to be corrected. Goods whose prices are determined by international markets are known as "tradable" goods and goods whose prices are determined by the domestic market are known as "nontradable" goods. The change in the relative prices of tradable and nontradable goods in a dollarized system is one of the possible approximations of the real exchange rate. An increase in the real exchange rate may be due to a decline in productivity in the production of tradable goods as well as to an increase in prices for nontradable goods. In Ecuador, after dollarization, the productivity ratio of these two sectors deteriorated, primarily affecting the tradables sector. At the same time, the ratio of relative prices for tradable/nontradable goods rose in 2000, propelled by an increase in prices for tradable goods that were affected by the sharp depreciation in the sucre. However, it subsequently fell because of constant, although smaller, increases in prices for nontradable goods (Figure 11).[11] The result of both trends has been an appreciation in the real exchange rate (see Figure 2). Note that estimated real appreciation is much lower when calculated on the basis of unit labor costs (8.1 percent) than when calculated on the basis of consumer price indexes (62 percent), in the case, for example, of Ecuador's principal trade partner—the United States—between 2000 and 2002 (Figure 12). In any case, this change in relative prices is a manifestation of a deterioration in Ecuador's external competitiveness that should be corrected.[12]

---

11. The labor productivity series (product/labor) are constructed using data on urban employment rather than national employment because the latter is only available for 2000 and 2001, whereas product is national in that there are no urban product series. The price series use the BCE's producer price index for tradable goods and the urban consumer price index, also produced by the BCE, for nontradable goods. Thus, both indexes are approximations of real values.

12. Another manifestation of the loss of competitiveness was the evolution of nontraditional exports, which reached an annual growth rate of 20 percent in 2001, but a rate close to

Figure 10. Ecuadoran Migration and Family Remittances

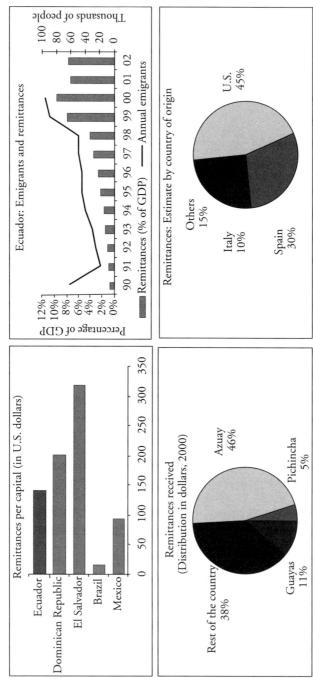

Source: BCE and World Bank estimates.

Figure 11. Relationship between Productivity and Relative Prices of Tradable/Nontradable Goods

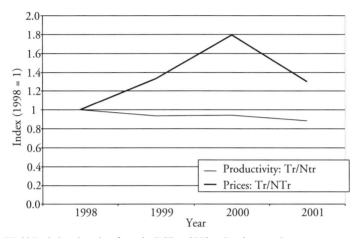

Source: World Bank, based on data from the BCE and Urban Employment Surveys.

Figure 12. Real Bilateral Exchange Rate with the United States, Based on CPI and Unit Labor Costs (1994 = 100)

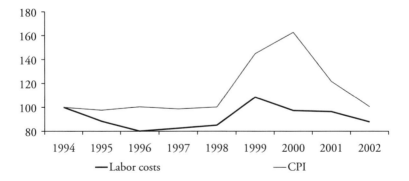

Source: World Bank, based on data from the BCE and Urban Employment Surveys.

zero in 2002. The tax authorities indicated that the latter figure reflects to some extent a significant underassessment of exports, which is explained by tax evasion.

The external position is weak. Given the inflexibility of the exchange rate, Ecuador must also find alternative mechanisms for absorbing real and financial shocks. Its high degree of dependency on a few primary products makes it more vulnerable to deterioration in its terms of trade. In addition, the development of mechanisms for absorbing financial shocks, typical of a dollarized economy, is nonexistent. There are three options: "abundant" international reserves in the Central Bank; contingent credit lines with multilateral agencies; and resources from a countercyclical stabilization fund.

- **The level of Freely Disposable International Reserves is declining**. Although the amount of international reserves required under dollarization is lower than under a flexible exchange rate system, because the monetary supply is always greater than the monetary base and the traditional role of the lender of last resort no longer exists, it is advisable to increase this amount in order to avoid minor contingencies.[13] "Excess" freely disposable reserves in Ecuador recovered slowly in 2000 with multilateral support and debt restructuring but the current level is low (close to $US400 million) and the trend downward (see the annex).[14]
- **After the crisis in Argentina, the possibilities for obtaining contingency lines from abroad are minimal**. Nor has the United States shown any interest in implicitly sharing its seniorage with dollarized countries.
- **The recently created Petroleum Fund will not have any significant money until 2004 and the amount it can be expected to have to meet contingencies is marginal**. The Fund for Stabilization, Social and Productive Investment, and Reduction of Public Debt (FEIREP) was created with the recently approved tax law. According to the law, the funds that go to FEIREP will be primarily funds from the OCP that do not derive from lower utilization of the Trans-Ecuadoran Pipeline (SOTE) for light petroleum. Given the delay in completing the construction of the OCP until late 2003, this means

---

13. Note that the role of lender of last resort was unsuccessful in avoiding the banking crisis prior to dollarization. We speak of "minor" contingencies that do not include the possibility of a large number of depositors withdrawing their deposits from the banks. Should that happen, either interest rates would have to rise to extremely high rates in an attempt to recapture deposits or another banking crisis would occur.
14. "Excess" reserves, a concept that is appropriate to a dollarized system, results from deducting from the total amount of freely disposable reserves from the internal liabilities of the Central Bank, which include the currency and paper it issues as well as the deposits of commercial banks in the Bank. Excess reserves increase in particular when the government makes deposits to the Single Treasury Account, and thus these deposits become a key variable/goal of the macroeconomic program.

that a very small amount of funds will be transferred in 2004 and thereafter to FEIREP. In addition, according to the law, only 20 percent of the funds in FEIREP will have a countercyclical function, and thus the amount for contingencies will be marginal.

The financial system remains vulnerable. The Ecuadoran financial system has made a remarkable recovery since the crisis of 1999, with stable growth in deposits in the banking system and credit to the private sector since the negative levels of 1999. However, there are still various critical areas that need improvement. Some key problems are as follows (Figure 13):[15]

- **Real active interest rates are slightly positive, while passive rates remain negative and do not strengthen financial intermediation.** Real active interest rates were negative during the hyperinflationary episode and only became marginally positive again starting in 2002.
- **The decline in nominal interest rates after dollarization has been late in coming and limited, and has not provided sufficient stimulus for economic recovery**. With dollarization, the elimination of exchange risk should have allowed for a rapid and significant decline in nominal interest rates, but this did not happen. Between April 2000 and late 2002, the decline was slight—barely 3–4 percentage points, and less than the nearly 5 percentage point decline in international interest rates.[16] However, as inflation has fallen and the financial system has been strengthened, the rates have gradually fallen. As of late 2002, with a lending rate of 12 percent and inflation at 9 percent, Ecuador's real active rates are slightly lower than the prime rate in the United States.
- **The liquidity of commercial banks remains high and continues to fluctuate**. The net liquidity of the banks (the ratio of funds available to deposits up to 90 days) recovered noticeably in late 2000, but since that time has fluctuated in a high and broad range of 30–45 percent. This behavior reflects the banks' preoccupation with having provisions that would allow them to meet their obligations in the event of a run on deposits.
- **The delinquent portfolio percentage is high and credit for housing or microenterprise remains stagnant**. Ten percent of the portfolio is delinquent. This average conceals the difficult situation that some commercial

---

15. Chapter 4 on the Banking System analyzes this subject in detail.
16. At the end of an inflationary episode, commercial banks tend to raise real interest rates in order to generate greater revenues and recover part of the losses from the decapitalization, in real terms, that occurred during the episode. This happens because interest rates never increase as much as prices during crises.

Figure 13. Financial System Indicators

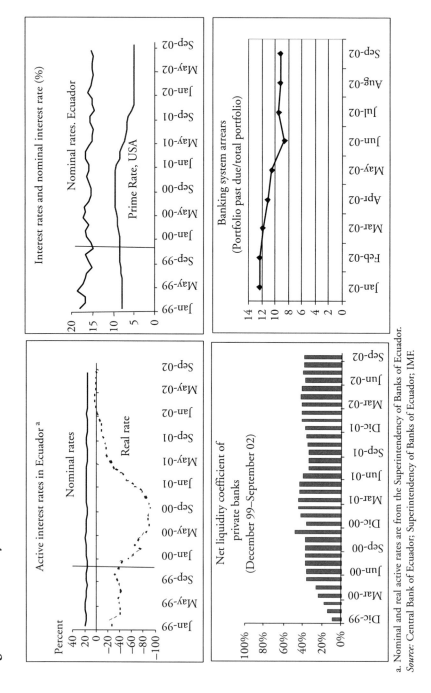

a. Nominal and real active rates are from the Superintendency of Banks of Ecuador.
Source: Central Bank of Ecuador; Superintendency of Banks of Ecuador; IMF.

banks went through with extremely high levels of delinquency. The highest proportion of credit continues to be concentrated in the segment with the most delinquency—commercial credit—with only a marginal amount (less than 10 percent) goes to housing or microenterprise, two sectors that make intensive use of unskilled labor, and whose reactivation would encourage economic recovery (Multiplica 2002). Both trends reflect, on the one hand, the difficulty that economic agents encounter in meeting their debts and not seeking rollovers and, on the other, the banking system's limited trust in granting medium-term credit, despite dollarization.

External competitiveness has not improved and the investment climate continues to be discouraging. Perhaps the other element that is key to dollarization in Ecuador in the medium term is growing gaps in competitiveness and rigidities in the country's factors markets. Earlier we analyzed the loss of competitiveness due to the trend toward real exchange appreciation as a result of the decline in the ratio between prices for tradable and nontradable goods. Another option is to focus on the global analyses of a country's competitiveness. Generally, global classifications and their rates should not be a source of great concern, but this is not the case in Ecuador. Almost all indicators provide evidence that the country's competitiveness gaps are significant and growing in most areas in comparison with other medium-income countries—and there is no evidence that domestic conditions are conducive to reversing these trends. For example, the Global Competitiveness Report of the World Economic Forum provides an overview of a country's basic competitiveness in terms of its macroeconomic situation, public institutions (corruption, contracts, and respect for law), the quality of its business environment, technological innovation, and computer technology. In 1999, Ecuador ranked 54th out of the 62 countries rated. In 2001, it ranked 68th of the 75 countries evaluated, with a relatively higher grade (59th) for innovation, and lower grades for the quality of its business environment (72nd) and for contracts and respect for law (73rd). This trend continued to deteriorate in 2002 when Ecuador ranked 73rd of the 80 countries considered. Similar indicators are found in the Heritage Foundation's Index of Economic Freedom, which also shows a deterioration in the country's relative position, which went from 72nd in 1999 to 117th in 2002, ranking ahead of only Cuba and Venezuela in the region (Table 2). The breakdown of the index's components indicates that the country's situation has worsened, particularly in terms of its investment climate and property rights, and has improved slightly in terms of its fiscal situation.

The rigidities in labor markets represent another important challenge. Labor flexibility is critical to the sustainability of dollarization, particularly as a mechanism for adjusting to unfavorable shocks. Initially, the private sector labor market became somewhat more flexible after the crisis of 1999. The approval of the Economic Transformation Law made it possible both to diversify hiring methods and to unify the many benefits based on one's base salary in the private sector, thus setting a good

Table 2. Index of Economic Freedom

	Relative position		Tax burden		Monetary policy		Foreign direct. investment		Property rights	
	1999	2002	1999	2002	1999	2002	1999	2002	1999	2002
Argentina	14	38	2.0	3.0	2.0	1.0	2.0	2.0	2.0	3.0
Bolivia	49	45	3.5	3.5	3.0	2.0	2.0	1.0	3.0	4.0
Brazil	95	79	3.0	3.5	5.0	3.0	3.0	3.0	3.0	3.0
Chile	14	9	3.0	3.0	3.0	2.0	2.0	2.0	1.0	1.0
Colombia	55	58	3.0	3.0	4.0	3.0	2.0	2.0	3.0	4.0
Costa Rica	69	43	3.0	3.0	4.0	3.0	2.0	2.0	3.0	3.0
Cuba	158	153	3.5	3.5	5.0	5.0	5.0	5.0	5.0	5.0
Ecuador	**72**	**117**	**3.0**	**2.5**	**5.0**	**5.0**	**2.0**	**3.0**	**3.0**	**4.0**
El Salvador	19	17	1.5	2.0	3.0	1.0	1.0	2.0	2.0	3.0
Guatemala	43	55	1.5	2.0	3.0	2.0	3.0	3.0	3.0	4.0
Honduras	106	88	2.5	2.5	5.0	3.0	3.0	3.0	3.0	3.0
Nicaragua	118	88	3.0	3.5	5.0	3.0	2.0	2.0	4.0	4.0
Panama	35	45	3.0	3.5	1.0	1.0	2.0	2.0	3.0	4.0
Paraguay	62	79	2.0	2.0	3.0	3.0	1.0	2.0	4.0	4.0
Peru	39	53	3.0	2.5	4.0	2.0	2.0	2.0	2.0	4.0
Dominican Republic	80	72	2.0	1.5	3.0	3.0	3.0	3.0	4.0	4.0
Uruguay	43	41	3.5	3.5	5.0	3.0	2.0	2.0	2.0	2.0
Venezuela	95	130	2.0	2.5	5.0	5.0	3.0	3.0	3.0	4.0

Note: the range from 1 to 5 goes from best to worst.
Source: Heritage Foundation.

precedent for the public sector, but reform in the latter did not happen. Labor law on Ecuador's civil service is still focused on promoting labor stability rather than on encouraging the efficient delivery of services, which would encourage growth and competitiveness. This is particularly true of the civil service, which has two areas that urgently need improvement: salary policy and the number of public employees. In general, salaries are not freely determined in the informal markets, but rather by a National Salary Council. The result is that real salaries have not fallen during the postdollarization period, despite the downward trend in labor productivity (see the annex). In addition, in civil service in particular, because of the proliferation of allocations (general and specific), each official increase in the base salary of a public employee sets off a chain of complex multiplier effects. This makes it impossible to precisely estimate in advance the cumulative effect of official increases. Nonetheless, it is estimated that salary increases have been high, from 60 to 110 percent above the preceding salary level (see chapter 16 on the Labor Market and Civil Service in Ecuador). For its part, public employment is without any effective controls. The exact number of public employees is unknown. Because there is no centralized control of payroll, the number is approximated indirectly based on budgetary allocations. The state's authority to manage civil service has deteriorated completely since the Secretariat for National Administrative Development (SENDA) was dissolved in 1998. The lack of central control also applies to state companies, decentralized agencies, and sectional governments.

D. Policy Recommendations

Perhaps the greatest achievement of dollarization in the medium term has been to eliminate the "veil of money" and reveal problems in the fiscal, real, and financial sectors more convincingly. With the suppression of monetary policy, the gradual elimination of the distortions caused by hyperinflation, and the assumption of contingent liabilities from the banking crisis, the fiscal, currency exchange, and price "illusions" have to a great extent disappeared, forcing the authorities to deal with correcting fiscal imbalances. This is why under a dollarized scheme, financial leveraging is the first and only way to gain credibility and keep inflationary expectations low. In turn, dollarization made even clearer the need for the program of structural reforms that Ecuador has postponed for decades.

Combining fiscal discipline with the implementation of structural reforms is no longer just an option. Indeed, it is a critical requirement for consolidating macroeconomic stability and reactivating the economy by strengthening the financial system, improving competitiveness, and eliminating market distortions in the medium term. A credible approach to correcting fiscal imbalances by improving prudential supervision, eliminating trade barriers, and introducing flexibility in factors markets is the best route in terms of economic policy. These reforms would have been essential for Ecuador even if the country had not dollarized, and will continue to be so even if the government should voluntarily decide to "de-dollarize" in the future. The previous section identified the principal problems. We present below the principal recommendations for overcoming these obstacles and holding on to the achievements attained.

The government's first macrofiscal priority is to deal with the economy's illiquidity and develop a plan to close the country's financial gap for 2003. In 2003, Ecuador has total net financial requirements[17] in the amount of $US2.150 billion, which after including already scheduled financing, leaves a gap of financing to be identified of $US871 million (Table 3). The heaviest burden comes from multilateral and bilateral debts, which together represent more than 90 percent of total external debt amortization and two-thirds of total public debt amortization over the

---

17. This is stated as "net" because it does not include $US827 million in interest on public debt, half of which is for payment of AGD and National Development Corporation bonds.

next three years. Given the specific composition of its debt, it is clear that the liquidity of Ecuador's public finances is critically dependent on (i) developing and carrying out a sound and credible macroeconomic program; (ii) implementing a program of structural reforms that will allow the country to obtain rapidly disbursing and freely disposable funds from the multilateral agencies, which could close the gap; and (iii) rescheduling its bilateral external debt with the Paris Club. One of the objectives of this rescheduling should be the prompt elimination of all pending arrears in 2003.

Table 3. The Financial Gap of the Nonfinancial Public Sector

	2001	2002	2003	2004	2005
Financing required	**1915**	**2150**	**2116**	**1534**	**1534**
NFPS deficit	0	0	0	0	0
NFPS deposits [f]	49	0	100	100	100
Amortization	1121	1105	1294	1304	1304
External	731	672	816	904	865
Internal	390	433	479	400	439
Other	745	1045	722	130	130
Arrears	285	655	181		
Accounts payable		122	541		
Assist., banking sector	300	268	0		
Other [a, b]	160	0	0	130	130
Financing identified	**1915**	**2150**	**1245**	**1087**	**1031**
NFPS surplus [f]	155	215	237	259	137
Internal financing [c]	335	278	130	237	259
External disbursements [d]	584	472	873	578	613
Governments		85	148	100	100
IDB		92	111	124	124
WB		26	71	94	129
CAF		96	250	175	175
IMF		143	150	0	0
Others		30	144	85	85
Other	841	1185	5	13	22
Cumulative arrears	407	181			
Floating debt	122	541			
Other [b, e]	312	463			
Financing gap	**0**	**0**	**871**	**447**	**503**

Notes:
a. Includes payments to IESS.
b. Excludes $US240M in 2002 for advance purchase of petroleum, which became a financing requirement in 2003.
c. Internal financing means domestic bonds and disbursements.
d. Since 2003, data from BCE.
e. Financing gap.
f. Starting in 2003, possible goals to be negotiated with the IMF.
Source: BCE and World Bank estimates.

The government's second macrofiscal priority is to deal with its insolvency risk, taking steps that will allow it to obtain the high primary surpluses needed to pay interest on its debt. Ecuador has scheduled interest payments that will fluctuate at about $US800–900 million (3.5 percent of GDP) over the next four years. Meeting these payments is synonymous with complying with a fiscal standard: the recently approved Law on Responsibility, Stabilization, and Fiscal Transparency (Box 2). The two fundamental objectives of this law are to achieve a goal of sustainable public debt in the medium term (40 percent of GDP)—with an intermediate reduction goal of 16 percentage points of GDP in the next four years—and to create the FEIREP, the petroleum fund designed to repurchase commercial debt (12- and 30-year Global bonds) and to play an countercyclical fiscal role. Under a basic scenario, a debt sustainability analysis indicates that the primary fiscal surplus needed to achieve the intermediate goal of reducing the debt is above 5 percent of GDP in 2003 and 2004 (see chapter 3 on Debt Administration and Sustainability). Note that although the law does not specify what fiscal efforts would lead to achieving this goal, it does at least suggest combining a number of countercyclical fiscal resources, equal to 2.5 percent of GDP (the intermediate value in the range of revenue variation in recent years).

Given that the law lacks any essential elements for leveraging the fiscal surplus goal, a third priority is to supplement it. On the revenue side, a tax reform is suggested for the purpose of **increasing the level of nonpetroleum receipts by a minimum of 2.5 percent of GDP**, the amount suggested by the tax law. This will require at least three actions: (i) approving a series of tax policy measures that will generate approximately 1.4 percent of GDP, based primarily on limiting VAT exemptions exclusively to unprocessed basic foods and home rental and eliminating all other exemptions, particularly those on income tax and customs duties, with an estimated effect on collections of about 1 percent of GDP (see chapter 2 on Tax Administration and Policy); (ii) increasing the rate of the VAT given the possibility that petroleum prices will fall to their "normal" historic levels—below $US18/barrel—considering that each additional point in the rate would generate increased collections of about 0.7 percent of GDP; and finally but no less important, (iii) not approving the "tax relief" measures proposed by the outgoing government in the last quarter, including donating 25 percent of income tax (ISR) to municipalities, reducing the withholding at the source percentage on the VAT from 1 to 0.1 percent, and reducing to zero the duty on 158 products.

A fourth priority is to adjust and reallocate spending and make it transparent. The lessons learned in the three years of transition should be utilized so as not to continue postponing fiscal adjustment of spending. The only way to achieve significant primary surpluses is to adjust current and capital spending, redirecting the savings to key priorities of the government's strategy. There are three aspects to a reform of government spending.

- **It is recommended that an emergency budget phase be declared in order to contain spending.** The 2003 budget should be declared a national emer-

Box 2. The Law on Responsibility, Stabilization, and Fiscal Transparency

This legislation was approved in late 2002. It has several objectives: to reduce public debt, contribute to stabilization and fiscal sustainability, use the savings by directing it to investments that encourage economic and social development, and establish regulations on public finances and transparency for efficient management and effective citizen oversight. The law approves the following commitments:

- There will be a multiyear plan at the start of each government for a period of four months to guide spending and investment and establish quarterly goals for each institution in the NFPS that can be monitored.
- Central primary spending may not grow by more than a real rate of 3.5 percent per year.
- The total central government deficit, without petroleum export revenues, will be reduced by 0.2 percent each year.
- The debt/GDP ratio will fall 16 percentage points during the period 2003–06, and a similar provision will be applied to subsequent years until the ratio reaches 40 percent.
- The real value of the state's debt to the Ecuadoran Social Security Institute (IESS) will be paid off in four years.
- For sectional (provincial and municipal) governments: Total annual liabilities must not be greater than 100 percent of revenues, and debt service must be less than 40 percent of total revenues.
- Resources from the budget surplus and revenues from the OCP (incremental based on the not lower utilization of the SOTE for light petroleums) will be the principal source of the FEIREP.
- FEIREP resources will be distributed as follows: 70 percent to repurchase external debt and pay off debt to the IESS, 20 percent to stabilize petroleum revenues until reaching 2.5 percent of GDP and to cover emergencies, and 10 percent to education and health.
- The MEF will establish an official information and dissemination system, as will the sectional governments.
- The annual budget will include the quarterly projection of revenues and tax spending (and budget headings to offset it), the list of productive and unproductive assets, contingent liabilities and fiscal risks, and an estimate of profits from state companies and autonomous systems.

gency budget and developed under strict austerity rules. This means confronting rigidities in spending. Various measures are suggested for achieving this: (i) limiting increases in spending to zero in real terms in 2003, which means establishing limits (possibly negative limits in nominal terms) on spending for salaries, goods and services, and investments; (ii) immediately suspending the application of the mechanism that automatically indexes salaries to projected (rather than actual) inflation that is used by the National Council on Public Sector Remuneration (CONAREM) and replacing it with a new restrictive mechanism; (iii) approving a Salary Unification Law with a neutral tax cost, which can lead to finding extraordinary external financing; (iv) immediately freezing the hiring of new permanent public employees and reviewing existing positions; and (v) using FEIREP funds to repurchase the most expensive debt in Global Bonds so as to reduce annual interest payments.

- **It is recommended that fragmented spending be consolidated and redirected to priorities**. This will require (i) explicitly prohibiting any new preallocation of revenues or expenditures; (ii) eliminating all existing preallocations, except that for the Ecuadoran Social Security Institute (IESS); (iii) consider freezing the current transfer of 10-11 percent to sectional governments during the emergency budget period, and (iv) condition future transfers (once the emergency budget has ended) on the concomitant transfer of responsibilities, the auditing of sub-national debt, and the requirement of evaluation by independent rating agencies before allowing further debt by large cities.
- **It is recommended that budgetary transparency be institutionalized at all levels of government and that it be strengthened with modern tools**. Having approved the law, it is now urgent to design and implement a modern and consolidated version of the SIGEF, its principal instrument. The tax law also calls on sectional governments to "establish their own information systems for citizen oversight and reporting to the Ministry of Economy and Finance (MEF)." However, the implementation of a similar provision has proven to be chaotic in other Latin American countries that have seen a proliferation of incompatible systems supported by different computer platforms. The future version of SIGEF, supported by a single modern computer technology, must consolidate the accounts of the nonfinancial public sector—including the decentralized agencies and the sectional governments—and provide not only user-friendly access to the budget through a virtual user network but also bet-

---

18. Another of the law's problems is that the process for preparing the indicated multiyear budget (as of January 31 of the month when the new government takes office) is inappropriate given the serious problems with closing out the budget for 2001 and 2002, with late preparation of the 2003 annual budget, and the lack of transparency in spending. It

ter control of compliance with established physical and financial policy goals.[18]

For the future, a fifth priority will be to amend the law to leverage greater fiscal discipline and reduce the burden of external debt. The law has various goals that are not sufficiently restrictive. For example:

- The goal of reducing the nonpetroleum central deficit by 0.2 percent of GDP per year has a marginal impact. This deficit was –5.2 percent of GDP in 2002, and it would take decades to eliminate the deficit. This low annual objective could be increased.
- The goal of 3.5 percent growth in central primary spending is inconsistent with a policy of spending austerity. In addition, productivity trends in the tradable goods sectors are negative and do not justify this. This goal should be reduced.
- The law should reestablish a provision on the primary earnings of sectional governments and place limits on the their internal indebtedness. In addition, the law's limits on external indebtedness for the sectional governments (100 percent of total revenues for debt, and 40 percent of total revenues for debt service) are too high. International practice suggests 100 percent in the first case, but with respect to current revenues only (thus eliminating capital revenues that are usually extraordinary), and 25 percent in the second case.
- The potential revenues of the FEIREP over the next four years are too limited to efficiently perform a countercyclical function: less than $US100 million each year projected for the period 2004–07.[19] Thus, we suggest that it would be better to allocate these funds exclusively to the debt repurchase fund.

A sixth priority is the required strengthening of the external position. The downward trend in excess freely disposable reserves increases the vulnerability of a recently dollarized system with a banking system that is still being restructured. To turn this situation around, it would be highly advisable to gradually accumulate a reserve "cushion" of about $US900–1,000 million.[20] This would make it possible to provide extraordinary financing should it be needed to deal with situations such as a sharp drop in petroleum prices, a regionalized outflow of private capital, or mini-

---

would be best to postpone budget preparation until mid-2003, with a plan to approve it for the period 2004–07, in conjunction with preparation of the year 2004 budget. The possibility of preparing the budget on a participatory basis, as Peru is already doing, could be explored.

19. This estimated amount does not include the funds that the Congress allocated to FEIREP to cover the state's debt to the IESS.

20. Note that the financial projection envisions an annual increase of $US100 million in government deposits in the Single Account of the Nation, which deposits are in turn part of "excess freely disposable reserves."

deposit runs on bank in the process of restructuring. Given that the projected FEIREP funds are minimal, that the recommendation is that they be used exclusively for debt repurchase, and that the chances of obtaining contingent credit lines overseas are nil, a possible alternative for financing this cushion would be to use a portion of the future revenues from the pending privatization program, which currently go exclusively to the Solidarity Fund (see chapter 7 on Basic Infrastructure).

A seventh priority is to mitigate the change in relative prices. Improving external competitiveness requires eliminating the bias against exports, promoting the diversification of nontraditional exports. In recent years, Ecuador has seen an **appreciation** in its real rate of exchange that is not favorable to its exports. There is a series of mutually consistent policies that Ecuadoran authorities could implement to generate a **depreciation** in the real rate of exchange, which would be favorable to its exports. These policies include (i) reducing government resource requirements with fiscal consolidation, which would lower interest rates and stimulate private investment; (ii) accelerating trade liberalization in order to increase the demand for tradable goods (see chapter 6 on Trade Policy and Competition); (iii) increasing national savings with a total reorganization of the financial system (see chapter 4 on the Banking System), development of the capital market, and reform of the social security system (see chapter 11 on the Social Assistance System); and (iv) promoting global external competitiveness with the measures indicated below. To the extent that this pro-export agenda is implemented, it will also be possible to achieve a reduction in the deficit in the trade balance and in the current account of the balance of payments.

The eighth priority is to implement an effective agenda of external competitiveness. In consultation with the private sector, the authorities have proposed a Competitiveness Agenda with eight themes (BCE 2002a). The agenda is comprehensive, but its priorities and sequence still need to be defined and consensus must still be built with the private sector, making it difficult to implement the agenda. Asking for simultaneous progress in so many areas weakens its content in practical terms. This is why one of the first steps the new administration should take is to develop a trimmed-back agenda of policy and laws to strengthen competitiveness, to be completed in the first 12 to 18 months. This agenda should give priority to reformulation of the Law on Competitiveness adopted by Congress and vetoed by the past president (Box 3). The agenda could include measures needed to support the financial system, trade policy, and private participation in infrastructure as mentioned above, in addition to measures on developing human capital (see chapter 9 on Education) and rural development (see chapter 13 on Rural Development). Added to this are activities in three specific areas: internal competition among companies, entry into the market, and labor markets. These areas include the following measures:

- **Promoting domestic competition.** In the vetoed Law on Competition, the concept of competition should be clarified, the autonomy of the Competition Council should be improved, and the role of the Consultative Council, currently in the Ministry of External Trade, Industrialization, Fishing and Competitiveness (MICIP), should be clarified.

- **Eliminating barriers to entering the market**. Attracting new companies promotes technology and new investment. However, a recent survey established the existence of 62 different steps that are needed to register a business in Ecuador, certainly one of the highest figures in Latin America. A drastic regulatory and administrative simplification is needed to lower the legal and operational barriers to the creation of new businesses, which extends to the agencies responsible for the registration of businesses, taxes, employment, health, and environmental licenses.
- **Flexibilization of labor markets**. Chapter 16 on the Labor Market and Civil Service in Ecuador examines the reforms needed to improve salary policy, labor mobility, and the redeployment of the labor force among firms, and between the public and private sectors. In addition to this are reforms to the public vocational training system, which should encourage training in firms so that they can attain the necessary technical and administrative standards that are essential to their competitiveness.

Beyond focusing on specific policies, an effective agenda must be one that can be monitored as a process. This means an explicit determination of intercompany competitiveness goals—defined primarily in terms of changes in product/service design, quality, cost, and delivery times. Corporate cluster organizations use a similar methodology to establish standards and monitor the evaluation of goals by the Competitiveness Council, analyzing policy options to improve its impact.

E. Conclusion

Ecuador's stability and recovery are promising, but fragile. Its fiscal and external position is vulnerable, in part because of its structural characteristics of high volatility in response to real or financial external shocks, in part because of the still heavy burden of its external indebtedness, and in part because of the persistence of expansive spending policies that have resulted in meager fiscal surpluses and high current account deficits.

The probability that dollarization will collapse in the medium term is not negligible. Factors such as a drop in petroleum prices, loss of neighboring markets due to competitive exchange rate depreciations, or regional capital flight which indirectly impact the Ecuadoran economy are some of the foreseeable external shocks which would affect the economy to a greater or lesser degree, depending on how prepared the country is to face them. Thus, the future credibility of the country's economic program will not be achieved by the mere existence of a foreign exchange provision, but rather through a combination of consistent and credible policies that make it possible to provide appropriate management of the waning of the current petroleum boom, which may happen at any moment.

Box 3. Suggestions on a Draft of the Vetoed Law on Competition in Ecuador

The vetoed law represents an excellent starting point for an initiative designed to strengthen Ecuador's private sector. However, from an international perspective, certain aspects of the initiative need to be developed further and made clearer:

- Types of conduct that are considered "illegal *per se*" (Art. 6) are not clearly differentiated from those that are to be considered punishable under the "rule of reason" (Art. 8). In effect, some behaviors (such as price discrimination and linked purchases) are examples used in both articles. It is highly recommended that "cartel" type conduct by companies be clearly distinguished from behaviors considered as abuse of a dominant position.
- Institutionally, neither the independence of the government's antimonopoly authority (*Consejo Ecuatoriano de la Competencia*—CECON) nor its separation from the investigative and prosecutory body (the *Superintendencia de Compañías* through the *Intendencia de Competencia*) is clearly established. For example, one of the functions of CECON (Art. 19) is to "establish national policies for the promotion and defense of competition, in accordance with the guidelines established by the President of the Republic…" In addition, the Director of the Secretariat has a subordinary Superintendency—**the Superintendency of Companies**—and also presides over CECON. International experience indicates that this type of institutional design increases the risk of state "capture" and reduces effective compliance with the law.
- Clarification of the role of the **Consultative Council** (Art. 20) and its relationship with CECON should prevent an overburdening of the agency and its mandate (Art. 7). The European Union and the antimonopoly authority of the Netherlands have tried to reformulate a similar provision.

After the presidential veto and reformulation of the law, the new administration should make these revisions and proceed to discuss them with the private sector.

Without seeking to be exhaustive, this chapter provides key elements for a sound and credible program for the next four years. It is essential to close Ecuador's immediate financial gap and resolve the insolvency of its debt position. Both tasks require the strong leveraging of the economy's fiscal discipline with tax reform, an austere national emergency budget, and the repurchase of the debt using funds from FEIREP as prerequisites for fiscal sustainability. Improving prudential supervision of the financial system and strengthening the country's external position will also allow Ecuador to create a financial "cushion" of contingent resources for liquidity pressures on the banking system or outflows of capital owing to regional movements. In real terms, the objective is to adjust the relative prices of tradable and nontradable goods in order to promote a depreciation of Ecuador's real rate of exchange. This means, on the one hand, a comprehensive reform of its trade policy to eliminate the anti-export bias and correct the many and chronic distortions that still "protect" its economy—and on the other, closing competitiveness gaps by stimulating the factors of production: making labor markets more flexible, eliminating barriers to the domestic market in order to attract technology, and promoting human resources training and development.

The risk of a failure to reform the real sector is that, given the existence of inflexible markets—such as the formal labor market—adjustments to shocks will occur primarily through reductions in production, with the corresponding contraction in demand derived from inputs, particularly labor. This potential situation will not only create pressure to "abandon" the model, in view of increased unemployment, but will also contribute to an increase in commercial bank arrears, as a result of the decline in general economic activity. This in turn would make achieving the goals of both fiscal adjustment and recovery of the banking system less feasible—creating a vicious circle that would be difficult to break. In summary, the *sine qua non* conditions for sustaining dollarization are to achieve and then deepen fiscal solvency, introduce flexibility in goods and services markets, and increase the productivity of the factors of production.

Policy Matrix

Problem	Measures		Progress indicators	Objectives/goals
	Short term (first six months)	Medium term		
High illiquidity and large financial gap	Design and implement a sound and credible macroeconomic program	Meet program goals during all management	Program performance indicators	Maintain stability, gain credibility, obtain multilateral financing, and open Paris Club negotiations
Risk of insolvency of medium-term debt		Achieve primary fiscal surplus of at least 5 percent of GDP in 2003–04	Goal achieved	Reduce debt/GDP by a minimum of 16 percentage points as of 2007
Low, volatile, and procyclical fiscal resources	Approve tax reform Review inherited tax relief measures		Tax laws submitted to and approved by Congress	Raise the nonpetroleum tax burden by at least 2.5 percent of GDP
Excessive, fragmented spending that is not transparent	Declare a 2003 national emergency budget Establish spending limits (zero real growth in 2003) Suspend indefinitely automatic salary indexation mechanism Prohibit new pre-allocations and exemptions, and submit bill to	Prohibit any new hiring of permanent public employees and evaluate existing positions Repurchase Global Bonds Transfer resources based on assumption of new functions, plan to reschedule subnational debt (contingent included)	Real salary indexation equal to 0 percent Amendments to law submitted to and approved by Congress Gradual transfer of resources to subnational governments as they comply with the new national investment policy	Adjust, consolidate, and redirect spending in a context of greater budget transparency and an established poverty reduction strategy

(Matrix continues on the following page.)

Policy Matrix (*continued*)

Problem	Measures		Progress indicators	Objectives/goals
	Short term (first six months)	*Medium term*		
	eliminate most preallocations and exemptions that are not constitutional Suspend during emergency phase of subnational transfers in excess of 10 percent of current revenues if there is no information on their use, and transfer functions in conjunction with resources Approve an improved SIGEF.	and new rules for future debts contracted by large cities Modernize SIGEF		
Tax law is not sufficiently restrictive, does not have potential for collecting countercyclical funds, but does have potential for debt repurchase		Prepare amendments to the Law Use FEIREP to repurchase debt	Amendments to the law submitted to and approved by Congress	Strengthen fiscal discipline and reduce the burden of external debt
The change in relative prices in favor of	Approve fiscal measures	Complete financial reorganization		Contain greater appreciation in the real rate of exchange

Problem	Action	Action	Indicator	Objective
prices for non-tradable goods (trending to appreciation in the real rate of exchange) harms external competitiveness	Eliminate customs and noncustoms barriers	Develop capital market Reform social security		Create a contingent liquidity cushion of $US1 billion
Vulnerable external position		Establish annual goal for increase in NFPS deposits in the Single Account (at least $US100M)	Goal achieved	
Low competitiveness and poor investment climate	Select three to five key priorities of the agenda Approve Law on Internal Competition		New agenda and laws submitted to and approved by Congress	Establish the priorities of the Competitiveness Agenda
	Complete an inventory of existing barriers and the institutional reform plan	Create the single window for recording and approving new regulations	Window in operation in early 2004	Eliminate barriers to the creation of businesses
	Approve the Salary Unification Law Design plan for company training	Amend labor laws Develop plans	Law submitted to and approved by Congress Plans underway	Increase the flexibility of labor markets and provide training through firms

Annex

Ecuador: Selected Economic Indicators

(As a percentage of GDP, unless otherwise indicated)	1997	1998	1999	2000	Est. 2001	Est. 2002	Proj. 2003
I. National Accounts							
Gross National Investment	21.5	25.3	14.7	20.1	25.7	27.2	26.4
Gross National Savings	18.4	15.9	20.5	26.4	23.2	20.6	20.1
Financing Gap	3.0	9.3	−5.7	−6.3	2.4	6.6	6.3
Government Investment	3.1	3.6	3.8	2.9	3.5	4.5	3.7
Government Savings	3.5	0.4	0.9	6.9	7.5	7.3	7.9
Government Savings Gap	−0.4	3.2	2.9	−4.0	−3.9	−2.8	−4.2
Private Investment	18.4	21.7	11.0	17.2	22.1	22.7	22.7
Private Savings	14.9	15.5	19.6	19.5	15.8	13.4	12.2
Private Savings Gap	3.4	6.1	−8.6	−2.3	6.3	9.4	10.5
II. Nonfinancial Public Sector							
Current Revenues	21.6	19.1	22.5	27.6	24.7	25.7	26.6
Taxes	7.8	8.5	9.1	11.7	12.3	12.3	12.3
Petroleum Revenues	5.4	3.9	6.2	9.2	6.4	5.7	6.5
Current Spending	18.2	18.9	21.2	21.0	17.3	18.5	18.7
Interest	4.3	4.2	8.1	6.6	4.7	3.6	3.6
Capital Spending	5.5	5.2	6.0	5.5	6.7	6.5	5.5
Primary Balance	2.2	−0.9	3.4	7.7	4.6	4.0	5.4
Global Balance	−2.1	−5.1	−4.6	1.0	−0.1	0.4	1.8
NFPS Balance without Petroleum	−7.5	−9.0	−10.9	−8.1	−6.5	−5.2	−4.7
III. Balance of Payments							
GNFS Exports	25.8	21.5	31.6	37.1	27.1	24.3	22.2
GNFS Imports	24.4	27.2	22.1	28.2	29.0	30.9	28.9

Trade Balance	2.5	-4.3	10.0	9.2	-1.4	-5.3	-5.6
Remittances	2.7	3.4	6.5	8.3	5.8	5.4	5.4
Current Account Balance	-3.0	-9.3	5.7	6.3	-2.4	-6.6	-6.3
Current Account Balance without Petroleum	-5.4	-9.5	-0.2	-5.6	-7.2	-11.4	-10.5
Direct Investment	2.9	3.6	3.8	4.5	6.3	4.9	4.3
Reserves*	—	—	-1.5	4.9	2.8	1.6	2.3
IV. Indicators of credit capacity **							
Total External Debt/GDP	63.9	70.5	97.6	85.1	68.5	65.7	60.8
Total External Debt/Exports	248.1	327.5	309.4	229.4	252.9	270.7	273.5
Total External Debt Service/Exports	97.6	151.3	125.0	202.4	118.6	114.9	124.8
Memo:							
GDP Growth	4.1	2.1	-6.3	2.8	5.1	3.0	3.5–4.0
GDP in $US	$23,636	$23,255	$16,674	$15,934	$21,024	$24,507	$26,725

—. No data available.

*Excess freely disposable international reserves.

** Includes arrears and adjustment for exchange rate variation and differs from records in balance of payments in that the latter does not include earlier payments or refinancing.

Source: Central Bank of Ecuador, MEF, and IMF. Information updated as of January 22, 2003.

2

Tax Policy and Administration[1]

Osvaldo Schenone

The three principal tax policy problems in Ecuador are lack of simplicity, a small tax base, and an inefficient use of resources. The reasons behind these problems are, first, the proliferation of taxes, a trend that lacks transparency and hides inequity and inefficiency in the allocation of resources. A second reason is the tax exemptions, which introduce distortions and do not comply with any of the tax policy objectives, especially with respect to redistribution in the case of the Value-Added Tax (VAT)(Impuesto al Valor Agregado—IVA) and are inefficient in achieving the goal of promoting socially equitable undertakings in the case of ISR (Impuesto Sobre la Renta—Income Tax) exemptions or import duties. Finally, a third reason is the tax revenue preallocations, which do not allow for the efficient use of tax resources and discourage the collection effort by those jurisdictions that prefer to count on transfers from the central government. A tax simplification—by abolishing minor taxes; broadening of the base through the elimination of exemptions; and reorienting taxes, through the elimination of preallocations—would result in lower administrative costs for collecting taxes, an increase in tax revenues, and more efficient allocations. Regarding tax administration, the two most serious problems are the inadequate institutional design of the Internal Revenue Service (Servicio de Rentas Internas—SRI), which makes it vulnerable to constant pressures from private interests, and the poor anti-evasion efforts by Customs, which has not been reformed and, consequently, has not had the same dynamism as SRI, in spite of the fact that they share the same computer system. Good practice would suggest reinforcing the independence of the SRI and merging with Customs under a single authority.

---

1. Osvaldo Schenone is a tax specialist and World Bank consultant. He is professor of economics at the Universidad de San Andrés, Bueonis Aires, Argentina.

A. Background

The advent of the new millennium not only brought a new monetary system—that is, dollarization—to Ecuador, but also put an end to the deficit in the Nonfinancial Public Sector (NFPS, SPNF in Spanish), which characterized the final decades of the last century, by generating a primary surplus through primary cost containment (as a percentage of GDP) and an increase in tax revenues, primarily VAT.

The NFPS comprises the central government, the municipal governments, the Ecuadorian Social Security Institute (*Instituto Ecuatoriano de Seguridad Social—IESS*), and a multitude of other public enterprises. The income from taxes and non-taxes (primarily from oil) of the NFPS have, during recent years, amounted to 22 percent of GDP, with a recent tendency to increase, as indicated in Table 1. This table also shows the portion of the income received by the central government under the headings of income from oil and income from taxes. The income from taxes, in turn, are shown in the table, separating, on the one hand, the taxes collected outside the SRI and, and on the other hand, the taxes collected by this Service—that is, ISR, VAT, ICE (*Impuesto a los Consumos Especiales*—Special Consumption Tax), and others.

As indicated in Table 1, the increased income by the central government and, in general, by the entire Nonfinancial Public Sector is primarily due to the increase in VAT revenues, since the increase in ISR, ICE, and others were significantly less, in terms of percentage of GDP, as of the middle of the last decade. VAT revenues account for more than 60 percent of all SRI collections.

Table 1. Total Income by the Nonfinancial Public Sector and the Central Government, 1995–2002 (expressed as a percentage of the GDP)

		Central Government							
				Taxes					
						Within the SRI			
Year	Non-financial Public Sector	Total	Oil	Outside the SRI	Total	ISR	VAT	ICE	Other
1995	22.7	15.5	5.9	3.7	6.0	2.0	3.0	0.5	0.4
1996	21.8	15.7	7.3	2.7	5.6	1.9	3.0	0.4	0.4
1997	19.9	13.8	5.3	2.5	6.0	1.8	3.2	0.7	0.4
1998	17.2	13.2	3.8	3.2	6.2	1.8	3.6	0.5	0.3
1999	20.8	13.2	4.4	1.3	7.6	0.6	3.4	0.5	3.0
2000	25.8	17.4	6.7	1.1	9.6	1.6	5.4	0.6	2.0
2001	23.4	17.9	5.8	1.5	10.6	2.6	6.8	0.8	0.4
2002(e) .	24.2	18.0	6.0	1.4	10.6	2.5	6.9	0.9	0.4

(e). Estimate.
Source: Actual preparation from the database of the Ministry of Economy and Finance, SRI, in F. Andic and A. Mann, *Report on the Internal Revenue Service of Ecuador. Tax Revenue and Administrative Policy* (Salto Project), May 2002; and J. Bour, D. Artana, and F. Navajas, *Fiscal Problems in Ecuador* (International Development Bank), September 2002.

At present, the tax income of the central government not administered by the SRI consists primarily of customs tariffs, collected by CAE (*Corporación Aduanero de Ecuador*—Ecuadorian Customs Corporation).[2] The SRI director is a member of the CAE board, in what may be interpreted as an indicator of the intention to merge the two institutions, which, up until this date, has not yet occurred.

The fact that the improvement in the VAT collection efforts has not been accompanied by a parallel improvement in ISR may be attributed to several factors, one of which is the zigzagging policy of first abolishing and then re-adopting the ISR in 1999. Another factor is that, as indicated in a later section, in recent years the ISR has suffered the effects of repeated and varying exemption proposals with greater severity than other taxes.

The tax administration also shows a change in orientation during the final years of the last decade. The SRI was created in December 1997 as a replacement for the discredited Internal Revenue Office. Likewise, in 1998, the CAE was created as a replacement of the previous National Customs Office. At the time of its creation, the SRI did not have a central taxpayers' registry—only several registries at the different regional offices throughout the country. This used to make it possible for a delinquent or tardy taxpayer to simply register at another regional office, and avoid punishment for previous delinquencies.

A number of improvements have been made since then. A centralized taxpayers registry (*Registro Único de Contribuyentes—RUC*) has been created, with 1.1 million registrants (80 percent of them individuals and 20 percent legal entities). The number of personnel was reduced and training was increased. More than 95 percent of the print shops authorized to print sales and withholding receipts were verified in 2002 (with an electronic authorization system for printing invoices, which reduces the time duration of the process—including taxpayer verification—to just a few minutes). The large taxpayers (approximately 3,000 companies, which generate around 80 percent of SRI revenues) are subject to special procedures, since a special unit for attending to their needs is not considered necessary. And finally, the management indicators show satisfactory levels for 2001 and 2002, as indicated in Table 2.

The SRI is making use of third-party information to increase taxpayer compliance. Cross-checks performed during 2001 and 2002 detected approximately 100,000 persons not registered in the RUC. The fact that companies and public entities are subject to VAT, offers excellent possibilities for cross-checking information, because when these entities request a reimbursement of VAT credits, they automatically reveal their identities to their suppliers. Because of the large volume of purchases made by the state, the volume of resultant cross-checked information is also very large.

---

2. Other sources of tax income, which are of lesser significance in terms of size, are two taxes on transportation and oil by *Sistema de Oleoducto Transecuatoriano* (TransEcuadoran Pipeline Systen [SOTE]), administered by the Central Bank, and the taxes on lubricants and aviation fuel for international service and the airport tax, administered by the Civil Aviation Office.

Table 2. Some SRI Management Indicators

	2001	2002
Debt collected versus outstanding debt	23%	41%
Forced collections versus collections under management	1.7%	2.8%
Taxpayers who declare nothing versus taxpayers who declare a gain	47.2%	41.4%
Taxpayers who declare versus taxpayers who should declare	43.4%	33.5%
Notifications to actual non-filers versus (special) non-filers	94%	89%
Notified taxpayers with cross-checked differences versus planned notifications	47%	91%

Source: SRI.

As a result of cross-checking the information, however, delays have been created that have to be resolved. The cross-checked information of ISR and VAT declarations by one taxpayer and the various taxpayers who buy and sell among themselves, have been delayed and the results from the cross-checked declarations of 2000 are not yet available.

The SRI is a proponent of the strategy of limiting to a minimum any visits to companies, in order to avoid needless discussions (which, it is feared, could lead to opportunities for corruption) among its auditors and the accountants of the companies, and has replaced said visits with information cross-checks and subsequent notifications of irregularities to the taxpayers.

Even though the SRI has the legal power to contract private collection agencies, it refrains from using them because a large number of the delinquent accounts come from the old Internal Revenue Office and it has not yet been possible to verify the legitimacy of the claims.

The so-called Ecuadorian Simplified Tax System (*Régimen Impositivo Simplificado Ecuatoriano—RISE*), an initiative for small producers and informal vendors, is pending legislative action. According to this initiative, these taxpayers would pay a monthly sum based on their estimated income, and they would not be obligated to maintain an accounting system, but they must issue and receive invoices. The SRI estimates an annual income from this of approximately $US20 million, or 0.1 percent of GDP.

B. The Three Primary Problems of the Tax Policy

The main difficulty of Ecuadorian economic policy is its subordination to immediate political urgencies. The Economic and Public Investment Balance from January 2000 to January 2003 provides a good example: "Once the goal of economic stability was reached, the national political front became complicated again. By not having a political party or a majority in Congress, the government was obliged to incur expenses and recruit economic authorities that provided it with greater discretionary space. This produced a reduction in the primary fiscal surplus which would have been better used as a contingency fund, but which unfortunately was used to guarantee the short term political governability in the absence of a long-term national pact."[3]

In the specific issue of tax policy, this subordination led to the creation of multiple taxes to satisfy the demands of different interest groups, while at the same time conceding exemptions for the same purpose. With the same desire to expand interest group accommodation, what remains of tax revenues after exemptions is preallocated to different beneficiaries. This delicate balancing act leaves few resources for the government to be able to provide public goods and infrastructure to benefit the entire population, rather than a few interest groups.

Even though various problems exist with the Ecuadorian tax system, three stand out owing to their importance and the urgency with which they require a resolution. They are the proliferation of taxes, tax exemptions, and preallocation of tax revenues.

Among the problems not chosen for detailed treatment in this chapter—despite their importance—are the limited progressiveness of personal income tax and the collection repercussions of reduced customs tariffs.[4]

The Problem of the Proliferation of Taxes

Even though nearly all of the country's tax revenues stem from 10 different taxes, and half of them (VAT, ISR, ICE, customs tariffs, and the vehicle tax) generate more than 75 percent of the tax revenues, the SRI has identified more than 80 taxes according to the classification shown in Table 3.

This situation implies unnecessarily high administrative costs for both the taxpayers and the administration. It discourages payment on the part of the taxpayers, and supervision on the part of the tax authority.

The proliferation of taxes demonstrates the need to "fine-tuning" the tax policy, carefully selecting which sector must pay the benefits received by the ones selected— which also requires detailed exemptions and, possibly, also exceptions to the exemptions. This type of tax policy lacks transparency and hides inequity and inefficiency in the allocation of resources. Without pretending to be an exhaustive list, some well-known examples are as follows: (1) the tax on company assets by the Superintendency of Companies, which then receives and uses those same taxes; (2) financial societies also being subject to the asset tax, which is allocated to the Superintendency

---

3. D. Badillo and R. Salazar, *Economic and Public Investment Balance from January 2000 to January 2003* (Ministry of Economy and Finance, November 2002), p. 5.
4. The reasons why the customs tariffs must be reduced and made more uniform are treated in the chapter on Commerce and Competitiveness.

Table 3. The Structure of the Tax System

| Type of Tax | Number of Taxes | Beneficiaries | | | |
		Central Gov.	Munici-palities	Prov.	Others
Income and Capital Earnings Tax	5	3	1	1	
Payroll Tax	1			1	
Property and Net Worth Tax	26	1	11	2	12
Real Estate Transfer Tax	24		8	2	14
Financial Asset Tax	6	1			5
Sales Tax on Goods and Services	17	7	3		7
VAT	1	1			
ICE	7	6			1
Telecommunications	1				1
Electricity	4				4
Public Entertainment	3				1
Betting	1		2		
Foreign Trade Tax	1	1			
Various Taxes	4	2	1	1	
Totals	84	15	24	4	41

Note: The *Others* category is composed of an enormous variety of institutions. For example, the Guayaquil Beneficence Council, the State University of Guayaquil, the Guayas Transit Commission, the Ecuadorian Social Security Institute, the Osvaldo Loor Foundations, the Potable Water Company, the National Promotion and Development of Sports, the Superintendency of Companies, the Superintendency of Banks, the Ecuadorian Tourism Corporation, the National Children's Fund, and so on.
Source: SRI.

of Banks; (3) the tax on the total assets of Act 006-88, which is allocated to the municipalities; (4) the tax on luxury and first-class hotel assets, which is allocated to the Ecuadorian Tourism Corporation (CETUR); and (5) the additional tax of Act 92-88 on bank profits of Act 92-88 whose tax revenues are allocated to the National Children's Fund (FONDIFA).

The Recurring Problem of Exemptions

Tax policy is constantly confronted by the challenge of exemptions. Despite the difficulty in eliminating them, Ecuador has been successful in reducing exemptions between 1999 and the first half of 2001. But following this period, within the space of a little more than one year, renewed efforts have been made to reinstate them.

During the first period, the ISR exemption was eliminated for the financial sector on the income from securities and shares issued by the government, for cooper-

---

3. It should be noted that some of those "reforms of the state," while necessary, would reduce fiscal costs only in the medium- and long-term (and may increase them in the short-run, for example, because of related severance payments).

atives and provident societies (except for the ones established by farmers or officially recognized indigenous people) and the for promoting development (directed primarily at tourism and industrial endeavors). As well, the list of items subject to VAT was replaced with a tax list of VAT-exempt services (fundamentally, housing rentals and financial services)—which, therefore, leaves all other services subject to VAT.

Nevertheless, since the middle of 2001, initiatives to create new exemptions have become more intense. The most important of these are as follows:

- To exempt interest on mortgage loans from ISR.
- To defer the VAT payments on the import of goods until the sale or use of such goods generate a tax debit against which the VAT can be credited.
- To reinstate exemptions in the tourism sector (with the feature—still under discussion—of allowing the acquisition of shares in a tourism project to be deductible from the ISR to be paid by the purchaser of the shares).
- "Tax-free zones" of large geographic dimensions (significant parts of a province or county) in which companies would be exempt from most taxes, regardless of the final destination of their products (internal market or export).[5]
- The Export and Investment Promotion Corporation (*Corporación de Promoción de Exportaciones e Inversiones—CORPEI*) granting a subsidy up to 5 percent on the freight on board (FOB) value of the exports.
- A reduction of 1 to 0.1 percent of the retention that the buyers of agricultural goods for export charge the producers, at the expense of the ISR to be paid by the latter.
- Generous deductions on the payment of ISR.

The SRI has called this set of initiatives "the dismantling of the tax base." In spite of the importance with which the authorities perceive the problem of the ISR and VAT exemptions, a tax cost calculation of these tax expenditures has not been made. A team of outside consultants began a quantification study on this matter in mid-November, 2002.

Aside from the results that may be obtained through these estimates, provisional calculations of the internal VAT exemptions can be made right now (that is, excluding the VAT on imports) on the basis of a sample of 3,055 large taxpayers during 2001, which represents 84 percent of the SRI tax revenues. This provisional estimate is presented in Table 4, and indicates a tax cost on account of the internal VAT exemptions of approximately $US237 million; or 1.1 percent of GDP for the year 2001. Approximately half of this comes from the commerce and industry sectors.

---

5. Hence the quote marks around the expression "tax-free zone," since the term is usually reserved for places where goods are produced only for export.

Table 4. Estimated Tax Cost of the Internal VAT Exemptions, 2001 (in millions of U.S. dollars)

Sector	Total Income	Export of goods and services	income before exemptions	Income actually taxed	Taxable Exempted estimated income	Tax credit on purchases	Fiscal cost
Agriculture	1,339	363	976	86.6	889.4	533.6	42.7
Commerce	7,162	507	6,655	5,148.6	1,506.4	903.8	72.3
Construction	523	1	522	467.8	54.2	32.5	2.6
Energy and gas	572	0	572	89.9	482.1	289.3	23.1
Energy and mining	571	431	140	65.3	74.7	44.8	3.6
Finance and insur.	1,499	63	1,436	1,190.0	246.0	147.6	11.8
Industry	5,468	899	4,569	3,469.9	1,099.1	659.5	52.8
Others	25	1	24	13.0	11.0	6.7	0.5
Comm. Services	3,089	909	2,180	1,982.4	197.6	118.6	9.5
Transp. and comm.	1,405	30	1,375	998.7	376.3	225.8	18.1
Total	21,654	3,204	18,450	13,512.4	4,936.6	2,962.2	237.0

Notes:
(1) The tax credit for purchases was estimated as 60 percent of the estimated exempt income.
(2) The fiscal cost was calculated as 12 percent of the difference between the estimated exempt income and the tax credit for purchases.
Source: Ministry of Economy and Finance.

An alternative estimate is shown in the annex, using National Accounts data, giving as the combined result of the exemptions and tax evasion a tax cost of 1.9 percent of GDP. This result is not inconsistent with a tax cost of the exemptions of 1.1 percent of the GDP.

Attributing the tax cost to the exemption on the basic food items and relating that to the entire agricultural sector (and admitting that this is an overestimate), it can be concluded that the remainder of the exemptions imply a tax cost of at least $US195 million for 2001, or approximately 0.9 percent of GDP.

The exemptions on customs tariffs and VAT on imports,[6] according to an estimate for 2000 and 2001, are concentrated in five tax codes which account for 93 percent of these types of exemptions, shown in Table 5. Their tax cost represents approximately $US123 and 148 million (for 2000 and 2001, respectively), or 0.7 percent of the GDP of these years, without including the exemptions for commer-

---

6. The exemption of VAT on imports has a limited tax revenue effect, since the majority of the import operations are not performed by end users, but by wholesalers, with the result that when they pay VAT they would claim the corresponding tax credit when they sell the products to retailers. In this way, the net VAT collection on import operations tends to disappear and show up as VAT on domestic operations (that is, in the retail sales to the end consumer).

Table 5. Tax Cost of Exemptions on Customs Tariffs and on the VAT on Imports, 2000 and 2001 (mlns $US)

Code number and name of the exemption	Cost and Freight (CIF) Value of imports		Tax cost rate			
	2000	*2001*	*Tariff*	*VAT*	*2000*	*2001*
407—Exempt from VAT	712.8	848.4		12%	85.5	101.8
395—Pharmaceutical products	29.0	27.0	5%	12%	5.0	4.6
464—Public sector	115.2	161.9	10%	12%	25.3	35.6
343—Public sector donations	1.8	11.6	10%	12%	0.4	2.6
413—Exempt from VAT (Public sector)	59.1	30.5		12%	7.1	3.7
Total	917.9	1,079.4			123.3	148.3

Note: The tariff is the average of the tariff positions involved.
Source: Ministry of Economy and Finance.

cial agreements, such as the Andean Community Nations *(Comunidad Andina de Naciones—CAN),* or the Aladi, as indicated in the same table.

Nevertheless, as explained in the footnote, it would be an overestimate of the tax cost of the exemptions to include the VAT exempted from imports. Leaving only the exempted tariffs in the previous calculation, the final cost of the exemptions are estimated at 5 and 10 percent, respectively, for 2000 and 2001, on the imports under Codes 395, 464, and 343. This makes for a total tax cost of between $US13 and 18 million, or approximately 0.1 percent of the GDP, for 2000 and 2001, respectively.

The exemptions based on trade agreements, on the other hand, represented a tax cost, in 2001, of approximately 90 percent of the tariff revenues of that year—or 1.4 percent of GDP—broken down as:

- Exemptions by CAN: $US247 million;
- Exemptions for trade with Chile: $US18 million;
- Exemptions for trade with Mexico: $US11.2 million;
- Exemptions for trade with Argentina: $US6.2 million; and
- Exemptions for trade with Brazil: $US12.8 million.

The promoters of exemptions generally draw on two arguments. First, the exemptions promote certain select activities whose competitiveness must, presumably, be safeguarded and increased through tax or tariff policies; and second, the argument of equity. The first argument is generally used when exemptions to the ISR or to the customs tariffs are proposed, while the second argument is used for proposing exemptions on VAT, for a variety of products.

Neither of the two arguments are particularly valid. Promoting business through tax or tariff exemptions requires the identification of those ventures whose promotion would be beneficial to the society as a whole and not only to the investors involved. The errors of identification that might result would be too costly for taxpayers who were not selected. Furthermore, there is no mechanism to ensure that only involuntary and honest mistakes would be committed which thereby opens up opportunities for corruption and is another disadvantage of the exemption policy. Exemptions on customs tariffs have, in general, strongly prejudicial effects on the economic efficiency, as they can generate widespread protection and, therefore, can create business opportunities that may be be profitable, but are disastrous to the national economy.[7]

The equity argument in favor of exemptions also has limited validity. VAT exemptions on popular consumer goods constitute a highly inefficient way of introducing progressiveness into the tax system. Although it is generally true that the exempted consumption represents a greater percentage of the total consumption by poorer families, it is the richer homes that benefit more from the exemptions. In the case of Ecuador, it was calculated in 1999 that out of every 100 sucres the tax office did not collect because of the exemptions on education, books, health, transportation, water, and electricity (in other words, except basic food items, house rental and financial services) 43 sucres benefited the richest 25 percent of the population and only 14 sucres benefited the poorest 25 percent.[8] Techniques have to be found to get the 14 sucres to the poorest sector, without, automatically, having to award the richest sector with 43 sucres.

Moreover, VAT exemptions complicate the tax administration for the taxpayers and the SRI alike. Taxpayers who sell exempted products as well as taxed products have to attribute the credits for VAT paid on their purchases on some of their sales, thereby complicating the accounting system of the business. Furthermore, the exemption creates a temptation to claim all of the VAT credits, as if all of the purchases were dedicated to the supply of taxed products. This greatly complicates the taxation task of the SRI and the CAE.

The Problem of Preallocations

Income preallocations, whether they are from tax revenues or oil, are found scattered throughout 50 pieces of legislation—laws, decrees, or ministerial agreements. In 2001 there were 32 preallocations from tax revenues and 25 preallocations from oil income.

The amount of preallocated tax revenues for that year were $US303 million, that is, 1.4 percent of GDP, of which 81 percent corresponded to VAT and ISR ($US112 million to VAT and $US133 million to ISR).

---

7. This matter is discussed in detail in the Commercial and Competitiveness chapter.
8. G. Kopits, E. Haindl, E. Ley, and J. Toro, *Ecuador: Modernization of the Tax System* (International Monetary Fund, Department of Public Finances, November 1999), p. 24.

The percentage of the preallocated VAT revenues is 12 percent (1.5 percent to SRI, 10 percent to the Permanent Fund for University and Polytechnic Development (FOPEDEUPO), and 0.5 percent to the state universities), which is approximately equal to the average percentage of the preallocation of all taxes, which, for 2001, reached 14.3 percent of total tax revenues.[9]

In the case of the ISR, the percentage of preallocation is at least equal to 28.5 percent of the tax revenues designated for various purposes. But furthermore, each taxpayer has the right to request, in writing to the tax authority, that up to 25 percent of the tax said taxpayer pays be transferred to the municipality where he or she maintains his or her home. If all of the taxpayers would make use of this right, 53.5 percent of the ISR's tax revenues would be preallocated.

Preliminary data for 2002 indicate that, possibly because of the use the taxpayers make of this right, the average percentage of preallocation of all taxes increased to approximately 19 percent of the total tax revenues.

As an example, the ICE preallocations are shown in Table 6. Of the six categories of goods and services subject to taxes, only one (telecommunications) does not provide any income for to the central government. All of the others provide income that fluctuates between 83.5 percent and 89.5 percent of their respective tax revenues, as can be observed in the last row of the table.

The preallocations of the customs tariffs consist of 3 percent for the Water Resources Council and 3 percent for the CAE. The other 94 percent goes to the central government.

Preallocation procedure prohibits the tax resources from being oriented to where their productivity is greatest. It promotes inefficient, and possibly also inequitable, use of the tax resources. The problem is particularly dire in the case of the funds allocated

Table 6. Preallocation Percentages of the ICE Tax Revenues

	Cigarettes	Beer	Soft drinks	Alcohol	Telecomm.	Luxuries
Hospital Equipment	10	10	10	10	—	10
Free Maternity Care	3	3	3	3	—	—
Osvaldo Loor Foundation	—	—	—	2	—	—
Internal Revenue Service	1.5	1.5	1.5	1.5	1.5	1.5
Potable Water Company	—	—	—	—	65.67	—
National Sports	—	—	—	—	32.83	—
Central Government	85.5	85.5	85.5	83.5	—	88.5

Source: Ministry of Economy and Finance.

9. See J. Gallardo, *Tax Reform: Guaranty for the New Generations* (Ministry of Economy and Finance, August 2001), p. 53.

to regional governments, since the automatic transfers discourage these governments from collecting their own taxes, thereby promoting irresponsible expenditure behavior, since the governments do not have to face the political costs of collecting taxes.

In March 2001, the government sent the parliament a bill for a Fiscal Discipline and Prudence Act, whose Article 22 abolishes "the preallocations in the same way in which they were established." Likewise, the bill legislated that "the General State Budget for the year 2002 would compensate, in the same amount, the Public Sector entities or organisms for the allocation actually received by them during the previous year."

The proposed preallocation elimination mechanism attempted to soften the transition, preventing the public sector entities or organizations from suddenly experiencing a shortage of financing.[10] Nevertheless, this component of the bill was not approved, leaving the preallocation regime unchanged.

C. Two Priority Problems for the Tax Administration

After the SRI and CAE reforms at the end of the last decade, a notable improvement was observed in the tax evasion control of the former, while the latter did not show evidence of significant improvement. The institutional designs of the SRI and the CAE are the most pressing issues of the tax administration.

Other matters are less urgent and of a more operational nature, such as the adoption of a checking account for each taxpayer, and for each type of tax, so that payments and reimbursements may function in the same way as a bank account. As a result, tax evasion control should improve, since the payments of each taxpayer and for each type of tax could be electronically reported to the SRI without delay. The delay in processing the information cross-checks needs to be resolved, as the results of the tax returns of 2000 are still not available. Likewise, in the tax returns of 2001, filed in April 2002, taxpayers have been detected who wrongly calculated the reinvestment deduction into the ISR, but at this writing (November 2002), they have not been notified yet. Finally, a prompt adoption of filing tax returns via the Internet must be taken into consideration.

---

10. Kopits and others, *Ecuador: Modernization of the Tax System* (International Monetary Fund, Department of Public Finances, November 1999), p. 14. This proposal is consistent with the recommendation included in this study: not exceeding the proportion of preallocated revenues by the Constitution to the sectional governments effectively reached in 1999 (9 percent of the current income, instead of 15 percent preallocated), and not exceeding the preallocation for educational expenses above the effectively reached percentage in 1999 (12.5 percent of the current income, instead of 30 percent preallocated). Finally, the abolition of all other revenues preallocated by law was recommended, except the revenues of the Ecuadorian Social Security Institute.

The Independence of the SRI

The SRI board consists of six members with voice and vote, and the executive director of the SRI, with voice but no vote. The members of the board are as follows: The Minister of Finance (with two votes in case of a tie); the Superintendent of Companies; the Superintendent of Banks; the Undersecretary of the Budget; the Minister of Industrialization, Commerce, Integration, Fishing and Competitiveness; and one representative of the private sector.

This board needs to be reinforced to put it into a better position to resist pressures (from the public sector itself and, naturally, from the private sector) that tend, without breaking the law, to satisfy objectives outside of the scope of collecting taxes—such making a profit promoting the competitiveness of a given sector, or improving the equity of the distribution of tax revenues. These may all be noble aims, but they are outside the objective of tax collection—which should be the exclusive goal of the SRI—and may impede its effective.

The Efforts of the CAE

The anti-evasion efforts of the CAE has not had the same dynamism as that of the SRI, in spite of the fact that it shares the computer system that was upgraded and modernized by the SRI before sharing it with the CAE. This includes online information from the moment the merchandise is shipped from the point of origin, in such a manner that the taxes can be paid and the merchandise liberated from customs at the moment of arrival in the port, preventing all storage problems and their corresponding delays.[11]

CAE has not been completely reconstructed, as was the case for the SRI, which practically replaced all of its personnel. CAE failed to replace hardly anyone, since the labor regulations prevent the dismissal of employees, unless the department within the CAE is abolished in which the employees work. (The managers, for example, are appointed for four years and cannot be removed by the board, even for negligence or other type of substandard performance).

The possibility of overhauling the CAE should be considered, or an evaluation should be made concerning the advantages of merging this institution with the SRI, without endangering the efforts of the latter. The tax reform legislation of March 2001 merged the two institutions, but Congress rejected this initiative as a result of strong pressure from the importation sector. Later, in November 2001, the participation of the executive director of the SRI as president of the CAE board was approved by law.

---

11. Payment by the taxpayer is immediately recorded in the network of banks, which also prevents possible fraud at the bank counters. This computer system also provides better control of temporary admission mechanisms and tax deposits for merchandise.

A bill is currently before Congress on the Reform of the Internal Customs Act, which incorporates labor reforms that would allow a personnel restructuring similar to that of the SRI.

Law 41 of 1999 provides that the merchandise in warehouses or storage areas may be inspected to verify whether the property is backed by documents proving merchandise ownership (commercial invoice if it is national, or a shipping bill in the case of international shipments). These documents must also be shown by transporters who move the merchandise from one place to another. The absence of these documents provides permission for seizure of the merchandise and to uncover cases of evasion of VAT or contraband. This procedure has **practically** not been used in Ecuador.

Decided official backing for the observance of this law coupled with an adequate reform of the Internal Customs Act could be a substitute for the disappearance of the Customs Office and its merging with the SRI.

D. Recommendations

The tax revenue value of this set of recommended tax and administration policies would be approximately 1.2 percent of GDP. If this increase in tax revenues were not sufficient for the macroeconomic balance, it would be recommended to increase the VAT rate, since each percentage point (within the scope of an existing rate) added to this rate is estimated to generate an increase in tax revenues of approximately 0.6 percent of GDP.

The adoption of these recommendations would produce a less complicated tax system that is broad-based and consistent with an efficiently functioning economy.

ELIMINATION OF MINOR TAXES. We recommend that the collection and disbursement of these minor taxes be eliminated. It is well known that the financial effects of their elimination would be of little significance, but the design of an orderly elimination strategy would require more detailed knowledge of the structure of each of these taxes. Their elimination would allow the tax authority and taxpayers to reduce administrative costs and to concentrate on the truly important taxes. The tax revenue effect is ambiguous, since an improved compliance with the important taxes may provide greater tax revenues than the one generated by the minor taxes whose elimination we are recommending.

ELIMINATION OF EXEMPTIONS. We recommend that VAT exemptions only be applied to unprocessed basic food items and residential rentals that are in addition to a primary home. Consequently, we recommend the elimination of exemptions on agricultural input items (such as seeds, balanced feed, tractors, fungicides, herbicides, plows, harrows, and so on); on financial services; different types of paper, books, and magazines; medicines and their raw materials; on transportation services, electricity, water, and sewage; public entertainment events; professional services; tolls; fumigation services; on the cooling and storage of foods and on all other services used in the preparation of foods or other goods. This list is not exhaustive, but it illustrates the exemptions to be eliminated in order to leave only on unprocessed basic foods and residential rentals that are not people's only home. The tax revenue increase of this elimination is estimated at 0.9 percent of GDP.

We also recommend the elimination of the ISR exemptions. The calculations of the tax revenue effect of this elimination have not yet been performed, but the Ministry of Economy and Finance, the Central Bank, and the SRI are committed to gathering the necessary information.

Likewise, we recommend the elimination of the customs tariff exemptions. Although the primary purpose of this elimination is not an increase in tax revenues but to reduce protection, an additional estimated tax income of 0.1 percent of GDP would be obtained.

ELIMINATION OF PREALLOCATIONS. We recommend the elimination of the majority, if not all of the preallocations, except for the payroll tax, which is allocated to the Ecuadoran Social Security Institute (see the chapter on the Policy on Preserving Fiscal Stability and Competitiveness). The gradual application of this measure could take place in the manner described in Article 22 of the Discipline and Fiscal Prudence Act of March 2001.

This measure would have the effect of permitting (although not guaranteeing) a more productive use of tax resources. The amount involved in 2001 is $US112 million of VAT and $US133 of ISR, plus other preallocated taxes up to a total of $US303 million (1.4 percent of GDP). This is in addition to a better use of these tax resources based on greater productivity for the public sector and for the economy as a whole. In this manner, the total benefit of the elimination of preallocations may be estimated as the productivity increase multiplied by the total amount of preallocated funds.

If the increase in productivity consists of 10 percentage points, the elimination of the preallocations will be equivalent to having more resources in an amount that is equal to 0.15 percent of GDP.

Tax Administration Recommendations

APPROVE THE RISE (ECUADORAN SIMPLIFIED TAX SYSTEM) LEGISLATION. This measure would allow greater control over the suppliers of small taxpayers in the system, because they have to have invoices from their suppliers. As the number of taxpayers in RISE grows, it will be more difficult for the suppliers to avoid registration with the SRI, since the demand for invoices will be greater for sales made to taxpayers in the RISE. It is estimated that at the outset of its implementation, this measure will generate a tax revenue of $US20 million, or 0.1 percent of GDP.

CORRECT DELAYS IN INTERNAL PROCESSES. Delays on account of information cross-checking (among different taxes of the same taxpayer and among different taxpayers) must be reduced, as must the delays in sending notifications to taxpayers regarding incorrect tax returns.

REINFORCE THE INDEPENDENCE OF THE SRI BOARD. The purpose for this recommendation is to prevent the SRI resolutions from being used as instruments for introducing discriminatory and distorted tax treatments. The SRI must not get involved in satisfying any objective other than the strict collection of the taxes created by law. In particular, the competitiveness of any sector, or the promotion of industry, agriculture, or a given region should never be an element of judgment in the deliberations of the SRI board of directors.

CONSIDER THE MERGER OF THE SRI WITH THE CAE. Because VAT contributors make up the major part of taxpayers who pay customs duties, and because they are satisfactorily controlled by the SRI, this institution could take advantage of economies of scale to also supervise the collection of customs duties from the same group of taxpayers. Certainly, this result could also be undertaken through a narrow collaboration between SRI and CAE. The question is whether this collaboration could be more easily obtained under a single authority that governs both institutions.[12]

AMEND THE CUSTOMS ACT. The Customs Office labor system should be reformed, which would permit a restructuring similar to the one that has worked so well at the SRI.

PROMOTE A STRICT COMPLIANCE WITH LAW 41 OF 1999. This evasion control mechanism of VAT and contraband requires official backing at the highest level so that it can be applied without exceptions or discretion.

Summary Table of the Tax Revenue Effects of the Recommendations (in percentage of GDP)

Reduction of VAT exemptions	0.86
Reduction of customs duty exemptions	0.09
Elimination of preallocations	0.15
Ecuadoran Simplified Tax System	0.09
Total	1.19

---

12. In 1999 the International Monetary Fund recommended the evaluation of this merger. See Kopits and others, *Ecuador: Modernization of the Tax System* (International Monetary Fund, Department of Public Finances, November 1999), p. 9.

Summary Table of the Order of Priorities of the Recommendations

Essential and Immediate Recommendations	Medium-Term Recommendations (during 2003/2004)
– Elimination of exemptions – Elimination of preallocations – Correction of the delays in cross-checking information in the SRI – Reinforcing the independence of the SRI board of directors – Amending the labor system of the Customs Act	– Elimination of minor taxes – Considering the SRI-CAE merger – Promoting the strict compliance with Law 41 of 1999 – Approval of the RISE

Recommendation Matrix

Problems (including annual tax cost—if applicable)	Policy Measures		Progress Indicators	Objectives/Goals
	Short Term (Until June 2003)	Medium Term (2003–07)		
Exaggerated number of minor taxes, of low tax revenues and preallocations.	Eliminate the minor taxes and their corresponding collections.	Gradually eliminate the minor taxes.	Approval of repealed laws.	Reduce administrative costs for the tax authority and for the taxpayers.
Exemptions of ISR, VAT (except unprocessed basic foods, financial services, and home rental), and customs tariffs.	Eliminate the ones that create less conflict politically.	Completely eliminate exemptions (except unprocessed foods, financial services, and home rentals).	Approval of repealed laws.	Reduce distortions in the economy; increase the tax revenues by 0.95 percent of GDP.
Preallocation of taxes (except preallocations to the Ecuadorian Social Security Institute).	Eliminate the ones that create less conflict politically.	Completely eliminate preallocation (except the Ecuadoran Social Security Institute—IESS).	Approval of repealed laws.	Increase productivity of the use of fiscal resources by 0.15 percent of GDP.
Small producers and merchants that are not taxpayers.	Adopt the Ecuadoran Simplified Tax System (RISE).		Approval of the law.	Reduce the informality and generate tax revenues of 0.09 percent of GDP.
Vulnerability of the SRI to private interest pressures.	Strengthen the SRI institutionally.			Prevent erosion of the tax base through administrative means.
Stagnation of CAE efforts.	Evaluate the merger between the CAE and the SRI.			Improve contraband control.

Delays in information cross-checks and in sending out notifications to taxpayers.	Start resolving the delays.	Complete elimination of the delays and prevent causing new delays.
Labor System of the Customs Act.	Approve a legal reform that allows the restructuring of the personnel situation.	Restructure Customs personnel, similar to the way it was done at the SRI.

Annex

An alternative estimation of the tax cost of the VAT exemptions is presented here.

Utilizing the information from the Final Consumption of Households on the National Accounts, a maximum potential VAT income can be estimated, which will be different from the tax income observed, for two reasons: exemptions and evasion.

Final Consumption of Households	Value in millions of dollars	Potential Tax Revenues
Bananas, coffee, and cacao	53.88	6.47
Grains	54.00	6.48
Flowers	18.45	2.21
Other crops	408.24	48.99
Breeding animals	229.14	27.50
Forestry and lumber	14.26	1.71
Fish and shellfish	183.40	21.99
Mineral products	2.63	0.32
Meat and meat products	728.71	87.45
Processed fish and shellfish	104.31	12.56
Oil and fats	204.83	24.58
Milk products	236.01	28.32
Grain milling and bakery products	549.04	65.89
Refined sugar	127.93	15.35
Candies and chocolates	67.99	8.16
Other foods	185.18	2.22
Drinks	384.12	46.09
Tobacco and cigarettes	52.21	6.27
Textiles and clothing	844.93	101.39
Wood products	26.24	3.15
Paper and related products	184.88	22.19
Petroleum products	197.02	23.64
Chemical products	620.41	74.45
Rubber and plastic products	109.06	13.09
Nonmetal minerals	39.45	4.73
Products made of metal	209.83	25.18
Machinery and equipment	319.75	38.37
Transportation equipment	201.40	24.17
Other manufactured items	401.86	48.22
Electricity and water	142.20	17.06
Hotels and restaurants	438.23	52.59
Shipping and storage	1,216.34	145.96
Mail and telecommunications	329.15	39.50
Financial and insurance services	130.98	15.71
Home rentals	683.88	82.07
Other activities	51.24	6.15
Public administration	10.36	1.24
Education	274.80	32.98

Final Consumption of Households	Value in millions of dollars	Potential Tax Revenues
Social and health services	182.05	21.85
Other social, personal, and domestic services	138.88	16.66
TOTAL	10,357.52	1,242.90

Source: Central Bank of Ecuador.

Using the 2000 data, it is calculated that the tax income results together with exemptions and evasion end up being equal to the difference between $US1,242.90 million and the effective tax income for this year, $US893.4 million; that is, $US349.5 million, or approximately 2.2 percent of GDP. The estimated amounts in the text of this report, which attributes a tax cost of 1.3 percent of GDP to the exemptions, is not inconsistent with the results of this annex.

3

Debt Administration and Sustainability[1]

Elaine Tinsley

Ecuador is no stranger to inefficient public debt management; during the last 30 years it has been struggling to control the enormous burden of servicing its debt. Part of the problem lies in the fiscal structure the country inherited from the military regime: a big bureaucracy coupled with dependence upon highly volatile oil revenues, subsidies, and earmarked expenditures. However, there are other reasons: persistent bad fiscal management practices, including sizable wage hikes in the public sector; inflation; and the distorted exchange policies of the past. All of these factors have conjoined to make fiscal accounts especially vulnerable to external crises, compelling the country to restructure its debt on two occasions. The first was in 1994, after a seven-year suspension of debt service, with the introduction of Brady bonds, and the second in 1998, when the government became the first country to default on its Brady bonds, necessitating restructuring in the form of global bonds. Any new external debt policy will be irrelevant without fiscal discipline, which means achieving significant primary surpluses in the next few years. If this prerequisite is met, good debt administration will be the other side of the coin of successfully attaining efficient management and lowering debt profile and financial cost. Proper debt management will improve credibility on the basis of the following: a strict fiscal discipline will reduce Ecuador's currently very high sovereign risk classification, which in turn impacts private sector competitiveness; it will buy back debt or reschedule the existing debt service, especially that which is most onerous to the fiscal accounts; and modernize the country's debt management team.

1. Elaine Tinsley is an economic policy analyst for the World Bank. The author wishes to thank the following individuals from the World Bank: Lenin Parreño, Katy Yánez, Alfredo Astorga, and Silvia Burbano—and especially, from the Public Credit Office of the Ministry of Economy and Finance, Mauricio Pareja and Gino Minoli.

A. Background

Ecuador's present public debt problems can be traced back to the 1970s, when large-scale oil exports enabled the military government of the time to finance large investments and boost public sector employment. Oil revenues also made it possible to provide subsidies to the electricity sector and to domestic oil consumption. As a result, public expenditure experienced a sharp increase between 1972 and 1975. In 1975, owing to a number of external shocks, including El Niño and the low prices of crude oil, public revenues declined. Instead of raising taxes or reducing expenditures, the government attempted to cover its deficit by borrowing, which led to a rapid increase in the volume of public debt. In the early 1980s, in the aftermath of monetary tightening in the United States, the situation worsened because of the resulting high interest rates on variable debt and increased public wages. In 1982, the combination of high interest rates, the recession, and the deterioration of fiscal accounts, compelled the government to devalue its exchange rate, which in turn generated a series of devaluations that increased the external debt service obligations of the private sector (mainly commercial banks). In 1983, to relieve pressure arising from the banking sector's debt burden, the government assumed most of the private external debt, swapping it for a debt in sucres , a move that considerably increased the volume of public debt. In the following years, economic volatility and poor fiscal management generated high fiscal deficits, which finally led to the suspension of public debt service from 1987 to 1994. During that period debt slowly climbed, mainly through accumulation of arrears. In 1994, the authorities reached an agreement with its private creditors to restructure the debt with the issuance of $US6 billion in Brady bonds, an agreement supported by the multilateral agencies which helped by financing the guarantee for the bonds. After the restructuring, Ecuador's external public debt totaled $US13.5 billion or 80 percent of GDP, making it one of the highest debt burdens in Latin America and the Caribbean (Figure 1).

In 1998, the high debt situation, combined with the collapse of oil prices, the effects of El Niño, and the resulting banking crisis led to a loss of confidence in the economy and a downward spiral of the exchange rate. Although each devaluation enabled the government to garner more petrodollars to service its deteriorating fiscal account, the increase in the dollar denominated debt stock counteracted whatever benefits the devaluation could generate. The situation became unsustainable and in August 1999, Ecuador defaulted on its debt obligations, making it the first country to default on its Brady bonds.

After the default, in July 2000, Ecuador offered to swap its Brady bonds and Euro bonds, valued at $US0.60 on the dollar, for new 12- and 30-year bonds. The thirty-year global bonds would pay an initial coupon of 4 percent, increasing by one percentage point annually up to a maximum of 10 percent in 2006. In exchange for an additional discount on the value of the debt, 12-year bonds were offered at a 12 percent fixed coupon. The offer was accepted and the debt stock in bonds dropped from $US6.5 billion to $US3.9 billion.

Figure 1. Composition of Public Debt

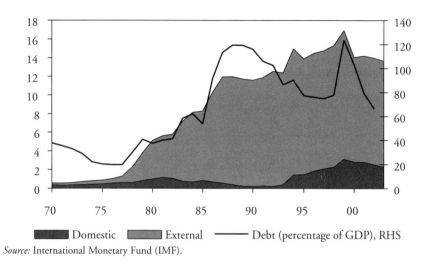

Source: International Monetary Fund (IMF).

This chapter examines some of the main topics relating to public debt management in Ecuador. The second section describes the structure of the public debt. The third section suggests some guidelines for a debt reduction plan based on a debt sustainability analysis model. Finally, the fourth section offers recommendations aimed at improving the level and administration of the public debt.

B. Present Debt Structure

Ecuador's total external debt amounts to $US15.7 billion (64 percent of GDP). Of this amount, 71 percent is public debt and 29 percent is private. While nearly all of the official external debt is medium- or long-term, short-term debt is only significant in the composition of the private debt (45 percent). Thus, although private sector debt is relatively small, its short-term debt represents 13 percent of total external debt, and accordingly could impact the economy to some degree in the event of regional capital flight.

Public debt is $US14 billion. About 80 percent is external debt, and 20 percent internal. Almost all of the external debt is medium- or long-term, and only 7 percent short-term. Thus, only 1.4 percent of total public debt is short-term. This long-term debt maturity structure avoids some of the risks associated with the refinancing of short-term debt, though its high interest rate results in a much heavier debt load. Despite renegotiation of its debt, Ecuador continues to have the highest public debt/GDP ratio in the region after Argentina. Net debt service of the country's debt (including disbursements) consumes about 35 percent of the budget.

PUBLIC EXTERNAL DEBT. Since the 1990s, public external debt from multilateral loans has practically doubled, while bilateral debt has remained almost constant. Taken together, the two represent 60 percent of external debt. Brady bonds (the main component of external debt to the private sector) represent another 36 percent (Figure 2). Before 2000, about 60 percent of external debt was at variable interest rates and the remaining 40 percent was fixed. Renegotiation of the Brady bonds reversed these percentages: at present 75 percent of the external debt is fixed and 25 percent is variable. Though the foregoing helps reduce volatility of debt service, the government must still bear high interest rates for a long period unless restructured.

It is estimated that interest payments on the external debt will total $US581 million in 2002, or 2.4 percent of GDP, and the global bonds represent half that amount and one-third of total external debt (Figure 3). This is not surprising, considering that Brady bonds are the most onerous in terms of interest.

Of the public external debt, the Central Government is the primary debtor responsible for 88 percent of the debt, while the public financial sector represents 9 percent, and public companies and subnational entities account for the remaining 3 percent (see Figure 4). Subnational entities have little chance of mobilizing external funding, partly because of limited administrative capability, but also because of the country's non-payment culture. Since all payments in the Nonfinancial Public Sector (NFPS) are channeled through the Public Credit Office of the Ministry of Economy and Finance (MEF), the government is ultimately responsible for ensuring that these payments are made. Although many entities are punctual in their payments, others, especially electrical utilities, either do not pay or are consistently late.

Figure 2. External Debt

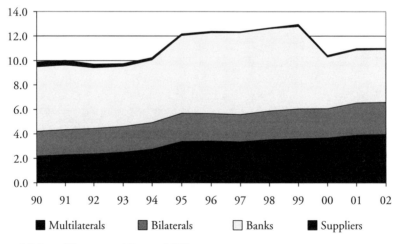

Source: Ministry of Economy and Finance (MEF).

Figure 3. External Debt and Interest Payments by Creditor

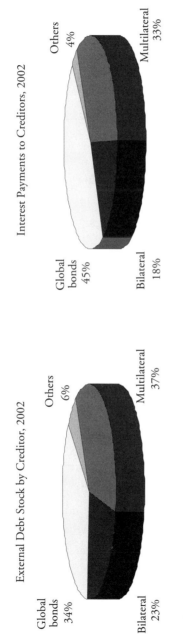

External Debt Stock by Creditor, 2002

Global bonds 34%

Others 6%

Multilateral 37%

Bilateral 23%

Interest Payments to Creditors, 2002

Others 4%

Multilateral 33%

Global bonds 45%

Bilateral 18%

Source: BCE, MEF.

Figure 4. External Debt by Debtor, 2002

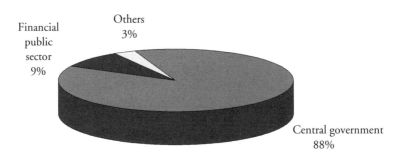

Source: MEF, Statistical Bulletin 68.

PUBLIC DOMESTIC DEBT. Of the $US2.7 billion public domestic debt, almost half ($US1.2 billion) relates to the Deposit Guarantee Agency *(Agencia de Garantía de Depósitos–AGD),* created to rescue the banking system during its crisis. With a nominal interest rate of 9.4 percent, AGD bonds are the most onerous of the internal public debt and they mature in 2014. The holder of this debt is the Central Bank (BCE) and the interest payments on these bonds constitute that entity's main source of income. The second source of debt is dollar bonds. The public domestic debt figures do not include debt to the Ecuadoran Social Security Institute *(Instituto Ecuatoriano de Seguridad Social–IESS),* which is estimated at $US2 billion.

Unlike other countries, Ecuador's public domestic debt is not especially vulnerable, since almost 50 percent of it is with the Central Bank and only 7 percent is short-term. This debt, however, is more sensitive to changes in interest rates: approximately 58 percent of the domestic debt bears a fixed rate, 30 percent is linked to LIBOR, and 12 percent has other variable rates. Overall, interest rates on the domestic debt stock vary from around 5 percent to 12.5 percent, with an average of 8.7 percent for fixed rate and 8.8 percent for variable. (See Figure 5.)

While the current structure of the domestic debt is adequate, it still faces vulnerabilities. Cash management problems compel the government to stretch legal limits to the maximum on issuing Treasury Certificates (currently this is capped at 1 percent of the previous year's GDP). Moreover, owing to the country's low capacity to absorb such issues and the concentration of a small number of buyers, the government's situation remains vulnerable and desperate, forcing it to accept high interest rates in order to cover its cash flow problems.

DEBT SERVICE. Public debt service in 2003 and 2004, exceeding $US2 billion, or approximately 33 percent of revenues each year, is troublingly high (Figure 6). Of the total public debt service for 2003–04, multi- and bilateral payments constitute almost 50 percent of the load, domestic debt nearly 30 percent, and global bonds

Figure 5. Public Domestic Debt (October 2002)

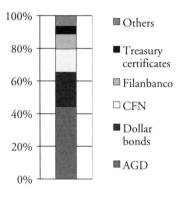

Source: MEF.

about 20 percent. On the other hand, Ecuador is facing serious liquidity problems. The intensive amortization of domestic debt for the capitalization of Filanbanco and medium-term dollar bonds will be particularly high, at $US478 million in 2003, though it will drop to $US270 million in 2004.

In the medium term, external amortizations will rise sharply in 2007, when the buy-back of 10 percent or more of 2012 global bonds is due to kick in, representing $US125 million each year until maturity. This amount is equivalent to 15 percent of current amortizations and its burden must be handled with timely planning. In the short term, interest payment on global bonds represents a sizable proportion of debt service. Every quarter a Brady bond payment comes due, causing peaks in total debt payments (for example, these abruptly jump from $US22 million to $US123 million from one month to the next), with traumatic impact on cash flow management.

C. Ecuador's Debt Reduction Plan

In approaching the high levels of public indebtedness, the Law on Government Fiscal Responsibility outlines the core goal of a debt reduction plan: reduce debt to 40 percent of GDP by the year 2010 (Box 1). The law fails to indicate how this goal is to be achieved, but includes two complementary measures to reduce the debt. The first is to limit spending in order to restrict any future indebtedness, and the second is to buy back its debt with surplus oil revenues generated from the second oil pipeline.

The law provides two approaches to reduce the debt, the first is by limit spending and the second by repurchasing expensive debt. The first approach limits spending by two rules. The first rule place a cap of 3.5 percent on real non-interest expen-

Figure 6. Debt Service for Current Debts, 2003–15 (mlns $US)

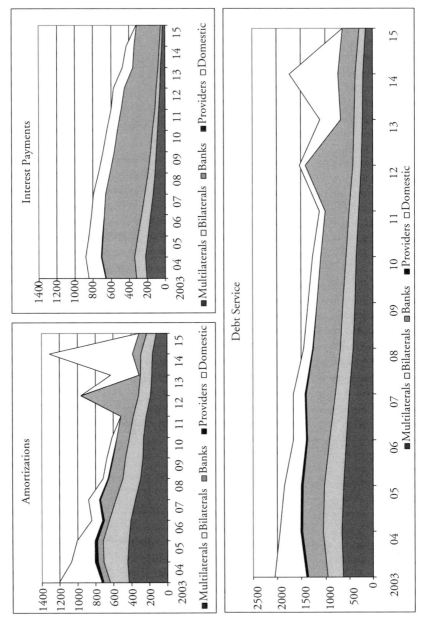

Source: MEF, BCE.

Box 1. On Public Indebtedness in the Organic Law on Fiscal Responsibility, Stabilization, and Transparency

Art. 5 Reduction and limitation of public indebtedness.

- The Ministry of Economy and Finance will implement a permanent public debt reduction policy, aimed at a minimum 16 percentage point reduction in the ratio between the total public debt balance and the GDP during the four-year governmental period reckoned from January 15, 2003. The same policy shall apply to subsequent four-year periods until a debt/GDP ratio of 40 percent is achieved.
- Once it reaches the 40 percent debt/GDP ratio, the level of public indebtedness will not be allowed to exceed this limit or percentage.

Source: Law No. 72. RO/589 of June 4, 2002.

---

diture growth. Since this rate is equivalent to our medium-term GDP projections, in essence, the cap will maintain expenditures as a fixed proportion of GDP, except in years of high growth when this proportion will diminish or vice-versa. The second rule requires that the non-oil-related fiscal deficit be reduced by 0.2 percent per year until it reaches zero. However, given that the present non-oil-fiscal deficit is 4.5 percent, it will not reach zero for 22 years, which renders the rules irrelevant. The two rules thus bring little pressure to bear to contain spending.

The second approach reduces the debt by placing the royalties derived from the marginal increase in private production (that is, over and above what is being currently transferred via the first pipeline) into the oil fund (FREIRIP). Of these amounts, 70 percent will be allocated to buy back debt, 20 percent will go into an oil stabilization fund, and the remaining 10 percent will go to social and health spending. Of the 70 percent earmarked for buy-back of the debt, only up to 15 percent can be used to reimburse social security debt. The remaining 85 percent would be used to buy back external debt, that is, the 2012 Brady bonds, which are currently the most expensive debt. In addition, once the oil stabilization fund reaches 2.5 percent of GDP, these funds will also be applied to debt repurchasing. FREIRIP funds are not expected to materialize until 2004.

Within the framework of the Law on Fiscal Responsibility, the Ministry will present its Debt Reduction Plan next February. At the same time, the Law provides that the Technical Secretariat, in this case the Central Bank, will support this task by (a) supplying the figures; (b) submitting technical reports with recommendations for policies to be adopted with respect to the debt, such as the debt buy-back policy; (c) submitting reports to Congress; and (d) implementing a transparent debt buy back system.

Debt Sustainability Analysis

Based on the medium-term goal stipulated by the law, our debt sustainability analysis determines what primary deficit is required to attain a debt level of 40 percent of GDP, which also could combine with reasonable, attainable financing parameters. The model includes maximum non-interest expenditure growth of 3.5 percent and debt buy-back with resources from the oil fund. We have also verified that the model meets the condition of the plan to reduce the non-oil-related fiscal balance by an average 0.2 percent annually. Box 2 lists the assumptions of the base scenario.

THE MODEL. The model starts with the government's amortization plan. Interest payment is calculated from the current level of debt and newly contracted debt. A public spending path is projected (on the basis of the fiscal law) and non-oil income (set as 20 percent of GDP), making it possible to arrive at an initial primary surplus. Then the target primary surplus corresponding to the declining annual debt/GDP ratio is calculated. Next, the difference between the target and initial primary surpluses is calculated as the **additional fiscal effort required**, which can take the form either of reduced spending or higher taxation. Finally, after subtracting amortizations from the total fiscal balance (corresponding to the target primary surplus), the remainder represents the extra financing required. The additional fiscal effort and the extra financing are substitutive, that is, a lower additional fiscal effort means greater financing requirements and vice-versa.

RESULTS. In order to reduce the debt/GDP ratio from 57 percent to 51 percent in 2003, the government needs an estimated primary surplus of 4.4 percent of GDP and extra financing of 3.4 percent. Neither this fiscal adjustment nor the necessary amount of financing are by any means figures to be taken lightly. The picture is similar for 2004.

Because of the recent adjustment in GDP, it is quite probable that Ecuador will achieve its goal of 40 percent of GDP before 2010, as the country also has an aggressive amortization plan. Nonetheless, in order to accomplish that goal, the country must obtain successive primary surpluses of approximately 3.7 percent of GDP over the years 2005–08. (See Table 1.)

Thus, Ecuador's debt problem is one both of solvency and of liquidity. Though prospects for 2003 seem daunting, this is partly due to the existing debt, which increases financing needs for 2003. It should be noted that as the debt stock diminishes, the debt service/GDP ratio also gradually decreases. The upside of the fiscal law is that it places a ceiling on spending; however, as has been noted, this ceiling is not sufficiently restrictive, requiring an additional fiscal effort, either via increasing revenues or reducing expenditures, and this is only possible with a solid policy commitment.

Our analysis also shows that the oil fund will have a marginal impact on debt buy-back. First, the government has modified what it believes will be maximum use of the pipelines to 600,000 barrels per day, that is, 200,000 barrels fewer than its

---

Box 2. Base Scenario Assumptions

1. GDP growth will be 4 percent for 2004 and 2005, and 3.5 percent for the 2006-10 projection period.
2. Inflation is exogenous and will decline to 2 percent over the long term.
3. Debt buy-back will begin in 2004 with the 2012 global bonds, which are the most onerous part of the debt, as they carry an interest rate of 12 percent.
4. Complete rollover of the domestic debt, which assumes disbursements from domestic debt equivalent to 1 percent of the GDP of the previous year will be reimbursed the following year. This is in keeping with current directives stipulating that treasury certificates cannot total more than 1 percent of the GDP of the previous year.
5. Average price of oil will be $US18 per barrel for 2003–10.
6. The new pipeline will go on line and start contributing to the oil fund in 2004.
7. Debt to the IESS is not included in internal debt, although resources from the fund will be diverted to pay it.
8. Non-oil-dependent fiscal revenues will be kept constant at 20 percent of GDP.
9. Nonfinancial spending will comply with the new law and will not climb to more than 3.5 percent annually in real terms (though this law applies to nonfinancial spending of the central government, it is also being applied as a spending limit for the nonfinancial public sector).
10. The conflict concerning the oil VAT rebate will delay investments by private companies by one year. Production by these companies will reach 108 million barrels or 295,000 barrels per day in 2007, which represents the use of only 65 percent of the heavy crude oil pipeline's (OCP) capacity. Petroecuador will increase its investment by $US140 million per year, its operating costs will rise 4 percent, and its production will reach 91 million barrels in 2007. The gas subsidy will be eliminated as of 2003.
11. Of the 70 percent earmarked for debt reduction, a maximum of 15 percent will be used to reimburse the IESS.

---

original projections. This will inevitably reduce the expected windfall in government oil revenues. Second, the fund's resources will depend on the marginal increases in oil production over those of the existing pipeline. Third, the problems that have arisen in resolving the controversy surrounding the VAT rebate dispute between the government and the oil companies have delayed investments in the oil fields, caus-

Table 1. Results of the Public Debt Sustainability Model

BASE CASE	2002	2003	2004	2005	2006	2007	2008	2009	2010
Key Assumptions	Prelim.	Proj. ⟶							
Nominal GDP									
(bln $US)	24.5	26.7	28.3	30.1	31.7	33.5	35.4	37.4	39.4
Real growth (%)	3.0	3.5	4.0	4.0	3.5	3.5	3.5	3.5	3.5
GDP deflator (%)	13.1	5.4	2.0	2.0	2.0	2.0	2.0	2.0	2.0
Key Results (as a percentage of GDP)									
Primary balance	**4.0**	**4.4**	**4.5**	**3.9**	**3.8**	**3.7**	**3.5**	**3.3**	**3.1**
of which fiscal effort		0.4	1.0	0.4	0.4	0.4	0.5	0.5	0.5
Interest payments	3.6	3.4	3.5	3.4	3.3	3.2	3.0	2.8	2.6
Overall fiscal balance	0.4	1.0	1.0	0.5	0.5	0.5	0.5	0.5	0.5
Balance less oil exports	-3.8	-2.8	-2.4	-2.8	-2.7	-2.6	-2.4	-2.2	-2.0
Required financing	**0.0**	**3.4**	**2.7**	**3.2**	**2.5**	**2.4**	**1.7**	**1.5**	**1.3**
Total debt/GDP ratio	57.1	51.4	47.4	44.2	41.4	38.7	36.1	33.7	31.5
Total debt service/									
GDP ratio	8.0	7.8	7.3	7.1	6.3	6.1	5.3	4.8	4.4

Source: MEF, IMF, and the World Bank.

ing a marginal increase in production than initially expected. Thus, at $US294 million, buy-back of the external debt will be more modest during 2004–07 than the originally estimated $US712 million.

D. Policy Recommendations

Management of the public debt is an important indicator for predicting the economic future of a country, since a government's debt portfolio is usually the biggest portfolio and hence can pose a considerable risk to the general balance sheet of the government and the financial stability of the country. Although it is possible that debt will not be the initial cause of a crisis, the structure, currency, and composition of its maturity can contribute enormously to aggravating a crisis. The better a country can manage its debt, the less vulnerable it will be to external crises capable of destabilizing an economy. This is even more critical in a dollarized system, since there are few alternative policies to absorb the impacts. And, since solid management of the public debt is not sufficient in and of itself, it must be complemented by prudent fiscal policies.

The transformation of Ecuador's public debt management style must pass through two main stages. The initial stage consists of strengthening investors' confidence in the new government's commitment to pay its debt. The second stage consists of modernizing management of the public debt, which brings with it reduction of the debt and the burden of servicing it. Accompanied by steady fiscal discipline, this should lead to reopening access to international markets in, one hopes, a not-too-distant future.

First Stage: Recouping Credibility

A number of rating agencies reduced their risk classifications of Ecuador in recent months owing to problems they foresee for the country in covering its financial needs, which are indeed significant for 2003 and 2004. Amortizations alone will consume on average about 4 percent of GDP, and interest payments another 3.5 percent. Further complicating the situation is the fact that the local market is highly saturated with domestic bonds, meaning the government has few available instruments to raise additional funds. In this environment, accessing new debt will be more expensive, particularly if markets perceive a high probability of default.

For this reason, the sooner the government succeeds in obtaining a contingency agreement with the International Monetary Fund, the stronger the signal to the investment community that it can cover its financial requirements in the next two years. An agreement with the Fund will allow new multilateral disbursements to help cover capital amortizations and open the possibility of debt rescheduling with the Paris Club. Based on that fact, the government must maintain an austere fiscal regime to meet its financing needs if it wishes to achieve the primary surpluses mentioned above. It should be observed that an average oil price higher than $US18 will partially reduce the value of the required additional fiscal effort or financing need and vice-versa.

On the other hand, since most of the government's bilateral debt comprises debts with the Paris Club, a conversion or rescheduling is feasible. With regard to global bond and fixed-interest debt, the government should concentrate on rescheduling or buying back the most onerous debt with new borrowings. In view of recent uncertainties in the country, bond prices are low, hence it is a good opportunity to buy back. Logically, both recent initiatives can be implemented once the government has signed the agreement with the IMF and improved its credibility sufficiently to be granted more advantageous conditions.

Second Stage: Modernizing Debt Management

Although the focus of Ecuador's current public debt management is on its immediate reduction, the country will also have to strengthen its administrative capability to manage it. The government needs to develop the institutional capability to manage and direct the debt portfolio in such a way as to take its cue from the goals of New Zealand's debt management goals: "identify a low-risk portfolio of liabilities consistent with the government's aversion to risk and negotiate efficiently to achieve and maintain that portfolio"—that is, reduce the cost of debt.

Ecuador's present public debt management is at a rudimentary stage when compared to other countries of Latin America and the Caribbean. The Public Credit Office of the Ministry of Economy and Finance is in charge of debt operations, in terms of both issuance and authorization of payments. Its function is primarily operational and it performs practically no analysis of risk management. The Public Credit Office responds to the financial needs of the Budget Office *(Oficina de Presupuesto)*, either issuing bonds or Treasury certificates to help cover the financing deficit and loans sought by the government. Given the weaknesses of this office, the Central Bank is the entity responsible for debt analysis. Before the office can process any debt, the Central Bank must approve it, with the exception of debts issued among public sector entities. The Central Bank issues a report examining conditions and assessing the macroeconomic effect of the potential new debt. Though it generally approves most debt requests, the BCE has on occasion rejected some and forced the government to find alternative financing, including ordering the suspension of deposit accumulations, drawing down the deposits, or requesting funds from other public institutions that have deposits. Debt analysis is therefore done at the micro level – one loan at a time and only prior to approval. The Central Bank does not analyze the overall debt profile, nor does it evaluate contingency options in case of external shocks.

Weak institutional capability is common in public debt management within emerging economies. To confront it, one initial step is to create clear and strategic directives to manage the debt profile other than establishing reference levels for liquidity, interest rates, and, to a lesser degree, their exchange composition. For example, Colombia has reference levels for liquidity (less than 15 percent of unsolved debt must mature within one year, while average maturity must be five years or more); interest rates (less than 13 percent must carry a floating rate); and composition of the debt (83 percent in $US, 13 percent in euros, and 4 percent in yens). Ecuador, on the other hand, has practically no guidelines or norms limiting the level of its domestic debt, although in practice the debt is limited by the relative saturation of the market. The issuance of debt in Ecuador is exclusively to satisfy immediate financial needs, as opposed to creating a sustainable medium-term debt profile.

As a second step to modernize debt management, a debt manager position could be created, to monitor compliance and also to advise on adjustments to the debt structure when necessary. Because it is important that the government commits to maintain a certain public debt structure, the manager should be given a high degree of independence. At present, the team in charge of debt responds to the needs of the Treasury and of the budget offices, no matter how precarious the evolution of the debt profile. In the end this is a counterproductive arrangement. The debt manager, though he or she must be sensitive to the needs of the country, must have the authority to protect the integrity of the debt structure. Thus, fiscal policies must be coordinated with the debt manager to limit spending growth based on the country's manageable debt capacity.

A third step would be the creation of a highly professional team responsible for debt management. Appropriate for the second most indebted country in Latin America, its creation would help to improve the government's credibility, especially considering that there have been no institutional changes in debt management since the country's default in 1999. The lack of a debt management team is an impediment not only to the possible reduction of the cost of debt, but also to the identification of risks and their anticipation, which helps create a more stable profile for public debt. So far, political support for the formation of this team has been small. It is, however, a necessary step toward achieving best practices for debt management.

Finally, Ecuador could work out alternative strategies to lessen the effects of economic volatility, such as issuance of anti-cyclical bonds—that is, bonds that are readjustable according to the price of oil (following Mexico's example) or bonds that are readjustable according to the GDP (following Bulgaria's example)—whose payments are made only when oil prices or the country's growth show positive development, thus reducing returns when the former show poor performance. Though the premium of this kind of insurance can be high, it could help relieve Ecuador's vulnerability to fluctuations in the price of oil.

If the government is able to meet the above-described stages and continues to demonstrates solid fiscal management, Ecuador should be able to access international markets, in which case it would obtain various benefits that would improve the conditions of its public debt. First of all, placing on international markets would enable the country to access a wider pool of buyers. This would eliminate some of the monopolistic pressures that it currently confronts from only having access to a few national institutional actors. Second, the government would not crowd out the private sector in the domestic market, which would facilitate access to credit and would lower business costs.

Recommendations for the Short Term

- Secure the financing plan for the year 2003 by creating a solid, credible macroeconomic program. Renegotiate outstanding arrears with the Paris Club. Supplement these measures with possible debt buy-back or rescheduling of the most onerous debt.
- Increase the liquidity cushion of public finances with a fiscal adjustment that eliminates the uncertainties affecting public debt management.
- Improve the transparency of the debt structure and payments. These must be public knowledge. The change would accomplish a number of things: first, it would enable citizens to monitor the performance of public servants; second, it would demonstrate future financial requirements; and third, it would improve the country's credit image among foreign investors, who maybe over penalizing the country.

Recommendations for the Medium Term

- Create guidelines and reference levels to generate a debt profile that is appropriate for a dollarized, oil-dependent country.
- Create a highly professional and politically independent team charged with managing the debt, headed by an independent debt manager and explicitly charged with the task of reducing the cost of debt service and developing an appropriate performance curve (as in the examples of Chile and Brazil). This includes improving the technical capability of the Ministry of Economy and Finance, in particular the Office of Public Credit.

Policy Matrix

Problems	Policy measures		Progress indicators	Objectives/goals
	Short term (to June 2003)	Medium term (2003–07)		
Very high debt service during 2003–04.	Approve solid macroeconomic program. Identify sources of additional financing and urgent cutback measures in spending or increase in revenues.		Punctuality in payments.	Gain initial credibility with foreign investors.
High level of indebtedness.	Maintain high fiscal surpluses, limit increases in spending. Reduce debt stock with Paris Club.	Buy back onerous external debt. Improve cash flow management to prevent bond saturation in local market. Develop capital market.	Decrease in interest payments/revenue over time. Evolution of credit indicators.	Reduce debt/GDP ratio by at least 16 percent in 2007. Reduce global bond debt as percentage of total debt.
Inadequate strategy for medium-term debt management. (Gains derived from good debt management could cover greater personnel costs.)	Ensure timely payment of debt and elimination of arrears. Regularly publish public debt indicators, increasing their transparency.	Create guidelines to determine objective indebtedness structure. Create the job of Debt Manager Create a professional team to administer the debt and improve the technical capability of the Office of Public Credit.	Reduction of the spread on the country's debt. Greater transparency in the decisionmaking process with regard to debt strategy.	Reduce risk and the cost of public debt. Decrease debt risk premium. Recoup international credibility and obtain access to international markets.

Annex
Public Debt Dynamics

	2002	2003	2004	2005	2006	2007	2008	2009	2010
	Est.	Proj.	Proj.	Proj.	Proj.	Proj.	Proj.	Proj.	Proj.
Assumptions									
GDP (Bln $US)	24.5	26.7	28.3	30.1	31.7	33.5	35.4	37.4	39.4
Real GDP growth (%)	3.0	3.5	4.0	4.0	3.5	3.5	3.5	3.5	3.5
GDP deflator (%)	13.1	5.4	2.0	2.0	2.0	2.0	2.0	2.0	2.0
Interest rate on new debt		8.0	8.0	8.0	8.0	8.0	8.0	8.0	8.0
Oil price ($US per barrel)	21.30	18.00	18.00	18.00	18.00	18.00	18.00	18.00	18.00
Results (percentage of GDP)									
Primary balance	**4.0**	**4.4**	**4.5**	**3.9**	**3.8**	**3.7**	**3.5**	**3.3**	**3.1**
Additional fiscal effort		0.4	1.0	0.4	0.4	0.4	0.5	0.5	0.5
Interest payments	3.6	3.4	3.5	3.4	3.3	3.2	3.0	2.8	2.6
Fiscal balance	**0.4**	**1.0**	**1.0**	**0.5**	**0.5**	**0.5**	**0.5**	**0.5**	**0.5**
Balance less petrol revenues	–3.8	–2.8	–2.4	–2.8	–2.7	–2.6	–2.4	–2.2	–2.0
Financing required		**3.4**	**2.7**	**3.2**	**2.5**	**2.4**	**1.7**	**1.5**	**1.3**
Total debt	**57.1**	**51.4**	**47.4**	**44.2**	**41.4**	**38.7**	**36.1**	**33.7**	**31.5**
Debt service	**8.0**	**7.8**	**7.3**	**7.1**	**6.3**	**6.1**	**5.3**	**4.8**	**4.4**
Model									
Primary balance	971	1,177	1,279	1,180	1,211	1,246	1,241	1,238	1,239
Interest payments	873	918	995	1,029	1,052	1,078	1,064	1,051	1,042
Interest payments, existing debt	873	881	892	856	810	771	700	640	589
Interest payments, new debt	0	36	104	173	243	307	364	411	453
Fiscal balance	98	259	283	150	159	168	177	187	197
Net amortization of existing debt	109	1,164	1,063	1,102	959	971	795	747	691
Financing (new debt issue)	10	905	779	951	800	803	618	560	493
Debt service	982	2,082	2,058	2,131	2,012	2,049	1,859	1,798	1,733
Implicit interest rate	**6.2**	**6.7**	**7.4**	**7.7**	**8.0**	**8.3**	**8.3**	**8.3**	**8.4**

Level of Public Debt (Mln $US)	13,985	13,725	13,442	13,292	13,133	12,965	12,788	12,602	12,404
New debt		905	1,684	2,636	3,436	4,239	4,857	5,418	5,911
Existing debt	13,985	12,820	11,758	10,656	9,697	8,726	7,931	7,184	6,493
Domestic	2,521	2,172	2,040	1,854	1,746	1,645	1,606	1,562	1,529
External	11,464	10,648	9,718	8,802	7,951	7,081	6,325	5,621	4,964
Debt buy-back	0	0	26	51	76	97	97	97	97
Fiscal Accounts (Mln $US)									
Primary balance	971	1,177	1,279	1,180	1,211	1,246	1,241	1,238	1,239
Additional fiscal effort		94	0	132	136	144	160	178	202
Core primary balance projected		1,083	1,004	1,047	1,075	1,101	1,081	1,060	1,037
Petrol revenues		1,427	1,340	1,373	1,419	1,465	1,465	1,465	1,465
Non-petrol revenues	4,915	5,345	5,670	6,015	6,350	6,703	7,077	7,471	7,887
Primary expenditures	5,217	5,689	6,006	6,341	6,694	7,067	7,460	7,876	8,314
Non-petrol primary balance	-419	-251	-61	-194	-208	-219	-224	-227	-225
Non-petrol primary balance (percentage of GDP)	-1.71	-0.94	-0.22	-0.64	-0.65	-0.65	-0.63	-0.61	-0.57
Petrol revenues (Mln $US)	1,390	1,427	1,383	1,459	1,547	1,628	1,628	1,628	1,628
Petrol revenues - to Fund	0	0	43	85	128	164	164	164	164
Petrol revenues - to Budget	1,390	1,427	1,340	1,373	1,419	1,465	1,465	1,465	1,465
Production (million barrels)	148	150	162	175	188	199	199	199	199
PetroEcuador	82	84	86	88	89	91	91	91	91
Private	66	66	77	88	99	108	108	108	108
FEIREP details									
Royalties from OCP (FEIREP)	0	0	43	85	128	164	164	164	164
=>20 percent to stabilization fund	0	0	9	17	26	33	33	33	33
=>70 percent to debt buy-back	0	0	30	60	90	115	115	115	115
to IESS	0	0	5	9	13	17	17	17	17
External debt buy-back	0	0	26	51	76	97	97	97	97
=>10 percent to social spending	0	0	4	9	13	16	16	16	16

4

The Banking System[1]

Mario Guadamillas, Giovanni Majnoni, and Yira Mascaró

Ecuador's financial system has been recovering from the serious crisis of 1998 and 1999 and adapting to the changes involved in the dollarization of the economy in early 2000, which eliminated the sucre as the local currency (and thus formalized the system's de facto heavy dollarization). Nevertheless, the characteristics of the system that emerged from the crisis differ from those of the past, not only in their impact on individual banks, but also in the dollarization's effect on the institutional framework. The crisis has drastically reduced the number of active financial institutions, while dollarization and associated changes have led surviving institutions to hold their assets in a more liquid form owing to the absence of a lender of last resort, and depositors have consequently preferred more liquid deposits. This change in asset composition has also led to a greater concentration of the banking sector, as the institutions seek to compensate the high proportion of low-yield liquid assets through larger-scale operations. The country is coming to the end of the most dramatic period of the postcrisis restructuring process that led to the adoption of a new regulatory framework and more efficient supervision. The structure and responsibilities of the supervisory authorities have also changed. Not only has the process of restructuring the banking system been a trial by fire for the agency in charge of deposit insurance, the Deposit Guarantee Agency (Agencia de Garantía de Depósitos—AGD) and for the Superintendency of Banking and Insurance (Superintendencia de Banca y Seguros—SBS), but dollarization has also changed the traditional role of Ecuador's

---

1. This chapter was written by Mario Guadamillas, Giovanni Majnoni, and Yira Mascaró, with the research assistance of Ilias Skamnelos (all with the World Bank). The authors acknowledge the collaboration of the Ecuadorian authorities and the useful comments of Macdonald Benjamín, Fernando Montes-Negret, and the participants in the seminar in Quito on Economic Policy Notes.

*Central Bank (*Banco Central de Ecuador—BCE*). Now, instead of functioning as a director of monetary policy, with dollarization, the Central Bank has the role of central manager of the system's liquidity, to ensure that the payments system functions well and to provide liquidity under conditions similar to those of a last resort lender.*

This chapter documents the progress of Ecuador's banking system over the last two years, highlighting economic policy actions that can help consolidate the progress achieved and lay the foundations for a stronger system. Section A describes the effects of the crisis on the structure of Ecuador's financial system, with a particular focus on the banking sector and its greater concentration as a result of the restructuring process. It also provides an estimate of the cost of the restructuring process that includes the management of the AGDand other parallel efforts such as the recent asset recovery process by the Credit Restructuring Unit (*Unidad de Reestructuración de Créditos—URC*) with its single representative. Section B analyzes the trends in balances and yield of private banks and their present prospects. Section C evaluates policy issues that authorities are currently considering to strengthen the banking system's capacity to resist exposure to the external shocks typically involved in dollarization. The main theme is proper management of the system's overall liquidity position by strengthening the existing liquidity fund to make it more effective. Section D considers the actions required to ensure that the banking sector truly functions as a principal provider of means of payment within the new dollarized economy. Section E briefly analyzes the characteristics of the safety net that will be in place once the liquidity fund is reformed and the AGD is restructured. Section F concludes with a list of policy actions included in the matrix of recommendations.

A. The Postcrisis Financial System: Structure and Depth

Ecuador's financial system underwent a serious, twin crisis (financial and exchange) in 1998 and 1999, which drastically reduced its size. The total number of 82 financial institutions in 2002 is down 30 percent from 1998 (Table 1). Specifically, 12 of the 38 private banks that were in business four years ago are now under AGD administration, along with 4 finance companies, for a total of 16 institutions. These banks, along with Filanbanco (the system's largest in 1998) and other institutions now closed, held 50 percent of the system's total deposits in 1998.[2] This reduction brought the level of the system's intermediation in October 2002 to half its 1998 value (measured as total assets over the GDP—see Figure 1), and the reduction was especially marked following the closing of Filanbanco in 2001 (in liquidation since July 2002). The value of the performing loan portfolio dropped to 11 percent of GDP, with only two-thirds channeled to the commercial and industrial sector.

---

2. SBS Annual Report, 2001.

Table 1. Number of Institutions in the Financial System

	Dec. 1998	Dec. 1999	Dec. 2000	Dec. 2001	Mar. 2002
Financial intermediation	**114**	**104**	**89**	**85**	**82**
Private banks					
Operating*	38	28	26	21	21
Operating with public capital				2	2
Offshore	15	18	10	8	6
Operating abroad	4	4	4	4	4
State-owned banks					
Operating	1	1	1	1	1
Second tier	1	1	1	2	2
Finance companies	23	19	14	13	12
Savings and loan associations	25	26	26	27	27
Mutual associations	7	7	7	7	7
Other institutions in the financial					
system	**72**	**68**	**67**	**61**	**62**
Exchange houses	13	13	13	8	8
Bonded warehouses	8	7	7	7	7
Public institutions	5	5	5	4	4
Credit cards	1	1	1	1	1
Securitization houses	1	1	1	1	1
Insurance companies	42	39	38	38	39
Reinsurance companies	2	2	2	2	2
Institutions under reorganization	**4**	**15**	**16**	**16**	**16**
Banks	1	12	12	12	12
Finance companies	2	3	4	4	4
Mutual associations	1				
Institutions in liquidation	**22**	**24**	**29**	**33**	**34**
Banks	3	2	2	2	2
Finance companies	9	9	12	12	13
Mutual associations	3	4	4	4	4
Saving associations	2	2	2	2	2
Exchange houses	1	1	2	6	6
Bonded warehouses	3	4	4	4	4
Insurance companies	1	2	3	3	3
Total general	**212**	**211**	**201**	**195**	**194**

* Includes Filanbanco, which entered liquidation beginning in July 2002.
Source: SBS.

The crisis had high fiscal costs aside from its direct effects on the system, with serious macroeconomic consequences such as the drastic fall in GDP (see the section on macroeconomics). The Deposit Guarantee Agency (AGD)—created in December 1998 as a result of the difficulties experienced by Filanbanco (in the first round)—has been managing the financial institutions that entered a reorganization

Figure 1. Total Bank Assets over GDP

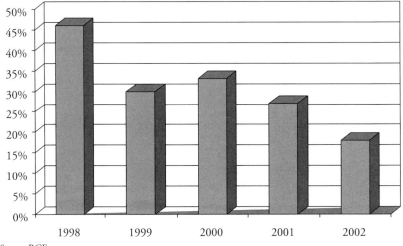

Source: BCE.

process after the crisis to recover or sell off assets to pay the deposit insurance.[3] By late October, the AGD had paid at least the first $US25,000 of all individual deposits in the institutions it is managing, for a total payment of over $US800 million (Table 2). Based on preliminary figures for the assets and liabilities of banks under AGD management, plus the cost of capitalizing Filanbanco (which was ultimately handled outside the AGD) and Banco Pacífico (open), the total outlay to date is estimated at $US2 billion (approximately 12 percent of the 2001 GDP). This does not take into account the opportunity cost of money that resulted from the freezing of deposits in early 1999, or other costs of the negative impact on the economy in various areas. The Credit Restructuring Unit (URC) made progress in recovering the portfolios of banks under reorganization and by December, after six months work, had managed to restructure approximately half of the total $US400 million representing the value of the largest loans. The cost may be lower, depending on how many additional assets can be recovered or sold off, although time makes

---

3. The AGD was created with broad powers for restructuring banks with access to deposit insurance, but this capacity was transferred to the SBS by two laws enacted in 2000 (the Ecuadorian Economic Transformation Act and the Investment and Citizen Participation Promotion Act). In January 2000, several characteristics of deposit insurance were also modified, including the elimination of the existing unlimited coverage, imposing a maximum coverage limit equivalent to four times the per capita GDP, while excluding deposits in offshore institutions.

**Table 2. The Costs of Restructuring the Banking System
(mlns $US)**

AGD	Assets	Liabilities
Total assets	2,154	
Assets to be sold*	800	
Auctions implemented**	100	
Recovered portfolio***	599	
Recoverable portfolio	655	
Total liabilities		1,601
Debts paid		832
Debts outstanding****		769
Capitalization of banks		1,350
Banco del Pacífico		250
Filanbanco		1,100
Actual cost at in December 2002		2,251
EXPECTED COST (Appraising Assets assets at 100%)		797

Notes: *   Estimated. Mainly includes buildings.
      **   Excludes allocated assets awaiting sale.
      *** As of October 31, 2002.
      **** Includes: primary and secondary depositors; debts for foreign trade, not guaranteed by the risk central; amounts owed to other institutions (open and closed).
Source: The authors' estimates based on AGD and SBS data.

this process increasingly more difficult (see the section on recent institutional efforts at debt restructuring).

The Structure of the Banking System

By October 2002, the 22 existing private banks had 82 percent of the total financial assets in the country (Table 3), concentrated in turn in the four largest banks (which held 63 percent of the total assets in private banks). These banks include Banco Pacífico (the largest in 1998), which is state-owned (by the BCE) as a result of its restructuring, but has been under the administration of a team of international bankers that has improved its operations.[4] The total private banks also include two mid-size foreign banks (Citibank and Lloyds) that remained in Ecuador. Another two foreign banks left the system by selling their assets to other banks or through mergers (ABN-

---

4. The restructuring of this bank's operations is still in progress, but has already logged significant achievements. It continues to work with two consultants from the international team that managed the bank until October.

AMRO and ING), owing to the high risk they faced following the crisis (aggravated by a climate of high instability and heavy banking losses by foreign banks in neighboring countries) and because they had not achieved sufficient scale to justify operating as retail banks. The remaining institutions have a small share in the system, particularly the state-owned banks—Corporación Financiera Nacional (CFN), Banco Nacional de Fomento (BNF), Banco del Estado, and Banco Ecuatoriano de la Vivienda—whose operations are directed toward specialized areas of production. Given the structure of the sector, the consolidation process is likely to continue.

In addition to the concentration of the banking subsystem, the majority of institutions are members of financial groups, which further concentrates the financial system as a whole. These groups include private banks (typically a group's main component), foreign branches, finance companies, securities houses, fund administrators, real estate companies, insurance companies, bonded warehouses, and computer service companies. The offshore banking that had predominated prior to the crisis and contributed to the system's deterioration, lost importance with the exit of almost half the private banks to which it was associated, via reorganization, merger, or liquidation. By the end of 2002, the four offshore banks that were still open belonged to the largest banks in the system,[5] although their growth was limited by the new restriction that each offshore bank had to keep assets under their levels of March 2000. Four new foreign banks have entered the system, operating almost exclusively abroad—as opposed to the offshore banks, which focused on operations with Ecuadorian banks—and are under the supervision of the authorities of the countries in which they are based (namely, Colombia and Peru). These four institutions belong to the financial group of the largest private national bank, Pichincha (which holds 27 percent of total assets in private banks), which in turn owns two other, small, private banks through one of these institutions operating abroad. Owing to Pichincha's rapid growth by acquiring banks that experienced troubles during the restructuring process and to foreign banks' deciding to leave the system over the last few years, the Pichincha group is now the system's largest, with 35 percent of the total assets of the financial groups. The owners of this group also own the system's largest finance company (Diners Card), with 64 percent of all finance company assets, which reveals the high degree of concentration resulting from the crisis management.

B. Trends in Bank Balances, Solvency, and Yield

Balance Trends

Balance sheets show that banks have recovered since the period following the crisis, to a large extent through an improved macroeconomic environment that brought

---

5. Formally, there are five offshore banks (see Table 1) if one includes Banco Continental, which is not operating.

Table 3. Number and Size of Institutions in the Financial System in October 2002

	Number	Total assets		Net credit portfolio		Investments net		Deposits with the public	
		Thousands of $US	%	Thousands of $US	%	Thousands of $US	%	Thousands of $US	%
Total in the country	**69**	**6,951,074**	**100%**	**3,559,719**	**100%**	**996,496**	**100%**	**4,919,225**	**100%**
Private banks	22	5,726,339	82%	2,683,543	75%	890,550	89%	4,242,060	86%
o/w									
PICHINCHA		1,529,505	22%	707,217	20%	195,905	20%	1,189,434	24%
GUAYAQUIL		841,932	12%	353,185	10%	136,744	14%	567,203	12%
PACIFICO*		621,985	9%	154,366	4%	190,377	19%	325,709	7%
PRODUBANCO		601,615	9%	314,666	9%	89,569	9%	463,060	9%
State-owned banks**	2	493,020	7%	310,365	9%	54,842	6%	192,464	4%
Finance companies	11	327,201	5%	231,689	7%	16,459	2%	199,872	4%
Savings and loan associations	27	246,481	4%	176,089	5%	19,715	2%	169,091	3%
Mutual associations	7	158,033	2%	158,033	4%	14,930	1%	115,739	2%
Total institutions abroad	**9**	**1,284,057**	**100%**	**571,169**	**100%**	**393,683**	**100%**	**946,248**	**100%**
Offshore	5	476,937	37%	222,260	39%	146,467	37%	367,113	39%
Operating abroad	4	807,120	63%	348,910	61%	247,215	63%	579,135	61%
Total	**78**	**8,235,131**		4,130,888		1,390,179		5,865,474	
Memoriam:									
Second- tier state-owned banks	2	433,634		73,637		181,711		1,351	

Notes: * Pacifico with public capital.
   ** Does not include second tier.

Source: SBS.

higher GDP growth and lower inflation (see the Chapter 1). Nevertheless, credit growth is still restricted owing—on the supply side—to the banks' need to maintain liquidity surpluses against the macroeconomic uncertainty heightened in this election year and to the greater caution of the banks that survived the crisis and experienced a severe deterioration of their portfolios. On the other hand, the gradual improvement in portfolio quality has been reflected in greater yields for banks.

Total assets of private banking rose by 16 percent over the first 10 months of 2002, reaching $US5.726 billion by October (Table 4). Productive assets (loan and investment portfolios) rose slightly to 63 percent of total assets (in other countries they are 80–90 percent), while **investments** accounted for 25 percent of the banks' total productive assets. Approximately half of all investments are in the public sector, largely as a result of the crisis resolution process.[6] The buyers (large banks) received bonds from the government as productive assets, in the absence of a quality portfolio. The government's debt exposure is concentrated in large banks (particularly in Banco Pacífico, with a 28 percent share of its assets). This increases the risk for these banks in the event the fiscal situation deteriorates.

Private investments are mostly placed abroad (close to 100 percent of total investments with the private sector, according to data from the largest banks), as are available funds (including cash, bank deposits, and reserves in the Central Bank), in order to keep the high liquidity that allows them to deal with potential bank runs.[7] The 2002 election campaign and the lack of a true last resort lender in the system increased the perception of a high risk of liquidity for the banks, resulting in the maintenance of a liquidity "cushion" that reached $US1.1 billion in October 2002. These liquid assets accounted for 23 percent of total assets, restricting portfolio growth during the year and negatively affecting yields. The banks reported their intention to restrict portfolio growth at least until the second quarter of 2003, continuing the high liquidity that prevailed during 2002, until the new government better defines its economic policies.

The **total gross portfolio** grew by 16 percent during the first 10 months of 2002, in contrast to a 3 percent decrease for the prior year, and remained concentrated (62 percent) in the commercial sector, although the year saw a healthy

---

6. This is the result of either the government bonds that some banks, such as Pacífico, received as capital contributions, or of the acquisitions or mergers by some large banks that absorbed others experiencing difficulties.

7. For example, by mid 2002 the system's largest bank had 19 percent of its deposits withdrawn in one month owing to a perception of system instability, but it was able to manage with the surplus liquid funds it regularly maintains. The run on Pichincha may have had more to do with the perception of macroeconomic and political risk than with a particular risk of the bank, because during the crisis it had been on the receiving end of the "flight to quality" along with other surviving banks. Pichincha also has by far the greatest number of branches in the system (almost 150), which facilitates massive withdrawals.

Table 4. Private Banks*: Balance Sheet
(thds $US and percentages of Total Assets)

	Dec. 2001		Oct. 2002	
TOTAL ASSETS	4,928,812	100%	5,726,339	100%
AVAILABLE FUNDS	1,077,508	22%	1,115,639	19%
INTERBANK OPERATIONS	1,480	0%	3,120	0%
NET INVESTMENTS	729,046	15%	890,550	16%
With the private sector	304,394	6%	336,632	6%
With the public sector	306,152	6%	436,913	8%
Of limited availability	146,976	3%	131,025	2%
NET CREDIT PORTFOLIO	2,151,682	44%	2,683,543	47%
Gross portfolio	2,601,952	53%	3,016,617	53%
Commercial	1,826,930	37%	1,879,947	33%
Consumer	529,981	11%	863,406	15%
Housing	245,041	5%	237,632	4%
Microenterprise	0	0%	35,632	1%
(Provisions for bad debts)	-450,270	-9%	-333,074	-6%
FIXED ASSETS	255,637	5%	324,905	6%
OTHER ASSETS	713,459	14%	708,582	12%
o/w: Allocated goods	42,874	1%	88,164	2%
TOTAL LIABILITIES	4,549,522	92%	5,143,995	90%
DEBTS TO THE PUBLIC	3,669,223	74%	4,265,304	74%
Sight deposits	2,530,676	51%	2,929,933	51%
Term and other deposits	1,138,546	23%	1,335,371	23%
INTERBANK OPERATIONS	51,412	1%	4,000	0%
OTHER LIABILITIES WITH COST	442,211	9%	462,831	8%
o/w: Foreign lines	256,283	5%	222,584	4%
CONVERTIBLE OBLIGATIONS & CONTRIBUTIONS FOR CAPITALIZATION	169,717	3%	194,655	3%
OTHER LIABILITIES	216,960	4%	217,205	4%
NET WORTH	**379,290**	**8%**	**582,344**	**10%**
TOTAL LIABILITIES & NET WORTH	4,928,812	100%	5,726,339	100%
TOTAL UNPRODUCTIVE PORTFOLIO:	456,882	9%	287,213	5%
Commercial	297,578	6%	204,809	4%
Consumer	45,655	1%	62,293	1%
Housing	113,649	2%	18,281	0%
Microenterprise	0	0%	1,829	0%

Notes: *Includes Pacífico, with public capital. Data to October is preliminary.
Source: SBS.

increase in financing for the consumer sector (Table 4). Banks focused their new loans on the consumer sector, which had grown more than 60 percent by October 2002. This growth was largely because large companies—including many multinational companies that accounted for much of the banks' commercial portfolio—had chosen to take direct lines of credit from abroad as international interest rates dropped. The improved economic growth also favored the consumer portfolio. The housing portfolio decreased, reflecting the banks' preference for shorter-term placements. These patterns predominated for banks of all sizes. The microfinance portfolio also benefited from the year's macroeconomic recovery, but remained at low as a proportion of the system's total portfolio.[8]

The quality of the net portfolio improved significantly. The nonperforming proportion of the portfolio (problem loans plus portfolio not earning interest) to gross portfolio dropped from 17.5 percent in December 2001 to 9.5 percent in October 2002 (Table 6). This was due to the increase in the **productive portfolio** during the year and to the sustained increase in provisions that cover 116 percent of the nonperforming portfolio (up from 99 percent coverage in December 2001).[9] By type of loan, the nonperforming portfolio (problem loans plus portfolio not earning interest) is concentrated in commercial loans, but less than its share in the total gross portfolio. Furthermore, both the commercial and the housing portfolios, stable in absolute value, saw their share in this total decrease, while the mature consumer portfolio doubled its share—reaching 20 percent of the total nonperforming portfolio.

During 2002, the improvement in portfolio quality also benefited from the activities of the Credit Restructuring Unit (URC).[10] Since late 2001, the URC had made use of a single representative to facilitate the restructuring of cases for $US1.357 billion (45 percent of the Filanbanco portfolio, 14 percent of the Pacífico portfolio, and 18 percent of the total portfolio of the banks administered by the AGD). By early December the URC had restructured 85 percent of the total portfolio value and estimates predicted that 95 percent of the debts transferred to the URC would be restructured by the December 20, 2002 deadline. Debts restructured in the last few weeks are mainly those of Filanbanco (which accounted for 40 percent of the unstructured debt in mid-November). The accounts that make up these restructured debts are few but sizeable.

In terms of **funding**, private banks continue to have little access to foreign lines of credit, as in the crisis period (Figure 2). Only six banks had positive balances by

---

8. The microfinance sector is mainly covered by two banks (Pichincha and Solidario), which account for 75 percent of the total, followed by one savings association (Ecuatorial), which accounts for 13 percent. Authorities are focusing on the recent rise in microfinance, particularly considering that the savings associations are the institutions that best survived the crisis. Furthermore, a study done by the International Project Consult (IPC) found great market potential for rural agricultural financing through saving associations and banks interested in the sector (see Proposed Strategic Plan for Long-Term Development for Ecuador, 2002).

9. Using as a reference the portfolio classified as C, D, and E as the system's most risky, the present coverage of constituted provisions is 83 percent and the deadline has passed for constituting the provisions required by the latest increase in the provisions rule in 2001.

10. Supported by the World Bank's technical assistance loan to the financial sector.

Table 5. Private Banks*: Profit and Loss Statement (thds $US)

	Oct. 2001	Oct. 2002
Interest and discounts earned	383,857	173,954
Interest accrued	158,588	49,588
NET MARGIN OF INTEREST	225,268	124,366
Income and commissions for service	160,167	67,879
Expenses and commissions paid	69,808	14,606
GROSS FINANCIAL MARGIN	315,627	177,639
Operating expenses	348,336	150,361
Other net operating income	61,309	25,469
NET OPERATIONAL MARGIN BEFORE PROVISIONS	28,600	52,746
Provisions	123,250	27,851
NET OPERATIONAL MARGIN	−94,650	24,895
Net extraordinary income	69,050	28,270
PRE-TAX PROFITS	−25,600	53,165
Taxes and employee profit-sharing	—	10,371
EARNINGS OR LOSS FOR THE BUSINESS YEAR	−25,599	42,794
Memorandum:		
Operating expenses/gross financial margin	1.10	0.85
Provisions/gross financial margin	0.39	0.16

Notes: *Includes Pacífico, with public capital.
Source: SBS.

the end of 2002,[11] while deposits from the general public were concentrated in sight deposits (70 percent of the total), revealing the preference for short-term assets owing to recent political and macroeconomic uncertainty. In fact, by mid-year high volatility was evident in system deposits, with withdrawals concentrated in mid-size banks, including foreign banks. The drop in deposits with foreign banks was largely due to the loss of a few, but large, accounts (some of them multinational companies). Driven by the marked increase in sight deposits, the majority of system deposits are at terms of under 90 days, and a high percentage are in deposits of under $US5,000 (63 percent of sight deposits). The average volatility remains high, and is even higher for at least one of the foreign banks and other small banks.[12] Consequently, the ratio of liquid assets to total assets was at a high 20 percent, sufficient

11. Including only one small bank, Solidario, which focuses on the microfinance sector and maintains broad access to foreign lines of credit from multilateral agencies.
12. The SBS calculates the average volatility based on monthly data on variations in each component of deposit liabilities in the last 18 months, weighted by their percentage of the total. Volatility reached 18 percent in 97 percent of the cases, with certain banks having much higher volatility rates (24 percent for Citibank).

Figure 2. Financing Lines Abroad (mlns $US)

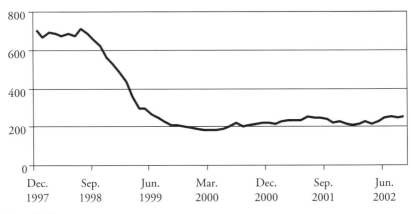

Source: BCE.

to withstand a monthly withdrawal of 30 percent of banks' liquid liabilities, although the liquidity index (liquid assets over liquid liabilities, as defined by the SBS) was at its lowest level of the last 12 months.

Solvency

Banks have also improved their solvency by capitalizing profits, in some cases (as with the second largest bank, Banco Guayaquil) with significant contributions of new capital from shareholders.[13] The strengthening of bank capital resulted in solvency indexes above the 9 percent regulatory minimum for all banks, with 11.8 percent for the system by October 2002. This index is also positive considering the time schedule imposed for reducing the ratio of primary to secondary capital, which must be brought to the 1:1 ratio established by Basel by March 2003. Several banks have already met, or are close to meeting, this ratio, while the system as a whole maintains a ratio of 1:1.10.

Yield

The management of private banking during the first 10 months of the year brought an improvement in profit generation as well as improved levels of solvency. This was evident despite the maintenance of high liquid balances, partly attributable to much lower expenses for provisions in 2002 as compared to 2001 (from 39 to 15 percent of the gross financial margin—see Table 5). Interest expenses were also significantly

---

13. This includes the capitalizations of Banco Pacífico since 2001, which came to $US250 million in February 2002, including contributions for future capitalization of $US152 million—which will double the present paid capital of $US155 million.

Table 6. Private Banks*: Financial Indicators

Oct. 2002	
Solvency	
Required capital / assets weighted by risk	11.80%
Primary capital/ assets weighted by risk	6.40%
Capital/ assets	9.40%
Quality of the assets	
Portfolio C, D & E / gross portfolio	13.40%
Unproductive portfolio */ gross portfolio	9.50%
Provisions/ portfolio C, D & E	82.70%
Liquidity	
Liquid assets (1st.) / total assets	22.50%
Liquid assets (2nd.) / total assets	23.90%
Liquid assets (1st.) / liquid liabilities (1st.)	30.40%
Liquid assets (2nd.) / liquid liabilities (2nd.)	29.00%
Net portfolio/ deposits	62.90%
Yield	
Net margin of interest / gross income	40.00%
Operating cost / gross income	48.30%
Operating cost / average assets	3.40%
Return on average assets ROAA	1.00%
Return on average equity ROAE	11.20%

Notes: *Includes Pacífico, with public capital.
Source: SBS (preliminary data) and the authors' estimates.

lower, partly through the effect of lower international deposit rates, although income from interest in October 2002 was also down, but to a lesser extent.

Profits approximated $US42.8 million in the first 10 months of the year, compared to a loss of $US25.6 million in December 2001, which was affected by the enormous losses of the Banco Pacífico—reversed in 2002 through its capitalization and rationalization of expenses.[14] Improved yield levels are partly attributable to the fact that coverage of the nonperforming portfolio had already increased significantly in 2001, requiring lower expenditures for provisions in 2002. Nevertheless, the high cost of maintaining liquidity continues to decrease the banks' capacity for profit generation, which in turn restricts the reduction of lending rates (to be addressed later in this document).

Banks have dealt with the crisis by diversifying their sources of income generation, increasing income from commissions (which is more stable), and offsetting the lower relative growth of their loan portfolios. In some banks extraordinary income

---

14. The return on average equity (ROAE) was 11.2 percent, while the return on average assets (ROAA) was 1 percent.

was particularly significant, especially income from the recovery of asset write-offs that were able to offset the expense for provisions. In effect, Figure 3 shows the total expenses for provisions and the same expenses after income from recoveries—with negative balances indicating a net income, illustrating the effect of high recoveries for some banks. This could reflect a very aggressive portfolio write-off policy, or unexpected recoveries via the debt restructuring plans undertaken during the year.

Between December 2001 and October 2002, the spread (measured as the difference between the average lending and borrowing rates, and excluding Filanbanco) dropped from 10 to 8 percent, owing largely to a marked reduction in operating costs. In effect, during this period operating costs (including personnel expenses) as a percentage of average assets were reduced from 7 percent to 3.4 percent. This reduction in operating costs is crucial because, as with most countries in the region, operating costs make up the principal component of the spread and are partially offset by greater operating income not originating in interest.[15]

Figure 3. Gross and Net Recovery Provision Expenditures (mlns $US)

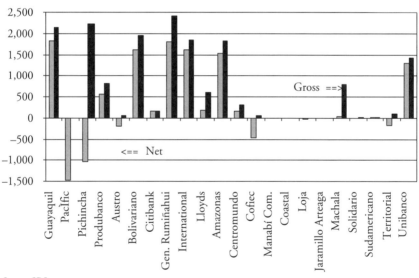

Source: SBS.

---

15. The accounting breakdown of the spread was done with reference rates instead of with average rates (flows from interest /inventory of loans or deposits) because of inconsistencies in the data with the recent change of the accounting plan. This exercise reveals that operating costs account for over half the spread and are offset in part by non-interest income (fee income). These patterns are similar to those in other countries in the region (see Dick, "Banking Spreads in Central America: Evolution, Structure, and Behavior," Harvard Institute for International Development, Discussion Paper No. 694, April 1999.

C. Strengthening Individual and System Risk Management

Institutional Structure and Management of Cash Risk

The need for a high proportion of liquid assets and the corresponding concentration of the banks' investment portfolio in foreign bonds are closely associated with the official dollarization of January 2000. Nevertheless, the maintenance of these high liquidity ratios is also typical in countries that have a high *de facto* dollarization, as Ecuador had prior to 2000, with over 60 percent of the banking portfolio denominated in dollars in 1998 and 1999 (Figure 4). The progressive loss of monetary effectiveness in processes of high dollarization[16] reduces the monetary authority's capacity to protect the economy from external shocks and leads banks to maintain their assets in more liquid forms.

In Ecuador, **excessive liquid holdings** have at least two negative effects on the economy. The first is that they reduce the funds available for long-term investment, which has negative effects on bank yield. Second, the need to keep these liquid assets abroad reduces the amount of internal savings that can be invested domestically. For both reasons this issue has become an important economic policy question: How can banks reduce holdings in liquid assets beyond the level required by a dollarized economy? The remainder of this section addresses this question.

Figure 4. "Onshore" Credit (percentage granted in $US)

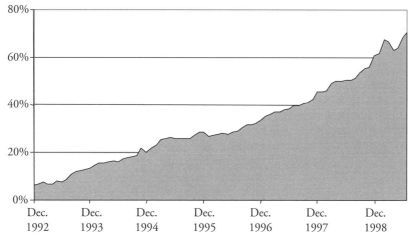

Source: SBS.

---

16. See Patrick Honohan and Anquing Shi, "Deposit Dollarization and the Financial Sector," World Bank, WPS 2748, October 2001.

Owing to the difficulty of establishing precisely the proper level of liquidity the system needs, the following exercise is based on a level of liquid reserves similar to that already maintained by the banks as a whole. Nevertheless, the exercise seeks to achieve a more efficient way to manage liquidity in the system, based on the alternatives currently under consideration by the Central Bank. Table 7 presents the value of banks' liquid assets in December 2001, which exceeded 25 percent of total reservable deposits. The Central Bank was also maintaining deposits equivalent to an additional 7 percent as a result of the required 4 percent mandatory reserves and funds in the liquidity fund (2.9 percent).

In general, the reduction of the liquid assets that banks maintain could result in lower lending rates (for a given margin of net interest) or greater bank yield (keeping the lending rate constant). In the former case, improved credit conditions would tend to increase access to credit, while in the latter, a greater bank yield would tend to reinforce the soundness of the system. The right side of Table 7 presents a different allocation of the liquidity that could result from access to reserves managed by the Latin American Reserve Fund (FLAR by its Spanish acronym) via a contingent line of credit, which could be as high as $US410 million (based on Ecuador's current participation in the FLAR).

A centralized management of liquidity could offer the opportunity to invest, for example, the $US410 million in high yield bonds, permitting a reduction of the lending interest rate. On the other hand, if banks were to decide to keep lending rates constant, they could achieve a better bank yield. Based on a 5 percent spread

Table 7. Liquidity in the Banking System

	Situation in Dec. 2001		Hypothetical scheme	
	Mill. $US	% deposits	Mill. $US	% deposits
Private funds	**932**	**25.7%**	**522**	**14.4%**
Voluntary reserves	54	1.5%	54	1.5%
Available funds (net of reserves)	878	24.2%	468	12.9%
Public funds	**251**	**6.9%**	**661**	**18.2%**
Reserves (mandatory)	145	4.0%	145	4.0%
Liquidity fund	106	2.9%	106	2.9%
Contribution from Corporación Andina de Fomento	70	1.9%	70	1.9%
Contribution from the banks	36	1.0%	36	1.0%
Contingent credit	0	0.0%	410	11.3%
Total liquidity	**1,183**	**32.7%**	**1,183**	**32.7%**
Memorandum:				
Reservable deposits	*3,623*	*100.0%*	*3,623*	*100.0%*

Source: SBS, BCE, and the authors' estimates.

between portfolio yield and the yield of liquid assets, profits could increase by $US20 million. The overall result would probably be even stronger than foreseen here. In fact, a centralized reserve fund would bring the total quantity of liquidity reserves lower than its level of early 2003.

A public scheme of greater liquidity provisions, however, faces two fundamental difficulties that must not be underestimated because they require changes in the legal framework. The first requirement for the viability of a greater "Liquidity Fund" is to instill, in the commercial banks, full confidence in the Central Bank's capacity to manage this fund with the required level of confidentiality. Furthermore, to date, the legal restriction that prevents the Central Bank from managing trusts has made it necessary to delegate management of the liquidity fund to the CFN, a state-owned bank experiencing problems in its balances. In addition, the Central Bank's share in ownership of the third-largest bank in the system (Banco Pacífico) makes the former subject to potentially significant conflicts of interest that could potentially hinder the full effectiveness of the liquidity fund. A second requirement is the need for close monitoring of the liquidity fund's investment policies, which could be delegated to a reputable financial institution that would act as trustee and even as administrator of these funds.

The reform of the liquidity fund centers on addressing the need for a more efficient management of the liquidity "supply" and therefore does not directly solve the problems resulting from a volatile liquidity "demand." One of the factors that could most stabilize this demand is effective supervision of the banks' liquidity position and of bank solvency in general. In fact, one of the more relevant reasons behind bank liquidity squeezes is when the banks have losses while they are at the bottom of the cycle. These affect their capital position and lead them to sell off their most liquid assets. Consequently the stabilization of the banks' demand for liquidity could be improved with procyclical provisioning policies that increase the volume of reserves against portfolio losses during periods of high portfolio growth (and high bank yield) and reduce it during periods of weak or negative growth (and low bank yield).

Over the last two years, the high level of provisions created to deal with the excessive nonperforming portfolio following the crisis has prevented Ecuador from considering the requirement of additional procyclical provisions. Even so, for an economy such as Ecuador's, with high exposure to cyclical variations in oil prices, a procyclical provisioning policy is an important option to consider. Based on Spain's successful experience, a dynamic provisioning process causes banks to put aside larger amounts during periods of expansion up to a given level. Using these accumulated reserves in low periods would avoid reductions of capital and liquid assets and, consequently, reductions of credit.

Efficient management of liquidity depends, to a great extent, on the existence of excellent relations with foreign correspondent banks, considering the low liquidity of Ecuador's financial activities and the considerable quantity of liquid investment that the country's banks maintain abroad. That is why it is very important that legislation on money laundering be established before a negative assessment of existing regulations can generate a sudden cooling of relations with foreign correspondent banks.

Strengthening Supervision and Regulation

In the last two years, the SBS has been immersed in an important plan to improve supervision of the banking system, including the introduction of a new Standard Chart of Accounts (in operation since July 2002), which provides a clearer and more reliable source of information on the financial position of the banks. On-site and off-site supervision procedures have been reviewed in detail (including recently a CAMEL analysis that laid the foundations for an early warning system that helps expedite taking corrective measures), with a focus on risk analysis that is more in line with the best international practices. Resolutions were issued for market risk analysis, concentrating first on putting into effect liquidity risk analysis, with reports from the banks beginning in January 2003 (a three-month testing period). The next areas of concentration are (new) operational risk and credit risk (improving practices implemented in the past). The SBS has also been moving toward a consolidated approach to supervision, but this is still in progress.

In addition, the SBS has restructured its organization to provide a greater harmony between its supervision practices for all the institutions it oversees. In doing so, it has been able to better coordinate its on-site and off-site supervision, which are not integrated into the new structure, and to seek a more timely intervention or investigation into issues brought to light by either of the two areas working together. System monitoring seems to have improved with the new inspections performed this year under new criteria centered on risks, and the SBS hopes to be able to perform at least one supervision of each bank per year. (It has already completed the arduous process of training its personnel in the new rules of play). To complement these efforts and improve transparency by increasing the reporting by the authorities, we recommend that the SBS provide a detailed report of its activities in its annual report. On the other hand, the effort to improve bank supervision has led the SBS to give less attention to problems in other sectors, particularly the insurance sector (which the authorities acknowledge). Because there is a high degree of concentration in the system between banking and nonbanking institutions, it is important to strengthen supervision of the latter and other institutions, despite their smaller size.

D. Issues in the Settlement of Payments and Securities[17]

An analysis of a more efficient management of bank liquidity must not neglect consideration of its effects on the functioning of the payments system. The system's effectiveness and security level for large transactions, along with the dematerializa-

---

17. This section was prepared on the basis of the report, "Assessment and Observations on the Payments and Securities Clearance and Settlement Systems of Ecuador," September 2002, which was produced in the context of the Initiative on Compensation and Clearance of

tion and easy transfer of financial assets used as (enforceable) collateral, are fundamental elements for reversing the incentives for foreign investment to obtain basic liquidity services. Nevertheless, Ecuador's payments system is characterized by the lack of Real Time Gross Settlement (RTGS), as well as the lack of an effective asset depository that can allow for an effective method of Delivery Versus Payment (DVP). The security of financial transactions and assets could be increased significantly by putting into effect some policy actions, such as those discussed below.

Cash and checks are the means of payment most commonly used in Ecuador. In addition to the check clearinghouse, the Central Bank operates a funds transfer system through its current accounts, either through SWIFT or over the counter with a mix of manual and automatic procedures. Those systems are being reformed at present. In addition to operating low-value payments, the check clearinghouse also processes high-value payments, which entails considerable risk for the payments system. One of the purposes of reforming the payments system is to launch a RTGS system to reduce the main risk in high-value transactions. However, this system in turn requires a highly efficient management of liquidity to prevent liquidity risk and the problems associated with a gridlock in the system.

To eliminate principal risk in high-value transactions, it is not enough to launch and run the RTGS. The Central Bank, in cooperation with private financial intermediaries, must take an active approach, establishing adequate incentives for high-value payments to be cleared through the RTGS and not through the check clearinghouse. One fundamental requirement for this to occur is increased efficiency of the payments system as a whole and, specifically, endowment of the RTGS with the proper characteristics. The following is a list (though not exhaustive) of issues to be considered: scarcity of total liquidity in the system; unequal distribution of liquidity, limited functioning of the interbank monetary market; lack of intraday credit; the Central Bank's limited capacity under the current monetary and exchange framework to deal with liquidity problems; and possible preference of institutions for a net settlement system or, in a gross system, for end-of-day deferral of payments.[18] The reform also calls for establishing two high-value systems, the RTGS and the Net Value Payments System, which doesn't seem to be an efficient solution for a country with Ecuador's characteristics. A net system of high value would not reduce principal risk, unless it establishes costly mechanisms to mitigate the risk, nor would it lead to payments in real time.

In addition, the securities market in Ecuador is clearly dominated by public securities, fundamentally government bonds and Treasury certificates. The settlement of

---

Payments and Securities of the Western Hemisphere (IHO, see **http://www.ipho-whpi.org/**). For detailed aspects of the evaluation of these systems, we recommend consulting the above-cited document.

18. Some specific proposals to resolve some of the problems mentioned here can be found in the report mentioned in the previous footnote.

securities is far from efficient because they are transferred through the delivery of physical certificates. The depository institution, DECEVALE S.A., created in 1994 by the two stock exchanges, has not been operating except for a very specific issue of CFN securities and the securities regulator has recently suspended its operations because of financial troubles. Nevertheless, the Central Bank is only capable of transferring ownership of securities apart from their payment. In other words, it does not have a DVP system. This fact is not only relevant for the settlement of capital market transactions, but also for the management of liquidity in the financial system. Specifically, it hampers the development of a collateralized interbank monetary market for which the settlement of securities through DVP is fundamental and which requires a connection between the deposit of securities and the RTGS system.

The efficient establishment of a securities depository requires dealing with a number of urgent issues—which institution(s) should be the depositor(s), what ownership structure should the depositor have, and so on. The lack of consensus on these basic questions usually leads to a significant delay in the improvement of systems, as has occurred in Ecuador, with negative consequences for the development of the financial system. Because of public interest in this issue due to its implications for fiscal and monetary policy, systemic liquidity management and risk management, and capital market development, the pertinent government authorities (Central Bank, the securities regulator, and the Ministry of Finance) must take the lead in defining, establishing, and implementing a centralized securities depository. The proposed solution must be adapted to the existing legal framework (or the latter must be modified if the chosen course does not fit it) and must carefully consider the subject of corporate governance to ensure that the system functions efficiently and allows equal access to all participants.

The 4 percent reserves for eligible deposits plus the existing 1 percent on the part of the liquidity fund could be insufficient to provide the liquidity required for the proper functioning of the payments system. Also, in the context of reform of the payments system, the launching of a RTGS system that has the virtue of eliminating principal risk increases the system's liquidity needs and requires meticulous management. The interbank monetary market is not very active and system liquidity is distributed through a system facilitated by the Central Bank. Each quarter, the Monetary Council approves the quantity of Central Bank securities that can be issued ($US30 million for the third quarter of 2002), using a formula that takes into account the level of international reserves. This quantity is in turn the quantity of funds that the Central Bank is authorized to inject into the market through open market operations (basically using securities issued by the government as collateral), thus permitting the redistribution of liquidity between the banks. This liquidity distribution system may not be sufficient for the functioning of the new payments infrastructure.

The reform of the payments system currently in process must take into account not only the objective of improving the provision of payments services, but also broader objectives such as improving the system's liquidity distribution through an efficient working of the interbank monetary market and the development of the securities market, among others. Preparing a strategic vision document that identifies these and other objectives would help to expand the sphere of influence of the payments system reform and would thereby improve the security and efficiency of the financial system. It's not only the operating aspects that are important; the reform must also consider providing a proper legal and regulatory framework and establishing a function of oversight of the settlement systems, which is normally the responsibility of the Central Bank.

This entails a far-reaching reform involving many participants. It requires a high degree of coordination among regulators and cooperation with the private sector and with all stakeholders in general. Some organizational change with regard to the existing arrangements through the Central Bank's interinstitutional committee could help. Therefore, the Central Bank's coordination with other participants could change from being merely informational, as it now is, to a more active participation in the discussion and design of the reform, which is very important in broadening the reform's framework. It is necessary to bring the users of the new systems into the process. The Central Bank must be prepared to establish and exercise, with the proper legal basis, the function of oversight of the payments systems. It is not enough to launch and implement the reform; the Central Bank must seek a way to continuously improve the systems and be attentive at all times to its proper operation owing to the implications of systemic risk and efficiency of the financial system.

E. The Financial Safety Net

This discussion of liquidity management has already introduced the more general question of how Ecuador could adapt its "financial safety net" to the needs of a dollarized economy. The new role of the Central Bank and of the SBS in managing and stabilizing liquidity requirements is only part of a more general problem, which this section will analyze.

The three main components of the safety net are usually identified as (a) lender of last resort, (b) deposit insurance, and (c) banking supervision. In Ecuador the three government institutions discussed above (BCE, AGD, and SBS) have been profoundly affected by the crisis. Their roles in the new dollarized financial structure has also been changed several times, while alternatives are being evaluated for each one's future role in the system. Under the alternative that seems to have the highest degree of consensus among the authorities,[19] the Central Bank could keep its central posi-

---

19. The main elements of this are addressed in the document, "Una propuesta de plan estratégico de desarrollo de largo plazo para el Ecuador," prepared in July 2002 as part of a joint committee that is analyzing the new architecture in Ecuador, composed of the Central Bank, the SBS, and the Ministry of Economy and Finance.

tion in the management of the payments system and of the system's liquidity needs, the AGD could be reduced to a pay box that delegates the settlement and solution of responsibilities to the SBS, while the SBS would maintain only responsibility for individual—but not systemic—interventions in the financial sector.

Under the new scheme, the Central Bank would be responsible for managing the overall liquidity of the economy, including being responsible for supervising the payments system and managing system liquidity. The main obstacles to the successful functioning of the payments system appear to be technical in nature, such as the dematerialization of the financial paper. There are also several legal matters with regard to system liquidity that would have to be resolved in order to ensure that this management can be delegated to the Central Bank. Also, the Central Bank's management role could be affected by the potential conflict of interest associated with its ownership of Banco del Pacífico. The Central Bank is aware of this issue and has delegated the administration of Pacífico to international consultants and is awaiting a change in the trend of withdrawal of foreign investment from Latin American banks, which could facilitate the privatization of Banco del Pacífico.

The alternative that is being explored, to reduce the AGD to a pay-box mechanism, could be accelerated if the AGD is relieved of responsibility for managing the remaining assets in banks under reorganization. In this case, the AGD would focus on strengthening the deposit insurance fund (with the premiums that are being charged to active banks), instead of having to use these premiums to pay the debts of banks under reorganization. The resolution of banks outside of the AGD was already put into practice at the time of the response to Filanbanco's second and final fall, which ended with its placement in liquidation in July 2002. Meanwhile, other schemes under consideration call for the possibility of the AGD handing over the management of the portfolio and the sale of allocated goods and buildings to an international professional administrator. This could expedite the collection of the portfolio based on scale issues (and better technologies) and on the lack of a relationship between this potential institution and the system's debtors (particularly the largest).

Finally, the SBS has had a greater sphere of activity with regard to the restructuring of banking. The strengthening of its internal processes of supervision and the use of new manuals for on-site and off-site supervision in its recent inspections is having positive effects on the institution's reputation—which is crucial to increasing confidence in the system—and thereby giving support to the institutional project of liquidity management proposed by the monetary authorities.[20] Another important matter is ensuring that supervisors have legal protection against lawsuits having to do with the performance of their duties. The high turnover in personnel in recent years is probably linked to the lack of this protection. (There

---

20. These efforts have been supported by the World Bank's technical assistance loan to the financial sector.

have been about two superintendents per year, despite the fact that the position has a six-year term.

Another crucial requirement is that improving the quality of banking supervision requires strengthening the legal framework governing the process of bankruptcy in the corporate sector and increasing the protection currently provided to creditors (within Latin America, only Haiti provides less protection than Ecuador[21]), as well as the bankruptcy law and the law concerning chattel and real property collateral. This would also increase incentives for lending, as has been the case with the improved availability of information provided by the credit register, although the credit register could be complemented by a credit bureau that also analyzes data from the real sector (especially with the rise of consumer loans). Within the legal sphere, it is also important to develop an antitrust law in keeping with the best international practices, to provide effective protection of the market.

F. Policy Recommendations

The double impact of the twin crises and the official dollarization of the system have required, and will continue to require, important institutional and operational adjustments to the financial system. The main issues to be addressed are summarized below.

- **The need to improve banks' prudent credit activities, providing greater access.** Large loans, frequently made to related parties, form a high proportion of the nonperforming loan portfolio. The broad coverage of deposit insurance for many of the banks undergoing processes of resolution distorted incentives for debtors, promoting a "nonpayment culture." The result has been a heavily deteriorated portfolio quality (with the ratio of credit portfolio to GDP at half its precrisis level); the cost of lending has risen, while small debtors have had much fewer opportunities for access to credit even considering that typically have less access to the formal sector. The challenge of increasing access to credit is even greater in dollarized economies owing to the circumstances described earlier, but this access could be improved by means of the policies discussed below.

- **A more efficient management of banking liquidity.** The reduced possibility of softening external shocks via economic policy makes dollarized economies more exposed to shocks resulting from exchange or of international interest rates. This vulnerability, together with the lack of a lender of last resort, leads banks to maintain a higher level of liquid assets. However, an

---

21. See Galindo, Arturo, "Creditor Rights and the Credit Markets: Where Do We Stand?" IADB Working Paper. March 2001.

efficient management of system liquidity could free up some of these assets, which would permit increasing the quantity of resources available for productive uses. Centralized management of system liquidity could also permit access to contingent lines of credit on better terms. The Central Bank is a natural candidate for this central role owing to its present responsibility for the payments system. Separating this function from the responsibility of centralized management of liquidity does not appear to be efficient and could negatively affect the provision of a public good such as liquidity. Therefore it is crucial to reduce the legal impediments and to eliminate the potential conflict of interest that could weaken the effectiveness of the Central Bank's actions.

- **Reforms of the payment systems.** The provision of liquidity cannot be successful if there is not an effective payments system. Consequently, the sequence of policies needed to reform the payments system must be codified in a public document. The essential steps include the following: introducing the Real Time Gross Settlement (RTGS) system; ensuring availability of a security deposit to achieve the dematerialization and which allows for carrying out DVP procedures; and, finally, defining a single net clearance system for check transactions. A delay in reforming the payments system will inevitably lead to the change of position of the country's payments services in a time horizon that, for a dollarized economy, may not be very long and would deprive the local banking system of an additional source of profit.

- **Banking supervision and regulation.** The banks' large holdings of liquid assets cannot be reduced solely through interventions related directly to liquidity, because one of the principal reasons behind bank runs is a lack of confidence in the quality of bank assets (aside from reasons of macroeconomic instability). Therefore it is vital that the SBS continue to improve its procedures, especially in relation to the evaluation of credit risks (urging banks to also modernize these processes) and in relation to the rules of portfolio provisioning. Accordingly, it is important to consider the possibility of establishing procyclical provisions as Spain has done, seeing that Ecuador's economy has characteristics of high volatility. Legal protection for SBS authorities in the performance of their functions is also vital, as are legal changes that allow for the improvement of the systems of bank resolution and liquidation. At the same time, the SBS's reporting must be strengthened. Finally, to increase confidence in the system and to prevent potentially dramatic consequences for the management of system liquidity—such as the suspension of correspondent reports between national and foreign banks—will require full compliance with international standards to prevent money laundering (coordinating efforts with the pertinent authorities), ensuring that the SBS can carry out legal actions in this regard within a fully integrated legal system.

- **Codification of exit mechanisms for banks.** The formalization of the role of the SBS and of the AGD in the process of bank resolution and liquidation must be strengthened and the AGD's functions must be revised, considering the alternative of converting it into a pay box. The latter would consider the resolution of the management of assets of banks undergoing reorganization through a specialized foreign agency, to permit a greater return and less erosion of the debtors' will to pay.

- **Reform of state-owned banks.** Owing to the difficult equilibrium that state-owned banks must establish in their dual commercial and social function, it is important to consider reforming the existing banks (particular the first-tier banks), limiting their activity to focalized areas where subsidies, if needed, are transparent and minimal. This effort would have to include an evaluation of alternatives for the development of the microfinance market that has been undergoing development (particularly with the greater success of the savings and loan associations in surviving the crisis) and of rural financing. This last option presents good market potential, which could motivate institutions (even formal ones) already leaning toward these sectors to improve sustainable access to credit and other financial services, based on extensive international experience (as in Bolivia, for instance).

Policy Matrix

Areas of focus and goals	Policy measures and progress indicators	
	Short Term (to June 2003)	Medium Term (2003–07)
LIQUIDITY FUND		
Legal authorization permitting the BCE to manage trusts. The present law does not permit this, which is why the CFN was assigned the role of trustee for management of the liquidity fund.	Transfer of management to the BCE could increase public confidence in the Liquidity Fund.	
Definition of a new organizational structure for management of the liquidity fund. Coordinator of responsibilities between the lender of last resort and the bank supervisor.	Create the Financial System Oversight Committee comprising the BCE, SBS, and the Ministry of Economy and Finance.	Create an agency to manage the technical part of the liquidity fund.
Efficient exchange of information between the BCE, SBS, AGD, and the oversight committee (to be created).	Prepare for the creation of a "data bank" that the different agencies can access.	
Reduction of the Central Bank's conflict of interest as owner of Banco Pacífico.	Sustain progress in the bank's restructuring plan.	Revise the plan for the bank's privatization in the medium term.
AGD		
Finalization of AGD activities related to the crisis. Payment of outstanding liabilities, sale of portfolio and other assets.		Contract with external consultants to sell assets to prevent their rapid erosion, permitting the payment of pending accounts.
Restructuring of the AGD. Allowing it to focus on partial deposit insurance.	Revise its structure, consider converting it into a pay box.	

SUPERINTENDENCY OF BANKING

Legal protection for the superintendent and other functionaries in performing their duties.	Modify the Banking Act, to include explicit protection.	
Improvement of the SBS's reporting	Include a section in its Annual Report with statistics that reflect the oversight activity of the SBS.	
Compliance with international standards against money laundering (coordinating efforts with the related authorities). Guaranteeing that the SBS can carry out legal actions in this sphere within a fully integrated legal system.	Introduce a law to bring the country into compliance with Financial Action Task Force (FATF) principles of money laundering.	Introduce regulations to be carried out by banks and insurance companies.
Strengthening of mechanisms for credit risk analysis, for both on-site and off-site inspections (to improve analysis systems in banks).		

PROTECTION FOR DEBTORS

Introduction of Bankruptcy Act in line with the best international practices. Redefine the legal framework for the property rights of creditors in the restructuring of debts.	Perform an analysis of corporate insolvency (*Insolvency Report on the Observance of Standards and Codes* [ROSC]).

PAYMENTS SYSTEM

Formulation of a strategic vision of the payments system beyond operational aspects, focused on improving payment	Formulate a strategic vision of a report from the Central Bank for the settlement of payments and securities that is comprehensive and goes

(Matrix continues on the following page)

Policy Matrix (*continued*)

Areas of focus and goals	Policy measures and progress indicators	
	Short Term (to June 2003)	*Medium Term (2003–07)*
services. Extend the scope of the reform to include legal issues, the oversight function, securities, government payments, and so on.	beyond operational aspects.	
Legal aspects: protection of the payments systems against individual bankruptcy, purpose of liquidation, legal basis for collateral, legal recognition of the estimation of net balances, and so on.	Perform in-depth review of the legal framework for a payments system and design a plan of action for implementing the necessary reforms. Incorporate into the legal framework all aspects identified for increasing the soundness of the payments system.	
Creation of a system of Real Time Gross Settlement. Significant risks because high-value payments are made through checks. The funds transfer system between Central Bank accounts still contains manual processes that reduce its effectiveness.		Follow the guidelines set down in the strategic vision document to establish the different elements necessary for modernizing the payments system.
Securities depository. The failure to develop the function of securities depository does not allow a Delivery Versus Payment (DVP) system. This puts limitations on management of system liquidity because the lack of this function hinders the development of an interbank monetary market with collateral.		Establish the function of securities depository based on the guidelines set down in the strategic vision document, with a connection to the high-value funds transfer system.

Establishment by the Central Bank of the oversight function. There is no legal capacity and no practical oversight of the payments system by the Central Bank. A reform cannot be considered complete unless this function has been activated, which permits controlling the risks and periodically checking that the liquidation arrangements are efficient and secure at all times.	Have the Central Bank establish the function of oversight of the payments system and coordinate with other regulators (on the subject of securities, for example).
Coordination by the Central Bank with other related parties. There is room for improvement in the existing organizational arrangements through the Central Bank's Interinstitutional Committee.	Establish a mid-level committee that provides better liaison between the high-level committee and the present technical committees.

5

Petroleum Policy[1]

Eleodoro Mayorga

The importance of the petroleum sector to the Ecuadoran economy is undeniable. Given the weight of external debt and the need to generate fiscal resources, there is an urgent need to increase exports and reduce inefficiencies in this sector. The country has considerable proven reserves, and by the end of 2003 will also have acquired the greater transport infrastructure it needs. However, the sector still suffers from serious structural problems: a legal, contractual and institutional framework that preserves PetroEcuador's monopoly and limits access to capital and technology; distortions in the management of oil profits; high costs resulting from low operational efficiency in the state enterprise; low quality products sent to market at a high cost; and a socio-environmental record that needs resolution in order to open vast regions of the country to sustainable development. The new government needs to undertake profound sectoral reforms. The most urgent actions include solving the problem of Value-Added Tax (VAT) reimbursement, the lack of stability in the judicial system for investors, the elimination of the gas subsidy, and the adoption of a formula to allow PetroEcuador to form partnerships with private companies for operations in its most important oil fields.

A. The Evolution of the Petroleum Sector and Legal Framework

The importance of the petroleum sector to the Ecuadoran economy cannot be overstated, as it comprises approximately 15 percent of GDP and a third of state revenues. Petroleum and its derivatives account for an average of 40 percent of total exports, a

---

1. This chapter was elaborated by Eleodoro Mayorga Alba, the World Bank's main petroleum economist, and Horacio Yepez, World Bank consultant.

number expected to rise in future years given the productive potential of this sector. Table 1 reveals the fragility of the trade balance, and in general of Ecuador's economy as export volume and oil prices fluctuate on the international market. It is probable that the year 2002 will close with acceptable gains because of sustained oil prices.

Since 1971, the year in which the first Law on Hydrocarbons was passed, the state has taken on a major role in sectoral management and operations. With the exception of exploration and production activities that are also carried out by private companies, PetroEcuador maintains a monopoly over wholesale industrialization and commercialization of petroleum derivatives. However, PetroEcuador's investments are subject to the dispositions of the Finance Ministry within the state's general budget. Annex 1 contains a historical chronology, as well as a detailed description of the sector.

Proven reserves are estimated at 4.6 billion barrels, of which Petroproducción— PetroEcuador's affiliate for exploration and oil and gas development—controls nearly 75 percent, including the majority of light crude oil fields. The state enterprises' production has decreased markedly from a maximum of 120 million barrels (bbl) in 1994 to 80 million bbl per year owing to a lack of investment and transport capacity. Private sector support for national production is nearly 65 million bbl. This means a national daily average of 400,000 barrels per day (BPD), limited by pipeline capacity with Petroproducción accounting for 56 percent, and private com-

Table 1. Importance of the Petroleum Sector to the Economy (blns/mlns $US)

	1995	1996	1997	1998	1999	2000	2001
Crude oil exports	1.395bl	1.520bl	1.411bl	789m	1.312bl	2.144bl	1.722bl
Export of petroleum derivatives (in millions)	134.5	227.9	145.9	134.0	167.4	298.4	177.7
Total crude exports and derivatives	1.529bl	1.748bl	1.557bl	922.9 m	1.479bl	2.442bl	1.9bl
Percentage of exports	34.9	35.9	29.6	22.0	33.2	49.6	40.6
Percentage of GDP*	14.6	14.0	14.0	13.5	14.6	15.0	14.6
Total Petroleum Revenues	1.329bl	1.574bl	1.269bl	912.9m	1,048bl	1.460bl	1.347bl
Revenues from crude exports (millions)	683.2	939.4	625.5	249.5	745.6	1.286bl	990.1
Revenues from sale of derivatives (millions)	645.8	635.1	644.4	663.4	303.1	173.1	357.2
Percentage of public revenues	29.0	33.8	26.9	22.7	29.8	35.4	27.4

* Includes mining, which makes an insignificant contribution to the petroleum sector.
Source: Central Bank Statistical Information and PetroEcuador Statistics.

panies for 44 percent. When comparing reserves to production, one observes that private companies own 25 percent of reserves, and yet currently contribute nearly half of total production.

The majority of private investment in exploration and development of new reserves is carried out through participation contracts. This modality, which was incorporated in the Law on Hydrocarbons in 1993, has allowed contracts in which private companies assume all risks, investments and costs, and share production with the state at a proportion of approximately 75 percent and 25 percent, respectively. In 1993, the modality of Contracts for Marginal Fields was also adopted which utilizes the participation model, while allowing private companies access to reserves discovered in small fields (which make up less than 1 percent of national production). In 1998 the former administration tried to incorporate the Joint Ventures modality into the law, in order to allow private companies to partner with Petroproducción to operate large fields. Although the National Congress supported this initiative, its initial economic conditions were modified and it was later declared partially unconstitutional—and became null and void.

During recent years there have been few initiatives to seek new private investment. The Operational Alliances was one such initiative, and was utilized to develop two Petroproducción fields in which private enterprise provided a variety of services and financing in return for payment—making the viability of the alliance dependent on increased production. The most recent attempt at contracting the management of producing fields is the proposal to Chile's National Petroleum Enterprise (*ENAP—Empresa Nacional del Petróleo*). There was no call for tenders, based on the privilege of state companies to sign specific service contracts directly. The government sent a reform bill to Congress to try to incorporate this privilege into the law, but apart from a specific contract with ENAP, the reform was rejected.

For 10 years petroleum production has been limited by transport capabilities. With the exception of the small AGIP pipeline, PetroEcuador and the private companies are using the TransEcuadoran Pipeline System (*SOTE—Sistema de Oleoducto Transecuatoriano*), with a capacity of 390,000 BPD of petroleum with a gravity of 23.7° API.[2] In addition, PetroEcuador can transport a volume of nearly 50,000 BPD in agreement with the Colombian Petroleum Company (*ECOPETROL— Empresa Colombiana de Petróleo*), to Tumaco via the TransAndean Pipeline. The crude transported via this pipeline is 29° API, the quality level required by the La Libertad refinery. Transport from Tumaco to la Libertad is by ship. Limitations on pipeline capabilities have made it necessary to mix light and heavy crudes.

In order to end these limitations, in February 2001 the government authorized the construction of a heavy oil pipeline (OCP) through a consortium composed of

---

2. The API grades are an *American Petroleum Institute* measurement used to define the specific gravity of oil. The greater the API, the lighter the product, meaning the higher the content in gasoline, diesel, and white products, the higher the price.

the main private companies operating in the country. The OCP will be able to transport up to 518,000 BPD of 18 to 24° API. It mainly follows the SOTE route and flows into a new sea terminal as in Balao Esmeraldas. In contractual terms, OCP construction should wrap up in June 2003, but owing to work stoppages caused by environmental groups and local communities, it is expected to begin operating in September 2003. Available transport capacity will increase to approximately 960,000 BPD with the OCP.

The state monopoly and lack of investments have also seriously affected activities. Primary refining capacity is currently 175,000 BPD. Refining production in the hands of Petroindustrial does not completely meet domestic demand (135,000 BPD), meaning the state must import gasoline, diesel, and LPG. The Amazon and La Libertad refineries only have atmospheric distilling units, and even though the Esmeraldas refinery has some conversion capacity, production of residuals in the three refineries exceeds local demand. These residuals are exported at a low price.

Petroindustrial derivatives and imports are distributed through the internal market by Petrocomercial, the owner of the network of ducts and terminals for storage and distribution. Petrocomercial provides products to vendors at the same price fixed by the President of the Republic in all terminals. As regards sale price to the consumer, the presidential decree establishes a maximum margin of 18 percent on the sale price in the terminal, applied by nearly all distributors, without price or margin competition.

In terms of environmental and social management, industry activities are regulated by the environmental standards for hydrocarbon operations approved in February 2001. The main modification to this code was to raise environmental standards to international standards, with special emphasis on re-injection of formation water, emissions monitoring, flaring of associated gas, and permanent environmental auditing. The Department of Environmental Protection in the Ministry of Energy and Mining (*Dirección de Protección Ambiental del Ministerio de Energía y Minas—MEM*) is the entity that supervises compliance with these standards.

The law establishes the right of indigenous peoples and communities to participate in consultations. The legal dispositions to support application of this right have just recently been promulgated. To date, companies have been managing social issues through direct negotiations with communities. The lack of a code of standards compounded by the enormous socioeconomic needs in petroleum zones that have not been met by the government, has forced firms to carry out public works and distribute resources in order to be able to operate and avoid suffering costly delays in their work. And this is despite the fact that companies already pay an Ecodevelopment tax to benefit these regions. The tax amounts to $US0.35/bbl and will reach $US0.50/bbl by 2005 in the eastern fields. There is no evidence that the taxes paid or the support provided by companies has significantly contributed to development in the oil-producing region.

In 2002, oil profits amounted to more than $US1.5 billion, and this sector's contribution to the state budget averaged 28 percent. Revenues distribution has become more complicated because of the series of preallocations established for each revenue segment: exemptions, former consortium production, service contracts, and so on. The lack of transparency in resource management, which takes place outside the framework of the state budget, is a serious problem. Starting in 2003, however, the large preallocation to the Armed Forces from oil royalties will be eliminated.

The Fund for Petroleum Stabilization was one effort to develop a contingencies fund, and it accumulated resources when the price of crude exceeded $US20 per bbl. However, these resources have also been subject to preallocations. Finally, given the expected increase in production when the OCP begins operations, a Fund for Stabilization, Social and Productive Investment, and Reduction of Public Debt *(FEIREP— Fondo de Estabilización, Inversión Social y Productiva, y Reducción del Endeudamiento Público)* has been established. FEIREP's goal is to repurchase external public debt at market value, and stabilize revenues earmarked for health and education.

B. The Main Problems of the Petroleum Industry in Ecuador

The petroleum sector in Ecuador suffers from inefficiencies and distortions that limit the country's economic growth. The first series of problems are related to the need to increase investments in exploration and production. These increases should come primarily from the private sector, given public sector limitations and in particular limitations on the state-owned company. The following measures are required in order to develop the production of proven reserves and to capitalize on the existence of increased transport capabilities by the end of 2003:

- Ensure legal and economic stability of contracts, beginning with the resolution of the VAT problem for oil companies operating in the country.
- Find a contractual formula within the framework of current laws that allows PetroEcuador to partner with private companies to develop reserves in the most important oil fields.
- Develop new reserves, as well as those already proven and those resulting from the exploration of new areas.

In commercialization and other activities, price and tax distortions should be eliminated, as should PetroEcuador's *de facto* monopoly, thus favoring competition both in refining (as opposed to importing products) and in product distribution and marketing. Without these improvements the state will lose tax revenues, and consumers will continue to pay high prices for low quality products. Some of these measures are as follows:

- Eliminate the LPG subsidy.
- Redefine the price and tax policy on consumption of fuels in a way that facilitates the entry of new companies.

- Seek private investments for refining activities.

Many of these measures are complementary and some can be taken without changing laws. In addition to these measures, other sectoral actions include:

- Revising the current petroleum revenues management scheme to ensure transparency, and eliminate corruption and the inefficient use of petroleum revenues.
- Revising the industry's legal and institutional framework, separating the role of the state—acting as guardian of the public interest by administrating revenues and as guarantor of a petroleum industry that is committed to sustainable development—from PetroEcuador's role, that should remain focused on maximizing the profitability of state assets in the sector.
- Improving the management of social and environmental impact. Ecuador is a country with very sensitive environments in petroleum zones, where a highly costly environmental liability has accumulated. Indigenous culture should be supported and the quality of life of indigenous peoples should be improved. These groups have been affected particularly negatively by industry activities.

The Problem of VAT Reimbursement and Contractual Stability

The VAT exemption on imports enjoyed by oil companies is contained in the Law on Hydrocarbons, while the exemption for petroleum services is in the Law on the Internal Tax Regime. In 1998, an interpretation of the Law on Hydrocarbons at the customs level resulted in companies being forced to pay sales tax on their imports. In 1999, the Tax Regime Law was reformed, with the elimination of the sales tax exemption for petroleum services, and the rate was increased from 10 to 12 percent. Until August 2001, companies received reimbursement of the value-added tax paid on crude exports, like any other exporter in the country. In that month, the Internal Revenue Service (SRI) introduced a reinterpretation of the tax law, differentiating, in terms of treatment, between the hydrocarbon industry and all other export industries. This meant that private oil companies stopped receiving the VAT reimbursement. The economic impact of this measure, according to the companies, will reach over $US200 million by the end of the year.

PetroEcuador has ignored the companies' complaints regarding this situation, even though it has a contractual obligation regarding retribution to the contractor in the event that the tax regime was changed. This should have been applied at least in order to compensate for the rise in the VAT rate from 10 to 12 percent.

With respect to the change in interpretation by the IRS, companies have presented administrative and legal complaints. They believe that the reimbursement of VAT should apply to all exporters because this tax should not be exported. The companies also oppose the revoked exemption on the fundamental basis that these contracts were established based on economies that did not take such a change into account.

At one time, the outgoing administration decided to let the SRI resolve the conflict. The SRI argues that the oil companies have been reporting costs illegally in some cases. There have been three judicial verdicts that have only taken into account the recognition of the 2 percent increase in the tax rate. In other words, the verdicts have ratified the nonreimbursement position, considering a rate increase, and not the entire revoked VAT exemption, as the only factor that affects the economic stability of contracts.

As the conflict continues, positions have lost clarity, mixing arguments such as the illegality of re-interpretation with accusations of tax evasion. With the goal of seeking a solution, the option of international arbitration has been proposed. The state has accepted the principle of arbitration with reservations, and still does not agree with Occidental Petroleum on how to proceed. Encana, a company that was negatively affected by the court ruling, has indicated its intention to seek international arbitration.

The negative impact of these tax measures on the country's economy, and specifically on the petroleum sector, is significant. The companies are downsizing their investment plans, which will directly affect production in both the short and medium terms. If the VAT problem is not resolved, this will also block revenues from new investment and will even affect company participation in the reactivation of Petroproducción's current oil fields.

Increasing Petroleum Production

Private Companies

At present, private firms maintain field operations that represent 26 percent of the country's reserves. The prospects of production by private companies has been affected by VAT problems, which is reflected in greater idle OCP capacity, at least in the short term. The following scenarios can be foreseen in the medium term:

- The first scenario corresponds to a low rate of growth of production that would increase from 180,000 BPD in 2002 to 240,000 BPD in 2004, reaching a level of 295,000 BPD in 2007. This scenario is based on a voluntary reduction of company investment because of the lack of stability in the judicial system in general, and particularly on a lack of resolution of the legal conflict over VAT.
- The second scenario—which assumes that the new government will resolve the VAT problem quickly during the first weeks of its mandate—would allow companies to accelerate the investment process, and production could jump from 180,000 BPD in 2002 to 290,000 BPD in 2004, and hit 420,000 BPD in 2007.

Considering that on average, 30 percent[3] of private production belongs to the state, the difference in the fiscal terms between these two scenarios is more than $US500 million—which translates to more than 45 million barrels that the state would no longer receive as part of its participation. This is sufficient reason for the government to urgently seek a solution to the VAT problem.

Petroproducción

During the last four years, the national company has been operating under restrictions that have caused a drop in production averaging 6.1 percent annually, costing the country over 45,000 BPD of petroleum, which represents nearly $US700 million in fiscal terms. If these limitations on PetroEcuador's financial and technological resources continue, based on the current 10 percent decline in production, only one-third of remaining proven reserves will be recovered in the next 20 years.

The drop in Petroproducción's production is not due to the geology of the oil fields (which have sufficient reserves), but due to the state's deficient management of an industry that is extremely technical. Political interference has been the norm, with emphasis on meeting short-term objectives and permitting different economic and social interest groups, as well as unions, to pressure the company. The company's maintenance of its facilities is very poor. It has lost key technical personnel over the years and has not gained access to new technologies. There is very little planning, and serious deficiencies exist in administration and operational capacity caused partly by the loss of financial autonomy because the entity is bound by the Public Budget Law. The collective contract, which covers all employees and establishes significant compensation in the case of either termination or resignation, is another factor that has diminished the efficiency of this state enterprise.

At the present time, PetroEcuador does not have the necessary technological know-how to execute, evaluate, and interpret the results of the perforation of horizontal wells, improved recovery, and 3D seismic campaigns. Investments in these activities have been only partially successful. However, no significant participation on the part of private companies, which have the capital and technology required, has been permitted. This is because political and labor union actor s have waved the flags of nationalism and identified this sector as "strategic," in order to block opening initiatives.

The little private participation in production development efforts is centered in five marginal oil fields and two medium-sized fields that are part of the Operative Alliance system. Meanwhile, the joint ventures option in large fields was thrown out following the distortions introduced in the National Congress during the approval of the Trolley Laws of 2001.

If Petroproducción continues to operate the most important reserves in the country with the same financial and technological restrictions, it probably will not be

---

3. This is over 30 percent even if state participation represents 25 percent in participation contracts, when participation in marginal oil fields and the equivalent of the AGIP contract is consolidated.

Figure 1. National Petroleum Production and Consumption

Millions of bbl.

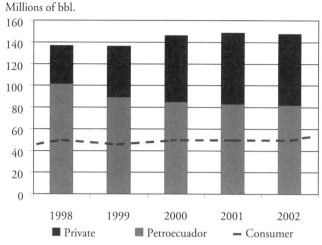

Source: PetroEcuador.

able to increase production. However, this scenario could change significantly if the private sector actively participates. If conditions are provided to attract private investment both in PetroEcuador's areas and the areas contracted out—that is, scenario 2 in Table 2—and restrictions on transport are lifted by the end of 2003, national production could double in the next four years.

Petroproducción's exploration activities have not achieved significant results in recent years. Reserves of fields not yet in production are not very promising (180 million bbl), and possible reserves are not substantial (75 million bbl). These fields contain many areas that are governed by environmental restrictions on exploration, with Imuya's prospects standing out.

Table 2. Projections for National Petroleum Production
(Mlns of bbl)

	2002	2003	2004	2005	2006	2007
NATIONAL TOTAL						
Scenario 1	148	150	173	179	183	191
Scenario 2	148	150	192	226	254	280
PETROPRODUCCIÓN						
Scenario 1	82	84	85	86	84	83
Scenario 2	82	84	86	93	106	127
PRIVATE COMPANIES						
Scenario 1	65	66	88	93	99	108
Scenario 2	66	66	106	133	148	153

The Case of the ITT Fields

In 1993, Petroproducción discovered heavy crude reserves in several fields called Ishpingo-Tambococha-Tiputini (ITT), in the central-eastern part of the Amazon. The last perforations and studies indicate the existence of a significant volume of reserves (1.4 billion bbl.). The geographic and environmental situation of ITT and the quality of crude oil with a high sulfur content means it is necessary to budget high levels of investment and to keep in mind that production cannot begin until seven years of investment have been completed. The interest of Petroproducción in becoming an active partner in the project, and determining the form of execution and deciding phases ofproduction, have delayed the project's definition. Both for this project and others, private investment requires operational autonomy.

Reserves

It is the state's responsibility to ensure that the flow of oil revenues in the long term equally benefits current and future generations of Ecuadorans. For this reason, it is necessary to begin new exploration, particularly when one considers that it takes from 5 to 10 years for reserves to reach the production stage. In the most favorable investment scenario, we can foresee significant production increases by 2007, based only on reserves already proven. After that date, there could be a reduction in production if the ITT fields are not being worked, and if there are no discoveries in other areas.

After the eighth round of bidding, carried out in 1998, no new blocks have been contracted. There are three blocks in the east that were adjudicated in the seventh and eighth rounds to the Burlington, CGC, and Tripetrol companies. These planned explorations have not begun because the first two companies have had problems with the communities, and because of legal problems in the case of the third company. Apart from the direct contracting carried out by Petroproducción with ENAP for the exploration and exploitation of the three medium-sized fields currently in production, it does not seem feasible or appropriate to carry out new direct contracts with state enterprises when this option has been expressly rejected by the National Congress.

The outgoing administration has delayed the ninth round, and modified its scope several times. The blocks up for bidding in the eastern region have been taken off the list, with the round being limited to blocks in the offshore region. In addition to the political waffling, the lack of specific regulations has made it impossible to carry out a consultation process with communities living in the blocks of the eastern region—a necessary prerequisite to begin the project. However, it is worth noting that thanks to the efforts to build consensus, the outgoing government has promulgated a regulation for community consultations that will facilitate initiating these processes in the new exploration and production zones.

General Subsidy for Liquid Petroleum

With the recent increase in oil prices and the prices of derivatives, the net effect of taxes paid by consumers and hidden subsidies that currently govern the sale of fuels has an estimated fiscal cost of more than $US300 million annually. This number includes the general subsidy for gas, as well as minor subsidies for diesel and fuel oil. Gasolines are the only products that are being taxed effectively.

A detailed estimate of the prices of current economic efficiency is presented in annex 2, along with a comparison with current prices. These calculations are based on crude prices in the West Texas Intermediate (WTI) of $US27,515/bbl, which are relatively high owing to the problems caused in the international market by the current situation in Venezuela.

LPG requires a karge percentile price increase to reach its price of economic efficiency[4] (347 percent). In addition to fiscal cost, the way the subsidy is currently applied to both LPG and other products means that the total value earmarked under this subsidy indiscriminately benefits the rich as well as the poor, without targeting to improve the quality of life of the most needy, which should be the priority objective.

Various governments have tried unsuccessfully to eliminate the gas subsidy, but they have not been able to implement compensatory measures that would convince the population to accept price increases. On some occasions, after deciding to increase the price of the product, governments have had to back down and reduce them in order to quell popular protest. There are various alternatives for targeting this subsidy. The outgoing administration has left a plan in place that would permit selling LPG at an economic price of import parity, while introducing a special coupon for the poor simultaneously. This way those in need of financial assistance can continue to buy the cylinder of LPG and pay the current subsidized price.

Price and Tax Policy, and Lack of Competition in the Derivatives Market

The state monopoly and the fixing of fuel prices by decree are the main characteristics of the petroleum derivative market in Ecuador. The elimination of the LPG subsidy opens the doors to efficiently organizing the tax system for fuels. This can be done without substantially changing the prices for the public, since the correction needed on diesel prices (16 percent) and fuel oil (13 percent) could be staggered while waiting for the international market to stabilize. The fundamental objective is to eliminate price fixing by the state, and basically letting prices respond to interna-

---

4. The economic efficiency price corresponds to the cost of opportunity. In this case the price is calculated taking into account the cost of importing each combustible fuel, plus the local costs of services until they are sent to the Petrocomercial terminal.

Figure 2. Price of Products in Terminal (incl. VAT)

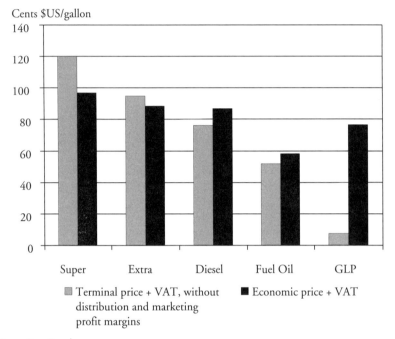

Cents $US/gallon

Terminal price + VAT, without distribution and marketing profit margins

Economic price + VAT

Source: PetroEcuador.

tional market variations. There are experiences with price adjustment mechanisms that allow the state to withdraw, and that absorb the inopportune price fluctuations on the international market, without affecting consumers.

Decisionmaking on taxes and profit margins of commercialization are closely linked to decisionmaking on prices. In Ecuador it is important to revise the value of the Special Consumption Tax (ICE) and liberalize the profit margins for product distribution and marketing in a way that permits the entry of private companies in a competitive manner. Commercialization activities of derivatives are carried out by Petrocomercial, with the private sector exclusively handling retail commercialization of derivatives at a fixed price established by the government. This is reflected in the absence of a competitive market, which forces the final user to accept rigid price and quality options.

Investments in Refining

In Ecuador, the consumption of derivatives is 135,000 BPD, compared with a refining capacity of 175,000 BPD. However, there is a national production deficit in gasoline, diesel, and LPG, and imports are needed to meet internal demand. At the same time, the excess production of residuals needs be exported. It is estimated that imports this year will hit $US360 million, a number that will continue to grow in future years.

Petroindustrial's refineries generate a high volume of residue to the detriment of production of white products, owing to its configuration and the crudes it processes. The quality of fuels is very low. Both gasoline and diesel have a high sulfur content, and gasolines are low in octane. In Ecuador, a diesel is sold containing up to 7,000 ppm of sulfur, while the Latin American average is approximately 400 ppm, and in western European and U.S. markets the goal is to have a ceiling of 30 ppm by 2005.

The refineries want to modernize their equipment to cut production costs and reduce the negative environmental impacts they are causing. In short, they should increase productivity. These actions have not been undertaken because of the lack of political decisionmaking, poor administration, low levels of investment, and pressure from labor unions. The current price policy does not provide incentives for investing in private refineries as prices are discretional rather than fixed by competition. This is compounded by limits on access to storage and transport infrastructure at reasonable rates for new wholesale companies. Without the possibility of integrating into the market, investors are not willing to participate in refining activities.

The state monopoly on refining activities and commercialization has generated costs for the Treasury, not only because of the existence of subsidies but also because of PetroEcuador's inefficiencies. Between the years 2000, 2001, and 2002, the accumulated losses of the sector were over $US1.7 billion.

Administrative System for Petroleum Revenues

From the beginning, the administration of the resources from the petroleum sector has been subject to inadequate and politicized management, converting collection and allocation of resources into a true labyrinth with each passing year. The government has found petroleum revenues to be a never-ending source of resources to meet all types of fiscal needs. In addition, revenues for the state budget are estimated based on high oil prices,[5] and total debits are adjusted to this estimate. This situation implies high risk during periods when oil prices are low because of the fiscal deficits produced. At the same time it does not permit rational management of ever-growing public expenditures.

The breakdown of petroleum revenue allocation for the period 1995–2000 illustrates that the management of profits from hydrocarbon activity is centralized (only 3.8 percent is directly allocated to sectional governments), and that preallocations

---

5. The price used in the state budget corresponds to the price of Eastern crude, which is the WTI price minus a quality differential. For the year 2003, an estimated price of between $US18 and 22/bbl. is being debated.

Table 3. Economic Results of Refining and Commercialization (thds $US)

	1998	1999	2000	2001	2002
REVENUES	1,174,474	964,941	1,156,661	1,321,511	1,491,115
Internal sales (*)	1,025,173	782,696	838,002	1,116,664	1,280,379
Export of derivatives	149,301	182,245	318,659	204,847	210,735
Debits	1,177,685	1,305,570	2,051,815	1,728,076	1,920,171
Import of derivatives (**)	440,105	302,722	320,135	347,581	361,904
Cost of crude (***)	474,919	724,878	1,457,029	1,084,899	1,225,500
Commerciali- zation costs	106,216	112,406	111,064	116,375	131,456
Industrialization costs	156,446	165,563	163,587	179,221	201,311
NET	–3,212	–340,629	–895,154	–406,565	–429,057

(*) Does not include value of VAT on products.
(**) In 1998, the compensation value of crude was considered.
(***) Refinery crude has been valued at international prices.
Source: Elaborated by the author based on PetroEcuador's statistics.

lack definition (a large quantity of resources allocated to various institutions is in the category "Others"). (See Table 4.)

In comparison with other countries of the Andean region, the Ecuadoran system of revenues distribution shows less transparency, and leads to inefficient management of petroleum revenues. For example, allocations to institutions outside of budgetary control in other countries are 2 percent less on average, while in Ecuador it is greater. The resources allocated to social funds in Ecuador are also clearly insufficient, at only 3.3 percent of total.

Table 4. Petroleum Revenues Distribution Structure (Average 1995–2000)

Central government	62.14%
Provinces	1.42%
Municipalities	2.40%
Social support funds	3.30%
Others	30.94%

Source: Population, Environment, and Energy Program (EAP), "Comparative Study of Distribution of Petroleum Revenues," Energy Sector Management Assistance Program (ESMAP), February 2002.

One of the measures already taken is the elimination of preallocation of resources for the Armed Forces, which now receive resources through the state's regular budget. However, there is still much to be done in order to improve the current system's transparency.

ECORAE, a fund created to help develop social programs and conserve the environment in the Amazon region, has not produced the expected results. Thirty percent of the revenues from this production-based fund is transferred to provincial councils of the region, 60 percent goes to municipalities, and 10 percent to the Institute for Regional Ecodevelopment in the Amazon (*Instituto para el Ecodesarrollo regional Amazónico*). The regional government has oriented its resources to maintain a bureaucratic system, and to develop urban areas, rather than specifically targeting zones affected by petroleum-related activities.

The Fund for Petroleum Stabilization was created along with other initiatives allocating resources to specific funds. The goal is to take precautions against external shocks that could result from a fall in crude prices, accumulating resources when crude prices go over $US20/bbl. This fund has not met its goal because revenues generated have also been preallocated to the Amazon Highway (35 percent) and the Public Investment Fund (65 percent). Finally, the current administration has established a new preallocation for a fund called Stabilization, Social and Productive Investment, and Reduction of Public Debt. The resources for this fund come from PetroEcuador's crude exports which are transported by the OCP, as long as they are not derived from lesser utilization of the SOTE. The fund will be used to repurchase external debt, to stabilize petroleum revenues, and for education and health. In this case, even though the Law's goal is worthy of praise, the amounts needed to fully comply with objectives do not match realistic expectations for production.

Legal and Institutional Framework

The sectoral law, in effect since 1978 and reformed many times, was structured based on the premise that the petroleum sector is strategic and that exploitation is the sole duty of the state. The state carries this out directly, and only exceptionally delegates the task to private companies. This is why the development of the country's petroleum sector depends on PetroEcuador's performance.

In the case of Petroproducción, operational costs have been rising continuously, since production is dropping and since there is no oversight and no accounts presented to the Ministry of Finance, which usually charges PetroEcuador on the basis of estimated costs. An even greater problem is that investments are not made in accordance with the approved budget, and projects are discretionally managed by the authorities of the day. (See Table 5.)

With the external commercialization of crude, contracts are adjudicated on the basis of premium that companies offer under a pre-established differential between eastern crude and the WTI. This differential is frequently modified, which is reasonable considering the fluctuating market conditions, but does not offer trans-

Table 5. Indicators of the Petroproducción Affiliate

		1998	1999	2000	2001	2002 (*)
Operational costs	$US/bbl	1.41	1.09	1.31	1.97	2.44
Production	MM bbl	101.4	89.5	85.0	82.9	82.2
Investments/budget		40%	77%	83%	55%	68%

(*) Estimated.
Source: Petroproducción's Economic Budget of expenditures and investment.

parency since it is based on PetroEcuador's internal studies, which often involve a large dose of subjectivity.

PetroEcuador's contracting system is slow and not very transparent. On average, six months are needed for contracting. Bidding processes are frequently canceled for lack of bidders, contracts are subscribed without a bidding process, and pressure is exerted on adjudicating bodies.

The assignment of a state role to PetroEcuador, as counterpart and control entity for petroleum contracts, has had a negative impact on the company's relationship with private companies and on the success of new initiatives with private participation. PetroEcuador, because it competes with the private sector for better projects, suffers from a conflict of interest and has tried to maintain the institutional status quo. In practice, this hurts the state's needs and plans.

The frequent change of administration, political intervention in company management, the lack of an auditing system for officials, and inefficient control mechanisms have all created a system where responsibility is low. All of these factors work against proper utilization of the country's hydrocarbon resources.

Ecuador is competing at a disadvantage compared to other countries in the region that have reformed their laws and have separated the roles of (i) the Ministry as the definer of sectoral policy; (ii) the regulating entities and/or the entities charged with representing the state in the definition of incentives and contractual frameworks that attract foreign investment to explore and produce hydrocarbons; and (iii) the national petroleum industry acting within a framework of financial autonomy and competition during all phases.

Environmental and Social Impact

The petroleum industry in Ecuador carries out activities in a fragile environmental and social context. Very little attention was paid to these matters during certain operations, and as a result, large environmental liabilities have accumulated. Perhaps the most notorious problem is the treatment and elimination of formation water that is a by-product of the production of crude oil. Crude spills are frequent, and mud perforation pools and/or pools of formation water are visible on eastern oil fields, and should be eliminated. Radical measures must be taken to prevent this problem from growing. Lessons can be learned from the experience of PetroEcuador's pilot project with the private company now charged with processing and re-injecting formation waters on the Shushufindi field.

The flaring of associated gases is also a pernicious practice on the production fields of PetroEcuador. The gas plant at Shushufindi has a idle capacity of 60 percent, equivalent to 15 million cubic feet of associated gas per day. This contrasts with the volume of gas that continues to burn in the Amazon, easily more than 50 million cubic feet daily. The negative consequences of gas flaring are environmental as well as economic. The full utilization of the Shushufindi gas plant will allow an annual 20 percent (1.2 million barrels) reduction in imports of LPG. Projects that take advantage of the LPG of associated gas and that improve electricity generation on oil fields should also be made feasible; as in the case of the Sacha field and others in the east.

Environmental regulations contemplate developing participatory-type monitoring of operations, but there is no capability to do this. It is important to evaluate the resources needed by the Sub-secretariat of Environmental Protection, and at the same time, seriously explore options for more participatory monitoring involving indigenous and local populations.

Government support for regions affected by petroleum exploitation in terms of preallocations is limited and not very transparent. Companies, in return for compensation, exchange permits to operate, and then carry out public works that are defined by the communities according to their immediate needs. In practice this does not translate into support for real sustainable development that increases the standard of living and that allows implementation of feasible sustainable projects in these regions.

C. Recommendations and Implementation

A series of recommendations are presented below, as well as a framework indicating priority, the entity responsible, and compliance indicators for the recommended activities.

A Solution to the VAT Problem

The VAT problem is in the hands of the new government and needs to be resolved as quickly as possible, whether by adopting international arbitration or another procedure. Measures that are adopted should be implemented administratively in the short term, and which will require rulings by the SRI make them operative.

If the government opts to return nonreimbursed amounts, we recommend negotiating a plan of financing with private firms, such as a payment linked to future production increases.

We suggest taking advantage of this situation to clarify the tax regime applicable to companies, not only in the present but also in the future, in such a way that

Ecuador provides transparency, clear rules, and security to current and new foreign investment. It would be useful to provide detailed information to the IRS in the case of new petroleum contracts, before they are signed.

Increasing the Production of PetroEcuador's Oil Fields

The new government should take immediate action to allow an increase in production. Private sector support is absolutely necessary given the business environment in Petroproducción. The Law on Hydrocarbons contains various legal provisions that can be applied in these cases, allowing the private sector to participate in petroleum-related activities with PetroEcuador.[6] The specific modality should satisfy the different sectors of public opinion and be attractive to investors. In order to ensure rapid implementation, this modality should be completed without the intervention of the National Congress.

One scheme that fits the needs described above is the establishment of joint venture companies, a form of contracting used by PetroEcuador when working with small firms (for example, Austrogas and Lojagas). This type of company acts as a limited liability company in which a state institution and a private company are stockholders. In each area of production (Sacha, Shushufindi, Aguarico, Auca, Lake Agrio, and Libertador—so of which cover several fields), a joint venture would be set up. Petroproducción would be the stockholder that capitalizes the firm with petroleum reserves, installations, and personnel, and obtains a percentage of shares. The search for a private stockholder could be done through international bidding, and would require at least three offers for each area thus guaranteeing transparency. The competing offers would be formulated as a single figure representing an annual bond fixed for several years. In calculations, the bond should include the cost of dealing with priority environmental liabilities.

Increasing Reserves

Once the problems affecting private investment are resolved, particularly those related to the legal security and stability of the tax regime, and once there is greater transport capacity combined with new regulations governing prior consultation with the local population, we recommend planning new tendering for blocks. Approximately 50 percent of the country with oil potential has not been explored, and there is a need to incorporate new reserves in coming years to make up for the decline in production.

---

6. It is estimated that investments potentially attracted by the optimization of current fields within the proposed framework could amount to more than $US1 billion, which would increase current production from 225,000 BPD to 347,000 BPD for the year 2007, or 60 percent more than current levels (see annex 3).

The launching of a new oil round requires the adoption of an appropriate contract model, and proceeding to the necessary consultation and environmental studies. We recommend the participatory contract model for bidding, because its application is immediate (it does not require legal modifications), the companies have accepted it, and it has not been questioned. It is significant that criticisms received have had to do with modified contracts.

This framework would allow the government to launch a broad round that includes the blocks identified in the east and on the coast, as well as a specific project to develop the ITT fields. This recommendation requires immediately initiating consultations with the communities in the area of influence of the blocks to be bid on, establishing principles for participation and concrete benefits for communities. These principles should be laid out in the terms of reference. In order to avoid questions about the validity of modified contracts, the new contracts should be standard and their final version should be the product of a consensus among the different actors—the Ministry of Energy, companies, the General Accounting Office, and the SRI.

Elimination of Indiscriminate Subsidies for Gas

An increase in the price of a cylinder of 15 kilos of LPG from its current value of $US1.60 to the estimated economic price of $US7.15[7] is recommended; at the same time a targeted direct subsidy should be established to compensate the poorest. No law is required for this adjustment since the fixing of fuel prices is the responsibility of the President of the Republic.

There are two alternatives for the proposed compensation. The first consists in the creation of a gas cash payment that would be paid along with a social cash payment currently in existence and that approximately 1,200,000 families are already receiving. This payment would be worth $US10 monthly, which would cover the increase in cost for gas usage equivalent to 21 cylinders annually per family. The second possibility is to hand out 21 coupons annually to these same families receiving the social cash payment, which would allow them to purchase a cylinder at the former price of $US1.60.

In consolidated fiscal terms, the elimination of the subsidy would save $US245 million, assuming that the benefit is received by the nearly 50 percent of the population that currently receives the Solidarity cash payment. After subtracting the cost of the gas cash payment of $US144 million annually; the state would reduce fiscal costs by $US101 million a year.

The increase in the LPG price to its efficiency price would considerably reduce the utilization of this fuel for purposes other than cooking, such as running motors

---

7. The economic price of $US5 per GLP cylinder mentioned frequently in the press is the average of the price of real opportunity ($US7.16/cylinder) for the volume of imported LPG (that is, two-thirds of the market), and an accounting cost price for national LPG production (that is, one-third of the market)

or heating water, for which other types of energy can be used (for instance, firewood). At the same time, contraband to neighboring countries would be eliminated making it highly probable that benefits would be greater.

New Price and Tax Policy

As in the case of subsidies, we recommend that the government make hidden taxes on products more transparent. This will require sending a legal reform to the National Congress to create a new tax on special consumption (ICE) in cents per gallon of the product. Table 6 presents the suggested ICE values by product and prices for the public.

With the exception of LPG, which will lose its indiscriminate subsidy, one advantage of the proposed scheme is that it does not imply a substantial modification of the price of gasolines, but simply adjustments in the prices of diesel and fuel oil that could be adjusted according to price fluctuations in the international market.

After adjustments in prices and the tax regime, we suggest continuing with the liberalization of the market. Tariffs on imports should be eliminated, which means opening the market to private imports of derivatives, with the possibility that private companies have access to transport infrastructure and storage facilities. In the short term they would utilize installations owned by Petrocomercial, and later their own installations resulting from new investment.

In order to make this proposal feasible, Petrocomercial must be forced to offer transport services via ducts, storage, and other means needed by firms interested in commercializing products. The Ministry of Energy and Mining would publish the transport and storage tariffs that Petrocomercial[8] would charge, and these should be competitive. Given the size of the Ecuadoran market, in order to avoid the establishment of private monopolies on distribution and commercialization, the qualifi-

Table 6. Suggested and Current Prices for the Public

	ICE suggested $US/gal.	Price suggested–current* $US/gal.	Commentary
Super	25.0	140.8–141.6	No change
Extra	7.0	111.7–112.1	No change
Diesel	0.0	97.0–83.6	Slight increase
Fuel Oil	0.0	61.5–54.6	Slight increase
LPG	0.0	97.5–21.8	Important increase

*Price for the Public = Terminal price + (VAT + ICE) + Margin for distribution and marketing.

---

8. According to the study, "An Analysis of Fuel Products Pipeline Tariff Structure for Transportation, Storage, and Maritime Terminal Usage," by Booner and Moore, 1999, prepared by CONAM.

cation of firms interested in activities should not be too rigorous in terms of size. On the other hand, in no way should this easing of requirements mean noncompliance with operational and environmental standards. These must be followed and supervised by the National Directorates of Hydrocarbons and Environmental Protection, respectively.

Producers and commercial agents would increase with the reduction of entry barriers and opening to imports. In the medium term this would surely result in improvements in the quality of products and services offered, as well as a reduction in profit margins for distribution and marketing that are currently too high—oscillating between 10 and 18 percent.

Investment in Refining

The establishment of joint venture companies is both politically and economically viable as an option to modernize refineries. The proposed scheme requires that the state cede a percentage of its property to qualified private companies, and in exchange these companies would make needed investments and cover operational costs, labor costs, and environmental measures. The private company would be selected through international bidding managed by the Special Bidding Committee (CEL), with a minimum of at least three offers. The company that offers the greatest economic value for the stocks offered would win the contract.

In terms of economic efficiency, it is more advantageous to build new refineries rather than increase imports to meet local demand. A local refinery can acquire raw material at lower prices and does not have to pay transport costs. Since refining is a competitive industry, the new refineries would require detailed economic feasibility studies, and these should only be done through private initiatives. In order to achieve this, the need for special authorization from the executive branch to implement these projects should be eliminated.

Improvements in the Administration of Petroleum Revenues

The incoming government should prepare a Law on Transparency of Petroleum Revenues that eliminates preallocations and classifies revenues in accordance with industry reality. The list of participants in preallocations should be submitted to the General State Budget and the resources to be allocated should respond to real needs. However, during a first stage, the amounts for preallocation would remain within the state budget until an evaluation is completed. This would reduce opposition to a project of this nature.

Distribution of petroleum revenues should respond to the following criteria, among others:

- Decentralization, which means part of the revenues goes to regional and local governments, with those affected by hydrocarbon activity having the greatest

weight. The parochial councils would be the first benefited by this, followed by municipalities and prefectures, thus modifying the current scheme.
• Development of indigenous communities. In the medium term, in order to be applied this case requires training and strengthening of indigenous organizations so that they can develop sustainable projects in which they invest the resources that they are administering.
• Stabilization Funds.

With respect to having a real Fund for Petroleum Stabilization, the government should adopt the policy of fixing a conservative price for the state budget, backed up by a legal reform.[9] All surpluses derived from a higher price should be used to capitalize this fund, which would help to mitigate the negative cyclical effects of the world petroleum market. The same reform should stipulate that this fund must be used to compensate for diminished revenues in periods of low prices and perhaps to lower the pressure of the foreign debt.

Legal dispositions should be established to ensure rigorous fiscal management that eliminates extrabudgetary spending, and to bind all state institutions to revenues calculated exclusively based on realistic prices and production during the period. All debt based on anticipated payments from crude sales should be prohibited. Finally, the law should contemplate the creation of a permanent information bank on revenues management that is universally accessible, in order to guarantee transparency.

New Legal and Institutional Framework

A structural reform for this sector is a priority in order to comply with the mandates of the constitution, which establishes that the state should exploit this natural resource through companies (public or private, national or foreign) that are efficient and competitive. Conditions should be created that spur competition, free enterprise, cooperation, and that penalize monopoly-type practices and any that distort or impede the market's free functioning. This means that state enterprises in the hydrocarbon sector cannot constitute monopolies. Their presence should not impede the participation of other companies in the sector under the same conditions.

The decision to carry out such a reform also means the elaboration of a new Law on Hydrocarbons and a new Law on PetroEcuador. The first law should make MEM the exclusive representative of the state, and provide continuity to the institutional strengthening of operational and environmental entities, while seeking to totally reduce political interference and promoting the execution of state plans and investments in the long term. On the other hand, the new law should assign PetroEcuador

---

9. It is suggested that the price remain under $US17/barrel.

the specific role of "oil company," with the same rights and obligations as any other private firm.

Structural reform of the sector should be widely debated and implemented in the medium term, without losing sight of the fact that the reform must comply with goals to increase national and foreign investment in the sector, increase fiscal revenues, generate employment in the industry, improve environmental and security conditions, and improve international competitiveness of all productive sectors either directly or indirectly linked with the hydrocarbon industry.

Management of Environmental and Social Impact

The new government should take actions that allow reparation of environmental liabilities. This opportunity could be used to introduce specific clauses in contracts with private firms to increase production. These clauses could fix a minimum amount of investment to be deducted from production bonds fixed for mixed enterprises. They should take into account the execution of priority environmental reparations. This recommendation is also applicable to refineries.

The MEM should establish a procedure that permits adequate utilization of gas and limitations on flaring, in accordance with the new regulations.

In social terms, it is important that the state develop an integral program to benefit communities, making them economic participants that would benefit from the operations. The channeling of economic resources should guarantee sustainability of development proposed in the long term, especially in the postpetroleum era. This implies a process of support for strengthening community organizations such as business entities capable of administering and generating their own resources, in addition to other actions.

Policy Matrix

Problems	Policy measures		Progress indicators	Objectives/goals
	Short term (by June 2003)	*Medium term (2003–07)*		
Reimbursement of petroleum-VAT and lack of fiscal stability.	Acceptance of international arbitration.		Signing of arbitration procedure.	Solve legal conflict in short term.
	Legal clarification of tax treatment of oil companies.		Legal disposition.	Provide legal and tax regime stability/Increase private investment.
	Agreement to pay VAT to companies.		Formation of a negotiations commission.	Distribute the fiscal cost of payments over time.
Low production in the fields with greatest reserves.	Presidential announcement of the opening of PetroEcuador fields to private investment.		Public announcement of the formula to be used.	Increase production, capturing private investment and new technologies without state investment.
		Preparation process for international bidding.	Expedition of regulations, bidding process and contracts.	
Low level of exploration activity.	Launching of a new round of bidding processes including the ITT project.		Resolution creating the CEL.	Engage in greater exploratory activity to replace oil reserves.
		Preparation for international bidding process including previous consultation.	Expedition of regulations, bidding process, and contracts.	

Indiscriminate LPG subsidy.	Increasing the cylinder price of LPG and create gas cash payment.		Presidential decree.	Reduce fiscal costs by more than $US100 million/year without affecting the poor.
Hidden taxes and lack of competition in activities.		Revision of tax on special consumption of combustibles.	Sending an "urgent" legal disposition to Congress, rectifying the creation of the ICE.	Offer higher quality products and allow the entry of competitors into the market.
		Obliging Petrocomercial to offer services to third parties and charge non-discriminatory tariffs.	Reform of laws governing Petrocomercial and MEM agreement on tariffs.	
Low refining capacity and inefficiency of current installations.	Eliminating need for executive authorization of new installations.	Preparation of international bidding process for private investment in refineries.	Legal disposition that eliminates the need for presidential authorization. Issuing of regulations, bidding process, and contracts.	Initiate new investments in refining, transport, and storage.
				Improve technological and productive capacity of current refineries.
Poor administration of petroleum-related revenues.	Presidential definition for a new law.	Elaboration of a draft of the Law on Transparency through broad consultation.	Public announcement.	Achieve equity in distribution, and better control and auditing systems.
		Allocation of petroleum-related benefits to affected communities.	Document turned in by CONAM to the Presidency and sent to National Congress. Proposal of the Ministry of Environment and Social Welfare.	Achieve sustainable development of the oil-producing region.

(Matrix continues on the following page.)

Policy Matrix (*continued*)

Problems	Policy measures		Progress indicators	Objectives/goals
	Short term (by June 2003)	Medium term (2003–07)		
Outdated legal and institutional framework of sector.	Presidential definition of a new legal and institutional framework to reform the sector.		Public announcement.	Define roles, modernize legislation, and dynamize sector.
		Elaboration of draft of Law on Hydrocarbons and PetroEcuador and discussion.	CONAM document submitted to the Presidency and sent to the National Congress.	
Poor management of environmental and social impact.		Quantifying the repair of environmental liabilities.	Inventory carried out by the Sub-secretariat of Environmental Protection.	Reduce environmental liabilities.
			Consideration in bidding tender.	Mitigate environmental impact of operations.
	Proposal to manage formation water in the eastern fields.	Proper use of rich gases in the oil fields of the Amazon.	Procedures manual published by the Ministry of Energy.	Eliminate contamination and give added value to gas.

D. Economic Results

The new government must try to resolve tax inefficiencies and distortions that block the entry of needed capital and technology. It must do this in order to capitalize on the advantages of this sector—such as proven reserves, the OCP, and the consultation law. There will be a substantial increase in this sector's contribution to the national economy if the VAT problem is solved, the generalized gas subsidy is eliminated, and a formal consensus is adopted that allows PetroEcuador to partner with private firms to operate the most important fields in the country.

To evaluate the result of the proposed measures, a model was developed to calculate how much the sector will contribute to the national economy over the next five years. Two scenarios were considered. The first assumes that the required measures are not taken, in particular the needed elimination of the LPG subsidy; that the VAT problem is not resolved; and that PetroEcuador continues to manage the largest petroleum reserves with its current limitations. The second scenario assumes that the subsidy is eliminated, the VAT problem is resolved, and a formula is established to permit the entry of private companies into the eastern oil fields. The details of this hypothesis and calculations are in annex 3.

Based on conservative estimates of oil prices ($US22 for a barrel of crude based on the WTI) and production projections based solely on proven reserves, the solution of short-term problems would raise production from 148 million barrels this year to nearly 280 million in 2007. Without counting the benefits from investments in terms of employment and regional development, the annual contribution of the sector to the Treasury would increase by 50 percent, from $US1.5 billion now to nearly $US2.4 billion in 2007. However, if the status quo is maintained and the solution to sectoral problems is delayed, the new government runs the risk of squandering the true potential of this important resource, and will continue to receive the same amount without any increase.

According to Figure 3, in accumulated terms the sector's contribution over the next five years (2003 through 2007) could rise from $US7.9 billion to $US10.1 billion.

In addition, if the conditions for oil prices remain high on the international market and the WTI average rises from 22 to 25 $US/bbl, the sector's contribution to the Treasury would still not increase significantly unless rules change in order to encourage private investment and the LPG subsidy is eliminated. In scenario 1, even with the highest prices there would only be a very insignificant average increase to the Treasury of $US130 million.

In scenario 2, however, despite a decrease in the price of crude on the international market, there would be a very significant increase in the sector's contribution to the Treasury, with the greater increase in production both on the PetroEcuador fields and on fields operated by contractors, combined with the elimination of the subsidy. In 2002, the Treasury received approximately $US1.6 billion, and this would rise to $US2.4 billion by 2007, coming from the cash

Figure 3. Petroleum Sector Support to the National Economy (projection through 2007)

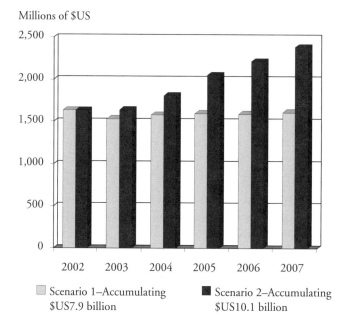

Millions of $US

Scenario 1–Accumulating
$US7.9 billion

Scenario 2–Accumulating
$US10.1 billion

flow produced by the private sector through greater production and annual bonds.[10]

As for benefits to petroleum revenues that can be attributed to the OCP, the first factor is state participation in the increase in production of companies that will be transported by the OCP, whose resources go to the FEIREP. Second, if SOTE freed up transport capacity, this would permit a production increase in the PetroEcuador fields mainly through new private investment.

The FEIREP is mainly capitalized with state revenues from crude transported by the OCP, which is not done at the expense of SOTE.[11] Seventy percent of the fund's value would go toward reducing external debt. There is no doubt that this fund has

10. Annual bonds come from private contributions for the establishment of mixed capital firms.
11. In order to calculate FEIREP's revenues, we take the production surplus from private companies for 2003 (180,000 BPD) as a percentage of state participation (30 percent), and deduct transport costs and the ECORAE tax.

a direct correlation with production levels. In scenario 2, where private investors participate more aggressively in the industry, 50 percent more is capitalized than in scenario 1. Given the high level of foreign debt (with a market value of over $US4 billion), the resources that the FEIREP can accumulate over the next five years—$US500 million in scenario 1 or $US1 billion in scenario 2—would still only marginally meet the fund's original goal. This reality makes it all the more necessary to undertake broader sectoral reform providing incentives for private investment in the petroleum sector, beginning with the exploration and development of new reserves, as well as other activities.

Annex 1
Historic Evolution and Description of the Sector

Petroleum production in Ecuador began in 1925. In 1971 the first Law on Hydrocarbons was expedited, which created the state company CEPE, which was responsible for the management of all petroleum-related activities including storage, transport, refining, and commercialization of derivatives. CEPE also was responsible for exploration and production phases at the same time as Texaco, along with other small companies operating through contracts with the state.

In 1989, PetroEcuador was created to replace CEPE, as well as its affiliates Petroproducción, Petroindustrial, and Petrocomercial, responsible for each stage of the industry. The goal was to create efficient enterprises, with financial, operational, and administrative autonomy, as well as their own contracting regulations for goods and services. With the exception of exploration and production activities that are also executed by private companies, PetroEcuador maintains a monopoly on the wholesale industrialization and commercialization of petroleum derivatives.

Since 1992, PetroEcuador's investments have been subject to the dispositions of the Ministry of Finance within the general state budget. The agencies that control the operational and environmental aspects of hydrocarbon activities are the National Directorate of Hydrocarbons and the Department of Environmental Protection, both responsible to MEM.

Petroleum Reserves

The proven reserves that can be recovered resulting from exploration in Ecuador are estimated at 7.7 billion barrels, of which 4.7 billion barrels remain to be extracted.

These reserves are calculated in MEM's official statistics with an average recovery factor of 36 percent for PetroEcuador and 22.5 percent for private companies. The difference in recovery factors between Petroproducción and the companies, despite the fact that the deposits are in the same basin, is due solely to political management rather than technical management of these factors. The type of amortization of investments used in contracts is based on production units over total reserves. This is why there is an interest in reducing the reserves held by private companies in order to accelerate the recovery of investments, and thus make future negotiations of contracts and fields possible.

As calculated in official statistics, most of the proven reserves belong to Petroproducción (74 percent). These are of a higher quality than the reserves in the hands of private companies, in terms of API gravity.

The undeveloped Ishpingo and Pungarayacu fields are among Petroproducción's prospective fields. The Edén-Yuturi and Palo Azul projects are also within areas where private companies operate and should also be developed. In addition, there are still 16 other fields with reserves oscillating between 1 and 30 million barrels of

Table A1. Reserves through December 31, 2001
(Blns/mlns of bbl)

	Petro-Producción	Private companies	Total
Proven	6.133 bln	1.561 bln	7.695 bln
Remaining	3.425 bln **74%** 1.204 bln **26%**	4.629 bln	
Oil fields in production	2.080 bln	775 mln	2.855 bln
Fields not in production	1.345 bln	428.6 mln	1.773 bln
Probably	259 mln	77.34 mln	336.46 mln
Possible	92.58 mln	344 mln	436.6 mln
Remaining reserves depending on gravity			
Less than 20° API	1.107 bln	760 mln	1.868 bln
Greater than 20° API	2.318 bln	443 mln	2.761 bln
Recovery factor	35.89%	22.50%	

Source: Figures for crude petroleum and gas reserves in the country through December 31, 2001, provided by the National Directorate of Hydrocarbons, Petroproducción, Administration of Oil Contracts.

low gravity crude. Finally there are possible reserves in prospective explorations that are under 100 million bbl, most below 20° API gravity.

The Amistad fields are the only ones with natural gas reserves, amounting to over 345 billion cubic feet. Greater amounts of gas continues to be produced in the Amazon, despite few initiatives for its utilization.

Exploration and Production

PetroEcuador

Since 1990, PetroEcuador has been responsible for the operation of areas in the PetroEcuador-Texaco Consortium—mainly the Sasha, Shushufindi, Auca, and Cononaco fields. This is in addition to the fields discovered through exploratory activity, particularly the Libertador field. PetroEcuador also maintains the option of broadening exploratory activities to zones that are not under contract with private companies.

In 1993, Petroproducción discovered heavy crude reserves in a series of ITT fields in the central-eastern zone of the Amazon. During 2000 and 2001, additional drilling confirmed reserves of 1.4 billion barrels, 14° API, according to statistics still not updated in official data. These reserves will require investments of approximately $US3.7 million for development. It is estimated that the ITT project could hit a production peak of 205,000 BPD.

Petroproducción's production has progressively decreased from a maximum of 120 million barrels in 1994 to a current level of 80 million barrels per year owing to the lack of transport capacity, the growing deterioration of its installations, and a lack of investment that would permit access to modern extraction methods. PetroEcuador possesses a large quantity of remaining reserves in fields in production, where technical operations are not at an adequate level.

The private sector share of national production is more than 60 million barrels. In other words, a national average of 400,000 barrels daily, or 56 percent of the total, can be attributed to PetroEcuador, and 44 percent to private companies. When we compare reserves to production, we find that private companies possess a quarter of the proven reserves and currently contribute nearly half of total production.

Contracting with Private Companies

The concession contract Texaco operated under and the partnership that City maintained for the Tarapoa block were characterized by high income tax (87.31 percent), and by relatively complex fiscal clauses. These contracts are not currently being applied: the Texaco contract ended in 1991 and the City contract was renegotiated and modified to a participation contract.

Between 1982 and 1988, under the "Service Provision modality," six rounds of bidding were carried out. These risk contracts were characterized by the reimbursement of investments and costs, and a service payment on each barrel of oil produced. Currently there is only one service provision contract in effect, with the AGIP company for Block 10.

In 1993, participation contracts were included in the Law on Hydrocarbons, with two bidding rounds administered by a high-level collegial body (Special Bidding Process Committee—CEL), which included the Armed Forces and the General Accounting Office. These rounds permitted the signing of nine contracts in

Table A2. Current Petroleum Production (BPD)

Company	August 2002		September 2002	
A. Petroproducción	219,860	56.5	223,870	56.0
B. Private	169,154	43.5	176,217	44.0
Marginal fields	21,994	5.7	21,961	5.5
Shared fields	16,091	4.1	14,946	3.7
Participation	99,545	25.6	104,923	26.2
Services	30,219	7.8	33,023	8.3
Peninsula	1305	0.3	1,363.6	0.3
Total (A + B)	38,9014	100.0	400,087	100.0

Source: Petroproducción Reports, 2002.

which state and private companies shared crude production in proportions of approximately 25 percent and 75 percent, respectively. The private company runs the risks, makes investments and pays costs. It should be pointed out that during the seventh round, the contract for the exploration and exploitation of gas in the gulf of Guayaquil, where reserves were discovered in 1982, was signed.

In several of the blocks in the hands of private companies, important deposits have been discovered that were shared with the Petroproducción blocks. Long negotiation processes have been required to establish the economic conditions for the exploitation of these blocks, and these processes have been criticized.

In 1993, the modality of Contracts for Marginal Fields was also incorporated into the Law on Hydrocarbons. This modality follows the participatory model, sharing the particularity that private companies can have access to the additional operation and exploration of small fields (that is, fields that represent less than 1 percent of national production) with reserves that have been discovered. In 1999, five contracts were signed that are currently being executed.

In 1998, the government decided to incorporate the Joint Ventures contract modality into the Law on Hydrocarbons, to permit partnerships between Petroproducción and private companies to operate in large fields—Sacha, Shushufindi, Libertador, Auca, and Cononaco. Although this initiative of the former government was approved by the National Congress, its initial economic conditions were modified. The decision was later declared partially unconstitutional, and the Joint Ventures modality became inapplicable.

During recent years, there have been few initiatives to attract private investment for exploration and production; although it is worth noting the process of operational alliances used to develop two fields in medium-sized Petroproducción fields. These alliances consist of contracting a firm that provides a wide range of services and financing, and the terms of payment for services depend on the increase in production.

The most recent attempt to develop a new form of contracting to manage PetroEcuador's fields under production was by the Chilean enterprise ENAP. This model adjudicated an exploration/production contract in three small fields not open to tender, based on the state company privilege that allows the state to sign specific service contracts directly. The government sent an urgent reform package to Congress to try to incorporate this new modality into the Law on Hydrocarbons. The reform project was rejected.

Crude Oil Transport

With the exception of the AGIP pipeline that ends in Baeza, PetroEcuador and the other companies use a series of secondary pipelines that flow to storage facilities at Lake Agrio to transport their production. From this point, the TransEcuadoran Pipeline System (SOTE), built by Texaco and turned over to PetroEcuador in 1989, begins. SOTE has a transport capacity of 390,000 barrels daily of oil that is 23.7° API grade, and includes storage facilities in Lake Agrio (with a capacity of 1.5 million barrels) and Port Balao Esmeraldas (with a capacity of 3.2 million barrels), plus the sea export terminal.

Also, in agreement with ECOPETROL, PetroEcuador can transport a production volume of approximately 50,000 barrels daily to Port Tumaco via the Transandean Pipeline. The crude transported by this pipeline is grade 29 API, the level of quality required by the La Libertad refinery. Transport from Tumaco to La Libertad is done by ship. The Transandean Pipeline is frequently and inconveniently paralyzed because of attacks by the Colombian guerrillas.

The private companies have a greater production capacity than their current output. However, this is a very heavy crude (below 20° API), which requires diluting to be transported through the SOTE. This situation, in addition to the fact that Petroproducción has significantly decreased its production of light crudes, is affecting the private companies.

The issue of mixing heavy crudes with light crudes is viewed as negative for the country because of various factors such as the following:

- A crude mix as a final product (eastern crude—23.8° API) has a price on the international market that is lower than the price obtained for light and heavy crudes sold separately. It is worth noting that the majority of private companies produce heavy crude, which would imply a mix that is detrimental to the state. However, no formal studies have been done to prove this.
- The majority of companies produce a heavy crude, and receive a lower quality crude in Port Balao. In order to estimate how many barrels equal the company's crude in barrels of eastern crude, the factor "k," a constant in petroleum contracts, is applied. This factor has been questioned because it is believed that it benefits companies while hurting PetroEcuador. To date, no government decision has been made on how to proceed with renegotiation.
- The Esmeraldas refinery receives crude that is 23–24° API, which is of lower quality than what should be processed (27–28° API). This situation leads to a smaller quantity of clean products being produced, and a greater quantity of residuals of lower commercial value.

In order to resolve this problem of the crude mix, and mainly to end the limitation on transport capacity that has lasted nearly 10 years, in February 2001, the government authorized the construction of a heavy crude pipeline (OCP), granting permission to a consortium made up of the main private oil companies operating in the country.

The OCP is designed to transport up to 518,000 barrels of oil daily with a gravity of 18 to 24° API. It mainly follows the SOTE route, and flows into a new sea terminal also at Port Balao Esmeraldas. Construction of the OCP should begin in June 2003 according to the contract; however, the work has been paralyzed because of the reaction of environmental groups and some local communities. It is hoped that operations will begin in September 2003. With the OCP, the available transport capacity of the country will reach over 960,000 barrels a day.

Refining

The current primary refining capacity is 175,000 BPD. This does not meet internal demand, meaning that gasoline, diesel, LPG, and high-octane naphtas are all imported. The Amazon and La Libertad refineries only have atmospheric distilling units. Even though the Esmeraldas refinery has a certain conversion capacity, production of residuals in the three refineries exceeds local demand and is exported at a low price.

The LPG plant in the Shushufindi complex has a capacity of 500 tons per day. It is now producing at 40 percent of its capacity because of the insufficient capture of gas from the oil fields. Even though Ecuador needs LPG, much of the gas associated with the oil rich in LPG is burned in the fields, mainly those run by Petroproducción.

In 2001, PetroEcuador set up a project so that private companies could invest in its three refineries, installing high conversion plants that allow the processing of atmospheric residuals and raise the level of production of light products (gasolines, diesel, and LPG). The project's bidding process has not been successful because of economic uncertainty.

Distribution, Commercialization, and Prices

The PetroEcuador crude that does not go to the refineries is sold by the International Commerce Management of this company, mainly done through traders.[12] The offers solicited from the traders use the West Texas Intermediate (WTI) crude price as a base, with an adjustment for differential of quality that PetroEcuador establishes based on monthly studies. The differential has fluctuated across a range of $US3 to 8 per barrel.

Petroindustrial's production of derivatives and the volume imported are distributed to the internal market by Petrocomercial. The affiliate owns practically the entire pipeline network, as well as storage and distribution terminals. Petrocomercial provides the products to buyers at the same sale price in all terminals, as fixed by the Pres-

Table A3. Refining Capacity

Refinery	BPD
Esmeraldas	110,000
Amazon –Shushufindi	20,000
La Libertad	45,000
Total	175,000

Source: PetroEcuador Statistics, 2001.

---

12. Traders are private firms dedicated to the sale of crude oil and petroleum derivatives.

ident of the Republic. The buyers are private companies with a network of distributors that also must be approved by Petrocomercial. They must comply with size demands—for example, a minimal national network of gasoline stations. As regards sale price to the consumer, the current presidential decree establishes a maximum margin of 18 percent on top of the terminal sale price. In practice, nearly all distributors sell at the terminal price plus 18 percent, and there is no price competition.

In the case of LPG, over 60 percent of demand is covered by imports. LPG is stored in tankers and then transported to the Tres Bocas terminal near the city of Guayaquil, and from there to the El Salitral terminal for storage and later distribution. Petrocomercial grants traders a global rate that includes transport in bulk, storage, packing, distribution, public sale, and replacement of cylinders and valves. The traders also have to be approved by Petrocomercial. The access of new competitors is limited by infrastructure and distribution network requirements, which include the capacity to sell at least 300 metric tons daily.

Environmental and Social Regulation

The development of petroleum industry activities involving environmental and social management is regulated by the Environmental Regulations on Hydrocarbon Operations, the latest version of which was approved in February 2001. The main modification introduced was the raising of environmental standards to international levels, with special emphasis on the injection of formation waters, emissions monitoring, and ongoing environmental auditing. The Directorate of Environmental Protection of the Ministry of Energy is the entity that supervises compliance with this legislation.

Since July 1999, a Law on Environmental Management has been in existence. Through the Ministry of the Environment, this law regulates the execution of industrial projects, mainly in protected areas, and requires that an environmental license be obtained.

The legal framework establishes the rights of local communities, particularly indigenous peoples, to consultation and participation. The regulations that ensure the orderly application of this right have been concluded thanks to a tripartite effort by the government, the industry, and communities. To date, social issues included in the regulations have been managed by different companies through direct negotiations with communities. The previous lack of a specific regulation, in addition to basic needs that the government is ignoring and that are evident in the zones of influence of petroleum activities, has forced firms to carry out public works and provide economic resources. This is the only way that they can develop activities without suffering costly setbacks because of community resistance to projects, resulting in delays.

This is the case despite the fact that oil companies are already paying an ecodevelopment tax to benefit oil zones. This year that tax is $US0.35 on each barrel produced, and it will reach $US0.50 on each barrel produced in eastern fields in 2005. The fruits of this financial support from companies is not evident in terms of any significant development.

Management of Petroleum Revenues

Annual petroleum sector revenues are over $US1.5 billion, with the main revenues coming from crude exports and sales to the internal derivatives market. The debits correspond to PetroEcuador's costs, and derivative imports. It is worth pointing out that this figure does not include taxes paid directly to the SRI by contractors.

The petroleum sector's contribution to the state budget is significant, averaging 28 percent. The distribution of petroleum revenues has become more complicated over the years, because of a series of preallocations that have been established by each revenues segment, whether they are exemptions, ex-consortium production, service contracts, tariffs on pipelines, or similar. The classification of oil revenues is broken down into 30 apparent revenue sources. Based on this analysis we can determine that these same sources could be reduced to eight real sources corresponding to con-tract type, type of Petroproducción activity, derivative exports, internal sales, and transport. The reason for this extensive classification is the multiple preallocations that have been legally established over the years. This classification continues to use revenue concepts that are out of synch with reality.

The lack of transparency in resource management, which operates outside the framework of the state budget, is the most detrimental aspect. However, starting in 2003, the significant preallocation of oil revenues to the Armed Forces will be elim-inated, alleviating this somewhat.

The Fund for Petroleum Stabilization was one of the efforts made to set up an economic contingency fund that accumulated resources when the price of crude went over $US20 a barrel. At the present time, resources from this fund are subject to a new preallocation. Finally, given the expectation that oil production will increase with the operation of the OCP, the FEIREP has been established to repur-chase public foreign debt at market value, and stabilize oil petroleum revenues ear-marked for education and health.

Table A4. PetroEcuador's Economic Performance (blns/mlns $US)

	1998	1999	2000	2001	2002(*)
Revenues (**)	1.839 bl	1.866 bl	2.289 bl	2.294 bl	2.535bl
Debits	926.7 ml	817.7 ml	829 ml	946 ml	1.052bl
Net balance	912.9 ml	1.048 bl	1.460 bl	1.347 bl	1.483bl
Percentage of national budget	22.7	29.8	35.4	27.4	25.0

(*) Estimates.
(**) The VAT from the domestic fuels market is not included in revenues.
Source: Author's own calculations based on PetroEcuador's statistics.

Table A5. Central Government Oil Revenues Headings

1	Revenues from service enterprises	18	Exports from marginal fields
2	Revenues from specific service enterprises	19	Company marketing; provision of services
3	Additional per barrel of exported crude	20	Export of petroleum derivatives
		21	Internal sale of petroleum derivatives
4	Crude export royalties	22	Liberation of debt resources
5	– PetroEcuador	23	SOTE transport fee
6	– State participation		Oil investment fund
7	– Marginal fields	24	– Pipeline export and transport
8	Ex-consortium PetroEcuador exports	25	– Domestic sale of derivatives
9	Northeastern PetroEcuador exports	26	Social and economic stabilization and development
	Exports with state participation:		
10	– With city	27	Surpluses
11	– With YPF	28	Others not specified
12	– With Canadá Grande	29	Law 24 (Corpei)
13	– With Keer McGee	30	Petroleum stabilization fund
14	– With Occidental		
15	– With Vintage Oil		
16	– With Pérez Company		
17	– With Lumbaqui Oil		

Source: State budget, 2002.

Table A6. Oil Revenues Distribution Scheme
Source: Petroproducción Reports, 2002.

Participants	Direct. export	Royalties	Export derivatives	SOTE fee	5 sucres bbl. exp.	Int. sale derivative	Addit. imports SOTE+ prod.	Decree 337
1. Central Government	XXX	XXX	XXX	XXX	XXX	XXX		XXX
1.1. Direct collection	X	X	X	X	X	X		X
1.2. Ministry of Health	X							
1.3. Ministry of Labor	X							
1.4. Law 02	X	X	X					
1.5. Law 18	X	X						
1.6. 100% of 15% royalties		X						
1.7. 10% oil investments	X		X	X		X		
1.8. Economic Stabilization, Agreement 107			X					
1.9. Law on Agricultural and Livestock			X					
Roadway Administration	X							
2. Descentralized Agencies	XXX	XXX	XXX				XXX	
2.1. ISSFA (LAW 169)	XX	X						
2.2. FAE	X	X						
2.3. Defense Council (JDN)	X	XX						
a. JDN 8% exports								
b. JDN others		X						
2.4. ECORAE (Law 20)	X						X	
2.5. State university participation	X							
2.6. Private univ.	X							
3. State Enterprises	XXX	XXX	XXX	XXX		XXX		
1. PetroEcuador	XXX	XXX	XXX	XXX		XXX		
Total PetroEcuador costs:	XX	XX	XX	XX		XX		
a. Restitution costs	X	X	X	X		X		

(Table continues on the following page.)

Table A6. (*continued*)

Participants	Direct. export	Royalties	Export deriva-tives	SOTE fee	5 sucres bbl. exp.	Int. sale deri-vative	Addit. imports SOTE+ prod.	Decree 337
b. Costs of services	X							
c. Costs of participation-specific services.	X							
d. 10% Petroleum invest.								
2. FERUM (Solidarity Fund)		X						
4. Sectional Bodies	XXX	XXX	XXX				XXX	
1. FODESEC	X							
2. Provincial councils		X	X					
3. Esmeraldas development	X	X						
Napo Esmeraldas and Sucumbíos Particip.		X					X	
4. Law 40								
5. Finance Sector								
1. State bank	X							
2. BEV	X							
3. Central Bank	X							
4. IECE	X							
6. Petroleum Stabilization Fund	X	X	X					

Source: State budget, 2002.

Annex 2
Updated Study on Taxes and Subsidies for Derivatives

Table A7. Prices FOB US-GULF

	$US/bbl	$US/gal.	According to original study
Super gasoline	31.995	76.18	69.19
Extra gasoline	29.353	69.89	64.19
Diesel	29.654	70.60	65.79
LPG	20.987	51.09	51.09
70% propane	19.736		
30% butane	23.905		
Fuel oil (2% S)	21.27	50.64	29.51
Residuals (exp.)	19.135		
WTI	27.515		
Eastern crude	21.735		

Source: PetroEcuador International Commerce, based on Platts, November 2002.

Table A8. Calculation of Parity Prices for Derivatives ($US/gal.)

	Price FOB export	Freight	Insurance	CIF	Leakage	Financial cost	Storage	Price of parity
Super gasoline	76.2	3.12	0.069	79.37	0.346	0.69	0.76	81.16
Extra gasoline	69.9	3.12	0.064	73.07	0.321	0.64	0.76	74.79
Diesel	70.6	3.59	0.066	74.26	0.263	0.66	0.76	75.94
LPG	51.1	20.00	0.051	71.14	0.409	0.51	1.15	73.21
Fuel oil	50.6			50.64				50.64

Source: Freight, insurance, leakage, and financial costs taken from international standards, according to previous World Bank studies.

Table A9. Calculation of Efficiency Prices in Terminal ($US/gal.)

	Parity price	Transport services and average storage (*)	Price terminal without taxes
Super gasoline	81.16	3.08	84.25
Extra gasoline	74.79	3.51	78.30
Diesel	75.94	2.76	78.70
LPG	73.21	3.13	76.34
Fuel oil	50.64	1.63	52.27

(*) According to a study on tariffs on services prepared by Booner and Moore for CONAM.
Note: Petrocomercial's present costs are not considered because it is a monopoly.
Source: World Bank calculations.

**Table A10. Tax Collection
Calculation of Taxes or Current Subsidies
($US/gal.)**

	Present terminal price	Efficiency terminal price without VAT	P	Present VAT	Tax (hidden) subsidy	Annual consump. thous. gals.	Value $US taxes (subsidies)
Super gasoline	120.00	84.25	35.75	12.86	22.89	63000	14,423,400
Extra gasoline	95.00	78.30	16.70	10.18	6.52	477540	31,151,526
Diesel	76.00	78.70	−2.70	8.14	−10.85	726180	(78,773,240)
LPG	7.51	76.34	−68.83	0.80	−69.63	352825.58	(245,682,026)
Fuel oil	52.00	52.27	−0.27	5.57	−5.84	436955.53	(25,536,929)
Total							**(304,417,269)**

Source: World Bank calculations.

Table A11. Public Efficiency Prices
Calculation of Terminal Prices Eliminating Subsidies
Applying VAT and Suggested Consumption Tax
($US/gal.)

	Efficiency terminal price without VAT	*VAT*	*Suggested consumption tax*	*Suggested terminal price*	*Average profit margin*	*Suggested public sale price*
Super gasoline	84.25	10.11	25.00	119.36	18%	140.84
Extra gasoline	78.30	9.40	7.00	94.69	18%	111.74
Diesel	78.70	9.44	0.00	88.15	10%	96.96
LPG	76.34	9.16	0.00	85.50	14%	97.47
Fuel oil	52.27	6.27	0.00	58.55	5%	61.47

Source: World Bank calculations.

Table A12. Comparison of Consumer Price Changes
($US/gal.)

	Suggested public sale price	*Current public sale price*	*Variation*	
			Net	*Percentage*
Super gasoline	140.84	141.60	–0.76	–0.53%
Extra gasoline	111.74	112.10	–0.36	–0.32%
Diesel	96.96	83.60	13.36	15.99%
LPG	97.47	21.80	75.67	347.11%
Fuel oil	61.47	54.60	6.87	12.59%
LPG 15 kg cylinder	**7.15**	**1.60**	**5.55**	

Source: World Bank calculations.

Annex 3
Economic Performance

General Terms

In order to evaluate the possible impact of recommendations, we present two scenarios of the possible evolution of the petroleum sector between 2003 and 2007. These scenarios are based on the following hypotheses and projected values:

- The price of crude is based on West Texas Intermediate (WTI), assuming that it will go down from the high values of the last three years, averaging $US22/barrel between 2003 and 2007.
- Eastern crude, the mix currently transported by SOTE (23.9° API) is estimated at $US18 per barrel, with a differential of $US4 per barrel of WTI.
- Light crude is defined as the new petroleum to be transported by SOTE, with a gravity around 28 ° API, and an estimated price of $US22 per barrel.
- Heavy crude will be transported by the OCP and has been estimated at $US15 per barrel, with a differential of at least $US8 per barrel, in relation to WTI.
- Import prices of derivatives will fluctuate with crude prices.
- There will be 4.5 percent annual growth in domestic demand for derivatives.
- The OCP's tariff for PetroEcuador will be $US1.50 per barrel.
- There will be no changes in refining capacity.
- The OCP will begin its operation at the end of 2003. Impact can be measured only at the start of 2004.
- The projection of production is based on proven reserves. Neither production at ITT fields (development will take at least an estimated seven years), nor production from new reserves (recent exploration) has been included.

Scenarios

Scenario 1

- Oil companies will not increase their investments because the VAT problem has not been resolved.
- Petroproducción will continue efforts to increase production under the current framework, and with exclusive state investment similar to current levels.
- The LPG subsidy will be maintained.

Scenario 2

- In the short term, the government will resolve the VAT problem, and with congressional approval, clarify tax treatment of oil companies in the short and long term. This will directly affect investment levels of private companies, increasing production.

- Petroproducción will enter into partnership with private companies through the legal disposition of joint venture enterprises, and receive new technology and investment for its productive fields.
- The LPG subsidy will be eliminated, compensating the poorest with a gas cash payment equivalent to the difference between the efficiency price and the current subsidized price.

Petroleum Production and Export Performance

If Petroproducción continues to produce under current conditions, there will be small increases that will help to avoid a natural decline of the fields currently in operation by 2007, and maintain current production levels. On the other hand, with the opening to the private sector, production levels could increase by over 50 percent with the incorporation of new technology—a recovery mainly attributable to reservoirs and an investment volume estimated at $US1 billion.

Private companies could increase their current production 1.3 times by 2007, if legal stability can be guaranteed for the investments that they would need to make. If this stability is not ensured, the rhythm of growth will be much slower, or 64 percent, which in daily production barrels amounts to 295,000. It is worth noting that by 2007, the OCP would only be operating at 60 percent of its capacity.

In terms of national production, the difference between these two scenarios by the year 2007 is an average of 245,000 BPD. Current daily production of 400,000 BPD would increase from 522,000 BPD in the first scenario to 767,000 BPD in the second scenario.

Table A13. Estimated Production of Private Companies (BPD)

| Companies | 2002 | 2004 (with OCP) | | 2007 | |
		Scenario 1	Scenario 2	Scenario 1	Scenario 2
Agip	35,000	40,000	40,000	40,000	40,000
Repsol	30,000	50,000	60,000	60,000	75,000
Encana	40,000	50,000	60,000	60,000	80,000
Oxy	30,000	45,000	60,000	65,000	100,000
Vintage	5,000	5,000	7,000	7,000	10,000
Perenco	15,000	15,000	18,000	18,000	28,000
Perez Company	3,000	13,000	18,000	18,000	58,000
Others	22,000	22,000	27,000	27,000	29,000
Total	**180,000**	**240,000**	**290,000**	**295,000**	**420,000**

Source: Author's estimates based on current production and reserves.

Table A14. Production Scenarios
(Thds of bbl)

	2002	2003	2004	2005	2006	2007
National Total						
Scenario 1	147,928	149,650	173,375	178,850	182,500	190,530
Scenario 2	147,928	149,650	191,625	226,300	253,675	279,955
Petroproducción						
Scenario 1	82,228	83,950	85,775	85,775	83,950	82,855
Scenario 2 (*)	82,228	83,950	85,775	93,075	105,850	126,655
Private Companies						
Scenario 1	65,700	65,700	87,600	93,075	98,550	107,675
Scenario 2	65,700	65,700	105,850	133,225	147,825	153,300

(*) As of 2005, this will include 100 percent of the production generated through the transformation into joint venture companies.
Source: World Bank calculations.

Export Balance

The total production by Petroproducción and state participation in the crude produced and refined by companies will generate an export balance that will increase starting in 2004, when the OCP begins operating. By 2007, in the case of scenario 1, there should be an increase of 13 million barrels.

In scenario 2, the export of state petroleum decreases, starting in 2005, because the model foresees the transformation of Petroproducción into joint venture companies, which would provide resources directly through a cash payment system. The bidding processes should take into account Petroindustrial's priority need to purchase the crude it requires for refineries at international prices, if it so desires.

Table A15. State Crude Exports
(Thds of bbl)

	2002	2003	2004	2005	2006	2007
National Total						
Scenario 1	44,938	46,660	55,055	56,698	56,515	58,158
Scenario 2	44,938	46,660	60,530	10,890	19,103	26,860
Petroproducción						
Scenario 1	82,228	83,950	85,775	85,775	83,950	82,855
Scenario 2 (*)	82,228	83,950	85,775	27,923	31,755	37,997
Private Company Support						
Scenario 1	19,710	19,710	26,280	27,923	29,565	32,303
Scenario 2	19,710	19,710	31,755	39,968	44,348	45,863
(–) Crude Refining	–57,000	–57,000	–57,000	–57,000	–57,000	–57,000

(*) Starting in 2005, we have considered 30 percent of their production, since they would be joint venture companies compensated with cash payments.
Source: World Bank calculations.

Petroleum Revenue Results

The following table presents performance in terms of contributions to the Treasury, including VAT received on the sale of derivatives. It excludes both income tax and VAT paid by oil contractors, as we have no information on this sector.

**Table A16. Petroleum Sector Support for the Treasury
(blns/mlns $US)**

	2002	2003	2004	2005	2006	2007	Total
Total							
Scenario 1	1,637	1,532	1,580	1,598	1,588	1,610	9,544
Scenario 2	1,637	1,638	1,807	2,053	2,215	2,385	11,733
Refining and							
Sale of							
Derivatives (*)							
Scenario 1	−275	−273	−286	−280	−262	−243	−1,620
Scenario 2	−275	−23	−28	−15	11	39	−292
Crude Production							
Scenario 1	1,912	1,805	1,866	1,878	1,850	1,852	11,164
Scenario 2	1,912	1,661	1,835	2,068	2,203	2,346	12,025
Gas Payment	0	−145	−145	−145	−145	−145	−723

(*) Includes VAT from the domestic derivatives market, at the terminal level.
Source: World Bank calculations.

In scenario 1, contributions to the Treasury are stable because the increase in PetroEcuador's revenues resulting from the rise in production and participation is lost (a) through the drop in crude prices on the international market, and (b) because of the increase in imports to meet growing internal consumption through subsidized prices. This is why contributions would fall from $US1.6 billion in 2002 to $US1.5 billion in 2003, and remain below $US1.6 billion until 2007.

If petroleum prices remain high on the international market and the WTI average is revalued to around 22 to 25 $US/bbl, sector support for the Treasury would not grow significantly in this scenario, since during the period 2003–07, there would only be an average increase of $US130 million annually.

**Table A17. Price Sensitivity of Treasury Support
(blns $US)**

	2002	2003	2004	2005	2006	2007	Total
Scenario 1							
(WTI = $ 22)	1.637	1.532	1.580	1.598	1.588	1.610	9.544
Scenario 1							
(WTI = $ 25)	1.637	1.671	1.712	1.727	1.711	1.731	10.189

Source: World Bank calculations.

This scenario is different from scenario 2. Despite the drop in crude prices on the international market, the large increase in production (both on PetroEcuador's fields and fields operated by contractors), coupled with the elimination of the subsidy, will generate a significant increase in tax contributions over the next five years. The Treasury received approximately $US1.6 billion in 2002. In 2007, it would receive the equivalent of $US2.3 billion, which would come from the cash flow produced by private companies through greater production and annual cash payments.[13]

Fund to Reduce Public Foreign Debt

One example of the benefits of oil revenues attributable to the OCP is state participation in the increase of production by companies that will transport their oil through the OCP. These resources will be allocated to FEIREP, as summarized below. Also, the liberation of transport capacity by SOTE will allow production increases in PetroEcuador's fields mainly through new private investment.

FEIREP is capitalized primarily through all state revenues coming from crude oil transported by the OCP, which do not result from reduced use of SOTE.[14] Seventy percent of the fund's value will be allocated to reducing foreign debt. There is no doubt that there is a direct correlation between this fund and production levels. As shown in Table A18, in scenario 1 less than 50 percent of the amount in scenario 2 is capitalized. In scenario 2, private investment participates much more aggressively in the oil industry. The surplus obtained for FEIREP in scenario 1 corresponds to 5 percent of fiscal contributions from the petroleum sector, and is 10 percent in scenario 2.

Table A18. Capitalization of FEIREP

	2002	2003	2004	2005	2006	2007	Total
Thousands of barrels							
Scenario 1	—	—	6,570	8,213	9,855	12,593	37,230
Scenario 2	—	—	12,045	20,258	24,638	26,280	83,220
Millions $US							
Scenario 1	0	0	85.7	106,8	128.1	163.7	484.3
Scenario 2	0	0	157.2	263.3	320.3	341.6	1,082.4

Source: World Bank calcuations.

Given the high level of foreign debt (with a market value of over $US4 billion), with the resources that the FEIREP can accumulate over the next five years ($US500 million in scenario 1 or $US1 billion in scenario 2), the fund would still only marginally meet its original goal. This reality highlights the need to adopt a much more aggressive private investment policy in the petroleum sector.

---

13. Annual cash payments come from private support to establish joint venture companies.
14. In order to calculate FEIREP revenues, we took the surplus of production from private companies for the year 2003, (180,000 BPD), as a percentage of state participation (30 percent), and deducted transport costs and the ECORAE tax.

6

Trade Policy and Competition[1]

Dominique Hachette

Ecuador's potential for future growth lies in its nontraditional exports as the country faces the prospect of exhausting its oil reserves in the 2020s. To boost nontraditional exports, the existing bias against exports must be significantly reduced. This bias originates in the competition for scarce resources where excessively protected subsectors are favored over imports in the agricultural, mining, and manufacturing sectors, and in the measures that directly affect Ecuadoran exports both within the country and in the countries to which products are exported. The protective blanket is disguised as tariff and nontariff barriers. The former include tariffs of all kinds (one of which is the price band); among the latter are regulations on origin, prohibitions, restrictions and licenses, safeguard measures, antidumping and compensatory measures, technical regulations, and policies contrary to competition. To eliminate the bias against exports it is necessary to reduce both the level and the dispersion of tariff barriers that exist today; carefully review ties with the Andean Community of Nations to determine to what extent membership in this club does not benefit the country in net terms; revise and continue to reduce agricultural price bands, licenses, and any other nontariff barrier that imposes eliminable direct or indirect costs on the production of exportable goods; and give "domestic treatment" to imports and foreign investment, which implies a profound review of the current application of technical regulations to guarantee a competitive framework for all productive activities in the country.

1. Dominique Hachette is a professor at the Pontificia Universidad Católica de Chile and World Bank consultant. The author would like to thank Fernando Suárez of the Ministry of Economy and Finance for his very valuable aid and José R. López-Cálix and McDonald Benjamin of the World Bank for their valuable comments and suggestions.

A. Precedents

Liberalization of the Ecuadoran Economy in the 1990s

Ecuador is increasingly participating in world trade. Exports and imports, as a percentage of GDP, increased from 53 percent in 1991 to 59 percent in 2001. Exports have diversified (Figure 1): the proportion of nontraditional products has increased, but the country continues to be highly dependent on oil (41 percent). Agricultural and agroindustrial exports represent 60 percent of non-oil exports. Imports of consumer goods have increased more than others, which is a clear sign of greater economic opening (see Figure 1). Markets for Ecuadoran exports have diversified to some extent, though the U.S. market continues to dominate. The Latin American Integration Association (ALADI) has overtaken the United States as the most important origin of imports but there have not been dramatic changes in the destination of exports.

The most significant change in the destinations and origins of trade flows may well be the greater presence of the Andean Community of Nations (CAN), which has become Ecuador's second most important trade partner. Specifically, Peru has become an important market for Ecuadoran exports and Colombia has become a major source of imports. Membership of these countries in the CAN has had deviating (negative) effects in Ecuador, but also positive ones in terms of generating trade, as well as acting as a significant force for the creation of markets.

Customs tariffs—which in turn are a variant of the Common External Tariff (CET) of the CAN—have stabilized at a range of nominal rates: 0, 3, 5, 10, 15, 20, and 35 percent. This scaling has been justified as an "incentive for added value,"[2] as it concentrates production input at low tariff rates and final consumer goods at high rates. This latter tariff is now being reviewed. What is covered by each rate is constantly changed by the impact of a great number of agreements and commitments in which Ecuador is involved. This is also the case of its CAN partners. The "effective tariff," as measured by fiscal income as a percentage of imported value, dropped from 10.6 percent in 1998 to 6.5 percent in 2001 (Figure 2). The 10.6 percent rate recorded for 1998 is atypically high, likely owing to the combination of the VAT and the Safeguard Clause (tariffs) established and eliminated the following year and possibly thanks to greater efficiency at customs (controlled at that time by the military). However, potential tax collection is above 6.5 percent and is likely closer to 9 percent since the weighted tariff for imports has been closer to this figure. However, as transactions within the CAN and with Chile have increased, this percentage today overvalues the fiscal ceiling for customs.

The simple average of the nominal rates of the other CAN countries is homogeneous, but the effective rates are not, ranging in the year 2000 from 7.5 percent in

---

2. It is interesting to note that in Ecuadoran practice, tariff levels are inversely proportional to the added value being protected.

Figure 1. Ecuador Trade Composition

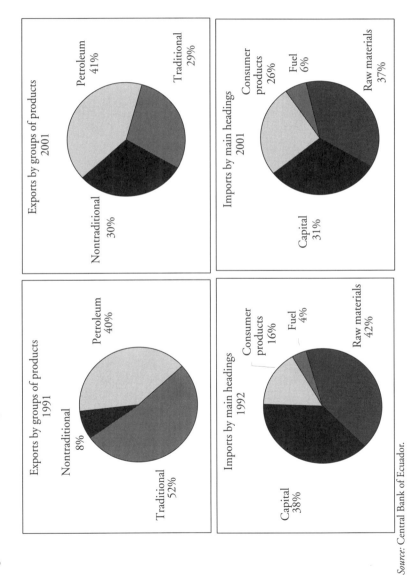

Exports by groups of products
2001

Petroleum
41%

Traditional
29%

Nontraditional
30%

Imports by main headings
2001

Consumer products
26%

Fuel
6%

Raw materials
37%

Capital
31%

Exports by groups of products
1991

Petroleum
40%

Nontraditional
8%

Traditional
52%

Imports by main headings
1992

Consumer products
16%

Fuel
4%

Raw materials
42%

Capital
38%

Source: Central Bank of Ecuador.

**Figure 2. Evolution of the Effective Rate of *Ad Valorem*
(VAT or Tariff/CIF Imports)**

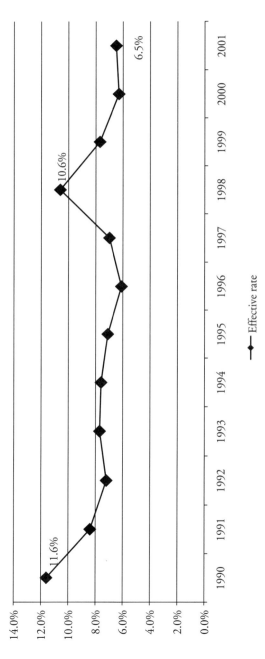

Source: Ministry of the Economy and Finance.

Colombia to 11.3 percent in Peru and 11.5 percent in Venezuela. Bolivia, with only two tariff rates (5 and 10 percent), collected an average 5.4 percent, similar to Ecuador, which has tariffs from 0 to 35 percent.

In 1994, through Decision 370 of the Cartagena Agreement, Ecuador adopted the CET, which establishes four levels—5, 10, 15, and 20 percent—and covers all tariff needs. And in 1995, the country formalized its membership in the World Trade Organization (WTO). Tariff ceilings were then established and in order to establish them in the WTO, the formula CET + 10 percentage points was used, except for automobiles, chemical products, and certain agricultural and agroindustrial products. Ecuador also acquired commitments in five main areas, most of which have now been met. However, the sensitivity of the agricultural sector led to the adoption of a mechanism for variable tariffs known as the Andean Price Band System (see section C of this chapter), which sets tariffs that fluctuate between 35 and 95 percent, depending on the product. This system is applied to 148 tariff subheadings.

The commitments acquired by Ecuador with the WTO regarding tariff contingencies were met before 2001. The country benefits from tariff concessions in the framework of the General System of Preferences (GSP) and the Global System of Preferences among developing countries, the objective of which is to favor processes of industrialization and accelerated growth.

Although the CET approved by three countries in the subregion (Colombia, Ecuador, and Venezuela) sets out essentially to standardize national tariff rates in order to consolidate a tariff union, in practice each country has presented a set of "differentiations" that effectively obliterate the content of Decision 370. For example, Ecuador applies differentiating factors[3] to 1,414 tariff subheadings under the "Not Produced" heading, to which tariffs between 0 and 15 percent are applied. This tariff is being reviewed and the CAN wants both Bolivia and Peru to participate in the definition and implementation of the new CET to strengthen the integration of Andean nations.

Exports have grown slowly (an annual average of 4.1 percent for 1990–2001), reaching their peak to date in 1997, at $US 5.3 billion, then falling owing to fluctuations in the price of oil, problems with banana marketing, and sanitary problems with shrimp production. Imports grew at an annual average of 3.4 percent in the same period and hit a record of $US 5.6 billion in 1998, before falling sharply to $US 3.0 billion in 1999 as a result of the economic crisis that struck the country (and the subsequent freezing of bank deposits), which was eliminated in 2000. Since then, there has been strong growth in imports—which, nonetheless, cannot be considered a new medium-term trend, but for now simply a recovery of previous levels.

The trends noted above have led to an increasingly negative balance of trade that naturally worries many Ecuadoran economic actors. Dollarization is considered by

---

3. Differences with respect to the CET agreed to between CAN and the rest of the world.

many to be the main culprit behind this trend. However, other important consider-ations cannot be ignored: fluctuations in the price of oil, problems in the banana market, recovery from the crisis of 1999 (which provides more incentives to imports than to exports), foreign remittances, the unfreezing of bank deposits in 2000, and statistical problems with the measurement of exports. These reasons do not imply that the negative trend (since 2000) in the real exchange rate (RER) has not played its part in the growing trade imbalance (elasticity in prices or real exchange rates for exports stands at 20, while at only 8.6 for imports).[4] Also, the long-term contracts that are typical of the oil market protect these exports from short-term fluctuations in the RER.

B. The Foundations of Ecuadoran Development

Given the poverty and poor distribution of income, Ecuador must increase its eco-nomic activity (measured by GDP).

Given the small size of its domestic markets and the limited technological capac-ity of its human and nonhuman capital, the country cannot depend only on indus-trial development to accelerate economic growth.

The country needs sectors that have potential for growth and that, on one hand, offer comparative advantages, and on the other, a large external market.

Ecuador has underutilized resources that can be used for export. These are to be found in overprotected and inefficient sectors (mostly in the manufacturing sector), in sectors with no comparative advantages (the automotive sector among others), in sectors that use resources inefficiently and manage them badly (public enterprises well known for their inefficiency), in poorly regulated or insufficiently controlled sectors (telecommunications), and even in corruption, which uses resources that cre-ate no added value productive employment.

However, to depend to a greater extent on exports, Ecuador must, as its first pri-ority, eliminate or at least significantly reduce the existing bias against exports.

This bias is generated by all the discriminatory support received by other pro-ductive sectors through trade policy that supports sectors that substitute imports through tariffs, as well as through nontariff barriers (NTBs) that are discriminatory in their purpose or in their application, such as prohibitions, technical regulations, customs procedures, customs valuations, rules on origin, safeguard measures, public purchases, and so on—all of which provide "support" or an implicit subsidy to cer-tain sectors or products to the detriment of the potential and existing exporting sec-tor. This is encapsulated in the concept of the effective protection rate (EPR), which differs from the nominal protection rate because input, raw materials, and capital

---

4. The price effect is stronger than the volume effect.

assets benefit from a lower tariff than that established for the final product. If the tariff on input to be used by the producer to manufacture the final product were the same as that paid for the final product when imported, the effective protection rate would coincide with the nominal tariff rate—which would indicate, in this case, the "real" degree of support for the production of the final product. If the Ecuadoran tariff system had a single tariff for all tariff subheadings, the effective protection rate would be the same for all domestic products, "final" or otherwise, and the EPR would be the same for producers of importable goods.

One important exception would remain: exportable products that cannot be protected domestically because of WTO restrictions and which would have to pay the single existing tariff on the use of their input. This would result in a negative EPR, while for other sectors it would be positive or equivalent to the nominal tariff. Discrimination against exports would therefore continue. The bias against exports would diminish, but would not disappear. Even the application of a "drawback" or simple payment (like the one recently created) would not entirely eliminate the bias against exports because positive support would remain reflected in the tariff, while the exportable product would receive zero support at best. In order to entirely eliminate discriminatory treatment and bias against exports, the single tariff rate must be zero.

Any barrier that favors one sector disfavors the other sectors. It is therefore ideal to have as neutral a trade policy as possible.

Given the above, some short- and medium-term trade policy recommendations for Ecuador in the general context of reducing the bias against exports follow. The most immediate goals are (i) greater efficiency in the allocation of resources, (ii) greater stimulation of non-oil exports, (iii) reduction of incentives to evade taxes and deal in contraband, (iv) greater simplification in order to eradicate corruption, and (v) greater transparency.

Recommendations

The main goal of tariff policy must be to reduce simultaneously the number and dispersion of tariffs in the coming years. The CAN countries are now renegotiating the CET and have considered maintaining 0, 5, 10, and 20 percent, transferring many input items and intermediary goods and capital (to which rates of 15 or 20 percent are now applied) to rates 0 or 5 percent. Although this reduction in dispersion is a step in the right direction, the change in the composition of coverage of tariff subheadings is a step toward increasing the average number of low-earning headings in terms of dispersion of the Effective Protection system, which is undesirable from the perspective of reducing the bias against exports. The CAN countries have negotiated 62 percent of tariffs, which covers only 33.4 percent of the combined gross national product. Therefore, the most important third of tariff subheadings is yet to be negotiated, since this affects two-thirds of national production. This is a good time to take a step in this direction. Furthermore, doing so would be a step toward the American Free Trade Agreement (AFTA), which today remains on the distant horizon, owing to Ecuador's failure to comply with several market access regulations (price bands, licenses, and so on).

Ecuador must also keep in mind that both Bolivia and Peru have maintained three and four tariff rates, respectively (10, 5, and 0 percent in the case of Bolivia and 4, 7, 12, and 20 percent in the case of Peru) and have not shown enthusiasm for the CET options discussed in the CAN.

We propose 5 and 10 percent[5] or some other option that is close to these figures. The proposal is coherent with the considerations discussed above but is not very attractive from the fiscal perspective, unless it is accompanied by serious efforts to reduce contraband and increase the efficiency of customs management (appendix 1). To the extent that these efforts are successful and the 0 percent rate is eliminated, the fiscal impact of this proposal will be neutral. It would not be fiscally neutral if the 0 percent rate were maintained. Although this is not the solution preferred by the Andean Community, Ecuador, together with Bolivia and Peru, has the weight to move the CET in the right direction. Also, Ecuador could take unilateral action in this area, making use of its status as a "less developed economy" within the Community and fall back on the "differentiations" allowed by Decision 370, which establishes the conditions by which each country establishes differences in the CET structure of the CAN. Bolivia did this and has a lower and less disperse tariff system than the existing Ecuadoran system.

Ecuador should make important adjustments to the price bands that have given the nonexporting agricultural sector significant protection (though less than that received by the manufacturing sector—about 10 percent, but very disperse) and have therefore made their contribution to the bias against exports. This issue of price bands will be dealt with in section C.

It will be useful, as long as a bias against exports remains, to continue strengthening special customs regimes such as temporary admission, industrial deposits, temporary exportation, commercial deposit, transit, and stock replenishment. The drawback system received more support in 2002, when an automatic returns system was created for up to 5 percent of gross exported value. Also, the drawback system is increasingly out of favor with the WTO and the most recent free trade agreements (FTAs) in Latin America. It has the inconvenience of being seen by some countries as an export subsidy and therefore must be used cautiously. Ecuador should eliminate or simplify prior authorizations, licenses, and permits for importation.

The country should carefully adjust tariff and nontariff barriers in order to eliminate their protectionist impact. A few of these still exist in Ecuador. Minimum prices exist in the context of price bands for agricultural products (see the following section). There are also bans on the importation of used automobiles and textiles. There is national legislation on compensatory safeguard measures (as part of the Law on Foreign Trade of 1997), on import licenses, and on technical regulations.

---

5. See Hachette (2000).

Ecuador should reduce the protectionist bias of licenses and of the institutions that issue them. Although automatic licenses have been abolished, some imports require prior authorization either by the Ministry of Trade, Industry and Integration; the Ministry of Agriculture; or the Consejo de Comercio Exterior e Inversiones (COMEXI)—and these bodies have sometimes refused to issue this authorization for the importation of rice, corn, other meats, dairy products, frozen fowl, turkey, and to a lesser extent, apples and fresh fruit. These institutions can (and do) prohibit or permit the importation of some of the sensitive products mentioned above (for example, sugar), under the contingencies system, charging the applicable VAT. Via contingencies, Ecuador allows limited entry of 17 agricultural products such as sorghum, wheat, corn, parts of fowl, turkey, powdered milk, and soy flour.[6]

Although this technique is attractively billed as "guaranteeing or stabilizing national consumption," it is protectionism in practice; therefore it should disappear entirely and be used only in circumstances duly justified before the COMEXI. Safeguards have also been imposed on the importation of industrial products such as matches, steel, and tires.

To make matters worse, importers of agricultural products must obtain two permits to import agricultural products: one from the Ministry of Agriculture and the other from the Ecuadoran Animal and Plant Inspection Service (SESA), which carries out zoo-phyto-sanitary control. Despite the usefulness of this, on the whole it has been used in such a way that it is often considered protectionist. SESA has also banned the importation of agricultural and meat products that use modern biotechnology. The purpose of this ban is unclear and appears to be an example of SESA's support of a protectionist policy in favor of Ecuadoran agriculture.

Pre-embarkation inspections, though necessary, result in longer delays than those caused by customs inspections. Spot checks are also carried out. These actions cause delays of six to eight weeks while merchandise is being held, which raises the cost of input for all productive sectors and reduces the competitiveness of exports, since it is equivalent to an additional tax on exports and imports, with predictable protectionist results.

The commitments acquired by Ecuador when it gained entry into the World Trade Organization require eliminating the existing bans on the importation of certain used articles (automobiles, tires, clothing). Although Congress is studying a draft law to eliminate the ban on importing used automobiles, this law has not yet been passed. The environmental concerns relating to this are well founded. However, the most efficient way of facing them is to require that used cars meet certain standards in order to enter the country (for example, as done by the Californian Environmental Protection Agency), rather than banning their importation.

---

6. For 2001, a contingency was established for hard corn and another for sorghum, very similar to the previous year.

These licenses represent a serious barrier to the transparency necessary in the rules of play; they have led to Ecuador's receiving a poor grade in the Economic Freedom index in recent years and delayed the country's preparations to enter ALCA. Ecuador has intensely and increasingly used this nontariff mechanism to manage its international trade. In September 2001, imports made under 1,424 tariff headings required prior authorization; this represented 21 percent of all tariff headings and were concentrated in the health and agriculture sectors. The Ministry of Health has exclusive control over authorizations for 614 tariff headings (43.1 percent of all headings requiring licenses), and the Ministry of Agriculture and Livestock handles 473 headings (33.2 percent of the total). This means that the two institutions are exclusively responsible for 76.3 percent of prior authorizations established in Ecuador (Table 1). In total, they affect about 9–10 percent of Ecuador's total trade (see Figure 3). There are no exportation licenses.

Between 1991 and 2000 there were no imports of goods under the 919 remaining tariff headings requiring authorization. Since this was not due to any *de facto* ban, these headings can be eliminated as unnecessary.

Table 1. Licenses Issued by Institutions

Institutions	Present situation	%	% Accumulated
Ministry of Public Health	614	43.1%	43.1%
Ministry of Agriculture and Livestock	473	33.2%	76.3%
National Council for the Control of Substances (CONSEP)	78	5.5%	81.8%
Ministry of Agriculture and Health	69	4.8%	86.7%
Armed Forces Joint Command	39	2.7%	89.4%
General Office of the Merchant Marine	32	2.2%	91.6%
Automotive Development Act	21	1.5%	93.1%
Ministry of Health and CONSEP	20	1.4%	94.5%
Atomic Energy Commission	16	1.1%	95.6%
Ministry of Health and COMEXI	15	1.1%	96.7%
Ministry of Public Works	14	1.0%	97.7%
Civil Aviation Office	11	0.8%	98.5%
Small Industries Development Act	6	0.4%	98.9%
Ministry of Energy and Mines	4	0.3%	99.2%
Ministry of Agriculture and CONSEP	3	0.2%	99.4%
Ministry of Agriculture and Joint Command	3	0.2%	99.6%
Ministry of Foreign Trade	3	0.2%	99.8%
Ministry of Health and Joint Command	1	0.1%	99.9%
Ministry of the Government	1	0.1%	99.9%
Ministry of Agriculture, Health, and CONSEP	1	0.1%	100.0%
Total	1,424	100.0%	

Source: MICIP, Sub-secretariat of Foreign Trade.

Figure 3. Percentage of Trade Requiring Prior Authorization

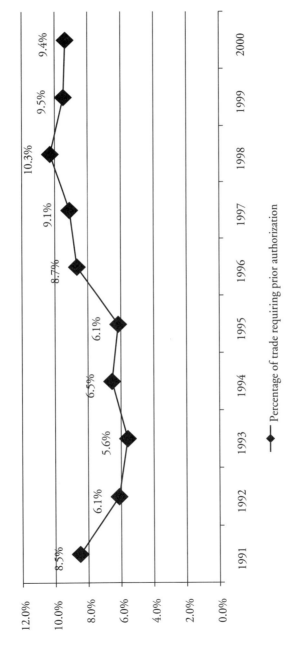

Source: MICIP.

It must also be kept in mind that a third of the tariff headings require an additional license at the same time, relating to health, zoo-phyto-sanitary, or national defense controls. No reasonable explanation has been found for this double procedure, each part of which is discretional and unclear.

Prior authorizations may be legitimately be used as a safety or security mechanism—for the health of the population or of the country's fauna and flora, or for national defense. However, they can also be used improperly as a protectionist instrument. It is difficult to classify the legitimate use of licenses because there are so many qualitative factors involved, but it is even more difficult to draw the line between legitimate and illegitimate uses. In any case, illegitimate use is equivalent to increasing the protection of products that substitute imports.[7] Making the application of the rules of play more transparent would help reduce the discretional use and calibrate their eventual impact on the protection of each sector.

According to licenses users, this mechanism is used to maintain public administration jobs (of those responsible for issuing the licenses), which generates unnecessary costs preventing free competition in the domestic market—as well as increasing the cost of imports, which is expressed in delays in the issuing of licenses or else bribes to reduce these delays. This also carries a social cost in terms of inefficiency, since there are fewer imports to benefit consumers owing to the effect of the tariff implicit in the license. These two costs come to about $US 37 million a year, about 13 percent of the value of the imports affected.[8] The largest surcharge for users was estimated at about $US 25 million a year, which represents the obligatory movement of users to the license-issuing mechanism; the difference represents the social or welfare cost.

Given the above, we recommend the following:

- Since they are redundant, prior authorizations that did not register commercial movement between 1991 and 2000 (that is, 919 tariff headings) should be eliminated.[9]
- Prior authorizations with specific prerequisites (health, phytosanitary, among others) should be immediately eliminated; a single license is sufficient.
- The other headings requiring prior authorization must undergo a process of technical analysis to justify their continued presence on the list of applicable

---

7. That is, to the extent that domestic products identical to imported ones are not subject to the same controls—then for lack of "domestic treatment" even a "legitimate" control becomes an implicit additional tariff.
8. Hachette (2001)' appendixes 1 and 2 of this chapter.
9. This recommendation is further justified as the current practice represents a potential threat to the protection of historically captive markets. Imported products whose importation is prohibited have been excluded from this analysis.

licenses. If they do not pass this test, they must be eliminated from the list of mandatory authorizations.

- Prior authorization must be maintained for products subject to importation prohibitions, as long as they meet the same obligation indicated in the previous paragraph within the same time frame.
- Free access to prior authorization should be guaranteed to any importer.
- Strengthening the Ecuadoran Agriculture and Livestock Service (SESA), which participates in issuing licenses, is necessary and urgent. The Service requires independence and a larger budget. Given the problem of SESA's limited infrastructure, a tendering process has begun with private laboratories. This is being carried out through the Methodology, Standardization, Accreditation, and Certification (MNAC) program with World Bank financing (see more details and recommendations in section D of this chapter devoted to Technical Regulations).

Other Recommendations

DOMESTIC COMPETITION. The liberalization of foreign trade will amount to no more than words if not accompanied by domestic liberalization. The benefit of liberalization is to be able to make use of input and final consumer goods at lower prices through commercial opening and greater domestic competition. However, monopolistic and discriminatory practices continue in Ecuador. The practice of exclusive trade arrangements appears to continue even though the Law on Foreign Trade and Investment (LEXI) banned it (Article 6). If importers are in connivance with domestic producers (or are representatives of products produced in the country) who do not want foreign competition, the result is maintaining the status quo in terms of protecting national production, or even increasing it (for example, the virtual ban of individuals bringing new cars into the country from abroad). There have also been cases in which the installation of a competitive foreign business (a foreign supermarket) has been arbitrarily blocked. The arbitrary application of technical regulations reinforces the monopolistic structure of Ecuadoran markets (see section D). A draft Law on Competition has recently been rejected by Congress, making it difficult to transparently, efficiently, and competitively open the market. The draft must be reconsidered as soon as legally possible.

Customs. There is considerable movement of contraband in Ecuador,[10] though estimates of its volume are subject to doubt and must be used with caution. Contraband indicates that the rules of play are too complicated and not transparent enough and highlights inefficient management of customs, ports, and airports and the lack of domestic competition. A Customs Act was passed in 2001. It does not get to the

---

10. Estimates range from 40 percent to 100 percent of imported value in the same year.

roots of the problem but at least makes it mandatory to report to the Internal Revenue Service (SRI); another law was in the hands of the previous President for his approval. Greater transparency and simplicity in the rules of play (lower and more homogeneous tariffs and the elimination of nontariff barriers) would help reduce the problem of corruption and increase fiscal income. This requires greater central control, perhaps through greater dependence on the Internal Revenue Service based on the principle that customs is a national service—that is, not only a provincial one—after a profound overhaul of the personnel involved. Random inspections by the fiscal police could be increased, as long as honesty is the outstanding quality of this corps. The authorities could study the experience of Mexico, which suffered similar endemic problems. There is no single solution except for a radical simplification of the VAT, which comes at a high fiscal cost.

We recommend establishing precise goals for increasing customs income. This could be 5 percent a year, duly corrected according to exchange rates.

The beneficial effects of tariff reform will be proportional to the flexibility and depth of reforms in the labor and financial markets, making foreign investment more attractive and improving infrastructure. Greater trade liberalization will have more positive and profound effects if the need for rapid reallocation of resources among products and sectors is not slowed by inefficient complementary markets (for example, lack of financing). These issues deserve more attention. The success of tariff reform depends to a great extent on profound reforms in the labor and capital markets, customs, infrastructure, and so forth. This is all the more urgent since, through dollarization, the country has lost a policy instrument—the nominal exchange rate.

Finally, international competitiveness depends on many variables that are prerequisites for successful exportation. The macroeconomic framework has improved since dollarization and the introduction of greater fiscal discipline. At the microeconomic level, the competitive atmosphere is lamentable; port services continue to be of low quality, with little innovative capacity; and industrial technology is unsophisticated since neither capital nor trained personnel are available (which is worsened by the emigration of skilled workers). Also, given their high level of protection, executives receive little systematic technical or professional training. This is particularly worrying in the case of state enterprises where incentives are often counterproductive and do not stimulate efficiency.

"The rule of law is fragile and does not provide adequate protection to property rights, according to the U.S. State Department, and judicial authority is subject to external pressures and corruption..."[11] State bureaucracy is complex, oversized, and often inefficient (see the issue of licenses discussed above). The banking and financial sectors have not emerged from the crisis that hit them in 1998 and 1999. This

---

11. Economic Freedom Index, 2002; Heritage Foundation; and others.

limits investment in the export sector, particularly investment involving risk. The Law on Foreign Investment of 1998 guarantees the same treatment for foreigners and for nationals, except for certain geographical limitations on foreigners in fishing and broadcasting. Ninety-six percent of recent investment has been in the oil and mining sectors. Ecuador's inflation rate, which is higher than the international average, continues to be an obstacle to the competitiveness of all of the country's present and potential exports. For these reasons, Ecuador receives a low grade and a low ranking in the Competition Index: 72nd of 75 countries studied.

C. Price Bands

THEORETICAL JUSTIFICATION. Agriculture is one of the main sectors of the Ecuadoran economy (12 percent of GDP). More than a third of the population depends directly on it; it is one of the main sources of employment in the country (7.3 percent of total employment in 1998); and it is socially important as it employs most of the indigenous population. It is also a sector with underutilized export potential and as the Ecuadoran economy has opened to the exterior, the domestic economy has become more sensitive to the outside world, whose prices, technology, and markets increasingly affect Ecuadoran agriculture. In fact, there are two kinds of agriculture: modern and traditional. The former is forceful, dynamic, highly productive, and makes flexible use of new technologies available in the rest of the world, making it competitive and therefore export-driven and able to stand up to competition from similar foreign products. However, this subsector remains small. Traditional agriculture, meanwhile, has low productivity and little modern input, which makes it impossible to achieve low costs; be flexible, dynamic, prosperous; or an engine for growth. It is also strongly protected, which has been an obstacle rather than an incentive for rapid modernization.

As part of national production agriculture must, like other sectors of the economy, respond to the challenges of economic opening to the outside world (see section A), guided mainly but not entirely by trade policy. Although it is desirable for trade policy to send out uniform signals to all productive sectors in order to take the best possible advantage of the few existing productive factors so that they can be allocated in the most productive and most efficient way, the range of trade policy tools applied to agricultural imports is more diverse than those applied to imports in other productive sectors. One of the reasons traditionally given for this is the need to moderate the volatility of prices and income.

Moderating the volatility of international prices is important, among other reasons, in order to improve the use of agricultural land, moderate undesirable fluctuations in agricultural income, reduce the risks inherent to the activity, and therefore, stimulate investment in the sector (product) thus increasing the productivity of the land. Price bands have generally been the main tool for moderating volatility, as is the case in Ecuador today.

The advantage of these bands is that, if applied transparently, symmetrically, and neutrally, they do not distort long-term signals aimed at better allocation of agricultural land.

Specifically, Ecuador, like the other CAN countries, has made use of them since 1996, within the Andean Price Band System, which justifies their use to (i) defend products and consumers against the natural instability of agricultural prices, (ii) defend products and consumers against price distortions in the international markets, and (iii) link domestic prices with international ones. Decision 371 (CAN) provides a detailed description of the price band mechanism.

This is a mechanism for stabilizing domestic prices by establishing a price "floor" and "ceiling" between which the cost of a specific product is to remain. Stabilization is theoretically achieved by applying a (variable) tariff surcharge when the importation (or reference) price plus the "standard" tariff is below the floor price, or reducing this tariff to zero when the price rises above the ceiling of the band. The mechanism used in the Andean Price Band System to stabilize the cost of imports is harmonized in the Andean subregion. Bands are applied to products from third countries that are not members of the Andean Community of Nations (CAN). They do not apply inside the CAN and are applied to 138 products. Twelve of these are benchmarks to which the rest are linked. Reference prices are established weekly by the Secretariat of the CAN and surcharges may not be greater than the difference between the VAT and the WTO consolidated tariff, that is, between 20 and 95 percent.

Although the six years that have passed since the creation of the bands may be too short a period to demonstrate whether or not their effect has been neutral, it is unlikely that this has been the case; rather, they have tended to be protectionist.[12] Although this is a sporadic measurement, it is unlikely that all the pertinent agricultural prices have been affected simultaneously by international events that have pushed up estimates of the effective protection of all the products involved. These figures are a call to attention, if nothing else.

To be neutral in the long term, price bands must not mix concerns regarding fluctuations with others regarding external subsidies, dumping, and other distortions that they are supposed to be combating. Such mixes hide high rates of protection at the cost of a more expensive basic food basket, while blocking the development of new agricultural exporting companies whose input includes products favored by the bands.

---

12. An example of this is that Ezquerra and Elorza (Andean Community) have estimated effective protection rates of 80.6 percent for production in agroindustrial bands and 66.5 percent for production in agricultural bands (cited by F. Suárez 2001). A protectionist bias can also be deduced from the fact that most reference prices plus taxes are higher than the band ceilings and that the consolidated tariff, which is higher than the legally applicable VAT is usually applied.

In practice, the CAN systematically applies a surcharge to the reference price, while taking care not to exceed the WTO consolidated tariff (see appendix 2, which gives examples of three price bands). The result is that the practical application of these bands in the CAN prevent them from being neutral, have a protectionist bias, and contradict their reason for being and even their very name. The reference price plus the variable surcharge calculated weekly by the CAN turn out in most cases to be independent of the existing band (that is, they fall outside the band—Table 2, column 6). However, for this reason, most of the bands do not have any practical purpose and could be eliminated without in the least changing the prices corrected by the VAT plus the surcharge.

If the price bands effectively played their part as a buffer against volatility, in the form in which they were designed and have been implemented in different countries, nearly 100 percent of the reference prices corrected by the VAT plus the pertinent surcharge would fall within them. However, as column 6 of Table 2 shows, 64 percent of pertinent prices fall outside these bands. Only two exceptions are to

Table 2. Variability in Ecuadoran Benchmark Prices, 1998–2001

Product	Standard deviation in the reference price	Relative variation coef. (reference price)	Standard deviation in the price plus taxes	Relative variation coef. (price plus taxes)	Coincidence[a] $P^{IMP} = P^{WTO}$ (% of cases)	P^{IMP} outside the price band (% of cases)
Palm oil	167.6	34.9	159.1	26.6	67.0	95.6
Soya oil	132.6	29.2	138.1	23.6	70.3	92.3
Rice 10% broken	55.2	19.6	34.7	8.2	37.4	76.9
White sugar	36.8	14.2	47.9	12.7	78.0	49.5
Pork	307.1	22.1	260.5	13.8	49.5	79.1
Barley #2	8.1	6.4	7.9	4.7	44.0	53.8
Powdered milk	140.5	7.3	85.4	3.1	0.0	100.0
Yellow corn	9.7	8.5	11.6	6.9	75.8	22.0
White corn	17.7	14.6	17.2	9.8	48.4	56.0
Soya beans	26.2	11.7	20.9	6.9	72.5	45.1
Durum wheat	11.7	8.3	11.7	6.1	82.0	9.8
Chicken parts	134.5	19.2	230.3	17.5	86.8	93.4

Notes:

PIMP corresponds to the reference price plus the applied tax.

PWTO corresponds to the price resulting from the application of the maximum allowable tax allowed according to agreements with the World Trade Organization (WTO).

a. Cases in which the maximum allowable tax according to WTO agreements was applied.

1. For all products, except durum wheat, 1991 statistics were used (two a month from January 1998 to September 2001 and one for October 2001). In the case of durum wheat, statistics include only the period from January 1998 to July 2000 (61 statistics).

2. Relative Variation Coefficients are the Standard Deviation divided by the average of the series and multiplied by 100. In this way, they can be interpreted as the percentile variation in terms of the average of the series of prices.

be found (yellow corn and durum wheat). The extreme case is that of powdered milk, with 100 percent of import prices falling outside the band; palm and soy oil and chicken parts are similar cases.[13] In addition to significantly reducing the "use" of the bands, this way of establishing import prices prevents, by definition, the desirable neutrality of the bands. This also makes them incompatible with current WTO regulations and probable ALCA regulations.

The high frequency of "coincidences" between import prices and prices corrected by the WTO consolidated tariff (second-last column of Table 2), without managing to "fit" prices into the corresponding band, indicates a lack of transparency in the use and estimation of surcharges. The CAN does not provide precise justification for this, except "the need to compensate for 'outside distortions.'" The arbitrariness hidden in the implementation of the system, as well as the comments above, cast doubts on the value of the price bands, since concerns about outside distortions seem to take precedence over concern for stability.

Nonetheless, the system that has been implemented has made prices more stable: variation in prices corrected with VAT and variable surcharges is 30 percent lower than for reference prices (columns 2 and 4, Table 2). The narrowness of the bands is also striking. This may be because prices fluctuated little in the past. If this hypothesis is correct, it would significantly reduce the justification of the bands. It is more likely that this narrowness is more the result of calculation mechanisms (see Decision 371).

Given the irrelevance of price bands, and despite the peculiarities of CAN methodology, the influence of medium-term price trends has not been reduced (see, for example, palm and soya oils and durum wheat in Hachette [2001, appendix V]). The inflexibility observed in the bands is the result of their long memory (more details can be found in appendix 2 of this chapter).

The application of surcharges to reference prices plus VAT that are above the floor price, *but within* a band, or above the ceiling price, illustrates the protectionist vocation of the bands (for example, broken rice in 1998, soya beans, and palm oil) and their irrelevance. This is also true of the application of surcharges—which, instead of being used to reach the floor of the band, reach its ceiling and even go above it (this is the case for all benchmarks). Given the above, there are several clear implications and recommendations.

Implications

It is unlikely that any single instrument such as bands can efficiently and simultaneously *correct* fluctuations in outside prices and in income: on average, they reduce both a little. Nor can bands simultaneously compensate for the "subsidies and other distortions in outside markets," "guarantee domestic availability," (arguments used by the Ministry of Agriculture to justify the bands), and also "link domestic prices

---

13. Details in Hachette (2001, appendix V).

to international ones." Most countries that use them also have antidumping tools or safeguards that they apply independently of price bands in cases of international distortions. This is approved in Article 8 of LEXI.[14] In the Ecuadoran case, in light of the handling of price bands, it is understandable that the lack of transparency in the mix of simultaneously applied instruments causes other countries to retaliate in the form of safeguards (exporter complaints).

The upward bias of the bands has hit Ecuadoran consumers hard, especially the poorest, since they spend more on food as a proportion of their income than the rich. This phenomenon has been especially severe since 1996.[15]

The fact that so many "related" substitutes and complements were included in the bands system provides the agroindustrial sector with an effective and extremely arbitrary structure and level of protection. Also, the more frequently surcharges are used and the longer the memory of the band is, the less domestic prices will be linked to international prices.

It is also important to distinguish between the "long-term" trend toward falling agricultural prices and short-term trends. Regarding the former, the reaction should be to modify agricultural production and not increase surcharges. This can happen only if the agricultural sector opens more to the outside world, so that international prices do not send false signals to domestic producers. The mechanisms discussed above are justified only in order to deal with the latter. These issues must be studied in depth. Agriculture is not a static sector; it depends on what happens in other sectors and, vice-versa, its development is important in order to efficiently substitute imports and develop new exports.

Recommendations

Ecuador should drastically reduce the number of bands. At least two-thirds of them do not pass the minimum tests of efficiency. Along with them, all references to related goods should be automatically eliminated. The great number of bands also presents administrative problems, makes the establishment of prices more rigid and may create pressures to maintain them for reasons of "self-sufficiency" (corn and sugar, for example), adding to the social cost of their inefficiency. If some bands are maintained, they should affect only commodities that have more open, complete, and efficient international markets (there is no sense in a band for

---

14. "(I)mports will not be subject any taxes other than tariffs, if applicable, value added tax, the tax on special consumption, compensatory rights or antidumping or the application of safeguard measures that may be temporarily adopted to prevent unfair trade practices in the framework of the WTO regulations..."

15. During 1985–95 (along with other agricultural policies) there was practically no bias in the bands applied; therefore, agricultural policy should not have had the redistributive effects of the kind mentioned above.

chicken pieces[16] and only importable goods. Bands should be eliminated if (1) their reference prices are stable; (2) they are not commodities; and (3) they are not importable. Examples include bands for powdered milk, durum wheat, palm oil (not importable), chicken pieces, pork, barley, rice (10 percent broken), soya oil, and goods related to these.

Ecuador should establish a clear and definitive separation of the objectives of the bands. The country should use the remaining bands only for balancing purposes (not protectionist ones) and use surcharges only in cases of dumping or foreign subsidies demonstrated on a case-by-case basis and only for a short time. This must be subject to an exhaustive review, which should be carried out by an organization not associated with the CAN in order to guarantee its objectivity. If some bands are maintained, they must be wide and flexible, with a short memory, and be subject to correction.

In order to guarantee long-term neutrality, it is unwise to mix considerations of variability with others regarding foreign subsidies, dumping, and other distortions. Such mixes hide high rates of protection at the cost of a more expensive basic food basket, while blocking the development of new agricultural exporting companies whose input includes products favored by the bands.

Ecuador must strengthen private or mixed insurance mechanisms such as futures markets (for commodities such as corn), options, long-term contracts, diversification of production, vertical integration, swaps, credit, and so on, either independently or in conjunction with other CAN countries or other third countries.

Independent of the above, there must be a permanent effort to increase competition in the agricultural sector, focused especially on small and medium-sized owners.

Joining the ALCA necessitates a profound review of the mechanisms that support agriculture. Given current WTO regulations, such as removing price bands, the only tools left are special (emergency) safeguards and WTO consolidated tariffs. The former, if negotiated taking full advantage of the Doha Round, could be applied to a small subset of the products to which they are now applied. Applying the consolidated tariff would increase the cost of the food basket (and of effective protection) according to the historical data used to estimate it. If this method were applied, the price with the WTO tax added would be higher than the effective price in 61 percent of the cases studied. This means that Ecuador, in the context of the Doha Round, should adjust both the level and the structure of the consolidated tariffs, reducing their deviation and their average level. This decision could be made in conjunction with the other CAN countries.

Ecuador does not appear willing to adjust the bands and other instruments as long as the United States does not ease its Farm Bill. The best case would be for rationality to prevail or that the weight of an agro-alliance among the CAN coun-

---

16. And less sense in bands for products related to chicken pieces—see Hachette (2001, appendix V).

tries, the Cairns group, the EU, and the WTO "convince" the United States that the future of globalization depends on greater liberalization of agriculture in the entire world.

D. Technical Regulations

A Lack of "Domestic Treatment"

Technical regulations began in Ecuador with the regulations for applying the Weights and Measures Act, laid out in Ministerial Agreement number 628 of March 1997, published in the official register in June of that year. These regulations, which could benefit Ecuadorans, have since then been a source of discrimination against imported products and a mechanism for reducing competition between domestic and foreign products.

Also, with the "Regulations Substituting the Regulations on Goods that must comply with Ecuadoran Technical Regulations, Codes of Practice, Regulations Resolutions and Mandatory Technical Regulations," published in June 1998 through Executive Decree number 1526, the Interinstitutional Committee is responsible for including the specific products that must comply with technical regulations.

There are 2,096 Ecuadoran Technical Regulations (NTEs): 757 are mandatory and 1,339 are optional. Five categories claim 53.7 percent of the total: food technology is the largest group (534 regulations, or 25.5 percent of the total); the others are construction materials, chemical technology, mechanical systems and components, and petroleum-related technology and other similar technology (Table 3). Unjustifiably, these are applied in a discriminatory fashion and only to imported products, making them another example of protection of the domestic sector.

INEN and WTO Regulations

When Ecuador joined the WTO, it officially adopted the Standardization Code. This code establishes that Technical Regulations are voluntary and must not constitute unnecessary obstacles to trade. Decree 401, the legal grounds for "Metrology, Standardization, Accreditation, and Certification" (MNAC), published in Official Register number 87 on Mary 30, 2000, establishes (i) in article 11, that the official standardization agency, the Ecuadoran Standardization Institute (INEN) will monitor compliance with the guidelines established in the Good Practices Code for the Preparation, Adoption, and Application of Regulations; and (ii) in article 13, that the Ministries must support standardization efforts under the guarantee and supervision of the National Standardization Agency (ONN).

Furthermore, Decision 419 (376) of the Andean Community ratifies the Voluntary Nature of the Andean Regulations and specifies that these must constitute unnecessary obstacles to trade. However, the effective application of the "Regulations

Table 3. Types of Ecuadoran Technical Regulations (to October 4, 2001)

ICS	Description	Ecuadorian Technical Regulation (NTE) number	%
67	Food technology	534	25.5
91	Construction and building materials	230	11.0
71	Chemical technology	132	6.3
21	Mechanical systems and components for general use	120	5.7
75	Petroleum and related technology	112	5.3
25	Manufacturing engineering	94	4.5
87	Painting and color industries	90	4.3
13	Environmental and health protection; Security	88	4.2
77	Metallurgy	75	3.6
23	Fluid systems and components for general use	74	3.5
59	Textile and tanning technology	62	3.0
65	Agriculture	52	2.5
29	Electrical engineering	45	2.1
43	Automotive engineering	42	2.0
83	Rubber and plastics industry	41	2.0
85	Paper technology	39	1.9
81	Glass and ceramic industry	31	1.5
97	Domestic economy; Entertainment; Sports	31	1.5
55	Packaging and distribution of articles	28	1.3
61	Clothing industry	28	1.3
7	Mathematics; Natural sciences	24	1.1
79	Wood technology	22	1.0
17	Metrology and measurement; Physical phenomena	21	1.0
1	General; Terminology; Standardization; Documentation	20	1.0
35	Information technology; Office equipment	16	0.8
11	Health care technology	15	0.7
3	Sociology; Services; Organization and management	14	0.7
93	Civil engineering	9	0.4
19	Testing	2	0.1
27	Energy and heat transfer engineering	2	0.1
53	Materials management equipment	2	0.1
100	Reserved	1	0.0
	Total	2,096	

Source: INEN.

Substituting the Regulations on Goods that must comply with Ecuadoran Technical Regulations, Codes of Practice, Regulations, Resolutions and Mandatory Technical Regulations," results in imported products not receiving domestic treatment. This means that INEN regulations amount to the discretional application of quasiprohibitive tariffs only to imports, since these regulations are not applied to similar domestic products. Therefore, this asymmetry constitutes the most damaging nontariff barrier applied by Ecuador to its imports.[17] This skewed application of WTO regulations, and the spirit in which it is done, implies a surreptitious use of different tariffs for imports that suffer from the mandatory application of INEN regulations, which adds social costs to those already created by tariff policy and by other nontariff barriers. It also reinforces the monopolistic power of domestic industries (whichever one holds the capital), significantly limiting competition in the country's markets. Even if the mandatory regulations applied were "transparent," this would not eliminate the discrimination against foreign products as compared to domestic products. It would be preferable (that is, more transparent) to establish a tariff equivalent to the cost of this discrimination and add it to the existing customs barriers.

The other invisible effect of this discrimination is the loss of state control over the commercial treatment of each imported product. It is now impossible to have a precise idea of the most probable overall impact of trade barriers (tariff and nontariff).

It is essential that Ecuador "disassemble" (deregulate) its current system of mandatory standardization in favor of a voluntary and optional standardization system regulated in accordance with WTO regulations. INEN regulations are based on considerations of risk (primarily security and health), while the application of "WTO Regulations," based on the same parameters, requires that a "technical justification" be issued. This "technical justification" makes it quite difficult to apply the barrier, thus making the market more flexible and open. Many of Ecuador's currently applicable regulations would not meet the requirements of "WTO Regulations."

It will be impossible for the Ministry of Foreign Trade, Industrialization, and the Fishery to come to Agreements on the Mutual Recognition of Certificates of Conformity to Regulations with the competent authorities of other countries—agreements that would facilitate Ecuadoran exports and imports.

Recommendations

The country should technically evaluate the 759 mandatory INEN Ecuadoran Trade Regulations to decide if they should be mandatory in the future. If they do not pass this test, they should automatically be declared optional. The same study should include an analysis of the impact of eventually moving from one category to another. It would be best for the regulations to be declared optional, *ipso facto,* with the possibility of once again becoming "mandatory" only after passing the pertinent test.

Along with the process of "deregulating or disassembling" mandatory regulations, preparation must be made for the process of "regulation or assembly" of the system of "WTO Regulations," notification, and information, as is stated in the pertinent legal documents.

---

17. It is true that the most developed countries with the most diverse imports have more technical regulations, but they are not mandatory.

The above recommendations suggest that Decree 401 must be quickly modified so as to make it transparent, so that through new regulations it can include the necessary elements to comply with WTO procedures, and to "regulate" its WTO application. The final objective of this must be to effectively apply "domestic treatment" to Ecuadoran imports and to eliminate everything that contradicts WTO Regulations.

Laboratories responsible to MNAC (Decree 401) must pass the ISO 17025 Standard test—a *sine qua non* condition for the "accreditation" required in order to guarantee international acceptance of the certificates they issue (see phyto-sanitary controls).

Also, with standard "WTO Regulations" commonly adopted, these requirements can be "homologated." This would allow products to enter Ecuador that cannot do so at present.

To the extent that certain mandatory standards are maintained, the Ministry of the Economy must be sure that these are also applied to domestic products classified under the same UIIC as imported products. If the domestic product does not comply, the imported product should automatically be exempted from the corresponding VAT. The relevant ministries and institutions should be responsible to the MNAC for compliance with the "domestic treatment" principle. The MNAC would act before the COMEXI in defense of importers and would be responsible for guaranteeing compliance with the above proposal. If applied, these suggestions would be the right step toward the greater competitiveness of Ecuadoran exports and compliance with WTO regulations.

Policy Matrix

Bias against exports	Policy measures		Progress indicators	Objectives/goals Δ- Bias against exports
	Short term (to June 2003)	Medium term (2003–07)		
Inefficiency due to high tariff level and great tariff dispersion. Fiscal neutrality with increased productivity at customs.		Apply two rates: 5 and 10%.	Tariff changes; lower average weighted level and standard deviation.	Improve allocation; reduce bias against exports.
Bands do not meet goals.	Eliminate ineffective bands: durum wheat, powdered milk, and so on.	Replace bands with mechanisms permitted by WTO.	List of eliminated bands.	Improve agricultural productivity.
Existence of licenses; use not transparent and managed discretionally.	Eliminate double licenses and licenses without importation registration. Free access to licenses.	Conduct technical analysis to justify remaining licenses.	List of eliminated licenses.	Add transparency, reduce bureaucracy and corruption, reduce importation cost.
Lack of competition in traditional agriculture.	Double volume of remaining contingencies.	Eliminate contingencies, bans, and other restrictions.	Indicators of contingencies given by WTO.	Achieve greater productivity.
Inefficiency and corruption at customs.	Increase effective control of imports at customs.	Continue efforts.	Δ^+ Fiscal income as percentage of imports by 5% a year.	Reduce contraband, corruption, and Δ^+ fiscal income.
Monopolized markets.	Present law on competition to Congress.	Create regulatory agency.	Monitored cases.	Boost competition.

Policy Matrix (*continued*)

Bias against exports	Policy measures		Progress indicators	Objectives/goals Δ- Bias against exports
	Short term (to June 2003)	Medium term (2003–07)		
"Domestic Treatment" not given when applying technical regulations.	Make "mandatory" regulations applicable to domestic products under the same UIIC.	Make "mandatory regulations" applicable to domestic products under the same UIIC.	Number of cases dealt with.	Establish domestic treatment.
Inadequate application of regulations.	Disassemble mandatory system and make it optional.	Complete disassembly.	Number of cases dealt with successfully.	Eliminate unnecessary mandatory character of regulations.
Capacity of control laboratories insufficient.		Approve ISO 17025 standard test for laboratories responsible to MNAC. Strengthen SESA.	Number of approvals.	Strengthen system, quality of service, and foreign confidence.

Annex 1
Estimate of the Social Cost of Licenses and Inefficiency at Customs

Licenses

We will explore three different costs: (i) the difference between the effective price of importation and the economic cost of the same product to the importer (including the cost of delays in issuing the license, or the opportunity cost of the imported goods—which here we will assume to be the same); (ii) the social cost of the inefficiency of licenses, which is traditionally measured by the triangle of welfare based on the demand for imports; and (iii) the transfer of the importer to "customs." This is directly proportional to the imports affected and to the financial cost of a hypothetically average six-month delay. Assumptions:

- Imports affected (8 percent of total imports—3400mm), that is, 292mm in 2000.
- Financial cost (17 percent annual interest rate).
  $292*0,17/2=25$mm
  (1) Social or Welfare Cost (CB), equivalent to
  $CB= R*\eta m*\Delta M$

Estimating elasticity in the demand for imports also requires certain assumptions. It is elasticity "derived" from the elasticity of domestic demand and of domestic supply, the former with the inverse proportion of the value of imports weighted in demand, and the latter weighted by the inverse value of imports as a percentage of supply: D/M = 5 (2000 value for domestic accounts) and O/M = 4 (difference with $1 - M=D - O$). If we also assume a unit value for the elasticity of demand and 0.2 for domestic supply, the results are as follows:

Where R=0.17/2   Surcharge   O: Supply
M=292mm   Imports D: Demand
ηm=5.8   Elasticity of demand for imports
$\Delta M=M*\eta m*R=144$
$CB=(R*\Delta M)/2=12$
TOTAL ANNUAL COST OF LICENSES IN $US mm: 25+12=37

Customs

The methodology is similar to that used to estimate the cost of inefficiency of licenses: they are variants on the same theme, that is, a surcharge on imported value (and in this case, exports as well). Another difficulty is coverage. Here, coverage is the sum of total nonpetroleum imports and exports. Since R could not be estimated in $US, a welfare cost (CB) could not be obtained and therefore the result is an underestimate of the sum of the costs caused by both inefficiencies. However, the first cost we call "transfer cost" applies only to importers subject to license in the preceding paragraph, while here it applies both to importers and exporters. This is the only estimate made here resulting in an underestimate of the real cost of inefficiency at customs.

The transfer of the importer and exporter to "Customs" is directly proportional to total nonpetroleum imports and exports in a single year (2000) affected by and bearing the financial cost of a delay assumed to be six months on average. The cost of "transfer" is simply

CT= [X+Mnp]*R   CT: cost of transfer
X+Mnp=5884 X: exports; Mnp: nonpetroleum imports
R : or surcharge due to inefficiency;

The information provided by import and export agents indicated that the surcharge of costs owing to inefficiency at customs was in the order of 15 percent. Since it was difficult to confirm this, we prefer to present scenarios:

R Alternative Surcharges (%):	1	5	10	15
CT (million)	59	294	588	883

The most realistic scenario, according to the author, would be an arithmetic average of the two main scenarios:

(294 + 588) /2 = 441 per year

Annex 2

The three bands shown in Figures A1 through A3 clearly illustrate several of the points explained in the text:

Soya oil:

 a) This illustrates, at least, the incompatibility of long memory and maintaining the link between domestic and international prices.
 b) A protectionist bias is present from the moment when the tariff placed on the reference price coincides with the WTO consolidated tariff.
 c) Furthermore, only 8 of 48 examples fall within the band, which shows the irrelevance of the band.

Recommendations:

 • Eliminate the band or at least make it much more flexible (shorter and broader memory)

Powdered milk:

 a) No example (reference price plus tax) falls inside the band.
 b) The outside price is very stable, meaning there is no justification for applying an instrument for reducing volatility and, therefore, for a band.
 c) Extremely high tariff with no justification.

Recommendations:

 • Eliminate the band.
 • Lower the consolidated tariff.

Palm oil:

 a) Comments and recommendations similar to those applicable to the soya oil band.
 b) It is difficult to imagine how the price band has "defended producers and consumers against the distortions of prevailing prices in the international markets."

Figure A1. Soya Oil

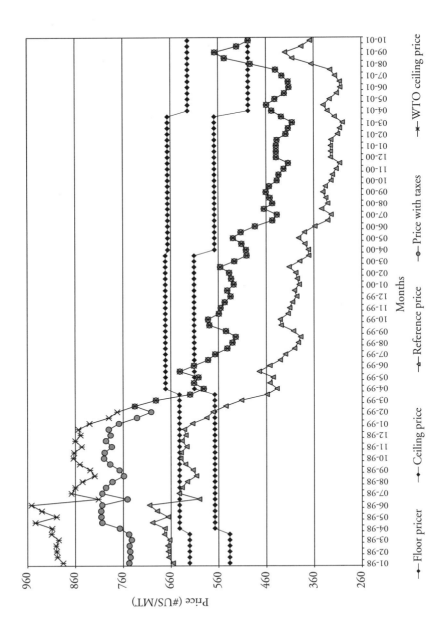

Source: World Bank calculations.

Figure A2. Powdered Milk

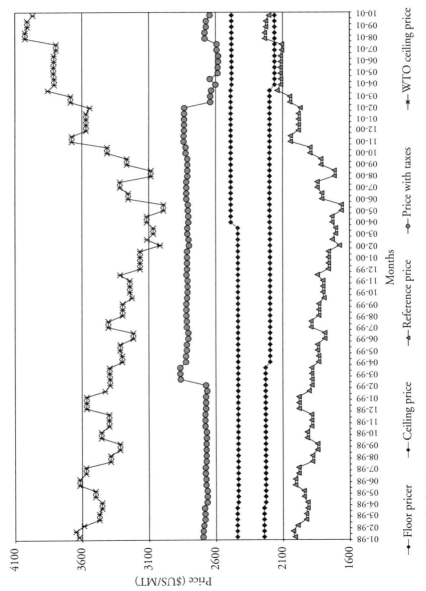

Source: World Bank calculations.

Figure A3. Palm Oil

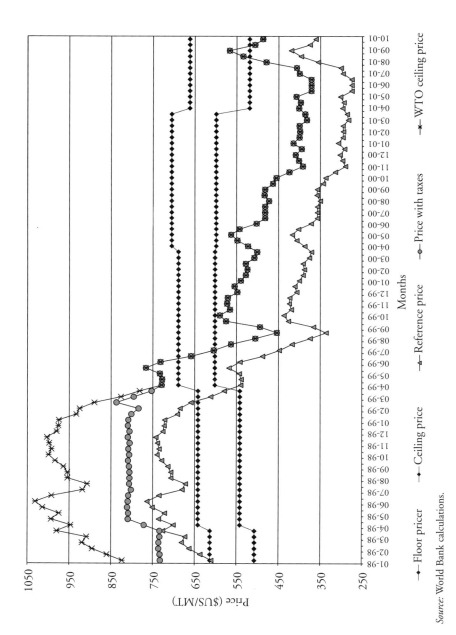

Source: World Bank calculations.

7

Basic Infrastructure: Water and Sanitation, Electricity, Telecommunications, and Transport[1]

Franz Drees, Philippe Durand, Eloy Vidal, and Emmanuel James

The water and sanitation, electricity, telecommunications, and transport sectors face problems of poor coverage (especially in rural areas), inefficiency and poor quality of services, insufficient resources for new investment and—with the exception of the electrical sector—incomplete regulatory and institutional frameworks. In general, the national government must face these challenges by encouraging greater local, national, and international private sector participation, by consolidating institutional and legal frameworkds and—especially in the water supply/sanitation and transport sectors—using resource transfers from the central government to encourage service providers to improve services and coverage.

In addition to these problems, the water and sanitation sector is characterized by poor recovery of costs through tariffs, and high dependence on transfers from the central government to cover deficits. An integrated national water resource management system is also lacking. Since all water and sanitation services are provided by decentralized providers that depend on municipal governments, the central government has two main tools at its disposal to improve the quality and efficiency of services, and to extend coverage to urban and rural populations not yet served; It can leverage central government transfers to encourage cost-effectiveness among service providers, and it can improve the institutional and legal framework.

1. This chapter was prepared by Franz Drees (coordinator, senior sanitary engineer), Eloy Vidal (lead telecommunications engineer), Emmanuel James (senior financial analyst, transport), and Philippe Durand (lead energy specialist). Carlos Gómez (telecommunications assistant), and Fernando Lecaros (World Bank energy consultant) made key contributions. The authors would like to thank María Angélica Sotomayor, Oscar Alvarado, Musa Asad, Samuel Taffesse, and Ernesto Sánchez-Triana for their support.

195

The most significant problems in the electricity sector include the ineffectiveness of an incomplete reform process; institutional vulnerability; the questionable sustainability of the wholesale electricity market; the need for rate adjustments to ensure the sector's financial sustainability; and the incomplete implementation of the environmental policy applicable to the sector. To face these challenges, it is essential to reactivate private sector participation in distribution and generation; modernize or eliminate state interference in the CONELEC regulatory authority; regulate the financial situation of the wholesale electricity market; reinitiate rate adjustments with appropriate "lifeline" protection for low-income households; deal with the problem of EMELEC; develop a rural energy strategy; and consolidate environmental planning and management systems in the sector, particularly in the Ministry of Energy and Mining and in CONELEC.

Beyond the general problems shared by various infrastructure subsectors, the telecommunications sector faces specific challenges including artificially low, unsustainable local rates for fixed telephone service; lack of competition in the cellular market, resulting in user costs that are among the highest in the region; and very limited Internet access. It is essential that the government consolidate the institutional and legal framework and promote greater private sector participation, attracting private capital to Andinatel and Pacifictel so that they can make the large investments that the sector requires, and in order to break the duopoly in the cellular market.

The challenges in the transport sector include the poor state of the highway system; the poor state of rural roads and the lack of transport services in rural areas; environmental problems; inconsistent and deficient sectoral and modal planning; and insufficient capacity and resources at the local government level to maintain provincial highways and local roads in the context of the decentralization process. The central government should contract maintenance services on the basis of results and promote private sector participation through microenterprises that maintain and pave rural roads, fomenting the creation of mixed capital cooperatives for rural transport and performance incentives for local governments. It should also improve the environmental management of the sector, and transform the Ministry of Public Works into a new Ministry of Transport with normative and planning functions.

A. Introduction

The development of basic infrastructure is a fundamental challenge for Ecuador. An improvement in the quality of life for the population depends on it, as does economic growth. This chapter presents a summary of the situation facing Ecuador at the end of the year 2002 in four key sectors that comprise a significant part of its public infrastructure: water and sanitation, electricity, telecommunications, and transport (highways and roads, railroads, ports, and airports). This section provides an overview of the sectors, including their actors, legal and regulatory framework. The following section then summarizes the main challenges facing the four sectors. Finally, policy recommendations are given for each of these sectors and for rural community infrastructure. The main recommendations are summarized in a short- and medium-term action plan.

Several of the challenges facing the sectors (especially coverage and service quality) are closely linked both to *urban growth* and the country's *urban-rural population structure*. On one hand, between 1995 and 2000, Ecuador had an urban growth rate of 3.6 percent, compared to the 2.1 percent average for South America. On the other, despite strong population growth in urban areas, Ecuador continues to be one of the most rural countries in South America, with only 63 percent of its population living in urban areas, compared to the regional average of 80 percent. These two facts pose a double challenge: first, the need to mobilize significant investment for rural areas, where the coverage of services is generally lower than in urban areas; and second, the urgent need to restructure urban service providers (including public utilities) in all infrastructure sectors, so that they are able to efficiently meet the technical and financial challenges posed by rapid urban growth (see chapter 8 on Urban Development Policy).

Description of the Sectors

Water and Sanitation

HISTORY. The structure of the water and sanitation sector in Ecuador from the 1950s to the 1980s was characterized by centralized planning, primarily by the Ecuadoran Institute for Water and Sanitation Works (IEOS). From the time of its creation in 1965 until its abolition in the mid-1990s, the IEOS built, operated and maintained potable water systems at the national level, financed by central government resources coming mostly from oil exports. When these resources diminished in the early 1990s, the central government decided to transfer the systems it had built to municipalities and communities. These communities would operate and maintain the system as part of a broader nationwide decentralization and modernization process. The IEOS was replaced by the Sub-secretariat of Potable Water and Basic Sanitation (SAPYSB) of the Ministry of Urban Development and Housing (MIDUVI), and its staff was sharply cut from about 2,500 public employees in the early 1990s to 148 in August 2002. Along with this reduction and supported by two studies by external consultants in 1999 and 2002, the SAPYSB began a still unfinished transformation of its role from that of a *direct implementing agency* to that of a *sector promoter and facilitator*. Its new role meant it was in charge of planning the development of the sector; establishing policies and setting standards; providing technical assistance to municipalities, communities, and operators; and developing and maintaining a sector information system.

THE INSTITUTIONAL STRUCTURE AT THE CENTRAL GOVERNMENT LEVEL. In addition to the SAPYSB, several other institutions have overlapping functions related to the sector (see Table 1):

Table 1. Institutions Related to the Water and Sanitation Sector

Institution	Functions
MIDUVI/SAPYSB	Formulates sectoral policies, establishes norms, and defines the development strategy for the sector at the national level.
Ministry of Public Health	Regulates the quality of potable water.
Ministry of the Environment	Responsible for environmental protection and conservation and for controlling of water pollution.
National Council on Water Resources (CNRH)	The CNRH comprises 8 regional development authorities responsible for water resource management including granting water abstraction rights.
Ecuadoran Development Bank (BEDE)	Channels resources to municipalities.

SERVICE PROVIDERS (SPs). As a result of decentralization in the 1990s, Ecuador today has a very large number of SPs, with utilities in big and medium-size cities, and municipal water and sanitation services in small cities (see Table 2). A few small municipalities have created SPs legally independent of municipal government (and theoretically with financial autonomy). However, most have decided to provide water and sanitation services to in cantonal capitals directly via municipal departments, whose staff is frequently shared with other services whose income and expenditures are not separated from the municipality's overall budget. In rural areas, water and sanitation committees (JASS) provide water supply (and sometime sanitation) in small communities, usually with very limited technical support from the municipal government.

Table 2. Water and Sanitation Service Providers (SPs)

Population	Number of municipalities	Type of SP	Pop. (millions)	Pop. growth in the 1990s
> 1 million	Guayaquil, 1.7 million;	Guayaquil: Concession (INTERAGUA— International Water Services)	3.35	+2.3%
	Quito, 1.6 million]	Quito: Municipal utility (EMAAP)		
100,000–300,000	12	11 municipal utilities and 1 municipal department (Loja)	1.92	+7.8%
30,000–100,000	37	8 municipal utilities and 29 municipal departments	0.80	−2.2%
< 30,000	169	Municipal departments	1.30	+3.5%
Rural areas	n.a.	Approx. 2,000 JASS	4.72	+0.9%
TOTAL	220		12.09	+2.1%

Electricity

MAIN FEATURES OF THE SECTOR. According to the census of November 2001, 96.6 percent of the urban population of Ecuador has electrical service, compared to only 77.8 percent of the rural population and the overall national average of 89.7 percent. In December 2001, nominal installed generating capacity for public service was 3,270 MW, of which 53.1 percent come from hydroelectric power plants and the rest from thermal power plants burning bunker or diesel fuel. In December 2000, 660.5 MW installed capacity was registered for independent generators.[2] In 2001, total gross production was 11,072 GWh (excluding production by independent generators). The 8,103 GWh of energy that was billed was divided as follows: residential sector (35.8 percent), industrial sector (26.1 percent), commercial sector (17.4 percent), public lighting (7.8 percent), other uses (11.2 percent), and large consumers (1.7 percent). Energy demand grew at an average of 5 percent a year between 1990 and 2001, and an average 4–5 percent yearly increase in demand is projected over the next 10 years. Distribution losses are very high—23 percent in 2001—and have remained practically constant throughout the past decade. The national transmission system consists of two 230 kV rings and 138kV radial lines. The transmission system operates under difficult conditions, owing to congestion and weaknesses in certain parts of the system. There are 20 distribution companies, the largest of which are the *Empresa Eléctrica Quito* (EEQ) with 26 percent of total billed electricity, and the Municipal Electricity Company (EMELEC) in Guayaquil, with 28 percent of total invoiced electricity. In addition to the national grid, there are two small independent distribution systems (Sucumbíos and Galapagos). The average electrical rate for consumers in June 2002 was 8.6 cents per kWh.[3] There is a cross subsidy for low-income residential customers who consume less than the residential average for each distribution company. This residential average ranges from a low of 48 kWh/consumer month (*Empresa Eléctrica Bolívar*) to 190 kWh/consumer month (EMELEC).[4] Table 3 provides a comparison of the electricity sector in selected Latin American countries.

SECTORAL REFORM. The reform of the electricity sector goes back to 1996, when the Electricities Sector Act was passed. The achievements to date include:

- **Restructuring of generation.** Seven new generating companies (Hidropaute, Hidroagoyan, Hidropucara, Termoesmeraldas, Termopichincha, Elecaustro, and Electroguayas) have been created from the assets of the former INECEL,

---

2. National Electrification Plan 2002–11, CONELEC.
3. Source: CONELEC statistics for 2001 and first half of 2002.
4. Source: Chart of distribution by frequencies, issued October 2001, CONELEC.

Table 3. Comparison of Selected Electricity Sectors in Latin America and the Caribbean

| Country | Population 2001 (millions) | Per capita GDP ($US) 2001 $US | System owner* | Electricity Coverage 2001(%) | | | Total installed capacity 2001 (MW) | Thermo-hydro generation (%) | Per capita consumption kWh/year/person | Average electricity prices June 2002 (US cents/kWh) | | |
				Urb.	Rural	Total				Resi-dential	Commer-cial	Indus-trial
Bolivia	8.5	990	P	78	25	57	1227	0.9	407	5.8	9.2	4.6
Chile	15.2	4590	P	100	80	97	10269	1.0	2599	8.1	7.7	5.4
Colombia	43.1	2020	P/G				13141	0.4	817	7.7	6.8	6.8
Costa Rica	3.9	3810	G	100		97	1715	0.2	1533	6.5	9.4	7.4
Cuba	11.2		G			95	4411	15.4	1068	12.6	10.0	7.6
Ecuador	*12.2*	*2130*	*G/P*	*97*	*78*	*90*	*3136*	*0.6*	*667*	*8.7*	*8.6*	*8.1*
El Salvador	6.4	2000	P/G	99	45	76	1135	1.5	587	12.3	13.6	3.6
Paraguay	5.6	1440	G			83	7429	0	796	5.2	5.5	3.5
Peru	26.1	2080	P/G			75	5906	0.18	700	9.3	6.3	5.9
Dom. Rep.	8.6	2130	P/G				3081	6.8	809	8.2	8.3	9.7
Uruguay	3.3	6000	G				2105	0	1918	11.2	9.8	5.5

*P = Private; G = Government.

Source: OLADE.

which was liquidated. While these companies were established as public limited companies, the State still holds the majority stake through the Solidarity Fund (FS). Moreover, EMAAP (the utility of Quito) owns a small electrical plant. In addition to the above, there are three private power providers (IPP) including Electroecuador Inc., Electroquil, and Machala Power, which represented 16.5 percent of installed capacity and 18.4 percent of annual production in October 2002.

- **Transmission.** A national transmission company, Transelectric S.A., was created to develop the national power grid.
- **Distribution.** INECEL's stake in the existing distribution companies was transferred to the FS. EMELEC, a private company since 1925, had to be placed under the administration of the Regulatory Authority because of its financial and legal problems.
- **Creation of a wholesale electricity market.** In April 1999, a wholesale electricity market was created in which contracts are made between generators and distributors and, the system operates on the basis of cost statements made by the generators. The CENACE (National Center for Energy Control) is responsible for standards and procedures.
- **Legal and regulatory framework.** After its founding, CONELEC (the regulatory and supervisory authority), with the support of the National Modernization Council CONAM, prepared all the essential technical regulations for the functioning of the sector. It also developed several detailed procedures necessary for the functioning of the wholesale electricity market, and for monitoring service quality.
- **Organization of a regulatory authority.** The regulations governing the wholesale electricity market and the components of the electrical rates that do not depend on market processes (transmission and distribution), are regulated by CONELEC.
- **Preparation for privatized distribution.** In 2001 and 2002, the groundwork was laid for the privatization of 17 distribution companies in four groups. This process reached an advanced stage (data gathering, preparation of bidding documents, and valuation of the four groups of companies), but was not completed for a variety of political, institutional, and regulatory reasons, and also because of unfavorable regional conditions that limited the interest of international investors in distribution companies. In fact, even when the companies were regrouped into only two blocks, (the Highlands and the Coast), there were only three prequalified investors. This process was handled by CONAM, the authority that has led sector reform.

As a result, the current state of the sector is somewhat peculiar, composed almost entirely by state-owned companies (except for the three independent power providers [IPP]), and subject to legislation inspired by principles that are essentially applicable to private companies.

Telecommunications

STRUCTURE OF THE SECTOR AND MAIN PLAYERS. The telecommunications sector in Ecuador continues to be one of the least developed in Latin America and has been among the last to open up to competition. The liberalization and privatization of the sector have not been consolidated owing to the failure to sell part of the operators on several occasions, and to Congress' unwillingness to pass new legislation that would strengthen and bring greater transparency to the sector. The local fixed telephony market is still controlled by Andinatel and Pacifictel, in the highland and the coastal areas, respectively. The exception is ETAPA, a municipal company that provides services exclusively in the city of Cuenca. Recent progress was made in the form of competitive bidding for three licenses for local wireless service (known as "WLL" (Wireless Local Loop), which connects the telephone switchboard with the subscriber via radio signals instead of wires). Although this technology will increase the coverage of local service, its short geographic reach and relatively high operating costs means it will have little overall impact on the market. These licenses were granted to two local companies—Consorcio TV Cable and Ecuador Telecom—while the third license was not issued for lack of interested parties. The cellular telephone market remains under the duopoly of Otecel (Bell South Ecuador) and Conecel (América Móvil), and although it has grown an average of 50 percent in the past two years, it has not yet demonstrated the penetration and rate reductions seen in other countries in the region. In November 2002, both operators obtained a court order to suspend tenders for a third license, arguing that the new player would receive undue privileges. The lack of additional competitors has constrained the growth of the market.

LEGAL AND REGULATORY FRAMEWORK. In general, it has not been possible to consolidate the reform of the telecommunications sector. The lack of political support has meant that despite several attempts at legal reform over the past seven years, no new law has been passed. According to the most recent ranking of the telecommunications sector by the Pyramid Research consultancy firm, the regulatory framework and the level of competition in Ecuador is one of the poorest in the region. Of the 18 countries studied, Ecuador ranks 16th and 13th in those two categories, respectively. The main challenges now are the existence of contradictory regulations, delays in the approval of the new Telecommunications Act, and finally, the confusion and overlap of responsibilities among the three regulatory authorities. Although it is argued that each of these has a different function, there is in fact a great deal of confusion regarding their functions and responsibilities: the National Telecommunications Council (CONATEL) is responsible for setting state policy in the sector and establishing interconnection regulations and the terms for concessions; the Telecommunications Authority (SUPTEL) is by law the only independent body responsible for the control of telecommunications in the country; and the National Secretariat of Telecommunications (SENATEL) prepares the National Telecommunications Development Plan and signs concessions contracts in the sector. International experience shows that having a single regulatory authority, independent of any operator and with sufficient power to supervise private operators in the sector, is the best way to ensure transparency, boost private investment, and support sector development. As far as tariff regulation is concerned, CONATEL has approved the adjustment of rates. However, in late 2002, the executive branch of government ordered a rate freeze for the rest of the year, which will delay the January 2003 target date of the adjustment plan. Another pending issue is interconnection, which is essential in order for competition to exist in the international long-distance, cellular, and WLL markets. Although interconnection regulations were only recently issued, they nonetheless contradict other regulations on several points.

Transport

CHARACTERISTICS OF THE SECTOR. The transport sector represents 6.2 percent of GDP, a percentage that remained relatively constant from 1995 to 2001. Like GDP at the national level, transport activity declined sharply in 1999. Seven percent of the state's general budget for 2002, prepared by the Ministry of Economy and Finance (MEF), was allocated to the transport sector. Furthermore, almost 10 percent of transfer payments to provincial and municipal governments (called local governments—LGs) are also earmarked for the transport sector.

INSTITUTIONAL FRAMEWORK. Various government bodies, with different degrees and levels of interdependence, are responsible for the planning, construction, maintenance, and operation of the transport system in Ecuador. At the national government level, several ministries and therefore several councils and commissions are involved. Among the most important in terms of highways is the Ministry of Public Works (MOP), which is responsible at the national level for building and maintaining the *national highway* network. At the moment, certain stretches of the state highway network (the main network) are operated under concession to private companies working in different regions of the country. As for *rural roads*, provincial and municipal councils, the Ministry of Social Welfare, the FISE (the Ecuadoran Social Investment Fund), CORPECUADOR (a regional development corporation), and now, the MOP, with its Local Road Works Unit (UCV), are all involved in building and repairing rural roads in different provinces throughout the country. At the provincial level, provincial councils are responsible for highway construction, maintenance, and rehabilitation.

The Civil Aviation Office (DAC) is responsible for the construction and maintenance of the national airports. Although the construction of private runways is very common, only the DAC can authorize this. Construction projects for new airports in the cities of Quito and Guayaquil are under the management and responsibility of CONAM and the respective bodies created by the municipal councils of these cities. DIGMER is responsible for *maritime transport*, administrating and controlling the largest ports, such as Esmeraldas, Manta, Guayaquil and Port Bolívar. DIGMER is also responsible for regulating river traffic on the navigable rivers of the coast, the mountains, and the eastern regions of the country. ENFE, the National Railway Company, is responsible for *the railway sector*. This form of transport is not heavily used, and is not really significant at the national level. Its tracks and trains are obsolete, service is poor, and certain lines of service have been suspended.

REGULATION AND CONTROL OF THE TRANSPORT SERVICES: Passenger and cargo transport by highway, both nationally and internationally, is handled by the National Land Transit and Transport Council (CNTTT), which regulates passenger rates. The CNTTT is attached to the Ministry of the Interior and has 14 members. At the national level, a rate was established for popular (basic) transport. Freight charges are not subject to established regulations and depend on the free market and each transport company. Air freight rates are established by the National Civil Aviation Council and by the Civil Aviation Authority. Rail transport rates are established by ENFE, with different fares for national and foreign passengers. At the regional level, the 20 Provincial Land Transit and Transport Councils, the Guayas Transit Commission, and the Quito Metropolitan Transport Service and Administration Company are all involved. Finally, the National Merchant Marine and Ports Council determines policies and regulations for this form of transport.

B. Diagnosis of the Main Problems and Challenges

Water Supply and Sanitation Sector

CHARACTERISTICS OF THE SECTOR. The water supply and sanitation sector in Ecuador is characterized by (i) low levels of coverage, especially in rural areas; (ii) low quality of services and inefficiency; (iii) low recovery of costs through tariffs and high dependence on transfer payments from the central government to cover operating deficits; (iv) an incomplete legal and regulatory framework, leading to overlapping functions and confusion within the national government and among different levels of government regarding the role of different actors; and (v) the lack of an integrated national water resource management system.

COVERAGE. Despite significant improvements made over the past decades (total water and sanitation coverage rose from 48 and 43 percent in 1980 to 67 and 57 percent, respectively, in 1999), water supply and sanitation coverage in Ecuador remains relatively low compared to other South American countries, even when this coverage is adjusted to take into account differences in per capita GDP in the region. Figure 1 shows that current levels of coverage for adequate water and sanitation services are particularly low for water supply (both urban and rural) and for rural sanitation. On the other hand, urban sanitation stands out as a subsector with relatively

Figure 1. Water Supply and Sanitation Coverage in Latin America (in percentage, compared with per capita GDP)

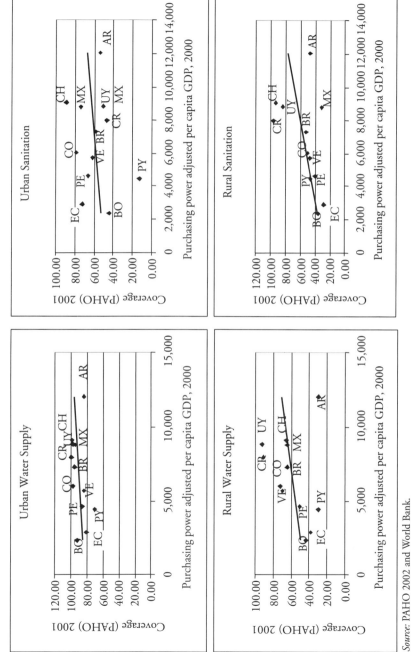

Source: PAHO 2002 and World Bank.

high coverage. *Water supply*[5] coverage is 82 percent in urban areas and 39 percent in rural areas; and *sanitation*[6] coverage is 73 percent in urban areas and 29 percent in rural areas.

INEQUALITIES IN THE PROVISION OF SERVICES. Coverage of appropriate water and sanitation services is characterized by a number of inequalities in provisions.[7]

- **Regional inequalities**: As Table 4 shows, the lowest levels of potable water and sanitation coverage are on the coast and in the east of the country.
- **Inequalities between urban and rural areas**. In percentage terms, rates of coverage with an appropriate services are higher in urban areas than in rural ones (twice as high for water supply and 2.5 times as high for sanitation).
- **Inequalities in terms of income level**. Both in urban and rural areas, low-income families are those with the lowest levels of access to water and sanitation services (see Figure 2).

QUALITY OF SERVICES. At the national level, it is estimated that only half of potable water supply installations have disinfection systems and only 11 percent of urban

Table 4. Coverage of Potable Water and Sewage Services, 1999 (percent)

| Service | National | Region | | | |
		Highlands	Coast	East	Islands
Potable water	67				
Urban	82	90	**70**	**73**	98
Rural	39	56	**22**	**26**	48
Sanitation	57				
Urban[a]	73	83	**60**	**61**	**19**
Rural	29	34	30	**22**	**22**

Note: Boldface shows coverage under national average.
Source: MIDUVI; Coverage for piped water supply in urban areas, appropriate piped or point source supply in rural areas.

5. Potable water service available either via household connection or protected and easily accessible public sources (standpipes, wells, springs, rainwater collection systems).
6. Sanitation service either via sanitary sewerage system (untreated) or on-site disposal systems (dry latrines or pour-flush latrines).
7. "Plan Nacional de Desarrollo del Sector de Agua Potable y Saneamiento Básico," G. Yepes, B. Gómez, and E. Carvajal, December 2002; pp. 11–14.

Figure 2. Access to Potable Water Supply by Income Level

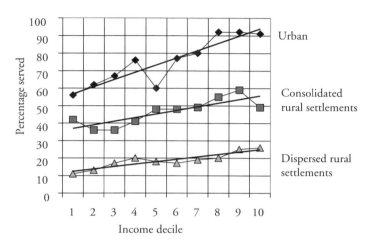

Note: 1 = lowest; 10 = highest.
Source: "Desigualdades en el acceso, uso y gasto con el agua potable en América Latina y el Caribe," Ecuador, Technical Report Series No. 5, Pan-American Health Organization (PAHO), Washington D.C., February 2001.

systems have full treatment plants.[8] Even in big cities such as Guayaquil there are still areas with intermittent water supply (12 hours of service in residential neighborhoods in the center and southern parts of the city) and low pressure (less than 0.5 Bar in the south, center, and poor outskirts). In Guayaquil, however, a concession contract with INTERAGUA establishes clear goals for achieving continuous service and guaranteed minimum pressure within five years.[9] This is not the case in the 12 medium-size cities (with populations between 100,000 and 300,000) administrated by 11 municipal utilities and 1 municipal water department. In these cities, the potable water supply is intermittent in 55 percent of urban systems and 60 percent of the water supply is not disinfected. The poor quality of water means extra costs for users who disinfect it at home, in addition to medical costs and lost time resulting from water-related illnesses—for lack of treatment. The poor quality of water in many systems has a particularly severe impact on the poor, since at the national level only 40 percent of families among the poorest one-tenth of the pop-

8. "Project Appraisal Document, Rural and Small Towns Water Supply and Sanitation Project (PRAGUAS)," World Bank, September 2000, p. 6.
9. "Proceso de Modernización de los Servicios Públicos de Agua Potable y Saneamiento de Guayaquil," ECAPAG, 2001.

ulation treat their water at home, compared to 90 percent of families among the richest one-tenth (see Figure 3).

EFFICIENCY OF SERVICE. The available figures suggest that water supply and sanitation services in the large and medium-sized cities of Ecuador are very inefficient given that the number of employees in almost all utilities (except Guayaquil/INTERAGUA) is 2 to 7 times as high per 1,000 water connections than the best levels in Latin America (see Table 5).

The conclusion is that in addition to low tariffs, excessive personnel costs also deprive companies of the resources they need to extend coverage to poor, unserved population groups. In 2001, for example, personnel costs at EMAAP/Quito were equivalent to 115 percent of income. Based on the little data available, it is difficult to reach a conclusion regarding the efficiency of service in small municipalities where employees are often shared with other services and separate accounts are not kept. However, regional experience suggests that the absence of economies of scale in these small systems (needed to maintain technically skilled personnel and specialized equipment) goes hand in hand with inefficient service.

Figure 3. In-home Water Treatment by Income

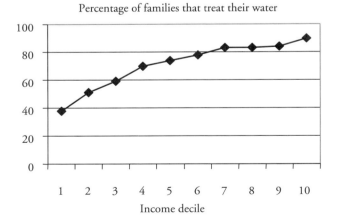

Note: 1 = poorest; 10 = richest.
Source: "Desigualdades en el acceso, uso y gasto con el agua potable en América Latina y el Caribe," Ecuador, Technical Report Series No. 5, Pan-American Health Organization (PAHO), Washington D.C., February 2001.

Table 5. Operational Efficiency of Water Utilities in Large and Medium-Size Cities

Company	Water connections (total)	Number of employees (N)	Employees (N) per 1,000 water connections
Cities with more than 1 million inhabitants			
Quito (EMAAP)	318,000	2,060	6.5
Guayaquil (INTERAGUA)	266,000 (estimate)	900 (estimate)	3.4 (estimate)
Cities with 100 to 300 thousand inhabitants (examples)			
Santo Domingo de los Colorados	20,375	196	9.6
Machala	29,685	173	5.8
Manta	29,000	220	7.6
Portoviejo	24,051	340	14.1
Duran	27,369	195	7.1
Ambato	34,741	300	8.6
Riobamba	30,122	180	6.0
Milagro	16,351	69	4.2
Ibarra	23,866	205	8.6
Esmeraldas	22,387	167	7.5
Examples of the best water supply companies in Latin America			
Santiago (Chile)	1,200,000		1.2
SANEPAR-Paraná (Brazil)	1,914,000		2.6

Source: MIDUVI and the World Bank.

OVERALL SECTOR FINANCING. The water and sanitation sector is characterized by generally low tariffs and high dependence on transfer payments from the central government and municipalities. At the national level, cumulative income from tariffs (approximately $US74 million in 2001) covers only 67 percent of the costs of adequate operation and routine maintenance. This drops to 58 percent if we consider debt service (approximately $US18 million a year). The deficit is closed by transfers to the water and sanitation sector by the national government (approximately $US114 million in 2001), and by the municipalities (approximately $US30 million in 2001). Of central government transfers, approximately $US64 million were made through MIDUVI in 2001 ($US6 million from the Solidarity Fund and $US58 million from its own budget), and $US50 million came from a telephone tax. These national and municipal transfers cover the deficit created by low tariff revenue in the companies and municipalities directly responsible for water and sanitation services, leaving about $US90 million a year for modest investments in 2001. These investments come to about $US40 per connection per year—which is less than is spent in other more developed Latin American countries (Brazil spends $US52 per water connection per year, and Uruguay $US59 per water connection per year). Figure 4 breaks down aggregate income and costs for providers of water supply services at the national level.

DISTRIBUTION OF SUBSIDIES. The importance of the different transfers to the sector varies according to the size of municipalities. In 2001, two cities (Quito and Guayaquil) received approximately 60 percent of all telephone tax transfer payments, though they represent only 28 percent of the country's population. In its present form, the special telephone tax—which has existed for nearly 40 years—is collected by the telephone companies. The companies then pass it on to the central government, which in turn distributes it among the potable water service providers in the area where the tax was generated. This form of distributing the income generated by the tax is apparently due more to tradition than to the letter of the law, which requires only that this income be used "... for the companies or local bodies that are responsible for providing potable water services, allocating this money

Figure 4. Aggregate Income and Costs of Water and Sanitation Services

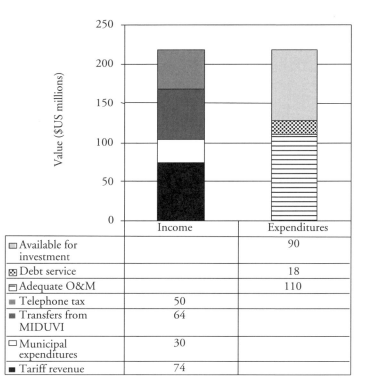

	Income	Expenditures
▫ Available for investment		90
▨ Debt service		18
▱ Adequate O&M		110
▨ Telephone tax	50	
▪ Transfers from MIDUVI	64	
▢ Municipal expenditures	30	
▪ Tariff revenue	74	

Source: Yepes, Gómez, and Carvajal 2002.

exclusively to potable water supply projects in all the cantons of the Republic."[10] To compensate for this imbalance in the distribution of the telephone tax, and given low revenue generation from tariffs, small municipal governments use a large part of their budgets to subsidize water and sanitation services, as can be seen in Table 6.

CRITERIA FOR ALLOCATING SUBSIDIES. Apart from the amounts transferred to the sector by the national government and the municipalities, it is important to consider that almost all of these resources are transfered without conditions that could encourage greater efficiency or quality of service to the public. In theory, resources from the telephone tax must be used for investment projects. In practice, however, they are often used by many service providers to finance operating costs that they cannot cover with income from tariffs. Even the SAPYSB—whose role as a body governing the water and sanitation sector makes it responsible for defining financial policy to support the sector—transferred 20 times more resources to service providers in 2002 (with no conditions of any kind) than was provided via the PRAGUAS project (Water and Sanitation Project for Rural Communities and Small Municipalities—financed by the World Bank through loan 7035-EC). The PRAGUAS project requires that both municipalities and rural communities comply with conditions aimed at improving the quality, coverage, and sustainability of their water supply services to qualify for project financing.

IMPACT OF TARIFFS AND TRANSFER PAYMENTS ON THE POOR. The poverty affecting a large part of the Ecuadoran population, as well as the fact that water is both a social and an economic good, is often involved as justification for low water tariffs. Unfor-

Table 6. Distribution of the Telephone Tax and Municipal Expenditure on Water and Sanitation ($US/inhabitant in 2001)

City	Telephone tax transfers	Total municipal expend.	Municipal W + S expend.	W+ S % total
Quito	8.40	31.80	0	0%
Guayaquil	4.69	63.80	0.18	0.2%
Cities of 100,000–300,000 inhabitants	2.27	56.50	2.80	5%
Cities of 30,000–100,000 inhabitants	2.52	68.40	7.90	12%
Cities with fewer than 30,000 inhabitants	1.91	91.10	9.60	11%

Source: Yepes, Gómez, and Carvajal 2002.

10. Law Reforming the Internal Tax Regime of May 2001, Article 38, added to Article 84 of the Tax Regime, which is partially quoted above. (Official Register number 325).

tunately, it is not the poorest who benefit from the lowest rates and transfer payments to the sector. As Figure 2 shows, almost 40 percent of the urban poor (lowest 3 income deciles) does not have access to piped water supply. The situation is even worse in consolidated rural settlements, where more than 60 percent of the poorest population (lowest 3 income deciles) does not have household connections. These people, who often get their water from untreated sources far from home (in rural areas) or from tank trucks (in peri-urban areas) spend much more time and money getting water of unreliable quality than their connected neighbors. In Machala,[11] (see Table 7), for example, it is estimated that a poor family connected to the water supply system spends only 0.4 percent of its monthly income to cover its water needs, while an unconnected family spends approximately 9 percent.

The World Health Organization recommends that no more than a maximum 5 percent of household income be spent on water supply. When the figures above are compared to this standard, it must be concluded that the current low tariffs deprive water and sanitation service providers of the resources they need to extend services to uncovered areas—areas that pay much more for water of unreliable quality. This deficit is only partly compensated by national and municipal transfer payments, which cover little more than operating and maintenance costs, and become a subsidy for the relatively privileged population that already has piped water supply.

INCOMPLETE REGULATORY AND LEGAL FRAMEWORK. Ecuador's National Water and Sanitation Policy (Executive Decree 2766 of July 30, 2002) establishes guidelines and basic principles to increase water and sanitation coverage. It also aims to

Table 7. Machala: Monthly Expenditure on Water Supply and Sanitation Services—Families with and without Home Connection

	User	
Item	With home connection	Supplied by tank truck
Monthly consumption, poor family (m³)	15[a]	4 to 5[b]
Monthly expenditure per family	1.20[c]	29.00
Monthly expenditure (percentage of family income)	0.4	9.0

a. World Bank estimates.
b. World Bank estimates based on approximately 30 liters/person/day.
c. The rate depends on the type of housing. The amount indicated is for the most inexpensive housing.

Source: World Bank.

---

11. "National Plan for the Development of the Potable Water and Basic Sanitation Sector," G. Yepes, B. Gómez, and E. Carvajal, October 2002; p. 13.

improve the quality of services provided and make more efficient use of water resources, all within a framework open to participation by the private sector and benefiting communities. However, the document does not take a clear position on key issues such as subsidies to the sector nor does it establish objective criteria for selecting the municipalities receiving them. Current legislation also does not establish an independent regulator of water and sanitation services—an issue that must be dealt with in the framework of a new Water and Sanitation Law, to be prepared by international consultants hired by the CONAM and monitored jointly by the CONAM and the SAPYSB. The new law should also more clearly define the responsibilities and functions of the various national bodies involved in the sector (see Table 1), and propose a clear division of sectoral responsibilities among the different levels of government.

Management of Water Resources

GENERAL SITUATION. Although in general Ecuador has sufficient water resources to cover its needs, there is constantly increasing competition for water use and greater conflict over its allocation. This leads to environmental degradation that affects poor and indigenous communities disproportionally. The efforts made to date by the government to protect water quality, promote efficient water use (especially in agriculture), increase the availability of water resources over the course of the year, and control flooding have been insufficient. The country needs a systematic long-term program to modernize the management of its water resources and to guarantee sustainable management both at the local and national levels.

MAIN CHALLENGES. The main problems affecting the sustainable management of water resources are as follows: (i) lack of updated information on the quantity, quality, and seasonal availability of water and its use by different subsectors (human consumption, agriculture, and so on), which impedes sectoral planning (stock was last taken of water resources in 1985); (ii) lack of political consensus regarding water as a social and economic good; (iii) weakness of the institutions responsible for managing water resources and overlapping functions among the National Council on Water Resources (CNRH), the ministry of agriculture, and the ministry of the environment, provincial councils, regional development corporations, and municipalities; (iv) degradation of water quality in several rivers (some already considered "dead") due to chemical discharges and pesticides; (v) flooding (especially on the coast) and erosion (accelerated by deforestation); (vi) sedimentation of hydroelectric reservoirs (the Paute station has lost approximately 20 percent of its generating capacity in the past decade); (vii) increasing conflict among different users of the resource, which is especially harmful to poor and indigenous groups; and (viii) lack of an integrated water resource management law and limited application of existing legislation.

Energy Sector

The main problems in this sector have been identified during previous Bank operations. They include (i) inefficient, incomplete reform; (ii) institutional vulnerability; (iii) doubtful sustainability of the wholesale electricity market (MEM); (iv) tariff adjustments necessary for financial sustainability that have yet to be made; (v) uncertain availability of resources for investment; (vi) insufficient coverage; and (vii) incomplete implementation of environmental policy in the sector.

INEFFICIENT, INCOMPLETE REFORM. Despite having implemented important structural changes, the sector remains practically the same as before the reforms. State-owned companies dominate, both in generation and distribution, and do not respond to economic and financial incentives, but rather to local or national political interests. This leads to low efficiency, which is reflected in the figures on losses and tariff collection, mainly in the area of distribution (see Table 8).

Losses came to 23 percent in 2001 at the national level, with large differences among companies. For example, EMELEC and Empresa Eléctrica Quito (EEQ) registered 25 percent and 16.1 percent, respectively, whereas Centro Sur, with a market that is five to six times smaller, registered only 11.4 percent. In general, the companies with high losses are characterized by high nontechnical losses, corresponding to unbilled energy (6 percent at EEQ, 15 percent at EMELEC, and only 2 percent at Centro Sur), which could be reduced with more concerted antifraud management.

Another important indicator is collection efficiency: the percentage of energy billed and effectively paid for by customers. At the national level, collection stood at an average of 90 percent in 2001; in competently managed companies this figure should be over 95 percent. Proof that this is possible is the fact that 4 companies have collection rates between 95 and 100 percent and 6 are between 90 and 95 percent, while 10 have lower rates. Losses and collection efficiency are factors that have a direct impact on the financial performance of these companies, almost all of which showed net losses for 2001.

The figures above indicate that of 100MWh delivered to distributors, 10MWh are lost in the network (technical losses) and 13MWh are consumed but not billed—and that of 77MWh billed, only 69MWh are collected. Efficient management should reduce nontechnical losses to less than 3 percent and should increase collection to above 95 percent. At these levels, instead of collecting the equivalent of 69MWh per 100MWh, the equivalent of 83MWh would be collected, with a corresponding 20 percent increase in income.

In the present context, there is little prospect that this inefficiency will be reduced, given the lack of an authority or agencies whose interests are directly affected by inefficient management. The current owner of the sector is the Solidarity Fund (FS), a body designed to administer proceeds from the sale of state-owned companies, and to allocate them to social sectors. The fund was not designed to

Table 8. Main Characteristics of Distribution Companies in 2001

	Technical indicators							Financial indicators		
								Liquidity	Solvency	Cost-effectiveness
Company	Electricity invoiced (MWh)	Electricity losses (%)	Peak demand (MW)	Load factor (%)	Average annual customers	Average price (¢/kWh)	% collected / invoices (a)	Current assets / short-term liabilities	Total liabilities / total assets	Returns / assets (b)
Ambato	229,577	14.0	63	52	136,014	7.7	94	2.75	0.20	(0.08)
Azogues	53,089	10.0	15	44	23,221	6.6	93	2.61	0.13	(0.09)
Bolívar	34,662	18.9	12	42	36,926	7.5	63	3.16	0.17	(0.14)
Centro Sur	443,962	11.4	102	56	210,868	6.8	101	1.73	0.12	(0.06)
Cotopaxi	141,025	17.8	38	51	70,392	7.9	88	3.02	0.07	(0.03)
El Oro	280,962	25.7	72	60	131,988	6.9	95	0.84	0.84	(1.66)
Emelec	2,246,711	25.0	526	65	340,595	5.8	91		0.51	(0.26)
Esmeraldas	188,523	27.2	47	63	56,713	8.0	75	0.79	0.08	(0.56)
Galapagos	14,443	11.4	4	48	4,665	6.3	85		0.58	(0.67)
Guayas-Los Ríos	506,945	34.0	137	64	134,595	7.8	76	0.62	0.69	(1.01)
Los Ríos	138,457	26.9	39	55	60,367	7.0	84	0.93	0.42	(0.32)
Manabí	504,317	27.6	130	61	171,522	7.5	70	0.79	0.53	(0.56)
Milagro	175,702	40.2	59	57	84,643	7.2	86	1.24	0.18	(0.19)
Norte	248,397	17.3	65	53	131,326	7.2	93	3.53	0.23	(0.12)
Quito	2,065,354	16.1	475	59	536,635	5.7	97	2.44	0.07	0.02
Riobamba	144,873	18.3	40	51	107,574	6.9	94			
Sta. Elena	184,958	25.8	56	51	59,414	7.7	90	2.55	0.30	(0.25)
Sto. Domingo	172,496	24.8	47	55	82,253	7.2	104	1.29	0.3	(0.19)
Sucumbíos	38,995	32.5	16	41	21,027	8.4	61		0.13	(0.25)
Sur	131,758	15.1	36	49	102,940	7.2	72	1.85	0.29	(0.11)
Total	7,945,209	22.6	1980	59	2,503,676	6.5	90			

(a) Amounts may be higher than 100 percent due to recovery of debts outstanding from previous years.

(b) A number in parenthesis indicates a negative result.

Sources: CONELEC 2001 statistics. Audited balances 2001, Solidarity Fund.

actually manage these companies. The FS has a budget of only $2 million a year to control the management of 19 distribution companies, five generators, and the transmission company. It is worth noting that the fundamental change introduced by private participation is the profit motive.[12] The impact of this change should not be confused with the effect of restructuring. The effort already made to restructure the sector will have been in vain if incentives are not introduced that ultimately produce the social benefits for which sector reform was undertaken in the first place. At present, despite its role as majority stakeholder, the hands of the FS are tied by local interests in the companies under its control.

INSTITUTIONAL VULNERABILITY. One of the main goals of reform in the sector is to attract private investment in energy generation and distribution. This requires a clear legal and institutional setting, one element of which is stability, both in terms of the rules and principles governing the functioning of the sector and the institutions that govern it. At present, this is not the case, particularly regarding the regulatory authority (CONELEC). While there is a consensus that CONELEC carries out rigorous technical studies, there is general distrust regarding the decisions made by its management, which is dominated by representatives of the executive branch whose disproportionate influence can block decisions of vital importance. Proof of this is the tariff freeze ordered in April 2002, which aborted a process of rate adjustment that would have finally raised rates to economically viable levels.

Furthermore, CONELEC also manages companies placed under the care of administrators, as one of its many functions. This function entails serious problems, as it leads to conflicts of interest, since the regulatory authority has an incentive to favor companies under its care, and to help them recover. An example of this conflict can be seen in the current intervention in EMELEC, the company with the largest market share in the country, which is not now subject to the same rules governing the transfer of operating revenue as the other distribution companies. This affects the wholesale electricity market and foments a perception of discretionality and unfairness in the decisions of the regulatory authority.

QUESTIONABLE SUSTAINABILITY OF THE WHOLESALE ELECTRICITY MARKET. The wholesale electricity market has been competently managed by CENACE, which projects an image of seriousness, transparency, and fairness, especially in the critical function of network operations and in market administration—its two main functions. Proof of this is the confidence it instills in market agents and the absence of lawsuits involving its actions, though it should be noted that until now the market has involved only public bodies, with very few exceptions. However—and perhaps in large part owing to this fact—the liquidation of transactions in the wholesale elec-

---

12. Robert Bacon, "Restructuring the Power Sector: The Case of Small Systems." The World Bank, FPD Note No.10, June 1994.

tricity market has not had satisfactory results, as distributors have (to date) accumulated debts of $US430 million, which is equivalent to eight months' billing for the entire sector. The wholesale electricity market's deficit originates in excessively low rates (applicable to all the distributors), in delays in payments (applicable specifically to EMELEC, which is the biggest MEM debtor), and in great inefficiency in distribution. Part of this deficit (about $US40 million in 2001) is financed by the government and involves thermal generators' debts to PetroEcuador.

Given the obviously insufficient collection of tariffs, the income of the distribution companies (with the notable exception of EMELEC) is managed through a trust that pays according to the following order of priority: (a) a percentage of added distribution value (ADV) for the distribution companies, (b) payments for supplies contracted with private thermal generators, (c) payments contracted through international interconnections, (d) payments for fuel used by state-owned companies, (e) remuneration of the transmission company, and (f) payments for transactions in the spot market, where most of the deficit accumulates. In the end, debt with generators translates into nonpayment of obligations contracted with Petrocomercial (a subsidiary of the government-owned PetroEcuador corporation) that does not cut off fuel supplies to the electricity sector, even when it is not paid. This accumulation of debt will most likely be dealt with by *ad hoc* measures that do not respond to economic principles. It is not financially healthy or useful for the debt level to rise above current levels.

TARIFF INCREASES NECESSARY FOR THE FINANCIAL SUSTAINABILITY OF THE SECTOR. The financial sustainability of the sector is intimately linked to the deficit in the spot market. The average rate for regulated customers in June 2002 was 8.6¢/Kwh and has been frozen there since April 2002. The efficient level of cost has been estimated at about 10.4¢/Kwh,[13] meaning that a hike of approximately 21 percent is needed to reach that goal. The difference is concentrated mostly among residential users, who paid an average rate of 8.7¢/Kwh in June 2002. This, however, hides a crossed subsidy that favors those who consume less than the average for each electric company. This subsidy covers a wide range of consumers (about 62 percent of consumers in October 2001) and is therefore not really focused on the neediest sectors of the population. In addition, the sector's financial problems are worsened by high technical and nontechnical losses, which accounted for 27 percent of the energy deliv-

---

13. Calculations by CONELEC and from the report, "Impacto de las Variaciones de los Precios de la Energía sobre el Costo de Vida y Costos de Producción Industrial" (Impact on Variations in Energy Prices on Inflation and Industrial Production Costs), February 2002, appendix 2.

It is worth mentioning that efficiency cost is sensitive to three main factors: hydroelectric production, international fuel prices, and hypothetical costs used to calculate the AVD.

ered to the wholesale electricity market in the first half of 2002. This is more than double the acceptable amount for an average, well-managed system. It is clearly possible to reduce these losses, considering that several distribution companies show good results in this area (see Table 8 above). The recovery of 50 percent of the losses (which is approximately equivalent to commercial losses due to energy delivered but not billed) would mean about 130 GWh a month, which would increase income in the sector by $11 million a month.

Regarding tariff increases, there are doubts regarding the calculation for added value of distribution (AVD), which can vary according to the characteristics of each company, but generally is in the 3 to 4¢/Kwh range. With a margin of 1¢/Kwh for transmission and generating costs of 5¢/Kwh, the reference cost comes to approximately 9–10¢/Kwh, which is near the desired rate of 10.5¢/Kwh. As has been mentioned, a significant part of the sector's problems involve inefficiency resulting in losses and a low collection rate. At present, the average wholesale electricity market price is around 5¢/Kwh; for every 100Kwh bought at a cost of $5, distributors collect the equivalent of only 69Kwh, which at current rates means income of about $5.9. Since their highest priority is to cover their own costs in terms of the AVD, a deficit with wholesale electricity markets is inevitable.

UNCERTAIN MOBILIZATION OF INVESTMENT RESOURCES. Gas production has recently begun (by Machala Power) in the Gulf of Guayaquil, which offers potential for the development of low-cost resources in the Ecuadoran system via combined cycle plants. At the same time, the national grid has been interconnected with Colombia, thereby providing access to a market where energy moves at lower cost than is now the case in Ecuador. Interconnections with Peru are also being prepared. These developments guarantee short-term supply (2003–04) for the system, but nagging questions remain regarding medium and long term sustainability. Transmission and distribution companies also face major difficulties in mobilizing financing for investments necessary for maintaining quality service (to say nothing of expanding service), owing to their financial situation and lack of access to capital markets. These difficulties are cause for concern in the case of the transmission company that is the heart of the electric system. Reform of this sector was focused on attracting private investors, but the problems associated with legal uncertainty and regulatory stability, in addition to smaller numbers of strategic international investors and changes in their investment strategies, threaten the mobilization of private investment. For example, the development of new power plants using gas from the Gulf of Guayaquil requires investment in new wells and new plants, which will not occur if doubts continue as to the stability of the legal framework and the sustainability of the wholesale electricity market. If institutional weaknesses are not dealt with, the state will likely face supply crises forcing it to take on investment risks, either through the companies in which it has a stake or as a guarantor of "PPA" contracts, which would contradict one of the goals of reform—that is, to substantially reduce the state's role in the provision of electrical services.

INSUFFICIENT COVERAGE. Electrification is now being carried out with the resources of the Rural and Peri-Urban Electrification Fund (FERUM), provided by commercial and industrial users, paid into the FS to later finance electrification projects proposed by the distribution companies. Most of these projects consist of extending networks and attending to the needs of the population in the area covered by the interconnected system. However, new initiative and alternative approaches are needed to extend service to the most remote rural areas, including mobilizing communities and local private agents to develop decentralized systems.

INCOMPLETE IMPLEMENTATION OF ENVIRONMENTAL POLICY IN THE SECTOR. In the framework of the Integrated Environmental Management System (SUMA), the Ministry of the Environment, in collaboration with the World Bank and the Inter-American Development Bank, prepared a draft decree regulating environmental impact studies, licensing, and environmental control and monitoring of the different sectors of the economy, including the energy sector. One of the components of the Bank's electricity and telecoms project (PROMEC) is to boost CONELEC's environmental planning and management in the electrical energy sector in order to comply with these mandates and to establish environmental regulations. Although the corresponding unit has been created, it is still not fully operational and does not have a work plan.

Telecommunications Sector

OVERVIEW OF THE SECTOR. During the past decade, Ecuador has practically tripled its number of fixed lines, reaching 1.35 million in September 2002, while doubling the density of telephone connections from 5 to 11 lines per 100 inhabitants. Compared to other countries in the region, Ecuador is below the Latin American average of 15 lines per 100 inhabitants. However, considering its per capita income, Ecuador has a higher level of penetration than other countries with the same level of development (see Figure 5). There are great differences in coverage within Ecuador: in the province of Pichincha (the capital of which is Quito), one out of five inhabitants has telephone service, while in provinces such as Orellana and Sucumbíos, there is one telephone line for every 30 inhabitants. This situation is similar to that faced by many other countries in Latin America, such as Mexico, Brazil, and Bolivia.

Countries with low fixed telephone line coverage, such as Paraguay, have seen a great increase in cellular telephones since this market was opened to free competition, at times quickly overtaking the number of fixed lines. In September 2002, Ecuador registered nearly 1.3 million cellular telephone subscribers, equivalent to 10 percent of the population. Compared to the region as a whole, Ecuador is below the average of 14 subscribers per 100 inhabitants and is behind other countries with a similar level of economic development (see Figure 6).

There are several factors that account for the poorly developed cellular market, particularly the scarce competition and late introduction of mobile phone technol-

Figure 5. Percentage of the Population with Fixed Telephone Line (2001)

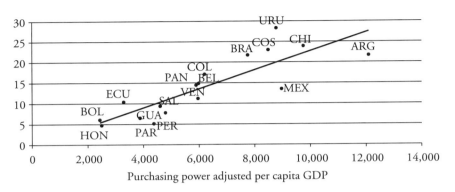

Source: World Bank.

Figure 6. Percentage of the Population with Cellular Phones (2001)

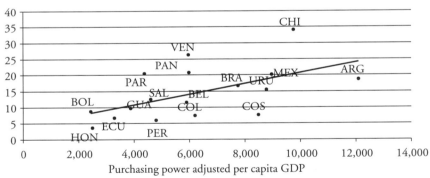

Source: World Bank.

ogy to Ecuador (in 1993), making it one of the last countries in the region to acquire it, ahead only of Panama and Honduras. It is significant that in 2001 (and during the first half of 2002), the cellular market grew by an average of 50 percent per year, because of the inability of fixed line companies to respond to demand and because of the threat to incumbent mobile phone operators, a third competitor would enter the market. The government has failed in its effort to attract private capital, international operators, and more competition to the fixed and mobile telephone markets, mainly because of scarce political support, financially unattractive contract structures, and a lack of clarity in the regulatory framework governing the sector.

The Chilean success story suggests that to reduce inequalities in access to telecommunications services, the most effective strategy for increasing low coverage in poor urban and rural areas is to introduce competition and private investment to the sector, and to create a development fund to which the companies themselves contribute. Although Ecuador has already created Fodetel, financing for this fund is not included in the law and it is therefore not operational for lack of resources. For this reason, the PROMEC project, which is financed by the World Bank, intends to install 160 rural telephone centers, including phone booths and computers with Internet access in order to provide government services in rural areas. Four pilot projects will also be implemented to support small and medium-sized enterprises (SMEs) and increase their production and export capacity. It must be kept in mind that as long as the basic telephone sector does not develop with private funds and does not open to competition, the viability of Fodetel will remain uncertain.

QUALITY AND EFFICIENCY OF SERVICE. The quality of fixed telephone service remains below the regional average. In 2000, there were 48 failures per 100 lines per year, compared to 39 for other countries in the region with the same level of development. It must be noted that low quality service has more to do with the provider being government-owned than with the level of a country's development. There is an average of 49 failures in countries where the local operator is in government hands, whereas the figure is 26 for countries with private sector operators. To take a specific example, Bolivia has a lower per capita income than Ecuador but its operator, ENTEL (privatized in 1996), registered only about 20 failures per 100 lines in 2000, while ICE in Costa Rica (with higher per capita income but a public phone company), registered an average of 65 failures in the same year. As long as the main local telephone operators do not operate with strict business discipline in a competitive market, there will be few incentives to improve the quality of service and availability of new products.

SUBSIDIES. Despite having opened the market to competition, serious distortions remain in the basic telecommunications services market. For several years, the basic telephone operator, EMETEL, and then Andinatel and Pacifictel, maintained a cross-subsidy to offer very low local service rates while maintaining artificially high international long distance charges far above the international average. This led to a large percentage of international calls being made via "by-pass" or the Internet, giving rise to a boom in cyber-cafés, some operated illegally. In 2000, CONATEL agreed to a rate adjustment plan to solve this problem and balance the market before the operators were privatized.

Nonetheless, this process was brought to a halt that same year when the executive branch of the government ordered a rate freeze. As a result, the local Pacifictel rate for the residential sector in November 2002 was 60 percent lower than originally planned in the adjustment program that should have concluded in January 2003. The cost of a local call is now one of the lowest in the region and both Andinatel and Pacifictel offer below-cost local service. Also, the long distance market has been opened to competition and international rates have dropped, meaning that both companies will begin to face financial difficulties if local rates are not adjusted to real costs. Adjusting rates is necessary so that both companies can operate efficiently and be ready to be bought or capitalized by an experienced operator. Both companies urgently need fresh capital to continue to make investments, build new networks, and install fixed lines, which are still a fundamental part of the basic structure for developing information and communications technology (ICT). The necessary increase in local rates will undoubtedly affect some population groups with the least economic resources, making it necessary to adopt a more effective strategy to continue subsidizing them. The present system of cheap rates is ineffective because it is based on the geographic location of individuals instead of their income level. One possibility would be to create a system of prepayment cards in which each individual has complete control over his or her spending.

LEVEL OF COMPETITION. In general, competition in the sector has risen continuously since it began in January 2002. The national and international long distance market is more competitive and rates have dropped sharply. A few years ago, it cost about $US1.30 a minute to phone the United States, whereas this can now be done for $US0.30. It is hoped that rates will continue dropping once the interconnection plan is clearer and the surtax on termination of traffic levied by incumbent operators is eliminated.

CONATEL seems to have opted for the presubscription system instead of the dial-up system for choosing a long distance operator. International experience indicates that markets become more competitive when consumers are more easily able to choose the operator that offers the best service and prices, which is facilitated by dial-up selection. This is particularly the case in markets such as Chile and in those recently opened to competition, for example Bolivia. Another problem that has arisen in countries that have opened up to competition but do not have an advanced and well-defined monitoring system involves illegal changes of operator, known as "slamming." The new national long distance regulations consider the possibility of implementing the dial-up system after two years, if this becomes economically viable. However, this strategy may be insufficient, given that once competition has become established and consumers have decided which service to subscribe to, a dominant operator is highly unlikely to lose its market share. This is the case of Telmex in Mexico, where after seven years of open competition, this company still controls about 70 percent of the long distance market. The presubscription system for choosing an operator tends to hold back competition, since it means that each customer has to change and consumers are generally not very proactive when it comes to taking this step.

The recent postponement of the third cellular license has sent a bad signal to the international markets. Compared to the rest of the region, Ecuador continues to have one of the lowest levels of competition in the cellular market, with few providers amd, consequently, with high prices (see Figures 7 and 8). However, so far this year, the mobile services market has grown approximately 50 percent and it is estimated that by the end of the year there will be as many subscribers with cellular phones as those with fixed lines. This significant growth is due in part to the fact that the operators Porta and BellSouth, threatened with the entry of a third competitor, recently decided to intensify their market strategy to attract as many customers as possible. Competitive bidding for a third license, or else granting one to Andinatel and to Pacifictel, so that they could partner with an experienced international operator, would undoubtedly improve current market conditions, benefiting low-income Ecuadorans in particular.

INTERNET ACCESS. According to the Office of the Superintendent of Telecommunications, only 2.47 percent of the population has direct Internet access. Statistics from the International Telecommunications Union (ITU) for 2001 show that Ecuador had 0.26 Internet servers per 1,000 inhabitants, ranking well below other

Figure 7. Competition in the Cellular Phone Market (Sept. 2002)

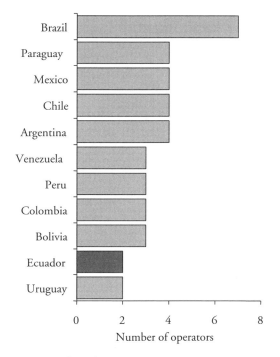

Source: EMC-Database.

Figure 8. Average Cost per Minute: Cellular Prepayment Plan (Nov. 2002)

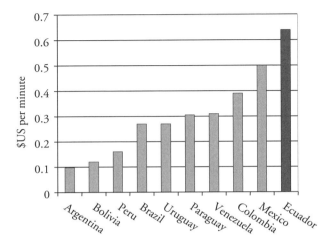

Source: National operators.

countries with a similar level of development, such as Colombia, Peru, and Paraguay, which have 1.33, 0.52, and 0.48 respectively. The low level of ICT in Ecuador is attributable to the fact that the basic telecommunications system remains seriously outdated, which prevents development of the value-added services sector. In response to this need, in August 2001 the national government ordered the creation of the National Connectivity Commission, responsible for formulating and developing state policy and programs aimed at increasing Ecuador's communications capacity through the effective use of ICT. This initiative includes various proposals to improve access to infrastructure; among the most important is a flat rate for Internet access and the development of network access points (NAPs) for local interconnection of Internet service providers (ISPs). The cost of Internet access is the key factor that determines the speed and scope of its development, and for this reason the implementation of a flat rate for Internet access through telephone lines is essential to reduce costs. Although Ecuador has the lowest local telephone rates in the region, a microenterprise that uses 20 hours' access a month still pays about $28 a month for calls and $22 for unlimited monthly access to the Internet. In terms of infrastructure, the lack of local NAPs makes it faster to send a data package via Miami than between two locally connected ISPs. The National Connectivity Commission needs greater decisionmaking and implementation power. Also, it must increase its dialogue with the government, Congress, and the general public to pass reforms to extend Internet access, which is considered a national priority within the National Development Plan.

Transport Sector

CHARACTERISTICS OF THE SECTOR. The transport system in Ecuador has never been systematically planned, but rather has developed in response to the specific needs, public demand, or government policy of the moment. The development of the different transport systems has never been coordinated and each one has acted independently of the others.

The problems in the sector arise from the inadequacy of the policies and strategies applied, and from a weak regulatory, legal, and institutional framework. These weaknesses then translate into operational, financial, and management problems. Investments and road maintenance are not adequately programmed, efficiency is low, and budget allocations to the sector remain below real investment and maintenance needs. Although the government dominates the sector in terms of formulating policy, acting as the regulatory authority and providing infrastructure and services, poor coordination among institutions prevents government plans from achieving the desired benefits. The provinces and municipalities have very little technical, administrative, and financial capacity to take on the new responsibilities imposed by the Special Law on Decentralization and Social Participation. At these administrative levels, political influences, poor training, and shortages of resources often contribute to paralysis.

Highway administration is generally a public sector function, with several institutions responsible, thus preventing proper planning and a clear division of responsibilities. Urban and rural cargo and passenger transport service is overwhelmingly managed by individuals and small private companies without proper planning or operational efficiency. This structure results in inefficiency to the detriment of users.

The following is a summary of the situation, as well as the key issues facing different transport subsectors.

ROAD TRANSPORT. All forms of transport are present in Ecuador but highway transport is the most important, accounting for 85 percent of domestic cargo and passengers. Though extensive, the road system is poorly operated and maintained. According to an inventory carried out by the Ministry of Public Works (MOP), Ecuador has about 43,200 km of roads, of which 8,161 km are paved, 23,055 km are gravel, and 12,000 km are dirt roads. Functionally, the national highway network is officially broken down by jurisdiction into (i) the State Highways Network (*Red Vial Estatal*), which includes roads managed by the MOP (8,682 km); (ii) the Provincial Highways Network (*Red Vial Provincial*), which includes the group of roads managed by each of the provincial councils; and (iii) the Cantonal Roadways Network (*Red Vial Cantonal*), which includes all the urban and interparochial roads managed by the provincial and cantonal councils. Approximately 51 percent of all the roadways in the country are local roads.

In terms of geographical coverage of roadways, there is a relatively extensive system of roads on the coast (except in Esmeraldas) and in the highlands: 16,492 km and

22,052 km, respectively. In the Amazon (or Eastern) region, there are only 4,470 km of roads, of which 89.3 percent are gravel or dirt roads. In the Galapagos Islands there are 184 km of roads, of which 92 percent are gravel. The eastern part of the country, characterized by a low level of development, sparse population and numerous rivers, is sparsely covered by roads. (See Table 9 for more figures on the highway system.)

The length of the road network, its functional distribution, and the type of surface applied are similar to other countries with similar levels of development. A total of 0.7 km paved and 3.6 km paved and unpaved roads per thousand inhabitants is typical of low/medium-income countries. Several factors, including the institutional environment, uncertain budgets, and the lay of the land contribute to the poor state of the highway network, resulting in long travel times and many accidents. Maintenance is poor throughout the network, especially the provincial and municipal rural network, only 30 percent of which is in good condition. In general, most of the primary network is paved, except in the eastern part of the country, where gravel and dirt roads predominate.

Difficult topography limits the technical quality of the network, and winding roads increase travel time. For example, the distance between Quito and Guayaquil is only 270 km as the crow flies, but the highway is 420 km long and travel time for

Table 9. Characteristics of the Ecuadoran Road System by Regions

Highway administration	Unit	Coast	Mountains	East	Islands	Total
Total length of roads	km	16,492	22,052	4,469	184	43,197
Population	inhabitants	5,989,543	5,463,934	546,602	18,555	12,018,634
Total km roads per 1,000 inhabitants	km/1,000 inhabitants	2.75	4.03	8.18	9.92	3.59
Jurisdiction						
Primary	km	1,830	2,586	1,120	72	5,608
Secondary	km	1,461	1,847	534	34	3,876
Tertiary	km	4,705	5,091	1,294	16	11,105
Residential	km	8,354	12,239	1,499	61	22,153
Local	km	141	290	21	0	452
Road surface						
Paved	km	4,040	3,628	478	14	8,160
Gravel	km	6,665	12,405	3,816	169	23,055
Dirt	km	5,787	6,019	175	0	11,981

Sources:
MOP, "Planning and Decentralization of the National Roadways Administration," Isra and Majón, 1997.
National Bank, Rural Roads Team, July 2002.

a heavy vehicle is over 8 hours. These great lengths also make highways more vulnerable to rockslides, floods, landslides, land sinkage, and earthquakes, as well as to interruptions due to other causes (public demonstrations, strikes, and so on).

Road-building practices used until recently have caused environmental problems in areas such as those near the Cuenca-Molleturo-Naranjal highway or the Borbón-Punta Peñas highway. Given the topographic and geological conditions in the Andes, action is required to mitigate environmental degradation.

In summary, the length and coverage of the network is sufficient, but the road surfaces are in poor shape due to lack of maintenance and institutional weakness. An extensive program of routine and periodic maintenance of the main MOP network is now necessary; at present, the MOP has plans for a routine maintenance program to be carried out by microenterprises. It is also absolutely essential to prepare and implement a comprehensive maintenance and repair program for the secondary and rural system, the state of which is so bad that many rural communities are cut off for weeks at a time during the rainy season.

VEHICLES AND TRAFFIC. The number of vehicles and the volume of vehicle traffic are also within the range to be expected in a country with Ecuador's per capita GDP. In 1999, there were a total of 624,924 registered vehicles in four groups: (i) Light: 559,691, including cars, jeeps, passenger vans, motorcycles, pick-up trucks, and cargo vans; (ii) Buses: 9,917, consisting of buses and other large passenger vehicles; (iii) Heavy: 54,233, corresponding to trucks, tank trucks, dump trucks, and truck trailers; (iv) Others: 1,083. The distribution of motorized vehicles is not uniform, with the greatest concentration in the provinces of Pichincha (34.5 percent) and Guayas (30.6 percent). 80 percent of registered cargo vehicles are of small capacity (weighing under 3 tons) and only 6,000 vehicles have a capacity of more than 15 tons. However, the number of these large trucks is increasing faster than the smaller ones, indicating a trend toward greater efficiency in cargo transport.

Traffic volumes are not very high, with most stretches of trunk highway carrying an annual average daily traffic (AADT) of 6,500 vehicles a day, but there are four stretches with 10,000 vehicles a day. Most stretches with high volumes of traffic are located near big cities and are held in concession or are in the process of being concessioned. In practice, there are periodic problems of traffic congestion owing to the state of the roads, special holidays, and the presence of slow trucks on mountain highways, but the main limiting factors involve the structure and condition of the highways. The volume of gas emissions generated by the transport sector and the atmospheric conditions of cities such as Quito lead to high levels of air pollution in densely populated areas. Air quality monitoring systems are being installed in some of these cities.

RAIL TRANSPORT. Ecuador's rail network has a total length of 964.6 km, of which 30.61 percent is in service. The network is divided into three sectors: Southern Division (Durán–Quito, 445.8 km); Northern Division (Quito–San Lorenzo 373.4 km); and Southern Branch (Sibambe–Cuenca, 145.4 km). The system is operated by the Ecuadoran National Railway Company (ENFE). This means of transport is used mainly by tourists. The most recent figures available, from 1999, show a very significant drop in passenger transport, with 94,029 passengers travelling by rail that year, compared to 197,855 passengers in 1996. ENFE is now involved in the process of legalizing its new name: *Empresa de Ferrocarriles Ecuatorianos* (Ecuadoran Railways Company).

AIRPORTS AND AIR TRANSPORT: Ecuador has about 200 runways, aerodromes, and airports, five of which are international airports: the Mariscal Sucre (Quito), the Simón Bolívar (Guayaquil), the Manta, the Tulcán, and the Esmeraldas airports. There are also 23 important airports for domestic flights. In 2000, 2.6 million passengers were transported—more than 1.5 million on international flights. Owing to the increase in passengers at the country's two main airports (Quito and Guayaquil), combined with increasing noise and urban pollution levels and the need to modernize and relocate the airports, a process has begun to build or grant new concessions in both cities. In the case of the Quito airport, an agreement was formalized on July 22, 2002, between the Municipality of Quito and the Canadian government. The Canadian Trade Consortium agreed to build a new airport (investing about 300 million dollars) and also to manage and operate the Mariscal Sucre airport for five years. Work will begin on March 15, 2003. The total concession period will be 35 years—5 for construction, followed by 30 years of operation.

PORTS AND MARITIME TRAFFIC: It is estimated that 8 million tons of cargo were moved at the country's main ports in 2001. The largest port is at Guayaquil, which handles 70 percent of the country's foreign trade. The national government has decided to grant concessions for the management of four state-owned commercial ports, through "landlord" contracts, by which the concessionaire assumes all responsibility and risk for the administration of existing infrastructure and for any investments that may be required, depending on the activities. At present, the national port authorities are not unionized and are free of labor liabilities. Services are currently provided by operators with short-term contracts, pending award of long-term concessions in the coming phase port modernization.

URBAN TRANSPORT: Except in Quito, urban transport in most cities is organized, planned and controlled by the CNTTT. Specific urban transport plans for Ecuadoran cities are rare and in most cases nonexistent. In most cases official information does not even exist. The only city government that has an official plan is the Municipality of the Metropolitan District of Quito (MDMQ). This body has the authority to plan, regulate, and coordinate everything to do with public and private transit and transport in its area of jurisdiction. In Quito, urban transport has many problems, but has undergone relative improvements in recent years, since the MDMQ has implemented projects such as the trolleybus system that has partially rationalized public transport on its main route. In May 2002, the Master Plan for Transport in the Metropolitan District of Quito was launched, setting out actions to be taken over the next 20 years.

The MDMQ covers 4,228 km² and has about 1.45 million inhabitants. There are about 10 inhabitants per vehicle. Public transit/transport demand is approximately 1.6 million trips a day, of which the trolleybus system handles 185,000 trips a day and Ecovía handles 24,000 trips a day. These two services are managed by the MDMQ through the Trolleybus System Operating Unit (UOST). There is a high concentration of public transport on the main routes, where the services overlap and generate congestion. Service is poor, routes are poorly organized, environmental impact due to exhaust emissions is high, and regulations and standards are not properly monitored. Eighty-two percent of movements on public transport are handled by private operators, representing 1.25 million urban trips. Forty-one percent of buses are less than 5 years old, 48 percent are between 5 and 10 years old, and only 11 percent have been operating for more than 10 years. This means that the fleet is relatively new, though there is a great diversity of makes and models. Transport in Quito is divided into 132 routes and includes about 55 operators.

GENERAL FRAMEWORK OF THE RATES SYSTEM: The national rates system for transport is established by the CNTTT, except in the cities of Quito and Guayaquil, where this is handled, respectively, by the Municipality of Quito and by the Guayas Transport Commission. In general, urban passenger transport rates depend on the type of vehicle used. Prices vary between 10 and 36 cents (U.S.). As for interprovincial transport rates, because there is a great variety of companies and cooperatives with routes throughout the country, there is fierce competition and prices are too low to renovate the fleet.

SUBSIDIES. In the highways sector, user charges include taxes on fuel, on vehicle imports, on tires, and on spare parts, plus charges for driving licenses and vehicle license plates. In Ecuador in July 2002, the price of gasoline ($1.12 a gallon for regular and $1.42 for super) was higher than the price of diesel fuel ($0.89 a gallon). Therefore, although the total amount collected from users is greater than the cost of maintaining the network, there is clearly a cross-subsidy for heavy vehicles using diesel fuel, which cause the most damage to the road network.

Highway Safety

There is an adequate Traffic Code included in the Law on Land Traffic and Transport of 1966. However, a number of institutions share the responsibility for traffic safety, and the management of this sector is not properly coordinated. There is a high rate of traffic accidents, almost all trucks fail to obey laws on weight limits, theft of cargo *en route* is very common, and secondary and rural roads are practically abandoned in terms of signposting and highway safety.

C. Sectoral Policy Recommendations

Recommendations vary depending on the maturity of existing institutional and legal arrangements and the degree to which the central government controls each sector. The *electricity* sector, for example, already has a modern institutional and legal framework (vertical separation of the functions of generation, transmission, and distribution and an adequate sectoral law). The main challenges include increasing operational efficiency and tariff collection through greater private sector participation, the necessary increases in rates, and increased coverage in rural areas. These measures depend mostly on the central government, which controls most of the distribution, transmission, and generation companies. In the *telecommunications* sector, on the other hand, the legal and regulatory framework is still incomplete, since a framework law appropriate to the sector is still lacking, as is a clear designation of regulatory responsibilities (several bodies have overlapping responsibilities). Improved coverage and quality of services also depend on greater private sector participation, for which a legal and regulatory framework must first be put in place. Since the central government controls the companies Andinatel and Pacifictel and also controls the issuing of licenses, improvements in the telecommunications sector also depend mostly on the central government. In the *water/sanitation* and *transport* sectors, a large part of the services is provided by decentralized providers that depend on provincial or municipal governments. Here too, the central government must finish an incomplete institutional, regulatory, and legal framework and promote better provision of services, using fiscal transfers as an incentive. In both sectors, improvements in the quality and coverage of services depend on greater private sector participation in the design, construction, and operation of the services (water/sanitation and transport) or the delegation of services to independent public and private operators (water/sanitation). Finally, regarding *rural community infrastructure* (construction of schools, health centers, bridges, local roads, and so on), Ecuador faces the challenge of generalizing a demand-driven approach (see section 4) with communities and municipalities in the driver's seat. This approach already exists in several isolated projects, such as PROLOCAL and PRAGUAS, for example, but is still not widespread.

CONTEXT OF DECENTRALIZATION. The recommendations summarized in the following subsections are given in the context of the general process of political, financial, and administrative decentralization that Ecuador has been carrying out since the country's return to democracy in 1978. The scope of this process is summarized in a separate document prepared by the World Bank (see chapter 17 on Decentralization in this volume). Only 7 percent of public spending in the country is now made by provincial councils and municipalities. However, it is significant that since 2001, agreements have been signed between the national government and 22 provinces and 140 municipalities to decentralize specific responsibilities in the environmental, tourism, agriculture, and public works sectors, including roads. As of this date, no agreements have been signed with the multiple *autonomous bodies* responsible to the central government (regional development authorities, social funds, institutes, implementation units, and agencies attached to municipalities). These independent bodies manage about $US1.5 billion a year and participate in various infrastructure sectors (including roads, water, and sanitation), implementing their own policies. These policies are not well coordinated with the sectoral policies of government ministries. This context is important, since the following subsections (especially those on the water supply/sanitation and transport sectors) recommend that the national government use financial transfers to the various sectors to encourage improvements by service providers. This makes sense only if the autonomous bodies operate clearly in accordance with the sectoral policies established by the ministries responsible.

ENVIRONMENTAL CONTEXT. There is a pressing need for an Integrated Environmental Management System (SUMA), established through a government decress that regulates environmental impact studies, licensing, and the control and environmental monitoring of all parts of the economy, including the infrastructure sectors.

Water Supply and Sanitation Sector

USING CENTRAL GOVERNMENT TRANSFERS TO PROMOTE IMPROVEMENTS. Earlier studies prepared by the World Bank have identified disperse, discretional transfer payments (made under 18 special laws) as being among the basic fiscal obstacles to the success of the decentralization process in Ecuador. The success of intergovernmental transfers depends on at least a minimal relationship between responsibility and resources, something that is nonexistent today. As for transfers to specific sectors, it is particularly recommended that mathematical formulas be used to link the physical and financial performance of the service provider (or of the sector) with the size of the transfers made by the central government.[14]

Since the country's water supply and sanitation services are municipal, the main instrument available to the central government to encourage improved performance by service providers is financial transfers. These transfers may be used so that municipalities adopt (i) adequate tariffs, with due protection for the poor; and (ii) modern structures for providing services. The following steps could be followed to turn financial transfers into development tools for the sector:

- Calculate and publish the resources effectively transferred by the central government to service providers and municipalities via either general transfers

---

14. The World Bank, "Decentralization Reform Agenda in Ecuador," May 11, 2001, pp. v, 42.

(the 15 percent law) or transfers linked directly to the water and sanitation sector (transfer of telephone tax, solidarity fund, and the like);

- Design a model formula linking the size of transfers to the water and sanitation sector to a set of variables (poverty, present coverage, performance and autonomy of the service provider, and so on);
- Apply this formula to a pilot group of water companies and municipalities of different sizes and characteristics, in order to refine criteria and goals and to determine their impact;
- Extend the use of the final formula to all providers of water and sanitation services. During this stage, the sector's multiple, overlapping sources of financing would be unified in a single Water Fund, which would make payments on the basis of the established formula. An alternative would be to adopt a single financing formula for all of the sector's present sources of financing (or for a small number of sources that would have the right to invest in the sector).

COMPLETING THE INSTITUTIONAL AND LEGAL FRAMEWORK. The development of the water supply and sanitation sector in the coming years depends to a great extent on a reform of the existing legal and institutional framework. Sectoral legislation is required to (i) clearly define and specify the functions of the different national and municipal actors in the sector; (ii) establish an independent national regulatory authority for the water supply and sanitation sector and grant it the minimum necessary functions to operate in a decentralized country; (iii) create conditions for the municipalities to delegate the operation of their systems to independent (public and private) operators; and (iv) promote private sector participation in the operation of water systems under clear, transparent contracts that guarantee the greatest possible benefits for the most vulnerable segments of the population. The proposed Water Supply and Sanitation Law, to be prepared by international consultants contracted by CONAM and jointly monitored by CONAM and SAPYSB, is an important opportunity to reform sectoral legislation. Along with the preparation of a new Water Supply and Sanitation Law, it will be important to establish an updated National Water Supply and Sanitation Policy that clarifies key issues such as the sector's policy on subsidies, and the criteria by which service providers can receive them.

IMPROVING THE QUALITY AND EFFICIENCY OF SERVICES. Along with the reform of subsidies policy and of the legal and institutional framework for the sector, a modernization of service providers (SPs) will be necessary to achieve a significant improvement in the coverage and the quality of water supply and sanitation services. The best way to modernize the SPs will depend on the size of each and on the specific characteristics of the municipalities involved:

- **Quito and Guayaquil**. On August 9, 2001, Guayaquil transferred responsibility for providing its water supply and sanitation services for 30 years to a private company, International Water Services (Guayaquil)—known as INTER-AGUA. The Empresa Cantonal de Agua Potable y Alcantarillado de Guayaquil (ECAPAG, the previous public operator) became the regulatory authority for the contract. A year after the transfer, the operator is meeting its contractual obligations and has achieved (i) better customer service via its "telephone hot-lines"; (ii) an increase in registered users (from 230,000 to 266,000); and (iii) an increase in the collection rate from 60 percent to 70 percent. The additional income from these measures are fundamental for connecting more than 55,000 more families to the water and sewage systems in the first five years of the con-tract. In addition to investments in the water and sewage system, the presence of a new private operator has enabled new schemes to be developed for tack-ling the issue of urban rainwater drainage, a problem that affects many munic-ipalities in the country (especially on the coast) threatened by frequent flood-ing (see Box 1). In Quito, the municipality is preparing more limited private sector participation with the concession of approximately 300,000 connections to the private sector in the eastern districts. In general, both of the largest cities in the country are working to modernize their structures.

- **Cities with between 100,000 and 300,000 inhabitants.** The 12 cities in this group, which have the fastest growing populations in the country—an annual increase of 7.8 percent—have not taken serious steps to begin the moderniza-tion process. It is essential that there be some form of private sector partici-pation (PSP)—national, regional, or international—in the operation, renova-tion, and extension of the systems. PSP should include some investment requirements in the future to attend to the great number of users who will be needing services, while improving the poor quality of existing supply.

- **Cities with between 30,000 and 100,000 inhabitants.** Of the 37 cities that make up this group, 29 do not even have an independent water supply and sanitation service, and the great majority operate their service directly from the municipality. The priority must be to delegate services to administratively and financially independent operators, who in turn could, if they wanted, look for private sector participation. Pedro Moncayo and Caluma are inter-esting examples: Pedro Moncayo has created a municipal company headed by a manager who will administer a management contract with a small private company which will operate the system. Caluma has created a "mixed" com-pany (two municipal representatives and three users on the executive board) in order to operate its water supply system in a nonpolitical manner.

- **Cities with fewer than 30,000 inhabitants.** The 169 municipalities that make up this group are home to 11 percent of the population of Ecuador, and are growing well above the national average (3.5 percent a year versus 2.1 per-cent nationally). All of them administer their water services (and sometimes sewage) directly. In addition to delegating to independent operators, the main challenge for this group of municipalities is to create multicantonal enterprises that allow for economies of scale in order to be able to hire skilled technical staff and acquire proper maintenance equipment. The consolidation of small water supply services has been very successful in other countries in the region (Brazil, Chile) and in other parts of the world (England), but has not yet taken shape in Ecuador.

To support all municipalities (especially the small and medium-sized ones) that wish to delegate their water supply and sanitation service to independent operators, it is essential to strengthen the capacity of the SAPYSB to provide quick, high quality technical support. It is also important to involve the Association of Municipalities of Ecuador (AME) to boost the process of delegating services to convince the smallest municipalities (fewer than 30,000 inhabitants) to create multicantonal water supply and sanitation enterprises.

IMPROVING THE MANAGEMENT OF WATER RESOURCES. The sustainability of the quality and quantity of the water supply to urban and rural communities depends on

---

Box 1. Stormwater Drainage—A User Surcharge for Improvements in the Context of a Concession Contract

In August 2001, the firm International Water took responsibility for water supply and sanitation services in Guayaquil, while the former company, ECAPAG, became the regulatory authority for the service. However, the contract with the concessionaire did not initially include drainage service, which is to be considered in the fifth year of operations. To solve the drainage problem, in part motivated by the coming rainy season and the resulting flooding, the city established a plan for building and financing drainage based on the contract with the operator and on a *special surcharge for improvements*. Through this plan, previously approved by the Municipal Council, the concessionaire is to build the requested works and recover its costs, by charging beneficiaries for the costs separately on their water bills in the form of a special surcharge for improvements, with a three-year payment period. To test this system, a $US500,000 emergency works operation was successfully carried out.

Given the success of this operation, the city has recently approved a second *surcharge for improvements* program, this time worth $11.0 million dollars, to finance the construction of a priority drainage plan for the next four years. To maintain manageable cash flow, the works will be carried out at the same rate that beneficiaries make payments. In this way, Guayaquil is headed toward significant improvement in these services—and perhaps toward becoming a management and financing model for the rest of Latin America.

integrated management of the resource at the river basin level, where all users (including rural municipalities and communities) can openly discuss the use, management, and prioritization of the resource. The management of water resources at the level of water basins is fundamental, especially in places where one municipality's sewage (or agricultural effluents) has a significant impact on raw water quality in other municipalities downstream. Two short- and medium-term measures are recommended:

- **Monitoring water basins**. In water basins where there are already conflicts over use or significant risks of flooding, it is important that the CNRH (supported by regional development corporations, provincial councils, and municipalities) monitor both the supply and the demand for surface and underground water and evaluate its quality to prepare more systematic management in the medium term.
- **Legal framework**. Although Ecuador already has a National Strategy for the Management of Water Resources, it is important that the government review the country's legal framework in this regard, in order to establish a more efficient and fairer system for managing river basins and allocating water resources. The World Bank is now evaluating the best way to support this process, perhaps in the framework of a new Project for the Management of Water Resources.

Energy Sector

The priorities identified for the electrical sector include (i) reactivating private sector participation; (ii) limiting or eliminating state interference in the regulatory authority; (iii) reinitiating tariff adjustments; (iv) regularizing the financial situation of the wholesale electricity market; (v) facing the EMELEC problem; (vi) developing a rural energy strategy; and (vii) starting up the environmental division of CONELEC.

REACTIVATING PRIVATE PARTICIPATION. This aspect of the reform could begin with the incorporation of private interests into the generation of electricity and, more importantly, into its distribution. Given the factors that prevented the sale of distribution companies in the past, and which will likely remain in the near future, it will be necessary to look for new ways to include private participation, such as granting concessions for state-owned assets, capitalization schemes (particularly in the case of the transmission company), or administration contracts that reward the administrator according to its performance and the achievement of clearly established quantitative goals. Such contracts would introduce the profit motive into this activity, motivating better business management through cost reductions, recovery of losses, and more efficient collection. It must be noted, however, that in the experience of the electrical sectors of other countries, such contracts generally do not lead to significant or lasting gains in corporate efficiency, owing to the difficulty in guaranteeing the private partner sufficient control over investments and company employees. It would also be desirable to encourage private sector participation in electrical generation, where the presence of new investors, besides increasing competition and envigorating the wholesale electricity market, would send out a positive signal for the allocation of new resources.

Support should also be given to the development of projects based on renewable energies leading to the reduction of carbon gas emissions. These projects, generally promoted by private investors, could benefit from financing under the Clean Development Mechanism, in particular the Community Development Carbon Fund.

REDUCING STATE INTERFERENCE. State influence in the regulatory authority completely distorts the incentives perceived by existing and potential investors. An initiative is therefore needed that would send a signal of legal stability to the market, whether through regulations that provide greater permanence (and thus assign greater responsibility) to directors of CONELEC, eliminating the possibility that these public employees can be freely transferred to other posts or, in the longer term, by amending the law in this regard.

REINITIATING RATES ADJUSTMENTS. This is a prerequisite for realizing the benefits of the reform, guaranteeing that the companies can meet their financial obligations and enabling the wholesale electricity market to operate without accumulating deficits. This adjustment will consist of maintaining a "lifeline" subsidy aimed only at the lowest-income households, for example, for consumption of less than 150–200 kWh/month. However, a simple increase in rates without clear budget restrictions (which would be obtained with the incorporation of private management—see above) would not guarantee efficient operations, especially in the case of the distribution companies.

FINANCIAL SITUATION OF THE WHOLESALE ELECTRICITY MARKET. The wholesale electricity market's continuous accumulation of deficits is not sustainable and requires a solution on the part of the government. The measures to be taken are related to the rates issue (so that the distributors can cancel their debts with the wholesale electricity market), the efficient operation of the trust and, most important, the normalization of EMELEC management, as is explained below.

FACING THE EMELEC PROBLEM. This private company has a service concession in the Guayaquil area and is the biggest distributor in Ecuador. However, its financial and legal problems with the state go back many years and it is now being administrated by CONELEC. Solving its problems may involve long and complicated negotiations and disputes, especially regarding the company's demands in terms of the state's obligation to guarantee it a certain level of cost-effectiveness. Therefore, although deeper problems may remain latent for a long time to come—beyond the term of the new government—it would useful to develop a strategy to normalize the company's current operations. This requires strong intervention by CONELEC to impose administrative discipline regarding obligations to the wholesale electricity market, as well as guaranteeing short- and medium-term implementation of the investments required to maintain the quality of service in the city.

DEVELOPING A RURAL ENERGY STRATEGY. The resources of the Rural and Peri-Urban Electrification Fund (FERUM) must not only be devoted to programs for extending networks, but must also support measures to take energy to isolated communities, using a broad-based approach to look for comprehensive solutions to their energy problems, either by extending networks or through decentralized systems. The first step in this direction is to develop a strategy for reaching these communities and studying the viability of different ways of implementing the strategy. The PROMEC project could be an important instrument for this endeavor. The rural energy strategy should include these main features: a rural electrification plan that makes the extension of the network compatible with decentralized systems (mini-networks, individual systems, and the like); determining the legal and regulatory changes and the financial mechanisms necessary to support the strategy (for example, increasing the sources for financing FERUM and their extension to decentralized systems); determining the instruments for providing rural electrification service, such as distribution companies, private operators, local organizations, and so forth.

ENVIRONMENTAL PLANNING AND MANAGEMENT IN THE ELECTRICAL SECTOR. To guarantee that environmental planning and management systems are set up for the sector, sector authorities must be strengthened institutionally. This includes the Ministry of Energy and Mining and CONELEC, whose environmental unit must be strengthened.

Telecommunications Sector

REGULATORY AND POLICYMAKING AGENCIES. To provide greater solidity to the institutional and regulatory framework, the organizational structure that regulates and sets policy in the sector must be reformed. There is great confusion regarding the functions of each agency. For example, SUPTEL controls and monitors the use of the radio frequency spectrum, SENATEL administrates and manages it, and CONATEL approves the frequencies plan and uses of the spectrum. The difficulty in defining the lines of authority and responsibilities make investors hesitant and uncertain. The consolidation of CONATEL, SUPTEL and SENATEL in two agencies with sufficient authority and functional capacity—one for regulatory functions and the other to set policy in the sector—will provide the simplicity and clarity necessary for a dynamic, competent sector. While the international trend is toward the convergence of telecommunications services, the Ecuadoran telecommunications sector is still extremely fragmented, beginning with the organization of the regulatory agencies.

LEGAL FRAMEWORK. A new legal framework must be found to replace the existing one based on regulations characterized by duplications, inconsistencies, and a lack of clarity. For example, Article 15 of the General Regulations prohibits private networks being connected to public ones, while Article 36 allows it. Furthermore, this same article indicates that operators of public networks must lease their infrastructure to third parties, but limits this leasing to a maximum of two years; however, Article 7 of the Interconnection Regulations requires that the network and other elements be broken up with no time limits.

ENERGIZING THE NATIONAL CONNECTIVITY AGENDA. It would be advisable for the new government to strengthen the National Connectivity Commission, providing it with a direct link with the executive branch of government. This could be achieved by proposing a new director of the commission with a high enough rank to be able to promote the Agenda, while remaining independent of any other government agency. Likewise, the Commission must include representatives of the private sector and of other levels of government, which are essential allies in this effort.

IMPROVING QUALITY. The cellular market is a serious threat to both current local telephone operators, which need capital and efficient administration to make the large investments the sector requires. Although there have already been several attempts to attract private capital to Andinatel and Pacifictel, the strategy has not been sufficiently clear, nor have the necessary incentives been offered. A package must now be put together that is attractive enough to convince international operators and investors. Unfortunately, the global telecommunications sector is now depressed and most companies are not in a position to invest in new markets, especially in fixed line operators. Cellular technology has proven to be the most attractive option for developing countries today, since it has the potential to attract a larger sector of the population at a lower cost. As a result, two possible strategies are recommended for Andinatel and Pacifictel:

- The first alternative is offering (by public tender) the sale of new shares in both companies to a strategic investor, including a management contract for both operators. A cellular telephone license would be included as the most attractive feature of the package. Thus, as the private operator invests in the companies, its capital stock would gradually increase and service would improve as investments are made to extend services.
- An alternative would be to offer (by public tender) a management contract to a well-known international operator that would manage one or both companies, and would gradually sell the companies' shares on the local and international stock markets. As in the previous alternative, both companies would have a cellular license to expand services.

Either of these options would solve the problem of the duopoly in the cellular market and would attract an operator with international experience and fresh capital. This operator could meet the sector's investment needs in terms of improved quality, increased coverage, and the introduction of new technology. It is important that before another tendering process is begun, rates must be adjusted and CONA-TEL must become consolidated as the regulatory authority for the sector, since certainty and transparency are generally highly valued by investors.

Transport Sector

Institutionally, the agencies responsible for planning, regulation, and control of transport are spread out among different ministries at different administrative levels, generally without proper coordination. Medium- and long-term sectoral and modal planning is deficient. In the short term, agencies try to solve immediate problems in an inappropriate framework, with insufficient resources. In this regard, there is a clear lack of leadership; better planning is also absent at the provincial and municipal levels. An exception is the metropolitan district of Quito, which has a properly functioning planning unit. Deficient planning is partially compensated for by CONAM, but this is not sustainable in the medium or long term. The greatest need is to complete institutional restructuring in the sector. This could include turning the MOP into a Ministry of Transport in charge of planning, regulating, and controlling the different forms of transport—functions now in the hands of different ministries. In this scheme, independent agencies would be responsible for the administration of each form of transport, with greater private sector participation in the creation of infrastructure. A Concessions Superintendency could even be established to administrate all projects of this kind in the sector, and improve the sector's institutional framework.

DECENTRALIZATION. As was mentioned earlier, Ecuador is deeply immersed in a long and difficult process of decentralization with significant implications for the transport sector. At present, there is a theoretical consensus on the definition of the types of network (primary, secondary, and tertiary) but administrative responsibilities are not clear. This issue also involves strengthening regional councils; financing provincial highways; maintaining and improving local roads, concessions, tolls; and environmental and social management. The case of local roads merits special comment, since national agencies have participated in their financing and construction and now their maintenance will theoretically be turned over to the municipalities. However, provinces and municipalities have little technical, administrative, or financial capacity to take on the new responsibilities imposed by the Special Law on Decentralization. At these levels of government, political pressures, insufficient training, and a critical lack of resources conspire to prevent change in the situation.

Linked to decentralization is the functioning of the system for transferring 15 percent of the total government budget to the local governments. A fundamental problem is that this system of transfer payments is nearly automatic and there are no incentives to link transfers with efficient use of the funds by local governments. The other problem is that local governments claim that the system is not adequate for managing the transferred infrastructure and, furthermore, that at the end of each year the central government typically transfers only 10 percent. The government cannot change the 15 percent transfer and should take steps to fund it. However, transfers above this level must be devoted to (i) projects focused on special issues such as the fight against poverty, and (ii) local governments that demonstrate good ability to manage resources and to plan and implement projects. This approach provides double benefits: the efficient use of resources and an incentive for weak local governments to improve their performance.

The transport sector will not be successfully modernized without greater private sector participation in various forms: in concessions (not only highways, but also concessions of maritime infrastructure, urban transport, and railways), the design and implementation of infrastructure works, and the provision of transport services. To do this, clear rules and appropriate project management are essential.

RURAL ROADS. Unquestionably, one of the main problems faced by rural and indigenous communities is the poor state of local roads (both for motorized and nonmotorized vehicles), as well as poor coverage by transport services. The combination of these factors in rural areas makes economic production more expensive and threatens government programs aimed at poor areas. Considering the goals of the decentralization process, the need for social participation by the rural population and the needs of the transport sector, emphasis should be placed on satisfying the transportation needs of rural communities. For rural transport, Ecuador could experiment with small truck cooperatives created with mixed capital (municipal, community-raised, and supplied by individual companies), as well as other more traditional forms of mixed capital ventures for operating stretches of railway.

MAIN NETWORK. The MOP has decided to substantially improve its highway maintenance system by contracting maintenance services on the basis of performance, rather than bu force account. In this context, a routine maintenance pilot project has already been implemented with 14 microenterprises in the province of Loja. Results have been positive, and there are plans to use this approach for the routine maintenance of the entire main network.

Community Infrastructure

THE ROLE OF THE COMMUNITY IN RURAL INFRASTRUCTURE SERVICES. Rural communities play an active role in the demand, planning, implementation, and administration of their own infrastructure services. Infrastructure service coverage is lower in rural areas than in urban settings, in terms of access to water supply and sanitation, electricity, transport, and telephone services. This lack of services affects all aspects of daily life and the general wellbeing of the rural population, making it difficult to rise out of poverty and develop economic productivity. Economies of scale and administrative involvement make large independent companies more efficient for taking on the management of certain infrastructure services, such as telecom-munications and electric energy. However, other services such as water supply and sanitation, independent energy systems, rural roads, and computer centers are more efficient when decentralized. Whenever rural communities and small companies have been given the opportunity and proper training, they have proven themselves capable of taking on the management of decentralized services. For example, rural water supply systems are successfully managed by water boards throughout Ecuador. There are also numerous examples of small companies contracted for highway main-tenance, managing computer centers, and supplying off-grid energy.

FOCUS ON DEMAND. A common feature of all infrastructure services is that they must be continuously paid for and maintained. In addition to the initial investment costs, all these services involve operational and maintenance costs. User tariffs are the best way to finance water supply, sanitation, energy, and telecommunications services. At the same time, community members make daily decisions by consum-ing services on the basis of their cost and their ability to pay. This information on the consumer is the starting point for determining the level of service to be provided. However, it is important to consider that in each infrastructure sector there is a range of technical options and different levels of service that can be designed to meet consumers' ability to pay. Projects must include a social intermediation program to help organize the community and inform residents about the different levels of serv-ice and their associated costs and management models, while helping the commu-nity make an informed decision about which option to choose.

FINANCING. Regarding the financing of community services involving rural infra-structure, tariffs should entirely cover operating and maintenance costs. In certain situations of poverty, the government can provide an initial subsidy for financing the investment. The design of the subsidy system is quite important and the following should be considered: (a) the importance of community participation, demonstrat-ing demand and willingness to pay; (b) participation by the municipal government as the agency responsible for providing the service, depending on its municipal development priorities; and (c) the central government's contribution to the trans-parency, fairness, and fiscal impact of the subsidy in the context of the sectoral goal of extending service at the national level. An ideal scheme for subsidizing rural infra-structure programs provides a per capita subsidy up to an established limit, which encourages additional contributions from the community and the private sector.

Community participation should go beyond assessing initial demand and plan-ning services; it should enable the community to participate in all stages of the implementation of the project. Community members can reduce their financial contribution by making contributions in kind, such as labor or local materials. Fur-thermore, it is during the infrastructure construction and installation stage that the community organization can develop its capacity to administer contracts and imple-ment works. At the same time as the technical aspects of the project are implemented, it is essential that a training program be developed enabling the community to establish an organization responsible for managing services and determining a tariff scheme. This organization should also have the technical capacity to operate and maintain the services, either directly or through a contracted company.

SERVICE PROVIDERS AND NECESSARY TECHNICAL ASSISTANCE. Decentralized rural infrastructure services must be provided by community organizations and small companies according to the same principles as those followed by centralized services—thus constituting a viable financing system that provides quality services sufficiently and sustainably. Community-based service providers require long-term technical assistance and training in business management skills. The government must provide this technical assistance either directly or through third parties—for example, through a contract with the urban services company. Supervision of the performance of community operators is also important and must be carried out within a simple, municipally based regulatory framework, with emphasis on financial concerns and quality of service.

SECTORAL POLICIES. Finally, sectoral policies for infrastructure are extremely important and must include legal provisions that allow for participation by community organizations and small companies as a viable alternative for providing services in rural areas. At the same time, the government must consider the need to establish a sustainable business model aimed at providing services over the long term, and not simply focus on the construction of infrastructure. This approach is possible if clear rules are established regarding financial policy, the role of the community and the extent of its contribution, the legal framework, and the technical standards applicable to each sector. It is important that these rules be followed by all programs that channel financial resources for the supply of rural infrastructure services. The policy on subsidies must be transparent and well-focused, supporting contributions to new investments to benefit those who do not receive services—and not used to cover maintenance or other recurring costs. The Water and Sanitation in Rural Areas and Small Municipalities (PRAGUAS) program, implemented by SAPYSB and financed by the World Bank (through loan 7035-EC), is an example of a demand-based project that (i) gives communities and municipalities the leading role in choosing water supply and sanitation systems that satisfy their needs and correspond to their ability to maintain them; (ii) requires financial contributions from municipalities and communities, as well as a commitment to provide the labor necessary to guarantee the sustainability of new infrastructure; and (iii) provides long-term technical assistance to communities (through the municipalities) for operating the systems. Finally, it is important that infrastructure services be considered an integral part of a broader vision of rural development involving increased productivity and growth of the rural economy.

SUPPORTING THE DECENTRALIZATION OF THE COUNTRY. According to other World Bank studies, the main problem with decentralization in Ecuador is "the many autonomous agencies responsible to the central government, but which do not have clear jurisdictions and responsibilities," such as the "regional development agencies, social funds, and the many institutes, implementation units, and agencies attached to ministries." These entities invest in many areas of rural infrastructure such as rural roads, potable water, and sanitation, without involving local governments (municipalities and provinces) in the process of prioritizing, planning, and implementing the investments. In addition to preventing true decentralization in the country, this tendency reduces the sustainability of the investments made, since the most complex examples of community infrastructure (rural roads, water supply systems, and so on) depend on long-term technical assistance from the municipalities. This assistance is often not provided when municipalities do not feel associated with the project from the start. For this reason, the Bank recommends that both municipalities and communities (and provinces, if appropriate) be involved in the process of planning and implementing community infrastructure.

Sectoral Action Plan

Problem	Policy measures		Progress indicators	Objectives/goals
	Short term (to June 2003)	Medium term (2003–07)		
		WATER SUPPLY AND SANITATION		
The sector's dependence on subsidies slows modernization of service providers.	Publish the list of resources effectively transferred by the central government and municipalities to service providers. Design a model formula linking the size of transfers to the sector to a set of variables (poverty, existing coverage, performance and autonomy of the service provider, and so on).	Apply the model formula to a pilot group of water supply companies and municipalities. Extend the use of the final formula to all providers of water supply and sanitation services.	Amount of transfers published. Model formula designed. Model formula applied to a group of water supply companies and municipalities. Formula extended to all providers of water supply and sanitation services.	Have service providers with modern, efficient structures and with the proper tariff-based resources to extend coverage and improve the quality of the service provided.
Incomplete regulatory and legal framework.	Prepare and pass a new Water Supply and Sanitation Law. Update Sectoral Policy Document.	Establish an independent regulatory authority for water supply and sanitation.	Draft law prepared. Law passed. Regulatory authority operating. Policy published.	Clear regulatory framework that encourages modernization of services and private investment.
Lack of transparency, in terms of performance,	Develop a sectoral information system.	Gather data on service providers.	Information system designed and operating,	

of companies in the sector.			Performance indictors of providers published ("benchmarking").	
Mismanagement of water resources.	Unify and modernize the legal and institutional framework for water resources management.	Improve and modernize the administration and management of available water resources (and related water infrastructure) in priority river basins.	Implementation of the new legal and institutional framework underway at the national level and in at least one priority river basin.	Implement an integrated water resources management system that includes a legal / institutional framework that is coherent at the national level, and has sufficiently decentralized administration and management.

ELECTRICITY

Incomplete reform.	Develop alternative strategies for private participation.	Implement the identified strategy (concession, capitalization, administration contracts, or others).	Production and discussion of the strategy; Companies with private participation.	Increase the efficiency of companies by introducing economic and financial incentives.
Institutional vulnerability.	Provide stability and independence to the posts of regulators using short-term administrative measures.	Amend the law to reduce state interference in regulation.	Decrees passed regarding the CONELEC Board of Directors; Amendments to the Law Confidence of regulated entities, allocation of investment resources.	Make the regulatory authority transparent and credible Make investors feel secure.
Unsustainable nature of the wholesale electricity market ($430 million deficit).	Restart tariff adjustments; include "lifeline" rate.	Implement deficit reduction strategy Implement corporate.	Reduction of wholesale electricity market deficit.	Guarantee the financial viability of the wholesale electricity market.

(*Sectoral Action Plan continues on the following page.*)

Sectoral Action Plan (*continued*)

Problem	Policy measures Short term (to June 2003)	Medium term (2003–07)	Progress indicators	Objectives/goals
	Normalize EMELEC payments. Develop strategy for reducing accumulated deficit.	payment plan. Improve EMELEC management.		Reduce impact on low-income households.
Unsustainable financial nature of the sector.	1. Adjust rates. 2. Develop strategy for private sector participation.	Implement private sector participation.	1. Rates set at objective levels. 2. Losses reduced to reference levels. 3. Private sector participation.	Implement financial restructuring of the sector. Achieve greater efficiency.
Poor allocation of investment resources.	1. Adjust rates. 2. Effect juridical stability (via reform of CONELEC).	Implement legal reform regarding CONELEC.	Private investors developing new generation plants.	Meet future demand.
Insufficient coverage of the service.	Develop a rural energy strategy.	Implement the rural energy strategy.	1. Strategy defined. 2. Pilot projects in implementation stage. 3. Legal and regulatory changes made.	Service isolated areas.
Flawed environmental policy.	Begin operation of CONELEC environmental unit.	Implement environmental policy.	1. Environmental and social impact studies developed.	

			2. Implementation of measures to limit environmental and social impact of future projects.	Ensure environmental protection and attenuation of social consequences in electrical energy projects.

TELECOMMUNICATIONS

Lack of competition and private investment in the sector.	Establish the bases for new tendering for private participation in Andinatel and Pacifictel, including new tendering for mobile telephone service.	Choose a bid for private participation in Andinatel and Pacifictel, including bid(s) for cellular telephone service.	1. Increased percentage of private participation in operators. 2. Increased number of operators in each market.	1. Foment competition in the market. 2. Promote investment and increase number of operators in the market.
Overlapping responsibilities and confusion regarding the role of each institution.	Create a structural plan for the new organization of regulatory institutions in the sector.	Implement institutional reorganization according to the plan.	1. Reduction in number of regulatory agencies. 2. Consolidation of authority and functions in a single regulatory authority.	Establish a single regulatory authority that is separate from the agency that dictates policy in the telecommunications sector.
Contradictions between regulations and confusing legal framework.	Prepare a new draft of a general law on telecommunications to eliminate legal inconsistencies in the existing regulatory framework.	Carry out negotiations and make agreements necessary for the draft law to be passed by Congress.	Approval of a new law on telecommunications that is comprehensive, clear and effective.	Establish transparent regulatory framework that encourages private investment.

(Sectoral Action Plan continues on the following page.)

Sectoral Action Plan *(continued)*

Problem	Policy measures		Progress indicators	Objectives/goals
	Short term (to June 2003)	*Medium term (2003–07)*		
Rates not fixed according to real costs.	Continue adjusting rates; complete this before opening bidding for private participation in the companies.		Rates established according to costs.	Eliminate distortions in the market that discourage private investment.
Low coverage in rural and peri-urban areas.		Receive bids to extend telecommunications services in rural areas through a minimum subsidy financed by Fodetel.	Private companies implementing investment contracts in rural areas.	Increase penetration of telecommunications services in rural and peri-urban areas.
Little use of ICT for development in Ecuador.	Appoint a director of the National Connectivity Commission with ministerial rank.	Implement the National Connectivity Agenda in accordance with its design.	Increased use of ICT in schools, health centers, agencies and national government ministries, municipalities, and so on.	Increase the use of ICT in business and education and extend government services through use of ICT.
TRANSPORT				
Poor highway maintenance.	Establish micro-enterprises to maintain the main network.	Prepare and implement a project for maintaining and improving the main network.	50 companies, formed, trained, and working throughout the main network.	Improve the state of the network. Increase the network's useful economic life. Increase highway safety. Generate employment for unskilled workers.

Necessity of institutional reform.	Form a committee to carry out sectoral reform.	Rationalize and clarify the role of management agencies in the highway sector.	Completion of the strategic plan for the sector.	Improve service. Reduce costs to users. Guarantee more efficient use of resources.
High rate of rural poverty.	Prepare a rural roads project with the World Bank and Inter-American Development Bank.	Implement the rural roads project.	Preparation of highway plans at the provincial level. Guaranteed budget for national participation.	Eliminate bottlenecks impeding economic growth. Provide isolated areas with social services. Provide employment. Stimulate agricultural production.

8

Urban Development[1]

Alexandra Ortiz

The urban population of Ecuador is growing at an increasing rate, not only in Guayaquil and Quito, but also in some smaller cities. In addition to natural urban growth and rural migration to urban zones, this process is being spurred by the international flow of persons displaced by the civil conflict in Colombia. The general deterioration of the macroeconomic situation in the country in combination with this heavy population increase in urban areas has resulted in a dramatic increase in urban poverty. The "urbanization" of poverty has caused the multiplication of squatter settlements that house over half of the population. In these marginal barrios, living conditions are precarious and residents are totally exposed to the elements. Often several families and a great number of individuals live in one dwelling, they lack basic sanitation and water connections, and access to servicesis very difficult. Part of the problem is that the price of housing solutions in the formal market is beyond the reach of the majority. While the price of partially urbanized land in established neighborhoods varies between $US50 and $ 60 per m², the price of land that has not been urbanized in illegal subdivisions is only $US4 per m², the only affordable option for the poor. The System of Incentives for Housing (SIV), introduced in 2000, is a direct subsidy system based on demand. Through the SIV, low-income families receive cash payments for housing based on transparent and established criteria. Unfortunately, however, families that are beneficiaries of the SIV do not have the purchasing power to acquire private sector housing. In order to confront this problem, a program of global urban improvement should be implemented to decrease the economic, social, and physical vulnerability of the poorest of Ecuador's urban poor. This program should also include preventive policies, particularly for the functioning of land markets and management of natural disasters.

---

1. Alexandra Ortiz is the World Bank's main urban economist. Valuable input and collaboration were provided by Marianne Fay and Thakoor Persaud, also with the World Bank.

A. Diagnostic Study

Urban development is of crucial importance to global economic development in Ecuador. Owing to the high percentage of residents living in urban areas and the fact that the population growth rate is greater than the regional average, the urbanization process is very dynamic in the country. Since industry and services, both typically urban activities, represent the largest share of GDP (34 percent and 59 percent, respectively) cities are the best places to implement effective development interventions. This chapter contains a summary of the main aspects involved in Ecuador's urban development. The first subsection presents statistical data to provide a typology of the population's urban nature, while the second offers a concise analysis of housing and land. The third subsection focuses on access, quality, and cost of basic urban services. The fourth briefly summarizes an analysis of the vulnerability of the poor in the face of an economic crisis and natural disasters. The document concludes with a second section containing specific recommendations.

Urbanization

Ecuador is one of the least urbanized countries of South America (see Figure 1). In 2001, 63 percent of the population lived in urban areas, compared to 76 percent in Latin America overall, and 80 percent in South America. However, this relatively lower level of urbanization is coupled with a population growth rate above the regional average: while South America's urban population increased an average of 2.1 percent annually between 1995 and 2000, the rate for Ecuador was 3.6 percent. During the next five years the rate is projected at 1.9 and 3 percent percent, respectively. Even more compelling is the fact that the increase in urban population accounts for 91 percent of total demographic growth in Ecuador between 1990 and 2000 (World Bank [several years]; United Nations [2000]).

Figure 1. Urbanization in Ecuador in Comparison with Latin America

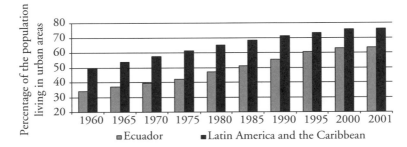

Source: World Bank, several years.

Another important characteristic of urbanization in Ecuador is that the population is concentrated in two cities, rather than in just one as is common in many countries of Latin America: Guayaquil, with an estimated population of 1.7 million in 1998, and Quito, the capital with approximately 1.6 million (Global Urban Observatory of the United Nations—GUO). Nearly half of the urban population—and a third of the entire population—is concentrated in these two cities. Guayaquil, in the coastal region, continues to be the country's most important commercial center, while Quito, in the Sierra region, is the center of political and administrative power.

While Guayaquil and Quito continue to grow at elevated rates,[2] some smaller cities (100,000 to 300,000 residents) and third-tier (30,000 to 100,000 residents), are growing even faster. In addition to natural urban growth and rural migration to urban areas, both important phenomena in Ecuador, foreigners are also arriving. The cities located in the north are the recipients of important waves of international immigrants, particularly people displaced by the civil conflict in Colombia.

When combined with the general economic deterioration, this heavy migration to urban areas has resulted in a dramatic increase in urban poverty. In 1995, 19 percent of the urban population was poor. By 1999, this percentage had jumped over 100 percent, reaching 42 percent. The high figures show that the urban proportion of poverty is growing rapidly, with an increase from 33 percent in 1995 to 48 percent in 1999 (SIISE). As shown in Figure 2,[3] other indicators that measure poverty levels also have worsened such as the poverty gap (the amount needed to lift the poor above the poverty line, as a percentage of the line), and the poverty severity index (which measures level of inequality between the population below the poverty line).

One of the consequences of the urbanization of poverty is the appearance of squatter settlements in the large and medium-sized cities. According to data from the Ministry of Urban Development and Housing (*Ministerio de Desarrollo Urbano y Vivienda*—MIDUVI), the percentage of households in these settlements rose to 64 percent in Guayaquil in 1994, of which 45 percent did not have property titles. These percentages are lower in Quito, but still high: 30 percent and 18 percent, respectively. In intermediate-size cities of the Sierra region, these percentages are also high, although they fluctuate widely between 25 and 13 percent. The worst conditions are in the medium-sized cities of the coastal region, where 70 percent of the population is concentrated in marginal barrios and where 56 percent of this popu-

---

2. The annual combined rate for the two cities was 2.3 percent during 1990–2001. However, other data from the United Nations and the Inter-American Development Bank indicates that during the five-year period 1993–98, Guayaquil grew 4.6 percent and Quito grew 2.8 percent annually.

3. The term recount in Figure 2 is equivalent to the incidence of poverty in Figure 2: percentage of inhabitants below the poverty line.

Figure 2. Urban Poverty in Ecuador, 1995–99

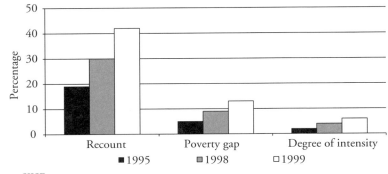

Source: SIISE.

lation lacks property titles. These numbers are very high and although the definition of "illegal occupants of barrios" differs greatly from one country to another, the data provided by the GUO demonstrates marked differences between Guayaquil and other cities similar in size within the region (see Table 1).[4]

Land and Housing in Urban Areas

Ecuador is characterized by a low rate of urban homeowners compared with other countries in the region (see Table 2), particularly among the poor. However, the

Table 1. Percentage of the Population without Formal Property Titles (1998)

City	Population	Percentage without formal property rights
Asunción (Paraguay)	1,080,000	9.8%
Córdoba (Argentina)	1,198,000	15%
Guayaquil (Ecuador)	2,166,000	54%
Recife (Brasil)	1,346,000	16.2%
Rosario (Argentina)	987,800	7.9%
Santa Cruz de la Sierra (Bolivia)	904,376	13%

Source: GUO.

4. Worldwide information is only available for a sample of 232 cities, including 53 cities in Latin America and the Caribbean. Of these cities, only a few have a population close to one million inhabitants, and complete information on the property regime is available for even fewer.

Table 2. Housing Ownership Rates in Ecuador and in Other Countries

	Ecuador	Argentina	Peru	Mexico	Chile	Colombia
All of the urban population	0.55	0.77	0.73	0.71	0.67	0.49
Income	1999	1998	1999	1999	2000	1999
1	0.53	0.78	0.65	0.63	0.62	0.30
2	0.48	0.72	0.72	0.65	0.64	0.44
3	0.53	0.73	0.71	0.69	0.68	0.54
4	0.58	0.79	0.77	0.77	0.72	0.58
5	0.63	0.83	0.82	0.81	0.68	0.58

Note: Sample only includes the urban population.
Source: World Bank estimates.

data presented in the table could also be overstated, since the poor tend to declare themselves as owners even when this is not the case on paper (legally), because of the fear of public measures to crack down on squatting. Since security of tenure is the main form of access to patrimony for the urban poor, this situation is cause for great concern. The root of the problem is the inability to make payments and lack of financing.

According to MIDUVI's analyses, urbanized and partially urbanized lots should only cost between $US660 and $1,330 (or $US6 and $ 11 per m² for lots of 120m²), so that the lowest income group can have access to them. Land for dwellings for medium-income households costs between $US50 and $ 60 per m², while partially urbanized lots in informal settlements cost between $US15 and $ 25 per m². On the other hand, lands that have not been urbanized cost $US4 per m² in illegal subdivisions. This has generated a progressive supply of informal housing: of total annual housing demand of approximately 54,000 units, the informal sector provides close to 31,000 each year, covering over 50 percent of the demand.

To improve this situation, in 2000, a direct subsidy system was introduced based on demand (the Housing Incentives System—SIV), one of the main programs administered by MIDUVI. The Ministry stopped participating in the direct execution of housing projects years ago, promoting private sector participation instead with the help of subsidies. The SIV system awards cash payments to low-income families through transparent and established criteria, and payments can be used to purchase new homes or improve old dwellings As of this date, 43 percent of the new homes built each year receive SIV support. Although during the 1990s the private sector only built houses for the highest income groups, the new system produced a change and the private sector now reaches the third income group with housing units that fluctuate between $US4,500 and $8,000. However, as shown in Table 3, these prices continue to be outside the range of the poorest urban Ecuadorans.

Table 3. Effects of the Subsidy on Purchasing Power for Housing

Group	Average monthly income (dollars)	Purchasing power in U.S. dollars	Purchase power with subsidy (dollars)
1	104	1,294	3,094
2	184	2,289	4,089
3	281	3,992	5,792
4	439	7,982	N/D
5	922	18,937	N/D

Source: IDB (2002).

The situation is even worse for the poorest households regarding the private financial sector. In the past, commercial banks performed an important role in financing housing for medium- and high-income groups, in particular during the oil boom period. But the economic crises, particularly the banking crisis of 1999, caused a sharp drop in the mortgage portfolios of banks. Even the Ecuadoran Housing Bank (Banco Ecuatoriano de la Vivienda, BEV) has suffered a reduction in its mortgage portfolio, despite a recent restructuring which has progressively transformed it from direct lender to second-tier financial institution. In light of this situation, the banking sector is not very interested in extending credit to low-income borrowers, since small loans are considered to carry a high risk as well as higher costs in relation to capital.

The municipalities also play an important role in this process, at least potentially. The decentralization laws establish that municipalities are responsible for urban planning functions and also must establish zoning prerequisites and approval processes for building. While municipalities can undertake local housing programs, they are not obligated to do so. Larger municipalities (Guayaquil and Quito) have joined forces with the private sector to turn over lots with basic services to low-income families, and they have also created programs to regularize property rights for those living in illegal settlements.

The accumulated housinghousing deficit is close to 850,000 homes, while the qualitative deficit is 350,000 (IDB 2002) if overcrowded shelters built with temporary materials, and without adequate sanitation and other characteristics are included. Table 4 shows that urban housinghousing conditions are worst in the coastal region.

Urban Services

In 1999, access to potable water inside houses in urban areas was 58 percent, five percentage points higher than in 1995. On the other hand, the statistic for sanitary services was calculated at 65% (Integrated System of Social Indicators of Ecuador—SIISE). Both percentages are low compared to standards in South America, and it is

Table 4. Housing Conditions in Urban Areas of Ecuador (1998) (percent)

Housing conditions	Coast	Sierra	East
Percentage with deficient housing conditions	29	22	19
Percentage with overcrowded conditions	44	24	26
Percentage of dwellings with walls built from temporary materials	19	0.7	0.2
Percentage without sanitation inside the dwelling	61	13.3	19.1

Notes:
1. Deficient dwellings include "renter's room," "mediaguas," "rancho, hut, or shack"
2. "Overcrowded conditions" refers to dwellings with more than three people per room.
Source: PHO (2001), based on surveys on living conditions.

estimated that they are dropping rapidly due to the crisis. However, these statistics conceal important differences between large and small cities in different regions. Table 5 shows that this situation is extremely serious in the coastal region, where less than half of the population has water connections in their dwelling, and less than 40 percent has sewage. The collection of solid wastes by municipal services is very spotty, particularly in the coastal region. In Guayaquil, the largest city in the region, an estimated 70 percent of the dwellings had water connections and 42 percent of homes had toilets inside in 1998, according to the Global Urban Observatory of the United Nations. These statistics indicate that 600,000 people in Guayaquil, a considerable number, had to find access to water through alternative means, which takes more time—and frequently this water is lower in quality and more expensive. More than one million people living in the city utilize latrines, septic pits, or simply dump sewage water into their back yard, on side streets or rivers nearby.

Table 5. Access to Water, Sanitation, and Trash Collection in Urban Areas of Ecuador (1998) (percent)

Indicator	Coast	Sierra	East
Water connection inside dwelling	42.1	69	66.1
Sanitation inside dwelling	39.2	86.8	81
Collection of solid wastes by municipal services	68.2	87.6	81
Access to electricity	99.6	99.6	98.6

Source: PHO (2001).

In addition to low coverage levels, the quality of services is deficient. In the case of water, residents without connections inside their dwellings spend an average of eight minutes in all urban areas (PHO 2001) trying to find this vital liquid, but it can increase to 12 minutes for those who utilize public faucets and up to 14 minutes when the water is taken from a river nearby. The water for all of these sources is of dubious quality, and up to 70 percent of urban Ecuadorans have to treat their water through various methods. Of this 70 percent, 26 percent have a home connection. The same source informs us that up to 25 percent of children five years old and under suffer from diarrhea during any given month. This statistic comprises 23 percent of the children without home connections, and 28 percent of the children in the opposite situation, which is not much of a difference. Other complaints refer to interruptions in service, inefficient services for the customer, and high water rates without accountability. The problems with sanitation services are even more serious: in Quito the same pipes are used to evacuate rain water and sewage, creating serious health risks during flooding. Another problem in Quito is the lack of treatment for sewage water. Flooding is the main problem in Guayaquil, particularly the poorest families living near the Guayas River.

The tariff and subsidy situation in Ecuador is similar to other Latin American countries—that is, (i) tariffs tend to be very low and they do not cover operational costs or investment costs (see Table 6); (ii) although tariffs are not regulated by the national government, they very rarely increase because of the fear that this would be an extremely unpopular measure; and (iii) subsidies are awarded based on consumption and not on purchasing power (IDB 2002; Yepes and Gómez 2002). This situation has had a negative impact on the finances of municipal water and sewage companies that have been charged with providing these services since decentralization was initiated. In order to relieve this problem, the companies in Guayaquil and Quito have begun to solicit private sector participation. In the case of Quito, Empresa Municipal de Alcantanillado y Agua Potable de Quita (EMAAP-Q) has delegated the updating and maintenance of the cadastral study to the private sector, as well as meter reading, billing, collection, and client services for certain contracts. The next step for EMAAP-Q will be the concession of the eastern area of Quito (Parroquias Orientales), an area with 100,000 medium- and high-income residents

Table 6. Tariff and Operation Costs for Water Companies in Ecuador, 2001 (millions of dollars)

Indicator	Guayaquil	Quito	Otras ciudades
Tariff revenue	21	34	19
Cost O&M	29	47	34
Debt service	13	13	5

Source: Yepes and Gómez, 2002.

and 16,000 connections. In Guayaquil, Empresa Cantonal de Agua Potable y Alcantanllado de Guayaquil (ECAPAG), with the help of the World Bank, has also increased private sector participation. The institutional framework, however, is still not clear because of duplication of management and regulatory functions between municipal enterprises and MIDUVI subsecretariats of water and sanitation.

Economic Vulnerability and Vulnerability to Natural Disasters

The urban poor in Ecuador face difficult conditions. The serious deficiencies in housing and basic services described in this chapter become problems of hygiene, health and sanitation, low educational levels, complex family relationships, and even violence and criminal activity. The problems are complicated further by the great vulnerability to any economic crisis or physical disaster. Perhaps most depressing, these circumstances constitute a vicious circle from which it is very difficult to escape.

In terms of economic vulnerability, the most serious problem is the high percentage of urban poor in need of employment. Among those who do have jobs, a large majority work in the informal sector without security or benefits. This situation forces them to adopt a series of survival strategies that affect individuals, particularly women and children, the family structure and budget, as well as interfamilial relationships. A study done by Moser (1997) for the Urban Development Program describes the situation of an extremely poor community of Guayaquil called Cisnes Dos. This study was done at the beginning of the 1990s, but its findings are still valid. Some of the most important results are: (i) mothers are forced to increase their participation in the working world and decrease the amount of time they spend taking care of their children; (ii) children of both sexes (12–14 years) also must work an average of 15 hours weekly in family businesses or taking care of their younger siblings; (iii) family nuclei are diminishing and being replaced by extended families with "nests" of relatives who live on the same land and help to take care of the children, and help with cooking and other reciprocal chores; (iv) there is a decrease in family spending and changes in composition, with greater priority given to education in the face of nutritional and health needs, or housing repairs; (v) increased sharing of assets between households, on exchange or credit; and (vi) there is greater participation at the community level in formal protection networks and greater dependency on these networks.

A second aspect of urban vulnerability is the high risk of natural disasters that characterizes the country. Quito, for example, is located in a valley surrounded by high mountains, both on the east as well as the west, several of which are active volcanoes. A number of creeks that feed the Machangara and Monjas rivers cross the city. There is the serious risk of flooding, landslide, and volcanic activity. And the poor, who normally live on the outskirts of the city and close to the creeks, are more exposed to thesedangers. The situation is particularly critical because rainwater and sewage are all carried by the same pipes. In Guayaquil, seismic activity poses the greatest risk, and the city has been affected by several earthquakes in the past which have destroyed the dwellings of the poorest inhabitants and cut off basic services. At the end of the 1990s, Ecuador was hit by ocean swells that affected the coast. In addition to injuries and loss of human life, El Niño destroyed many dwellings and seriously damaged productive infrastructure, roads, and services.

B. Recommendations

The situation of the poorest Ecuadorans living in urban areas is harsh, and threatens to become worse because of the rapid increase in poverty in all cities. We propose that this serious problem be treated through an urban improvement program in various cities, particularly in the coastal region. This would help to support and optimize actions undertaken by various municipalities, where property titles have been awarded, and it would also take advantage of the high level of social participation that exists in poor neighborhoods.[5] However, in order to go beyond the classic urban improvement program that is by nature corrective, it is necessary to understand the dynamics of the housing and real estate market, both for land as well as dwellings, and find a way to bring housing within reach of the poorest of the poor. In addition, since urban improvement means building or improving basic infrastructure, it is important to keep in mind the aspect of disaster prevention.

Because of this, the program of recommendations is two-fold, one part preventive and the other corrective. The preventative part has two main objectives: (i) understand completely how land markets work, and (ii) decrease vulnerability to natural disasters. Regarding land markets, there are techniques—such as price gradients and density, indexes of unplanned urban growth, prices and uses of land, impact of regularization of soil, spatial and temporal price analysis, densities, land use and building permits—that would all help to characterize formal and informal land markets. This analysis should result in the formulation of specific reforms that allow the poorest urban families to get access to formal land markets Regarding disaster vulnerability, the program should lend technical assistance to municipalities and communities in the form of geo-referenced information systems (such as vulnerability maps), institutional dispositions to prevent and mitigate disasters, programs to raise community awareness, and specific civic works.

The corrective part of the program should deal with housing and infrastructure deficiencies at the neighborhood level, such as the organization of land lots, invest-

---

5. The Bank has considerable experience with urban improvement programs all over the world, and can offer specialized knowledge to the Government of Ecuador. In Latin America, projects such as El Mezquital in Guatemala City and the CAMEBA project underway in Caracas, are good examples of direct intervention to improve living conditions for thousands of families.

ment in infrastructure, social development programs, and a pilot project to generate income. The territorial organization of land lots includes registering and turning over property titles, improving cadastral studies and municipal registries, and the process of awarding property titles, in addition to technical assistance to improve household conditions. One phenomenon that is well documented by studies·is that the awarding of property titles increases property value and thus represents a transfer of patrimony to the poor, increasing private investment in housing and strengthening the possibility of obtaining credit. The improvement of related information systems, particularly cadastral studies and registries, should translate into greater transparency in real estate transactions, and an increase in the municipal tax base. Investments in infrastructure should include water connections and sewage; improvement of roads and pedestrian access, ditches, and public lighting; as well as the construction of social centers and social infrastructure of other types. General support for community organization and extension, as well as education and training of communities in environmental matters will be decisive in order to ensure active participation in the design, implementation, and evaluation of programs. Finally, a pilot project to generate income through small businesses, better market information systems, and the formation of local capabilities is needed to complete an integral intervention program to combat urban poverty.

Ecuadoran municipalities have been in charge of water, sanitation, sewage, drainage, trash collection, roads, and urban transport since 1997. They are ready to directly implement these types of programs. The Special Law for State Decentralization and Social Participation also allows municipal governments to assume responsibility for social services, particularly health and education. Despite the incipient nature of the decentralization process, municipalities have progressed in this area during the last five years, especially in terms of diversifying their income sources and decreasing dependency on transferences from the national government. Important efforts are underway to boost local tax collection, and in the case of the most advanced municipalities, to improve access to credit.

Policy Matrix

Problems	Recommendations		Progress achievement indicators	Objectives/goals
	Short term (to June 2003)	Medium term (2003–07)		
Increase in the quantity of urban squatter settlements.	Analysis of urban land markets to determine reasons for failure.	Implementation of specific measures that result from analysis.	Prices of un-urbanized lands and urbanized lots in different areas of each city.	Deal with land market failures that are the fundamental cause of formation of squatter settlements.
Decrease in the quality of life in existing settlements.	Pilot project for urban improvement.	Extending scale of pilot project to turn it into an urban improvement project.	Water and sewage connections, kilometers of pedestrian and vehicular access.	Improve quality of life and productivity of poor urban residents and their integration into the formal city.
High vulnerability of urban poor to economic crisis and natural disasters.	Vulnerability analysis.	Technical assistance and infrastructure to decrease vulnerability.	Number and type of risk maps produced and interpreted, awareness campaigns, institutional framework to prevent and mitigate disasters.	Achieve greater awareness and preparation for natural disasters.

Part II

Boosting Sustainable and
Equitable Social Development

9

Education[1]

Carlos Rojas

The principal challenges facing education in Ecuador are extending the coverage of quality education, so that all boys and girls can receive 10 years of basic schooling, and financing the sector and improving its administration. Although the country has made significant progress in expanding the system's coverage, there are signs of inequity between urban and rural areas, and between the indigenous and nonindigenous populations. Coverage at the secondary level is limited, with a net school enrollment rate of 51 percent. In terms of quality, the results of the academic achievement tests known as APRENDO, indicate that third-, fifth-, and seventh-grade students have deficiencies in achievement and aptitude for language and mathematics. These deficiencies are especially pronounced among students who live in rural areas, who attend public schools, or who live in the coastal region. As for financing, spending on education was cut in half in the past decade. This has affected the provision of teaching materials, maintenance of school infrastructure, and teacher training and salaries. In terms of administration, it is still centralized. Thus, increased public and private investment in the sector will not have the desired impact unless the sector is decentralized. Clearly, in order to achieve the established coverage and quality goals, spending on education must be raised to at least 5 percent of the GDP. Furthermore, quality must be improved based on high-performance programs monitored through institutionalizing the APRENDO testing. Finally, it is imperative to review the structure and functions of the Ministry of Education, analyzing personnel selection processes, and further decentralizing education, so as to grant greater autonomy to the local level and increase parent participation.

---

1. Carlos Rojas is a specialist in education for the World Bank.

A. Introduction

Ecuador is one of 189 countries that have pledged to meet the eight "Millennium Development Goals" aimed at eradicating extreme poverty and at improving the living conditions of its people by the year 2015. One of these goals is universal elementary school education, which means that all boys and girls would complete elementary school. Given that investment in education has diminished in recent years to levels below 3 percent of the GDP, the attainment of this goal is in great jeopardy.

Access for children and young people to education in Ecuador has increased with each generation, resulting in higher average years of schooling. Persons born in 1933 were, on an average, functionally illiterate, with less than four years of schooling, while persons born in 1973 have an average of nine years of schooling. Estimates by the Integrated System of Social Indicators of Ecuador (*Sistema Integrado de Indicadores Sociales de Ecuador*—SIISE) indicate that the present generation of boys and girls will attain 11.5 years of schooling. In elementary school education, Ecuador, like the rest of the countries in the region, has made significant progress, steadily extending coverage. Despite these efforts, however, there are still large sectors of the population without access to education or that are prematurely forced out of the system. In 1999, the net enrollment rate for elementary schools was 90 percent. For secondary schools, coverage is still very limited, with a net school enrollment rate of 51 percent, and at the level of higher education, the net enrollment rate is just 14 percent. Only one out of every three children between ages four and five is enrolled in preschool.

Progress in coverage for the sector, particularly in elementary school education, is due, in great measure, to the Ecuadoran government's investments in education during the 1970s and 1980s. In the 1970s, spending on education averaged 4.4 percent of GDP. This percentage rose in the 1980s, to as much as 5.8 percent of GDP in 1988. Spending on education has gradually diminished since that time, reaching levels as low as 2.7 percent in 2000. Education spending is currently estimated at close to 3 percent of GDP. Unless investment in education is restored to the levels of the past decade, it will be difficult for Ecuador to meet the goal of universal elementary school education by the year 2015.

This chapter first presents the principal problems facing the educational system in Ecuador. It then summarizes some of the Ministry of Education's initiatives, actions, and measures to promote decentralization of the system. Also included is a summary of the 10-year plan adopted in 2000.Lastly, conclusions and policy recommendations are given, summarized in a policy matrix, which includes progress indicators.

B. The Educational System: Principal Problems

Ecuador has a complex institutional system (see Box 1). Several plans and initiatives have been developed during the 1990s and in the past few years (see Box 2). Yet many challenges still face the educational sector. The principal challenges are described below:

(*Text continues on page 271.*)

Box 1. Ecuador's Institutional Framework for the Education Sector

The Ministry of Education and Culture is responsible for formulating policies in the sector, administering the national education system, and managing and administering certain aspects of cultural and sports affairs. The Ministry of Education and Culture is also responsible for disseminating scientific and technological knowledge. Ecuador has a National Education Council comprising the Minister of Education or his/her representative, the president of an institution of higher education representing the National Council of Universities and Polytechnic Institutes, two members of the teachers' union, one representative for public schools and another for private schools, and a representative from the National Council on Development. The Ministry of Social Welfare and the Children's and Family Institute are responsible for early childhood education (zero to six years). These two institutions provide coverage to approximately 250,000 at-risk children. The National Council of Universities and Polytechnic Institutes, as an autonomous entity, regulates, coordinates, and administers higher education.

THE ORGANIZATIONAL STRUCTURE of the Ministry of Education and Culture includes four technical/administrative levels: executive, advisory, support, and operational. The system has four territorial levels: central, regional, provincial, and local (educational establishments and networks). There are also subsystems for "Spanish" education and "Intercultural Bilingual Education."

CENTRAL ADMINISTRATION. The executive level is responsible for setting policies, and for general administration and control of the educational and cultural system on the national, regional, provincial, and educational institution levels. The advisory level is responsible for overall planning in the educational system. The support level is in charge of the administration and provision of human, financial, material, and technological resources, and for providing services for carrying out the activities of the Ministry of Education and Culture. The operational level is responsible for educational and cultural development, and in said capacity administers, controls, supervises, and carries out activities aimed at meeting the objectives of the

(*Box continues on the following page.*)

Box 1. (*continued*)

Ministry of Education and Culture. There are three deconcentrated entities: The National Service for Books and Teaching Materials; the National Directorate on Physical Education, Sports, and Recreation; and the National Directorate on School Structures. There are also five decentralized entities: the National Directorate on Intercultural, Bilingual Education; the Ecuadoran Institute on Educational Loans and Scholarships; the National Institute on Cultural Heritage; the Ecuadoran Cultural Association (*Casa de la Cultura Ecuadoriana*); and the National Sports Forecasting Company.

PROVINCIAL ADMINISTRATION. The subsystem for "Spanish" education includes 22 Provincial Directorates of Education and Culture, 10 of which are under the technical and administrative control of the Office of the Assistant Secretary for Education, 6 of which are under the Regional Undersecretariat of the Coastline, and 6 of which of are under the control of the Undersecretariat for the Southern Region. These two regional undersecretariats have an organizational structure that replicates the structure of the central administration. The subsystem for intercultural, bilingual education, has Provincial Directorates in the 16 provinces with indigenous population.

FORMAL EDUCATION AND NONFORMAL EDUCATION. Intercultural Bilingual Education is also divided into formal education and nonformal education. Formal education includes 10 years of basic education (one year of preschool, six years of elementary school, and three years of basic middle school education); three years of specialized secondary education; technical institutes; and university education. Formal education contains three specific programs: (i) the regular program, which requires attendance in accordance with age groups, with a sequence of grades and a specific duration of courses; (ii) alternative programs for boys and girls who are not enrolled in regular programs, or who, for a variety of reasons, have not completed their programs (basic literacy and postbasic literacy is included in these programs); and (iii) special education programs. Nonformal education includes early childhood education (zero to six-year-olds) and educational, cultural, and technical instruction programs for boys and girls, youth, and adults. These programs are offered through both public and private institutions.

Box 2. Government Strategies and Initiatives

PROGRESS IN THE DECENTRALIZATION OF THE SYSTEM. In Ecuador, the legal framework for decentralization and deconcentration is found in the Constitution of the Republic and in a series of legal provisions. Despite the good intentions toward establishing a decentralized system, the efforts made in that direction are quite timid and incomplete. Current decentralization efforts are based in part on prior experiences, especially those of the 1990s, which were partially successful. Examples of these experiences include the Program for Better Quality Basic Education, which created 120 Educational Matrix Centers (*Centros Educativos Matrices*—CEM), with each CEM constituted by approximately 20 schools comprising a network; and the Autonomous Rural School Networks Program, known as *Redes Amigas*. The latter has as its objectives the following: (i) to grant autonomy to approximately 20 percent of the rural schools (close to 2,400 schools) for the management of their resources, with greater participation from parents and members of the community in school administration; and (ii) to improve teaching conditions in basic rural education (elementary school and middle school) in the beneficiary schools' zones of influence. A third example is the decentralization of approximately 1,800 secondary schools, which are managed as decentralized units and receive funds (cash transfers) directly from the Ministry of Economy and Finance. With the funds received, the school pays its teachers directly and covers campus utility bills and maintenance expenses. In the municipality of Quito, decentralized education currently covers 42 Municipal Educational Centers, more than 12,000 students, and 900 teachers. The Quito experience is a further example of actions that are conducive to providing autonomy and delegating functions to the various levels. The annex includes a summary of the progress mentioned above, which plays a fundamental role in future educational policy decisions.

PROGRESS IN PLANNING. Various plans have been delineated by past administrations to continue the process of extending coverage, improving the quality of services, and, in general, making services more efficient. In 2000, the Ministry of Education and Culture prepared and published a 10-year plan covering the various levels of the education sector. The plan sets forth policies to be followed, priorities for the sector, and strategies to be implemented. The fundamental objective of this plan is to ensure universal access to general education (that is, basic education, high school, and adult education), in accordance with the principle of equity. This plan contemplates a Ministry "converted

(Box continues on the following page.)

Box 2. (*continued*)

into an organization that functions as a leader; that is decentralized, efficient, and flexible; and whose management contributes to reducing inequities in access to educational services and in the distribution of knowledge..." (Ministry of Education and Culture 2001). The plan in question established the following policies and strategies to be implemented: (i) universal access to early childhood and basic education, while ensuring that students stay in school at those levels of education; (ii) improved quality of education, to ensure significant learning and the integral development of the students; (iii) strengthening of intercultural, bilingual education; and (iv) better conditions for teachers, along with regulation of the teacher training system for intercultural, bilingual education. In order to implement these actions, the Ministry of Education and Culture has considered the following measures: (i) decentralization and devolve authority, with specific strategies for each level of administration—central, provincial, and local; and (ii) changes in financial and budgetary administration that involve strengthening and integrating the planning and financing functions; (iii) monitoring and evaluating the use of financial resources; and (iv) a decentralized allocation of budgetary funds in order to generate autonomous school networks and schools.

THE "SOCIAL CONTRACT FOR EDUCATION." More recently (September 2002), the agencies of the United Nations system proposed what has been called the "Social Contract for Education," which sets forth the following goals: "…ensure that Ecuadoran girls and boys have access to and remain in school for 10 years of quality basic education; and adopt standards of quality in education, taking into consideration the ethnic and cultural diversity of the country, which would include training in ethical, moral, and civic values, so that Ecuador would become one of the countries with the best indicators in basic education within the region." The declaration also includes strategies that need to be followed to meet these goals, which can be summarized as follows: (i) training and continuing professional development for the teachers, and decent pay; (ii) an equitable distribution of human resources in accordance with the needs of the schools; (iii) compliance with curricula; (iv) establishments with adequate infrastructure and equipment; (v) an incentive policy based on the implementation of a national evaluation system; (vi) support to needy families (through scholarships and school meals, for instance); and (vii) ensuring that appropriate financial resources to meet the goals that have been established.

Limited and Unequal Access to Education

Considerable discrepancies and inequities are seen in the provision of services when comparing income quintiles or urban, rural or indigenous/non-indigenous populations. While the population of the poorest quintile in rural areas has less than 4 years of schooling, the population of the wealthiest quintile in urban areas has more than 12 years of schooling (World Bank World Development Report 2000). The results of the Living Conditions Survey of 1999 indicate that the indigenous population over the age of 24 living in the rural highland areas has an average of 2.4 years of schooling, compared to 5 years of schooling for the rural nonindigenous population in the same areas and 7.6 years of schooling on a national level. In 1999 the net school enrollment rate for basic middle school education among the poorest quintile of the population was 19 percent, while for specialized high school this figure was 11 percent. Among the wealthiest quintile of the population, these rates were 80 percent and 62 percent, respectively. Inequities are also reflected in higher education, as only 2 percent of the population among the poorest quintile has access to higher education, as compared to 38 percent among the wealthiest quintile. A summary is presented below of this situation as seen in early childhood education, preschool, elementary, secondary, and higher education.

EARLY CHILDHOOD EDUCATION. The supply of early childhood education is very limited. Only 7.3 percent of children up to four years of age in the three poorest quintiles of the population have access to these services. It is estimated that out of a target population of close to 1.2 million children, only 97,000 are serviced by the two national programs. There is no national policy or strategy that addresses this group of children.

PRESCHOOL EDUCATION. This level, which is considered to be the first year of the mandatory 10-year cycle (basic education), covers only half of children who are age five. Only 42 percent of children among the poorest quintile have access to preschool education, as compared to 86 percent among the wealthiest quintile. Rural enrollments at this level account for only 22 percent of the total, even though the number of children in rural areas represents 44 percent of all children between four and five years of age. Net enrollment at this level (33 percent) for children between four and five is similar to that of other countries of the region with similar income.

ELEMENTARY SCHOOL EDUCATION. The majority of children in urban and rural areas have access to elementary school education. In 1999, net enrollment was 90 percent and gross enrollment was 109 percent, demonstrating high coverage. Yet a significant number of students were either younger, or, as happens more often, older than what was expected for this cycle. According to a study conducted by the World Bank (2000), at age six, only 65 percent and 78.6 percent of children from the two lowest income quintiles, respectively, were enrolled in school, while 98.8 percent of children from the wealthiest quintile were enrolled. At age seven, children from the poorest quintile were the only ones with late-enrollment problems (82.9 percent enrolled), and at age eight, the enrollment rate was 92.5 percent. The study also indicated that delayed enrollment age was principally a problem in rural areas, where, at age six, slightly more than 70 percent of children were enrolled, while in urban areas this figure was 90 percent. (See Figure 1).

At the elementary school level, the enrollment rate nationwide grew by 7 percent between the 1994–95 school year and the 1999–2000 school year—that is, by two million students. In this estimate, bilingual schools are included. Yet enrollments only grew by 3.9 percent during that same period in the rural areas. The annual enrollment growth rate was lower than the estimated growth of the population (2 percent). Over a five-year period, the number of teachers grew by 25 percent in

Figure 1: Net Enrollment Rates, by Consumption Quintiles and by Educational Levels

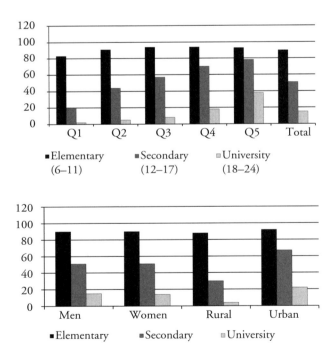

Source: Living Standards Measurement Study (LSMS) 1999), in Social Indicators System of Ecuador–SIISE) (*Sistema Integrado de Indicadores Sociales de Ecuador*—SIISE) (2000), and the author's calculations (using information based on consumption quintiles).

urban areas and 20 percent in rural areas, which reduced the student/teacher ratio from 26 to 23 during this period.

The Intercultural Bilingual Education subsystem, created in 1998, had slightly more than 85,000 students in 2000, which corresponds to 4.4 percent of the total enrollments in that year. This percentage is relatively small when one considers that between 12 and 25 percent[2] of the rural population is indigenous. Enrollments in bilingual schools increased by more than 100 percent in a decade. It is worth noting that the enrollment of males grew twice as much as the enrollment of females.

Close to one-third of elementary schools nationally (approximately 6,000) have only one teacher for the school. In the Amazon region the percentage of schools with one teacher is higher (53.5 percent). One-teacher schools cover an estimated 170,000 students or 9 percent of total elementary school enrollments. Since these schools are principally found in the country's poorest rural, isolated areas, they are at a disadvantage with respect to the rest of the public schools in the rural areas.

Despite significant reductions in grade repetition rates, these rates are still alarming, particularly in rural areas, where grade repetition rate is 13 percent during the first two grades, compared to 6 percent in urban areas. As well, the percentage of students in bilingual schools who are not promoted to the next grade has been shown to be almost double the number of students who are not promoted in "Spanish" schools.

BASIC MIDDLE SCHOOL AND SPECIALIZED HIGH SCHOOL EDUCATION. The nationwide enrollment rate at this educational level grew by 19 percent between school years 1994–95 and 1999–2000. During school year 1999–2000, the country had close to one million students enrolled in 3,473 schools. One out of every four students attended a private school, while educational institutions in rural areas accounted for only 14 percent of the students. This demonstrates that access to middle and high school is limited for poor and indigenous peoples. Enrollment in intercultural, bilingual education establishments amounts to less than 1 percent of total enrollments in middle and high school education. The net school enrollment rate is calculated at 50 percent. The student/teacher ratio is very low when compared to the average in Latin America.

Data from the Living Conditions Survey for the year 1995 indicate that the older the age-group, the less likely it is that youth will be enrolled in school. For example, 91 percent of youth who are 12 years of age were attending school, while in the same year, only 76 percent of 13-year-olds, 68 percent of 14-year-olds, 62 percent of 15-year-olds, 58 percent of 16-year-olds, and 55 percent of 17-year-olds were attending school. The gap between rich and poor is wider at this level than in the elementary grades. A study conducted by the World Bank, *Ecuador: Crisis, Poverty, and Social Conditions*, (2000) using data from the Living Conditions Survey of 1998 found

---

2. The percentage depends upon the source of information.

that the principal reason why 34 percent of children between 11 and 15 years of age were not attending an educational institution was the cost; 19 percent were not attending owing to a lack of interest, 16 percent because they had to work, 10 percent owing to lack of access, 4 percent because of sickness, and 3 percent because they had to do chores at home.

During school year 1998–99 almost 235,000 students, 14 percent of the population between 18 and 24 years of age, were enrolled in institutions of higher education. The percentage is very low when compared to Chile, which has a university enrollment of 21 percent, or Argentina which has a university enrollment of 27 percent. Eighty percent of the students enrolled attend public universities and the remaining 20 percent attend private universities. The *Universidad Central del Ecuador* and the *Universidad de Quito* account for almost 50 percent of university enrollments. Higher education is not equitable: Net enrollments are 4 percent in the country's rural areas and 22 percent in urban areas. Less than 1 percent of the population over 24 years of age has a university degree in the rural areas of the coastal region, compared to 8 percent in the cities. In the highlands region these percentages are 1.1 percent and 11.8 percent, respectively. By income quintiles, the percentages are 2 percent and 5 percent for the poorest quintiles and 38 percent for the wealthiest quintile of the population. In the highlands region, significant differences between genders are found: male population rates in institutions of higher learning are twice higher than female rates. Higher education is inefficient as it takes an average of 13.4 years of study for a person to graduate (including primary school years) at a cost of $US22,460. The rate of graduation at public universities is rarely more than 10 to 15 percent of the original freshman class (*Ecuador: Crisis, Poverty, and Social Conditions*, World Bank 2000).

In summary, inequities are seen at all levels of the system. It is clear that there are significant discrepancies among rural, indigenous, and urban populations and within income groups (See Figure 2). The school-age population of a poor, indigenous rural area is at a great disadvantage compared to non-poor, non-indigenous urban school-age children. Middle school, high school, and university education are principally aimed at the urban school population from the wealthiest quintiles, as the poor in rural areas have no possibility of enrolling in middle school. It is interesting to note that the analysis found no differences that could indicate problems of inequity between men and women in basic education.

Efforts to expand coverage have had positive results. It is important to note that illiteracy rates in the country have been significantly reduced. Currently it is estimated that 10.5 percent of the population over the age of 15 is illiterate. This illiteracy rate is only 3.2 percent among persons between 15 and 24, and 6.2 percent among 25- to 39-year-olds. As is to be expected, the greatest percentage of illiteracy is found among persons over the age of 65, among whom the illiteracy rate is 34.5 percent. It can also be noted that illiteracy is chiefly found in rural areas, and especially in indigenous regions.

Within the Ministry of Education, the National Directorate of Continuing Popular Education (*Dirección Nacional de Educación Popular Permanente*—DINEPP) is

Figure 2. Public Spending on Education by Consumption Quintile

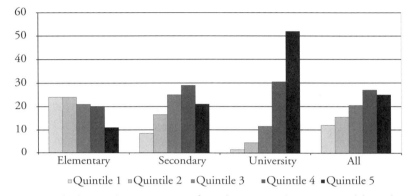

□Quintile 1 ▨Quintile 2 ▪Quintile 3   ▪Quintile 4 ▪Quintile 5

Source: National Educational Statistics System of Ecuador - SINEC (*Sistema Nacional de Estadísticas Educativas del Ecuador*—SINEC);, Living Conditions Survey, 1998,. iIn World Bank, (2000).

in charge of adult education. Currently it coordinates a plan aimed at improving the supply of formal and nonformal education for groups that for one reason or another have been excluded from the system. The progress report indicates that the plan lacks the political support and economic resources needed to put it into action.

Low Quality of the Education Imparted

Results from academic achievement tests (APRENDO) indicate deficiencies in the quality of teaching at the basic level. It is clear that the low quality of education is related to factors involving school campuses, the teaching staff, the family, and in general, to the socioeconomic conditions surrounding the students.

In 1996 the Ministry of Education and Culture implemented a system to measure the quality of education and ascertain student achievement in the areas of language and mathematics. This system was applied to students in second, sixth and ninth grades in public and private schools in the coastal region and the highlands. To date, the system has been applied four times (in 1996, 1997, 1998, and 2000). In general, results indicate deficiencies among the students in achievement and aptitude for language and mathematics, especially in the rural areas and among public school students.

Similarly, the deficient quality of education was noted in a survey conducted in Ecuador in 1998, known as *"Barómetro Latino"* ("Latin Barometer"). The survey's participants indicated that they considered the educational system in Ecuador to be one of the most deficient educational systems of the Americas. Researchers who conducted a survey of employers in 2001 for the World Economic Forum and Harvard University's Center for International Development (CID) reached the same conclusion. As is seen in Figure 3, the results for quality of education in Ecuador are the lowest from among 19 Latin American countries (Arellano 2002, pp. 75–76).

Figure 3. Quality of Schools, Based on the Opinion of the Business Sector

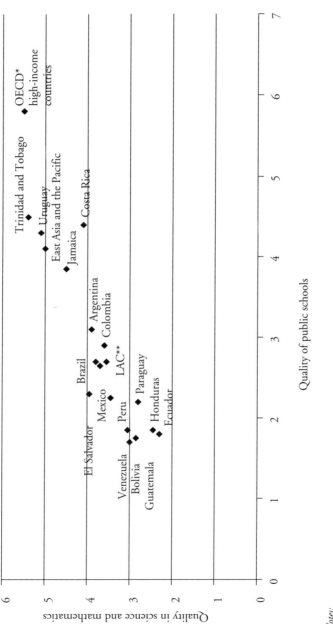

Notes:

* OECD = Organisation for Economic Co-operation and Development; ** LAC = Latin America and the Caribbean;

1 = Worse than most other countries; 7 = Among the best in the world.

Source: Global Competitiveness Report 2001–2002, Harvard University.

Among the principal causes that directly affect the quality of education, the following could be considered:

- Poor teacher training, particularly in the country's rural areas. Despite the efforts of the Ministry of Education to improve the quality of the teaching staff, teachers need more training, both in content and in teaching techniques. The majority of teachers in rural areas who have to work simultaneously with more than one grade or on more than one course (that is, in multigrade classrooms), have not been trained to handle such a situation. Similarly, there is still a long way to go in terms of teacher training for contexts of intercultural, bilingual education. A further problem is that teachers are using obsolete methodologies that are not conducive to furthering an effective teaching/learning process.
- Because of the economic crisis of the past few years, investment in teaching materials for students and the teaching staff is very limited or almost nil. It is common in rural areas to find students who do not have access to the most minimal school supplies (such as notebooks or pencils). It is also common, in both rural and urban areas, for school campuses to be in physically deplorable conditions that are not conducive to learning.
- Other factors affect the quality of education, related to child labor, absenteeism among children who work to help their parents, and other socioeconomic realities. It is important that future measurements under the APRENDO system include instruments to detect the influence of associated factors (family, school, teachers) in the students' academic achievement.

Serious Difficulties for Financing Education

Serious financial difficulties resulted in the funding cuts that made an impact on the educational sector. Teachers' salaries have been affected and families had to contribute more than they used to in the past to educational expenses. Some indicators are presented below:

Since the late 1980s, investments in education have been cut sharply as a result of the economic crisis. Available information suggests that spending on education dropped, on an average from 4.7 percent of GDP in the 1980s to 3.1 percent in 1998 and 2.7 percent in 2000. (See Figure 4).

As a result of the spending cuts, needed investments in education are not being made. Infrastructure maintenance is minimal and teachers' salaries have been reduced. This has contributed to a higher turnover rate, moonlighting, and absenteeism among teachers. Similarly, these pay cuts have probably reduced the interest taken in the profession by young people who would have wanted to be teachers. This situation could have serious consequences for the availability of well-trained teachers in the future.

Parents have had to increase their contribution to finance their children's education. For example, they have had to hire teachers to replace those who have aban-

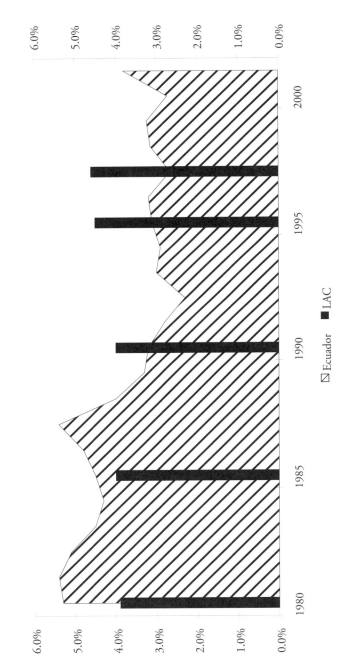

Figure 4. Spending on Education as a Percentage of the GDP in Ecuador and in Latin America and the Caribbean, 1980 to 2001

Sources: Data on Ecuador from 1980 to 1995 based on Social Indicators System of Ecuador (SIISE), 2000). Data, and from 1996 to 2001 from the Ministry of Finance and the Banco Central del Ecuador. Data on Latin America and the Caribbean (LAC) from the UNESCO database.

doned schools in isolated rural areas, or hire teachers for certain subject matters in secondary schools. The home survey conducted in 1998 indicates that 40 percent of parents from the poorest percentile contributed a monthly amount in fees and uniforms, both in elementary and secondary schools (excluding transportation, textbooks, and school supplies), that was almost equal to the monthly payment made by parents of private school students (*Ecuador: Crisis, Poverty, and Social Conditions*, World Bank 2000). Data from the most recent teacher census indicate that more than 1,000 public school teachers are paid with community funds (World Bank 2000).

During the years 2000 to 2001, higher education received 26 percent of the funds allocated to the educational sector, compared with 22 percent in 1995. In 2001, the budget for elementary and secondary education was the same as the amount allocated for these levels of education in 1995, while higher education received an increase in its budgetary allocation of almost 33 percent over that same period. From an equity point of view, these budgetary allocations are not advisable. Aggregate spending in education at all levels indicates that the lowest-income population quintile is allocated 12 percent of public spending on education, while the highest-income quintile is allocated 25 percent. The percentage of public spending on education that reaches the poorest sectors of the population is lower in Ecuador than in neighboring countries such as Peru, where 21 percent is channeled to the poorest population quintile, Bolivia (32 percent), or Chile (34 percent).

Problems in Sector Administration

Despite the magnitude of the educational sector's financial problems, one of the greatest challenges is the sector's administration. Greater public and private investment in education will not have a significant impact unless measures are taken to address administrative deficiencies. The principal issues are mentioned below, along with certain points that serve as indicators to illustrate the severity of the problem:

The Ministry of Education and Culture has an elevated turnover rate in its high-level authorities (ministers, assistant-ministers, provincial directors, and advisors). This situation impedes continuity in educational policies, makes it difficult to apply a long-term outlook for resolving problems in the sector, and also creates obstacles for teamwork within the Ministry. In its 118 years of existence, the Ministry of Education and Culture has had 113 ministers, 11 in the last 10 years alone.

In a recent analysis of the ministry's structure and functions (Moore and Rosales 2001), the administration was found to be excessively centralized, that there are too many administrative units with parallel functions and lacking coordination, that participation in decisionmaking at the local levels is almost inexistent, and that service to clients is deficient. Within the Ministry of Education and Culture, intercultural, bilingual education has been incorporated through the creation of a parallel system, meaning it and the "Spanish" system are nearly independent of one another.

Coordination is lacking throughout the sector. The Ministry and the Provincial Directorates have limited communication with the elementary and secondary schools. As a result, follow-up and control of activities at the school level are not effective. In addition, there is almost no follow-up or support from the Ministry for teachers, who are the most important resource in the educational process. Finally, early-childhood education is beyond the control and coordination of the Ministry of Education and Culture, since it is administered by the National Children's and Family Institute and by the Ministry of Social Welfare.

The administration of human resources, mainly teachers and principals, is deficient and must be improved. The screening, appointment, and promotion of teachers within the institution is a process that lacks transparency. Principals of elementary and secondary schools lack authority to select their personnel, or to take corrective measures when teachers engage in serious misconduct. Frequently, appointments depend on subjective criteria and not necessarily on the experience and qualifications of the teachers being considered for the position.

The system for assigning teachers contributes to the difficult situation, principally in rural schools. When there is a vacancy in a rural school, a teacher can be appointed to work in the school, but a few months later, can obtain a position in an urban school or in a Provincial Directorate, taking the appointment along with him or her, and leaving the school without an available position to fill with a replacement teacher.

Teachers and principals of elementary and secondary schools are appointed for an indefinite period. No mechanisms exist to ensure that they will retire when they reach a certain age. Because retirement income is significantly lower than salaries, very few persons opt for a voluntary retirement.

The rate of teacher absenteeism in schools is high, as teachers must visit the Provincial Directorates or the offices of their supervisors frequently regarding administrative matters. Moreover, during the past 15 years an estimated one month per year on average has been lost because of teacher strikes. At schools servicing the poorest populations, an average of nine days of work per month is lost.

The distribution of teachers is not adequate. There is a glut of teachers in some areas and a deficit in others. During the 1990s the student/teacher ratio declined and the inadequate distribution worsened.

Finally, the salary structure of the teachers has no correlation to the objective of improving the quality and equity of the system. For example, the "frontier bonus" received by teachers in isolated rural areas, which represents an amount equivalent to up to 25 percent of their salary, continues to be included in a teacher's salary even when the teacher stops working in the rural area and is transferred to an urban school.

The management of the budget as a tool to promote progress in the implementation of educational policy is inexistent. The budget of the Ministry of Education and Culture is administered by the Ministry of Finance, with limited participation from the former. There are delays in the transfer of funds and the educational authorities are not incorporating economic and financial variables into their policy decisions.

C. Recommendations

The new administration needs to find solutions to the problems detected in the areas of coverage, quality, financing, and administration of the sector. The principal challenge is attaining the goal of providing 10 years of basic quality schooling. This challenge is encompassed within the framework of the Millennium Development Goals. Programs aimed at extending coverage must be clearly focused on groups that have not been attended to, such as low-income persons and those in rural areas, particularly the indigenous areas. The Ministry of Education and Culture has had successful programs during recent years, and its coverage must be expanded. Particular attention must be paid to the schools known as one-teacher or multigrade classroom schools, so that in places where there are only one or two teachers, at least all elementary school grades would be offered.

Ecuador should consider other educational options such as the "Telesecondary" education model developed by Mexico, which is being successfully implemented in countries of the region such as Guatemala, Panama, Colombia, and Brazil, among others. Similarly, innovative strategies should be developed to offer the complete basic education cycle in areas that are far from major population centers, where there are no schools offering secondary education.

Given that the economic situation of families is a factor influencing whether students enroll and stay in school, the Ministry of Education and Culture should consider financing the most needy students through scholarships.

Regarding education quality, Ecuador has already made significant efforts to design and implement a quality measurement system, which can be improved and institutionalized. APRENDO can play a fundamental role as a measuring tool that makes it possible to: (i) identify schools with serious difficulties in attaining given standards; and (ii) provide follow-up to policies focused on solving certain identified problems.

As for training (continuing education) of the teaching staff, various options or strategies should be evaluated. The Ministry of Education, public and private universities, as well as teacher schools should all be involved in the training process. The most ideal institutions would be those devoted to teacher training. This process will be highly effective if the instruction, as well as the teacher training, are closely correlated to teacher promotions and thus increase remuneration.

The financing of the sector should be closely analyzed from an efficiency standpoint (size of the system at the central, provincial, and local levels), as well as that of resources needed to expand coverage and guarantee at least 10 years of basic education. Consideration should be given to financing demand for the service, through scholarships for students of the poorest families. An investment in infrastructure, textbooks, libraries, and teaching materials is fundamental to ensure, at least in part, the quality of the service being offered.

If the Ministry of Education and Culture fails to improve sector administration, it is quite possible that the funds allocated will not achieve the desired results. The structure of the Ministry should be reviewed, carefully analyzing processes for screening, appointing, and promoting personnel both in teaching and administrative positions. It is equally important to review experiences with decentralization and devolving authority, so as to give autonomy to individual schools and greater participation to parents.

Policy Matrix

Problems/challenges	Short-term policy measures (to June 2003)	Mid-term policy measures (2003–07)	Progress indicators
Access and equity:	*Define the strategy to be followed to ensure universalization of basic education and include the educational models.	*Target investments at all levels toward the poorest (rural and indigenous populations) to increase coverage at all levels.	*As is set forth in the Social Contract for Education: "Access for all Ecuadoran girls and boys to 10 years of basic education."
Elementary and basic middle school	*Evaluate different approaches to decentralization so as to determine what is working well and what aspects require adjustments. *Increase coverage in the rural and indigenous areas through various administrative and teaching options.	*Make sure that real decentralization has brought decisionmaking to local levels and promote rational, equitable management of resources at local levels. *Strengthen the evaluation system. *Take measures at the central, provincial, and local level to make sure that all boys and girls enter school at the appropriate age. *Grant scholarships to the most needy students in the rural areas. *Consider other educational options to extend coverage such as telesecondary education and postelementary education, among others.	*CEM networks and *Redes Amigas* Networks are strengthened and improved. *Evaluation system is being implemented. *Poorest students are receiving scholarships. *Net coverage has increased from 90 to 95 percent in elementary education.
High school	*Evaluate the current system of decentralized management in the secondary schools to determine which aspects need to be improved. *Develop and commence implementation of the plan to transfer decisionmaking and responsibility.	Create distance-learning programs (for example, telesecondary programs), especially in rural and indigenous areas, to increase access to services. *Transfer responsibility for decisionmaking, as well as resources for provision of services to the majority of secondary schools and to the community.	*Net coverage increases from 51 to 65 percent in five years. *Secondary schools are fully autonomous and receiving transfer of funds from the central level. *Poorest students are receiving scholarships.

(Matrix continues on the following page)

Policy Matrix (*continued*)

Problems/challenges	Short-term policy measures (to June 2003)	Mid-term policy measures (2003–07)	Progress indicators
		*Grant scholarships and subsidies to the best students from the poorest areas so that they can continue their education.	
Quality and relevance:	*Institutionalize the APRENDO academic achievement measurement system as a tool for monitoring the system's success at the various levels.	*Improve the academic achievement measurement system, making sure that all levels receive feedback so that they may take corrective measures that impact learning in the classroom. (At least two measurements should be conducted in grades 3, 5, 7, and 9.)	*Achievement tests have been applied and results returned to the individual schools.
Elementary and basic middle school	*Train all teachers of multigrade classroom schools in the use of APRENDO. *Revise teacher training programs. *Develop a continuing education plan for teachers that is correlated to their pay scale.	*Train bilingual teachers of all ethnic groups, so that they specialize in teaching at multigrade classroom schools. *Train teachers, utilizing new methods and technologies. *Promote teacher training at the level of the educational network or CEM.	*All rural teachers are trained in intercultural, bilingual education and education in multigrade classrooms.
Secondary school	*Revise the policy on specialized secondary education.	Reform education at this level to meet the needs of the labor market.	Concerted proposal for secondary education.
Financing of the sector:	*Determine financing requirements to respond to the demands for coverage and quality. *Design the model for a teachers' pay scale based on training and continuing education.	*Provide financing to the sector consistent with identified needs. *Implement the new promotion model, in which teacher remuneration is correlated with training and continuing education.	*Coverage and quality goals are met. *N basic elementary students from the poorest stratums are receiving scholarships.

| *Administration of the sector:* | *Define educational policies that improve the system's equity, quality, and efficiency, taking into account the resources available for doing so.
*Develop a plan to implement an efficient administrative and financial decentralization process.
*Initiate the process of reorganizing the Ministry of Education and Culture at all levels.
*Initiate gradual transfer of budget management to the deconcentrated entities of the Ministry of Education and Culture. | *Implement the decentralization plan, making sure that the monitoring system for the process is functioning properly.
*Utilize the budget as a tool to support educational policy.
*Implement the restructuring of the system at all levels to make it more efficient and equitable. | *Ministry of Education has been restructured.
*Provincial and local level has greater autonomy. |

Annex

Progress in the Decentralization of the Ministry of Education and Culture

In Ecuador, the legal framework for decentralization is found in the Constitution and a series of legal provisions that apply those constitutional principles. In addition, it should be noted as advantageous that the government has seriously embarked upon the process of decentralization, through the creation of the National Commission on Decentralization, Autonomy, and Territorial Limits. This body has formulated a Decentralization Plan based on the legal framework in effect, in which the scope and phases of decentralization are delineated. Current efforts toward decentralization are based in part on prior experiences, especially those of the 1990s, which were not always successful.

Program for Better Quality Basic Education (PROMECEB)

The Program for Better Quality Basic Education (*Programa de Mejoramiento de la Calidad de la Educación Básica*—PROMECEB) was created to provide an integral, long-term response to problems in basic education in the country. In its original design, the program's objective was to contribute to improving the efficiency and effectiveness of basic education, particularly in rural areas. In order to attain this objective, the program promotes administrative and teaching academic decentralization coupled with increased parental and community participation and control over the quality of education. Over time, however, the program has defined its objective as the creation of a quality educational environment so that children in the rural sector will learn effectively. To that end, the program has proposed a strategy to transform basic rural education. Three years of middle school have been added to the traditional six years of elementary school. Thus, basic education now comprises nine years of compulsory education, plus one year of preschool. Furthermore, based on the methodology and knowledge gained through school mapping, the plan proposes a clustering strategy, organizing intermediary institutional networks for administrative management and teaching collaboration among establishments. These are the Educational Matrix Centers (*Centros Educativos Matrices*—CEMs) located in selected rural areas.

In accordance with the program and its operating regulations, the CEMs are teaching academically and administratively decentralized, aimed at bettering the quality of basic education. These networks have been authorized to appoint their personnel, administer the financial resources allocated to them, and administer institutional educational plans. The CEMs are an institutional network formed by a central campus plus the public schools of a homogeneous or geographic area. The central campus is the educational unit for offering the 10 years of basic education, and is the headquarters that encourages the rest of the educational units of the CEM. In the year 2001 there were 119 CEMs (36 urban and 83 rural), with a total of 2,380 schools in the networks.

The objectives of the Educational Matrix Centers are as follows:

(i)   apply the policies formulated by the Ministry of Education and Culture for improving educational quality;

(ii)   decentralize budgetary, administrative, and technical teaching aspects of educational administration;

(iii)   expand opportunities for the population to obtain access to and remain in the educational system;

(iv)   organize and consolidate the supply of 10 years of education, conceived as basic education;

(v)   facilitate the educational supervision system's function as a resource that drives educational innovations and provides technical support to teachers;

(vi)   create conditions for the development and implementation of education based on school/community interaction;

(vii)   promote interaction among the communities comprising the CEMs and participate in the design and implementation of community development projects;

(viii) improve the capacity of the network's teaching and administrative personnel through continuing education;

(ix)   promote the production of teaching resources and auxiliary materials, by incorporating new educational technologies and using materials from the media;

(x)   collect useful information from the network for evaluation and research; and

(xi)   conduct teaching research that generates curriculum innovations.

Results of the Evaluation of PROMECEB[3]

The CEMs' experience with decentralization should be carefully reviewed to ensure that whatever model is implemented under the current circumstances will not repeat the same mistakes. Certain evidence indicates that a lack of clear strategies for the participation of parents and for the various players within the different levels of the Ministry of Education and Culture could limit possibilities for success in the decentralized management models.

One of the most serious problems in the implementation of the CEM networks has been a lack of administration and continuity, delays in the implementation of components, changes in priorities and in orientations for spending, lack of follow-

---

3. Juan Samaniego offers a model for strengthening the Model CEMs in "*Diseño de un Centro Educativo Matriz Demostrativo y Estrategia de Reingeniería de Siete Existentes* (Design of a Model Educational Matrix Center and Strategy for Reengineering Seven Existing Ones), December 2000. Processed.

up and monitoring, and conflicts with several of the country's sectors and institutions.

Another problem that existed from the start was the creation of an autonomous executive entity that was totally separate from the Ministry of Education and Culture, displacing traditional players. The agency within the Ministry of Education and Culture that was traditionally in charge of the administration and management of education felt excluded, marginalized, and relegated to performing insignificant functions.

The original design of PROMECEB failed to incorporate an adequate feasibility analysis. It also failed to consider the conflicts that a proposal of such a nature would generate among the various interest groups—regarding the degree of influence to be exerted by the educational system's centralized administrative organization; the technical capacity and openness to change of the Provincial Directorates and of the supervisors for implementing the program with autonomy; the lack of interest of the Teaching schools themselves for participating in a strategy of teaching change; and the legal and administrative complexity involved in operating the programmed activities, organizing bidding competitions, and engaging in adequate follow-up.

The majority of the investment was made in infrastructure and civil works, while the importance and visibility of the teaching dimension was lost. This investment was principally made in the matrix schools and not in the network schools, which had a negative impact on the possibility of constructing true networks and a good flow of communication and interchange with the schools.

The importance of the teaching dimension was revived when the program was reformulated in 1997. A movement was clearly directed toward teaching aspects of the program and the strengthening of the CEMs' decentralization and autonomy. Similarly, the implementation of a decentralized teacher-training system through nongovernmental organizations was a good response to the deficiencies seen in the program's prior phases. Yet the impact of these achievements in the model have been minor.

One flaw of the program is the lack of ongoing intermediary monitoring and evaluation activities nor progress balance sheets or reports that allow one to become rapidly familiar with each program component.

Serious problems exist regarding the personnel chosen to implement the project, principally with regard to their quality and motivation. There is also no performance incentive–based personnel policy, which would have contributed to obtaining better results.

The lessons learned lead to the conclusion, as set forth in the decentralization objectives, that the administration of resources and decisionmaking are supposed to be transferred to the local level. In that light, such a transfer should indeed be made and community interests and demands should be prioritized. Otherwise, the program will end up being an experiment administered centrally, which would further drain the educational system, erode the faith of local players, and waste resources.

Autonomous Rural School Networks (Redes Amigas)

This program is being conducted through a loan agreement signed by the Government of the Republic of Ecuador and the Inter-American Development Bank. The Ministry of Education and Culture is in charge of the program's implementation through the program's coordinating unit.

The Autonomous Rural School Networks, known as *Redes Amigas*, have as their objectives the following: (i) grant autonomy to approximately 20 percent of rural schools (close to 2,400 schools) for the management of their resources, with greater participation from parents and members of the community in school administration; and (ii) improve teaching conditions in rural basic education (elementary and middle school) in the beneficiary schools' zones of influence. A series of actions are contemplated, targeting approximately 120 school networks. It is characteristic of the program that the networks participate voluntarily.

The program seeks to strengthen the network's organizational capacity for exercising autonomy and participatory management, and will also finance projects to improve teaching. Based on its objectives, the program has three components: (i) support for the school autonomy process; (ii) betterment of teaching conditions in the networks; and (iii) follow-up and evaluation.

The school networks may directly contract approximately 30 of the technical support institutions called "Educational Support Units" (*Unidades de Apoyo Educativo*—UAE) out of the 60 certified UAEs. The contracted UAEs would primarily engage in activities related to (i) training for parents and communities to promote participation; (ii) training for the network's board members, administrators, and teaching staff; and (iii) advice and accompaniment to the networks to strengthen management capacity and to design and implement projects for their betterment. These actions will be combined with equipment purchases (computers, photocopiers, and so on) necessary to facilitate the networks' autonomous administration.

This component also carries out activities for the adjustment and institutional strengthening of the central agencies of the Ministry of Education and Culture and of the Provincial Directorates. This reinforcement of capacity is oriented toward improving the educational planning system, strengthening management evaluations and impact evaluations, updating the sector's statistical and financial information system, and training the respective agencies' personnel.

The Provincial Directorates should be strengthened so that they will efficiently take on the role of providing academic advice and verifying learning results. To do so, the program would contract consulting firms to reach agreements with the various sectors involved in the educational process and to promote active parent and community participation.

For the component of **Improved Teaching Conditions in the Networks**, the program will finance approximately 120 network projects to resolve problems involving physical infrastructure, the supply of teaching materials, and training for the teaching staff, among others. For that purpose, the needs diagnostic and design of the projects should involve the collaboration of parents, local communities, teachers, and board members, and should consider project options that the program offers. It is worth noting that the program calls for at least one-fourth of the projects financed as benefiting school networks that serve indigenous communities, given the high proportion of indigenous communities in rural areas.

A further component aims to provide **Incentives to Teachers** through two forms of monetary awards: (i) $US25.00 per month to teachers who have been at school every working day of the month, which would increase teachers' salaries, reduce teacher absenteeism, and improve the quality of the teaching; and (ii) an annual US $1,200 prize to one teacher in each network, which would stimulate the behavior of the teaching staff in a manner that benefits the academic life of the network's schools.

The **Follow-up and Evaluation** component is aimed at establishing and applying the mechanisms needed for ongoing follow-up and evaluation of the effective transfer of competencies and resources to the school networks, the resulting transformations, and their impact on administrative and academic improvements in the schools.

Decentralization of the Academies ("Colegios")

The approximately 1,800 primary and middle school academies in Ecuador known as "*colegios*" are currently managed as decentralized units. They are "implementation units." That is to say, they receive cash transfers directly from the Ministry of Economy and Finance. The academies directly pay teachers, utilities, and maintenance expenses. Given that the transferred funds are generally insufficient, schools typically request contributions from parents. In cases in which financing is required for investment in infrastructure or equipment, the academy's headmaster is in charge of directly negotiating with the Ministry of Economy and Finance to obtain the necessary funds.

Nonetheless, financial autonomy does not imply that the headmaster has autonomy for the management of the school. Transfers and contracting of the teaching staff are decided by the Provincial Administration. Likewise, the academy is subject to the directives issued by the Ministry of Education and Culture as regards curriculum and the school calendar. There is no evidence that the academies actually have greater participation from parents or have an accountability system.

Decentralization to the Municipalities: The Case of Quito

The municipality of Quito currently has 42 municipal educational centers, of which 8 cover early childhood education, 11 are basic education elementary and middle schools, 2 are high schools, and 21 are trade schools, with a total coverage of more than 12,000 students and 900 teachers. The municipal educational centers are the responsibility of the municipality's Directorate of Education and are financed through tax revenues. The teaching staff receives a significantly higher salary. On the other hand, promotions and supervision are still determined by the Provincial Directorate of Education. One-hundred and sixteen schools have requested to be transferred to the municipal system.

Although no evaluation has been made of children's performance in these municipal schools as compared to those in state schools, there are certain indications that the municipal schools are providing higher quality education, among them the number of actual days of classes imparted (198 versus 140 in school year 2000–01), the high rate of enrollment in higher education, the high demand for enrollment, and the award of the national mathematics and physics prizes.

The Municipality of Quito, in response to the national decentralization policy, is developing a Metropolitan Education Subsystem, for which it already has a model and a strategic development plan. Furthermore, a Municipal Education Commission exists, with prominent members of the local community meeting each week to approve and follow up on the actions of the Directorate of Education. The Ministry of Education and Culture, through a Ministerial Decree, has transferred authority and responsibilities over personnel status (including the hiring, continued employment, and promotion of teachers) and professional registration, the school calendar, the granting of degrees, training and continuing education of teachers, curriculum, and creation of educational establishments and educational supervision to the Directorate of Education of the Metropolitan Municipality of Quito. On the other hand, the municipality has issued a Municipal Ordinance, which limits the time in office of headmasters and principals to four years, although they can be reelected for one additional term. The Municipality of Quito hopes to see the approximately 800 educational establishments located in its jurisdiction transferred to the municipality. Nonetheless, it is felt that the transfer should be gradual, at a projected rate of approximately 100 establishments per year. The basic criteria for the transfers is that they be made voluntarily and that the schools be eligible for accreditation by the municipality (in other words, the municipality should determine that it has the capacity to receive the establishment).

The municipality will have to face a number of significant challenges to be able to receive the transferred schools while also ensuring that quality education is being provided. The principal challenge is financing. The municipality's own resources do not allow it to finance additional spending on education. Furthermore, the municipality will have to strengthen its capacity to manage and supervise the schools in its jurisdiction.

10

Health[1]

Marcelo Bortman

Despite recent efforts to encourage investment and decentralization, the health sector has not resolved its fundamental problems. These efforts were modest, and low population coverage, lack of access, and low quality of health services prevail. In addition, public spending on health continues to be insufficient, while private spending is inequitable. Approximately 30 percent of the population still has no access to basic health services. More than two-thirds of Ecuador's inhabitants have no formal health insurance, and the Ministry of Public Health (Ministerio de Salud Pública—MSP) and other public institutions are incapable of providing healthcare services to nearly half of them. Those who are left without service are precisely the persons with the worst health indicators. Childbirths without proper medical care and lack of access to basic healthcare are the principal factors responsible for an epidemiological profile marked by inequities. A direct consequence of the low levels of population coverage is seen in the high rates of infant, maternal, and premature mortality. Mortality rates due to infectious disease and cancer are also very high, with great disparities from one region to another. The reform of the health sector should include several measures: The Free Healthcare Maternity Act (Ley de Maternidad Gratuita—LMG) should include a targeting model to avoid double coverage, while also taking into consideration social and cultural issues that tend to limit the demand for basic services. The coverage of the Rural People's Social Security Program (Seguro Social Campesino—SSC) should be expanded and coordinated with coverage under the Free Healthcare Maternity Act. Basic health benefits should be incorporated into the Bono Solidario *Cash Subsidy Program for retired persons and the disabled. The essential functions of the Ministry*

1. Marcelo Bortman is a health specialist for the World Bank. The author thanks Daniel Dulitzky, Patricia Bernedo, Daniel Cotlear, and Pablo Gottret.

*of Public Health should be redesigned, with a new Organic Law for the national health system that modifies the system's role from that of a service provider to that of a regulating body. In said role, the Ministry of Public Health would take charge of mechanisms to accredit establishments, monitor the quality of services, create a health surveillance system, and provide training for situations of epidemiological risk, among other functions. As part of the redefinition of the Ministry of Public Health's functions, it should once again be coordinated with the Ecuadoran Social Security Institute (*Instituto Ecuatoriano de Seguridad Social—*IESS). Finally, a regulatory framework should be created to develop a system of regional health service networks, expanding the coverage of the SSC and possibly creating a new insurance for the low-income population to consolidate and gradually replace the benefits of the Free Healthcare Maternity Act and the* Bono Solidario *Cash Subsidy Program.*

A. Introduction

Despite the difficult economic and political conditions that Ecuador has confronted in recent years, the country's Human Development Index (HDI) has shown sustained improvement, increasing by 9 percent between 1980 and 2000. Nonetheless, even though new countries have been incorporated into the analysis, Ecuador's ranking has dropped, from 49th place in 1975 to 93rd place in 2000.[2]

During this period, Ecuador's health indicators have improved significantly. Life expectancy at birth, (one of the three components of the HDI), increased from 58.8 years in 1975 to 70 years in 2000—67.3 years in males and 73.5 in females. This represents an increase of 19 percent and an average of 11.2 additional years of life for each member of the population.

Infant mortality was reduced by two-thirds, from 87 per thousand in 1970 to 30 per thousand in 2000, and mortality in children under five was reduced by three-fourths, from 140 per thousand to 39 per thousand over that same period. Nonetheless, the changes seen at an overall national level were not evenly distributed in the country's interior.

This trend toward better health was seen in the majority of the countries in the region. Social, cultural, technological, economic, and environmental factors have all contributed to these changes, along with increased accessibility to and improved quality of health services. The relationship between a country's per capita income and its life expectancies follows a curve, with Ecuador located at the curve's mid-point (Figure 1). Some countries with income similar to that of Ecuador show greater life expectancies, such as Armenia, Syria, Sri Lanka, Suriname, and Jamaica, among others. Certain countries, however, such as Egypt,

---

2. UNDP, *Human Development Index*; statistics available at http://hdr.undp.org/statistics/default.cfm.

Figure 1. Relationship between Income and Life Expectancy, 2000

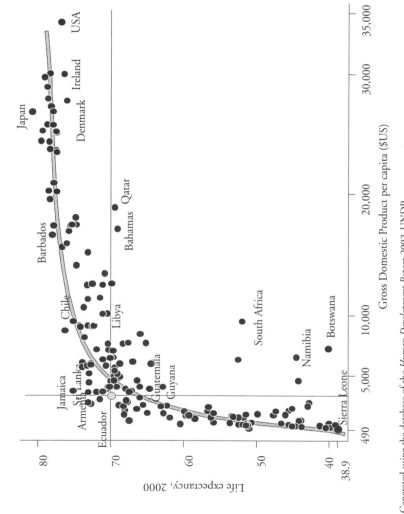

Source: Generated using the database of the *Human Development Report 2002,* UNDP.

Ukraine, Honduras, and Guatemala, with income also similar to that of Ecuador, have lower life expectancies.

Within Ecuador, demographic, cultural, and social heterogeneity has created fertile ground for the development of economic inequities and for disparities in health conditions and living standards.

In the province of Amazonía, life expectancy for 1995–2000 was 59.6 years,[3] and an estimated 21 percent of the population would not survive more than 40 years. At the other extreme, the population of Pichincha province had a life expectancy that was 14.9 years longer, and only 6.8 percent were expected to die before age 40. When life expectancies are compared with household consumption per capita, the relationship follows a similar curve to the country comparison graph. In this instance as well, the populations of "poor" provinces have a lower life expectancy than those of provinces with greater resources (Figure 2).

Figure 2. Correlation between Life Expectancy and Household Consumption, 1999

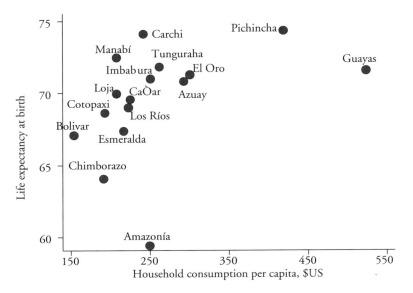

Source: UNDP, Human Development Indicators, Ecuador, 1999.

---

3. *Source:* UNDP, *Human Development Indicators*, Ecuador, 1999.

B. Ecuadoran Health: Characteristics and Diagnosis

Ecuador exhibits a polarized pattern of epidemiological transition, in which problems common to developed populations go hand in hand with problems typically seen in developing populations (high rates of mortality due to infectious disease or external causes, cervical cancer, infant mortality, deaths of children under five years of age and deaths related to pregnancy, childbirth or puerperal deaths). This does not mean that the same population is suffering from both types of problems. Rather, it suggests that certain population groups with better health indicators, longer life expectancies, and an epidemiological pattern more typical of a developed country, coexist with other population groups that, owing to adverse conditions of life, situations of inequity, and lack of access to basic health services, suffer from premature mortality whose causes are preventable.

Problems with Record Keeping and Premature Mortality from Preventable Causes

Vital statistics record keeping in Ecuador does not yet provide reliable information, and mortality rates vary depending on one's data source. In 1995 it was estimated that mortality was being underreported by 25 percent, while, the Latin American Demography Center *(Centro Latinoamericano de Demografía*—CELADE) considered the underreporting to be even higher. Estimated mortality for 1999 was 5.9 per 1,000 inhabitants (6.8 in males and 4.9 in females). The deficit in medical certifications was 17 percent (11 percent in the coastal region and 37 percent in the Amazonian region). Furthermore, in 14 percent of the deaths for which medical certification was provided, the cause of the death was incorrectly defined.[4]

Deaths due to cardiovascular disease have increased by 31 percent compared to 1995 and continue to be the leading cause of death, with an adjusted rate, to correct for underreporting, of 155 per 100,000 inhabitants—166 in males, 143 in females (Figure 3). The second, third, and fourth most frequent causes of death, each with very similar rates, are cancer, external causes, and infectious disease. Lastly, at a rate of 180 per 100,000, are all other causes. Among deaths caused by cancer, the most frequent type in both sexes is stomach cancer, followed in males by lung cancer and prostate cancer, and in females by breast cancer, uterine cancer, and lung cancer. The rate of mortality for uterine cancer (surpassing that of lung cancer

---

4. Pan-American Health Organization, *Health in the Americas*, 2002 Edition.

Figure 3. Mortality by Types of Causes, 1999

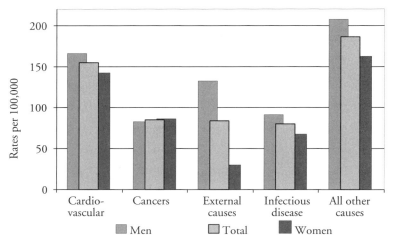

Source: Pan-American Health Organization, *Health in the Americas*, 2002 Edition.

and almost equal to that of breast cancer) is very high. It causes the death of approximately 700 women each year, which indicates the lack of effective preventive efforts.

Deaths from accidents, suicide, and homicide are four times as frequent among men (132 per 100,000) as among women. One fourth of these deaths are due to traffic accidents.

Diseases easily controlled through basic healthcare, such as respiratory infections and diarrhea, continue to cause the majority of deaths from infectious disease, especially in the population groups with the least access to health services.

Cholera cases have decreased, but rates for typhoid fever and food poisoning have gone up. The incidence of tuberculosis has gone down slightly, but rates for the provinces with the largest proportion of indigenous and rural populations are up to 10 times as much as those of the coastal provinces. In addition, it is estimated that the diagnosis and treatment of tuberculosis is accomplished in less than 60 percent of the actual cases.

Even though the actual incidence of AIDS is not accurately known, the greatest proportion of AIDS cases and HIV carriers are also clustered in the province of Guayas (83 percent of the country's total). The reporting of cases continues to grow, especially in women. Heterosexuals account for 62 percent of the cases, homosexuals account for 33 percent, and bisexuals account for 5 percent (Figure 4).

Slightly more than 50 percent of the country's population lives in malaria risk zones, and since 1996 the reporting of cases has increased annually, until reaching levels almost 10 times as high as 1996 in the years 2000 and 2001. There has also

Figure 4. Incidence of AIDS by Sex, 1990 to 2000

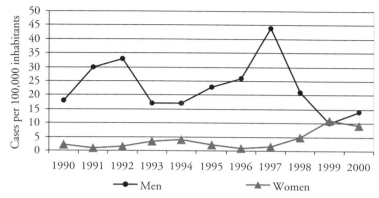

Source: Pan-American Health Organization, *Health in the Americas*, 2002 Edition.

been a notable increase in the incidence of dengue fever. From less than 1,000 cases per year between 1992 and 1995, the rate rose to more than 20,000 in 2000 (the majority centered in the province of Guayas). The four serotypes of the virus are now in circulation, and cases have been seen of dengue hemorrhagic fever. All this leads to a prediction that dengue will have a major short-term impact on the health of the population and on health services.

High Infant Mortality Rates

As in the case of general mortality, the figures on infant mortality obtained through vital statistics are lower than those obtained through surveys or estimates. For the period of 1994 to 1999, the mortality rate according to the Survey on Demographics and Maternal and Infant Health (*Encuesta Demográfica y de Salud Materna e Infantil*—ENDEMAIN III) was 30 per thousand. These values represent a decline of 24 percent as compared to the period of 1990 to 1994 (39.5 per thousand).

The rates estimated by the Pan-American Health Organization (PAHO) were even higher. Indeed, according to PAHO's estimates, the decline, over a longer period (1990 to 2000), was only 18 percent, that is, from 52.7 to 43.1 per thousand.[5]

The national infant mortality rates do not reveal existing internal variations. In the costal region, the rate for 1994–99 was 25 per thousand, in the highlands it was 34 per thousand, and in the Amazonian region it was 38 per thousand.

---

5. Pan-American Health Organization, *Special Program for Health Analysis*. Based on linear interpolation of World Population Prospects.

The differences are even more extreme if one takes into consideration the following:

- Place of residence: urban zones (22 per thousand), rural zones (40 per thousand).
- Educational Levels: no schooling (51), elementary (35), secondary (25), higher education(11).
- Income quintile: lowest (44.5), second (33.5), middle (23), fourth (15), highest (21.9).

High Prevalence of Risk Factors for Infant Mortality

Fertility rates have decreased over recent decades for all age groups, except in adolescents. The fertility rate in the 14–19 age group for the period from 1994 to 1999 was 58 per thousand in Quito, 76 per thousand in Guayaquil, and as high as 157 per thousand in the Amazonian provinces, exhibiting the gap in access to information and family planning methods among those populations.

Close to 20 percent of mothers deliver their children without any prenatal care (10.8 percent in urban zones and 28 percent in rural zones), with a wide disparity— 7 percent in Guayaquil compared to 34 percent in the Amazonian provinces. On a national level, 29 percent of childbirths are home deliveries, but in Guayaquil and Quito the rates are only 4.5 percent and 6.7 percent, respectively, as compared to 50 percent in the Amazonian region (60 percent in Chimborazo, in Bolívar, and Cotopaxi). Home deliveries are done by only 2.3 percent of mothers with a higher education, while for mothers with no schooling, the rate is 73.6 percent.

There is a high rate of newborns with a birth weight of less than 2,500 grams (16.1 percent). Indeed, a reduction in this indicator could produce a significant decline in infant mortality. More extensive provision of basic health services would not necessarily have a radical impact on this factor. Specific measures are required, such as an increase in the interval between pregnancies, nutritional control, and other factors related to fetal malnutrition or to premature childbirths. Finally, despite the Free Healthcare Maternity Act, there are major inequities in access to health services for care during the first year of life.

Mortality in children under five follows a pattern similar to that of infant mortality. According to the results of the ENDEMAIN-94 and ENDEMAIN-99 surveys, mortality rates for this group decreased from 55.7 per thousand to 37.1 per thousand (a 33.4 percent reduction). Nonetheless, estimates from the PAHO and the United Nations Population Division suggest higher rates and a decline between 1992 and 1999 of only 11.5 percent, from 65.2 to 57.7 per thousand.[6]

---

6. United Nations, Population Division, *Demographic Indicators 1950–2050*, Dataset 1999.

The distribution of mortality rates in children under five also follows a similar pattern to that of infant mortality, with a predominant role played by malnutrition and infectious disease.

The second Survey on Health and Nutrition in children under five, in 1986, determined that 37.5 percent of Ecuadoran children were underweight (below minus two standard deviations from median weight-for-age) and 49.4 percent had retarded growth (below minus two standard deviations from median height-for-age). Malnutrition was even more pronounced in the highland provinces (51.9 percent and 69.8 percent).[7] Twelve years later, the 1998 Living Conditions Survey estimated that the prevalence of chronic malnutrition had declined to 26 percent. This means that still, more than 350,000 children under five are suffering from malnutrition.

High Maternal Mortality Rates

The records on maternal mortality are even less precise. While the National Statistics and Census Institute of Ecuador (*Instituto Nacional de Estadística y Censos*—INEC) states that the rates for the years 1990, 1996, and 1998 were 117, 63, and 55 maternal deaths per 100,000 births, respectively, ENDEMAIN II has estimated that during the period from 1981 to 1994, there were an average of 220 maternal deaths for each 100,000 births (302 per 100,000 during 1981–87 and 159 per 100,000 during 1988–94).

The significant rate increase reported for the year 2000 in the Yearbook of Vital Statistics in comparison to 1998 could indicate improvements in the rate of underreporting.[8]

C. Problems in the Health Services System

More than two-thirds of the population has no formal health insurance, and the Ministry of Public Health and other public institutions are incapable of providing healthcare services to nearly half of the uninsured. Those who are left without service are precisely the persons with the worst health indicators. While the financing is insufficient to provide basic healthcare to this 30 percent of the population, average spending per person is US$70 on persons affiliated with the General Obligatory Insurance (*Seguro General Obligatorio*—SGO) of the IESS and barely one-fifth that on the affiliates of the SSC. These disparities are even greater if instead of considering national averages, the numbers are analyzed at a provincial level.

---

7. Food and Agriculture Organization (FAO), *Nutrition Country Profiles*, Ecuador, 2001.
8. INEC, *Anuario de Estadísticas Vitales*. Ecuador, 2000.

Background

In 1992 a process was commenced for the modernization of the national government. As part of that effort, the Ministry of Health promoted decentralization of services and community participation in the management model. In 1993 a project was launched that was known as FASBASE—"Strengthening and Expanding the Scope of Basic Health Services in Ecuador" (*Fortalecimiento y Ampliación de los Servicios Básicos de Salud en el Ecuador*). This project's activities, focused on the country's 71 poorest zones, was aimed at expanding the covered population and at increasing institutional capacity, so as to provide basic health, nutrition, and sanitation services and also improve the quality of health services for the population at greatest risk. In 1997, the Special Law on Decentralization of the State and Social Participation defined the conditions for a transfer of authority and resources to the municipalities and provincial councils. In 1998, the National Constitutional Assembly legally consecrated the right to health, with an integrated conception involving both health promotion and healthcare. At the same time, it reaffirmed the regulatory role of the state, the need to organize the national health system, and the need to implement a strategy of decentralizing governmental management. The reform also recognized the need to develop a new, competitive social security health care approach, based on universality, solidarity, and efficiency, while entrusting the IESS with the management of that system.

As a complement to FASBASE, a project was launched known as MODERSA—"Modernization and Development of Comprehensive Health Services Networks" (*Modernización y Desarrollo de Redes Integrales de Servicios de Salud*—with three strategic pillars: (a) to strengthen the Ministry of Health's regulatory and supervisory role, (b) to develop Decentralized Health Services that would function in networks, and (c) to promote the modernization of semiautonomous hospitals that could provide support to those networks.

In November 2001, the Social Security Act was passed. It was subsequently declared unconstitutional, however, in a legal process that has yet to be completed, and whose validity is not clear. One year later, the Organic Law on the National Health System was enacted, which guarantees equitable, universal access to comprehensive healthcare services for the entire population.[9] The law proposes to implement a Comprehensive Health Plan, which emphasizes primary care, basic services, and health promotion. The law guarantees the financing of the plan with government funds, and creates specific funds for protection against catastrophic diseases among the uninsured low-income population. Currently, regulations for the law are being drawn up.

---

9. *Organic Law of the National Health System*, Official Gazette No. 670, September 2002.

Fragmentary Organization and Underutilized Resources

Ecuador's health sector comprises a number of public and private institutions that have independent organizational structures and management mechanisms and little or no interaction and/or coordination. Thirty percent of the population lacks access to health services,[10] and despite efforts to increase access, this percentage has not significantly changed in recent years. Such deficiencies notwithstanding, Ecuador has ambulatory care and hospitals run by either the IESS or the private sector, although the geographic distribution of human resources is not uniform (see Box 1).

Box 1. Organization of the Health Sector

The public subsector comprises the Ministry of Public Health; the IESS with General Obligatory Insurance and Rural People's Social Security, the Health Service of the Armed Forces, and the Health Service of the Police (each with its own institutions). One can also consider some of the institutions of the Ministry of Social Welfare and certain municipal services as forming a part of this sector, along with those of some private, nonprofit institutions, such as the Welfare Council of Guayaquil, the Guayaquil Children's Protection Society, the Red Cross, and the Society for the Fight Against Cancer.

The Ministry of Public Health provides health services to approximately 31 percent of the population; the IESS to 18.0 percent (10 percent through SGO and 8 percent through the SSC); the Armed Forces cover close to 1 percent; and the rest of the institutions cover 10 percent. The private sector, with a number of independent institutions, covers 10 percent, while as much as 31 percent of the population (or more if one takes into consideration that part of the population covered by the IESS also receives services from the Ministry of Public Health), has no access to basic services. For the performance of its functions, the Ministry of Health has, in addition to service units, Health Directorates in each province and Health Areas for each municipality, which oversee municipal health posts, health centers, and hospitals.

The IESS is Ecuador's social security health system. It also covers pension programs, workmen's compensation, severance pay indemnifications, a funeral aid program, Illness and Maternity Care Insurance, and the SSC. Nonprofit institutions also exist, with a very long history and powerful influence in the sector.

(Box continues on the following page.)

---

10. Pan-American Health Organization, *Basic Country Health Profiles,* Summaries 1999, Ecuador.

Box 1. (*continued*)

In 1999 there were 3,518 health service units, of which 2,975 were ambulatory care units and 543 were hospital units.[11] The Ministry of Public Health accounted for 48 percent of the total establishments (52.5 percent of the ambulatory care units and 22.3 percent of the hospital units), while the IESS, through its General Obligatory Insurance and Rural People's Social Security Program, accounted for almost 30 percent (33.6 percent of the ambulatory units and 3.3 percent of the hospital units). The three groups of establishments function in parallel, and in many areas they provide an underutilized, inefficient installed capacity. This is particularly true among the establishments of the Ministry of Health and the General Obligatory Insurance. Utilization of hospital-bed capacity during 1990–99 fell by 25 percent, as a result of the decrease in the average hospital stay and a stable rate of 50 patient discharges for each thousand inhabitants. The private sector contributes 67.6 percent of the hospitals (148 institutions) but only 23 percent of the available beds (4,408 beds).

The availability of human resources, especially of physicians and professional nurses, has grown over the last decade, from 11.6 physicians and 3.7 nurses per 10,000 inhabitants in 1991 to 14.5 and 5 per 10,000, respectively, in 2000. In contrast, the number of auxiliary nurses during that period went down by 12.3 per 10,000 inhabitants to 10.5, as a consequence of the professionalization programs and a reduced supply of training programs for auxiliary nurses. The geographic distribution of human resources is not uniform. Urban centers and training centers have much higher concentrations than do the provinces of Amazonía, Esmeraldas, and Bolívar.

Insufficient Government Spending and Inequitable Private Spending on Health

According to recent estimates, after the dramatic 32 percent drop in overall spending on health in 1999, spending grew to US$1.5 billion in 2001 (US$123 per year per inhabitant), recovering 1998 values.[12] These values are greater than the ones estimated in the National Accounting Report,[13] which would indicate that private

---

11. Pan-American Health Organization, *Profile of the Health Services System of Ecuador*, 1999.
12. MODERSA, *Gasto y Financiamiento del Sistema Nacional de Salud* ("Expenditures and Financing for the National Health System"), 1995–2001.
13 *Cuentas Nacionales de Salud* ("National Health Accounts"), Final Report, Ecuador, 1997, Ministry of Public Health, National Statistics and Census Institute of Ecuador (INEC), and Partners for Health Reform (PHR), March 2001.

spending had been severely underestimated and that it probably accounted for 80 percent of total health expenditures. Government expenditures amounted to 1.7 percent of the GDP, somewhat higher than the 1.5 percent figure for 2002, but failed to regain the 2.2 percent level of 1997. As such, Ecuador is one of the countries of Latin America with the lowest proportion of its GDP earmarked for public health expenditures (only Haiti spends less). Owing to the crisis, the Ministry of Public Health cut its expenditures from US$197.6 million in 1997 to US$89.6 million in 1999. The recovery of the country's GDP allowed health expenditures to grow to US$145 million in 2001, however, of which one-fourth was earmarked for administration of the Ministry of Public Health and the Area Directorates.

By care level, the Ecuadoran health system allocates 34.2 percent of expenditure to primary care, 29.7 percent to secondary care, and 36.0 percent to tertiary care. In terms of structure, 34.4 percent of expenditures are earmarked for hospital services, 29.3 percent for medications, 23.6 percent for ambulatory care, 11.7 percent for public health services, and 0.9 percent for research.

The average expenditure of US$123 per inhabitant varies notably when viewed in terms of each provider's expenditure with respect to the population covered. The Ministry of Public Health, which covers approximately 31 percent of the population, spent approximately US$38.40 dollars per beneficiary in 2001, the IESS, through its SGO, spent US$84.8 million (US$70.50 per insured party), and US$14 million (US$14.80 per affiliate) through the SSC. The disparity between the expenditures on these two programs was even greater this year, since the level of spending for the SSC remained unchanged while spending on SGO is estimated to have almost doubled.

Moreover, the most recent Living Conditions Survey (1998) made it patently clear that the poorest of the poor are the group most impacted by out-of-pocket expenses. Among the decile with the least income, health expenses represent 40 percent of income, while among the decile with the highest income, they barely surpass 5 percent of income (Figure 5).

Nontransparent Financing

According to the National Accounting Report, approximately 51.3 percent of national spending on health is financed by public sources—that is, 23.7 percent from the general budget of the nation, a similar percentage (23.9 percent) through the social security health system, and the remaining 3.7 percent from other public sources. For its part, the private sector reportedly contributes 46.2 percent, of which 34.4 percent corresponds to the families' out-of-pocket expenses. The remaining 2.5 percent of national spending on health comes from external sources. Yet according to the study that MODERSA conducted, private financing is approximately 100 percent greater, which would reduce the percentages attributed to the national budget and the Social Security Health system by 50 percent.

Figure 5. Percentage of Income used for Out-of-Pocket Health Expenses, by deciles, 1998

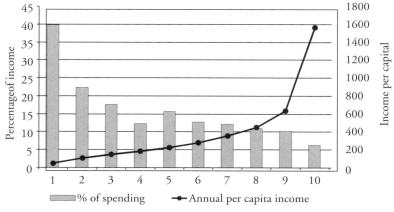

Source: INEC, Living Conditions Survey, 1998.

Limited Health Insurance Coverage

Ecuadorans, or a sector of them (22 percent), have four types of health insurance: General Obligatory Insurance (SGO), Rural People's Social Security (SSC), the Insurance of the Armed Forces and the Police, and insurance through prepaid healthcare companies.

General Obligatory Insurance is managed through the IESS. Persons with steady employment, as well as the majority of self-employed workers, are entitled to this insurance. Though SGO is now obligatory, a significant number of workers are not affiliated with it. SGO is an individual insurance that does not cover one's immediate family. The only exception is that for female affiliates, their children's healthcare is covered, but only during the first year of life. The Social Security Act, which extends coverage to one's dependents, is not, in fact, being applied. Nonetheless, the IESS has begun to extend the scope of coverage. Thus, children under the age of six and the wives of affiliates are expected to be included by the year 2003.

In 1999, 1,303,000 affiliates (10.7 percent of the population) were covered by this insurance, of which 1,092,000 were active affiliates and 211,000 were retired. In comparison to the number of active affiliates in 1990, the current figure represents a growth of 33.8 percent. Yet considering the increase in the economically active population during this period, this actually represented a growth in coverage of only 5 percent. With the incorporation of family members projected for late 2003, the number of affiliates would be two million, with 16.5 percent of the population covered by this insurance.

The health services are preferably provided through the IESS's own institutions, although expenses for services rendered at establishments with which agreements have been made are eventually compensated. The population generally considers this insurance to be of poor quality. Many people consider the insurance to be useful to them for situations necessitating major expenses, but not for minor health problems. In fact, many people have additional private insurance.

SGO had a financial deficit of close to 50 percent in 1997, 24 percent in 1998, and 29 percent in 1999, which was covered using investment returns. Under the dollarization of Ecuador's currency, and calculating contributions on the basis of the totality of revenues from private workers, the financing of SGO grew significantly, from US$59.8 million in 2000 to US$88.1 million in 2001 and approximately US$187 million in 2002. Revenues in 2003 are projected at US$237 million. The Social Security Act prohibits cross subsidies between the pension funds and the health funds of the IESS.

Rural People's Social Security Program. This insurance is also managed by the IESS. It is a voluntary family insurance that provides coverage to peasants who work for themselves or are organized into cooperatives, communes, or agrarian associations. The population covered in 1999 was 200,000 direct active affiliates, 13,000 passive affiliates, and 737,000 family members. As of 2002, these figures have remained unchanged, and an estimated 75 percent of the rural population (3 million persons) has not even applied for coverage. The insurance covers medical and pharmaceutical services, with no maximum limit, and includes prevention and health promotion activities. The services are provided through service centers in the rural zones, and for more complex healthcare problems through the IESS's General Obligatory Insurance establishments, as opposed to those of the Ministry of Public Health. The insurance is paid for through a symbolic contribution from the peasants of US$0.04 per month and through 1.0 percent of the wages of all workers affiliated with the IESS, prorated as follows: 0.30 percent is covered by the government; 0.35 percent by employers, and 0.35 percent by workers affiliated with the General Obligatory Insurance, in addition to the contribution of 1.0 percent of the minimum wage from heads of households.[14]

This insurance, which is older than the Ministry of Public Health itself, has a great deal of meaning for the peasants, who consider it to be a social victory. Unlike the General Obligatory Insurance, its affiliates consider it to be "good insurance." Nonetheless, the SSC is facing serious financing difficulties, along with problems in the provision of supplies and medications. Moreover, many of its service units require maintenance, and obsolete basic equipment also needs to be upgraded. The Social Security Act extended the application of the insurance to the entire rural population either working in the fields or involved in fishing.

---

14. IESS and World Bank, *Rural Social Security in Ecuador*.

Because of budgetary constraints, however, it has not been possible to actually extend the coverage. During 2003, an additional 100,000 affiliates are expected to be covered, with only 3.3 percent of the population remaining to be incorporated into the insurance program.

Insurance of the Armed Forces and the Police, for the personnel of the Armed Forces and the Police, and their direct relatives. This insurance covers approximately 1 percent of the population.

Finally, **private insurance**, according to records that are not very up-to-date, covers approximately 3 percent of the population.[15]

The Free Healthcare Maternity Act. This is not insurance *per se*, but nonetheless it guarantees 33 health services for expectant mothers and infants at no charge in 119 municipalities that have signed an agreement. The law was passed in 1998, but its regulations were only recently adopted, in 2002. Users can receive care from several different services, particularly those of the Ministry of Public Health, and the system reimburses providers through a fee schedule. Expenditures for 2002 are estimated at US$12 million,[16] and the budget for the coming year projects a financing of US$30 million. This financing is not dependent on demand, and many service providers complain that the fee schedule does not cover their costs. Furthermore, given the universal nature of the coverage under this law, double coverage is being provided to persons who already have some type of health insurance.

Inadequate Performance of the Essential Functions of the Ministry of Public Health, Shortfalls of the IESS, and Difficulties in Achieving the Millennium Development Goals

In October 2001, the Ministry of Public Health evaluated its performance in relation to its Essential Public Health Functions,[17] for which purpose it followed the protocol developed by the Pan-American Health Organization (PAHO). According to the evaluation's results, the performance of the Ministry of Health can be summarized as follows:

15. Pan-American Health Organization, *Profile of the Health Services System of Ecuador*, 1999.

16. Inter-American Development Bank, *Análisis de la ejecución de los Programas Sociales Prioritarios y del Instrumento de Focalización* SELBEN, 2001–2002 ("Analysis on the Implementation of Priority Social Programs and Targeting Instruments of SELBEN, the Ecuadoran Beneficiary Identification and Selection System").

17. Ministry of Public Health, Pan-American Health Organization, *Performance Measurement of Essential Public Health Functions*, October 2001.

Insufficient or minimal in:	Health surveillance, research, and control of risks
	Research in public health
	Policy development and capacity for planning and management
	Its regulation and auditing capacity
	Health promotion
	Development of human resources
	Guaranteeing and improving the quality of health services
Low in:	Monitoring, evaluating, and analyzing the health situation
	Promoting the participation of the citizenry in health issues
	Evaluating and promoting equitable access to health services
Very good in:	Reducing the impact of emergencies and disasters

These results illustrate the Ministry of Health's existing weaknesses in carrying out its planning, administration, monitoring, control, and evaluation functions. There is no single health information system, and each of the various subsystems, which in general are dependent on vertical programs, have different percentages of underreporting. Their efforts overlap and they fail to coordinate with one another. Health promotion, which was recently prioritized by the Ministry of Health, was qualified as being minimally developed. Participation of the citizenry is being encouraged through a general governmental initiative. The active community role in the Local Health Councils, in the context of developing Decentralized Health Services, is an important step in that direction. As for control activities, these vary depending on the zone. For example, in terms of the surveillance system, research and control activities for outbreaks of disease and epidemiological emergencies are very limited. On the other hand, even though one-fourth of the municipalities have not attained the goal of 95 percent coverage, the expanded immunizations program has succeeded in significantly lowering the number of cases of neonatal tetanus (24 in 1998, 14 in 1999 and only 6 in 2000), and no cases of diphtheria or measles have been recorded since 1998. The Ministry's capacity for reducing the impact of emergencies and disasters was the only aspect evaluated as very good. The government's emphasis on control and assistance in emergency situations, derived from the El Niño phenomenon, has probably been the determinant factor in this regard.

Limitations of the IESS Health Area

Although the Ecuadoran Constitution considers the IESS to be universally responsible for the administration of insurance, the proportion of the population that is insured continues to be low. The IESS provides inadequate, inequitable services, and the population is not satisfied with them, despite the fact that the IESS administers almost 50 percent of the public sector funds. The IESS health area is suffering from problems similar to those faced by the health system in general in Ecuador:

- **Lack of orientation and clear policies**. Constant changes in laws and regulations, conflicts of interest in its administrative functions (to direct, plan, and oversee the institution) and a long, unconcluded IESS restructuring process.
- **Deficient allocation of resources**. Mainly directed toward covering the expenses of the provider network, but without using resource allocation mechanisms to promote fairness and efficiency in their use.
- **Healthcare and hospitalization model**. Little content in terms of preventive care and health promotion, with the bulk of the resources concentrated on curative medicine. There is no reference and referral network, and demand is concentrated on Level II and III hospitals, which account for 65 percent of expenditures.
- **Deficient health services management model**. Adequate incentives do not exist, and there is no flexibility in resource management. No emphasis is placed on patient satisfaction, and there are no systems to monitor and evaluate the quality of the care.
- **Little coordination within the sector**. An absence of coordination with the Ministry of Public Health, which results in poor investment policies, duplication of supply, and low utilization of resources. The Ministry of Public Health fails to regulate the General Obligatory Insurance, which is needed to orient the Institute's health policies.

Difficulties in Achieving Millennium Development Goals

For Ecuador, achieving the Millennium Development Goals is a difficult challenge. Many of the needed changes are beyond the scope of the health sector, yet action to reform the sector from within is indeed required, especially in terms of narrowing gaps and reducing risk factors.[18] The goals are summarized below.

Reduce malnutrition between 1990 and 2015 by one-half.

Considering a prevalence of close to 40 percent of children under five with a weight-for-age that is below minus two standard deviations from the median as a baseline, the goal to be achieved by 2015 would be a prevalence of 20 percent. The latest survey, from 1998, estimated that the national average was 26 percent, which indicates that progress is being made in attaining this goal. Nonetheless, the national average could be deceiving, as the decline may not have been similar in all population groups.	**Goal** 20 percent

---

18. World Bank, *Measuring Progress Using the Poverty Reduction Strategy Framework*, Final Report, 2002.

Reduce by two-thirds the mortality rate among children under five.

Considering the data from the ENDEMAIN II survey as a starting point (55.7 per thousand), the goal would be 18.6 per thousand. According to data from the ENDEMAIN III survey, this indicator has already gone down by one-third. Nonetheless, during 1994–99, no individual province, and not even the highest income quintile, achieved the goal. Infant mortality is responsible for more than 75 percent of mortality in children under five, and in order to reach the goal, national infant mortality risk-factor values must go down to less than the corresponding values for the province with the lowest infant mortality rate (Guayas). This means that at a national level, the fertility rate in females between 15 and 19 years of age should be lower than 75 per thousand, that more than 90 percent of pregnancies should receive pre-natal care, that more than 87 percent of childbirths should take place at institutions, and that the percentage of under-weight children should be close to 13 percent.	**Goal** 18.6 per 1,000

Reduce maternal mortality by three–fourths.

Starting with an estimated rate for 1990 of 160 per 100,000 births, the goal should be a rate of 40 per 100,000. Many of the risk factors for maternal mortality are linked to infant mortality, especially institutionalized childbirth, prenatal care, and a lowering of fertility rates in high-risk groups.	**Goal** 40 per 100,000

Halt and begin to reverse the spread of the HIV/AIDS epidemic.
Halt and begin to reverse the incidence of tuberculosis, malaria, and other major transmittable diseases.

These diseases are still not under control. In fact, their incidence has been growing, particularly over the last half of the past decade. It is necessary to review the control programs, seeking intervention alternatives consistent with local needs and involving the community so that the efforts will be more effective.	**Goal** Rates in decline

D. Recommendations

Ecuador must overcome a difficult, complex epidemiological and social scenario, in which inequities are clearly present. In particular, it must meet the following challenges: attain the Millennium Development Goals regarding infant malnutrition and infant and maternal mortality (see Figures 6 and 7), as well as mortality in the young population; expand basic care coverage and formal health insurance coverage; increase public investment in health and seek formulas so that private spending will be more equitable and efficient; and develop a sectorial coordination between the Ministry of Public Health and the health area of the IESS.

Figure 6. Mortality in Children under Five Years of Age

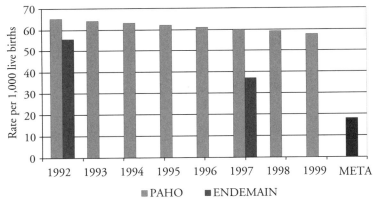

Source: PAHO and ENDEMAIN.

Figure 7. Maternal Mortality

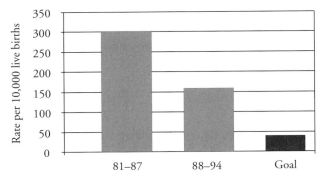

Source: ENDEMAIN II survey.

It is clear that public investment in health is insufficient and that certain areas and services require an investment in upgrades and development. Yet for want of coordination, there is also undesirable duplication of underutilized resources. Moreover, in addition to inequities in spending and in access to services, there are inequities in the quality of health services, and especially in their results. The universal programs approach (give everything to everyone) has limited the ability to set priorities, which has resulted in services of variable quality for a few, while many people receive no services at all.

Extension of Access to Basic Services

Universal coverage for all benefits and for the entire population is for now impossible, and such an aim has served to distort an equitable distribution of spending. The idea of a system that guarantees the provision of a series of basic services is a rapid, efficient alternative, and has already been implemented, albeit with certain difficulties, by the Free Healthcare Maternity Act. In order to improve this program, a targeting model should be used to avoid double coverage. In addition, actions should be taken to extend coverage, taking social and cultural aspects into consideration that limit the demand for basic services.

A package of basic activities and services should be developed and gradually expanded to cover the majority of the population, especially aimed at achieving the Millennium Development Goals (reduction of infant malnutrition, of mortality in children under five, and of maternal mortality). This should include promotion and prevention activities, in particular the promotion of prenatal care and institutionalized childbirth; the prevention of low birth weight, teenage pregnancy, and short intervals between pregnancies; and the provision of care to children under the age of six (addressing growth, development, and common childhood diseases).

Out of approximately 300,000 births per year, some 250,000 take place with no type of health insurance. The US$12 million from the 2002 budget for the Free Healthcare Maternity Act is equivalent to US$48 per birth, which would increase to US$120 with the US$30 million projected for 2003. This figure is still insufficient when one takes into account that in addition to the 250,000 births (pregnancies, childbirths, postpartum, and care during the first year of life), these funds must also finance healthcare activities for approximately one million children between one and five years of age who have no health insurance coverage, along with a series of programs to stimulate the demand for health services among this population and promote reproductive health.

If the Free Maternity Healthcare funds were exclusively earmarked for the uninsured population, estimating an average expenditure of US$90 per birth, (including prenatal care, childbirth, and postpartum, along with care during the first year of life), plus US$30 for each child between one and five years of age and for promotional programs, an additional US$22.5 million would be required in 2003.

The information system for the management of the Free Healthcare Maternity Act must also monitor indicators for the Millennium Development Goals and for their respective risk factors.

The possibility of progressively including children up to age 13 in the program should be evaluated. Health expenses for the population between 6 and 13 years of age is much less than for children under the age of six. Moreover, this group has no health coverage through other mechanisms.

In order to reach the population most in need, it is also essential that efforts to implement the Free Healthcare Maternity Act be integrated with the SSC. The Rural People's Social Security Program has financial limitations in the short term that prevent it from extending its coverage to the remaining three million targeted beneficiaries. Thus, the uninsured maternal and infant population depends on the Free Healthcare Maternity Act for its care—which is why a closer collaboration should be sought between SSC services and Free Healthcare Maternity activities, by creating mechanisms that allow Free Healthcare Maternity beneficiaries to be serviced at SSC establishments.

In order to extend access to basic services to include retired persons and the disabled, access should be made available through the *Bono Solidario* Cash Subsidy Program earmarked for this population. Such a mechanism could take advantage of part of that subsidy program's operating and targeting structure. In this way, coverage could be offered to approximately 230,000 retirees and 8,000 disabled persons who have no other healthcare resource. These services should include preventive and promotional activities, ambulatory care, and hospitalization for common acute diseases, as well as a basic package for chronic diseases and surgery. Estimating a cost per person of US$80, the additional cost of these services would be US$19 million. To arrive at a more accurate estimate, an actuarial calculation would have to be made, based on a profile of the population and a definition of the services.

As a mid- and long-term action, an attempt should be made to expand the population coverage of SSC and of SGO, while creating an insurance for the low-income population to gradually replace the benefits of the Free Healthcare Maternity Act and the services of the *Bono Solidario* Cash Subsidy Program.

Decentralization for a Better Supply of Health Services

The use of local managers and planners who are closer to the communities they serve would increase the possibilities for community involvement in decisionmaking regarding the design and operation of the services. Such community involvement is a factor that promotes demand.

That said, health services are still highly dependent on a Ministry provider. An accelerated decentralization would contribute to a deterioration in the supply of health services, and prior training efforts are needed. The decentralization of health services should be considered a first step in a long-term decentralization, and the Ministry of Health should continue moving this process along. In doing so, it should build on the experiences of MODERSA and utilize the decentralization to strengthen its administrative role. An evaluation should be made in each particular case of the operative conditions for the decentralization. In addition, encouragement should be given for health centers and hospitals to develop capabilities so that they can define their own baselines, priorities, objectives, and management commitment goals; formulate plans of action and budgets; and develop periodic, systematic evaluation mechanisms of their results.

Sectorial Coordination and the Future for the Ministry of Public Health and the IESS

Bearing in mind the opportunity for change that a new administration of government creates, consideration should be given in the short term to preparatory changes aimed at improved coordination of the health sector, so that the Ministry of Public Health can properly perform its essential public health functions, and so that the health area of the IESS can, in the long term, manage a national health coverage system.

The regulations for the Organic Law on the National Health System create an opportunity for this process. Given the lack of a clear regulatory framework for the Social Security health system, those regulations need to be rapidly defined and applied to the Organic Law.

The regulatory framework needs to be developed, and the groundwork needs to be laid for a system of regional health service networks structured into tiered levels of complexity, with participation from establishments affiliated with the Ministry of Public Health and decentralized establishments, as well as those affiliated with General Obligatory Insurance and the Rural People's Social Security Program. The local levels should focus their efforts on primary care and basic services programs, while specialized institutions and network hubs should focus on technical and logistic support to resolve more complex situations. The networks should operate with referral systems and a training program for human resources in primary care, promoting the concept of working as a network. The signing of management commitments should be encouraged. These management commitments should stimulate the demand for basic health services among the population and award the attainment of indicators that exhibit an increase in the quantity and quality of coverage.

While the process of decentralization is underway, the Ministry of Public Health should consider developing a comprehensive program for executing its functions as a regulating body, taking the following aspects into consideration: (a) implementation of an accreditation mechanism for establishments, bearing in mind their levels of complexity and the services they offer, along with systems for monitoring their production quality and results; (b) a review and modernization of the activities of the National Hygiene Institute (its procedures for record keeping, quality control, and approval of medications and medical supplies; as well as for the production of biologics and as a public health laboratory); (c) strengthening of control strategies for the enforcement of regulations on the treatment of solid waste generated by hospitals, as well as food safety, air quality, and potable water; (d) improvement of the vital statistics system to reduce underreporting and raise the quality of death certifications; (e) strengthening of the health surveillance system and capacity building for intervention in situations of epidemiological risk and disease outbreaks; (f) and the training of Human Resources employees.

Parallel to the above, a modernization program for the health area of the IESS should be developed incorporating both promotional and preventive activities which develops the following: (a) forms of service provisioning, contracting systems, and risk management systems; (b) mechanisms that allow the insured party to freely choose his or her provider; (c) systems to prevent increased costs; (d) mechanisms for coordination with the rest of the health system, especially the Ministry of Public Health; (e) changes in financial transactions, from historically budgeted funding to payment for services rendered, depending on the capacity for local management; (f) a human resources training program; (g) improved mechanisms for the contracting of services in order to promote competence, including capitation systems with management commitments; and (h) the implementation of a system to monitor and evaluate quality and results.

Policy Matrix

Problems	Policy measures — Short term (to June 2003)	Policy measures — Medium term (2003–07)	Progress indicators	Objectives/goals
Lack of access to basic health services for the vulnerable population. Need to meet Millennium Development Goals.	Definition of a package of basic health benefits for pregnant women and infants. Expanded application of the Free Healthcare Maternity Act. Basic health benefits using the *Bono Solidario* Cash Subsidy Program.	Definition of health priorities. Program for prevention and health promotion. Implementation of a program of the same type as the Integrated Management of Childhood Illness (IMCI). Expanded coverage of the SSC and SGO, and creation of an insurance for the low-income population.	Package of basic services agreed upon and implemented. Information system for the Free Healthcare Maternity Act in operation. Increase in the percentage of timely prenatal care, in the number of pregnancies receiving prenatal care, in the number of institutionalized childbirths, and in the number of children under five receiving healthcare. A 10 percent increase in the insured population.	100 percent of the population with access to basic health services. Promotion and prevention activities are incorporated throughout the sector. At least 95 percent of pregnant women have prenatal care. 90 percent of the childbirths take place at institutions. Reduction of mortality in children under five to 30 per 1,000. Reduction of maternal mortality to 80 per 10,000. 60 percent of the population has formal health insurance.
Lack of coordination in the sector.	Review of the regulatory framework for the Organic Law on the National Health System. Definition of regional services networks.	Definition of the regulatory framework of the Social Security health system in relation to the Organic Law on the National Health System.	Regulatory framework for the development of a system of health services networks. Development of reference and referral systems.	All regions have service networks of growing complexity. The reference and referral system is being regularly applied.

(*Matrix continues on the following page.*)

Policy Matrix (*continued*)

Problems	Policy measures		Objectives/goals
	Short term (to June 2003)	Medium term (2003–07)	
		Implementation of networks that integrate decentralized services with those of the Ministry of Public Health, of SGO, and of the SSC.	The supply of health services has grown as a result of the complementarity of resources.
Poor performance of Essential Public Health Functions (EPHF) by the Ministry of Public Health.	Elaboration of a program for carrying out the Essential Public Health Functions (EPHF) of the Ministry of Public Health.	Implementation of a program for the development of the Ministry of Public Health.	The Ministry of Public Health is properly fulfilling its administrative, regulation and control, and health surveillance functions, and so on.
			Development plan for the Ministry of Public Health and the National Hygiene Institute.
Limitations of the IESS health area.	Preparation of a program for developing the health area of the IESS.	Program implementation.	The health area of the IESS has the capacity to manage the health insurance of 50 percent of Ecuador's population.
			Development plan designed.

11

The Social Assistance System[1]

Daniel Dulitzky

This chapter presents a synthesis of the current state of Ecuador's social assistance system. With $US264 million spent in 2001, Ecuador's spending on social assistance, as a percentage of GDP, is average among the countries of the region. Despite the crisis, Ecuador has maintained a system with programs that assist a large number of persons. Some of these programs have clear objectives and a certain degree of targeting, yet with more than 22 programs, the system is extremely fragmented. The are administered by several different entities and their objectives and beneficiary population overlap one another. Three principal problems are present. First, the system is very inflexible, in terms of its budget, design, and coverage, as it has no mechanisms to increase the number of beneficiaries in times of crisis. Second, the social programs, in general, lack consistent targeting criteria. The universal programs, such as subsidies to public utilities, tend to be regressive, while the targeted programs fail to address particularly vulnerable groups, such as children between zero and five years of age at risk of malnutrition or pregnant women. Third, the Bono Solidario Cash Subsidy Program, which currently has the largest budget and is one of the most significant programs in terms of coverage, is plagued by numerous problems. The program fails to update its beneficiary base, lacks clear objectives, has inadequate targeting mechanisms, and grants a low level of benefits. Through restructuring, the social assistance system should become more flexible, using budgetary contingency funds to provide special funding increases to specific social programs in times of crisis. A mechanism should also be designed that will allow a program's beneficiary base to be updated.

---

1. Daniel Dulitzky is a social protection specialist for the World Bank. The author thanks Carolina Sánchez-Páramo and Norbert Schady for their valuable participation in defining the chapter's content and structure, and also thanks Marcelo Bortman and José Roberto López Cálix for their excellent comments on the preliminary versions.

Furthermore, if funds are available, an anticyclic program should be created—for example, a public works program targeted to principally assist individuals in temporary situations of poverty. There is also a need to improve coordination, protect the budget, and better target existing priority programs, applying a single targeting instrument to each of them. The objectives and beneficiary population of the programs should be reviewed, and consideration should be given to eliminating programs that are outright regressive. Finally, the Bono Solidario *Cash Subsidy Program should be transformed into a program of conditioned subsidies, oriented toward protecting the health and nutrition of children and pregnant women who live in poverty. The benefit to the elderly and to expectant mothers should be recalculated as a function of some criterion that reflects the beneficiary population and the program's objective.*

A. Introduction

The Ecuadoran economy has recently undergone a major economic crisis. It is therefore imperative that the performance of the country's social assistance system be evaluated. In fact, the economic crisis of the late 1990s was the worst such crisis over the past one hundred years, if measured in terms of reductions in GDP. Between 1997 and 1999, Ecuador's GDP fell by 10.4 percent (Frente Social 2002). Though the economy has since recuperated, exhibiting positive growth rates, the country's GDP has yet to attain precrisis levels.

This crisis resulted from a combination of economic problems and natural disasters. The damage caused by the El Niño phenomenon in 1997 and 1998 is estimated between 2.7 and 13.6 percent of GDP, depending on the source one consults. The situation was further aggravated by a series of exogenous impacts, such as the drop in oil prices, increases in the fiscal deficit, instability of the exchange rate, and unsustainable growth of the external debt, which unleashed an economic crisis of unprecedented impact.

The economic crisis of the late 1990s has increased the pressure felt by social protection programs. The poverty rate jumped in a period of only three years (1995 to 1998) from 34 to 56 percent of the population (World Bank 2000). The poverty rate is higher in rural zones, but its relative change has been greater in urban zones: in the latter, the poverty rate rose from 19 to 42 percent, while in the former, 77 percent of the population was considered poor in 1998, up from 56 percent in 1995. Extreme poverty, nonetheless, continues to be a principally rural phenomenon.

Increased inflation rates, the decline in real wages, and the rise in unemployment have had a cumulative effect, creating a new group of families in need of temporary social assistance. In addition, some groups, with even fewer protections, face chronic problems of poverty. The system must therefore be reviewed in light of this new demand for social assistance, contemplating the need to have certain flexible programs that can provide protection not only in a permanent manner, but also on a temporary basis to those in need during times of crisis.

Recovery from the crisis, dollarization, and political changes on the country's horizon are creating a favorable climate to redefine the features of the social assistance system in light of the needs of the population. With approximately 1.5 percent of GDP allocated to social assistance—without including insurance programs aimed at helping the poorest of the poor, such as the Rural People's Social Security Program (SSC)—Ecuador has succeeded in maintaining a system that aids a large number of persons in vulnerable population groups. Some of its programs have clear objectives and a certain degree of targeting, and the country has managed to protect a good part of social assistance budgets over recent years. Nonetheless, the system is still very fragmented, and in several programs, targeting and coordination could be improved.

This chapter describes the most prominent aspects of the social assistance system. Problems and risks faced by different population groups—those that will potentially be in demand of social assistance—are indicated, and the most severe problems in the system's current structure are identified. Based on this analysis, the chapter culminates with a series of recommendations for the short and medium terms, aimed at improving the system's functionality. An analysis of the social security healthcare system and programs such as the SSC goes beyond the scope of this report (see Chapters 10 and 12, on Health and on the Pension System, respectively). Such programs have a social assistance component, but since they are insurance, they do not constitute social assistance *per se*.

B. Principal Features of the Social Assistance System

A social assistance system can be defined as a set of programs designed to protect vulnerable population groups (whose vulnerability may be chronic or temporary) against specific risks that threaten their well-being. Such a system should be comprise structural elements as well as anticyclic elements. Programs of the structural type attempt to raise the standard of living and well-being of persons in situations of chronic poverty, that is, persons who face a prolonged impossibility of subsisting or generating an adequate level of income on their own. Anticyclic programs aim to protect individuals against temporary reductions in their income or well-being, and are fundamental in times of crisis, when the number of poor increases as a consequence of temporary impacts on major sectors of the population. A typical example of a classically anticyclic program—although it is actually insurance—is unemployment insurance. In times of crisis, when the number of unemployed increases, the base of the insurance also expands; once the crisis is over, the base of the insurance contracts.

A system can be composed of a great variety of programs. There are programs for the supply of goods and services, such as in-kind transfers and subsidies on the consumption of certain goods; demand-based programs, such as money transfers; and programs that help generate income in families by providing temporary employment. Many of these programs are represented in the Ecuador's social assistance system. In fact, the country has 22 social assistance programs designated as Priority Programs by the *Frente Social* (the "Social Front")—an entity that attempts to coordinate the social assistance activities of the ministries of Education, Health, Social Welfare, and Urban Development and Housing, which administer these priority programs.[2] The Priority Programs came into being in 2000 with the design of the Emergency Social Plan in an attempt to confront the crisis.

Table 1 summarizes the principal features of the Priority Programs. In 2001, Ecuador spent close to $US264 million on its Priority Programs, or approximately 1.5 percent of its GDP. Out of that sum, approximately 60 percent is represented by two money-transfer programs, the *Bono Solidario* Cash Subsidy Program and the Scholarship Program ("*Beca Escolar*"), the latter of which has a minimal budget as it is at an experimental stage. The rest involve food and nutrition, education, childcare for children between zero and six years of age, healthcare, and construction of housing. This list does not include subsidies on gas and gasoline consumption, which, according to Gutiérrez Santos, *et al.*, cited in Pérez (2002), represented approximately $US350 million in transfers to households in 2000, and almost $US500 million in total.

Table 2 summarizes the outstanding features of the most significant social assistance programs. In terms of coverage and budget, the two foremost programs are the School Breakfast and Lunch program, with an implemented budget of $US25.4 million in 2001, and the *Bono Solidario* Cash Subsidy Program, with a budget of $US154.5 million in 2001. In general, the system is made up of a great number of programs—some of which overlap one another in terms of their objectives and the population they cover. In addition, the programs are administered by many different players. Some recent programs, such as the Scholarship Program, represent a fundamental change. Indeed, this program pioneered the use of a clear targeting tool, a system known as SELBEN, the Ecuadorian Beneficiary Identification and Selection System (*Sistema de Identificación y Selección de Beneficiarios*), and it also provides money transfers in an attempt to influence the behavior of the beneficiaries.

C. Supply and Demand for Social Assistance

Vulnerable Groups

One methodological framework for evaluating social protection programs is known as the Social Risk Management Framework.[3] The concept of Social Risk Manage-

---

2. The 22 programs designated as Priority Programs are not an exhaustive list of social assistance programs. In addition, there are the programs administered by the National Children and Family Institute (*Instituto Nacional del Niño y la Familia*—INNFA), an autonomous entity historically directed by the First Lady. Several NGOs also provide decentralized social assistance.
3. "Social Risk Management Framework," in World Bank (2001).

Table 1. Selected Features of the Social Assistance System's Priority Programs[a] for 2000–01

Number of programs	22
Approved budget for 2001	$US295.7 million
Implemented budget for 2001	$US263.8 million
Money transfer programs	2
Percentage of the budget for money transfers	58%
Programs that provide food	5
Percentage of the budget	20.9%
Energy subsidy for households, 2000	$US341 million

a. Social Assistance Programs created in April 2000 as a part of the Emergency Social Plan. These include *Redes Amigas* ("Girls' Networks of Friends"); *Mochila Escolar* ("Backpack for School"); Improvement of Intercultural Bilingual Schools; School Meals; *Nuestros Niños* ("Our Children"); *Operación Rescate Infantil* ("Children's Rescue Operation"); *"Beca Escolar"* ("The Scholarship Program"); *Crédito Productivo* ("Productive Credit"); the *Bono Solidario* Cash Subsidy Program; Community Kitchens; Generic Medications; Mobile Health Units; Free Maternity Healthcare; National Food and Nutrition Program (PANN) 2000; Extended Immunizations Plan; Epidemiological Control: Tuberculosis; Epidemiological Control: Malaria and Dengue; Peasant Housing; Urban Low-Income Housing; Housing for Beneficiaries of the *Bono Solidario* Cash Subsidy Program; and Potable Water and Environmental Sanitation.
Source: Frente Social (2002).

ment is based on the idea that individuals are subject to unexpected shocks that affect their capacity to generate income. In some cases, the shock is permanent in nature, while in others it is purely temporary. Optimal risk management consists of a series of mechanisms to prevent and mitigate the risk in question, and, as a last resort, activities to aid those affected, so that they can minimize the adverse effects of the shocks. The mechanisms so utilized include social security health systems and social assistance systems.

This framework for evaluating the social assistance system involves the following steps: First, a determination is made of the potential demand for social assistance, as a function of the risks associated with the various population groups. Second, an evaluation is made of the mechanisms that these groups employ in order to cope with those risks, and how such mechanisms could affect the well-being of the respective groups. Third, a survey is conducted among the groups that face a high-risk of temporary impacts as a consequence of a crisis, or of permanent impacts due to a chronic impossibility of generating income. Fourth, an evaluation is made of the features of the current social assistance programs in light of the needs of the population, especially the needs of vulnerable groups as determined above. Finally, a decision is made regarding measures to be implemented, aimed at improving the contribution of programs to the well-being of groups who are in need of social assistance.

(*Text continues on page 328.*)

Table 2. Outstanding Features of the Most Significant Social Assistance Programs

Program	Type of assistance	Risks addressed	Administration	Coverage	Targeting	Implemented budget in 2001 (million $US)
Bono Solidario Cash Subsidy Program	Money transfer	Low income, poverty	Autonomous entity associated with the Ministry of Social Welfare	1,216,222 direct beneficiaries 4,500,000 total beneficiaries	Self-screening, validated by churches Error of exclusion: 21.2% Error of inclusion: 18.3%	154.5
Free Maternity Healthcare	Provision of healthcare to pregnant women at units of the Ministry of Health	Maternal and infantile mortality	Ministry of Health	743,000 women receiving prenatal care 93,000 normal childbirths	Universal	—
National Micronutrients Program	Provision of iron and Vitamin A supplements to children under five years of age, pregnant and nursing women	—	Ministry of Health	—	—	—
Children's Development Program	Day care, nutrition for children from six months to six years of age, whose parents are working outside the home	Early childhood development	National Children's and Family Institute (*Instituto Nacional de la Niñez y la Familia*—INNFA)	47,000 children ages zero to six	65% beneficiaries in quintiles 1 and 2	—

Program	Description	Category	Ministry	Beneficiaries	Targeting	
Operation Children's Rescue (*Operación de Rescate Infantil*—ORI)	Day care, nutrition, healthcare for poor children under six years of age	Early childhood development	Ministry of Social Welfare	50,296	41% beneficiaries in quintiles 1 and 2	14.1
National Pre-school Education Program (*Programa Nacional de Educación Preescolar*—PRONEPE)	Day care for children from four to six years of age who have no access to preschool education	Early childhood development	Ministry of Education	18,027	—	—
Supplementary Food Program for Mothers and Infants (*Programa de Alimentación Complementaria Materna-Infantil*—PACMI)	Nutritional supplements for children and under-nourished pregnant women	Early childhood development	Ministry of Health	14,930 (5% of the group objective)	73% beneficiaries in quintiles 1 and 2	—
Nuestros Niños ("Our Children")	Complement to INNFA, ORI, and other programs for children from zero to six years of age	Early childhood development	Ministry of Social Welfare	82,300	—	7.9

(*Table continues on the following page.*)

Table 2. (*continued*)

Program	Type of assistance	Risks addressed	Administration	Coverage	Targeting	Implemented budget in 2001 (million $US)
School Snacks and Lunches	Food supplement for poor children in public schools	School dropout rate, accumulation of human capital	Ministry of Education	1,251,000 (76% of the total children enrolled in elementary schools)	Poorest 40% receive 53% of the benefit Almost universal	25.4
Redes Amigas (Girls' Networks of Friends")	Teacher training, school books, creation of school networks	—	Ministry of Education	128,469 (16% of students in rural zones)	58% of beneficiaries in the poorest municipalities	7.9
Child Workers' Program	Scholarships, tutors, familiar education	Accumulation of human capital	INNFA	12,335 (In Ecuador there are 330,000 children between the ages of five to nine who are working)	—	32.8
Community Kitchens	Supplemental food to the population	Chronic poverty	Ministry of Social Welfare	238,000 persons	—	4.7
National Food and Nutrition Program (PANN) 2000	Education and supplemental nutrition to pregnant women and to children ages 6 to 24 months	Malnutrition	Ministry of Health	102,000 pregnant women and 117,000 children	Poorest townships	2.4

Subsidies on gas and fuel	Subsidy for gas and gasoline consumption	Low income	—	Universal	The poorest 20% receives 8% of the subsidy	341.0
Scholarship Program	Subsidy in money conditioned upon school attendance	School dropout rate	Ministry of Social Welfare	35,000 children	Use of SELBEN for targeting	1.0
Crédito Productivo (Productive Credit)	Financing of microbusiness projects	Low family income	Ministry of Social Welfare	3,000 persons	—	3.5

Sources: Frente Social (2002), Cely (2002), UNICEF (2002).

A study of poverty in Ecuador (León 2002) maintains that "recent" poverty in Ecuador doubled between 1998 and 1999. "Recent" poverty refers to households that are below the poverty line, but whose basic needs are satisfied. This means that the households in question are confronting a situation of temporary poverty, in which their standard of living has been reduced, but not for so long that their basic needs are affected. When households live in poverty over a long period of time, their basic needs go unsatisfied. The population of Ecuador living in conditions of poverty qualified as "chronic" increased from 28 to 36 percent between 1995 and 1999. Interestingly, the increase in temporary or recent poverty was principally seen in urban zones, while the increase in chronic poverty is both an urban and a rural phenomenon.

The unemployment rate also increased notably during the period of crisis. While for the 15- to 28-year-old age group, unemployment rose from 15.3 to 27.8 percent between 1998 to 1999, unemployment for the 29- to 44-year-old age group rose from 5.4 to 11 percent. In total, the unemployment rate doubled, from 8.5 percent in May 1998 to 16.9 percent in August 1999. Underemployment also increased significantly.

The increase in the inflation rate, the depreciation of the sucre, and the subsequent dollarization of the economy may have increased the number of recent poor. The inflation rate was 52 percent in 1999 and 96.1 percent in 2000. Many families who were not poor at the beginning of the period may have been affected by the depreciation of the sucre if they had debts in dollars. At the same time, those with savings in sucres suffered from the freeze on deposits ordered by the government in March 1999 and the high inflation and depreciation rates that eroded the value of their savings. According to the survey of households of 1998, approximately 25 percent of the families in the third quintile of consumption had savings accounts.

The most vulnerable age groups in Ecuadoran society are poor children and pre-teens, pregnant women in conditions of poverty, and elderly persons with no formal income. In fact, families with children under two years of age, and to a lesser extent families that include older children or elderly persons, have a higher probability of being poor. Indigent families include, on average, a higher number of elderly persons and children between zero and two years of age (World Bank 2000).

According to the Living Conditions Survey of 1998, the percentage of chronic malnutrition among children between zero and two years of age in the first income quintile was 32.5 percent, while the percentage of low weight-for-age was 24.3 percent. Both these figures are far above average for that age group. This situation was also seen, to an even worse extent, in the group of children between three and five years of age, where the percentage of chronic malnutrition was 44 percent in the lowest quintile, as compared to an average of 29 percent in the general population. Among this group, the percentage of low weight-for-age was 23.3 percent as compared to 14 percent overall. The National Children's and Family Institute (INNFA) reports that approximately 660,000 children between zero and five years of age show signs of acute, chronic malnutrition.

The group of school-age children in the poorest quintile is also subject to numerous risks, especially malnutrition and limited formation of human capital. Preschool education for this group is very low, with levels of attendance at 10 percent (compared to 30 percent for the highest quintile). The disparity between levels of income is particularly notable for secondary schools, with net attendance rates of 44 percent for the country as a whole, but only 19 percent for the lowest quintile. A parallel phenomenon to low school attendance is that of children who work, with 21 percent of children between the ages of 10 and 15 working and not attending school in 1998. According to data from the Integrated Social Indicators System of Ecuador (*Sistema Integrado de Indicadores Sociales de Ecuador*—SIISE), there are 1,050,802 Ecuadoran children who work, 32.5 percent of whom are between five and nine years of age, and the rest of whom are between 10 and 17.

According to the Demographic Survey and the Survey on Maternal and Infantile Health, there were no significant changes in the percentage of children who received healthcare and follow-up during the first five years of life between 1994 and 1999. Though the prevalence of diseases such as diarrhea and acute respiratory infections went down for the country as a whole, an a increase was seen in the incidence of both these ailments for the group of mothers without schooling, which is an approximate indicator of low levels of income. A similar trend was seen for vaccination rates. When observing the percentages of children under one year of age who received complete vaccinations, a significant deterioration was seen between 1994 and 1999, especially in rural zones and in families in which the mother has no schooling. In these families, the percentage who received complete vaccinations declined from 26 to 16 percent. This might reflect a deterioration of healthcare conditions as a consequence of the crisis.

The elderly without coverage are an especially vulnerable group. Poverty statistics indicate that families with elderly persons in their nuclear family unit have a 13 percent greater probability than the average population of being poor (World Bank 2002). From 1990 to 2001, the proportion of persons older than 60 rose from 6 to 9 percent, and in 1999, illiteracy was seen in 34 percent of the elderly. Five out of every 100 poor persons were elderly (SIISE 2002). The coverage of the social security health system is minimal, as only 23 percent of Ecuadorans over 60 are affiliated with the IESS. In this context, many elderly persons belong to multigenerational households (54 percent of the elderly live in this type of household). A social assistance program does target this population group, as according to the Living Conditions Survey of 1999, 30 percent of Ecuadorans over 65 were receiving the *Bono Solidario* Cash Subsidy. Currently the subsidy is approximately $US7 per month, representing between 15 and 30 percent of the value of the average pension.

Social Risk Management Strategies

The Living Conditions Survey and information from a qualitative study aimed at determining the effects of the crisis in Ecuador reveal a series of behaviors that could be considered to constitute social risk management (World Bank 2000). Many of the behaviors that households are employing to manage risk could have a negative impact on the future well-being of their members, and the social assistance system aims in part to prevent these behaviors from being maintained for prolonged periods of time:

- Child labor: According to a 2001 UNICEF study (based on the Living Conditions Survey of 1999), there were 136,700 children in Ecuador between five and nine years of age and 914,000 between 10 and 17 years of age who were working.[4] This is not necessarily due to the crisis, and may have already existed, but some households have indeed coped with the crisis by incorporating more members of the family into the labor market to generate income. The percentage of children between 10 and 15 who were working and not studying remained more or less constant between 1998 and 1999, and the same constancy was seen in the gross attendance rate. Nonetheless, the number of days absent from school almost doubled, from 5.4 to 10.5 days per month. This may reflect a deterioration in the supply of education or problems with transportation and other social services, on account of which it has become more difficult to attend school, but it may also be due to the alternative use of time by children on temporary jobs. In many cases, even where no drop has been seen in school attendance, the quality of the education received, which is much more difficult to measure, could have been affected as a result of the crisis.
- Reduction in consumption: A recent IDB study (2002) cites data from 1999, which indicates that 95 percent of the beneficiary households of the *Bono Solidario* Cash Subsidy Program have reduced their consumption of food, and 58 percent have reduced their number of meals per day. Information is also found in interviews with focus groups conducted in July 1999 (World Bank 2000), which reported a drop in the consumption of proteins and minerals, and an increase in the consumption of carbohydrates and cheaper foods of poorer quality. In small local markets, a decline was reported in the sale of fruits and vegetables, cheese, eggs, and meat.
- Debt: This strategy is more common in—but not exclusive to—households that face a situation of temporary poverty. One out of every two beneficiaries of the *Bono Solidario* Cash Subsidy Program applied for a loan in 1998; one in four beneficiaries fell behind in rent payments, and one in five had to buy on credit in neighborhood stores or sell belongings (Carrera 1999, cited in Pérez 2002).
- Deferred healthcare: According to a World Bank report (2000), the percentage of households that report that they deferred healthcare for some member of the family because they could not afford it rose from 51.5 to 72 percent.

---

4. INNFA reports significantly higher numbers, based on information from the SIISE.

- Migration: Several newspaper articles have reported an increase in the number of persons who have left the country and not returned. While in 1997 the total number of migrants was 18,000, in 2001 160,000 persons left the country without returning. Moreover, during the past five years 451,143 Ecuadorans have migrated (Pérez 2002). Money sent from abroad is becoming an important source of income for many Ecuadorans.

D. Problems of the Social Assistance System

LACK OF FLEXIBILITY. With a budget of between 1 and 1.5 percent of GDP earmarked for social assistance, spending on social assistance in Ecuador is average for the region.[5] Nonetheless, the system does not seem to have the capacity to adapt to the needs of the population, that is to say, to expand in times of crisis and contract under normal circumstances. The system's lack of flexibility is a result of the nature of its budget, problems related to coverage, and the design of its programs.

FLEXIBILITY IN THE BUDGET. In a recent analysis of trends in social spending between 1970 and 2002, Vos and others (2002) argue that social spending as a whole has been procyclic, although volatility varies according to the category of the expenditure—education, health, social security healthcare, and social assistance. In the case of social assistance, the trend is principally noncyclical, as it is characterized by a relatively inflexible budget that is not correlated to the needs of social protection of vulnerable groups during times of crisis. Over the past two years, social assistance spending has increased, to the detriment of spending on health and education. This is primarily a consequence of the creation of money transfer programs such as the *Bono Solidario* Cash Subsidy Program. Nonetheless, the trend over the past two decades has been a decline in social spending as a whole.

It is not only necessary to keep the social assistance budget flexible—and wherever possible anticyclic—but also to protect the budgets of certain priority programs in order to guarantee their long-term sustainability. If minimum floors were established—in terms of absolute value—for the budgets of some programs, this in fact would add an anticyclic component to the social assistance system. Currently there are no guarantees regarding the continuity of several social programs, as the budgets are not protected in the future. Although the World Bank Structural Adjustment Loan for the year 2000 included a commitment from the government to maintain minimum floors for social programs in terms of absolute value for 2000 and 2001, there are no similar figures for 2002 and the following years.

---

5. For example, in 1999 Argentina spent approximately 0.9 percent, Mexico 1.1 percent, Nicaragua 1.1 percent, Peru 1.4 percent, and Venezuela 1 percent (Dulitzky, Gragnolati, and Lindert 2001).

FLEXIBILITY IN COVERAGE. The programs do not have an automatic mechanism that allows them to be rapidly updated. This is especially necessary for anticyclic programs aimed at providing temporary social assistance in times of crisis. In these cases, it is necessary to be able to enroll beneficiaries at various times during the life of the program, and, in the same manner, remove beneficiaries from the system when they no longer require assistance. For example, the *Bono Solidario* Cash Subsidy Program enrolled beneficiaries only at the time of its launch in 1998. In successive years the beneficiary base was screened and noneligible households were eliminated, yet no mechanism was ever designed to enroll new beneficiaries. Some supply-based programs are updated, which allows for the enrollment of new beneficiaries, but no systematic mechanism exists. Rather, the review of the beneficiary base is made on an *ad hoc* basis.

FLEXIBILITY IN DESIGN. At this time there is no program that is classically anticyclic. Anticyclic programs contain automatic adjustment mechanisms that allow the beneficiary base to be increased in times of crisis. For example, programs that provide temporary employment with a self-targeting criterion and sufficiently low wages are clearly anticyclic, as only during a crisis is the opportunity cost of taking such employment sufficiently low, and therefore the beneficiary base increases.

ABSENCE OF CONSISTENT TARGETING CRITERIA AND REGRESSIVITY IN THE SYSTEM'S PROGRAMS. The social assistance system in Ecuador includes both universal and targeted programs. In general, it is observed that many of the universal programs tend to be regressive, as a high percentage of the expenditure on those programs ends up benefiting the higher-level income quintiles. The targeted programs vary in their effective outreach to the lower quintiles, and furthermore, do not utilize consistent targeting criteria. This generates duplications and dilutes their effectiveness even further. Several programs—for instance, those in place to protect children from zero to two years of age against the risk of malnutrition—also have insufficient coverage, and in many cases fail to address important risks for certain vulnerable groups.

TARGETING AND REGRESSIVITY. The social assistance system includes certain highly regressive programs. For example, subsidies for electricity, gas, and gasoline amounted to $US541 million in 2000, almost 4 percent of GDP, of which households received 63.5 percent (Gutiérrez Santos 2002, cited in Pérez 2002). These subsidies are highly regressive, as they are correlated to the consumption of fuel, which increases with income. It is estimated that the total subsidy per capita—on electricity, gas, and gasoline—is five times as large among the wealthiest quintile as among the poorest (Gutiérrez Santos 2002, cited in Pérez 2002). Nonetheless, the subsidy represents a fundamental source of aid for the poorest of the poor. The study in question argues that without the subsidies, the poorest sectors would see their income reduced by 7 percent annually.

Vos and others (2002) estimate the percentage of benefit of various social assistance programs in terms of the population quintiles benefited. This can be represented graphically through concentration curves, such those in Figure 1. A progressive program would have a concentration curve higher than the 45 degree curve, indicating that the poorest quintiles receive a more than proportional benefit. Figure 1 illustrates that some social assistance programs are progressive, but even in those programs, a high percentage of the benefit reaches the wealthiest population quintiles. For example, 45 percent of the benefits of the *Bono Solidario* Cash Subsidy Program is received by families in the three highest quintiles (The annex contains the exact percentages of benefits reaching the various population quintiles).

INSUFFICIENT COVERAGE. The coverage of the social assistance system is inadequate. This is not necessarily due to a lack of budget, for, as was mentioned above, Ecuador's spending on social assistance is average among the countries of Latin America for which information is available. Yet due to the lack of a consistent targeting criterion and the overlapping of programs, in many cases funds are diverted toward groups that do not need them. The group of children under the age of six offers a clear example. There are at least five programs that target this population

Figure 1. Concentration Curves for Some Social Assistance Programs

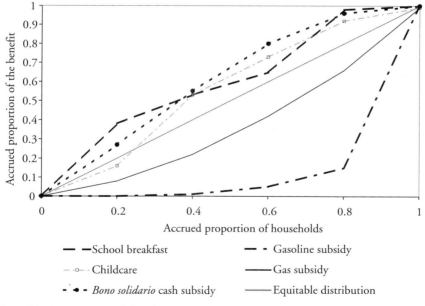

Source: Vos, Ponce, León, et al. (2002).

group, and according to INNFA (2000), the programs administered by the Ministry of Education, of Social Welfare, and INNFA itself cover approximately 139,000 children—that is, approximately 7 percent of all children, and 11 percent of children in poverty, in that age group. According to INNFA 1999, 40.3 percent of the population was undernourished in Ecuador in 1999—comprehensively and chronically. In other words, out of 1,304,920 children under five, approximately 525,800 showed some sign of malnutrition. This illustrates that the programs for this age and risk group are far from ideal. Other vulnerable groups, such as the elderly, are covered by social assistance programs, but the benefit received is insufficient to meet their needs.

The near universality of certain programs limits the field of action of the social assistance system. The Free Maternity Healthcare program provides free medical assistance to pregnant women through childbirth, even for women covered by IESS health insurance. It is imperative to review the targeting criteria, coverage, and benefits of the system's most significant programs.

SHORTCOMINGS OF THE *BONO SOLIDARIO* CASH SUBSIDY PROGRAM. The *Bono Solidario* Cash Subsidy Program is the most significant endeavor in the social assistance system. If Ecuador could only administer a single assistance program, this would be a natural candidate, given its broad beneficiary base, its high budget within the system, its scope, and the possibilities it offers. Nonetheless, the program has numerous organizational and implementation problems that must be addressed.

ENROLLMENT OF BENEFICIARIES. To date there is no mechanism that allows for the enrollment of new beneficiaries. The beneficiary base is being screened, and the number of beneficiaries has been reduced from approximately 1.7 to 1.2 million through this mechanism. Yet new beneficiaries have not been allowed to enroll since the commencement of the program. This is particularly serious if one bears in mind that the program's initial targeting did not utilize any consistent instrument beyond an enrollment form verified by local churches and parishes.

QUESTIONABLE VALIDATION CRITERIA. The original beneficiary base has been gradually screened, using a series of criteria. For example, the elimination from the beneficiary base of all individuals affiliated with Social Security Insurance creates disincentives to affiliating with this program. Although the idea of approximating beneficiaries' income levels through closely-correlated indicators is adequate, such indicators must be selected with care in order to minimize disincentives.

INADEQUATE TARGETING. At present, the *Bono Solidario* Cash Subsidy Program is a self-targeted program, given that, as mentioned above, enrollments were made through an enrollment slip validated by local parishes and churches. A World Bank analysis conducted in 2000 demonstrated that the coverage rate of the program was 88 percent of the poor. Yet according to that same study, many individuals who met the requirements for the subsidy were not actually receiving it, while many who were receiving it failed to meet all the requirements. Table 3 shows the number of mothers and the elderly who were receiving the *Bono Solidario* Cash Subsidy in 1999 according to the Living Conditions Survey, as compared to the potential number of beneficiaries. It is seen that the number of persons who are not receiving the subsidy despite meeting all its requirements is high—59 percent of those eligible—while ineligible persons who nonetheless receive the subsidy represent 54 percent of the total number of beneficiaries.

INADEQUATE BENEFIT LEVELS. Currently mothers with children under 18 years of age receive $US11.50 per month, the elderly $US7 and the disabled $US7. These levels of benefits were determined in keeping with the initial purpose of the *Bono Solidario* Cash Subsidy Program: to aid families with the costs of gas and electricity, given the elimination of energy subsidies. Nonetheless, the energy subsidies were later reinstated, and the program, which was supposedly a replacement for them, was never eliminated. The calculation of the benefit is based on a historical criterion, and does not accurately correlate to the way beneficiaries use it. Factors such as the poverty line, the opportunity cost of accumulating human capital, the cost of basic healthcare, and the effects of dollarization and inflation on the income of the beneficiaries were not borne in mind for the calculation.

INSTITUTIONAL PROBLEMS. Currently, the *Bono Solidario* Cash Subsidy Program is an entity with financial autonomy, associated with the Ministry of Social Welfare. Nonetheless, the payments are made by the Ministry of Economy and Finance. This means that there is no single responsible entity. Rather, different administrative aspects of the program are under the dominion of different administrative bodies. Such a state of affairs creates confusion and problems of coordination. Other institutional aspects should also be reviewed. For example, the system uses the private banking system, intensely clustered in urban zones, to effect payment of the benefit. The banks verify the identity of the payment recipients, but are not obligated to convey that information to the government. There are also problems with the manner in which payments are made (such as times of service and long waits at private banks).

Table 3. Targeting of the *Bono Solidario* Cash Subsidy Program (Individual Beneficiaries)

	Eligible	Ineligible	Total
Receive the subsidy	590,955	692,985	1,283,940
Do not receive the subsidy	856,442	1,417,795	2,274,237
Total	1,447,397	2,110,780	3,558,177

Source: World Bank (2000).

FAILURE TO EVALUATE THE PROGRAM'S IMPACT. No evaluation is made of the impact of the *Bono Solidario* Cash Subsidy Program in terms of its effectiveness. The closest approximation to such an evaluation was a baseline survey of the program, conducted in August 2002, which attempted to determine how the beneficiaries were using the money. Yet, just as occurs with the rest of the programs in the social assistance system, no serious evaluation is being made of the subsidy's effects.

LACK OF CLEAR OBJECTIVES. As was mentioned above, the historical reason for which the *Bono Solidario* Cash Subsidy Program was created—that subsidies on energy consumption were being eliminated—is no longer valid, as the energy subsidies have since been reinstated. The *Bono Solidario* is currently a money transfer program with no stated purpose. This compromises other dimensions of the program, such as targeting and determination of the level of benefits.

LACK OF AIM TO INFLUENCE BEHAVIOR. In many cases, the most effective social assistance programs are those that attempt to influence changes in the behavior of their beneficiaries. A good example would be the education of mothers on aspects of nutrition, which is considered more effective and longer lasting than food distribution programs. The *Bono Solidario* Cash Subsidy Program is nothing more than a money transfer. It does not seek to influence behavior, and thus entails a risk of generating dependency among its beneficiaries.

E. Recommendations

Ecuador's social assistance system is plagued with numerous faults that the new administration needs to address. The principal problem is not a lack of funds for social assistance—rather, it is that social assistance is not well targeted, and that several programs are regressive, and therefore do not reach the population most in need.

The recommendations of this chapter can be grouped into three categories. In the first place, the flexibility of the social assistance system needs to be increased, using some mechanism to ensure that the system can adapt in times of crisis, when the number of persons demanding social assistance grows. In second place, a series of distortions in the current social assistance system must be corrected. This will require a review of the benefits, targeting criteria, objectives, and administration of certain programs. Changes such as these demand a major political commitment and are not easy to implement. An evaluation of the impact of the measures adopted is therefore imperative. The third recommendation involves Ecuador's largest assistance program, the *Bono Solidario* Cash Subsidy Program. The new administration should focus its efforts on ways to take advantage of the program's structure, which has a broad outreach and could serve as the backbone of the social assistance system. In this sense, numerous changes are needed, which are described below.

Increase the Flexibility of the Social Assistance System

As was stated above, creating flexibility in the social assistance system entails the creation of mechanisms so that it can expand in times of crisis and contract under normal circumstances, when the demand for social assistance goes down. For said purpose, the following is recommended:

PROTECT THE BUDGET OF PRIORITY SOCIAL ASSISTANCE PROGRAMS. It is recommended that minimum statutory budgets be created for certain social assistance programs. The social assistance system should have a basic budget that is protected, at least in the case of certain programs. In this sense, the inclusion of clauses in the agreements made with multilateral entities to guarantee the protection of these funds is an option that has been utilized in the past, which has allowed certain priority programs to stay in operation.

DESIGN A SYSTEM THAT ALLOWS FOR AN UPDATING OF PROGRAM BENEFICIARIES. To date, the most significant targeted programs are not allowing new beneficiaries to enroll. This means that during a crisis, those who require temporary social assistance have no access to it. A mechanism must be conceived that will allow new beneficiaries to enroll at various times of the year. One way to accomplish this is to periodically verify the eligibility of potential beneficiaries, particularly during a crisis. Another possibility is to consider a functional decentralization of certain programs. If their administration were in the hands of provinces or municipalities, which would be closer to the potential beneficiaries, it would be easier to evaluate the needs of the population.

CONSIDER THE CREATION OF A PUBLIC WORKS PROGRAM OR OTHER ANTICYCLIC PROGRAM. Public works programs provide income to unemployed persons who are unable to obtain work during a crisis, while simultaneously contributing to the creation of infrastructure. The advantage offered by these programs is that they are purely anticyclic and temporary. Indeed, it is only during a crisis that a major group of individuals will exist who will be looking for work and unable to find it. In general, these programs are self-targeted, as they offer low wages that only attract very poor persons who are truly in need. Furthermore, the benefit granted is usually short in duration. The programs tend to be expensive, but part of the financing for a program of this type could be made available through rationalizing or adapting many other existing programs, such as the energy subsidies.

Improve Coordination and Targeting in Existing Programs

Ideally, a social assistance system should focus on a few programs with specific objectives and consistent targeting instruments. In the case of Ecuador, the system could cover vulnerable groups and the most immediate risks to which these groups are subjected through the *Bono Solidario* Cash Subsidy Program, the Scholarship Program, and an anticyclic program such as public works employment. This would entail a reform of the *Bono Solidario* Cash Subsidy Program (the recommendations for which are included in the next point). This program should be reoriented toward protecting very young children and pregnant women against the risks of malnutrition. At the same time, the influence of other programs that offer in-kind transfers should be reduced. Given that the elimination of programs can be very costly from a political point of view, an attempt should at least be made to improve coordination among the programs already in existence, so as to avoid the temptation of creating more programs than are recommended. It is recommended that the following measures be studied:

ADOPT CONSISTENT TARGETING CRITERIA. As was explained in the preceding section, there is evidence that the present social assistance programs do not always reach those most in need. It is suggested that a single criterion be adopted for targeting the most significant social assistance programs. There are at least two possibilities. On the one hand, surveys of households can be used to determine which ones are the most needy, in order to entitle those households to a series of benefits. That system would be periodically reviewed to allow the enrollment of new households and to validate the information obtained on households that are already receiving benefits, thus minimizing errors of inclusion or exclusion. There are numerous examples of this type of targeting criterion, such as Colombia's Beneficiary Selection System (*Sistema de Selección de Beneficiarios*—SISBEN), and the Ecuadorian Beneficiary Identification and Selection System (*Sistema de Identificación y Selección de Beneficiarios*—SELBEN), which is now being developed. This system tends to be very onerous and difficult to administer. Thus, in several cases, it has been decided to utilize poverty maps to grant benefits. The benefits are granted to all the inhabitants of a given community considered to be very poor. Such a system is easier to administer, but in principle can generate errors of exclusion if the mapping is not sufficiently precise, that is to say, concerning the lowest geopolitical division of the population (in the case of Ecuador, that would be the sub-township level).

IMPROVE THE COORDINATION OF EXISTING PROGRAMS. The objective of the programs on which the most emphasis is placed must be clearly defined. This means that their targeted population must be identified, as well as the eligibility criteria and the risks against which the beneficiaries would be protected, in order to prevent an overlapping of programs that benefit one and the same household and address one and the same problem. In this sense, it will be necessary, for example, to reconsider the role of the School Meals Program, as it addresses risks that are similar to those covered by other programs. The School Meals Program has an approved budget for 2002 of $US46 million, and provides nutritional supplements to school-age children, both elementary and secondary. The program uses an approximate poverty map determined by the Social Vulnerability Index. Yet this program's benefit clearly reaches beyond those who are the poorest. Indeed, in 2001 supplements were granted to approximately 1.4 million school-age children, yet in 1999 Ecuador had 1,629,065 children enrolled in elementary schools. Furthermore, like all programs that grant in-kind transfers through schools, those who are the poorest do not receive the benefit, because they are outside the formal educational system. As for the objective of programs such as these, it is clear that they do not solve the problems of infant malnutrition, as such a goal would require interventions at a very early age. Although the School Meals Program does act as an incentive to school attendance, it also competes with the *Bono Solidario* Cash Subsidy Program. In fact, recent surveys have determined that 60 percent of the beneficiaries of the *Bono Solidario* Cash Subsidy use all or a significant portion of that money to buy food. The School Meals Program also competes with the Scholarship Program, whose objective is to promote school attendance through a cash subsidy to families that send their children to school.

CONSIDER THE ELIMINATION OF SUBSIDIES ON ENERGY CONSUMPTION. It has been demonstrated that this program is highly regressive and costly for the government.

EVALUATE THE IMPACT OF THE MOST SIGNIFICANT PROGRAMS. All decisions to make changes in current programs should be founded on a cost/benefit study and on a measure of their impact.

PRIORITIZE DEMAND-BASED PROGRAMS SUCH AS CONDITIONED SUBSIDIES. This will also require the improvement of the supply of related health and education services to make it easier for beneficiaries to meet the requirements.

Reorient the Bono Solidario *Cash Subsidy Program toward Becoming a Program of Conditioned Subsidies*

The *Bono Solidario* Cash Subsidy Program, which represents approximately half of the government's social assistance budget, has the tools it needs to become the central program of the social assistance system. Nonetheless, a series of changes need to be made to it, including a review of its objectives, a recalculation of its benefits based on clear criteria, and an improvement in its targeting. Specifically, the following measures are recommended:

TRANSFORM THE *BONO SOLIDARIO* CASH SUBSIDY PROGRAM INTO A CONDITIONED SUBSIDY PROGRAM, ORIENTED TOWARD PROTECTING THE HEALTH OF CHILDREN AND PREGNANT WOMEN WHO LIVE IN POVERTY. Children's nutrition programs have very limited coverage. It is estimated that there are 1.3 million boys and girls in Ecuador between zero and five years of age. Programs targeting this vulnerable group only provide services to approximately 200,000 children, even though, according to SIISE data, approximately 600,000 children are suffering from chronic malnutrition. Clearly the coverage of the programs aiming to alleviate this problem is insufficient and inadequate. The *Bono Solidario* Cash Subsidy Program is a good potential channel for promoting control of children's nutrition and health in exchange for a transfer in money. This approach is already functioning in other countries, such as Colombia and Mexico. The conversion of the *Bono Solidario* Cash Subsidy Program would entail an analysis, among other things, of the possibility of including pregnant women in the system; the type of control that would be required of mothers; and the exclusion of persons who are receiving benefits from other programs such as the ORI, PDI, or the PANN.[6] An approach must also be developed for mothers with children over the age of five, for whom the type of control and the objective of the program would be different.

MAINTAIN BENEFITS FOR THE ELDERLY, OR PROGRESSIVELY REPLACE THEM WITH A NONCONTRIBUTIVE PENSION FOR THE ELDERLY POOR. As explained in section C, the elderly are a vulnerable group, especially those elderly persons who do not receive pensions from the social security system (in other words, the majority). The *Bono Solidario* Cash Subsidy Program is thus the only program that mitigates the lack of income in this demographic group. Nonetheless, there needs to be coordination with the Social Security System, so that this program does not compete with a possible noncontributive pension under the IESS reform plans (see Chapter on the Social Security System). Also, elderly persons who live with beneficiary families of the *Bono Solidario* Cash Subsidy Program should not receive a separate benefit under that same subsidy amounting to a double benefit for those families. One possibility in such a case is to consider a reduction in the benefit, rather than its complete elimination.

IMPROVE TARGETING CRITERIA. In the first place, the beneficiary base should be screened, using a criterion consistent with those of the other most significant social assistance programs. In the second place, new beneficiaries should eventually be allowed to enroll, provided that they meet the respective eligibility criteria. In the third place, clear targeting criteria should be chosen. For said purpose, the advantages and disadvantages of systems such as surveys or poverty maps should be studied. A possible combination of these methods with self-targeting criteria should also be considered.

REVIEW THE AMOUNT OF BENEFIT GRANTED. In good measure, the amount would depend on the program's objective and beneficiary population. For example, the benefit amount to protect children against problems of malnutrition would be very

---

6. Children's Rescue Operation *(Operación Rescate Infantil)*, Children's Development Program *(Programa de Desarrollo Infantil)*, and the National Food and Nutrition Program *(Programa Nacional de Alimentación y Nutrición)*, respectively.

different from the amount granted to protect families from temporary reductions in their levels of income or to protect children from possible losses in the development of their human capital. Benefits must be based on clear criteria and must respect budgetary limitations. For example, increasing the benefit to mothers so that their income would reach 50 percent of the poverty line would require a doubling of the budget. Considering the budgetary limitations, these funds could be made available through a reorganization of existing programs or an elimination of certain beneficiaries based on such targeting criteria as may be adopted. Rofman (2002) estimates the additional costs of increasing benefits and enrolling additional beneficiaries under various scenarios.

REVIEW ADMINISTRATIVE ASPECTS OF THE PROGRAM. This includes reevaluating the contracts with private banks for handling benefit payments, confirming the beneficiaries' identity, and studying possible delays in project budget implementation.

EVALUATE THE IMPACT OF THE PROGRAM. An impact evaluation plan should be included in the design of the new program.

F. Conclusions

The political changes on the horizon in Ecuador create an opportunity to lay the groundwork for a more efficient and equitable social assistance system. The economy has been recuperating in recent years, but the effects of dollarization and a possible repeat of the El Niño phenomenon necessitate a profound analysis of the social assistance programs. It has been emphasized in this chapter that many of the changes do not require budget increases, but simply a firm political commitment to improve the well-being of Ecuador's vulnerable population groups.

Policy Matrix

Problems	Policy measures		Progress indicators	Objectives/goals
	Short term (to June 2003)	Medium term (2003–07)		
1. The social assistance system is inflexible				
The social assistance budget is inflexible, and is not dependent on the social protection needs of vulnerable groups.	Propose new minimum floors for certain social assistance programs.	Protect the social assistance budget of the most significant programs.	Budgets of social assistance programs. Agreements with multi-lateral entities, specifying minimum floors for social assistance. Stabilization Fund in operation.	Provide the social assistance system with greater flexibility, so that it can respond to situations of crisis through anticyclic changes in its budget.
The social assistance programs do not contain mechanisms to update the beneficiary base.	Evaluate possible mechanisms for updating at least three of the most significant social assistance programs.	Implement the plan to update the beneficiary database in at least three of the most significant programs.	Beneficiary database.	Allow individuals in temporary situations of vulnerability to benefit from social assistance programs.
There are no anticyclic programs.	Evaluate the costs of implementing various anticyclic programs.	Reorient funds from the most regressive social assistance pro-grams toward the creation of an anticyclic program.	Report that simulates various anticyclic programs.	Improve the social assistance system's response capacity to emergency situations.
2. Absence of consistent targeting criteria and problems of regressivity				
Various social assistance programs	Redefine objectives and the beneficiary popu-	Evaluate various targeting mechanisms.	Reports on social assistance programs'	Improve the targeting of the social assistance programs.

are regressive or inadequately targeted.	lation in the most significant programs. Evaluate the impact of the social assistance system's most significant programs.	Adopt a unified targeting mechanism for the most significant programs, in a coordinated manner.	objectives and beneficiary population. Reports with impact evaluations. Report on targeting mechanisms. Executive order, law, or regulations that adopt unified targeting criteria.	
There is little coverage for certain key risks.	Analyze gaps in the social assistance system in terms of vulnerable groups and risks that are not being correctly addressed.	Coordinate existing programs to minimize overlapping and to ensure that benefits are granted to the groups that need them.	Plan that addresses the coordination of the most significant programs. Plan aimed at reorienting programs in order to cover risks that are not currently addressed.	Improve the scope and effectiveness of the social assistance system.

3. Faults in the Bono Solidario Cash Subsidy Program

The targeting of the subsidy is inadequate. Self-targeting was used when the program was launched, and new beneficiaries have not been incorporated.	Examine the possibility of enrolling new beneficiaries while continuing to screen the beneficiary database.	Reorient the *Bono Solidario* Cash Subsidy Program toward the objective of combating malnutrition, transforming the benefit into a conditioned subsidy.	Changes in the operating regulations of the *Bono Solidario* Cash Subsidy Program.	Improve the effectiveness of the *Bono Solidario* Cash Subsidy Program.
The level of benefits is not based on clear criteria, and is very low.	Establish clear eligibility criteria for the benefit. If the *Bono Solidario* becomes	Update the benefits based on the criteria established.	Changes in the operating manual of the *Bono Solidario* Cash Subsidy Program.	Improve the beneficiaries' level of income as a function of the program's objective.

(Matrix continues on the following page.)

Policy Matrix (*continued*)

| | Policy measures | | |
Problems	Short term (to June 2003)	Medium term (2003–07)	Progress indicators	Objectives/goals
	a conditioned subsidy, the benefit should be related to the poverty line or the cost of a basic family food budget.			
There is no evaluation of impacts and the program's objective is not clear.		Conduct periodic impact evaluations.	Report that includes impact evaluations.	Allow for corrections in the *Bono Solidario* Cash Subsidy Program as a function of their impact on the beneficiaries.

Annex: Incidence of Social Assistance Programs (Selected)

Quintiles	Consumption per capita	School breakfast	Free food programs	Childcare programs	Bono Solidario Cash Subsidy Program	Gasoline subsidy	Gas subsidies
Poorest	5	38	17	16	27	0	8
Second	9	15	18	37	28	1	14
Third	13	12	46	20	25	4	20
Fourth	20	33	19	19	16	10	24
Wealthiest	53	2	0	7	4	85	33

Source: Vos and others (2002).

12

The Pension System[1]

Rafael Rofman

*The Ecuadoran pension system has three types of problem in its design, management, and institutional makeup, which need to be resolved in the short and medium terms. The **first** problem involves the program's effective coverage. The proportion of the economically active population and the elderly who are protected by the Obligatory Insurance of the Ecuadoran Social Security Institute (IESS) is one of the lowest in the region. Noncontributive programs, such as Rural People's Social Security (SSC) or the Bono Solidario Cash Subsidy, extend coverage, but with benefits that are too low to provide effective protection for old age. A **second** problem is in the financial management of the IESS. On the one hand, the state has failed to pay certain contributions to the IESS for more than a decade. Yet according to the Institute's accounting, this debt is listed as an asset. The amount of the debt differs significantly, depending on whether it is calculated by the IESS or by the Ministry of Economy and Finance. The discrepancy in question has a major impact on the actual size of the reserves. Furthermore, reserves are not clearly separated in accordance with the uses for which they are earmarked. Thus, undetected cross-subsidies may exist. Finally, the state is mandated by law to contribute 40 percent of the benefits of retired persons each year, even though the pension program of the IESS clearly has a surplus. As such, unnecessary pressure is placed on government revenues. A **third** type of problem is in the system's legal situation. With the enactment of the Reform Act in November 2001, a new organizational design was to have been implemented within the institution. However, the law's full application was blocked by a decision of*

---

1. Rafael Rofman is a senior economist and specialist in pension systems at the World Bank. The author thanks McDonald Benjamin, Christopher Chamberlin, Daniel Dulitzky, José R. López Cáliz, and Anita Schwarz for their comments, and also thanks the officials of the government of Ecuador and of the World Bank's Quito office for their kind support.

the Constitutional Court, which in turn is being challenged in the court system. As a consequence, the new law's validity is debatable. The IESS has opted to apply some aspects of the law while ignoring others, at its own discretion. Even if the law were eventually implemented, there are serious problems in its language, particularly with respect to the role of the Technical Commission on Investments in relation to private pension funds. The law also contains certain inappropriate rules for handling those funds. All this must be corrected before the law goes into effect. This chapter proposes measures for broadening the scope of coverage of the insured, in a manner that is fiscally and socially responsible, while improving the financial management of the IESS and strengthening the system's institutional stability.

A. System Diagnostic

The Institutional Organization of Ecuador's Pension System

Ecuador's system for the protection of the elderly's income comprises three contributive type programs; a fourth program that, though nominally contributive, has a major subsidy component; and a fifth, noncontributive program. The principal contributive program is Obligatory Social Security (*Seguro Social Obligatorio*— SGO), which covers workers from the formal sector of the economy. The other two are the pension systems of the Armed Forces and of the police. The Rural People's Social Security Program (*Seguro Social Campesino*—SSC), which covers peasants who work independently or are members of communes, cooperatives, or other community organizations, is nominally contributive, but the contributions made by the beneficiaries cover only a minimal part of expenses. Finally, the fifth program, which was not created as part of the pension system but in practice plays an important role in the economic safety net for old age, is the *Bono Solidario* Cash Subsidy Program.

Obligatory Social Security began in the first two decades of the 20th century, when certain government workers obtained the right to receive pensions upon retirement. This program expanded to further sectors of public servants and private employees in the following decade, and other coverage was added, including sick pay, maternity benefits, disability insurance, death benefits, workman's compensation, and severance pay. Obligatory Social Security has been administered by the IESS since the early 1970s. The IESS also administers the SSC, which was created a little more than 20 years ago with the goal of extending social security coverage to families belonging to communes or other social peasant organizations. This program has been financed through contributions from workers and employers enrolled in Obligatory Social Security, as well as contributions from the state and minimal contributions from the participants themselves. Benefits under the SSC are lower than benefits to persons covered by Obligatory Social Security.

Members of the Armed Forces and the police force enjoy a protection similar to that of Obligatory Social Security, through programs administered by independent institutions—the Social Security Institute of the Armed Forces (ISSFA) and the Social Security Institute of the Police (ISSPOL). Finally, the *Bono Solidario* Cash Subsidy Program, which grants a noncontributive monetary subsidy to low-income elderly persons, is administered through the Ministry of Social Welfare.

Structure of the Pension System Prior to the Reform

Prior to the reform of late 2001, Obligatory Social Security protected its affiliates against the risks of disability, old age, and death, as well as risks related to health, maternity, workman's compensation, and job loss. Participation in the program was obligatory for all public and private sector employees. Its financing was accomplished through personal contributions from workers and employers. In addition, the state contributed the equivalent of 40 percent of the pensions paid by the IESS. Total contributions from workers and employers were made at the rate of 20.5 percent of the wage base, out of which approximately 8.4 percent was earmarked to cover disability, old age, and death benefits. Finally, pursuant to the Labor Code, the IESS administered a reserve fund generated through a monthly contribution from employers equivalent to one-twelfth of monthly wages. The contribution was credited to an individual account of the worker, and could be recovered upon termination of the labor relationship with the employer or after three years.

Workers of both sexes could retire at age 55, provided they had 30 years of contributions credited. The two limits (age and years of contributions) were flexible. For example, a person with 40 years of contributions could retire regardless of the age limit, while persons who had less than 30 years of contributions could retire with a minimum of 10 years of contributions at age 70.

The monthly old-age retirement benefit was proportional to the average of the five best years of the worker's contributions, and was further determined based on the number of years of contributions. Thus, a person with 10 years of contributions at the time of retirement (regardless of age), would receive 50 percent of his or her former wages. That percentage would increase by 1.25 points for each additional year, up to 81.25 percent with 35 years of contributions, and up to a maximum of 100 percent with 40 years of contributions.

Although one's employment had to terminate in order to receive retirement benefits, there was no restriction against obtaining employment after retirement. This means that a worker could simultaneously receive a pension and a salary or wages. Furthermore, the corresponding additional contributions subsequent to retirement increased one's benefit by 0.8 to 3 percent per year of additional contribution, depending on one's age. Finally, a special reduced retirement allowed benefits to be received at 45 years of age with 25 years of contributions, and with a proportional reduction in the benefit amount.

Disability and death benefits had their own structure. The amounts of these benefits were not established as an automatic percentage of prior wages, they increased as a function of the age of the disabled or deceased person. In the case of disability, workers with a minimum of 60 monthly contributions had a right to a pension once they were declared disabled by the IESS. The corresponding pension was calculated using the same criterion as retirement, with a minimum of 43.75 percent of wages for beneficiaries who had made a minimum of five years of contributions. Death benefits were made to a widow or female cohabitant, and to a widower or male cohabitant if he were disabled and a dependent of the decedent, as well as to children who were under 18 years of age or disabled. Death benefits for widows, widowers, or cohabitants were 40 percent of the pension that the deceased had been receiving or would have been entitled to collect, and 20 percent of that amount for each child. The rules and regulations also provided for benefits to other family members under exceptional circumstances.

Contribution rates and benefits were both determined on the basis of "taxable wages." This only reflected a part of the workers' actual income—as, in recent decades, workers' wages have tended to be adjusted not through direct increases to their pay, but through the creation of new forms of remuneration that formed a part of the worker's total income but were not considered taxable wages. This practice was especially pronounced in the public sector, in which there were 28 items for which compensation was received, but contributions were only made on base wages. The complementary remunerations, which represented 36.5 percent of total remunerations in 1990, grew to the point at which they reached up to 92.5 percent in 1999 (IESS 2001). The trend started to reverse in 2000, and private estimates indicate that taxable income now represents 82.5 percent of total remuneration in the private sector and 25 percent of total remuneration in the public sector. The distortion that this phenomenon introduced into the system is twofold. On the one hand, it severely reduced the resources available to the IESS for financing benefits. At the same time, it affected (though to a lesser degree) the future benefits of those making contributions during those years.

The Rural People's Social Security Program, in contrast to Obligatory Social Security, required minimal contributions for benefit entitlement. Heads of households contributed 1 percent of the basic minimum wage to finance worker benefits. Workers and employers enrolled in Obligatory Social Security were required to contribute 0.35 percent of wages. In addition, 0.30 percent of that same wage base was provided as a contribution from the state, and the state also made another direct contribution. Enrollment in the SSC entitled the beneficiary to health services for his or her family unit. The head of the household was also entitled to disability or old-age benefits, equivalent to 75 percent of the basic minimum wage. The right to an old age pension was acquired at age 65, provided that the beneficiary had made at least 10 years of contributions. This requirement was gradually phased out starting at 71 years of age, and at age 75 or above, only five years of contributions were required.

Finally, the *Bono Solidario* Cash Subsidy Program offered a benefit in the form of assistance granted through the Ministry of Social Welfare. The subsidy was created in 1998 to replace subsidies on consumption energy, which were eliminated that same year (although the energy subsidies were reestablished shortly afterwards). This program targeted mothers of minor children, the disabled, and low-income persons over 65 years of age. In the case of the elderly, eligibility to obtain the benefit was determined through meeting the requirements of reaching the established minimum age and having a family income of less than $US20 per month and no job. This program is closed—to be precise, at the time it was created a mass enrollment took place, but since then no new beneficiaries have been admitted.

Financial Situation

The financial situation of the pension system in Ecuador is difficult to evaluate, owing to various factors. For one, the IESS has not maintained a separate administration or accounting of the various types of insurance. One therefore has to make a series of estimates to obtain an approximation of trends in insurance for old age, disability, and death over the past decade. Furthermore, the flow of revenues has varied considerably, as the result of the fluctuations in taxable wages described in the previous section, the state's failure to perform its obligations as an employer and as a direct contributor, and the acute fluctuations in variables provoked by inflation and dollarization in 2000.

The IESS, in recent years, has had a surplus. The surplus was smallest in 1999, when it amounted to only 0.2 percent of the GDP, and largest in 2001, when it amounted to 1.7 percent. The surplus for 2002 is projected at 2 percent (Figure 1). These results reflect the combined effect of the various insurances, foremost among which are health insurance and old age insurance. The recent growth in revenues is because the state has now commenced to pay its obligations.

An analysis of trends in insurance for old age, disability, and death is more complex because, as mentioned above, the IESS did not keep a separate accounting of the various funds. Nonetheless, estimated values indicate a surplus since 1993, with balances ranging from 0.16 percent of GDP in 1999 to 0.74 percent in 2001. It is interesting to note that the trend in 2002 indicates a leveling of revenues (in terms of GDP), while expenditures continue to grow. Thus, the surplus is expected to decline by 0.25 percent of GDP (Figure 2).

Figure 2 shows the estimated results for the Obligatory Social Security pension system, without considering transfers from the government. If the total results of policies aimed at generating income for the elderly were included, the estimated surplus would be smaller, as disbursements are also made from the military and police retirement systems (with expenditures of $US60 million and a deficit of 50 percent of that amount), pensions granted through Rural Social Security (less than $US1 million annually), and the *Bono Solidario* Cash Subsidy Program for the elderly ($US20 million). Thus, the total disbursements of programs that transfer revenues to the elderly in 2002 would be in the neighborhood of 1.1 percent of GDP and the aggregate financial surplus would only be 0.15 percent of GDP. Also, it should be noted that at the end of 2002, the state reportedly transferred some $US80 million in additional funds, or 0.4 percent of GDP, to the system.

**Figure 1. Financial Trends in the IESS
(as a percentage of GDP, 1993–2002)**

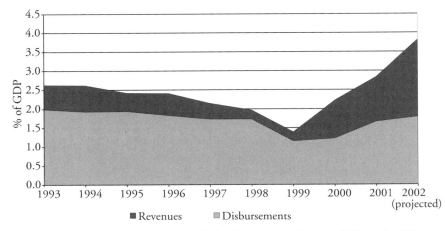

Source: Generated by the author, based on IESS data for 2001 to 2002 and on IMF data for 2002.

**Figure 2. Financial Trends: Insurance for Disability, Old Age, and Death
(as a percentage of GDP, 1993–2002)**

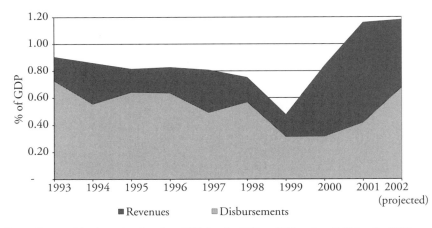

Source: Generated by the author, based on IESS data for 2001 to 2002 and on IMF data for 2002.

The improvement in capturing revenues as of 2000 is due to two reasons. First, since March 2000, a wage standardization process has begun, which tends to simplify the structure of remunerations and to classify the majority of wages as taxable income for purposes of social security contributions. Second, since 2001 the government has started paying the contributions it owes as an employer and as a third party, thus collected revenues have rapidly increased.

The positive results obtained by the IESS have led to an accumulation of reserves. In late 2001 the General Insurance reserve (which includes disability, old age, death, and health), according to the Institute's own accounting, was $US1.092 billion, and the reserve grew during the first nine months of 2002 by approximately $US300 million. It is also important to point out that the IESS, in its accounting statements as of December 2001, has included a debt owed by the national government in the amount of $US2.085 billion among the assets supporting these reserves. The government has not acknowledged that amount, and estimates the debt at approximately $US400 million. As a result, the actual size of the reserves is unknown.

The Level of the Benefits

One of the reasons why the IESS has been able to maintain a certain degree of financial stability despite the problems discussed in the previous section is that benefit amounts were severely affected by macroeconomic dynamics. The average benefit, which in the mid 1990s was approximately $US100 per month (after accounting for special payments), fell rapidly between 1998 and 2000, to less than $US30. As of 2001 the IESS has been restoring benefit levels. Thus in the third quarter of 2002, the average was approximately 70 dollars per month (Figure 3).

Although the average benefit payment has increased in the past year, it is still significantly less than as promised under the law. In fact, in accordance with the legislation, workers who retire because of old age should receive benefits equivalent to approximately 75 percent of the average of their best five years of wages. Nonetheless, the average salary of an IESS affiliate in mid-2002 was $US171, and the average retirement was approximately 30 percent of that amount. There are several reasons for this great disparity, including the absence of automatic mechanisms to adjust benefit payments, as well as the methodology of calculating the initial benefit, which fails to consider the current value of the wages when calculating the average of the best five years.

Retirees eligible for the SSC, in accordance with the law, receive a benefit payment equivalent to 75 percent of the basic minimum wage, but the amount has not been adjusted since the dollarization. The average pensions under this program in the mid 1990s were slightly greater than $US20 monthly, but then the amounts fell, in a similar manner to what occurred with benefits under Obligatory Social Security, reaching levels of less than $US3 monthly in 2000. The amount has yet to be corrected.

Figure 3. Average Benefit per Month per Person, in Dollars, Insurance for Disability, Old Age, and Death: Rural People's Social Security Program; and the *Bono Solidario* Cash Subsidy 1995–2002

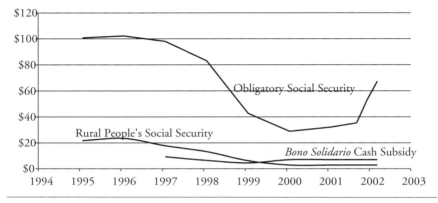

Source: Generated by the author, based on IESS data for 2001 and 2002, data from the Social Protection Program (*Programa de Protección Social*—PPS) for 2002, and IMF data for 2002.

Finally, beneficiaries of the *Bono Solidario* Cash Subsidy Program have been receiving $US7 per month since December 2000. This represents an increase as compared to the $US3 benefit paid at the time of the dollarization, and is approximately equal to the amount originally granted in 1998.

Coverage

The core objective of a pension system is to provide income for persons who, by reasons of age (or disability or death), are unable to generate the income they need for their subsistence and the subsistence of their family group. Therefore, a system's coverage is a central issue. A pension system that fails to protect a significant proportion of the population has failed to meet its principal objective.

The coverage of Ecuador's pension system is one of the lowest in South America. The coverage indicators customarily utilized (such as the proportion of the economically active population that pays into the contributive system, or the proportion of persons of age 60 or above with benefits) indicate values that are much lower than those of other countries in the region. Indeed, only Bolivia has a lower percentage of contributors (Figure 4).

The problem of low coverage in Ecuador has worsened in recent years, given that macroeconomic difficulties affected the degree to which workers had formal employment. This provoked a stagnation in the number of contributors to Obligatory Social Security in the mid-1990s, at a time when the economically active pop-

Figure 4. Percentage of the Labor Force Participating in Contributive Pension Programs in South America in and about the Year 2000

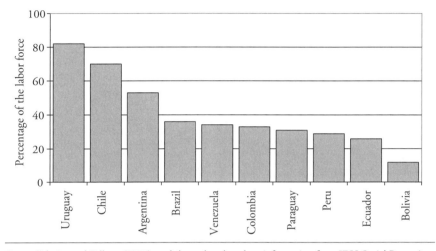

Source: Palacios and Pallares (2000), and the author, based on information from IESS Social Protection Program (PPS).

ulation was growing steadily. As a consequence, the proportion of the economically active population covered by Obligatory Social Security declined between 1995 and 2002 from 34 percent to 26 percent. This fall reflects the incapacity of the formal labor market to expand at the same rate of growth as the population (Figure 5).

Trends in the Rural People's Social Security Program during this same period were similar. The SSC grew rapidly during the first decade of its existence. In 1995, however, the number of heads of households registered in the program started to stabilize, and the program's impact diminished in terms of the benefited percentage of the economically active population.

The low coverage of Obligatory Social Security among active workers is also reflected among elder workers. Indeed, the coverage of this program among persons over 55 years of age (the minimum required age for retirement) is 13 percent. Coverage for the *Bono Solidario* Cash Subsidy Program, by contrast, is 30 percent. Other programs have little effect, either because they are relatively new (in the case of the SSC) or because they are small and/or cover a younger population, given the characteristics of the programs themselves (for example, the retirement systems of the police force and the Armed Forces). An analysis of coverage by age group shows that even though the minimum retirement age is 55, relatively few persons actually retire at that age. Coverage, as would be expected, grows with age, reaching 70 percent for the 70–74 age group. The coverage indicated for the 80-and-above age group is strikingly high—but that value may have been affected by errors in the data (Figure 6).

Figure 5. Participation of Active Workers in Ecuador's Pension Systems
(as a percentage of the economically active population in each program and
in the system as a whole, 1965–2002)

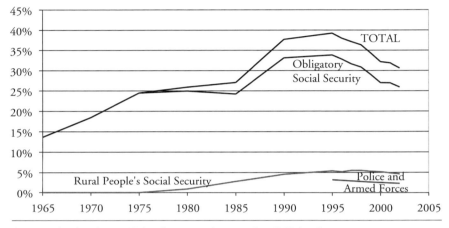

Source: Author, based on IESS data for 2002 and 2002 and on IMF data for 2002.

Figure 6. Coverage of Pension Systems with Respect to the Population Age 55
and Older
(by age group and in total, 2002)

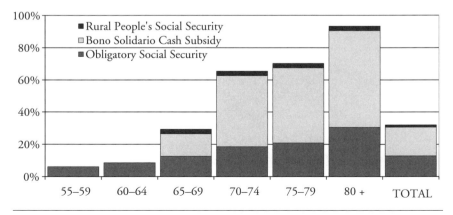

Source: Generated by the author, based on data from the IESS, PPS, and the Latin American
Demography Center (*Centro Latinoamericano de Demografía*—CELADE).

The Reform

After a prolonged debate, the National Congress passed a new Social Security Act in November 2001. Application of this law is being legally challenged, as we shall discuss below. The new Social Security Act fully supersedes the old law, created 60 years earlier, and modifies the system's basic structure, through changes in parameters, in the system's structure, and in the system's institutional organization. Some of the principal reforms introduced are summarized below.

Reforms to Parameters

The new law changes several parameters of the Obligatory Social Security system, in order to adapt them to the current situation. These changes include the following:

- The minimum retirement age is raised to 60, and (as of 2006) the possibility of retiring with 40 years of contributions regardless of age is eliminated. In addition, in an innovation that is unprecedented in the world, the law provides that in the future, the minimum age shall be corrected as a function of life expectancy at the time of retirement.
- Formal coverage is expanded to encompass all workers, including the self-employed and employers.
- The method of calculating pensions in cases of disability or death is changed. They are now set as a percentage of the base calculation, and are no longer proportional to the number of years of previous contributions.
- The rate of contributions to the pension system has been indirectly increased, since contributions to the reserve fund (8.33 percent of the wages) shall now be capitalized in individual accounts and may only be recovered upon retirement, disability, or death (although affiliates may use this fund to secure debt and may withdraw it in its totality upon retirement).

Structural Reforms

- A multitier approach is taken, with a structure similar to that of the reform carried out in Uruguay. As such, all workers must participate in a first "Obligatory Solidarity Regimen," for which they must make contributions based on their income up to the sum of $US165 per month. At the same time, the totality of employer contributions and personal contributions corresponding to wages in excess of $US500 are earmarked to finance this regimen.
- The second tier, or "Obligatory Savings Regimen," consists of capitalizing personal contributions on wages between $US165 and $US500, in individual accounts. These contributions shall be administered by Pension Savings Deposit Institutions *(Entidades Depositarias del Ahorro Previsional*—EDAP), for which purpose a bidding competition shall be conducted by the IESS Technical Commission on Investments *(Comisión Técnica de Inversiones*—CTI).

- A new noncontributive assistance benefit is created for individuals over the age of 70 who have no other funds, and it is financed by the General Budget of the state. The features of this benefit are similar to those of the *Bono Solidario* Cash Subsidy Program, but the two programs are kept separate.

Institutional Reforms

- The new law requires a separate reserve for each fund administered by the IESS, and prohibits the use of funds from one program to finance another.
- A dual control system is created for companies administering pension funds. The Technical Commission is assigned the ultimate responsibility for managing the funds. At the same time, supervisory authority is delegated to the Superintendency of Banks. The new law also grants the CTI an imprecise degree of autonomy, as it sets forth that the Commission's members shall be designated by the state, the insured, and the employers, in a tripartite fashion.

Predicting the fiscal effects of the reform is a complex task, as this depends, in good measure, on variables that could be (and have been) discretionally altered. Informal estimates based on data available as of December 2000 indicate that only 9.5 percent of the contributors to the IESS (that is, slightly more than 2 percent of the workforce) will be making contributions to the pension funds. This estimate needs to be corrected to account for the effect of wage standardization in the private sector, but even so, it clearly seems that at least in the first few years, the magnitude of the private system, and therefore the fiscal cost of the reform, will be minor.

The validity of the new law was challenged in the Constitutional Court. The court ruled that several of the law's articles were unconstitutional, among them Article 176, which sets income ranges for participation in the various tiers of the new system. As a consequence, the court prohibited application of the individual accounts mechanism provided for in the law. Nonetheless, a further court action blocked the official publication of the Constitutional Court's decision. Thus, the decision currently has no formal effect. This dispute remains unresolved to date, which increases confusion as to what constitutes applicable law. The national government has not issued the necessary regulations for the law's application, although the IESS and the Superintendency of Banks have started to set their own rules and selectively apply certain aspects of the law.

B. Proposed Solutions

The current state of the pension system raises several issues that require attention. A general problem is the institutional weakness of the sector, which is attributable, in part, to the fact that there is no high-ranking entity within the national government that is politically responsible for designing strategies, coordinating their implementation, and evaluating their execution. Such an entity must have the budgetary and technical resources it needs and should maintain an active policy of coordinating the various programs aimed at economically protecting the elderly. Furthermore, there are various specific issues on which action should be taken. These include but are not limited to the following.

Problems of Coverage, in Terms of Broadness and Depth

If we include the *Bono Solidario* Cash Subsidy Program for the elderly in our analysis of the system to protect the elderly, it is clear that the current system still provides a low level of coverage among the age groups that actively participate in the economy. Nonetheless, the coverage increases considerably among the elderly, especially among those over the age of 70, for whom coverage surpasses 60 percent and approaches levels that could be considered satisfactory.

There are various problems of magnitude, however, that ought to be considered. On the one hand, the limited coverage of Obligatory Social Security makes coverage among persons under 70 very low. Furthermore, the *Bono Solidario* Cash Subsidy Program for the elderly, created in 1998, has not permitted new enrollments since that time. As a result, the number of beneficiaries of that program has slowly but surely diminished since its creation. Even more important is the problem of "depth" of coverage. The fact that people are formally enrolled as beneficiaries is positive, but if the benefits received are minimal, the practical effect is also minimal. The current monthly benefit payment of the *Bono Solidario* Cash Subsidy Program for the elderly is $US7, while, under the Rural People's Social Security Program, the retirement benefit is only $US3 per month. The benefits of Obligatory Social Security are greater, and have been increasing considerably since 2001, but even so, the average benefit of the old-age pension, as of June 2002, was only around $US70 per month, with 30 percent of the beneficiaries receiving $US20 or less.

The poverty line for the country's population is estimated at $US47 per person. This means that close to 57 percent of the beneficiaries are receiving pensions at less than 15 percent of the poverty line (recipients of the *Bono Solidario* Cash Subsidy Program and of pensions through the SSC), while another 13 percent are receiving pensions at less than 50 percent of the poverty line.

The Ecuadoran government should make efforts to extend nominal and effective coverage to the majority of the population. Five actions in particular could be recommended:

DEVELOPING A RIGOROUS METHODOLOGY FOR ANALYZING PENSION POLICIES. This first action is relevant in terms of applying the other recommended actions. It consists of preparing a methodological framework and delineating a critical path along which to implement measures aimed at broadening the coverage proposed below. For that purpose, the fiscal cost (as well as the savings) generated by the reform and by the proposed measures in the short term need to be evaluated, to plan for their gradual implementation.[2]

BROADENING THE SCOPE OF COVERAGE OF OBLIGATORY SOCIAL SECURITY. The new Social Security Act calls for mandatory participation of all workers in Obligatory Social Security, including the self-employed and employers. In order for this provision to be effective, regulations need to be drawn up that establish enrollment procedures, the method for paying contributions, and so on. This action must be taken in the short term, in order to enroll new beneficiaries as soon as possible. Furthermore, in order to ensure effectiveness, contribution payment mechanisms and procedures for control of evasion among new affiliates need to be designed and implemented. This measure has no fiscal cost whatsoever in the short term. Rather, it will immediately increase revenue collections.

BROADENING THE SCOPE OF COVERAGE OF THE SSC. The Rural People's Social Security Program currently covers close to 25 percent of its target population, estimated at one million families. The IESS should develop a mechanism to broaden coverage, bringing in new families, individuals, and communities. To do so, an expansion plan must be designed, defining a geographical targeting mechanism that identifies the zones with the greatest need so as to commence the expansion effort in a targeted manner. Although this action does entail a fiscal cost, it would be limited, considering the low cost of the system at present. A 20 percent increase in the current coverage per year would result in an additional cost of approximately $US2 million per year.

REGULATION AND GRANTING OF NONCONTRIBUTIVE AID. The new law also provides for the granting of noncontributive benefits to persons over the age of 70 who lack adequate resources of their own. These pensions should gradually replace the *Bono Solidario* Cash Subsidy, by bringing the informal sector into the social protection system. For this purpose, the government needs to issue the respective regulations and start granting the benefits. Given the potential fiscal cost of this program, the government should consider a phased-in implementation of the program, targeting access based on minimum age criteria until the totality of the target population is included.

CORRECTION OF BENEFIT PAYMENTS FOR RETIREES UNDER THE SSC AND FOR BENEFICIARIES OF THE *BONO SOLIDARIO* CASH SUBSIDY PROGRAM. As mentioned above, the benefit payments received by these two groups are very low. It is positive that a min-

---

2. The World Bank has offered to provide support using a methodological simulation tool called Pension Reform Options Simulation Toolkit (PROST). This software evaluates the effects of various policies, based on the system's relevant variables. With this objective, the new administration of government may be requested to provide a training course regarding its use of technical administration personnel.

imum coverage is being offered to them, and indeed, in order to preserve a reasonable incentive, benefits under these programs ought to be lower than Obligatory Social Security benefits. Nonetheless, the current amount seems to be insufficient. The problem is particularly serious for the SSC, which provides a retirement benefit of only $US3 per month. The amount of the benefit under both programs should be established using a rigorous criterion, such as a percentage of the poverty line, considering the capacity of the state to finance the assistance. In this sense, it is worth noting that raising the benefits of the SSC up to the level of the *Bono Solidario* Cash Subsidy Program would entail an increase in spending of $US850,000 per year, and as a result, the cost of increasing benefits under the SSC and the *Bono Solidario* Cash Subsidy Program by one dollar per beneficiary would be $US3 million per year.

Table 1 provides an estimate of implicit costs considering different scenarios of modifying benefit payments and coverage under the SSC and the *Bono Solidario* Cash Subsidy Program. It should be mentioned that the figures indicated refer exclusively to retirement benefits under the SSC and to subsidies for the elderly in the case of the *Bono Solidario*, as other benefits under those programs are addressed in chapters 10 and 11 on Health and Social Assistance, respectively. In this context, it is worth noting that the $US85 million earmarked by the state as an additional contribution for the IESS during 2002 would be sufficient, for example, to raise benefits in this entire category to 50 percent of the poverty line, and at the same time, broaden the scope of coverage by 20 percent.

Table 1. Cost of Increasing Coverage or Benefits under Rural Social Security and under the *Bono Solidario* Cash Subsidy Program for the Elderly (absolute values and as percentage of GDP)

| | | Number of beneficiaries | | |
		Current	20% increase	50% increase
Amount of benefit	*Current*	$US20,023,200 0.10%	$US24,027,840 0.11%	$US30,034,800 0.14%
	Raising the SSC to the level of the *Bono Solidario* for the elderly ($US7/month)	$US20,848,800 0.10%	$US5,018,560 0.12%	$US31,273,200 0.15%
	Raising all benefits to the level of the *Bono Solidario* for mothers ($US11.50/month)	$US34,251,600 0.16%	$US41,101,920 0.20%	$US51,377,400 0.24%
	Raising all benefits to 50% of the poverty line ($US23.50/month)	$US69,992,400 0.33%	$US83,990,880 0.40%	$US14,988,600 0.50%

Source: Generated by the author, based on IESS, PPS, and IMF data, all for 2002.

The Financial Management of the IESS

The IESS administers reserves for the various insurance programs it offers its affiliates. The management of these reserves is critical for the smooth functioning of the system, as they guarantee the payment of future benefits. Certain problems exist with respect to these reserves that should be carefully considered, as they could have adverse effects. They include the following:

THE DEBT OWED BY THE STATE TO THE IESS. Between 1984 and 2000, the state stopped paying its two obligations with respect to Obligatory Social Security: the contributions corresponding to its role as an employer and the contribution for 40 percent of the pensions, as required by law. The amount accrued is significant. The IESS estimates it at $US2.085 billion (as of December 2001), while the Ministry of Economy and Finance estimates it at less than $US400 million. The discrepancy results from applying different criteria to adjust the amount to current money values. The IESS has included the $US2.085 billion as part of its assets in its accounting—therefore at least a portion of its reserves is based on assets whose collectability is doubtful. The IESS should correct its accounting to bring its estimate of the debt in line with that of the Ministry of Economy and Finance. For its part, the Ministry should document the debt through the issuance and delivery of a specific certificate of debt to the IESS, with interest and dates certain of payment.

ADMINISTRATIVE SEPARATION OF THE INSURANCE PROGRAMS. The Obligatory Social Security reserves, which include the health and pension programs, are not differentiated, nor are the Institute's administrative expenses. This situation diminishes the transparency of the programs' financial management, since one cannot establish each program's situation with precision. The IESS should immediately differentiate the various programs, both in accounting and in administrative terms, identifying each program's revenue sources, disbursements for benefits, administrative expenses, assets, and equity.

THE CONTRIBUTION FROM THE STATE. Laws regarding the social security system indicate that the state has an obligation to contribute 40 percent of the Institute's pension-payment expenditures, so as to stabilize the Institute's actuarial balance. This percentage is required under the previous legislation as well as the legislation passed in 2001, since it was believed that the IESS lacked sufficient funds to meet its obligations in the long term. Nonetheless, it is important to note that this contribution is not needed at present, given the IESS's current financial situation. In practice, during the first nine months of 2002, revenue collections from contributions to the pension program surpassed benefit payments and administrative expenditures by approximately $US110 million. The state made additional contributions as well, for a total of $US65 million so far in 2002, which are expected to total $US85 million by the close of the year. Thus, IESS reserves have increased significantly. The state's obligation to contribute 40 percent of benefit disbursements should be reviewed, as that practice has several negative implications. For one, this contribution is a major fiscal burden, in a context in which the state is facing financial difficulties. Furthermore, the transfer is clearly regressive in nature, as it consists of a subsidy from the general revenues to the affiliates of the IESS, who comprise 25 percent of the labor force and whose features clearly identify them as middle-income level, since they are public servants or employees in the formal urban sector. If the flow of revenues and disbursements of the IESS shows a deficit in the future, the proper policy should be to correct the system's parameters in order to reverse that trend, or, if it is considered justified within the priorities of the state's social policy, the IESS could be subsidized by the rest of society. It is not clear that such a discussion has taken place (and indeed, it appears more reasonable to allocate this subsidy to more vulnerable sectors of society). Yet even if a social consensus and political agreement existed, the mechanism of "presubsidizing" the pension system would be considered inefficient. If the state wishes to grant a subsidy to workers in the formal sector of the economy through a pension system, that subsidy should be transferred when needed, and not accumulated in the reserves of the IESS. Of course, eliminating this transfer requires amendments to the law and would generate a major political debate, but the policy must be immediately reviewed, given the pressure it exerts on the fiscal balance.

Partial Implementation of the Reform of the Social Security System

The law enacted in November 2001 included certain significant improvements in the system, in particular regarding changes in eligibility requirements for retirement, the administration of the funds accrued, and the management of the IESS. At the same time, some aspects of the law are confusing or inapplicable (especially those involving the operating rules of the Pension Savings Deposit Institutions—EDAP), and should be reviewed to ensure the smooth operation of the system.

THE COURT CONFLICT. The new law was challenged before the Constitutional Court, yet institutional problems have prevented the court from issuing a clear, applicable ruling. This situation has created a particularly distressing legal void, considering that a pension system's efficiency is affected by its mid- and long-term stability. The resulting institutional confusion must be overcome, as various entities have adopted their own interpretations of the legal situation. For example, the Superintendency of Banks has started issuing resolutions regarding the management of the IESS reserves (which the IESS does not apply). It has even issued resolutions as to whether the IESS executive officers are fit for their jobs, along with resolutions regarding the creation of the EDAP. For its part, the IESS has modified criteria regarding the application of the reserve funds, as it no longer returns them to workers after three years. Yet it has not applied other changes embodied in the law, some of which were not even ruled against by the Constitutional Court, such as the requirement to separate reserves by type of insurance or extend the formal coverage of Obligatory Social Security.

LACK OF A WELL-DEFINED ROLE FOR THE TECHNICAL COMMISSION ON INVESTMENTS. The new law grants a central role to the Technical Commission, giving it political autonomy and the ability to significantly influence the investment strategies of the EDAP. Furthermore, certain of its functions would seem to contradict those of the Superintendency of Banks.

PROBLEMS IN REGULATING THE EDAP. The new law makes several references to operating rules for the pension savings institutions. These rules should be reviewed, as the current language is confusing or inapplicable. One example is the requirement to guarantee minimum profitability, while leaving the definition of this concept in the hands of each institution. Thus, unless the possibilities are restricted through regulations, the lack of standardization could make comparisons impossible, and the guarantees, in practice, might not offer any protection whatsoever. Similarly, the requirement that the EDAP maintain an equity stake in the amount of 10 percent of the administered fund is impractical and unnecessary. Minimum equity requirements in other countries are much lower, and generally correlated in some way to the minimum profitability guaranty. In contrast, such equity requirements are pointless if their objective is simply to make participation more costly and create obstacles for the entry of new participants in the market.

Policy Matrix

Problems	Policy measures		Progress indicators	Objectives/goals
	Short term (to June 2003)	Medium term (2003–07)		
1. The institutional structure of the Social Security System				
There is no hierarchical entity within the national government that is responsible for designing policies and evaluating the pension system.	Creation of a hierarchical entity responsible for planning, designing, coordinating, and evaluating the income protection system for the elderly.	Full functionality of the entity, with responsibility for drafting regulations and for the systematic dissemination of evaluations.	Issuance of the formal regulations created by this entity, which define its organizational structure and budget. Drafting of proposed legislation and regular publication of reports.	To improve the institutional and technical capacity of the state in proposing and developing pensions policies.
2. The effective coverage of the system				
No rigorous methodology exists for evaluating the fiscal effect of the measures to be implemented under the Social Security System reforms, in particular in the short term.	Evaluation of the costs and savings entailed by the reform. This evaluation would include the defining of a critical path for the implementation of coverage-expansion efforts.	Follow-up on the implementation process, with periodic cost evaluations.	Preparation of a short-term progress report. Issuance of a periodic report indicating the fiscal results of the various measures and possible future trends.	To develop the capacity for designing policies that seek to improve the level and depth of the coverage, without placing excessive pressure on government revenues in the short term.
Obligatory Social Security has low coverage within the economically active population.	Regulations for the new Social Security Act that make participation obligatory for new types of workers.	Implementation of captation and control compliance mechanisms among the new workers who have compulsory coverage.	Increase in the rate of coverage among the economically active population.	To increase the participation of groups who are in an economic condition to do so.

(Matrix continues on the following page.)

Policy Matrix (*continued*)

Problems	Policy measures		Progress indicators	Objectives/goals
	Short term (to June 2003)	Medium term (2003–07)		
Rural People's Social Security covers 25 percent of the potential economically active population.	Definition of a program to expand the Rural People's Social Security Program, with explicit quantitative goals.	Expansion of coverage.	Increase in the percentage of coverage among the peasants.	To improve the protection of the sectors that do not participate in the formal labor market.
Access to the non-contributive pensions or the *Bono Solidario* Cash Subsidy Program for the elderly is blocked.	Regulation and implementation of the noncontributive benefits provided for in the new Social Security Act.	Enrolling elderly workers from the informal sector as beneficiaries.	Increase in the rate of coverage of elderly workers from the informal sector.	To offer effective protection to those who have been unable to participate in the formal labor market.
The amounts that retirees receive from Rural People's Social Security and the *Bono Solidario* are very low.	Immediate corrective adjustment of retirement benefits under the SSC and the *Bono Solidario* Cash Subsidy Program.	Gradual increase in these benefits until they reach the level of the noncontributive assistance.	Increase in the buying power of the beneficiaries.	To offer effective protection, with income that brings improvements to the quality of life.
3. Financial Management of the IESS				
IESS accounting, as of December 2001, has included a debt	Development of suitable accounting criteria, so that the	Application of the new accounting criteria and issuance of the debt	Publication of the corrected accounting statements of the IESS.	To increase transparency in the management of the IESS funds.

owed by the state in the amount of $US2.085 billion, while the Ministry of Economy and Finance estimates said debt at less than $US400 million.	estimates of the debt calculated by the IESS and by the Ministry of Economy and Finance will be consistent with one another; designing of a debt instrument for the payment thereof.	instrument to the IESS.		
The Health Insurance reserve is not differentiated from the pension reserve.	Immediate separation of the reserves, both in terms of their accounting and their effective assets.		Continual publication of the equity statement for each insurance, itemizing assets.	To increase transparency in the management of the IESS funds.
The state has an obligation to contribute 40 percent of the pension disbursements, which amounted to approximately $US85 million in 2002, when the system had a surplus even without that contribution.	Drafting and passage of a proposed legislative reform to eliminate the 40 percent contribution.	Application of the new law.	Enactment and application of the legal reform.	To free funds that are being unnecessarily allocated to the IESS, so that they may be used for other purposes.
4. Institutional instability of the system				
Application of the new Social Security Act is partial owing to a court conflict.	Drafting and passage of a legislative bill that allows for resolution of the court conflict, while	Application of the new law.	Enactment and application of the legal reform, without court restrictions.	Generate a climate of legal security, which is needed for the system to run smoothly.

(Matrix continues on the following page.)

Policy Matrix (*continued*)

Problems	Policy measures		Progress indicators	Objectives/goals
	Short term (to June 2003)	Medium term (2003–07)		
The new law has several ambiguities and contradictions in its language with respect to the role of the Technical Commission on Investments and the autonomy of that Commission. Several articles regarding the Pension Savings Deposit Institutions are vague or inapplicable, such as the absence of a definition regarding the minimum profitability guaranty or the requirement to maintain an equity in the amount of 10 percent of the administered funds.	also correcting several technical problems in the law.			Allow the Pension Savings Deposit Institutions to design their own investment policy; place restrictions on discretionality in the management of IESS assets. Reducing the equity requirement will make the Pension Savings Deposit Institutions viable. Likewise, if the minimum profitability requirements in the law are specified, that would increase transparency and legal security.

13

Rural Development[1]

María Donoso-Clark

Three fundamental factors highlight the importance of rural development for Ecuador: the high dependence of the economy on natural resources, particularly from agriculture, hydrocarbons, forestry and mining; the concentration of poverty in predominantly rural areas; and the great natural, social, and cultural wealth and diversity in rural Ecuador. Despite this importance, rural development in this country has suffered from poor coordination and excessive centralization, resulting in inefficient public and private investment. Many rural policies have concentrated on the agricultural sector, with little attention to other activities. A set of policies must be established to guarantee natural resource sustainability, reduce rural poverty, and take into account the cultural and natural wealth of the rural sector. The emphasis on agricultural production as the engine for rural development has been changing in favor of also recognizing the importance of occupational diversification, of the links between rural regions and cities, of access to markets as an engine for growth, and of developing local capabilities. However, the agricultural sector will continue to play a key role in rural development, requiring major adjustments in order to meet challenges involving a demand for greater productivity, the consolidation of lands, a reduction in the labor force due to migration, and the transition toward products of greater value. Furthermore, centralized administration must be replaced by processes guided by demand and local-level decisionmaking, so that the beneficiaries of antipoverty strategies can themselves discover and implement these strategies in their own surroundings. In this context—with an eye on decentralized economic growth and relief

---

1. María Donoso-Clark is regional sector leader for Environment and Sustainable Social Development at the World Bank. Jorge Caballero (FAO), Matthew A. Mcmahon, Francisco Pichon, Jorge Uquillas, and Pierre Werbrouck, World Bank specialists in rural development, helped the author in the preparation of this chapter.

of rural poverty— it will be necessary to prepare a strategy for multisectoral, diversified, and spatially-focused rural development. This strategy should have three main objectives: economic and social cohesion through the development of local space; changes in agriculture and rural economic diversification; and environmental protection. Ecuador's geographic, economic, and sociocultural diversity require that this strategy be based on policies that support a participative approach to development based on jurisdiction or rural spaces; the diversification of the rural economy; agricultural adjustments aimed at increasing competitiveness in the agricultural sector through new technology and research; and the promotion of environmental conservation through better land zoning and use of natural resources. This strategy will also require an institutional structure that facilitates complementarity among the roles of the different actors. International rules guiding this effort must promote the convergence of key objectives of the national public sector, the private sector, civil society, municipalities, provincial governments and parochial boards; stimulate coherence among the regulations and activities of the various institutions that are involved; and define a program based on the strategic plans of each jurisdiction and establish financial allocations, based on the concept of "additionality" to encourage the implementation of strategic plans. This chapter is limited to a proposal for a conceptual framework and some policy points for the preparation of a rural development strategy that recognizes the great potential of Ecuador's geographic, social, and cultural diversity.²

A. Introduction

Three fundamental factors highlight the importance of rural development for Ecuador: the high dependence of the economy on natural resources, particularly from agriculture, hydrocarbons, forestry, and mining; the concentration of poverty in predominantly rural areas; and the great natural, social, and cultural wealth and diversity of rural Ecuador.

Four sectors—agriculture, mining, forestry, and hydrocarbons—contribute about 40 percent of the country's GDP.³ However, these resources are not exploited with enough care for the environment, and the resulting profits are not fairly distributed. The result is an accelerating degradation of land, rivers, and coasts, and great economic inequality between rural and urban areas.

Rural poverty in Ecuador was estimated at 56 percent of the population in 1995 and 77 percent in 1998, versus 34 percent and 46 percent, respectively, in the coun-

---

2. The World Bank, in collaboration with the government of Ecuador and other national organisms, is preparing a rural development study in which the proposals presented here will be dealt with in greater detail.

3. These sectors cover agriculture, livestock breeding, silviculture, fishing, mining, hydrocarbons, food products, and leather and wood goods.

try as a whole, with the rural population representing 40 percent of the country's population. Extreme poverty at the end of the 1990s was four times as high in rural areas as in the cities and according to data from the Survey on Employment, Unemployment, and Underemployment (INEC), rural dwellers and indigenous people are more exposed to social exclusion than people living in the cities. Rural poverty in Ecuador is diverse and varies by region, but is generally linked to five factors: (i) lack of work in activities off the land or in the formal sector, (ii) a low school attendance rate, (iii) little available land, (iv) limited access to markets, and (v) the fact that many heads of households speak only an indigenous language. All of these are the results of social exclusion related to centralist, narrow policies that prevent integrated development at the community level, efficient markets, and the development of local potential.

At the same time, rural areas where poverty is concentrated are very often also areas with community and cultural practices that offer potential for development and economic diversification. Ecuador has great ethnic and natural diversity with equally diverse cultural and social practices that have very often served as starting points for decentralized economic development, for example in the province of Imbabura, where crafts made by the Otavaleño indigenous people; the natural landscape, with the lakes of San Pablo and Cuicocha; flower plantations; and local customs have all served to support the development of a diversified and complementary economy. This diversity stems from the country's geographic diversity, and therefore requires diverse development strategies.

The rural sector in Ecuador has undergone several transformations since the decline of the feudal and semifeudal haciendas in the mountains and the plantations on the coast before the 1970s. First came the subdivision and fragmentation resulting from the reform of the agrarian and inheritance systems (Jokisch 2002), and more recently, the move toward more intensive agriculture—the result of rural policies contained in the Law on Agricultural Development of 1994. The policies contained in this 1994 law are aimed at favoring intensive modern agriculture and have had a positive impact on export-oriented coastal agriculture and on some subsectors in the highlands, such as fruit growing, horticulture, and floriculture. Export-oriented agriculture reveals acceptable levels of productivity in some categories, compared to industrial and service sectors, according to a Central Bank report (2002a). Even so, agriculture dropped from 12 percent of total GDP in 1994 to 10.5 percent in 2002 and the productivity and cost-effectiveness of small and medium-sized agricultural operations has been dropping continuously (Figures 1 and 2).

Meanwhile, the agricultural sector continues to be subject to various exogenous factors that increase its vulnerability, including natural disasters, the El Niño phenomenon, the recent Reventador volcano eruption that destroyed hundreds of hectares of flower plantations and hit livestock hard, and low world market prices—such as the case of coffee. (See Figure 3).

Being highly market-dependent and subject to macroeconomic and trade policies and international agreements, the agricultural sector is vulnerable and requires great

Figure 1. Yield per Hectare in 2002 (tons)

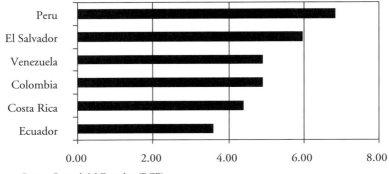

Source: Banco Central del Ecuador (BCE).

Figure 2. Agricultural GDP/Total GDP

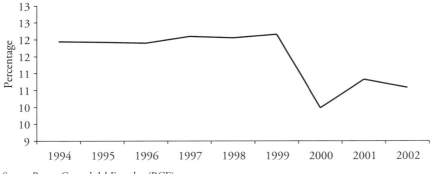

Source: Banco Central del Ecuador (BCE).

dynamism. Lower prices for domestically marketed agricultural products and depressed international prices mean that national production loses cost-effectiveness (through prices—see Figure 3 and Table 1). The rural poor, who produce for example potatoes, corn, rice and nonexportable vegetables, are facing especially unfavorable terms of exchange with neighboring countries. Competition with imported (and subsidized) products is very strong and production costs tend to rise. Compared to other countries, dollarization has had a significant impact on the marketing of products in Ecuador.

Migration from the countryside to the cities and abroad has been an important strategy for escaping poverty. Remittances from abroad (principally from Spain) are

Figure 3. Producer Price Index

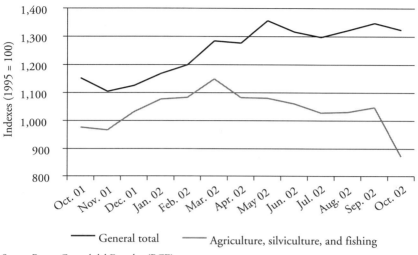

Source: Banco Central del Ecuador (BCE).

Table 1. Ecuador's Agricultural Trade Balance with Colombia and Peru

Year	Columbia	Peru
1997	59,742.86	6,795.87
1998	−41,597.92	−10,128.14
1999	52,826.07	15,030.13
2000	61,879.82	6,950.05
2001	93,851.06	6,101.18
2002	18,022.27	−15,639.15

Source: Banco Central del Ecuador (BCE).

now estimated at $US1.4 billion a year, a clearly significant amount if compared with total exports in 2001 ($US4.474 billion) or petroleum and banana exports ($US1.722 and $US827 million, respectively), which are the country's two largest exports.

As a result, the emphasis on agricultural production as the engine for rural development has been changing in favor of also recognizing the importance of occupational diversification, of the links between rural regions and the cities, of access to markets as an engine for growth, and of developing local capabilities. Nonagricultural income continues to gain importance, especially in highland areas populated by poor indigenous communities, where agriculture is no longer the main source of income but is supplemented by a mix of crafts, wood products, services, and other occupations.

Likewise, centralized approaches are being replaced by processes focused on demand and local decisionmaking, in which the beneficiaries of antipoverty strategies can themselves discover and implement these strategies in their own surroundings. The importance of "social and institutional capital" and the role of women in development are also both increasingly recognized. The PROLOCAL and PRODEPINE projects, financed by the World Bank, have a decentralized, multisectoral approach with local participation in development and are providing important lessons for a national rural development strategy.

B. Three Strategic Goals for Rural Development

In this context, the first step toward decentralized economic growth and relieving rural poverty must be to prepare a diversified, multisectoral rural development strategy with a territorial focus. This strategy should focus on three main goals: (i) economic and social cohesion through development of the local space; (ii) adjustments to agriculture and rural economic diversification; and (iii) environmental protection.[4]

ECONOMIC AND SOCIAL COHESION. Ecuador's topographic, climatic, and sociocultural diversity require different development strategies, each of which take advantage of social capital and the various organizational forms that characterize the country. To do so, the goal is foment the local development based on territorial units such as municipalities and micro-regions through local participative planning, strengthening local institutions, identifying shortcomings in physical and social infrastructure, nurturing economic opportunities specific to each local area and their competitive advantages, and reducing local obstacles to making use of them. Convergence among national and provincial agencies, municipalities, and economic and social actors toward common development priorities is important in order to create economic corridors for rural-urban development, maximize the use of resources and other local or regional development instruments, reduce the cost of public investment, and promote national economic growth. To accomplish this, policies must be established to set the conditions for convergence. For example, the allocation of resources for rural infrastructure projects should depend on an agreement between municipalities, communities, and the private sector—and based on operative criteria that define the rural space, the priority action for that space and the role of each of the actors. The PRODEPINE project offers a successful experience that can be

---

4. This strategic model has been highly effective in disadvantaged areas in the south of Italy and Spain as part of the European Union's rural development policy. See "Estrategias, Instituciones y Políticas de Desarrollo Rural en la Unión Europea" by José M. Sumpsi.

extended. In its four years, the project supported 210 local development plans prepared by 194 organizations involved in a population of more than 1.4 million people. Ninety-eight percent of the subprojects financed by PRODEPINE responded
to goals and priorities detailed in the strategic plans and were cofinanced by the
communities, with municipal collaboration in some cases. Second- and third-degree
organizations acquired the capacity to prepare local development plans through participation with the communities, thus institutionalizing the planning, monitoring,
evaluation, and systematization of their experiences as management-oriented practice. The project has fomented intercultural cooperation, establishing strategic
alliances for promoting local development.[5]

AGRICULTURAL REFORM AND THE ECONOMIC DIVERSIFICATION OF RURAL AREAS. The
agricultural sector will continue to play a key role in rural development, requiring
major reform to respond to challenges such as the demand for greater productivity,
land consolidation, the reduction of the labor force due to migration, and the transition toward products of greater value. At the same time, rural economic activity
will have to extend beyond agriculture. This will require two main types of intervention: (i) increasing the competitiveness of the agricultural sector by increasing
access to new technology, training, and other inputs such as land, credit, more
attractive markets, remote education, and new information sources; (ii) promoting
economic diversification through systems for extension and innovation, and building on nonagricultural potential in each territorial unit, including cultural capital,
biodiversity, and development of services or industries derived from agriculture or
livestock breeding. Successful development of the agricultural sector depends on a
macroeconomic framework favorable to investment, but its competitiveness will also
depend on its capacity for technological adaptation and on the availability of—and
access to—this technology. Many poor rural people could become successful producers if they had access to the most efficient technological options, training opportunities, and other input such as land, credit, and more attractive markets. These
inputs can be provided through favorable institutional arrangements such as strategic alliances, remote education, and other information sources. We predict, however,
that agricultural activity will continue to decline. Rural inhabitants will therefore
need economic alternatives preferably derived from their cultural and natural
resources—for example, crafts, cultural tourism, and environmental services.

ENVIRONMENTAL PROTECTION. The sustainability of Ecuador's economic foundations depends entirely on its ability to conserve its soils and its rich biodiversity and
natural wealth. The expansion of the commercial agricultural sector and the economic future of rural areas also requires the correct use of land and water, and the

---

5. Final Report on the Development Project for Indigenous and Black Peoples of Ecuador
   (PRODEPINE).

protection of forests and other important ecosystems. The development approach for rural areas where commercial agriculture predominates must focus mainly on the use of conservation measures and appropriate management of soil, water, forests, mangrove swamps, and other ecosystems. In areas with less agricultural activity, environmental policy must focus on recovering degraded soil through conservationist activity and small-scale value-added production associated with other activities such as tourism.

Within the proposed strategic framework, an initial plan for rural development policy should include recognition of Ecuador's natural and socioeconomic diversity. This first requires that rural areas be classified according to their different features— for example, as modern rural areas, changing rural areas, or marginal rural areas. With this spatial and community focus, the application of a combination of policies will vary depending on the features of each territory. For example, in areas with predominantly modern and export-oriented agricultural activities, such as the Ecuadoran coast and some highland areas, land zoning and environmental protection policies would be implemented; in changing areas with high rates of migration, such as certain areas of the provinces of Azuay and Azoguez, economic diversification policies would be implemented; and in marginal, relatively depopulated areas, strategies would be implemented to conserve activities such as agriculture, forestry, the environment, and cultural heritage. All this would be based on strategic plans developed at the territorial level with the participation of local social and economic actors. The wealth of information and data available from the Ecuadorian Agricultural Census will facilitate the classification of rural areas through operative criteria.

C. Key Issues in Rural Development in Ecuador

Although interventions in the different territorial areas will vary according to their natural, economic, and social features and potential, certain key issues will appear in one way or another as implementational challenges to any community rural development strategy, and thus demand immediate attention. It should be noted, however, that rural development will be effective only through an integrated, multisectoral strategy, developed with active participation by local actors and supported by a well-organized system of incentives and state services.

The problem areas considered most relevant for rural development in all of Ecuador are (i) rural education and technological progress, (ii) land ownership and administration, (iii) water resources and water basins, (iv) rural financing, (v) synergies with rural infrastructure initiatives, (vi) commodities markets, (vii) diversification strategies involving nonagricultural rural activities, and (viii) regional development and rural-urban development corridors.

RURAL EDUCATION AND TECHNOLOGICAL PROGRESS. The rural labor market is characterized by a poorly qualified labor force with low productivity. Specifically regarding education, at the end of the past decade the rural population received two-thirds as much formal schooling as the urban population, and its illiteracy rate was three times as high on average (6 percent urban and 19 percent rural). The agricultural census of 2001 indicates that the percentage of people without any kind of education among small producers is between 23 and 27 percent, dropping proportionally as the size of their agricultural production units rises (up to 6 percent). The national illiteracy rate for rural women is 23 percent. (See Table 2)

Raising rural educational levels in accordance with local customs and socioeconomic features is a key to any rural development model. Educational policy must give priority to raising educational levels in rural areas through a varied combination of educational methodologies and tools, with a curriculum relevant to the real experience of rural inhabitants and built on their cultural wealth. Experiences in several developing countries show that rural education programs are successful when their content corresponds to the reality of the rural world.

Formal technical agricultural training is lacking in the area of research and development. Agricultural technology exists only in specific areas, for specific export crops or subject to contracts. It is generally deficient at all levels, especially on small land holdings. Producers with more than 100 hectares report technical training rates of between 7 and 12 percent, while only 1 percent of those with fewer than 10 hectares have any technical training. Technical training and business management skills are essential for rural inhabitants to boost rural development. Higher educational levels also enable the poor to look for better opportunities in the urban and rural labor markets, diversify their sources of income, and create conditions to raise productivity in agriculture and microenterprises.

In recent years, the PROMSA and SICA programs have provided the country with important experiences in technological innovation and information. These experiences have given the country the opportunity to modernize these services. It is important to use this beginning to build a new institutional framework consisting of a competitive system for offering agricultural services. This would imply changing the public sector monopoly on the provision of services to a pluralist model that includes the private sector, NGOs, public and private institutes, public agencies, producers' organizations, and universities. In this framework, the role of the public

Table 2. Illiteracy Rates, 1999
(percentage of population over age 15)

Sector	Women	Men	Total
National	13	9	11
Urban	7	4	6
Rural	23	15	19
Indigenous	53	31	43

Source: SIISE.

sector would be to finance public assets, strengthen institutions, and control the quality of services. The challenges of establishing a new institutional framework will include (i) improving the ministry's management capacity, (ii) achieving more effective participation by small producers, (iii) establishing efficient institutions, (iv) establishing a mechanism for more sustainable financing, and (v) increasing the capacity of producers' organizations (that is, corporate capital).

LAND OWNERSHIP AND ADMINISTRATION. The high concentration of land ownership (in the highlands 2.6 percent of landholders own 50 percent of the land, while on the coast, where there are more medium-sized operations than in the highlands, 4 percent own 55 percent of the land) is associated with the development of a dynamic exporting sector, especially on the coast, and with a sector of small and medium-sized commercial producers focused mainly on the domestic market in the highlands (dairy farmers, flower growers, vegetable growers, and so on) and to a lesser extent on the coast. There is also an enormous number of families with very small production units, including the traditional indigenous communities, which under present conditions are hardly economically viable. For example, 30 percent of agricultural production units are under a hectare in size and occupy only 0.8 percent of the nation's land. In some cases, agriculture is not the most recommendable activity; however, there are dynamic groups of small farmers who need better access to land. There have been several unsuccessful land ownership reform initiatives. In recent years access to land has improved in several Latin American countries through agricultural reform programs based on market mechanisms, land purchases, and the recognition of forms of traditional community land ownership. Some programs require major financing by the state. In this framework of land ownership and economic activity, the combination of measures to be adopted will depend on the territorial area in question.

In addition to the concentration and fragmentation of land ownership, the main causes for concern in the land market are the lack of a rural land register, problems involving titles and registry, and the nonfulfillment of ownership contracts. When the agricultural census was carried out, only 8 percent of producers (56,000) said they held ownership deeds. Fifty-nine percent of occupied deedless land is concentrated among 6,000 producers with more than 50 hectares, while the 50,000 remaining producers have less than 3 hectares.

To face these problems, the World Bank's 1998 Policy Notes recommended investing in a rural land register, as well as rationalizing and strengthening the legal framework. Currently the problems of legal and administrative irregularities involving land ownership are being dealt with under the pilot PRAT project, which includes improvements to the rural land register in nine cantons and 20,000 titles granted by the INDA. Also, the PRODEPINE I project has managed to title 252,000 hectares of ancestral land. It is hoped that this process will continue under the PRODEPINE II project, which is now under consideration.

WATER RESOURCES AND WATER BASINS. The distribution of water and the rights to its use (for human consumption and industrial and agricultural uses) are a source of conflict in Ecuador. The biggest users are urban municipalities, large producers on the coast, and flower producers in the highlands, while small rural producers and indigenous groups claim that they do not receive their fair share of available water. Policies on water use in urban areas are dealt with as separate water supply and sanitation policies. In terms of rural development, the approach to water management is based on water basins and on the rights to the use of water resources, including irrigation systems. There is no updated information on the availability of water in each basin or on water quality. The latest study of the water situation was in 1985. Integrated management of water basins is important for environmental conservation and economic diversification through the provision of environmental services (reforestation, ecotourism, and others deserve urgent attention). Also, completing the transfer of irrigation systems to groups of users must continue to be a water management priority. Of the 8.1 million hectares of permanently or periodically cultivated land, 853,332 (or 10.6 percent) are irrigated. However, Ecuador potentially has an estimated 3.1 million hectares of land appropriate for irrigation, meaning that the area now irrigated represents barely 27.3 percent of the country's potential. Of the total irrigated area, nearly 170,000 hectares are on government land and the rest are collectively (communally) owned. Irrigated agriculture represents an estimated 70 percent of the country's agricultural production, and is five times as productive as feeding crops with rainwater.

In addition, the legal framework for water resources needs to be examined in order to establish a more efficient and fair system for managing water basins and allocating water resources. These initiatives are part of a much broader program for the integrated management of all resources in water basins. Several studies and proposals for pilot projects have already been presented.

RURAL FINANCING. Rural credit is restricted by the difficulties many producers have meeting the administrative and guarantee requirements of financial institutions. The *Banco Nacional de Fomento*'s practice of writing off debts has created a widespread habit among the rural population of not repaying debts, as well as hesitation among formal financial agents to grant loans in rural areas.

According to the agricultural census, only 7 percent of agricultural producers have access to any kind of credit (including commercial credit; bank loans; and credit from savings and loan cooperatives, from NGOs, or from informal agents such as intermediaries and family members who can provide loans). Informal credit is most common: 41 percent of producers who receive credit, especially owners of small and medium-small operations, receive it from informal sources. Bank loans are concentrated among producers with more than 50 hectares. Savings and loan co-ops are an important source of financing for small producers: 25 percent of producers with fewer than 3 hectares who receive credit are assisted by savings and loan cooperatives.

More than 600 rural savings and loan cooperatives and other institutions have been formed in rural areas and operate on the basis of direct intermediation with community associations, families, and the like. These institutions have existed for years, but more recently have evolved into centers of financial activity in rural areas. They are becoming the embryo of an alternative market for rural capital.

After the recent conflict over the government's intention to abolish cooperatives that did not qualify to be regulated by the Bank Superintendence for lack of sufficient capital (a conflict resolved by placing all these small institutions under the umbrella of the Cooperatives Office of the Ministry of Social Welfare), there is now a renewed interest in setting up a national microfinancing system.

In order to respond to this demand, several alternatives should be considered: (a) promoting greater competition within the national financial sector; (b) strengthening the cooperative movement by establishing (from the grassroots, not from the top) a network of cooperatives and credit institutions; (c) establishing connections among women's credit groups (*cajas solidarias*) and formal financial institutions; (d) establishing laws and new regulations to permit the easy use of rural family assets such as land or livestock as guarantees for loans; e) allowing agricultural middlemen to use the input they acquire as guarantees for bank loans; and (f) offering a legal guarantee—in the Brazilian fashion—for a "rural protection certificate" for future sales, in order to reduce the risk of price drops and to enable farmers to take out loans with their future crops as a guarantee. This instrument could have a secondary market (stock market); instead of a public system of loan guarantees—which has not worked anywhere—a lottery would be established for private insurance: those who buy the ticket would be eligible to receive a prize upon independent confirmation that more or less than the prespecified amount of rain fell in a specified period of time. This system would be open to everyone who buys a ticket—the price and conditions of which would have been established beforehand. No verification would be required by an insurance agent, since payment would be based on an objective and verifiable indicator. This scheme covers an important aspect of production risks and when combined with a system of insurance against low future sales prices through the "rural protection certificate," a large part of the producer's risk is eliminated. Although these mechanisms take some time to become established, they are sustainable interventions and would be available to a much larger group of producers.

SYNERGIES WITH RURAL INFRASTRUCTURE INITIATIVES. The poor state of infrastructure (rural roads and marketing) and of public services (communications and electricity) creates a dependency on traditional intermediation, which increases transaction costs. The availability of rural roads, by contrast, helps prevent the prices of locally transported goods from rising too much in situations of increasing aggregate demand, by promoting external competition and reducing transaction costs between urban and rural areas. Furthermore, improving rural infrastructure and communications would help stabilize prices during times of economic expansion and would reduce the privileges of certain local agents that prevent a more equitable distribution of agricultural income. Investments in infrastructure, particularly roads, also contribute to generating external economies to attract companies that transform or market agricultural products, as do many other related services in rural areas, thus aiding economic diversification. Rural infrastructure initiatives must be based on local strategic plans, with active participation by the local population through microenterprises that generate employment and financing shared by the central government, municipalities, the private sector, and communities. Chapter 7 on Basic Infrastructure describes the policy options for rural infrastructure that may be considered as part of a rural development strategy.

COMMODITIES MARKETS. Commodities markets have structures that are unfavorable to the rural poor. Some have a very dense intermediary structure with high mark-ups (corn, potatoes, and similar), while others fix prices under oligopolistic conditions (the banana market). Production and marketing contracts are commonly broken and it is not easy to have them legally enforced. Those most affected are small producers who must continually accept unfavorable transactions. The markets could be more efficient with a better legal framework, and if the Law on Competition were passed, provide penalties for anticompetitive practices—which would be unprecedented.

In addition are the transaction costs and the traditional intermediation associated with poor infrastructure. However, as soon as these traditional systems are integrated in commercial circuits dominated by cities and other populated centers, opportunities arise for small producers to penetrate attractive markets and capture a large share of the added value of their products. In the highlands, COSUDE is successfully applying (with producers of vegetables, dairy products, and legumes) a model for providing aid aimed at strengthening the link between production and marketing and increasing the share of added value captured by producers. Another important factor allowing continued high mark-ups by middlemen is the imbalance in access to information on local and world prices. Wide publication and broadcasting of the information collected by SICA would provide an opportunity to inform producers about opportunities for their products.

This marketing strategy contributes to improved risk management by maintaining a portfolio of products and diversifying buyers; appropriately managing market information in order to anticipate events, both favorable and unfavorable; and facilitating the contracting of collective crop insurance with private insurance companies (this has been done in the case of broccoli). This latter mechanism has barely been developed in Ecuador at present.

DIVERSIFICATION STRATEGIES. The agricultural census indicates that at the national level agricultural producers obtain 33 percent of their income from nonagricultural sources. Small producers obtain 60–70 percent from other sources. A study carried out in 12 Integrated Regional Development areas in 1993 (Martínez 1995) showed that "...areas with a predominance of non-agricultural income are located in the highlands populated by poor indigenous communities with few resources, where agriculture is no longer the main source of income and occupational diversification crosses families longitudinally. At the other extreme, the only areas where agricultural income clearly predominates are on the humid coast of the Guayas basin. Rural people here continue with agriculture to the extent that good quality land is available to them."

REGIONAL-LOCAL DEVELOPMENT AND RURAL-URBAN DEVELOPMENT CORRIDORS. The diversity of rural spaces in Ecuador requires a variety of interventions that support the potential of each local jurisdiction through participative plans and strategic alliances. There are already some experiences that can serve as a starting point. The PROLOCAL program, financed by the World Bank, sets out to relieve poverty by increasing local development management capacity in the cantons and provinces and by supplying financial resources, training services, and technical assistance. The following institutional strategy has been proposed: strengthening local capacity for planning (participative preparation of local development plans) and implementing projects; further advances toward decentralization of public administration; strengthening the institutional capacity of local actors; organizing action by public and private institutions; and broad participation by grassroots communities. The PRODEPINE project pursues goals similar to those of PROLOCAL, but unlike the latter, which works with nonindigenous rural communities, PRODEPINE deals exclusively with ethnic and Afro-Peruvian groups.

Local planning involves all actors (communities, parishes, municipalities, the private sector, and the public sector) and the implementation of plans is a very powerful instrument for achieving rural development goals. The implementation of local plans

Martínez (2002) reports that in the province of Tungurahua, where the commercial dynamics of the city of Ambato and its privileged location in the center of the country have coincided with rural conditions such as a less concentrated agricultural structure and better access to basic education, "a dense network of productive movements has been created, the focal point of which is the internal market" (clothing industries, small agricultural industries, and so on), which has benefited the poor population, including indigenous people. Also, the existence of rural infrastructure and public services (electric energy, roads, and the like) has enabled other rural communities to take advantage of this dynamic, "which in turn extends into the deepest rural areas." The author adds that this process has been boosted by the presence of Integrated Rural Development projects. This experience demonstrates the possibilities of regional-local development and the potential of urban-rural links through medium-sized cities, as well as the relevance of investment in education, rural infrastructure, and basic public services.

created by local agents allows a growth dynamic to develop, based on the comparative advantages of each area, during the attempt to diversify the local economy through small and microenterprises. The conditions for attracting and keeping private investment can be attained only if an investment program is also put in place for public services such as communications, electricity, transport, and market infrastructure.

On the basis of concerted local planning, "economic corridors" can be created, linking rural areas with other rural areas and with urban areas through local highway infrastructure projects, developing comparative advantages (niches for products and know-how) and entrepreneurial and business training programs.

D. The Institutional Framework of Rural Development

The system for promoting rural development is institutionally complex in the sense that it includes a great number of public and nongovernmental organizations working in an uncoordinated fashion and channeling resources according to objectives that are not always in line with the needs of the beneficiaries.

At the central government level, we find the Ministry of Social Welfare, the Rural Development division of which presides over the PROLOCAL council; the Ministry of Agriculture, which has agricultural and rural planning functions, and the autonomous institutions responsible for technology, training and agricultural development; the Planning Office (ODEPLAN) responsible to the President's Office, which promotes a national system of decentralized participative planning; and the Ministry of Education and Culture, with responsibilities in its respective sector. There is also the Council for the Development of the Indigenous Nations and Peoples of Ecuador (CODENPE), which is responsible for implementing the PRODE-PINE project, for which purpose it makes agreements with institutions such as INDA on the regularization of land rights and with financial intermediaries for the implementation of sub-projects.

The National Council on Hydraulic Resources (CNRH) governs the use of water for irrigation, drinking, and hydroelectric energy generation. Since INERHI was eliminated, there is no central body involved in irrigation policy. Irrigation is managed by a set of actors with different functions, including regional development corporations, provincial councils, and users' boards. The Agricultural Census (SICA) project is another important actor working to improve the availability, consistency, validity, and usefulness of information in the agricultural sector in order to facilitate decisionmaking in the private and public sectors.

Provincial councils, municipalities, and parochial boards share responsibilities for rural development in their respective jurisdictions, as established by each autonomous sectional government system. Parishes are the basic geographic and social unit in the local development process and the parochial boards can play a leading role in guaranteeing popular participation and initiative in the management of official development policy. At the provincial, municipal, and parochial levels are sufficient mechanisms for discussion and agreement among state institutions and civil society, though membership in these bodies could in some cases be adjusted to reflect the importance of the social actors involved. As is enshrined in the constitution, resources destined to operating local entities consist of income generated by the entities themselves plus the transfer of at least 15 percent of the total current income of the central government budget. Finally, the nine regional development corporations also carry out development activities, mostly involving irrigation, rural road infrastructure, and other infrastructure.

Given the limited public resources at the central and local levels, civil organizations and NGOs have occupied part of the space for cooperation not covered by the state. Complete information on their activities is not available, though it is quite clear that there is no coordination among so many institutions working in rural development.

An effective rural development policy that favors a spatial, multisectoral, participative approach and supports economic diversification will also require institutional architecture that facilitates complementarity among the roles of the different actors. The institutional rules that guide this effort must be based on (i) cooperation among the central public sector, the private sector, civil society, municipalities and provincial governments, parochial boards, savings and loan banks, and so on; (ii) coherence among the regulations and activities of the different institutions; (iii) programming based on the strategic plans of each jurisdiction; and (iv) financial allocations based on the concept of "additionality" as incentives for guaranteeing the implementation of the strategic plans. This means that state contributions will complement contributions made by other actors with similar goals.

E. Conclusions and Recommendations

Rural development in Ecuador suffers from a lack of coordination and excessive centralization, resulting in inefficient public and private investment. Many rural policies concentrate on the agricultural sector and little attention is given to nonagricultural activities. Community development experiences such as PRODEPINE offer a good starting point for strengthening the rural sector but require concerted action on a larger scale.

Ecuador's geographic, economic, and sociocultural diversity requires a varied rural development based on policies that support (i) a participative approach to development focused on jurisdictions or rural spaces, in order to foment economic and social cohesion; (ii) diversification of the rural economy, the creation of nonagricultural employment through investment in rural and social infrastructure, and greater competitiveness in the agricultural sector through new technology and research; and (iii) the promotion of environmental conservation through better land zoning, the recovery of soil conservation methods, and other uses of natural resources.

Creating a rural development strategy using this new approach could take a new government the better part of its first year. Rural needs demand immediate action; therefore, these recommendations are of two kinds: (i) actions leading to the preparation of an integrated strategy for social development; and (ii) actions that must continue or begin immediately in order to deal with the problems identified above.

Recommendations

BEGIN PREPARING A RURAL DEVELOPMENT STRATEGY that supports the decentralization process and is based on participative processes and strategic alliances within each territorial jurisdiction; promotes economic diversification in the agricultural sector; and strengthens environmental protection. This will require classifying territorial jurisdictions on the basis of operative criteria; identifying participative process for the preparation of integrated local development plans; identifying the different actors at the national, provincial, municipal, and community levels; developing criteria for eligibility for the development funds supporting the strategic plans; clarifying the roles and responsibilities of the different actors, especially in the various sectors that already operate in rural areas; and creating a program of incentives for preparing strategic alliances, chains of production, and innovative local proposals. In the meantime, the following priority actions will facilitate the move toward rural development with the features mentioned above.

PRIORITIZE INVESTMENT IN EDUCATION IN RURAL AREAS. This requires immediate action since the potential of rural Ecuador depends to a great extent on the educational level of its people. Basic rural education must be in keeping with rural reality and the cultural characteristics of its people (see chapter 9 on Education).

IMPROVE RESEARCH AND TECHNICAL TRAINING, not only in the agricultural sector, but also in nonagricultural sectors such as crafts and tourism. This requires continuing and expanding existing research and development programs and developing alternatives for spreading technology in a broad and decentralized way in areas with agricultural potential, based on an evaluation of the state of the institutions in charge of these activities. Immediate action that could be taken includes supporting (i) the National Professional Training Service in collaboration with agricultural colleges; (ii) the National Institute for the Training of Rural Farm Workers (*Capacitación Campesina*), which the Ministry of Agriculture and Livestock operates on a decentralized basis; and (iii) the institutionalization of a modern research and development system based on the principles of diversity, cofinancing, and competitiveness, such as the one being developed by PROMSA. This kind of system requires the creation of real demand through the participation of the beneficiaries and a redefinition of the role of the INIAP. The Consulting Councils of the SICA project could serve as key points of contact to develop an effective research and development project.

CONTINUE LAND TITLING AND ZONING. Any rural development strategy will require that private and community land ownership and their respective legal guarantees be clearly determined. When the PRAT pilot project has been completed and evaluated, it will be necessary to look for options to extend the experience and coverage of rural land registry and titling. Also, it is hoped that the PRODEPINE II project will continue advancing with the land titling process begun during PRODEPINE I. It will also be necessary to examine alternatives for improving access for the rural poor through market mechanisms. If it is feasible and if the cost is acceptable, pilot programs should be initiated in certain key areas, aimed at implementing land zoning schemes, regulations for land use, and support for economic diversification outside the agricultural sector.

MONITOR WATER BASINS AND TRANSFER IRRIGATION SYSTEMS TO USERS' BOARDS. Begin monitoring water basins where the greatest conflicts have occurred and those with the greatest risk of flooding in order to determine the supply and demand for surface and underground water, to evaluate water quality, and to determine alternative action. The CNRH would be responsible for such monitoring, in collaboration with development corporations and provincial councils. Future action related to water basin management must be determined as part of the strategic plan of each territorial jurisdiction. The Ministry of Agriculture should also continue with the transfer of irrigation systems to users' boards.

RURAL FINANCING. Strengthen the national network of savings and loan cooperatives for the rural sector, as well as other options that could be applied during a pilot stage of projects aimed at extending access to financial services in rural areas if these pilot stages are successful. Explore innovative risk protection mechanisms such as the "rural production certificate" and the lottery system for insurance against low prices. Links should also be established between informal credit models (such as women's credit groups) and the formal financial system.

IMPROVE RURAL PUBLIC INFRASTRUCTURE (see chapter 7 on Basic Infrastructure). Increase public investment in rural areas that have the greatest potential for economic diversification or economic corridors; the highest transaction costs for marketing their products; and the best opportunities to form alliances with communities and the private sector for financing, building, and maintaining infrastructure.

REVISE THE REGULATIONS THAT REGULATE COMMERCIAL RELATIONS IN RURAL MARKETS. This will require wide-reaching measures such as revising and updating current legislation (the current commercial code dates back to 1904). As a start, a technical commission could be established to carry out an inventory and evaluation of existing regulations that have an effect on juridical security in the rural markets.

BOOST A MARKETING ASSISTANCE PLAN as a pilot project based on the following services for supporting associated producers: business management, organization, credit, market research, chains of production, and alliances with the agroindustrial sector. The goal is to attract producers toward an expansive dynamic and support improvements to the productive base in order to increase productivity and diversification. In principle, this would be implemented in one or two areas with good potential for gaining access to urban or export markets, in conjunction with investment in rural infrastructure.

INVESTIGATE EXISTING AND POTENTIAL DIVERSIFICATION STRATEGIES for communities in order to provide them with the appropriate investment and support. This is especially true of indigenous people, many of whom have proven themselves to be successful business and craftspeople.

EXPERIMENT WITH PILOT PROJECTS TO DEVELOP RURAL SPACES AND PRODUCTION CHAINS (jurisdictions) based on the principles of (i) participative local planning, (ii) implementation of locally concerted public investment, (iii) support for private investment, (iv) strategic alliances, and (v) the establishment of economic corridors aimed at diversifying the local economy.

Policy Matrix

Problem (including annual fiscal cost, if any)	Policy measures Short term (to June 2003)	Progress indicators Medium term (2003–07)	Objectives/goals
Lack of a comprehensive rural development strategy that recognizes the geographic, economic, and sociocultural diversity of of the rural sector and its need for economic diversification.	Develop a strategic framework for rural development Establish operative criteria for classifying rural spaces as modern rural areas, less favored areas, and marginal areas, also using Agricultural Census data and other sources of information. Develop participative strategic plans at the level of territorial jurisdictions (municipalities, micro-regions). Establish policies that encourage the convergence of the objectives of the different actors toward a common goal—for example, additional budget allocations for projects, based on transparent and inclusive strategic alliances.	Implement the strategy in areas marked for priority intervention, based on compliance with basic requirements such as the strategic plans and territorial agreements among the various actors in the areas and innovative local action plans.	Applying the new rural development policy in five pilot areas with different geographic, economic, and sociocultural characteristics. Reducing poverty, strengthening the decentralization process, and promoting diversified rural development, while strengthening local institutions and strategic alliances.
Low level of education and training among the rural population. Low productivity of small and medium-sized agricultural production units.	Prioritize investment in education toward rural areas and adjust education to the local cultural context. Increase support of National Professional Training Service in an alliance with agricultural colleges, and National Institute	(Based on chapter 9, Education Policy) Evaluate the state of rural research and training. Adopt and implement measures to strengthen training institutions. Establish a minimum of	Increasing school attendance rate and the percentage of the population with technical training. Increasing technical and management levels not only in the agricultural sector but also in other rural economic sectors. Increasing research capacity in

	for the Training of Rural Farm Workers (Capacitación Campesina) Initiate strategic alliances with national and international research institutions Demand reasonable performance by the INIAP under an accountability system that guarantees its effectiveness Involve the Consulting Councils of the SICA project in the development of an effective research and development program.	five strategic alliances nationally and internationally. INIAP either functioning in accordance with the provisions of the PROMSA project or else restructured. Develop and implement appropriate alternatives; undertake massive, decentralized distribution of technology.	biology, genetics, and other areas of importance to agriculture. Increasing the number of farmers participating in development activities. Raising rural productivity and real wages, increasing rural added value captured by the poor, and increasing the competitiveness of the agricultural sector.
Lack of rural land register and problems with land titling and registration.	Continue with the PRAT pilot program and begin the second stage of the PRODEPINE project.	Extend the reach and coverage of the PRAT project and continue with the PRODEPINE land titling program.	Establishing rural land registers in municipalities, issuing deeds, updating registers, and so on. Making land ownership more secure and facilitating the capitalization of land holdings.
Difficulty experienced by small farmers in gaining access to land.	Evaluate the possibility of improving access to land through market mechanisms.	Develop the appropriate market mechanism and launch pilot projects.	Facilitating agricultural expansion in areas with productive potential and facilitating the consolidation of small land holdings with low productive value. Increasing opportunities for access to land for small producers.
Inappropriate and inequitable management of water resources.	Identify the water basins with the most conflictive situations or risk of flooding, to determine the supply	Identify basins and bring action plan to implementation stage. Revise and approve the necessary	Reducing conflict over water; rationalizing its use (see water policy)

(Matrix continues on the following page.)

Policy Matrix (*continued*)

Problem (including annual fiscal cost, if any)	Policy measures Short term (to June 2003)	Progress indicators Medium term (2003–07)	Objectives/goals
Social conflict involving water use for industry, irrigation, and human consumption.	and demand for surface and underground water, evaluate water quality and determine alternative action. Revise the current legal framework (Water Act). Continue with the program for transferring irrigation systems to users' boards.	changes to the Water Act. Transfer all irrigation systems to users' boards.	Completing the process of transferring irrigation systems. Protection of natural resources and increase in the productive capacity of small farmers.
Questionable viability of many agricultural production units. Insufficient agricultural activity to employ the rural poor.	Investigate strategies and potential for economic diversification based on the cultural and natural potential of the different rural areas in the country: the coast, the highlands, and the east.	Implement an economic diversification program based on local innovation or alliances among actors in three pilot areas. Aim rural programs toward the goal of diversification.	Building the economic base on local potential outside the agricultural sector. Increasing the efficiency of existing programs for supporting rural areas. Increasing occupational diversification and generating employment.
Lack of capital for the development of rural microenterprises and for rural diversification.	Strengthen the cooperative movement through a network of grassroots cooperatives supported by credit institutions. Establish formal connections among women's credit groups (*cajas solidarias*) and formal financial institutions. Explore innovative mechanisms for financially supporting the rural	Begin establishing the network in three provinces. Link 50 percent of *cajas solidarias* (savings banks) to formal financial institutions. Implement pilot projects with new mechanisms for supporting micro-credit, rural financing, and risk management.	Reaching a point at which the network is structured and operating. Achieving 50 percent increase in access to credit among small producers. Increasing productive investment and diversification in rural areas.

	...sector such as rural production certificates and private insurance lottery. Establish laws and regulations on the use of family assets (land, livestock) as a guarantee for loans.	Increase income among small farmers in selected areas through risk reduction.	Increasing juridical stability in contractual and commercial relations among rural producers and entrepreneurs. Stabilizing the income of producers.
Production and marketing contracts frequently broken; inefficient mechanisms for enforcing them.	Establish a commission to evaluate regulations on rural markets; begin work.	Implement the most urgent measures among the recommendations of the mixed technical commission.	
High mark-ups by middlemen and low competitiveness.	Design a pilot program for supporting rural marketing, based on business management, organization, credit, chains of production, and alliances with the agroindustrial sector. Prioritize rural public investment for areas that have the greatest potential for economic diversification or economic corridors; the highest transactional costs; and the best opportunities to form alliances with communities and the private sector for financing, building, and maintaining infrastructure.	Implement the program in two areas with potential for gaining access to urban or export markets, in conjunction with investment in rural infrastructure.	Achieving goals with regard to: functioning structures for cooperation with producers' groups, number of people trained, alliances established with the private sector. Increasing the competitiveness of the rural economy
Economic marginalization of rural areas and weak rural-urban links.	Using operative criteria, identify areas with potential for developing local and regional development programs; engage in participative planning in collaboration with all actors in the area; and create economic corridors.	Implement a pilot program for integrated development in three areas, with links to the urban sector.	Developing alternative economic activities linked with rural areas. Creation of virtuous circles of development among the rural poor.

14

The Environment and
Sustainable Development[1]

Ernesto Sánchez-Triana and Juan Quintero

The poverty endured by more than 60 percent of the population is the most critical problem confronting Ecuador. Poverty is caused and exacerbated by two priority environmental problems: environmental pollution and natural disasters. In 2000, the major diseases associated with environmental pollution were (i) acute respiratory infections (697,254 cases); (ii) diseases associated with water pollution (225,734 cases), particularly diarrheal diseases; and (iii) vector-borne diseases (97,007 cases), such as malaria and dengue fever, that are associated with sanitary deficiencies. In addition, natural disasters (floods in coastal areas, seismic and volcanic phenomena, landslides and erosion in the Andean area, and blights), primarily the El Niño phenomenon and other climatic changes represent one of the major limitations on reducing poverty in Ecuador. For example, the 1997–98 El Niño produced floods in coastal areas leading to economic losses in excess of $US2 billion. On that occasion, floods affected 2,500 kilometers of major highways and 40,000 kilometers of secondary roads throughout the country. Floods also destroyed 1,600 homes and affected another 7,500. Storms in recent years, including 2002, have increased in frequency and intensity, leaving unparalleled devastation in their wake.

Environmental policy must confront these priority problems associated with poverty—that is, control pollution and prevent the effects of natural disasters on the population. To develop an environmental policy, the state has two basic forms of intervention at its dis-

---

1. This chapter was prepared by Ernesto Sánchez-Triana (senior environmental engineer, LCSES) and Juan David Quintero (lead environmental specialist, LCSES). The authors appreciate the comments, suggestions, and information provided by Minister of the Environment, Edgar Isch, and by Maria Donoso-Clark, Gabriela Arcos, Kulsum Ahmed, George Ledec, and Peter Brandiss.

posal: environmental regulation and investment in the environment. To control environmental pollution, the government issued Executive Decrees 3399 and 3516 in December 2002, plus secondary environmental legislation that includes environmental regulations providing for different instruments, notably economic and administrative procedures and direct regulation. The short-term challenge in this area is to ensure the implementation, supervision, and monitoring of these regulations. To reduce rural vulnerability to natural disasters, investments are urgently needed in structural and nonstructural risk prevention measures. Structural measures include the resettlement of populations living on floodplains, flood control projects, the use of wetlands to alleviate rising waters, and erosion control and bank stabilization projects. Nonstructural measures include establishing soil use zones, designing emergency response and assistance programs, and equipping and preparing citizens for such events. Investments in road infrastructure; potable water; and in the agricultural, health, or energy sectors necessitate incorporating environmental considerations in order to ensure the efficiency, equity, and effectiveness of such investments. Finally, investments in conservation and protected areas should target areas that have the greatest potential for nature tourism.

A. Introduction

This chapter starts with the premise that any strategy for economic growth and social development in the country will be contingent upon the control of degradation in the biophysical environment and the sustainable management of natural resources. In this respect, we discuss the principal environmental issues associated with economic growth and the fight against poverty, and propose a series of institutional options intended to consolidate the government's efforts on the path to sustainable development.

The chapter is divided into five sections. The second section identifies the most important environmental problems faced by Ecuador, including those associated with the population's morbidity and mortality rates. It also discusses the limitations that natural disasters place on growth. The third section analyzes environmental management activities currently underway in the country and examines the opportunities for converting the management of natural resources into a variable that consolidates Ecuador's competitive advantages. Finally, the fourth section presents a series of conclusions and suggests policy options designed to institutionalize the path of sustainable development.

B. Poverty and the Environment

Between 1995 and 1999, the incidence of poverty in Ecuador increased from 34 to 56 percent—making the poverty endured by the highest percentage of the population the critical problem facing the country. Poverty exists and is exacerbated as a

Figure 1. Poverty Deciles in Ecuador's Cantons

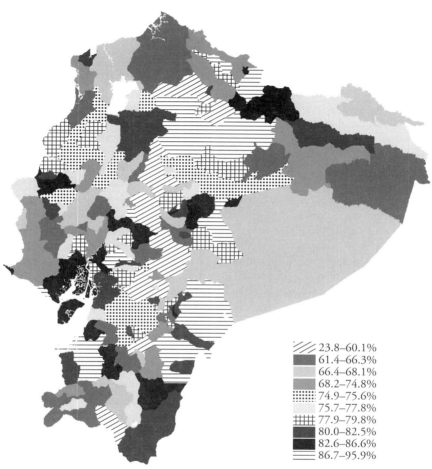

23.8–60.1%
61.4–66.3%
66.4–68.1%
68.2–74.8%
74.9–75.6%
75.7–77.8%
77.9–79.8%
80.0–82.5%
82.6–86.6%
86.7–95.9%

Source: Henninger and Hammond (2002).

result of two predominant environmental variables: environmental pollution and natural disasters. Controlling pollution and preventing the effects of natural disasters on the population must both be given the highest priority and attention by environmental authorities.

Environmental Pollution

One of the principal factors exacerbating poverty in Ecuador is the drastic increase in the rates of morbidity and mortality from diseases directly related to environmental pollution. In 2000, the major reportable diseases were (i) acute respiratory infections (697,254 cases); (ii) diseases associated with water pollution (225,734 cases); particularly diarrheal diseases; and (iii) vector-borne diseases (97,007 cases), such as malaria and dengue fever, that are associated with sanitary deficiencies (PAHO 2002). The economic cost of these diseases is hundreds of millions of dollars and the social and individual cost is even higher.

Air pollution, particularly pollution created indoors, is associated with acute respiratory infections (Harding and Staton 2002). This type of pollution is caused by incomplete combustion of firewood and other fossil fuels inside both rural and urban homes (Smith 1986). In 2001, approximately 18 percent of the energy consumed in the country came from firewood and other traditional fossil fuels. This is 2 percentage points higher than the average consumption in Latin America and the Caribbean (IBRD 2001).

Air pollution is one of the principal causes of respiratory diseases in Ecuador. Children under the age of five are those who are most at risk, owing both to air pollution inside buildings and atmospheric contamination in urban areas near roadways or industrial corridors. Air pollution is particularly critical in cities more than 2000 meters above sea level such as Quito, Cuenca, and Ambato (Jurado and Southgate 1999). The rates of atmospheric contamination in urban environments such as the historic center of Quito are made worse by high altitude conditions and weather conditions associated with thermal inversion. The effects of atmospheric pollutants are significant in areas where populations with the lowest incomes live. In these areas, high population densities, incomplete combustion of fossil fuels, motor emissions, and the topography itself synergetically increase the concentrations of pollutants with the resulting effects on human health. A study of school-aged children in Quito identified four times more episodes of asthma per year in children of the same age as in cities in the United States that had a higher number of automobiles (John Boldt 1998, cited by Fundación Natura and Universidad Central del Ecuador 2000).

Air pollution inhibits lung development, aggravates asthma, and contributes to chronic lung diseases. It also reduces worker productivity. A study conducted in 1996 estimated annual losses of approximately $28 million dollars owing to absence from work and the treatment of respiratory diseases associated with the elevated presence of particles in the air. Vehicles are the major generators of atmospheric pollution due to suspended particles, carbon monoxide, and ozone precursors, particularly in urban centers. Sulfur oxide and nitrogen oxide emissions come primarily from fixed sources. In cities such as Quito, fixed sources include textile factories, leather-tanning operations, and industries involved in the processing of food and beverages (Southgate and others 1996).

Public health problems due to water-borne diseases are associated with deficiencies in the coverage and quality of potable water services and with inadequate hygiene. The incidence of diarrhea in the infant population is estimated at more than six million per year and the country has an infant mortality rate in children under the age of five higher than the average for Latin America (UNDP 1999). For example, in the coastal cities barely 21.9 percent of the population has access to residential drinking water. (INFOPLAN 1999).

Morbidity and mortality rates due to poisonings or diseases caused by carcinogenic and teratogenic agents correlate with the improper handling and disposal of hazardous wastes. Some existing data show the intensive use of substances that are precursors of hazardous wastes (Ministry of the Environment, IDB, and PAHO 2002). The use of agrochemicals in Ecuador is higher than the average for Latin America. According to data from the World Resources Institute (2000), during the period 1996–98 Ecuador held fourth place in the consumption of pesticides among 12 South American countries. In a study of exposure risks, Britton (2000) found concentrations of 44.3 g/day of heptachloride and 11.0 g/day of aldrin. The health effects of high concentrations of these organic compounds in food are associated with cancer risks of 0.3 to 9.1 x 10-3, which means an additional 150 cases of cancer each year.

Deficiencies in the handling and disposal of waste and deficiencies in sanitation in general are also associated with morbidity and mortality owing to diseases spread by vectors such as insects and rodents. The production of waste in Ecuador is estimated at 8,000 tons per day (PAHO 1998). Eighty percent of this waste is disposed in open-air dumps. Garbage collectors live with their families in all of these dumps. Industrial wastes containing hazardous wastes are handled along with household waste. The daily production of industrial waste in 1996 was estimated at close to 400 tons, 75 percent of which was produced in Guayaquil and Quito (Southgate and others 1996). Waste disposal problems have worsened in cities such as Quito, where in late 2002 the waste disposal site was filled to capacity and alternatives are being sought for temporary and subsequent permanent waste disposal.

Natural Disasters

Natural disasters (floods in coastal areas, seismic and volcanic phenomena, landslides and erosion in the Andean area, and blights), primarily El Niño and other climatic changes have caused the reappearance of diseases such as dengue fever and malaria. As mentioned earlier, natural disasters are one of the major limitations on reducing the conditions of poverty in Ecuador. The population's vulnerability to natural disasters has increased owing to the accelerated process of urbanization in recent decades. A characteristic of this process is the occupation, particularly by the poorest populations, of areas that are most susceptible to floods, erosion, landslides, and seismic movements.

Natural disasters are associated with significant reductions in GNP growth. Economic growth has been significantly affected in proportion to the magnitude and

Figure 2. GDP and Natural Disasters

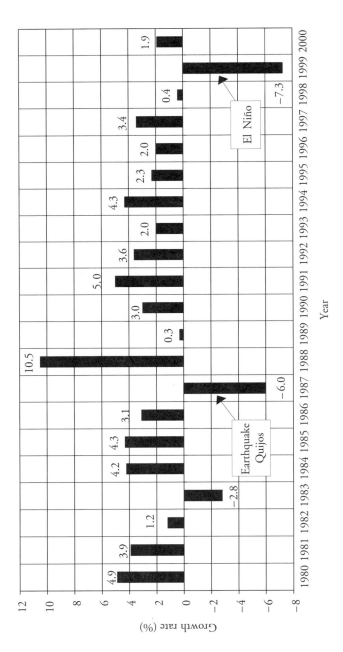

intensity of natural disasters. Some of these disasters have been particularly destructive. For example, in 1987 an earthquake affected the area of Quijos in Napo Province, interrupting the transport of hydrocarbons from the east to Esmeralda; in 1997 and 1998, the El Niño phenomenon had a significant impact on the country (Benavides and Solberg 2003).

The El Niño phenomenon of 1997–98 produced floods in the coastal areas with economic losses in excess of $US2.869 million or close to 15 percent of GDP in 1999. On that occasion, floods affected 2,500 kilometers of major highways and 40,000 kilometers of secondary roads throughout the country. Floods also destroyed 1,600 homes and affected another 7,500. Recent storms have increased in frequency and intensity, leaving unparalleled devastation in their wake. With the El Niño phenomenon and other climatic changes there has also been a reemergence of diseases such as dengue fever and malaria. Earthquakes and ash storms due to the eruption of volcanoes such as Pichincha or Revolcón have caused significant interruptions in the country's economic activities. Landslides, floods, and mudflows that occur on the hillsides of Quito and other cities in the Andean area have also caused great damage to local economies.

The high costs of natural disasters are associated with the great vulnerability of human settlements, particularly low-income populations, located on floodplains, areas with high seismic activity, and hillsides with geotechnical problems. Various governmental and nongovernmental organizations are engaged in disaster response and reconstruction activities. National legislation assigns the responsibility for coordinating emergency assistance and response to Civil Defense. In addition, organizations such as the Coordinator of the Emergency Program to Cope with the El Niño Phenomenon (COPEFEN), established in 1997, are responsible for coordinating reconstruction activities in conjunction with Ministries such as Housing (MIVI) or Public Works (MOP). In 2002, the government expanded the scope of COPEFEN so that it would act as the Coordinating Unit of the Emergency Program to Cope with Natural Phenomena. In addition, CORPECUADOR was given the responsibility of supervising the rehabilitation of infrastructures affected by natural disasters. However, to date Ecuador has no organizations for coordinating disaster prevention through actions to reduce vulnerability by means of economic instruments or land management schemes.

C. Sustainable Development

Environmental issues cut across the various sectors of Ecuador's economy and society. Responsibility for sustainable development lies not only with the Ministry of the Environment and the environmental authorities but also with the various public and private agents. Both the public and private sectors are responsible for establishing comprehensive environmental management schemes. The incorporation of environmental considerations in the economic sectors and the efficient management of natural resources are essential for ensuring sustainable development in the country. Comprehensive resource planning and management ensures both equity in investment projects and the effectiveness of the solutions planned—and is the basis for sustainable development in that it incorporates environmental considerations in policies, plans, and programs. In addition, natural resource management and conservation in Ecuador are basic elements for ensuring the development of sectors such as nature tourism that offer competitive advantages in the international market.

Comprehensive Resource Planning and Management

Ecuador's economic growth and social development depend on variables such as sectoral investments, increased productivity, governance, and macroeconomic stability. These variables become operational when environmental considerations are incorporated in comprehensive resource planning. Investments in sectors such as road infrastructure, potable water and sanitation, agriculture, health, and energy require that environmental considerations be incorporated in order to ensure the efficiency, equity, and effectiveness of such investments. Increased productivity in sectors such as industry and agriculture correlates with the adoption of clean production practices. Governance, as a mechanism for obtaining consensus and unifying efforts behind a common vision, is strengthened when decisionmaking processes are opened up to public scrutiny through procedures such as public hearings and environmental assessments. In addition, macroeconomic stability is guaranteed when there are clear and unchanging rules of the game that avoid distortions in pricing systems, internalize externalities, and promote efficiency in the use of resources.

Investments in key sectors of Ecuador's economy, such as transportation, tourism, energy, mining, health, and agriculture, require the incorporation of environmental considerations to ensure their efficiency, equity, effectiveness, and sustainability. The road transportation sector demonstrates how the problems of the majority of the rural population can be resolved through environmentally sound investments such as adapting lanes and paths for nonmotorized traffic. Options for defining these projects require including communities in the processes of design, construction, operation, and maintenance. When environmental considerations have not been incorporated in the definition or implementation of such solutions, significant problems have been created for the population and the natural environment. Experience in road projects such as La Virgen-Papallacta, Cuenca-Molleturo-Naranjal, and northeastern Esmeraldas make clear the need to incorporate environmental considerations from the outset when sectoral investments are conceived. Economically important roadways such as La Virgen-Papallacta and Cuenca-Molleturo-Naranjal were constructed in areas with geotechnical problems as well as without technical environmental specifications. Problems with landslides and blocked roads have meant spending considerable amounts on maintenance and rehabilitation, as well as on mitigating the environmental impacts on neighboring communities.

The hydrocarbons sector also illustrates the need to have a precise environmental regulatory framework to ensure that citizens are included in decisionmaking processes. In the design and implementation of large hydrocarbon exploration and transport projects, the lack of a precise regulatory framework has required those carrying them out to adopt international environmental technical specifications whose monitoring and control go beyond the scope of existing national standards. In this case, and as in other hydrocarbons projects, it is necessary to ensure that environmental considerations are fully incorporated from the moment such investments are conceptualized.

In the agriculture and fishing sectors, the destruction of natural capital and the use of deficient phytosanitary practices have also contributed to significant productivity reductions. For example, the destruction of the mangrove forest and the spread of blights have created environmental and economic problems for productive sectors such as the shrimping industry. In 1999, this industry was devastated by the white spot virus; 90,000 jobs were lost and the total losses exceeded $US600 million in 2000.

Natural Resource Management and Economic Growth

Ecuador is one of 17 "megadiverse" countries in the world thanks to its great biological and cultural wealth and diversity. The country has high species density (9.2 species/1,000 km) and high flora density, with 25,000 species of vascular plants, which is equal to 10 percent of the world's species. There are nearly 1,600 species of birds, and 12 of them are endemic. There are 301 known mammal species. In order to protect this great biological wealth, protected areas have been established in 43.6 percent of national territory. This figure is significantly higher than the average in Latin America and the Caribbean (7.4 percent). Unfortunately, the rate of deforestation is one of the highest in South America, amounting to 1.2 percent of a forest cover area of 106,000 square kilometers. The sustainable management of natural resources is essential to ensure economic growth in Ecuador. In this respect, the results of the study conducted by the Native Andean Forests Program (PROBONA) point to promoting the management of conflicts in soil usage through systematic efforts to guarantee the sustainable use of resources (Henninger and Hammond 2002). The national biodiversity strategy prepared by the Ministry of the Environment indicates that national agriculture and ecotourism are based on the existence of a high level of biodiversity.

Population groups, including many indigenous peoples and nationalities, base their livelihood on the use of natural biological riches. Biodiversity can be the basis of food security, particularly for the rural population. Deforestation and the destruction of products associated with the forest help to exacerbate the conditions of poverty in which such groups live. The high rate at which the forest cover is being destroyed limits opportunities for reducing poverty and for raising the living standards of population groups with ancestral cultures. It would be advisable to ensure that efforts to consolidate the system of protected areas are directed toward ensuring the livelihood and raising the living standard of these groups as well as of the majority of the rural population.

Ecuador's economy has been strengthened, among other things, by the generation of foreign exchange from tourism in natural areas. For example, the Galapagos Islands contribute about $US100 million per year to the Ecuadoran economy. The potential for increasing employment and generating greater opportunities for growth based on tourism in natural areas is yet to be developed in areas such as the Andean plateaus and the Amazon area in eastern Ecuador.

In areas with high tourism potential such as the Galapagos and protected areas in the Amazon, deforestation and over-utilization of natural capital can affect the incomes of the poor. In such cases, it is essential to guarantee investments in conservation or in the eradication of foreign species, so that natural capital is preserved.

In addition, a series of actions must be taken to confront global environmental issues such as climate change, the destruction of the ozone layer, and the preservation of biodiversity. The international community's high level of interest in resolving these problems justifies fully using the financial resources and assistance of the international community while following the guidelines of national authorities. The limited resources available locally should be allocated to dealing with the priority environmental problems identified earlier. With regard to the preservation of biodiversity, international funds should supplement local efforts to manage protected areas for the sustainable management of watersheds, flood protection, and promotion of ecotourism.

In terms of environmental management policy (see Box 1), the preference for actions and investments to preserve protected areas and biodiversity is clear in the actions financed by international bodies and multilateral financing agencies.[2]

---

2. To support the preservation of biodiversity in Ecuador, the Global Environmental Facility (GEF) is financing the Comprehensive Program for the Control of Species Introduced in the Galapagos as well as the formulation of the National Biodiversity Strategy, while the United Nations Fund is providing cooperation for the preservation of biodiversity in the Galapagos. The European Union financed the PETRAMAZ project with emphasis on the utilization and conservation of the Amazon region, as well as the identification of economic potential in the sustainable use of natural resources in the Amazon. The United States Agency for International Development (USAID) is providing support for the Sustainable Management of Biological Resources project in Esmeraldas. Other bilateral partners, principally the Netherlands, Switzerland, Germany, and Spain, have allocated resources for projects for the conservation of native forests, management of protected areas, management of watersheds, and pilot sustainable development programs. The IDB has granted loans to the government for the conservation and utilization of biodiversity in

Box 1. Environmental Policy and Management

The National Constitution enacted in 1998 establishes that the state must recognize and guarantee the people's right to live in a healthy, ecologically balanced, and pollution-free environment. The Constitution also establishes that the state must defend the country's natural and cultural heritage and protect the environment. The mandate to defend the natural heritage has taken precedence over other mandates. Since 2000, the Ministry of the Environment has had an Environmental Strategy for the Sustainable Development of Ecuador. This strategy emphasizes the preservation of fragile ecosystems, the consolidation of a system of protected areas, and the conservation of biodiversity. Regarding this last subject, the Ministry of the Environment developed and established the National Biodiversity Strategy in 2001.

The environmental policy that Ecuador has designed and implemented in the last two decades has given preference to natural resource conservation and management programs because specialized governmental agencies, particularly the Ministry of the Environment, are dependent on the financial and technical support of the international community. In recent years, governmental efforts to formulate policy have been directed to preparing the Draft Biodiversity Law and the Draft Forest Development Law.

To balance actions relating to poverty and environmental management with actions to preserve protected areas and biodiversity, a policy must be developed that revolves around two basic elements: environmental regulation and investment. Environmental regulation includes developing command and control standards, economic instruments, land management and soil use zoning, administrative procedures, and legal mechanisms. The priority for investment programs would be to strengthen the government's regulatory ability and to prevent disasters. Financing of investment in activities such as consolidating the system of protected areas, research on and protection of biodiversity, emissions control, climate change, and other global problems must be based on international support and assistance.

the Galapagos and the Amazon, as well as for the conservation and management of coastal resources. The World Bank (through the PATRA project) granted a loan to the government in 1996 to support institutional strengthening and environmental management in the Amazon and in the coastal region. The Bank is also the executing agency for the "National System of Protected Areas in Ecuador" Project, financed by the GEF. The principal objective of this project is to ensure the preservation of the country's biodiversity for sustainable development by strengthening the National System of Protected Areas.

D. Recommendations

The increase in poverty among the Ecuadoran population associated with the growing environmental deterioration requires active and effective state intervention, supported by efficient environmental action by civil society and the private sector. The conditions causing poverty in Ecuador, as noted above, are rooted in the environmental problems of pollution and natural disasters. In this sense, the intervention priorities of environmental policy should be directed to coping with critical problems. By way of conclusion, this section presents intervention priorities and recommends environmental regulation and intervention actions designed to deal with the critical problems that have been identified.

In developing its environmental policy, the state can basically intervene in two ways—environmental regulation and environmental management and investment. Environmental regulation includes various tools, notably economic instruments, direct regulation, and administrative procedures. Environmental management and investment include the management of state assets on the one hand, and on the other, environmental investment in sectors that are facing the environmental conditions associated with poverty in Ecuador.

As discussed earlier, Ecuador's poverty is directly related to critical environmental problems, particularly the problems of pollution, which are associated with morbidity and mortality among the population, and the effects of natural disasters. These problems must be given the highest priority and attention in the short and medium terms. The incorporation of environmental considerations in the private sector also merits special attention. Local investment in the preservation of natural resources is justified to the extent that such resources generate conditions for growth in economic sectors such as ecotourism in which Ecuador has clear competitive advantages.

The allocation of scarce resources to environmental objectives not directly related to the eradication of poverty in Ecuador should be relegated to a secondary level. In this sense, investments in activities that aim to minimize the creation of global environmental problems should be financed exclusively through the use of international donations, nonreimbursable transfers, support, and assistance.

Environmental Regulation

The options for environmental regulation tools include command and control standards, economic instruments, administrative procedures, reconciliation and arbitration systems, and legal instruments. Among these options, the development and strengthening of command and control regulations merit special attention, particularly regulations on land management and land use zoning. The application, control, and monitoring of these regulations is an urgent matter. Priority must be given to developing regulations to ensure land management planning in areas that are vulnerable to natural disasters, particularly landslides, floods, or earthquakes. The basic variable for land management, particularly in the coastal provinces, is drainage. The definition of high water levels with periods of return beyond two years requires special emphasis. It is essential to establish resettlement programs for all settlements located on the floodplains. This resettlement should be voluntary, as involuntary resettlement are generally more costly and lead to conflict. Similarly, land management plans must ensure the relocation of settlements that are located in areas close to geological faults or areas subject to landslides.

In December 2002, the national government issued Executive Decrees 3399 and 3516, with secondary environmental legislation. These Executive Decrees established the provisions for the Single Environmental Management System (SUMA), pollution rates, water and air quality control, hazardous waste management, and final disposal of solid wastes. The instrument par excellence among the administrative procedures is the Environmental Impact Assessment. Priority must be given to implementing the recent executive decrees that provide regulations for these environmental assessments. In the context of the SUMA, the Ministry of the Environment, pursuant to the regulations issued, has the central role in certifying environmental impact assessments, licensing, supervision, and monitoring of the economy's various sectors.

Among environmental regulation options, the new regulations develop the use of economic instruments, particularly the imposition of taxes for the use of natural resources or the degradation of the environment. These taxes are established as incentives for the placement of buildings, the efficient use of resources, and clean production. In addition, the use of economic instruments may become a source of significant tax revenues. It is advisable to take advantage of Quito's recent experience with the collection of taxes for water management and conservation programs and the establishment of funds to finance sanitation projects. The use of levies or taxes for the use or licensing of water is a mechanism that guarantees the resolution of conflicts over the use of water resources. Setting up and imposing these taxes is particularly important in the country's Andean area and in the agricultural area of the coastal provinces. It is similarly advisable to apply pollution taxes on pathogenic, toxic, inflammable, reactive, corrosive, and radioactive products and wastes.

With respect to legal instruments and arbitration and conciliation instruments, Executive Decrees 3399 and 3516 should be used to strengthen social control mechanisms such as public hearings, the right to request and access public information, and public action.

Strategic environmental assessment instruments are used internationally to define the priorities for sectoral or regional environmental regulations. It would be advisable to develop assessments of this type for the most important sectors of the Ecuadoran economy—hydrocarbons and energy, agriculture, potable water and sanitation, and transportation. The implementation of these sectoral environmental assessments could be consolidated as a regular policy for all basic sectors of the national economy.

At the institutional level, it is essential to define mechanisms for coordinating actions to prevent disasters and minimize vulnerability to them. The Ministry of the

Environment and the MIVI could take a more active role in these measures. The supervision and monitoring of compliance with soil use regulations and building codes such as those that relate to earthquake tolerances should be given greater importance. In addition, based on the recommendation of Benavides and Solberg (2003), it would be advisable to establish incentives in public works design, construction, concession, operation, and/or maintenance contracts in order to ensure high quality and to incorporate technical environmental specifications that minimize the vulnerability of public infrastructure.

Figure 3. Soil Use Conflicts

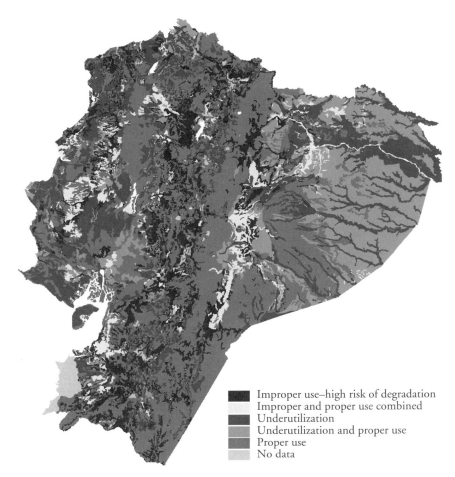

Improper use–high risk of degradation
Improper and proper use combined
Underutilization
Underutilization and proper use
Proper use
No data

Source: Henninger and Hammond (2002).

Environmental Investment

Strategic environmental assessment instruments are also used internationally to determine the priorities for environmental investment in different sectors. Developing these analyses will make it possible to establish environmental investment priorities in sectors such as drinking water and sanitation, transportation, health, agriculture, industry, urban development, and tourism. To ensure that the analyses use reliable information, investments must be made in setting up an environmental information system that includes environmental quality monitoring systems as well as soil use monitoring systems. The air quality monitoring systems in Quito should be completed and started up, as should air and water quality monitoring systems around the country's most important urban and industrial centers.

Investment is urgently need in structural and nonstructural damage prevention measures in order to reduce rural vulnerability to natural disasters. Structural measures include the resettlement of populations located on the floodplains, flood control projects, the use of wetlands to alleviate rising waters, and erosion control and bank stabilization projects. Nonstructural measures include soil use zoning, designing programs to respond to and deal with emergencies, and equipping and preparing citizens for such events. Action is needed in the short term to strengthen and consolidate the ability of the state and communities to reduce vulnerability. Pre-investment activities in the coastal provinces involve the measurement and modeling of hydrometeorological and seismic phenomena and the design of structural and nonstructural methods in areas such as flood control.

Investment in some sectors is given priority in dealing with environmental problems that cause poverty in Ecuador. For example, the increased coverage and quality of potable water services represent priorities for action in the short term. The situation is similar in the case of the management and final disposal of solid wastes in the country's principal urban centers, including Quito. In sectors such as manufacturing and health, there is an urgent need to promote clean production programs that reduce the production of waste, particularly hazardous wastes that are pathogenic, toxic, or radioactive. Along these lines, efforts of this type that are being started up in the Clean Production Center must be given continuity and strengthened.

It is also important in other sectors to promote environmental investments, particularly those coming from the private sector. For example, environmental practices, processes, and agricultural technologies can be improved in the agricultural sector, particularly through the promotion of organic farming, integrated management of soils and pests, and sustainable harvesting technologies for crops such as coffee and cacao. In the case of such crops, the export markets favor (with better prices) products certified as "biodiversity friendly," organic, and/or fair trade. In addition, the establishment of peasant and indigenous community management areas can be promoted in buffer areas for fragile ecosystems (such as the plateaus) in order to redirect the lines of settlement that are moving toward areas of high ecological fragility. This is particularly applicable in all the plateau ecosystems in the Andean area and around the protected areas in the east.

In the electrical energy sector, it is advisable to continue promoting unconventional sources for generating electricity and managing the final demand through increased energy efficiency as is being done through PROMEC. In the transportation sector, it is advisable to extend the mass transit systems that are being used successfully in Quito to the major urban centers such as Cuenca and Guayaquil and to improve the quality of fuels. In addition, the sustainability of investments in rural roads should be supported through community participation in the maintenance of rural roads, extending the investment program being carried out in this area by the Ministry of Public Works. In the urban development sector, actions should be carried out to recover public space and promote nonmotorized transportation (using bike paths and pedestrian lanes) in urban centers such as Cuenca, Guayaquil, Cumbayá, Esmeraldas, and Quito.

The tourism sector can receive direct benefits from investments in the preservation of natural resources and ecosystems. The areas where investment in tourism seems most favorable are the Amazon piedmont, the southeast Amazon, and the protected areas in the Andean area. Investment in ecotourism in the Galapagos could focus on ensuring that tourism in the archipelago targets specialized groups that maximize the generation of foreign exchange and the sustainability and conservation of the ecosystem. Interventions in nature tourism include stimulating tourism investment in protected areas, particularly in improving services and strengthening the participation of local populations in the provision of those services; identifying the tourism potential of protected areas and other scenic resources; and establishing systems for certifying sustainable tourism activities.

Part III

Building a Quality Government That Serves All Ecuadorans and Fights against Corruption

15

The Environment and
Governance and Corruption[1]

Mitchell A. Seligson and Francesca Recanatini

Ecuador's problems with poor governance and high corruption are legendary and lead to the deficient delivery of public services. In comparison with the rest of Latin America, most of Ecuador's recent indicators reflect deterioration, particularly in terms of the quality of its regulations, participation, the rule of law, and the responsibility and effectiveness of government. Specifically, Ecuador rates as the country with the least control over corruption in Latin America. Corruption is a very serious problem in Ecuador, as clearly reported by most citizens, and it is particularly frequent in obtaining government contracts and receiving public services. The frequency of bribery varies from one service to the next, but occurs less frequently at the subnational level of government. Corruption exacerbates poverty and inequality, discourages tax collection, and reduces the resources available to society. An estimated one-third of available public funds are improperly diverted for political reasons. A program of reforms must focus on the public sector and on civil service. In general terms, a multifaceted plan of reforms focusing on three pillars is needed: strengthening existing regulations and institutions in the fight against corruption; promoting education for the population on its oversight rights regarding the work of government, with the development of mechanisms to monitor and control public spending; and improving governance in order to prevent the various forms of corruption, whether administrative or associated with specific areas such as government procurement and contracting. Three measures are suggested for the short term: the creation of a Governance Pact between the state and civil society, civil service reform, and immediate transparency in the publication of government procurement bidding and contracts via the

---

1. Mitchell A. Seligson is the Daniel H. Wallace professor of Political Science at the University of Pittsburgh and a World Bank consultant. Francesca Recanatini is an economist with the World Bank.

Internet. Supplemental measures in the medium term would be modernizing budgetary information to provide access for citizens, the media, and Congress; regulating finances and contributions to political parties in political campaigns, strictly prohibiting the use of state funds for political campaigns; and strengthening the mechanisms for the administration, control, and social auditing of sectional governments. Finally, a National Transparency Campaign, carried out at the provincial, municipal, and local levels, would be part of a new culture of governance in the country.

A. Governance in Ecuador from a Comparative International Perspective

Although the growth of democracy in Latin America is a welcome trend ,the path followed has been neither smooth nor easy. Ecuador finds itself among the countries in the region for which democratization has been a particularly formidable challenge. In recent years, Ecuador has faced political instability, with serious consequences for its economic and social development. However, the government assuming power in 2003 has numerous opportunities to make rapid progress.

For various years, the World Bank Institute has gathered indicators to measure the quality of governance.[2] The set of current international data is from the year 2000 and covers some 170 countries (see Figure 1).[3]

A key component of the indicators is "Government Effectiveness." This measures the quality of public service provided and of the bureaucracy; the fitness of public employees; the independence of public administration from political pressures; and, finally, the credibility of the government's commitment to policies (Kaufmann, Kraay, and Zoido-Lobatón 1999a. Ecuador should be compared with other South American countries through analysis of the data seen in Figure 1. Within the context of Latin America, it is clear that the quality of governmental efficacy in Ecuador does not earn a good rating. In the international context, the country falls slightly below the 28th percentile, unlike Chile, which has a rating higher than 90. In effect, only two other countries in Latin America are in the "low" range in this regard: Venezuela and Paraguay.

---

2. The aggregate indicators constructed included data from 1997 and 1998. Assuming that institutional indicators do not change too much from year to year, these indicators provide a good measure of the 1990s. However, these indicators may not capture a true institutional improvement (or unfavorable evolution) in the same decade. Kaufmann, Kraay, and Zoido-Lobatón (1999a and b).

3. The thin lines associated with each bar in Figure 1 represent the margin of error in the calculations for a confidence interval of 95 percent. For more data on measurement procedures, see Kaufmann, Kraay, and Zoido-Lobatón (1999b).

Figure 1. Government Effectiveness
(Latin America and the Caribbean Region, 2000–01)

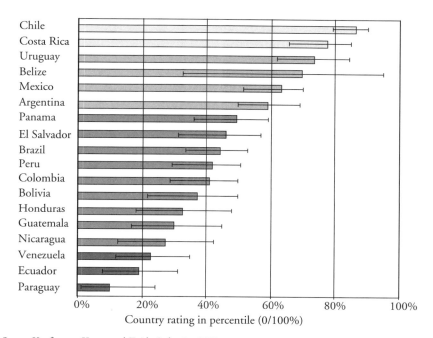

Source: Kaufmann, Kraay, and Zoido-Lobatón, 1999.

Why is governance so problematic in Ecuador? One reason is that the rule of law is very weak. Although its ranking is not as low as in the case of six other countries in the region, World Bank data indicate that Ecuador is in the lowest quartile in the world distribution of the rule of law. This can be seen in Figure 2.

The impact of limitations on the rule of law is, in turn, manifested quite concretely in high levels of corruption. As can be seen in Figure 3, the World Bank Institute's comparative data indicate that controlling corruption is a significant problem in Ecuador. In summary, Ecuador finds itself in a vicious circle of low government effectiveness and limited rule of law, both of which limit efforts to control corruption. As we will see below, all this in turn leads to a decline in investment and economic growth.

The fact that the trend of the indicators seen above has been negative is a cause for concern. As can be seen in Figure 4, which compares the measures of governance for 1997–98 with those for 2000–01, the significant challenges that Ecuador's economic and political system faced during the 1990s affected all measures of gover-

**Figure 2. The Rule of Law
(Latin America and the Caribbean Region, 2000–01)**

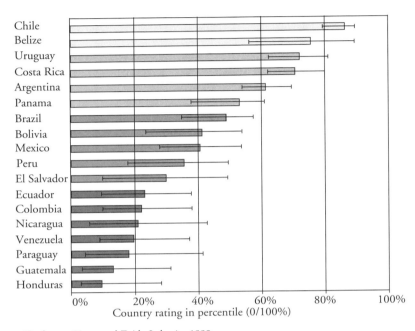

Source: Kaufmann, Kraay, and Zoido-Lobatón, 1999.

nance. In all cases, the most recent level is lower than the preceding one. It is possible that some stability may have been created in 2002, but there are still no data to corroborate this. However, the presidential campaign seems to have shown that both party elites and the general public have generally rejected the politicians of the past—whom they blame, perhaps with good reason, for the political and economic crisis of the late 1990s. It would seem that Ecuadorans want to begin from scratch.

B. Corruption and Its Impact

As noted above, the problem of corruption is very serious in Ecuador. Good governance is intimately associated with limitations on corruption. Corrupt undermine citizens' confidence in the political system. This section provides information that measures the cost of corruption and poor governance.

According to a survey conducted by the World Bank Institute in 2000, Ecuadoran households consider corruption to be a serious problem. When evaluating the

Figure 3. Control of Corruption
(Latin America and the Caribbean Region, 2000–01)

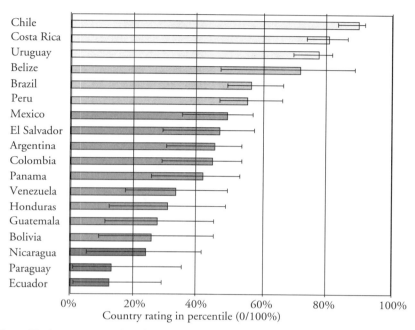

Country rating in percentile (0/100%)

Source: Kaufmann, Kraay, and Zoido-Lobatón, 1999.

seriousness of the country's problems, approximately 70 percent of those surveyed gave "corruption in the public sector" the worst rating possible. Companies also consider corruption to be the greatest obstacle to business development (see Figure 5). When rating the seriousness of a series of obstacles to business development, more than 50 percent of the companies surveyed gave the worst possible rating to corruption (as well as to the high cost of unofficial payments, inflation, crime, robbery, and unstable policies).

The Cost of Corruption

The increasing amount of data from empirical research emphasizes that poor governance and corruption reduce the standard of living and make the distribution of wealth among citizens more uneven. The channels through which corruption affects development are its prejudicial effects on the poor, negative impact on investment and growth, and negative effect on quality in and access to public services such as health and education. In this way, corruption hits companies and households hard.

Figure 4. Changes 1997–98 and 2000–01

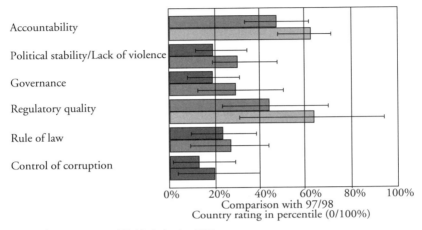

Source: Kaufmann, Kraay, and Zoido-Lobatón, 1999.

The data indicate that corruption perpetuates poverty, given that it acts as a regressive tax (see Figure 6). Households indicate that they allocate an average of 2 to 3 percent of their incomes to paying bribes in order to obtain access to public services. In the case of low-income households, the burden of corruption is heavier. On average, they spend up to 4 percent of their annual income on bribes, whereas the richest households spend less than 1.5 percent. However, Ecuador is not the only country that faces this problem. Data from surveys conducted in various countries suggest a similar scenario: corruption punishes the poorest and thus most vulnerable groups excessively, given that it acts as a regressive tax on users of public services.

There are other mechanisms through which corruption affects the well-being of poor citizens. Corruption contributes to discrimination in terms of access to public services. The survey indicates that the cost of corruption, in addition to the cost of illegal payments, is that numerous users stop asking for a service because they are unable to pay bribes.

However, individual citizens are not the only ones who are penalized by deficiencies in governance: companies also pay a high cost because of corruption. The data indicate that companies spend more in bribes and bureaucratic red tape than on security. Companies indicate that unofficial payments to public servants represent an average of 8 percent of their gross incomes. In contrast, companies indicate that they spend "only" 5 percent on bureaucratic red tape and 4 percent on security.

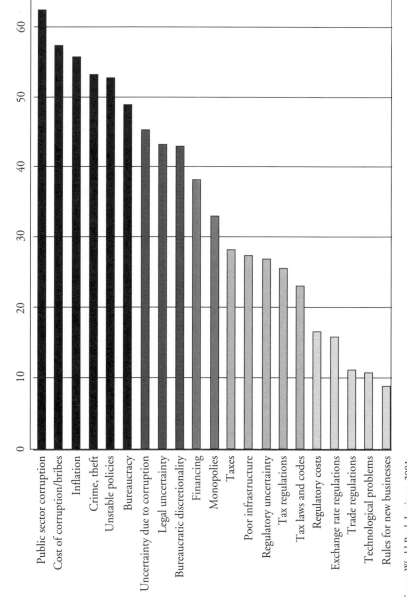

Figure 5. Opinion of Companies on Obstacles to the Development of Their Business

Source: World Bank Institute, 2001.

Figure 6. Corruption as a Regressive Tax on Users

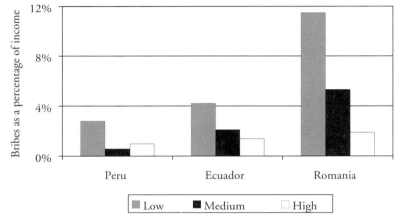

Source: World Bank Institute, 2000, 2001.

Small companies must spend more on bribes in terms of their monthly income than large companies. Microenterprises (with fewer than 10 employees) pay an average of 8 percent of their monthly income, while large companies (with more than 100 employees) pay less than 2 percent.

Nearly all companies (97 percent) that work with the public sector indicate that they must pay bribes to obtain purchase contracts. To bid successfully, they must pay an average of 15 percent of the total value of the contract.

The data indicate that corruption discourages private (particularly foreign) investment. Companies were asked whether they had ever decided not to make an investment they had already planned. The data show that companies for which the burden of bribes is highest are those that decide not to invest. In this sense, bribery frightens away investment. In particular, when the difference between local and foreign companies is analyzed, we see that foreign companies that decided not to invest in Ecuador are also those most affected by corruption. The consequences of this are particularly negative.

Corruption is widespread in public services, but some are more corrupt than others. For both households and companies, the likelihood of having to pay a bribe varies depending on the service. The data from the World Bank survey show that, of the services studied, those for which households will most likely have to pay bribes are public registry, running water, electricity, public hospitals, and public education. In the case of companies, the public services for which they will most likely have to pay bribes are customs, automobile registration, tax inspections, the traffic police, and the technical vehicle inspection agencies.[4]

The amount of the bribe varies considerably depending on the service. On average, households tend to pay relatively higher bribes to the traffic police, customs, the license department, and the national police. Each time they received a service from these institutions, they paid more than $US4. (Table 1). The average amount of bribes in public schools is $US11. Companies, on the other hand, usually pay relatively higher bribes to customs, for tax inspections, for import/export permits, and for construction permits. On each occasion, they paid more than $US40 (Table 2).

It is possible to analyze what service receives the major part of the "booty" if the frequency and amount of the bribes are taken into account. More than 80 percent of the bribes paid by households are for the traffic police, the telephone company, running water, public registry, customs, and the electrical company.[5] More than 80 percent of the bribes paid by companies are for customs, construction permits, tax inspections, the traffic police, and the national police. This means that the burden of bribes can be considerably reduced if efforts to combat corruption focus on these services from the outset.

The data from the survey conducted by the World Bank Institute in the year 2000 indicate that corruption reduces public resources considerably owing to uncollected taxes and tariffs and misappropriated public funds. On the other hand, both companies and households are willing to contribute money to eliminate corruption. More than 85 percent of the companies surveyed indicate that they would be willing to pay an additional share of their income if this would eliminate corruption. On average, they agreed to pay an additional amount equal to 9 percent of their income. Nearly 70 percent of households stated that they would be willing to pay an additional share of their income if this would eliminate corruption. They indicated that they would agree to pay an average additional amount equal to 12 percent of their income.

Corruption reduces the resources available to public institutions owing to the diversion of funds for political reasons. More than one-fourth of those who work in PetroEcuador (the national petroleum company) and in the National Land Traffic and Transportation Council indicate that public funds are misspent in these institutions. They estimated that between 40 and 50 percent of the funds available are diverted for political reasons. Overall, about 6 percent of public employees interviewed indicated that public funds are misspent in their institutions. They estimated that one-third of the available funds are diverted for political reasons.

---

4. In calculating the probability of paying bribes, the difference in the number of contacts with each public service is taken into account. For example, it is much more likely that a household will deal with a public hospital than with customs.

5. The expected amount of the bribe for each public service is calculated based on the frequency of contact, the frequency of the payment of bribes, and the amount.

**Table 1. Frequency and Amount of Bribes
(According to Citizens)**

Public services	Probability of paying a bribe (as a percentage)	Amount of bribe paid in each contact, contingent on payment of the bribe (in $US)	Frequency of payment of bribes contingent on contact (percentage that reports bribe)	Percentage of households with some contact
Public registry (identity document, passport)	10.5	2.72	11 (25)	42.4
Installation of running water	7.8	2.42	6 (14)	54.1
Electrical company	6.6	1.90	5 (12)	100.0
Public hospitals	5.1	2.32	11 (19)	99.7
Public educational institutions	4.9	1.74	5 (15)	32.6
National police	4.7	4.37	18 (39)	12.5
Telephone company	4.2	3.72	3 (12)	99.5
Traffic police	3.0	11.50	26 (36)	8.3
Customs	2.4	5.14	30 (50)	4.7
Tax collection offices	2.0	2.31	5 (10)	19.6
Department of drivers' licenses, permits, and so on	1.9	4.48	8 (19)	9.6
Trash collection	1.2	1.03	2 (5)	99.3
Offices that grant construction permits	0.7	3.68	6 (17)	3.9
Post offices	0.3	0.34	2 (4)	99.8
Social Security	0.3	2.87	1 (4)	99.5

Source: World Bank Institute survey conducted in 2000.

The data also reveal the close relationship between bribes and poor service quality. Poor service quality (according to the users' evaluation) is associated with the highest bribes (according to households and companies). The usual argument is that bribes help to speed up the delivery of public services or even increase the quality of the services provided. The data from Ecuador prove that, on average, the higher number of bribes does not result in better quality service provision. The opposite is very much the case: poor service quality and bribery go hand in hand. Households rate customs, the traffic police, the national police, and public registry as being extremely deficient in terms of both service quality and bribes. Similarly, companies give poor ratings to the traffic police, the national police, running water installation, border crossings, and construction authorities both in terms of service quality and corruption. In contrast, they gave good grades to fire inspection, property registry, and company registry.

Table 2. Frequency and Amount of Bribes (According to Companies)

Public services	Probability of paying a bribe (as a percentage)	Amount of bribe paid in each contact, contingent on payment of the bribe (in $US)	Frequency of payment of bribes contingent on contact (percentage that reports bribe)	Percentage of households with some contact
Customs crossing	11.3	83.06	19 (44)	34.3
Automobile registration	11.3	31.69	24 (42)	30.8
Tax inspections	10.0	66.08	16 (36)	42.2
Traffic police	6.1	22.88	46 (61)	11.3
Technical vehicle inspection	5.8	13.95	19 (35)	18.9
Registry of companies	4.8	29.90	8 (22)	26.4
Import/export permits	3.9	58.61	11 (31)	15.9
National police	3.9	24.74	33 (55)	8.6
Construction permits	3.7	49.67	22 (52)	9.2
Installation of electricity	3.7	14.91	18 (33)	12.3
Installation of running water	3.6	18.57	20 (45)	11.9
Health inspections	3.1	26.11	16 (31)	16.9
Property registry	2.8	31.99	6 (16)	17.8
Construction licenses	1.2	32.81	12 (27)	4.9
Fire inspections	1.0	17.89	11 (21)	7.7
Public credit	0.9	9.11	8 (35)	3.9

Source: World Bank Institute survey conducted in 2000.

It is no surprise that Ecuadorans perceive public corruption to be widespread. Taking the country as a whole as the basis, three-quarters of the population believe that corruption is very common or somewhat common (see Figure 7). The answer to this question varies considerably depending on the region. As perception moves on a scale from 0 to 100, we see that in Quito, the seat of the national government, the perception is significantly higher than in other areas of the country (see Figure 8).

By way of comparison, Ecuador's indicator is higher than that of any other country for which there are directly comparable data, with the exception of Paraguay. This means that national perception of the magnitude of corruption is higher in Ecuador than in the other Latin American countries, except for Paraguay.

In the survey, Ecuadorans had to rate a large variety of institutions based on a scale ranging from extremely corrupt (rating: 1) to extremely honest (rating: 10). Figure 9 shows the results. Although it may not be surprising, it is disturbing that members of Congress, ministers, and party leaders receive the lowest ratings. Nonetheless, it is to be noted that mayors obtain a considerably better grade. These findings have direct effects on any effort carried out in the fight against corruption.

Figure 7. How Common Is Payment of Bribes to Public Employees?

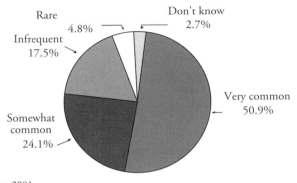

Source: Seligson, 2001.

Figure 8. How Common Is Corruption?
(by region)

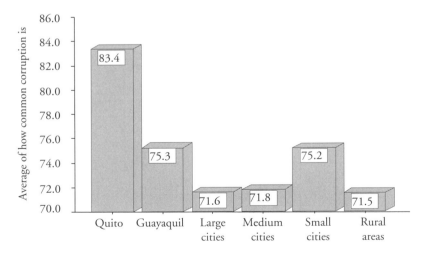

Source: Seligson, 2001.

Figure 9. Perception of Honesty

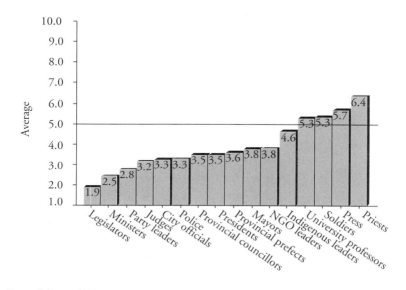

Source: Seligson, 2001.

Focusing the analysis directly on the level of corruption as such, rather than on perceived corruption, the surveyors asked the respondents about their experiences with corruption in the 12 months prior to the interview (see Figure 10). The survey covered a wide range of situations, including direct and personal experience and indirect experience, that is, seeing or hearing about corrupt acts. The most commonly experienced corrupt act is seeing a policeman ask for a bribe. More than one-third had this experience in the 12 months prior to the survey. Having seen a bribe paid to a civil servant ranks second. Sadly, the level is also high for some type of improper payment in the country's public education system: Nearly half of all those surveyed had a child in school in the year prior to the survey and 41.1 percent of these had experienced bribery. As seen in the figure, excluding those who had no children in school, 19 percent of Ecuadorans encountered corruption in this setting.[6] According to the survey, the fourth most frequent form of corruption occurs in hospitals or health clinics. Of those surveyed, 17 percent had an experience with

---

6. However, this figure should be interpreted carefully. As indicated above, the question asked about "payments exceeding those required by law." Schools may ask parents for

Figure 10. Forms of Corruption

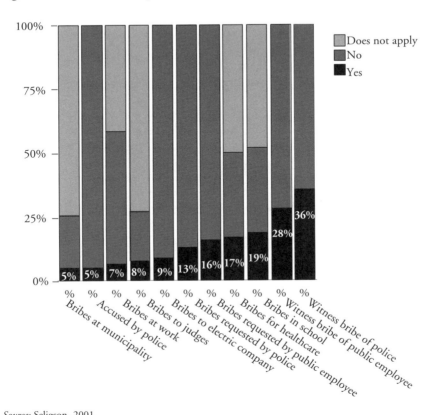

Source: Seligson, 2001.

bribery in these settings. Once again, not everyone used the health services. In effect, only 45 percent of those surveyed used the health services in the year before the survey, but 35 percent of these had to make some kind of improper payment. The remaining types of corruption are shown in the figure.

How do these levels of experience with corruption compare with those in other countries? The results of the World Bank indicators on controlling corruption noted at the beginning of this report put Ecuador almost at the end of the list for Latin America. Figure 11 shows survey results on experience with corruption, and we see that they are broadly consistent with the World Bank's results.

---

money to pay for books or other educational materials and actually use the money for that purpose. Thus, although these payments may not be required by law, they are not necessarily a clear case of corruption either.

Figure 11. Experience with Corruption

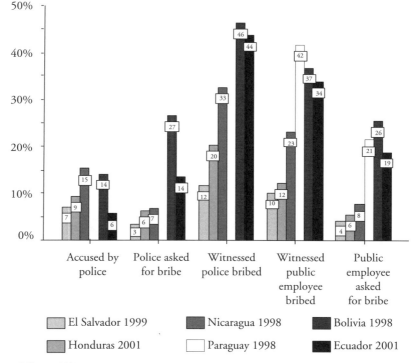

Source: Seligson, 2001.

A general index of victimization by corruption has been created by recording direct and personal experiences with corruption, setting aside observed or second-hand accounts. The index includes bribes paid to the police, to public and municipal employees, bribes at work, in the courts, in the public health services, in the schools, and bribes paid to obtain electrical service. The results show that 50 percent of Ecuadorans have had at least one experience of corruption in the 12 months preceding the survey. In addition, we see that one out of every four Ecuadorans has been the victim of a corrupt act, and that 25 percent have been the victim of more than one. In other words, on average Ecuadorans experienced about one act of corruption in the year prior to the survey.

Perhaps the most important reason for studying corruption is its potential influence on long-term democratic stability. Recent studies conducted in various Latin American countries have shown empirically that citizens who have been victims of corruption support their political systems less than those who have not (Seligson 2001, 2002). These findings come from studies conducted in Bolivia, El Salvador, Honduras, Nicaragua, and Paraguay. When the measure of support for the system (presented earlier in this work) is used as the dependent variable, the impact of corruption is very clear, as can be seen in Figure 12. The national survey showed that citizens who had not been the victim of corrupt acts during the preceding year were above average in support for the system, but the higher the number of corrupt acts experienced by the person surveyed, the more his or her support for the system was reduced.[7] The results do not vary when controls for gender, age, education, income, marital status, and city size are introduced. In addition, the effects of political parties were analyzed to check whether official party voters were less likely to report being victimized by corruption. No such effect was found. Corruption in Ecuador is clearly a matter of importance, as in other countries in the region.

Figure 12. The Impact of Being Victimized by Corruption (on support for the system)

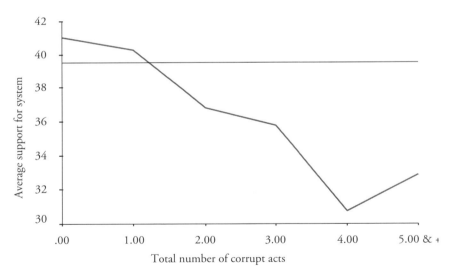

Source: Seligson, 2001.

---

7. The slight increase at the highest levels is statistically insignificant but could reflect the political power of the country's wealthiest groups and their ability to avoid the usual forms of bribery.

C. Local Government and Decentralization

During most of its history, Ecuador has been a highly centralized country. Local governments have been, and continue to be, highly dependent on transfers from the national government because of their limited ability to generate their own revenues. In recent years, the government decided to increase decentralization. As the National Modernization Council (CONAM) has declared, the Political Constitution of the Republic of Ecuador provides that public administration be organized and developed in a decentralized way, and that the central government will gradually transfer its functions, powers, jurisdiction, responsibilities, and resources to independent organizations or other regional organizations.

The data from the University of Pittsburgh/Cedatos-Gallup survey show what citizens consider to be the most serious problems of municipal governments at present. The results shown in Table 3 reveal some variation between regions. Road maintenance is an important problem throughout the country, but it seems much more serious in the rural highlands region. In contrast, problems relating to security and crime are common in urban areas but not in rural areas. We also see that deficient municipal administration is mentioned more frequently by citizens in the urban highlands area. In no region of the country are local corruption, the environment, or taxes considered important municipal problems. This does not mean that Ecuadorans are unconcerned about these problems (in the national context, for example, corruption is mentioned frequently), but rather that those surveyed do not consider these problems to be the most serious in the context of local government.

Problems require solutions. To what extent are Ecuadorans satisfied with the solutions provided by their local governments? Figure 13 shows the results of this question for the entire country.

Figure 14 shows the regional variation within Ecuador. We note that satisfaction is much higher in Guayaquil than in other regions of the country.

Participation is the essence of democracy, and nearly all programs that seek to strengthen local governments include citizen participation as a key mechanism for achieving their objective. As shown in Figure 15, Ecuador is at the very bottom of the list of Latin American countries in this regard.

Within Ecuador, urbanization and geographic location affect participation in municipal meetings. The results reveal a notable variation: participation is three times as high in small cities and rural areas than in Quito.

Ecuadorans recognize different levels of government, including local and national. Do they look at all levels the same way, as "just government"? It is clear they do not. Those surveyed were asked what level of government they considered more effective in resolving local problems. The question was, "In your opinion, which has provided the best response to help resolve problems in your community or neighborhood—the national government, Congress, or the municipality?" Figure 16 shows the results. Citizens responded overwhelmingly that the municipal government did best at resolving local problems.

Table 3. The Most Serious Problem Faced by the Municipality (by Region)

| | STRATUM | | | | Region | | |
	Urban coast	Rural coast	Urban highlands	Rural highlands	North-east	South-east	Total
In your opinion, what is the problem in your municipality?							
Lack of water	10.5%	14.9%	7.2%	17.8%	11.9%	10.6%	10.8%
Road maintenance	14.0%	13.7%	13.1%	20.2%	7.1%	10.6%	14.3%
Lack of security, crime	12.0%	8.1%	20.8%	5.5%	4.8%	2.1%	13.4%
Cleaning of public spaces	7.1%	2.0%	2.1%	.3%		2.1%	3.8%
Lack of services	12.5%	14.1%	7.4%	14.7%	11.9%	10.6%	11.2%
The economic situation	11.2%	8.1%	8.6%	11.7%	19.0%	23.4%	10.5%
Lack of funds	8.0%	18.1%	8.9%	9.8%	16.7%	19.1%	9.9%
Poor administration	11.3%	12.1%	21.1%	13.5%	14.3%	12.8%	15.0%
Corruption	1.4%	1.6%	2.4%	1.8%	2.4%	4.3%	1.9%
Lack of machinery and equipment	1.8%		.6%	2.8%	2.4%		1.3%
High taxes	.0%	.4%		.3%	2.4%		.2%
Abuse of mayor's power	.7%		.7%				.5%
Others	.4%		.1%	.3%			.2%
Total	1.7%	.8%	2.4%	.9%	2.4%	2.1%	1.8%
Total	100.0%	100.0%	100.0%	100.0%	100.0%	100.0%	100.0%

Source: University of Pittsburgh/Cedatos-Gallup.

Figure 13. Evaluation of Municipal Services

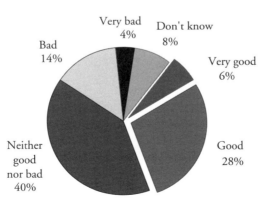

Source: University of Pittsburgh/Cedatos-Gallup.

Figure 14. Satisfaction with Municipal Services and Locality

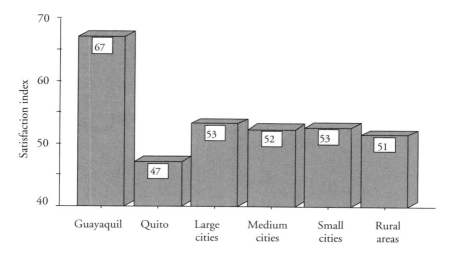

Source: Seligson, 2001.

Figure 15. Comparative Attendance at Municipal Meetings and Open Town Councils

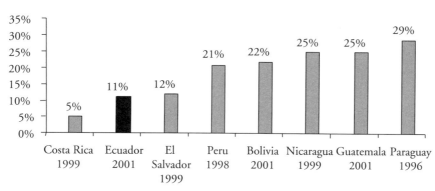

Source: Seligson, 2001.

**Figure 16. Who Responds Better to Local Problems
(by locality)**

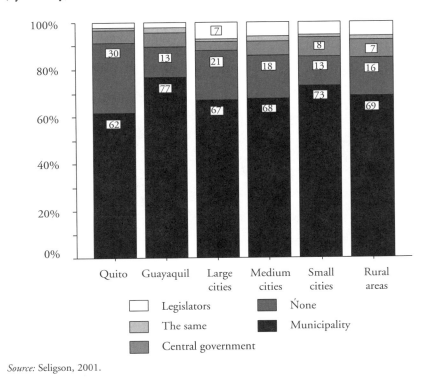

Source: Seligson, 2001.

Local governments in Ecuador face the problem of budgets that are inadequate for carrying out their numerous responsibilities. Those surveyed were asked whether they were willing to pay more taxes to obtain better services. Figure 17 shows that, in Ecuador, the willingness to pay more local taxes is low.

D. Institutional Vulnerability

This section is based on diagnostic work done by the World Bank Institute in 2000 and seeks to provide an initial exposition of the underlying institutional factors that could explain why corrupt behaviors and practices are concentrated in some institutions and not in others. The data from that survey identify the following 10 factors as most important for obtaining good performance and integrity indicators.

**Figure 17. Willingness to Pay More Municipal Taxes:
International Comparison**

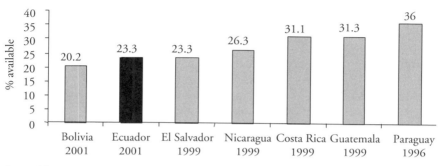

Source: Seligson, 2001.

- Procedures manuals that detail the duties and responsibilities of public employees—and that are available to personnel and effectively utilized in their training;
- Policies, guidelines, and regulations on budget management that are set down in writing;
- Suitable personnel not subject to constant changes in administration and who do not fear imminent replacement;
- Standards that allow precise measurement of performance that are implemented and monitored;
- Policies, guidelines, and regulations regarding the provision of services that leave little room for arbitrary or discretionary behaviors on the part of public employees;
- Personnel management practices that reward merit, professionalism, and performance;
- Mechanisms for reporting corruption that are accessible to all and give the accuser credible and effective protection;
- Information channels among organizations that promote good understanding and coordination of functions;
- Motivated civil servants who know their duties and responsibilities, the objectives and strategies of the organizations where they work, and who truly participate in decisionmaking processes; and
- A group of reformist leaders who have the support of upper management.

Another important accountability mechanism is existing systems for reporting corruption. The data indicate that mechanisms for reporting corruption, if effective and independent, can be effective tools for reducing corruption. In effect, in institutions with high grades for integrity, reporting corruption is less discouraged. The data also indicate that existing reporting mechanisms are generally unknown and extremely ineffective. More than half of the public employees interviewed (60 percent) do not know how to report corruption. This is equally true for most of the households interviewed (90 percent). Those who do know how to report corruption feel that the system for doing so is quite ineffective. Public employees fail to make reports primarily for fear of the consequences. This suggests that, at present, integrity is not an important value in the internal culture of government organizations and that there are few procedures for protecting those who make reports. The second most frequently provided reason is a lack of confidence that the report will actually be investigated and used to curb corruption.

E. Recommendations

The data indicate that Ecuador is facing an enormous challenge of governance. This chapter seeks to highlight the most serious governance problems that the new government must face. The country's central problem is the lack of credibility in key institutions of the central government. These problems are serious not only in absolute terms but also in the general context of Latin America, a region that also suffers from problems of governance. Furthermore, the problems have been growing, which is even more disturbing. In the last election, the citizens' rejection of the traditional parties and the acceptance of new faces is a clear signal that people are tired of the old and want to start anew. Corruption, as shown above, is also a very serious problem in Ecuador. Households and companies indicate that corruption is among the most important social challenges faced by the country and one of the greatest obstacles to business development.

The study also points directly to steps that must be taken to confront these issues. It has already been pointed out that the high level of corruption in daily life is a significant cause of the central government's problems with credibility and legitimacy. Finally, it has been shown that the population has more confidence in local institutions and that this confidence can be a starting point. Therefore, it seems necessary to implement three key measures.

First, the government should make its position against corruption very clear from the outset, which means a broad alliance in a National Governance Pact. Then, ministers must be selected from among public figures of indisputable honesty. These officials must meet the most rigorous criteria so that they do not even have the appearance of being corrupt. Third, going from the short to the medium term, explicit steps must be taken against corruption such as civil service reform to create incentives for honest administration and reporting of corrupt practices. Fourth, Ecuador must devote significant attention to strengthening local governments by giving them control and responsibility. Other policy recommendations will be explained in greater detail in the sections that follow.

The Climate for Reforms

It is easier to design an anticorruption strategy when the levels of resistance likely to be encountered are fully understood. Both surveys suggest that there is a high level of support for many types of reform. Companies and households tend to support the vigorous implementation of anticorruption laws, transparency measures, and strengthening the efficiency of public administration. However, the most notable factor is the overwhelming support for numerous types of reforms expressed by public employees.

The time has come to carry out an anticorruption campaign. The data suggest that although some institutions clearly benefit from the status quo, others are in favor of implementing reforms intended to improve governance and reduce corruption. The Office of the President is in a good position to head up efforts in the fight against corruption. The institutions in which the impulse toward reform is strongest can be turned into useful and powerful allies in the fight against corruption. In general, public employees believe that a public campaign can be an effective step in reducing corruption if it is accompanied by fundamental public sector reforms.

Openness, Transparency, and Accountability in Society

Transparency in government is synonymous with openness. In order to create transparency, the government must give the public (civil society organizations, communications media, or other interested parties) sufficient information about government activities so that the public can act as an effective control on abuses committed by government and public employees. Many countries have promulgated freedom of information laws that require their governments to provide information to the public unless there is a valid reason for keeping the information secret (such as a threat to national security). It is essential to establish clear guidelines for determining when information must be kept secret and to make the necessary investments to train public employees (see Edes 2000).

In a more general way, openness should not be limited to providing information. Civil society and the communications media could be effective allies of the state in working to reduce corruption and promote efficient government. A proactive approach that encourages vigilance in civil society and the media with respect to issues such as large-scale privatization or significant public bidding for contracts will be the most effective approach to creating true transparency and openness in government and reducing corruption.

Another possible reform pointed to by these studies is to increase transparency and vigilance with respect to public life. Many of the specific reforms in a particular government agency that were identified in the plan are aimed at promoting more transparent administrative practices in public life. Another recently popularized technique in Latin America is the scoring cards of public institutions, using surveys to regularly grade their performance and measure their perceived progress in different areas of governance.

Even though there is strong support for new laws regulating contributions to political parties and political elections, in many countries it is a complicated task to separate political interests from economic interests and at the same time maintain a dialogue between the private sector and the state. Although no political system can claim that it has been able to fully resolve this difficult question, the principle of transparency is certainly an essential first step in the right direction. Requiring transparency in the financing of political parties and their campaigns reveals the explicit and implicit links between politicians and the interests that support them. The practice of mandating the preparation and publication of detailed reports on the finances of all political organizations and identifying contributors and beneficiaries gives civil society, the media, and the general public tools that allow them to identify the sources of state capture. The survey results suggest that Ecuador is prepared for reforms of this type.

Prohibiting the use of state resources (funds, postal services, automobiles, and so on) for political purposes and generating public sector neutrality help to ensure that public employees serve the interests of society rather than the interests of politicians or some business in particular. Other measures include limiting the amount of money that can be spent in political campaigns, providing public financing, and prohibiting certain types of entities from making contributions to political campaigns.

Imperatives for Public Administration

Improved employee hiring practices and merit-based promotions can strengthen the ability of public agencies to provide quality services. The data show that the clarity with which staffing decisions are explained correlate closely to corruption. The dissemination of personnel management procedures and adherence to these procedures must be considered an imperative in combating corruption and not simply a form of good public administration. Similarly, insulating public employees from political changes will help to limit the scope of state capture.

The surveys also provide an important rationale for clarifying and broadly publicizing the rules and procedures of internal administration in general. State agencies in which the rules and procedures are clear, well supervised, and do not create excessive bureaucracy show the lowest levels of corruption.

Although establishing a meritocracy and strengthening the rules of internal administration were the measures that gained most support among public employees, there were other reforms in public administration that also received notable support and should be implemented immediately. Strengthening budget management systems, ensuring that public employees have the information they need to do their work, and providing a strong sense of mission and direction to the client are measures that will surely promote the development of a professional and honest public sector.

Corruption seems to be concentrated in high-revenue areas such as the customs service and the national petroleum company, in internal oversight areas such as the General Comptroller's Office, and Congress. However, the head of the country, the Presidency, and the institutions most recently reformed, such as the Internal Revenue Service, seem to be most free of corruption. In fact, the action plan that the government of Ecuador developed in 1999 included improved performance in the customs service and in PetroEcuador among its major objectives. However, data from the survey conducted by the World Bank Institute in the year 2000 once again underline the need to focus reforms on these two areas. Internal oversight mechanisms were the second focus area targeted by the plan. The 2000 survey and Ecuador's recent experience indicate that it is important to further strengthen these mechanisms.

In terms of the provision of public services and the administration of public resources, it is important to evaluate the actual impact that resources allocated to services have on citizens. This facet has not been explored as yet and should be studied in depth in order to ensure efficiency in the use and allocation of public resources.

A Broad and Inclusive Approach

The results presented in this chapter highlight the fact that corruption is not reduced simply through strong law enforcement, but rather through direct incentives given to public employees, companies, and households. Many reforms that are important in and of themselves (regulatory reforms, development of public administration, health sector reforms, and openness in government, to mention only a few) can also be considered components of an anticorruption campaign.

Although the process of developing and implementing an anticorruption strategy depends on the policies and priorities of each individual country (there is no single recipe for success), lasting efforts generally have two traits in common. First, the strategies recognize that the task of reducing corruption entails not only strict enforcement of regulations, but also implementation of social changes and improvements in public sector governance. Various countries, Honduras and Slovakia among them, have adopted variants of the tridirectional strategy of enforcing anticorruption statutes, educating the public on what rights they have when dealing with the public sector and on the damage done by corruption, and preventing corruption through improved governance in the public sector.

Second, durable anticorruption strategies follow the inclusive approach. Given that reducing corruption goes beyond enforcing the law, a broad approach to this problem must be accompanied by collaboration and participation in decisionmaking on the part of a broad spectrum of governmental and nongovernmental leaders. A high-level facilitating council, supported by a professional secretariat, can help bring together representatives from both central and local government agencies to develop specific action plans to implement the anticorruption strategy. Through the explicit inclusion of representatives outside government, facilitating councils can create greater credibility and at the same time add an important ally for reducing corruption.

Broad support for and coordination of the principles of an anticorruption strategy that includes prevention, education, and law enforcement are extremely important first steps. However, the implementation of that strategy may be an enormous challenge. In order to ensure progress, detailed actions plans for reducing corruption and improving the quality of the entire public sector are required, followed by strict oversight of their implementation. When no progress is made, external oversight creates accountability, but only if action plans are formal and public.

The climate in Ecuador is favorable for reform because broad support already exists among the three groups surveyed for many types of reforms that can help to reduce both state capture and administrative corruption, and because rigorous sanctions exist for violators. As the need to act and the support of the population are both clear, the key now is to capitalize on the growing momentum by developing and implementing a broad-based action plan. This plan should reflect the ideas of people both inside and outside of government and should not only consider aspects related to enforcing the law but prevention as well. Progress will be made only with a direct attack on the institutional weaknesses that encourage corruption.

Policy Matrix

Problems	Policy measures		Progress indicators	Objectives/goals
	Short term (to June 2003)	Medium term (2003–07)		
Lack of confidence in central government institutions.	1. Selection of ministers with indisputable record of honesty. 2. Virtual publication of all government procurement.	Creation of vigorous national campaign in favor of transparency, accompanied by incentives for reporting corrupt practices.		
Lack of confidence in central government institutions.	1. Signing of a Governance Pact between government and civil society to reach consensus on anticorruption strategy. 2. Design and implementation of a permanent program of scoring cards filled out by the public to rate the performance of Ecuador's institutions.	1. Conversion of Pact into permanent commission that can manage the protransparency campaign 2. Consolidation of Scoring Cards program. 3. Discussion of strategy in national and regional workshops.	1. Creation of Governance and Transparency Commission. 2. Results of institutional ratings exercise and definition of program goals. 3. National and regional workshops.	Joint development (government and civil society) of an anticorruption strategy.
High levels of corruption in daily life.		Strengthening local governments and the courts. Civil service reform.		

Annex
Governance in Ecuador:
Citizens and Public Employees Give Their Opinions

The preceding data provide a good overview of the quality of governance in Ecuador in international terms and suggest the existence of some serious problems. However, these data do not provide information on the specific dimensions of governance or on measures that could be taken to improve Ecuador's situation.[8] The intent is to fill in this gap through surveys, including the largest survey ever conducted in Ecuador, which investigated citizens' opinions regarding good governance (Seligson, Grijalva, and Córdova 2002), and a series of surveys conducted by the World Bank on corruption (World Bank Institute 2000). These surveys provided detailed information on how Ecuadorans evaluate the operation of their political system, corruption and its impact and costs, and the governance situation at the subnational level.[9]

Legitimacy of the Political System

The support of its citizens is a key factor in the stability of any country. The first question is, "Is there a political community in Ecuador?" The answer is emphatically "Yes." The overwhelming majority of Ecuadorans from all regions of the country are very proud to be Ecuadoran.

Although these results indicate that Ecuadorans overwhelmingly believe that they are part of a political community, this does not necessarily mean that they trust the institutions that govern them. In fact, as can be seen in Figure A1, there is a wide gap between pride in being Ecuadoran and pride in the Ecuadoran system of gov-

---

8. The World Bank's governance indicators are based on indicators taken from a variety of sources. Most of these indicators are surveys (or compilations) of experts' opinions in various research institutes such as *Freedom House* and *Economist Intelligence Unit*. The only Ecuadoran public opinion survey used in this set of indicators, *Latin Barometer*, includes a modestly sized sample (about 1,000) and does not allow for a breakdown by region. In addition, the raw data that allow for a detailed analysis are kept confidential by *Latin Barometer Corporation*.

9. The survey on efficient governance, which included more than 3,000 subjects, was carried out by the University of Pittsburgh in collaboration with CEDATOS/Gallup of Ecuador in late 2001. That survey covered all provinces except for Galapagos, which was excluded for budgetary reasons. The margin of error in this sample was very small (±1.8 percent). The World Bank Institute conducted separate surveys on public employees, companies, and households between April and June of 1999. It then prepared a preliminary report based on this exhaustive diagnosis and presented it to the government. The principal objective of this study was to contribute to the design and implementation of a detailed and participatory anticorruption strategy and action plan. The results of the World Bank Institute are based on surveys of 1,139 public employees, 1,164 companies, and 1,800 citizens.

ernment. While the former is close to the top on a scale from 1 to 100, the latter is well below 50. These results have an effect on governance as the degree of support for the political system is used to measure political legitimacy and without legitimacy there is no democratic political system that can remain stable for a long time. Furthermore, governments that try to govern without the support of the population are destined to encounter difficulties, as demonstrated by the Ecuadoran situation in recent years. Citizens must have confidence in their government's right to govern (which is the essence of a government's legitimacy).

The University of Pittsburgh (Seligson 2000) has developed a compound measure of support for the system that has been broadly applied and allows for international comparison. As shown in Figure A2, Ecuador does not have a good rating compared to other Latin American countries. Another noteworthy observation is that low support for the system is coupled with higher levels of education. This means that more educated Ecuadorans, who have better access to information from the media, are less likely to support the system. It is also clear that a major factor reducing support for the system is citizens' perception of the economy: those who feel that the economy is doing worse are those who support the political system less. These results would not be so disturbing if the perception of the economy were better than it is, but 62.9 percent of those surveyed maintained that the economy has been performing poorly or very poorly.

A more detailed look at specific institutions, both public and private (see Figure A3), indicates that citizens' confidence in them is extremely varied. The Catholic

Figure A1. Pride in the Ecuadorian Political System vs. Pride in Being Ecuadoran

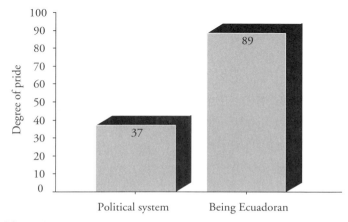

Source: Seligson, 2001.

Figure A2. Comparative Support for the System

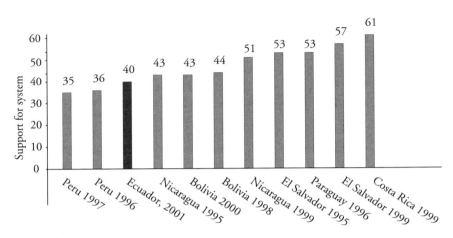

Source: Seligson, 2001.

Church has a high rating, as is usually the case in most countries of the region. It should be noted that the recently established "parish boards" also have a relatively high rating. However, it is disturbing that democratic institutions par excellence, namely the political parties, Congress, and the Supreme Court, enjoy very low levels of confidence.

On the other hand, it should be pointed out that the municipality as an institution has a comparatively good rating, much higher than national democratic institutions. This suggests that more importance is assigned to local government. At the same time, the study results indicate clearly that support for the national political system is very closely associated with the level of satisfaction with municipal services, indicating that one way to build the legitimacy of the national political system is to increase the effectiveness of local governments.

Participation of Civil Society and Governance in Ecuador

According to the writings of Alexis de Tocqueville (1875) on democracy in North America, an important factor in uniting citizens and their officials is an active civil society. A factor more directly related to this chapter is that social capital is considered to play an important role in economic growth (Helliwell and Putnam 2000). Recent events in Ecuador have made clear the extent of the impact that participation has on the political system. Ecuadoran citizens can organize themselves, and have in fact done so, in order to exert pressure and demand that their claims be heard.

Figure A3. Support for Institutions

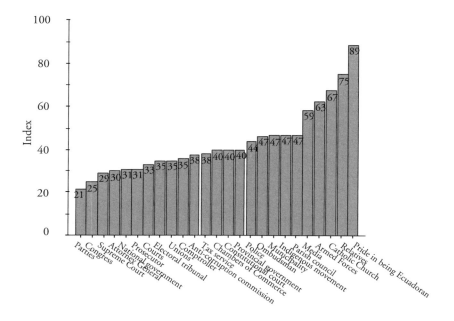

Source: Seligson, 2001.

To what extent is there active participation of civil society in Ecuador and what factors could be inhibiting that participation? On the positive side is the fact that Ecuadoran citizens participate in civil society in many ways such as in their resounding support for nonaggressive ways to express their needs, as can be seen in Figure A4. On a scale from 1 to 10, participation in community groups and electoral campaigns receives the most support. However, there is strong opposition to civil disobedience.

Participation is conditioned and limited by many factors and there is a wide gap between men and women in many countries in the region. Another factor that limits participation is crime. It is disturbing that crime is so common in Ecuador. In the year the survey was conducted, 20 percent of the population had been the victim of some form of crime. However, very few citizens report crime to the authorities. In turn, there is growing fear of crime that acts to limit participation, as shown in Figure A5. The decline in participation generated by fear of crime is regrettable because, as also indicated in Figure A6, there are direct links between participation at the community level and support for the system.

Figure A4. Approval of Conventional or Aggressive Forms of Political Participation

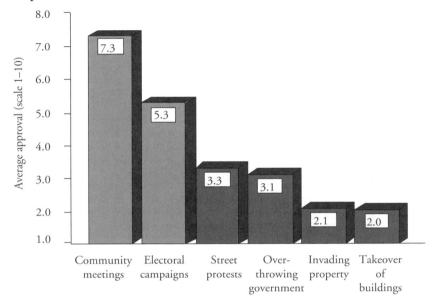

Source: Seligson, 2001.

Figure A5. Professional Participation and Fear of Crime

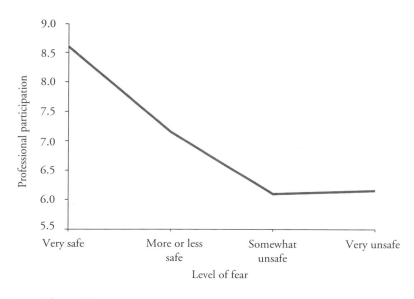

Source: Seligson, 2001.

Figure A6. Participation in a Parents' Committee and Support for the System

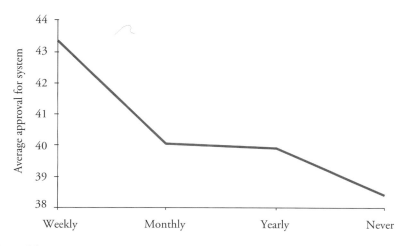

Source: Seligson, 2001.

16

The Labor Market and Civil Service in Ecuador[1]

Jeffrey Rinne and Carolina Sánchez-Páramo

Ecuador's dollarization carries with it a complete transformation of the role of labor markets—in that external and internal competitiveness no longer depend on devaluations. This has made flexibility and labor productivity central elements in economic growth. In addition, an efficient civil service is key to combating corruption and gaining noticeable improvements in the delivery of public services.

Labor indicators show a partial recovery from the impact of the crisis at the end of the last century. Formal employment fell until 2000, and later showed a tepid recovery to levels close to those of 1998. This partial recovery conceals deeper shocks such as high migration, with half a million Ecuadorans moving out of the country; continued migration from the country to the cities; and the fact that the rate of underemployment remains three times as high as the 1998 level, reflecting a growing number of workers who work fewer than 40 hours per week (visible underemployment) or are paid less than their stipulated salary (invisible underemployment). The evolution of real incomes and salaries has followed a similar trend.

Although the Economic Transformation Law simplified private sector salary policy and introduced new and more flexible hiring methods through hourly and temporary contracts, the system still contains excessive rigidities in its sectoral tables, the adjustments to which bear no relationship at all to productivity. The mechanism for indexing to projected inflation, which is logically desirable in the case of rapidly falling inflation, becomes a serious obstacle to competitiveness once inflation stabilizes close to international levels. In addition, the proliferation of temporary

---

1. Jeffrey Rinne is civil service specialist and Carolina Sánchez-Páramo is a labor markets specialist at the World Bank.

employment agencies means that they are not adequately monitored— the labor relationship deteriorates, and it is difficult to ensure compliance with minimum labor requirements when the task falls on the firms doing the hiring. Civil service also shows serious deficiencies: the proliferation of salary benefits and hiring methods makes it impossible to assess the exact number of workers and payrolls, significantly multiplies the cost of "base" salary increases granted by the government, and does not allow for control of the government payroll.

Given that one of the central objectives of the government is to promote job creation, particularly in the formal sector, special attention must be given to salary levels and the degree of labor flexibility. In the private sector, it is suggested that future salary increases be consistent with increases in labor productivity; that the current negotiation process be simplified by abandoning salary reviews based on projected inflation; that the requirement of increases decreed based on "sectoral tables" be eliminated; that a single minimum reference salary be established; that collective agreements as a mechanism for salary negotiation, rather than governmental dictates, be strengthened; that the use of temporary employment agencies be regulated and limited; and that the rule requiring that 15 percent of profits be redistributed to the workers be eliminated.

In civil service, the basic objective of the government should be to continue streamlining the public sector; to approve an improved draft law on salary unification; to maintain incentives based on geographic location for physicians and teachers so that minimum health and education services are guaranteed in remote areas; to combine salary unification with a process to restructure public employment, reducing staffing levels as much as possible; and to strengthen the system for controlling public contracting through a centralized registry within the Integrated Financial Management System (SIGEF) of the Ministry of Economy and Finance (and ensuring that this system is set up in the near future).

A. Introduction

The 1998 crisis and dollarization in 2000 have had profound and lasting repercussions for Ecuador's economy. Since dollarization, the country has been operating in an environment in which external and internal competitiveness can no longer be achieved through devaluations. In this context, labor flexibility and labor productivity have become key elements for maintaining economic growth. This chapter examines how labor markets in general and civil service employment in particular have been affected by these changes, and identifies what challenges are on the horizon in both areas. Given that the problems of each environment are different and thus the policy recommendations are different as well, we have decided to discuss each segment in a different section.

B. The Labor Market in Ecuador[2]

Employment and Unemployment

Macroeconomic developments in Ecuador, specifically the 1998 crisis and dollarization in 2000, have had profound repercussions for the labor market. The activity rate rose slightly in 1999, fell in 2000 in response to the economic crisis, and rose again in 2001 when it reached its highest level in the last four years. These changes applied to both men and women. The employment and unemployment rates followed a similar cyclical pattern. Employment fell and unemployment rose as a result of the crisis. Then the employment rate recovered in 2000 and suffered a small decline in 2001, while the unemployment rate fell and then rose to 11 percent, a figure similar to that for 1998 (Table 1).

Although according to this general trend the labor market situation in 2001 was slightly better than in 1998, suggesting that the negative effects of the crisis and dollarization may have only been temporary, other changes emerged during the same period that call that optimistic view into question. First, a large number of working-age Ecuadorans emigrated from the country and in this way relieved the pressure on the labor market. A clear reflection of this is that unemployment is below the national urban average in Cuenca and other cities that have had high outmigration rates.

Second, the rate of underemployment rose noticeably in 1999 and, while falling somewhat in 2001, it remained at a level three times as high as that of 1998. This increase indicates that a growing number of workers are involuntarily working fewer

Table 1. Active Work Force, Employment and Unemployment in Urban Areas, 1998–2001

| | Active labor force | | Employment | Unemployment |
	All	Women	rate	
1998	58.4	46.1	88.5	11.5
1999	60.0	47.8	85.6	14.4
2000	57.3	45.0	91.0	9.0
2001	63.1	52.5	89.1	10.9

Source: Survey of Employment, Unemployment, and Underemployment (INEC).

---

2. All figures on activity, employment, and unemployment discussed in this section are based on the Survey on Employment, Unemployment, and Underemployment (INEC). Independent experts and other users in Ecuador have expressed concern regarding the survey's sampling method and the comparability of its data over time. It would be useful to recalculate some of the data on the basis of the Central Bank of Ecuador's (BCE's) employment survey.

than 40 hours per week (visible underemployment) or, while still working 40 hours or more, are receiving less than the stipulated salary (invisible underemployment). Further, there was an increase in informal employment that coincided with the crisis and this did not later reverse itself (Table 2).

These changes generally suggest that to a large extent the recovery of the rate of employment described above was somewhat precarious. In fact, although total employment rose 17 percent between 1998 and 2001, formal employment rose only 11 percent while informal employment rose 24 percent (Table 3). It is striking that most of this growth was concentrated in the manufacturing (or marketable) sector and in construction, where employment grew more than 25 percent compared to 11 percent in the service (or nonmarketable) sector.

Table 2. Underemployment and Informal Employment in Urban Areas, 1998–2001
(as percentages of employed people)

	Rate of underemployment	Visible underemployment	Invisible underemployment	Informal employment
1998	5.5	2.5	3.0	42.2
1999	21.9	7.5	14.4	45.0
2000	22.1	6.4	15.7	44.4
2001	17.7	7.1	10.6	45.0

Notes:
Rate of underemployment: percentage of employed persons who involuntarily work fewer than 40 hours per week—that is, the legal work week—(visible underemployment) or who work 40 hours or more per week but receive wages below the legal minimum (invisible underemployment).
Informal employment: percentage of the work force classified as employers, independent workers, unsalaried workers, and salaried employees in companies with five employees or fewer, with the exception of those who engage in professional, intellectual, or scientific activities.
Source: Survey of Employment, Unemployment, and Underemployment (INEC).

Table 3. Growth of Urban Employment by Sector, 1998–2001
(percentage changes)

	All sectors	Manufacturing	Construction	Services
Total	16.6	31.9	26.4	11.0
Formal	11.6	28.4	12.1	5.8
Informal	24.1	35.0	38.6	19.7

Source: Survey of Employment, Unemployment, and Underemployment (INEC).

Labor Income and Salaries

The crisis and dollarization also had a profound effect on compensation in the work force in terms of both labor income and salaries. According to the most up-to-date data available, real labor income and salaries fell significantly (35 percent) as a result of the crisis, recovered in 2000 thanks in large part to the price stabilization achieved through dollarization, and fell slightly in 2001 because of inflation. The result of all these changes was a 20 percent increase in real labor income during the period 1998–2001 (Table 4).

However, these changes must be viewed with caution because the period between 1998 and 2001 in Ecuador was one of significant macroeconomic unrest, and these trends are the result of simultaneous changes in labor income and nominal salaries and changes in prices and the sucre-to-dollar exchange rate. In particular, alternative assumptions regarding the evolution of prices between 1998 and 2001 can create entirely different scenarios. The technical annex that appears at the end of this chapter discusses this subject in detail and presents alternative calculations for real labor income and salaries based on a different price deflator.[3]

It is striking that real labor income increased markedly more in the informal than in the formal sector, although the informal sector continued to pay less than the for-

Table 4. Real Monthly Labor Income in Urban Areas, 1998–2001 (at constant 1998 $US values)

	Total	*Formal*	*Informal*
1998	146.5	209.4	103.6
1999	96.0	138.6	70.6
2000	186.0	258.5	143.6
2001	177.2	240.2	135.9

Notes:
Labor income includes salaried income and the income of independent workers (INEC).
The calculations for 1998 and 1999 use the sucre/dollar exchange rate provided by BCE: 6,780 and 20,100, respectively.
Source: Calculations by the authors using BCE data.

---

3. Ecuador has just returned to calculating its National Accounts for the period 1993–2002 in dollar terms with technical assistance from the IMF. Thus, the data that appear in this chapter use the deflator created for this review, while the data presented in the annex uses the deflator published by BCE in October 2002. Given that the data in each of the series yield very different panoramas, we feel it is necessary to continue the discussion on the development of these price indexes. This is particularly important not only for the description of real salaries and their evolution but also for the poverty calculations.

mal sector. Real monthly labor income in urban areas increased by 30 percent in the informal sector compared to some 14 percent in the formal sector (Table 5). Apparently, the rounding up of prices was more common and widespread in the informal sector than in the formal sector after dollarization. This, added to the fact that self-employment occurs more frequently in the informal sector, could explain the difference.

This is confirmed by looking at changes in real earnings according to the employment situation. Although there is no information for the year 1998 and we thus cannot calculate the decline in real earnings associated with the crisis for the various groups, it is possible to see up to what point real income increased between 1999

Table 5. Monthly Labor Income in Urban Areas According to Employment Situation, 1998–2001
(in constant 1998 $US values)

			Total employees		
	Employers	*Independent workers*	*Salaried employees in the public sector*	*Salaried employees in the private sector*	*Others*
1998	—	—	—	—	—
1999	241.4	72.2	134.9	93.5	30.2
2000	583.6	172.3	251.0	176.9	59.0
2001	487.0	153.3	244.6	173.9	69.6
			Formal sector		
	Employers	*Independent workers*	*Salaried employees in the public sector*	*Salaried employees in the private sector*	*Others*
1998	—	—	—	—	
1999	405.3	198.3	134.9	115.3	
2000	774.1	391.6	251.0	220.7	
2001	728.3	275.0	244.6	205.4	
			Informal sector		
	Employers	*Independent workers*	*Salaried employees in the public sector*	*Salaried employees in the private sector*	*Others*
1998	—	—		—	
1999	170.0	71.0		55.7	
2000	455.1	167.8		99.8	
2001	337.0	147.8		122.8	

—. No data available.

Note: The calculations for 1998 and 1999 use the sucre/dollar exchange rate provided by BCE: 6,780 and 20,100, respectively.

Source: Calculations by authors using BCE data.

and 2001. On average, real labor income more than doubled for employers and self-employed workers, while it rose 80 percent for salaried workers in both the public and private sectors. However, this average conceals significant differences between the formal and informal sectors. Employers and self-employed workers in the formal sector enjoyed an increase of their real incomes of 79 and 40 percent respectively, compared to 98 and 100 percent in the informal sector. Similarly, salaried private-sector workers in the formal sector enjoyed an increase in their real salaries of 78 percent compared to 120 percent in the informal sector.

The real minimum salary increased 62 percent between 1998 and 2001: first it fell to half its value between 1998 and 1999 and then increased 200 percent between 1999 and 2001 (Table 6). This means that although the real minimum salary actually increased more than real labor income or than real salaries, it was also more volatile (that is, it fell more drastically after the crisis and recovered more between 2000 and 2001). This could affect the changes seen in poverty during this period, in that the minimum salary generally covers those workers who find themselves at the bottom of the salary distribution.

In summary, Ecuador's labor market was characterized by a tenuous creation of employment in the formal sector as a result of a notable deterioration in most of the indicators during the 1998 crisis, followed by a very timid recovery after 1999. This is particularly disturbing given that emigration increased noticeably after 1998 (approximately 200,000 people have emigrated during the last 3 years, doubling the number of Ecuadorans who live and work outside the country). This probably relieved the pressure on the labor market. In fact, calculations submitted by the SIISE indicate that the rate of unemployment might be between 0.5 and 2 percentage points higher than the current rate if all these people had not emigrated (SIISE. 2002).

Table 6. Labor Income, Average and Minimum Salary in the Private Sector in Urban Areas, 1998–2001

| | Labor income | | Average salary | | Minimum salary and basic supplements | |
	Nominal ($)	Real ($1998)	Nominal ($)	Real ($1998)	Nominal ($)	Real ($1998)
1998	146.5	146.5	—	—	84.5	84.5
1999	68.9	96.0	67.1	93.5	29.7	41.4
2000	123.0	186.0	117.0	176.9	91.9	138.9
2001	163.0	177.2	160.0	173.9	125.3	136.2

—. No data available.
Note: The calculations for 1998 and 1999 use the sucre/dollar exchange rate provided by BCE: 6,780 and 20,100, respectively.
Source: Calculations by authors using BCE data.

The data on real earnings are more confusing in that they depend on assumptions regarding inflation. If we do the calculations according to the latest revision submitted by BCE we see that real labor income increased an average of 20 percent during the period. The increases were higher than average for the informal sector and among employers and independent workers, and lower than average for the formal sector and for salaried workers.

Generally we can see deficient performance in terms of employment and a significant recovery in terms of real earnings during the 1998 crisis, with potential effects on competitiveness to the point that true changes in the productivity of the labor force would not be reflected. We will discuss these questions as well as the policy recommendations below. We will discuss employment and salaries first in the private sector and then in the civil service sector.

C. Problems in the Private Market

In this context of limited creation of employment in the formal sector and positive growth in real earnings, two aspects stand out that merit greater attention. First, salary negotiation is a complex process for Ecuador, both because it involves many agents who negotiate at different levels and times and because, until recently, salaries represented only a part, and sometimes a very small part, of what workers received, the rest consisting of supplements and allowances. Second, formal employment has over the last 10 years been subject to what is commonly called "outsourcing" or the growing use of so-called temporary employment agencies through which temporary employees are hired to do permanent work, thus avoiding the payment of the contractual obligations that a permanent employee entails.

Congressional ratification of Ecuador's Economic Transformation Law (also known as TROLE I) in 2000 sought to deal with these matters by simplifying pay policy in the private sector ("salary unification") and introducing more flexible and modern hiring methods, such as hourly and temporary contracts. The new Social Security Law also provides that all workers, regardless of the nature of their contracts, must contribute to Social Security, thus equalizing to some extent the contractual obligations of "regular" workers and those hired through temporary agencies. However, these measures may not have been enough.

Setting Salaries, Salary Unification, and Incentives for Creating Formal Jobs

Salaries are set at three different levels:

- The National Wages Council (CONADES) regulates the base salary and annual increases to it. When no agreement is reached between employers and workers' representatives within the CONADES framework, the Ministry of

Labor establishes an annual increase in the base salary equal to expected inflation in the upcoming year.

- Minimum salaries specific to each occupation (and thus the relative minimum salaries for each occupation) are established in each sector though fixed salary programs called "sectoral tables" that employers and workers' representatives renegotiate periodically. In the past, the tables had to be updated once a year, but this is no longer the case. Except in the petroleum, electricity, and telecommunications industries, the tables seem to be binding, that is, workers receive salaries according to the levels specified by the tables.
- Employers and workers' representatives can agree on additional salary increases through "collective agreements" by sector or by company.

The interaction between the tables and decisions made through CONADES and the agreements has multiple effects:

- The tables, by setting relative salaries, have the ability to automatically transmit the increase in the minimum salary to the entire salary distribution. This situation may or may not be desirable. Although it may be considered reasonable to index the minimum salary according to inflation in order to preserve the buying power of those less favored by the distribution, it is not clear that this is the best method for all salary levels.
- The tables do not reflect differences in productivity between companies in a single sector and thus create considerable salary rigidity at a time when dollarization has diminished the competitiveness of Ecuadoran companies. In addition, renegotiation could create a tool for unfair competition between large and small companies in the same sector given that the former are more productive than the latter, and have more negotiating power in the renegotiation process.
- Increases in the minimum salary that are indexed to projected inflation are desirable in a period of rapidly declining inflation, but once prices stabilize they can cause inflationary pressures. This situation could be exacerbated by the fact that the agreement can propose additional salary increases and at the same time follow what is stipulated by CONADES if the economic conditions of the sector and of the company so require.

In summary, the system is too rigid, leaves little room for differences in productivity to be reflected in salary differences, and makes it difficult to modify relative salaries between employees and companies. In this context, Congress approved salary unification in the year 2000 (TROLE I). The law establishes that, with the exception of the 13th and 14th salaries, all existing allowances should be incorporated in the minimum salary—an attempt to expand the tax base for Social Security and other employment-related taxes that are traditionally paid exclusively on the basis of salaries. Given that in practice these changes will increase the cost of employment for employers, they will be implemented over five years, so that in each year during that period the base salary will incorporate 20 percent of all nonsalary components of the workers' pay.

The effective increase in labor costs, combined with a somewhat rigid salary-setting system (which will be still more rigid once the discretionary element involved in the special allowances disappears), may partially explain why the creation of formal employment has been limited since 2000 in comparison with the creation of informal employment.

Outsourcing and Flexibility in the Labor Market

Since the emergence of temporary employment agencies, employers have made extensive use of them, far beyond their cyclical needs, to the point that some companies are now operating exclusively with "temporary workers." The result is that the country now has some 2,000 temporary employment agencies employing approximately 10,000 workers—that is, between 5 and 10 percent of formally employed workers.[4]

Termination costs in Ecuador are similar to those in Peru, Bolivia, and Colombia (approximately equal to 3.5–4 months of average monthly salary—see Pages and Heckman 2000), but much higher than termination costs in other countries in the region such as Argentina, Paraguay, and Uruguay (2–2.5 months of average monthly salary), most European countries, and the United States. Avoiding these costs may be part of the reason why temporary employments agencies are popular.

Another reason why companies use temporary employment agencies seems to be to avoid paying employees the profit sharing that is due to them by law (up to 15 percent of all company profits). Although all workers are entitled to this, regardless of whether they are temporary or permanent, the threat of losing work is enough to keep the demands of temporary workers to a minimum. This in turn explains why outsourcing did not decrease despite the introduction of hourly and temporary contracts in 2000 (although companies are allowed to hire temporary employees for up to 40 percent of their total work force, regardless of the company's type of activity).

In addition, temporary employees often receive salaries below the legal minimum and are completely denied special allowances. This could partially explain the increase noted in invisible underemployment.

Finally, the fear is that outsourcing has contributed to a general deterioration of relations between employers and employees, as well as to the decrease training and

---

4. Preliminary data obtained from Ecuador's representative to the International Labor Organization. To date, Ecuador has no reliable and systematic sources on information on outsourcing.

other types of company investments in human capital, although once again the quantitative data are limited. The second outcome could have serious consequences in an era when technology and skills complement each other and when growth in productivity seems to depend more on the simultaneous accumulation of both factors rather than the replacement of one by the other.

In summary, although outsourcing prevented later increases in informal employment, it does not have the principal characteristics of formal employment—namely, the right of workers to a minimum salary and some type of job protection, as well as the right to join unions and receive appropriate training.

D. Recommendations for the Private Labor Market

Recommendations for Setting Salaries

The process used to set salaries must be simplified so that salaries by sector and by company are more sensitive to the labor productivity changes. This would minimize potential negative effects on competitiveness. The three measures suggested below could make a contribution in this respect:

- Suspend the indexing of annual salary increases to projected inflation in order to prevent the emergence of inflationary pressures and greater deterioration in competitiveness.
- Make the recommendations of the sectoral tables optional. Specific values recommended should be used as a reference but should not be compulsory, particularly for the private sector. Although after dollarization the spread between the lowest and highest levels has diminished considerably in almost all of the tables, the tables still have the adverse effect of transmitting any increase in the minimum salary to the entire salary distribution. The Ministry of Labor has already taken some steps toward transforming the tables into a specific minimum salary for each sector, indicating the corrections in the tables in dollars and not in percentages (that is, all salaries in the table increase based on a $US multiple and not by a percentage). This compresses the distribution of the table by increasing the lowest salaries proportionally more than the highest salaries, and thus makes the table less relevant for workers at higher levels in the distribution. The new minimum salary should be a reference point but should not be compulsory.
- Follow the regulations on the basic salary and collective agreements in setting salaries. The collective agreements by sector and particularly the agreements by company should be the principal instruments for setting salaries that exceed base salary, so as to leave room for greater sensitivity to economic conditions.

Recommendations on Labor Market Flexibility

It is necessary to control the frequency of outsourcing and promote the replacement of temporary workers from agencies with formal workers governed by a flexible system that allows for temporary and hourly contracts. It is hoped that this change will have a favorable impact on income, labor relations, and training—without compromising labor market flexibility. Four types of measures should be implemented:

- Control the use of temporary employment agencies and monitor the work and pay conditions of temporary employees in order to ensure that they reflect the provisions of the law. This subject has already been discussed with the Minister of Labor and various employer representatives, but not much progress has been made. It would be interesting to review the proposals raised during their discussions.
- Reduce the costs to terminate formal permanent employees under new contracts.
- Eliminate rules on profit sharing. Given that this seems to be the principal cause of outsourcing and possibly also for reliance on the informal sector, it would be desirable to eliminate this clause in all new contracts. For economic policy reasons, it would be extremely difficult to take this step with existing contracts.
- Promote the use of temporary and hourly contracts when labor flexibility is needed. These contracts give the employer flexible arrangements and give workers formal employment and the benefits that go with it.

E. Civil Service in Ecuador

Number of Personnel

Since 1998, the number of central government positions, without counting autonomous and decentralized agencies, has remained stable at about 276,000 employees.[5] The number of employees in the police, health, and education departments has increased during the last five years by a total of more than 13,000. However, there has been a reduction of about the same amount in other areas of the central government.[6]

---

5. The data on employees in autonomous and decentralized agencies prior to the year 2001 are very difficult to obtain. However, it seems that employment rose a little, from approximately 32,500 in 2001 to 33,500 in 2002.
6. After the decline in 2000, the total number of central government employees (including autonomous and decentralized agencies) rose by several thousand in recent years. The increase was 2.4 percent during 2001–02. In 2002, the total number of central government employees plus the Armed Forces was approximately 328,700.

Policy Matrix for the Private Labor Market

Problems	Policy measures		Progress indicators	Objectives/goals
	Short term (to June 2003)	Medium term (2003–07)		
Salary setting mechanism that is too complex and rigid.	Go from revisions in percentages to revisions in dollars for the sectoral sectoral tables and make adherence to the tables optional (recommended) rather than compulsory. Strengthen the role of the minimum salary as a reference only—that is, ,not compulsory—and of negotiations by company as tools for setting salaries. Amend TROLE I to eliminate salary indexing tied to projected inflation.	Change the sectoral tables into noncompulsory minimum reference salaries by sector.	Reduction of salary spread in sectoral tables.	Establish salary-setting system that is more sensitive to labor productivity.
High termination costs. Need to go from precarious hiring methods (temporary employment agencies) to formal methods (temporary and hourly) in order to achieve labor flexibility.	Control the use of temporary workers. Improve the supervision of work and pay conditions for temporary workers. Promote the use of formal temporary contracts and hourly contracts instead of temporary workers.	Reduce termination costs in all new contracts for permanent formal workers. Eliminate in all new (temporary) contracts the rule that provides for paying workers 15 percent of profits.	Percentage of temporary workers hired by a single company. General incidence of outsourcing.	Promote the creation of formal employment. Increase labor flexibility without reducing workers' access to social security and other benefits.

As for the subnational governments, the officials in Quito calculate that Ecuador currently has 34,000 municipal and provincial council employees. The data on state companies are not easy to obtain but we have been told that they can be extracted from files in the hands of the Ministry of Labor and Human Resources. These data have not been given to us at this writing.[7]

Table 7 shows the annual figures on public employees in Ecuador and in other countries presented for purposes of comparison.

Table 7. Public Employees of Ecuador and Other Selected Countries

	Ecuador[1] (2002)		Bolivia[2] (1999)	Chile[3]	Honduras[4] (2001)	Nicaragua[3]
	No.	% pop.	% pop.	% pop.	% pop.	% pop.
Total public employees	—		2.8	3.1	1.9	—
State companies	—		0.1	0.2	0.3	—
Armed Forces	56,200	0.4	0.3	0.6	0.1	0.3
Central civil government	269,600	2.2	2.3	…	1.4	1.3
Education	112,600	0.9	1.3	0.8	0.7	0.3
Health	16,900	0.1	0.2	0.2	0.16	0.2
Police	26,000	0.2	—	0.23	—	—
Subnational government	34,000	0.3	0.2	…	0.1	0.1

—. No data available.
Note: A definition of the categories can be found in
http://www1.worldbank.org/publicsector/civilservice/cross.htm.
Sources:
1. Calculated based on data from the Ministry of Economy and Finance. The figure for subnational government is a calculation of actual employment. The remaining categories represent authorized positions, which quite probably exceed the actual number of public employees. In order to determine the number of employees in the health sector, the percentage of health professionals employed by the Ministry of Public Health was calculated in three provinces and this ratio was then applied to the country as a whole.
2. World Bank 2002.
3. World Bank data series on government employees and salaries, available at
http://www1.worldbank.org/publicsector/civilservice/cross.htm.
4. Data gathered by the author and the World Bank on government employees and salaries.

---

7. In 2000, some of the largest state companies in Ecuador (for example, PetroEcuador) did not respond to a request from the Ministry of Labor and Human Resources for data on their employees. Up to this point, it is not clear how accurately the Ministry can record data on employment in state companies.

Public Employee Systems in Ecuador

Civil service in Ecuador belongs to the largest framework in the public sector. The legal code for government employees (approximately 53,000) is the Civil Service and Administrative Career Law. The National Teaching Corps, regulated by the Teaching Career and Teaching Salary Scale Law, has approximately twice as many employees. Another 20,000 state employees are governed by the same law that applies to private company employees—the Labor Code (see Table 8).

Physicians are in the category of "Scheduled Professionals" but have their own salary schedule, while the other eight professions also in this category receive a single salary and have the same grade system. Although the total number of physicians employed is fewer than 7,000, the remaining professions together amount to less than 2,800.[8]

The Police and Armed Forces of Ecuador have their own salary schedules, as do the Judiciary, the Legislature, and Foreign Service personnel. Contract employees, amounting to 2,500 last year, are governed by the Law on Contracted Professionals Services.

Table 8. Number of Government Jobs under the Public Employees System, 2002

Employment system	No.	% total
Civil Service and Admin. Career Law	53,330	16.3%
Labor Code	23,865	7.3%
National Teaching Corps	112,790	34.5%
Armed Forces Personnel Law	57,440	17.6%
National Police	26,000	8.0%
Scheduled Professionals (excl. physicians)	3,075	0.9%
Physicians	6,940	2.1%
Judiciary	4,900	1.5%
Legislature	320	0.1%
Foreign Service Law	610	0.2%
Law on Contracted Professional Services	2,540	0.8%
Others	35,120	10.7%
TOTAL	326,930	100%

Source: Gathered using data from the Ministry of Economy and Finance.

---

8. The eight professions are attorney, administrator, architect, economist, civil engineer, chemical engineer, geologist engineer, and journalist.

Public Sector Salary Expenses

Although the number of public employees increased very slowly between 1998 and 2002, government salary expenses fluctuated noticeably during the same period. The principal reasons for this are relatively simple. The fiscal crisis of 1998–99 caused runaway inflation and a drastic decline (more than 70 percent) in the real value of the basic salary between 1997 and 1999.[9] Although GDP fell by more than 5 percent between 1998 and 2000, the personnel expenses of the central government shrank as a portion of the GDP from 7.7 percent to 5.2 percent.[10]

With dollarization in 2000, the deterioration in real salaries stopped and an opposite trend began to take hold. However, and despite significant salary increases in March and May of that year, the basic salary of public employees was equal to only half of its 1997 value in the case of the lowest salaries and one-third in the case of the highest salaries.[11] In early 2002, basic salaries rose another 50 percent, thus restoring the lost buying power, but government spending increased in any case. (Annex 1 provides a synopsis of the evolution of basic salaries for employees in the system governed by the Civil Service and Administrative Career Law).

It is much more complicated to measure changes in the total compensation of public employees in the late 1990s. Today's basic salaries typically represent barely a fraction of an employee's total compensation. Countless monetary allowances have been added over the years and have been accumulating. Consequently it is not uncommon for an employee's salary to include between 20 and 30 different items. Annex 2 shows a list of possible allowances. Table 9 shows the relative importance of the basic salary and the allowances in a sample from six ministries and government departments for which we have reliable data. Basic salaries represent no more than one-fourth of government spending on personnel in any of the six agencies. The highest percentage of spending goes to "supplemental payments" (for example, the 13th and 14th salaries and other bonuses).

Human Resources Management

In the Civil Service and Administrative Career Law (LSCCA) of 1964, the key human resource management functions were transferred to the National Personnel Directorate (DNP). These responsibilities included controlling hiring in government agencies, developing salary policies, and recording data on public employees. Although in principle it was created as an autonomous agency, the DNP later car-

---

9. This comparison of real salaries in Ecuador's public sector and subsequent comparisons are calculated according to the salary figures that appear in annexes 1 and 3; the sucre/$US exchange rate is from the Central Bank's *Boletín Anuario*, No. 24, 2002, p. 154.

10. Central Bank of Ecuador, *Boletín Anuario*, No. 24, 2002, p. 104.

11. As of April 2000, civil service salaries are paid in U.S. dollars.

ried out these same functions as a division of the Secretariat for National Administrative Development (SENDA).[12] However, in 1998, President Jamil Mahuad dissolved SENDA through Decree No. 41, and the DNP along with it. The decree stipulated that, from that point on, each government agency would be responsible for its own decisions on hiring and personnel management.[13] At the same time, a new government agency was created: the Civil Service and Institutional Development Office (OSCIDI), which is responsible for analyzing human resources policies and for providing guidelines on personnel management to government ministries, departments, and agencies (MDOGs). However, OSCIDI's authority and resources are meager in comparison with those of its predecessor.[14]

Salary Policy

In an attempt to reassert central control over public salaries, the Law on Reform of Public Finances (LRFP) of 1999 created the National Public Sector Compensation Council (CONAREM) to control total personnel spending in all government agencies.[15] However, the authority of CONAREM was immediately questioned by various autonomous agencies. These agencies made a presentation to the Office of the General Comptroller in which they asserted that CONAREM did not have authority over the salary policy it applied to their employees, given that they were autonomous institutions.[16] The Office of the Comptroller, also an autonomous agency of the central government, supported these petitions and, as a result, the autonomous agencies were free to design their own compensation policies.[17] In practice the only limits were those that the Ministry of Economy and Finance imposed on them through budget allocations.

---

12. Law No. 16 (R.O. 143, 17-3-1989).
13. Only the reclassification of positions and general pay policy were beyond the authority of the ministries and departments. (Executive Decree No. 41, Art. 5; RO-S 11, 25-8-98).
14. For example, the DNP had four separate divisions and SENDA, of which it was a part, had 388 employees. OSCIDI had only 44 employees in 1999 (OSCIDI 1999).
15. Law 99-24 (RO-S 181: 30-4-99). CONAREM was empowered to set ceilings on salary cost increases for each MDOG. Compensation includes wages, salaries, transportation, lunch subsidies, termination indemnity fund, and so on. The council has three voting members: the Minister of Economy and Finance (chairman), the Minister of Labor and Human Resources, and a member appointed by an electoral college of workers, employees, and teachers. Decisions are reached by consensus.
16. For example, the Office of the Attorney General and the Judiciary made presentations to the Office of the Comptroller in which they asserted that, because they were autonomous agencies, they were not under the authority of CONAREM.
17 As for the sectional agencies (namely, municipalities and provincial councils), the Office of the Comptroller determined that they were subject to the authority of CONAREM.

Table 9. Personnel Expenses by Type in Five Ministries and Departments, 2002[a]

Payments[b]	Office of the President and General Secretariat of the Administration		Office of the Vice President of the Republic		Ministry of Economy and Finance		Ministry of Agriculture and Livestock		Ministry of Social Welfare		Ministry of Tourism	
	% total spending on personnel	% increase 2001–02	% total spending on personnel	% increase 2001–02	% total spending on personnel	% increase 2001–02	% total spending on personnel	% increase 2001–02	% total spending on personnel	% increase 2001–02	% total spending on personnel	% increase 2001–02
Basic	21.2	9.5	24.0	47.2	10.7	73.7	17.8	39.2	16.5	55.6	24.1	9.9
Supplemental	46.7	17.9	49.5	59.8	66.0	130.7	50.0	54.3	51.4	78.1	51.3	40.8
Compensatory	19.1	45.7	21.7	97.3	6.0	34.9	28.2	21.8	21.9	38.6	20.7	38.9
Subsidies	0.4	4.4	0.3	8.6	0.3	97.0	0.9	53.0	0.4	–3.8	0.3	32.3
Temporary	8.9	15.5	1.7	–5.1	8.0	174.8	0.2	–57.2	7.0	329.8	0.0	0.0
Social Security Contributions	3.8	30.9	2.8	45.4	7.0	93.1	2.9	41.7	2.8	87.8	3.5	43.3
TOTAL		20.5		60.5		113.5		40.0		70.1		31.5

a. The percentage increase for 2001–02 is based on cumulative figures for 2000 and coded numbers for 2002.
b. Excludes payments for any type of indemnity.

Since 1999, CONAREM has issued more than 150 resolutions. Several of these have applied to all or most public employees, while others have been directed to a small group of employees to establish a particular benefit (for example, resolutions establishing or increasing the allocation of bonuses for physicians or civil engineers). Meanwhile, the ministries and autonomous agencies have sought the direct approval of the Ministry of Economy and Finance to obtain new or better allowances for their personnel.[18] Political leaders and bureaucrats have often acceded to these demands, either in order to gain support or based on their own conviction regarding the fairness of the claims. The ultimate result is a salary system with many separate components that make up a monthly salary and the consequent loss of control over salary policy.

F. Principal Problems

There are two areas that require attention. The first is salary policy. Base salaries for most public employees are still slightly below their 1997 equivalents. However, the proliferation of allowances (both general and specific to a sector) has led to alarming increases in salary expense. Certainly, increases that range from 60 percent to 110 percent cannot be sustained (see Table 9). It is difficult to anticipate the impact of a salary increase owing to the large number of allowances and their complex interconnections.

The second problem, related to the previous one, is the issue of human resources management authority over authorized positions (that is, the staffing list) and supervision of the selection and appointment of personnel. The state's authority to deal with these problems seems to have deteriorated significantly since the dissolution of SENDA. There is no government agency that has a complete overview of the number of public employees in each department, its positions, and categories. There is no department for tracking employees who have been terminated in the public sector (and who have received indemnities) and for ensuring that they have not returned to government employment through some other avenue. In addition, since the disappearance of the DNP, there is no agency working to ensure that the merits of the applicant are considered when vacancies are filled.

To be fair, we should point out that these two problems are addressed in the draft Law on Managing the Income of Public Servants that President Gustavo Noboa sent to Congress in November 2002 as a matter of urgency. In December, Congress rejected the bill, in part because of the transition phase the country was going through. Nonetheless, many are in agreement on the need for salary unification in the public sector.[19] The objectives of the draft law should be taken up again by the new government.

---

18. Of the general allowances established in the LRFP, the academic degree bonus is the only one that can vary (and in fact does so) depending on the MDOG.

19. See the newspapers "El Universo" and "El Hoy" for December 10 and 11, 2002.

The primary objective of the law is salary unification. The large number of elements that make up the salary of a public employee would be reduced to the basic salary, the 13th salary, the 14th salary, the time in service bonus, and bonuses for having relevant academic degrees that exceed the minimum required for the position. A new salary schedule was proposed that would be designed, quite appropriately, on the basis of the same 14-category schedule that was developed and approved by CONAREM in 2000.[20]

The 14-category schedule (with a base salary between four and five times greater than in the existing 21-category schedule) only applies in certain ministries and departments. Before adopting the new schedule, the government agency must go through an administrative restructuring process implemented by OSCIDI. This leads to the definition of processes, design of an appropriate structure, and the assignment of qualified human resources to that structure. Currently 11 ministries and 25 government agencies have gone through this process in OSCIDI. Nonetheless, these do not include the agencies with the highest concentrations of public employees (that is, those relating to agriculture, social insurance, health, and public works).

Annex 3 presents the current salary schedule and the schedule proposed by the law. However, it is difficult to calculate the impact of salary unification. The Ministry of Labor has calculated that making all public employees subject to the new schedule will cost $US240 million. This figure is twice what the Ministry of Economy and Finance calculated it would cost to make all public employees subject to the existing 14-category salary schedule.[21] The final cost will be determined by three variables, which are explored below.

- What is the true monthly salary that employees receive in a ministry or department on the eve of salary unification? The increase in the real salary would be considerably less than the difference between the current salary schedule and the future one given that the state is already paying salaries well above the current base salary owing to cumulative allowances. If an employee already receives a monthly salary (including allowances) higher than the one he or she would get under the new schedule, he or she will receive no salary increase.[22]

- Many employees would be reclassified during the salary unification process. But how many would there be and to what levels would they be assigned?

---

20. Resolution No. 46; 1-11-2000.

21. Memorandum No. SIP-DM-2002-236. The precise calculation was $US119.9 million.

22. The draft law sensibly recognizes that it will be neither legally nor politically possible to reduce the current salary of an employee. Therefore, the new base salary will be calculated by dividing by 12 all payments that an employee receives (setting aside the 13th salary, the 14th salary, the time-in-service bonus, and the bonus for a relevant academic degree) in order to arrive at the new base salary.

Employees with academic and work histories that do not correspond to the position they currently occupy would be placed in a lower or higher category, as applicable. Reducing their salaries would be very painful from both a political and administrative perspective. But they could be frozen until the position they occupy merited a salary increase beyond their current level. The OSCIDI calculates that in the ministries and departments that it has already restructured it has reclassified nearly half the staff.

- How many of the employees who are not needed to carry out the functions of the department can be terminated with an indemnity? How many would get the maximum indemnity of $US10,000? How many indemnities paid all at once can the state handle in the short term in order to reduce its long-term obligations in this way?

The possibilities for saving by reducing personnel (to mitigate the impact of the salary increase) and increasing efficiency through the reassignment of personnel are considerable. Nonetheless, in the 37 MDOGs that went through this restructuring process before the salary unification law was approved, staff cutbacks amounted to an average of only 3 percent. The cost of the indemnities is an important factor that limits the restructuring process (we will continue with this topic below).[23] Nonetheless, if the money is available, the human resources management (HRM) systems must be alert in order to ensure that those who have received indemnities do not reenter government employment through another channel.

The Law on Managing the Income of Public Servants provided for the strengthening of HRM systems by replacing OSCIDI with a new agency, the National Secretariat for Organizational Development of the Public Sector (SENDOSEP), with powers similar to those of the old DNP. In the draft law, this objective is not as vigorously promoted as the objective of streamlining the salary system. It is imperative to recreate the central government's internal capacity to analyze, design, administer, and supervise government human resources.

---

23. The OSCIDI is completing a restructuring plan for the General Civil Registry Directorate. This organization has more than 1,500 employees and the OSCIDI believes that only half are needed. However, the proposal indicates eliminating only 50 positions, in large part because the cost of hundreds of indemnities would be prohibitive. Public employees do not have a right to stability in employment, but they do have a right to an indemnity if their position is eliminated (LSCCA, Art. 59). The payment value is calculated as the average salary over the last 12 months, multiplied by the years of service (or fraction thereof) times four (L. No. 93, R.O. No. 340, June 16, 1998). This is a relatively generous benefit. One month of salary per year of service is much more common throughout the world. Since January 2001, there is a mandated limit of $US10,000 (CONAREM Resolution No. 70, R.O. No. 248, January 19, 2001).

G. Recommendations

Salary unification in the public sector is an appropriate initiative that seeks to resolve serious defects in public administration in Ecuador. How could this proposed reform be improved or broadened?

Recommendations on Salary Reform

- Restructuring is a way to counteract the impact of the salary increase by eliminating unnecessary personnel. Given that the list of positions that should be eliminated could remain in effect for various years (as indicated during conversations at the OSCIDI), it would be possible to terminate only a few people each year, as the funds for paying the indemnities become available. However, it is likely that the lists would become public knowledge, and the productivity of a public employee who knows he or she will be terminated will fall to zero (or worse). It would be unfortunate not to take advantage of the opportunity to discharge superfluous staff. The Bank would offer support through an adjustment or investment operation under appropriate circumstances.

- Although it is logical, in an effort to achieve salary unification and simplification, to incorporate nearly all allowances in the base salary, it might be better to continue the allowance for geographic location. In many communities throughout the world this allowance is used to ensure that physicians, teachers, and other providers of essential services set up in rural areas and help the poor. Almost invariably, urban areas have a disproportionate number of physicians and teachers, given that they are considered more attractive places to live. For this reason, many employees who were originally assigned to rural areas fight to negotiate a transfer to the cities. Monetary incentives can be used to at least retain service providers in rural areas where they are most needed.

- Physicians and teachers have their own employment laws. The unified schedule can be used as a reference point but not a rigid model. Perhaps the allowances for geographic location could be retained for these groups but not for other groups. What should be done with employees in the Galapagos? Maintaining the geographic allowance could be the lesser evil. However, if Ecuador decides to use this monetary tool, it is particularly important to set up strong HRM systems to check whether the employees transfer to urban areas and whether they continue collecting the rural area allowance.

- Salary compression: In 1997, the ratio of the highest base salary and the lowest base salary on the LSCCA schedule was 5.2:1. (Compressed salary ratios vary considerably from country to country, but the 5.2:1 ratio was in a good range). With the deterioration of real salaries in the late 1990s and their later recovery, the compression ratio fell to 3.6:1 in 2000. Further, according to the unified salary schedule in the law proposed by the government of Gustavo Noboa, the effective compressed ratio would be only 3:1.

- A highly compressed salary structure reduces public employees' incentives to pursue a long and successful career in civil service, in that it makes promotion less attractive. If it is neither possible nor desirable at this point to slightly lower the salary floor on the proposed salary schedule, it is then extremely important to resist any change in the salary schedule that would further increase salary compression. The fiscal cost of increasing salaries at the upper end of the salary schedule may be low, given that there are relatively few public employees with high salaries.

- Those charged with formulating policies in the government have expressed interest in proceeding rapidly (in just a few months) with the restructuring of all government ministries, departments, and agencies (MDOGs) and with applying the unified salary schedule to all of them (once a salary unification law is approved). Nonetheless, it would be advisable to act more calmly, establish priorities among the MDOGs, and complete the process over a period of one or two years.

Recommendations on Human Resources Management and SENDOSEP

- In view of all the energy that will likely be directed to salary reform, care should be taken to give this area of reform a lot of attention. Divisions should be developed within the new SENDOSEP (or similar agency) to collect and organize the data on personnel in all the ministries, departments, and agencies, *including the state companies*. This division will need visible support from the President in the initial phases of operation. Otherwise, it is likely that many state agencies will ignore the request for information (as happened in the past at PetroEcuador).

- The new position lists should be connected with the Integrated Financial Management System (SIGEF)—Ecuador's computerized payroll.

- Separate lists should be kept of those who have left civil service (voluntarily or otherwise) and those lists should be linked with the unit in charge of procedures for authorizing appointments, so that employees who have received indemnities do not return to civil service in the short or medium term.

- The application of merit-based principles for personnel hiring is perhaps the weakest area in the draft law. Article 12 (k) mentions that the new SENDOSEP will ensure that the MDOGs apply the pertinent statutes to their hiring practices. But no mention is made of how this will be achieved. The law may leave certain details to be resolved later, but a clause such as this could be considerably strengthened by briefly indicating in the text of the law how compliance mechanisms will be established and who will have the responsibility for verifying compliance with the mechanisms and the authority to enforce them.

Policy Matrix

Problems	Policy measures		Progress indicators	Objectives/goals
	Short term (to June 2003)	Medium term (2003–07)		
Overly complicated pay system that leads to lack of consistency and loss of control over salary policy in the public sector.	Approve a Unification Law. Study the funding sources for paying indemnities when restructuring the ministry or department.	Ensure that the education and health sectors, where the majority of public employees are concentrated, adapt their salary systems to the new policy, maintaining some flexibility to meet their special characteristics.	Seventy percent of all central government public employees subject to the new schedule.	Consistent and sustainable salary system in fiscal terms—target an average reduction of staff in the restructured ministries and departments of more than 5 percent (however, this objective should not be applied indiscriminately; keep the additional long-term cost below $US 100 million through selective reduction).
Lack of complete information in government on the number and location of public employees; lack of merit supervision.	Develop a separate division in an agency such as SENDOSEP that is assigned to each of these tasks.	Develop a complete database of public employees. Draw up and disseminate procedures for central supervision of vacancy appointments based on merit.	HRM data easily obtainable All appointments in higher categories, starting at grade 5, based on merit considerations	Limited civil service based on merit, with relatively well-paid employees (the size of the civil service, in each of its components, is a figure that those responsible for formulating policy in the central government can access easily).

Technical Annex
Determining Real Salaries in Ecuador, 1998–2001

The calculation of real salaries and labor income uses three types of information:

a) Consumer price index, two different series obtained from BCE (Table A1);
b) Sucre/dollar exchange rate, obtained from BCE (Table A1); and
c) Salaries (or labor income), obtained from the Survey of Employment, Unemployment, and Underemployment.

The evolution of consumer prices is considerably different depending on the deflator considered. While the deflator used up to October produces a high inflation scenario for the entire period, the corrected deflator indicates that prices fell between 1998 and 1999 and between 1999 and 2000, and rose only between 2000 and 2001.

It is not surprising then that, as indicated earlier in the chapter, the use of one deflator or the other would have significant implications in terms of the evolution of salaries and real labor income. While labor income seems to have risen some 20 percent between 1998 and 2001 when the corrected deflator is used (Table 4), real labor income would have fallen some 70 percent during the same period when the alternative deflator is used (Table A2).

Table A1. Price Index and Exchange Rate Series

	Price index		Exchange rate (sucre/$US)
	BCE (October) $US 1995	BCE (corrected) $US 2001	BCE
1998	221.1	108.7	6,780
1999	336.7	78.0	20,100
2000	660.2	71.9	
2001	908.9	100.0	

Source: Data obtained from BCE.

Table A2. Monthly Labor Income in Urban Areas, 1998–2001 (at constant 1998 $US values)

	Total	Formal	Informal
1998	146.5	209.4	103.6
1999	45.2	65.3	33.3
2000	41.2	57.3	31.8
2001	39.7	53.8	30.4

Note: Labor income includes salary income and independent worker income (INEC).
The calculations for 1998 and 1999 use the sucre/dollar exchange rate provided by BCE: 6,780 and 20,100, respectively.
Source: Calculations by the authors using data from BCE and MEF.

Given the different implications of the two scenarios in terms of economic policy recommendations as well as our understanding of the poverty trends, we feel it is absolutely necessary to explore in detail what the methodological differences are between the two deflators and to understand them.

Tables A3 and A4 below reproduce the calculations in Tables 5 and 6 of the chapter in order to facilitate the reader's analysis.

Table A3. Monthly Labor Income in Urban Areas by Employment Situation, 1998–2001
(at constant 1998 $US values)

| | *All employees* | | | | |
	Employers	*Independent workers*	*Salaried employees in the public sector*	*Salaried employees in the private sector*	*Others*
1998	—	—	—	—	—
1999	113.8	34.0	63.6	44.1	14.2
2000	129.3	38.2	55.6	39.2	13.1
2001	109.0	34.3	54.7	38.9	15.6
	Formal Sector				
	Employers	*Independent workers*	*Salaried employees in the public sector*	*Salaried employees in the private sector*	*Others*
1998	—	—	—	—	
1999	191.0	93.5	63.6	54.3	
2000	171.5	86.8	55.6	48.9	
2001	163.0	61.6	54.7	46.0	
	Informal Sector				
	Employees	*Independent workers*	*Salaried employees in the public sector*	*Salaried employees in the private sector*	*Others*
1998	—	—		—	
1999	80.1	33.5		26.3	
2000	100.8	37.2		22.1	
2001	75.4	33.1		27.5	

—. No data available.

Note: The calculations for 1998 and 1999 were done with the sucre/dollar exchange rate provided by BCE: 6,780 and 20,100, respectively.

Source: Calculations by the authors using data from BCE and MEF.

Table A4. Labor Income and Basic and Average Salaries in the Private Sector in Urban Areas, 1998–2001

	Labor income		Average salary		Basic salary and basic supplements	
	Nominal ($US)	Real ($US 1998)	Nominal (US$)	Real (1998 $US)	Nominal ($US)	Real (1998 $US)
1998	146.5	146.5	—	—	84.5	84.5
1999	68.9	45.2	67.1	44.1	29.68	19.5
2000	123.0	41.2	117.0	39.2	91.9	30.8
2001	163.0	39.7	160.0	38.9	125.3	30.5

—. No data available

Note: The calculations for 1998 and 1999 were done with the sucre/dollar exchange rate provided by BCE: 6,780 and 20,100, respectively.

Source: Calculations by the authors using data from BCE and MEF.

Annex 1
Civil Service and Administrative Career, Salary Schedules, 1997–2002

Category	Ministerial Agreement		CONAREM Resolutions			
	356 & 357; RO 133 (8-19-97)		01 RO 262 (08-25-99)		06 RO-S 350 (12-30-99)	
	A	B	A	B	A	B
1	260,000		330,000		380,000	
2	270,000		340,000		390,000	
3	280,000		350,000		400,000	
4	290,000		360,000		410,000	
5	320,000		380,000		430,000	
6	330,000		400,000		450,000	
7	350,000		420,000		470,000	
8	370,000		440,000		490,000	
9	390,000		470,000		520,000	
10	420,000		500,000		550,000	
11	450,000		540,000		590,000	
12	490,000		590,000		640,000	
13	520,000		620,000		670,000	
14	550,000		660,000		710,000	
15	580,000	290,000	690,000	350,000	750,000	350,000
16	600,000	300,000	720,000	360,000	780,000	360,000
17	620,000	310,000	760,000	370,000	820,000	370,000
18	650,000	325,000	800,000	390,000	860,000	390,000
19	820,000	410,000	1,000,000	490,000	1,060,000	490,000
20	1,100,000	550,000	1,300,000	660,000	1,360,000	660,000
21	1,350,000	675,000	1,600,000	810,000	1,660,000	810,000

A = Salaries (S/.)
B = Expenses and housing allowances (each one)

Category	CONAREM Resolutions							
	10 RO-S 48 (03-31-2000)		13 S.R.O. 88 (05-31-2000)				129 RO 545 (04-01-2002)	
	A	B	A	($US)	B	($US)	A	B
1	440,000		750,000	30.00			45.00	
2	450,000		765,000	30.60			45.90	
3	460,000		780,000	31.20			46.80	
4	470,000		800,000	32.00			48.00	
5	490,000		825,000	33.00			49.50	
6	510,000		850,000	34.00			51.00	
7	530,000		875,000	35.00			52.50	
8	550,000		900,000	36.00			54.00	
9	580,000		950,000	38.00			57.00	
10	620,000		1,000,000	40.00			60.00	
11	660,000		1,050,000	42.00			63.00	
12	710,000		1,100,000	44.00			66.00	
13	750,000		1,150,000	46.00			69.00	
14	780,000		1,200,000	48.00			72.00	
15	830,000	350,000	1,250,000	50.00	385,000	15.4	75.00	17.50
16	860,000	360,000	1,300,000	52.00	395,000	15.8	78.00	20.00
17	900,000	370,000	1,380,000	55.20	405,000	16.2	82.80	22.50
18	945,000	390,000	1,460,000	58.40	430,000	17.2	87.60	25.00
19	1,165,000	490,000	1,700,000	68.00	540,000	21.6	102.00	27.50
20	1,495,000	660,000	2,200,000	88.00	720,000	28.8	132.00	30.00
21	1,820,000	810,000	2,700,000	108.00	870,000	34.8	162.00	35.00

A = Salaries (S/.)

B = Expenses and housing allowances (each one)

Annex 2
Budgetary Classification of Expenditures

(RO-S 249: 22-1-2001)

Classification of current expenses			

5	1		Personnel expenses
5	1	01	BASIC COMPENSATION
		01	Wages
		02	Salaries
		03	Day wages
		04	Community workers
5	1	02	SUPPLEMENTAL COMPENSATION
		01	Bonus for years of service
		02	Responsibility bonus
		03	Thirteenth salary
		04	Fourteenth salary
		05	Fifteenth salary
		06	Sixteenth salary
		07	Supplemental bonus
		08	Bonus for academic degree, specialization, and special training
		09	Representation allowance
		10	Differentials and additional bonuses
		11	Monetary incentive
		12	Anniversary bonus
		13	Christmas bonus
		14	Functional percentage
		15	Addition to grade 10
		16	Teacher economic stimulus
		18	Monthly Galapagos bonus = 100% minimum salary or base salary
		19	75% additional for special Galapagos system
		20	Border bonus
		21	Dental bonus
		22	Medical bonus
		23	Physicians' Day bonus
		24	World Health Day bonus
		25	Nurses' bonus
		26	Annual economic bonus (administrative personnel)
		27	Amazon region addition
		28	30% supplemental Galapagos compensation
		29	Extracurricular activity in the Galapagos
5	1	03	COMPENSATORY PAYMENTS
		01	Residence allowances
		02	Subsidy for geographic circumstances
		03	Cost of living allowance
		04	Transportation allowance
		05	Overseas allowance
		06	Breaks
		07	Administrative office
		08	Education allowance
5	1	04	SUBSIDIES

			01	Family
			02	Education
			03	Maternity
			04	Death
			05	Daycare
			06	Vacation
			07	Economic incentive for years of service
			99	Other subsidies
5	1	05		TEMPORARY COMPENSATION
			04	Orders and substitutions
			05	Personnel replacements personal
			06	Remunerated license
			07	Fees
			08	Food
			09	Overtime and supplemental time
			10	Contracted personal services
			11	Night shift special compensation

OTHER PERSONNEL EXPENSES:

5	1	06		EMPLOYER CONTRIBUTIONS TO SOCIAL SECURITY
			01	Employer contribution
			02	Reserve fund
			03	Employer retirement fund
			04	Private termination indemnity
5	1	07		INDEMNITIES
			01	Compensation for voluntary resignation
			02	Elimination of position
			03	Untimely dismissal
			04	Compensation for dismissal
			05	Restoration of position
			06	Retirement
			99	Other labor indemnities
5	1	99		ALLOCATIONS TO BE DISTRIBUTED

Annex 3
Basic Salary Schedule for Public Employment Governments, 2002

Civil Service and Administrative Career Law		Human Resources Management System (14 Grades)		Scheduled Professionals[a]		Physicians		Senior Level Officials		Proposed Organic Law on Incomes of Civil Servants	
National Position Classification System											
Grade	Basic Salary	Grade	Basic Salary	Grade	Basic Salary	Grade	Basic Salary	Grade	Basic Salary	Grade	Basic Salary
1	45.00	Service Assistant	70.00	1	60.00	Resident Physician 1	120.00	Director of Govt. Inst.[b]	400.00	1 Service Assistant	210.00
2	45.90	Admin. Asst. A	80.00	2	67.20	Resident Physician 2	125.00	Director of Govt. Inst.[c]	500.00	2 Admin. Asst. A	240.00
3	46.80	Admin. Asst. B	85.00	3	75.26	Resident Physician 3	130.00	Under-secretary	850.00	3 Admin. Asst. B	255.00
4	48.00	Admin. Asst. C	90.00	4	84.30	Resident Physician 4	135.00	Vice Minister	1,100.00	4 Admin. Asst. C	270.00
5	49.50	Technician A	95.00	5	94.41	Resident Physician 5	140.00	Minister	1,500.00	5 Technician A	285.00
6	51.00	Technician B	100.00	6	105.74	Treating Physician 1	145.00	Vice President	2,400.00	6 Technician B	300.00
7	52.50	Pre-professional	110.00	7	118.43	Treating Physician 2	150.00	President of the Republic	3,200.00	7 Pre-professional	330.00
8	54.00	Professional 1	120.00	8	132.64	Treating Physician or Admin. 3	155.00			8 Professional 1	360.00

Grade	Salary	Professional / Director	Salary	Grade	Salary	Treating Physician or Admin.	Salary	Grade	Position	Salary
9	57.00	Professional 2	130.00	9	148.56	Treating Physician or Admin. 4	160.00	9	Professional 2	390.00
10	60.00	Professional 3	140.00	10	166.38	Treating Physician or Admin. 5	165.00	10	Professional 3	420.00
11	63.00	Professional 4	150.00	11	186.35	Treating Physician or Admin. 6	170.00	11	Professional 4	450.00
12	66.00	Professional 5	170.00	12	208.71	Treating Physician or Admin. 7	175.00	12	Professional 5	510.00
13	69.00	Professional 6	190.00			Treating Physician or Admin. 8	180.00	13	Professional 6	570.00
14	72.00	Director	210.00			Treating Physician or Admin. 9	185.00	14	Area Technical Director	630.00
15	75.00					Treating Physician or Admin. 10	190.00	15	National Director	1,050.00
16	78.00					Treating Physician or Admin. 11	195.00	16	Director of Govt. Inst.[b]	2,500.00
17	82.80					Treating Physician or Admin. 12	200.00	17	Director of Govt. Inst.[c]	3,000.00
18	87.60					Treating Physician or Admin. 13	204.00	18	Undersecretary	3,500.00
19	102.00					Treating Physician or Admin. 14	208.00	19	Vice Minister	4,000.00
20	132.00					Treating Physician or Admin. 15	210.00	20	Minister	5,000.00
21	162.00							21	Vice President	6,000.00
									President of the Republic	8,000.00

a. There are nine so-called scheduled professionals. These are physicians, attorneys, professional administrators, economists, civil engineers, geological/mining engineers, chemical engineers, architects, and journalists. Physicians have their own pay scale, which is shown separately. The other professionals have the same pay scale, except that the professional scales for architects, professional administrators, and chemical engineers only have the first 10 grades.
b. Region A.
c. Region B.

17

Decentralization[1]

Jonas Frank

To build an efficient and fiscally responsible decentralized government, Ecuador must face three challenges. The first is to clearly define the areas of responsibility of a second layer of public administration (functional decentralization)—made up of the regional development agencies, executing units, social funds, and attached entities—with respect to the provincial councils and municipalities. Given the magnitude of the resources these entities manage and their type of organization, they do not encourage accountability. The second challenge is to halt the transfers of resources that occur without being tied to the transfer of powers. This process is in high gear and has contributed to the fiscal pressures besetting the central government. The third challenge is to manage the indebtedness of local governments with fiscal responsibility, sustainability, and transparency. Without rules and a clear framework of incentives, decentralization has no foundation. In order to achieve it successfully, the four most important actions are: (i) undertake an intermediate (provincial) level transition strategy in which the decentralized entities of the lower-level system will be accountable to elected authorities, the Prefect, and the Provincial Council; (ii) amend the transfers stipulated by the "15 Percent Law" that are the major source of funding for local governments, making them contingent on the transfer of powers and the delivery of results; (iii) regulate and create transparency concerning the indebtedness of local governments in order to promote fiscal responsibility, which means entering into a rescheduling plan for existing debt with municipalities and provincial councils that are today overindebted, and establishing new regulations for the future indebtedness of the largest ones; and (iv) introduce provisions in the contractual system of transferring powers in order to clarify the responsibilities and rights of each level of government.

---

1. Jonas Frank is a decentralization specialist at the World Bank.

A. The Principal Problem and the Challenges of Decentralization

THE PRINCIPAL PROBLEM. In Ecuador, decentralization is one of the most significant and important challenges in reforming the state and society. The principal problem is that centralized decisionmaking has a negative effect on the quality of public services. The central government cannot provide solutions that are as creative as those provided by the provincial councils and municipalities, which currently execute only 7 percent of total public spending. Since they are closer to the problems, local governments[2] can direct spending to the community's most important needs. Under certain minimum circumstances, decentralization contributes to more efficient and effective services.

THREE CHALLENGES. Ecuador faces three challenges along the path to a more decentralized government: (i) adequately decentralize the autonomous entities of the central government which interact with local governments; (ii) change the process of decentralization, which is currently based solely on the transfer of resources, without the transfer of powers; (iii) control and regulate the debt of municipalities and provincial councils in order to promote fiscal responsibility.

THE FIRST CHALLENGE: PARALLEL PUBLIC ADMINISTRATION—"FUNCTIONAL DECENTRALIZATION." The current structure of public administration shows that the challenge of decentralization does not lie with the sectoral ministries, as is commonly thought. In reality, what affects local governments most today are the many autonomous entities that are part of the central government but do not have clear jurisdictions and responsibilities. Under this sort of "functional decentralization" would be grouped, for example, the regional development agencies, the social funds, and the many institutes, executing units, and agencies attached to the ministries.

These entities manage a total of about $US1.4 billion; for the regional development agencies alone this amounts to close to $US400 million per year (GTZ 2002a, 2002b, 2002c). These are considerable amounts compared to the resources that are currently being negotiated in the decentralization process in the context of the agreements that all 22 provincial councils and 140 municipalities have signed with four ministries (Roads, Environment, Tourism, Agriculture). Close to $US200,000 is being negotiated in the Ministry of the Environment; and less than $US100,000 is being negotiated in the Ministry of Tourism.[3]

The new government should evaluate how this second layer of administration

---

2. The term "local government" refers both to the provincial councils and the municipalities. We also use the term "subnational governments."

3. The Ministry of Public Works and Agriculture has not yet completed the costing phase, but it is estimated that the values in these cases are really higher.

affects the provincial councils and municipalities in terms of (a) evaluating which level of government provides services best; (b) accountability, given that there is a series of overlapping powers and a large majority of these entities answer to the central government; (c) fiscal sustainability, considering the enormous financial resources being managed, often based on credit; (d) the implementation of the government's policy, given that the form of financing and organization allows them to be managed with flexibility and discretion, a situation unlike that in ministries. Given how advanced and rapid the decentralization process is at present, these issues must be resolved in the short term.

THE SECOND CHALLENGE: TRANSFERS OF RESOURCES TO PROVINCIAL COUNCILS AND MUNICIPALITIES. Contrary to the general perception, in the last five years decentralization has made notable and rapid progress. Since 1997, significant resources have been transferred to subnational governments—up to 15 percent of the state's current revenues (the "15 Percent Law"),[4] and in 2002, 25 percent of income. However, a critical look at these transfers would also reveal that they are not based on the principles of decentralization:

- The transfers occur without being tied to an assumption of powers;
- Given that these transfers are not contingent on local governments' generating their own revenues, they have diminished the autonomy of local governments; municipalities, and provincial councils—which are now more dependent than they were in 1997, when the 15 Percent Law was adopted;
- There are significant discretionary transfers and these are sometimes concealed bailouts;
- Other transfers are uneven and favor specific municipalities and provincial councils; and finally
- Much of the decentralization is executed without affecting the structures of central government because the process channels only international credit resources to the local levels.[5]

Thus the challenge is to reverse this trend in fiscal decentralization that has contributed to the financial pressure besetting the central government and cannot be sustained over the long term.

---

4. The law's complete name is as follows: "Special Law on the Distribution of 15 Percent of Revenues from the Budget of the Central Government." With the exception of 2002, there has never been a transfer of more than 11 percent in a given year, or about $US500 million.

5. For example, the Municipal Development Program (PDM), which has been in operation since 1990, transferred $US300 million to the municipalities. For the administration of President Borja, that program has officially been *the* decentralization program.

THE THIRD CHALLENGE: INDEBTEDNESS AND FISCAL RESPONSIBILITY. Decentralization generally creates pressure to take on debt when the process is started. Not only new investment needs but also existing gaps between resources transferred and powers assumed are funded through credit. However, the country has a history of concealed bailouts that have led to moral hazard. Although access to credit at the Ecuadoran Development Bank (BEDE) is handled transparently, there are pressures to relax the payment conditions once credit is obtained. The data used to monitor indebtedness are not always reliable. The Municipal Development Program (PDM) has left most local governments overindebted. Today the challenge for the future administration is to manage indebtedness with clear rules that encourage fiscal responsibility.

Responsibility is affected because local governments are highly dependent on transfers from the central government. This leads to inefficient decisions on spending, because no budgetary restriction is more effective than that based on local governments' own revenues.

FOUR LINES OF ACTION. To confront these three principal challenges, we recommended developing four lines of action:

(i) **The structure of the state and of intergovernmental relations**: the search for the optimum number of levels of government, their jurisdictions, and political authorities;

(ii) **The transfer of powers**: the assignment of responsibilities to each level of government;

(iii) **Decentralization and fiscal responsibility**: determining the coordination and efficiency of spending in the context of the country's financial possibilities;

(iv) **Management of the decentralization process**: clarifying who is responsible for which activity in the process of change.

B. Diagnosis

Structure of the State and Intergovernmental Relations

Over recent decades, the structure of the Ecuadoran state has undergone unprecedented complications. The petroleum resources that have been available since the late 1960s contributed significantly to the increase in public spending and there are now a variety of entities with a duplicate responsibilities (Frank 2001; CONAM 1998a). This expansion of the state has had a negative effect on intergovernmental relations and the autonomy of subnational governments in many ways.

A marked tendency has been the growth of public spending through functional decentralization. There are entities that are autonomous in political, administrative, and financial terms and that maintain only a minimum level of coordination with the sectoral ministries. With no clear jurisdiction, they interfere not only in decentralized agencies of the central government but also in the municipalities and provincial councils as autonomous governments.

REGIONAL DEVELOPMENT AGENCIES. The regional development agencies are part of this group of functionally decentralized entities. They were created starting in the 1950s, an era when the state was seen as the promoter of development. These entities, including CREA, CEDEGE, CRM, CORPECUADOR, UDENOR,[6] and others, violate the principles of decentralization in at least three ways:

- *Their jurisdictions are ambiguous*: The regional level in Ecuador does not formally exist and each entity defines its own jurisdiction. Thus these entities cover many provinces or establish their limits irrespective of the legal-administrative division of the country.
- *Their powers are ambiguous*: They provide services in social sectors such as educational infrastructure, health; they have productive projects in fishing, forestry, and other areas; they invest in highways and rural roads. Reviewing this list of powers, we conclude that all could be decentralized under provincial councils and municipalities.[7]
- *They are accountable to the central government*: Their authority is assigned by the sectoral ministries, which do not answer to the users.

Given that they administer an enormous amount of resources, partially financed with international loans, the regional development agencies have grown in human[8] and financial resources to the point of exceeding the size of some of the ministries to which they report. Given the resources they manage, these agencies are autonomous and have no incentives coordinate at local levels. Thus, they work independently of the provincial councils and municipalities.

SOCIAL FUNDS. The social funds, conceived as programs to combat poverty with interventions at the local level, are another set of functionally autonomous entities. Programs such as FISE (Emergency Social Investment Fund) or the Comprehensive Rural Development Project (run by the Ministry of Social Welfare) finance social projects such as primary schools, basic health centers, centers for children and the

---

6. CREA (Center for the Economic Reconversion of Azuay); CEDEGE (Center for Development of the Guayas Basin); CRM (Center for the Reconversion of Manabí); UDENOR (Development Unit of the North).

7. The only justification for continuing to administer such powers at the "regional level" is economies of scale compared to the provincial level (where they exist).

8. For example, CREA maintains a staff of 700 people. In contrast, the Ministry of Education at the central level has a staff of about 600, and the Ministry of the Environment has a staff of 150.

elderly, potable water and basic sanitation projects, and rural roads.[9] Like the regional development agencies, the powers of the social funds could be decentralized. Only as an exception—infrastructure construction, for example—do they include the municipalities in the management of services. In practice they operate parallel to the municipality, making coordination difficult and working against efficiency in service delivery.

THE INTERMEDIATE LEVEL. In this complex institutional framework, the government level most affected is the provincial level, where institutional complexity creates an extremely counterproductive framework for the delivery of services and negatively affecting accountability. There are two authorities, one elected (the Prefect) and one appointed (the Governor), the ministers, and the regional development agencies.

PROVINCIAL COUNCILS. This complex institutional framework has had an extreme effect on the provincial councils. It can be shown that many of the councils' powers overlap those of other entities (Frank 2001). In addition, the legitimacy of the provincial councils suffers from another dilemma: the Constitution gives them jurisdiction in rural areas, although they are elected by citizens who live in both urban and rural areas. Thus, they provide services for only a minority of those who elect them, those living in rural areas. The fact that the majority of the council members come from urban neighborhoods further accentuates this dilemma of legitimacy.

The Constitutional reforms of 1998 sought to formalize the role of the provincial council as the link between the national and municipal levels. These reforms provide for indirect representation of the municipalities on the council. This leads to some coordination between municipalities and provincial councils, whereas their relationship previously had been antagonistic and competitive. Resources flow directly from the central government to each of the subnational governments, something that does not encourage collaboration between the provinces and cantons. The subnational elections of 2000 took place under this new rule but there were various attempts to declare indirect representation "unconstitutional." If this form of representation were eliminated, the provincial council and the municipalities would lose an important instrument of coordination.

---

9. Other programs include Friendly Networks, School Backpack, Improvement of Bilingual Intercultural Schools, School Meals, Our Children, Operation Child Rescue, School Scholarship, Producer Credit, Solidarity Bonus, Community Dining Halls, Generic Medicines, Mobile Health Units, Free Maternity Care, National Food and Nutrition Program (PANN) 2000, Expanded Program of Immunizations, Epidemiological Control–Tuberculosis, Epidemiological Control–Malaria and Dengue Fever, Peasant Housing, Marginal Urban Housing, Housing for Solidarity Bond Beneficiaries, and Potable Water and Environmental Sanitation.

MUNICIPALITIES. Since the reintroduction of a democratic system of government in 1978, the number of municipalities has more than doubled. While Ecuador used to have about 100 cantons, last year it had nearly 220. This means that the possibilities for providing services with economies of scale have been reduced, with a negative effect on efficiency. Thus, the municipalities' technical capacity on the one hand and financial capacity on the other have diminished. Nonetheless, Congress continues to approve requests from parishes to convert to municipalities. The situation is so serious that today 80 percent of the municipalities can be considered illegal because the Municipal Regime Law requires a minimum of 50,000 inhabitants for a community to become a municipal government.

PARISH BOARDS. The Constitutional reforms of 1998 represent a great effort to democratize the state. Part of this effort is changes in the status of parish boards, which to this day are appointed by the municipality and thus are without any legitimacy backed by the citizens. The Constitution provided for popular elections in rural parishes. However, the more radical measure was to convert them into "autonomous governments," whereby they were not only entitled to their own political authority but powers and financial resources as well. In this way, from one day to the next Ecuador created about "parish municipalities" because legally they are not well differentiated from the country's municipalities.[10] Still unclear are the financial consequences of this for the central governmenand how these parish boards will be financed. The country should ask itself whether it is in a position to pay for four levels of government. This legal ambiguity affects the government's relationship with the citizens as well as coordination with the municipality in the delivery of services.

JURISDICTIONS. Looking at intergovernmental relations as a whole, it does not appear that they provide a favorable context for decentralization. This situation seems more serious when we consider that there are currently as least seven border conflicts between provinces or between cantons. Nonetheless, having clear jurisdictions and authorities is a *sine qua non* to build a more decentralized system of government.

Administrative Decentralization: Transfer of Powers

The provincial councils and municipalities currently carry out only 7 percent of total spending. In international terms, this is relatively little if we use the example of countries such as Colombia, Argentina, and Brazil, where close to 40 percent of spending is decentralized. Further, Ecuador's data are probably overestimated

---

10. The Constitution is ambiguous here. According to the constitutional provision, provincial councils and municipalities have "full autonomy" as compared to the simple "autonomy" that parish boards have. This has been part of an extensive debate regarding the powers of this governmental body.

because they do not reveal the autonomy that local governments in Ecuador actually have over this spending. Cumbersome procedures, delayed transfers, and a lack of local decisionmaking are part of the centralist reality that provincial councils and municipalities continue to face.

In addition, since the end of the National Commission on Decentralization and Autonomy, the country has begun to define the powers that each level of government would have in four sectors: environment, tourism, agriculture, and public works. Motivated by the political pressure exerted by the provincial councils and municipalities because of the central government's failure to provide a concrete response, the process of organized negotiation among the three levels of government—national, provincial, and municipal—began in 2001. The first step was to define the existing situation regarding the existing powers. The second was an agreement between the executive branch and the "province," that is, between the provincial council and the municipalities, on the management of powers. The third was detailed negotiations between the provincial council and the municipalities. The fourth step, begun just recently, was the actual transfer agreements and the start-up of services.

This form of negotiation has no precedent in Latin America. It is happening in an organized context and with the participation of the ministries. It is proof that it is feasible to organize local governments around common objectives. Although there have been cases of local governments seeking their own advantage and wanting to withdraw from collection negotiations,[11] the process has been quite successful so far. All of the 22 provinces and 140 of the municipalities, representing two-thirds of the total, are participating—indicating the great desire that exists at local levels to go further with decentralization.

However, the risk of this procedure lies not in the way powers are defined, which seeks to minimize duplications and assign responsibilities according to the capacity of each local government, but rather in the contractual system. In addition, the particular traits that the process took on in Ecuador through the signing of a series of agreements—a "Promotion Agreement" and various separate "Transfer Agreements"—are a source of risks because they could be mutually incompatible.[12] In addition, the lack of provisions for penalties, of reversibility in the process, and of conflict solutions are other risk factors (World Bank 2002).

Further, in many cases it seems premature at this point to sign transfer agreements, given that there is still no complete clarity regarding the human resources,

---

11. The province of Esmeraldas is an example. CONAM and the GTZ have estimated that about 18,000 individual agreements would be created in the province if this collective negotiation scheme were not adopted. In addition, the evidence that local governments are less willing to engage in collective negotiation in the health and education sectors must be taken very seriously.

12. However, the signing of the "Promotion Agreement" in March 2001 was a political necessity and is an important milestone in the process in Ecuador.

financial resources, and infrastructure (assets) to be transferred in each case. Moreover, the Ministry of Economy and Finance is just beginning to participate in the preparation of these reforms.

The second risk lies in the political, financial, and administrative structure that provides the framework for the agreements. As we have mentioned, in Ecuador there are few conditions for accountable service delivery. This is due, on the one hand, to the existence of dual authorities at each level of government, the duplication of functions, and the complex arrangement of jurisdictions. On the other, it is due to the dispersed fiscal system that ultimately directs the local government spending. In this adverse context, the Committee on Powers has been created to settle conflicts in the administration of powers, but it does not have sufficient legal capacity because it is only an administrative body. In other words, in the legal hierarchy, its rulings are only "recommendations" to each of the parties, which in turn are not obligated to implement them.

Fiscal Decentralization: Transfer of Resources

In Ecuador, the fiscal system is at the center of the discussion regarding decentralization. Transfers of resources are the central tools that governments use to maintain their legitimacy, and political crises loom if resources are not transferred to the subnational governments. In other words, their legitimacy is volatile and fickle given that a legitimacy based on fiscal resources "cannot be saved up." This was Ecuador's experience in the fiscal crisis of 1999 when it ceded the flow of resources, and the coastal provinces in particular sought "autonomy," a legal status that had never been completely clarified in the debate about decentralization.[13]

The system of fiscal decentralization in Ecuador has some specific characteristics that merit careful study. We mention this not only because of its political repercussions but because to a great extent it determines the conditions for the delivery of services. It is not the decentralization laws that ensure coordination among levels of government, nor the transfer of powers agreements, but rather the financial system available to the subnational governments. We analyze it from the perspective of transfers, own revenues, debt, and fiscal responsibility.

TRANSFERS. The public finances system depends above all on transfers. However, the system has various deficiencies from several perspectives. First, it is a dispersed system

---

13. The differentiation between "decentralized provinces" and "autonomous provinces" has not been very helpful given that any process of decentralization involves a greater degree of autonomy. This is one of the reasons why those participating in decentralization in Ecuador cannot communicate very well with each other. However, symbols such as "autonomy" take on a political function within the process of decentralization that must be taken into account.

given that transfers to subnational governments derive from no less than 16 "special laws" (see the annex). Each begins from the concept of not allocating resources that are already assigned, that is, based on the notion that additional resources are created to protect "earned rights." Each law applies its own distribution principles and different spending conditions. It is a highly complex system that makes it impossible to create a framework conducive to efficient service delivery. Given that these are direct transfers from the central government to each of the country's provincial councils and municipalities, these levels of government have absolutely no incentive to coordinate their investments in a more reasonable manner.

A second characteristic of the system of transfers is that is allocates resources without the corresponding powers and thus violates a basic principle of decentralization. The most remarkable case is the 15 Percent Law, whose regulations expressly prohibit using these resources to assume new powers and thus set up a considerable amount of funds that have put a straightjacket on the central government. Given the amount of resources involved in this law, it constitutes a landmark in the demands for more resources by the country's regions, demands that were unleashed after the return to democracy in 1978. This has also contributed to the financial crisis the country is facing, although there has never been a transfer of more than 11 percent, something that regularly helps to distort intergovernmental relations.

As if these negative experiences were not enough, in September 2002 Congress approved a law that allocates up to 25 percent of income taxes to the country's municipalities, without any link to the assumption of powers.[14] Once again, this confirms that the country's provinces and cantons have strong ties in Congress that guarantee them access to the country's revenues.

Third, the system of transfers only puts the central government under pressure to finance powers that are to be decentralized. A process has been unleashed of meticulous definition of how much the central government "owes" each provincial council and municipality. Although this is understandable in the atmosphere of distrust that exists between the levels of government, this rule does not foster shared responsibility at local levels.

Fourth, the system does not apply the principles of partnership that sharing proportionally in the nation's revenues would imply. For example, in the case of the 15 Percent Law, only the resources approved in the budget at the start of the fiscal year are transferred. If revenues are later higher than projected in the budget, the central government does not use the actual revenues it has as a reference. Just as the possi-

---

14. The distribution system is also surprising. Each taxpayer can freely decide to which municipality the resources will be allocated, even though he or she may not live in that jurisdiction and receive certain services. This violates the principle of fiscal federalism that there should be a correspondence between taxes and the services that citizens receive in a specific locality.

bility of sharing "upwards" is excluded, so too is the possibility of "sharing down-ward" in times of economic contraction. The Constitution protects the subnational governments from having lower revenues from year to year. This creates a ratchet effect that also contributes to the financial pressures on the central government. The rigidity of the budget is also aggravated by a series of preallocations amounting to about 30 percent of tax and petroleum revenues.

Fifth, transfers are discretionary and ambiguous. The 15 Percent Law is again an example: it was approved based on the current revenues of the central govern-ment and then the 1998 Constitution amended it, using the general budget as a reference. This situation has not yet been clarified and the distribution base is not clear. In addition, and although there are no reliable data, a series of transfers are discretionary, favor particular municipalities and provinces, and are used as con-cealed bailouts for subnational governments and regional public companies, unleashing a series of similar actions owing to moral hazard. For example, in 1990 alone the central government assumed debts for about $US100 million, 80 per-cent of which belonged to ECAPAG, the water company for the city of Guayaquil (Figure 1).

Given this ambiguity in transfers, in the past the debate has focused on the inequities existing among localities, even though information is unreliable and coastal and mountain institutions have published their own data in an effort to

Figure 1. Subrogation of External Debt (1998)

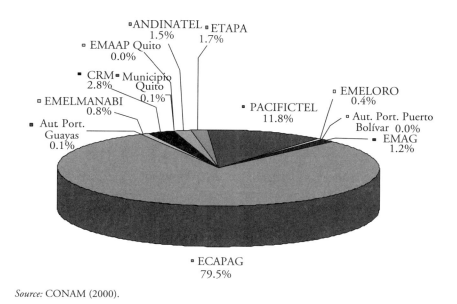

Source: CONAM (2000).

demonstrate the inequities. This debate—focused on what each locality receives and what each locality contributes—shows the high level of mistrust that exists in the country. No doubt the differences in fiscal capacities are enormous (CONAM 2000). On the other hand, based on the per capita transfers that each province receives, Ecuador's allocations are relatively equitable in comparison with international standards. Surprisingly, the provinces that receive the least include the most economically powerful provinces, such as Pichincha and Guayas (Figure 2).

However, only if the above-mentioned discretionary transfers are also counted is it possible to obtain a clear picture of what the provinces actually receive and on that basis build a new decentralized fiscal system.

OWN REVENUES. Local governments have own revenues, but these are either unproductive (as in the case of provincial councils) or subject to a series of administrative obstacles or exemptions that prevent more autonomous tax management. This is evident, for example, in the urban and rural property tax, the tax on vehicles, the patent tax, the tax on total assets, improvement contributions, levies, and others (CONAM 2001b). This precarious revenue situation is demonstrated by the fact that 96.3 percent of all tax revenues are still administered by the central government and only 3.7 percent by the municipalities (Wiesner 1999).

In addition, the transfers as they are currently applied do not encourage fiscal effort. They are not contingent on increases in the municipalities' and provincial councils' own revenues, and the continuous increase in transfers has led not only to a vertical imbalance in subnational governments but also to dependence on the central government:

- **Municipalities**: While in 1998 the municipalities had a dependency rate of 47 percent (transfers/total revenue; CONAM 2000), this figure was 74 percent in 2000 (MEF/CONAM 2002).
- **Provincial councils**: Although there are no recent data, in 1998 the dependency rate was 76 percent (CONAM 2000) and this has also probably worsened owing to the effect of transfers.

This leads to a series of problems in public finances and in the efficiency of spending: subnational governments incur oversized expenses. Given their dependence on transfers, there are incentives for them to overexploit the common resources (in other words, the free rider problem). In this situation, they do not feel any effective budgetary restriction. Such restrictions are more effective when based on the subnational governments' own revenues.

INDEBTEDNESS. The municipalities and provincial councils can take on debt with the BEDE in order to make investments. With a high rate of dependency and a high percentage of transfers, subnational governments also have incentives to contract

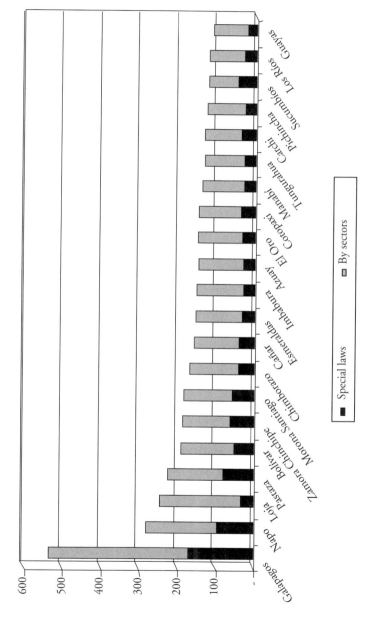

Figure 2. Per Capita Resources Received, by Province (in $US, 1998)

Special laws ■ By sectors

Source: CONAM (2000).

excessive debt. Although no credit push[15] can be seen as in other countries of the region (Colombia, for example), several local governments find themselves overindebted, in part as a result of the Municipal Development Program (PDM). The government has still not begun debt-restructuring reforms, which is compulsory under the Law on Transparency and Fiscal Responsibility.

In addition, the data and references that the government uses to determine the level of indebtedness must be revised and supplemented (MEF/CONAM 2002) in order to produce a more reliable view of the situation. The Ecuadoran system of government debt is difficult to monitor. Local governments do not produce reliable data and do not regularly send their financial reports to the central government. Although access to credit can be regulated transparently, the BEDE is often under pressure to make concessions to politically strong local governments. In addition, a system of indebtedness based on administrative principles—and not on market principles—creates monitoring requirements that cannot always be satisfied in an informal environment. Although the BEDE has begun to take credit risk into account with respect to municipalities and provincial councils, this situation is not changing significantly.

FISCAL RESPONSIBILITY. In this context of incentives created by the fiscal system, it is doubtful whether the measures proposed in the Law on Responsibility, Stabilization, and Fiscal Transparency of 2002 can actually help to bring public sector revenues and spending into line. The reasons for this assessment follow:

- Measuring the degree of indebtedness[16] does not determine the *actual ability* to pay in the future, given that the indicators are based solely on the past.
- Although indebtedness indicates the future payment on debts and the fiscal pressures on the debt portfolio, it does not reveal (i) the *risks* in the debt portfolio, (ii) the impact of the fiscal balance sheet on the *sustainability* of the debt, (iii) the *obligations* to be converted to debt, and (iv) the *budgetary flexibility* at the subnational level for meeting obligations.
- Although a broader notion of debt and its various forms is being introduced, the subnational financial data in Ecuador have never been all that reliable; various extrabudgetary activities continue to exist.
- In addition, the penalties imposed on individuals (such as mayors and prefects) do not take into account the pressure exerted by the provincial councils and municipal councils.

---

15. "Credit push" is understood to mean accelerated indebtedness.
16. Measured by the percentage relationship calculated each year between total liabilities and total annual revenues and the relationship between annual debt service and total revenues (Art. 7).

- Finally, the law opens the door to new debt given that the subnational governments—in the event of a budgetary cutback—"will have to approve credit changes in the expense budget equal to the value of the revenues not obtained" (Art. 41).

Management of the Decentralization Process

Except when working to draw up the transfer of powers agreements, provincial councils and municipalities do not currently participate in the decisionmaking on decentralization. The situation is radically different from 2000, when the National Commission on Decentralization and Autonomy represented both social forces and the subnational governments. The President of the Republic had a forum he could use and the members of the commission also found an atmosphere of open discussion regarding the future model of the state. The ability to call together a broad forum has been key to managing the decentralization process.

However, the National Commission on Decentralization now functions only as an internal agency of the central government in support of decisionmaking by the Office of the President. Without any type of representative function, the only participants are the Ministry of Economy and Finance, the Planning Office, and CONAM as the Technical Secretariat. Although the formal participation of the Decentralization Commission of the National Congress as a guest ("with a voice but no vote")[17] is a sign of enormous progress, the commission does not currently have sufficient legitimacy in the eyes of local governments. Moving the location of the commission's sessions from one of the country's major cities to another in order to lend a tinge of representativeness to the proceedings is not enough.

Furthermore, Ecuador still has no simple and practical system for monitoring decentralization. Various attempts have already been made to establish such a system, with support from ODEPLAN and CONAM. It is enormously useful to have this instrument so as to be able to verify whether decentralization is really meeting the high expectations that it creates in the country. This also means strengthening the open information policy that CONAM has had since the beginning of the National Commission on Decentralization and Autonomy. A link has been established between the institutions of decentralization, but this role must still be consolidated with the systematic and ongoing dissemination of information directed to the broadest target groups in society.

---

17. Recently, the chairman of the Congressional Commission on Decentralization chose not to participate in the sessions as a protest against the central government's "lack of political will" for supporting decentralization.

C. Policy Recommendations

Structure of the State and Intergovernmental Relations

Ecuador's complex institutional framework is not conducive to decentralization. Different levels of government, autonomous entities, and agencies compete among themselves without any clear reference point. In this context, no one is clearly responsible, which contradicts the principle of accountability. Making more financial transfers based on this institutional framework is risky, and thus reforms are needed in the various spheres of the government's structure.

REFORM OF THE INTERMEDIATE LEVEL. Reform of the intermediate level[18] will only be viable if it is designed as part of a slow strategy, with successive steps moving toward complete transfer to the provincial councils or municipalities. This must be organized as a transition strategy. To do this, it is extremely important to choose a starting point that potentially determines the remaining actions needed.

REGIONAL DEVELOPMENT AGENCIES. If the government is willing to give a strong signal of support for decentralization, it should focus on transferring powers and resources from the regional development agencies. As a first step, it is recommended that a new board be established for the development agencies. This would be made up of the provincial councils in provinces where the development agencies have jurisdiction, given that they cover various provinces. A neutral representative from the central government should also participate. This board would be responsible for managing services until proceeding to transfer them in a later phase. It would have to determine the human, material, and financial resources that belong to each of the provincial councils or municipalities in the province. Until the transfer is completed,[19] the new board should approve the annual budget of the Regional Development Agency.

DECENTRALIZED ENTITIES OF THE SUBORDINATE SYSTEM. The transition strategy also applies to the subordinate system at the provincial level. As a first step toward decentralization, a framework of incentives promoting coordination with the autonomous system (provincial councils and municipalities) should be created. Using Chile and Bolivia as a reference, a scheme could be considered in which the provincial directors currently appointed by the ministries (Ministries of Health, Education, and

---

18. Like Ecuador, several other countries in the region, including Venezuela, Colombia, Peru, Bolivia, and Chile, are also reforming or discussing the future functions of the intermediate level.

19. Based on international experience, transferring human resources in particular entails many problems.

others) would appoint a short list proposed by the provincial council. In this way, the provincial directors would owe their positions, at least in part, to the autonomous governments of the province or enjoy their confidence. A second measure would be to submit the ministries' operational plans to the provincial council for approval. Thus, although the central government would continue to develop operational plans, it would be possible to coordinate activities so that the provincial council would acquire a certain degree of control over the actions carried out by the ministries on a decentralized basis. As long as decentralization does not actually progress, this is the only way to arrive at a transition.

THE GOVERNOR. Another debate in Ecuador concerns the role of the provincial governor, who is currently appointed by the Ministry of the Interior. Although this governor is an authority in addition to the Prefect (elected), his or her involvement in public life is minimal given that his or her resources are extremely limited. A provincial cabinet has operated in only a few provinces. However, undertaking a reform of the governorships now would divert attention from the administration's more serious and important problems. The real problem lies in the multiple entities of the subordinate system that in the province of Guayas, for example, amount to 220 different agencies and in Azuay to 180 different agencies (CONAM 1998). Looking at them from this perspective, flashy reforms of the subordinate system such as the elimination of the governor are basically unimportant.[20]

If the government is successful in organizing the intermediate level in accordance with this phase of the transition, it will have made great progress toward decentralization. Any further steps would require a transfer of resources and powers within the framework of the negotiations that have been in progress since 2001.

Administrative Decentralization: Transfer of Powers

The transfer of powers should seek to produce the smallest possible fiscal impact and promote conditions for accountability. The agreements are the principal route whereby the transfer of powers is achieved in Ecuador and should continue to be used. In order for the agreements to fill in the gaps in decentralization, the following specific aspects should be taken into account:

---

20. In 1998, the administration of President Mahuad launched a project to strengthen the governor's offices based on the provincial cabinets (following the Chilean model) with the governor in charge of a territorial budget (CONAM 1998). If Ecuador is consistent in following the Spanish model of "provincial autonomies," it should retain the governors' offices, given that in Spain they also exist parallel to the elected authorities. On the other hand, the provincial councils have indicated that they should be the only governments in the province. A part of this clamor is the fact that some of them call themselves "provincial governments" in order to express the idea that they are actually the only legitimate government.

- The agreements may transfer resources appropriately only if intergovernmental transfers guarantee a minimum of correspondence between responsibility and resources.
- The agreements can establish a clear division of responsibilities only when (i) the labor problem is resolved (contracting, rights, labor liabilities) and (ii) clear jurisdictions and authorities are established.
- The agreements can contribute to the efficiency and quality of services only when (i) goals are set for the delivery of services and (ii) penalties are levied for failing to meet goals.

Ecuador's reform program should resolve these open issues. However, it is a *sine qua non* condition that the Ministry of Economy and Finance participate regularly, actively, and on a committed basis in the negotiations. Only then will we know whether the central government takes decentralization seriously and is committed to it. The intergovernmental agreements mentioned below could commit the Ministry in this respect.

MAKING ACCESS TO THE NEGOTIATIONS CONDITIONAL. Access to the transfer of powers program should be subject to subnational governments' meeting minimum standards of accountability and submitting financial reports. This is necessary because it is likely that not all of the 22 provincial councils and 140 municipalities that are participating can meet this minimum level of quality that will later contribute to responsible management.

PROVISIONS IN THE CONTRACTUAL SYSTEM. The government should work rapidly to generate sufficient provisions for the contractual system. The model agreements that have been designed still do not adequately address the many adverse situations that may occur. In particular, there should be more in-depth treatment of penalties in the event of noncompliance and of the reversibility of the process.[21]

PRODUCTION OF INFORMATION. Additional information should be produced for decisionmaking; the "Study of the Consequences of the Transfer of Powers" begun in 2000 should be carried out for each of the sectors. This is important because as of yet not all ministries—such as Roads, Tourism, Agriculture, and Environment—know the effects that decentralization would likely have. The Ministry of Education is the only central government agency that participated in the study.

---

21. In this regard, the work previously done by CONAM, AME, the Consortium of Provincial Councils of Ecuador (CONCOPE), and the World Bank can be a guide for completing the agreements (World Bank 2002). In addition, the Powers Commission should be empowered to be the final arbiter in resolving conflicts, perhaps with the support of the Attorney General, provided this arrangement is operative.

TRANSFER OF HUMAN RESOURCES. The institutions of the central and subnational governments still do not have sufficient knowledge of the labor issue. Experience in all the countries of Latin America shows that if human resources are not paid by the subnational governments, the central government continues to have influence on spending decisions at the local level. The government should hold strategic discussions with the unions in each of the sectors. There was an initial dialogue in the education sector but it would probably be more productive if there were concrete data on labor liabilities, indemnities, and the future rights of public employees.

INCLUDE THE ENTITIES OF "FUNCTIONAL DECENTRALIZATION." The agreements still focus on transferring powers from the sectoral ministries. As we have mentioned, the principal problem facing decentralization in Ecuador is the fact that an enormous amount of resources is administered outside the ministries in a second layer of administration made up of the regional development agencies, the social funds, and other entities. Thus, the entire transfer of powers process could fail to attack the central task of decentralization.

TRANSFERS OF POWERS SUBJECT TO RESULTS. In the sectors that have made the most progress in the negotiations, such as the environment and tourism, Ecuador should experiment with agreements based on results. As we mentioned, without clear goals that can be monitored there is no knowledge concerning the usefulness of decentralization, and the debate will continue to revolve around the amount of resources to be transferred, an important issue but not what is essential in a decentralization effort, which seeks improved efficiency and quality of services.

Fiscal Decentralization

Since the National Commission on Decentralization and Autonomy presented the "New Management Model" in 2000, there have been no new proposals for extensive reform of public finances. In 2001, the Ministry of Economy and Finance took the lead and developed the Fiscal Reform, which contains some ideas submitted by the National Commission. However, this reform has gradually encountered resistance both in the ministry and in Congress, and consequently it has not been possible to do much. One exception is the Law on Responsibility, Stabilization, and Fiscal Transparency, but this still needs to be put into practice. Thus, there are many other fiscal decentralization reforms that are still pending.

INFORMATION. Reforming public finances and adopting a new system of transfers presupposes having more reliable, complete, and transparent data. As a first step, we recommend quantifying not only the transfers that each provincial council and each municipality receives but also how much the central government spends in each province and canton through the following:[22]

---

22. The work done previously in the context of the National Commission on Decentralization and Autonomy is not sufficient.

- Ministries,
- Regional development agencies,
- Social funds,
- International loans, and
- Extrabudgetary allocations and discretionary transfers.

Only if these data are available and reliable will the debate about decentralization be more informed and the conditions right for making well-founded decisions. This is a condition for being able to adopt a new system of transfers. In addition, information could be produced—such as GDP generated in each province—that would measure the economic potential of the jurisdictions.[23]

This also means having budgetary management based on the principles of unity and universality, at both the national and local levels. The submission of reports by the subnational governments must be enforced—and probably the only way to do this is to exclude from the decentralization process those government entities that do not meet the minimum standards. Having more information on public finances also means having the instrument of SIGEF at subnational levels. Since 2000 there have been plans to expand the system to the municipalities and provincial councils. It has not yet been possible to consolidate these plans in the network of participating institutions such as the Comptroller's Office, AME, and the Consortium of Provincial Councils of Ecuador (CONCOPE). The parties must make a commitment to move ahead—in an initial phase—with pilot programs and later a gradual extension to other subnational governments.

TRANSFERS. Reforming transfers is one of the most important reforms that the new administration must undertake. This means defining the distribution bases and clear distribution criteria. For the future system of transfers, a vision should be developed that takes several considerations into account. The transfers of resources should be based on the delivery of results; without this rule is it impossible to say with certainty what impact resources would have in terms of service quality. If this condition is met, the rules on the use of resources for current expenses and investment can be less strict; these rules are generally difficult to monitor and it is best to encourage autonomous decisions by local governments rather than determine at the central level how resources are to be used. As well, a healthy balance should be struck between freely assignable resources and other resources for specific uses in each of the sectors (such as health and education). And finally, transfers should encourage the generation of local government's own resources.

Given that the financial system is so disperse, a first step should be to focus on what has the most impact—for example, the 15 Percent Law and the social funds—

---

23. On this subject the government should take the lead in order to avoid new discussions regarding the reliability of the data obtained by institutions from the different regions of the country—that is, the coast and the mountains.

leaving for a second phase the numerous transfers that benefit particular provinces. In addition, consideration should be given to establishing two matching grants at different levels of government.

THE 15 PERCENT LAW. The resources that the 15 Percent Law transfers—actually in violation of the principles of decentralization—are politically unrecoverable. In the event that the government decides to transfer more than the current 11 percent, any additional resources should be subject to the assumption of powers and the management of results. This would send an important signal to the local governments on the responsible management of finances. This reform would be viable only with changes in the law's regulations. Second, the calculation basis should be clearly defined. The difference between the Constitution, which takes the general budget as the reference, and the law, which refers to current revenues, should be resolved, reaffirming current revenues as the base. Third, the distribution criterion that distributes 10 percent of the law's resources in equal parts should be nullified. This rule has contributed substantially to the growth in the number of municipalities given that for a small parish (to be converted into a canton) these resources represent an enormous amount. Fourth, the transfers should be effected in proportion to the revenues actually obtained, whether they are higher or lower. With these rules, the principles of shared participation would be reaffirmed.

SOCIAL FUNDS. Under the current scheme, the many functionally decentralized agencies do not coordinate their actions with the provincial councils and municipalities. This is because in practice it is the financing systems—and not the decentralization laws—that determine the entities' powers. Thus, in the long term, social funds such as the FISE and others should be incorporated in current transfers from the central government to the municipalities and provincial councils. These funds should be contingent on a specific use.[24] In its first phase, a transition strategy should provide that operational plans be approved by the respective municipalities in which activities are carried out, and that the fund be managed with the participation of the provincial councils or municipalities.

MATCHING GRANTS. Given that resource flows are the most effective tool for improving intergovernmental relations, efforts should be made to establish links between the provincial councils and the municipalities. Except for their approaches to the negotiations on powers, the two levels have for the most part had an antagonistic relationship. In order to encourage greater cooperation between them, a matching grant could be set up and offered by the provincial councils[25] to the

---

24. However, any effort to place conditions on spending also implies having the ability to monitor their application.
25. The provincial councils are financially in a weaker position than the municipalities. But even so, the resources offered by the provincial councils to the municipality in a matching grant

municipalities for services with externalities. For example, in sectors such as health and highways, this grant could be funded with resources from existing transfers. In addition, there could be a matching grant between the central government and the provincial councils,[26] and directly between the central government and the municipalities. In this way, there would be a sufficient level of competition among the levels of government and greater cooperation would be ensured at the same time, provided that the rules were well defined.

OWN REVENUES. Given the high degree of dependency of the subnational governments on transfers, it is imperative that they improve their own revenues. The government has already begun to examine the principal obstacles to improving this situation (CONAM 2001b). It is important to reform the many administrative obstacles, particularly in the property tax, as this is the principal source of revenues for the municipalities. Making regular transfers contingent on increases in the subnational governments' own revenues can be an excellent way to encourage these reforms.

In addition, it is important, particularly for the provincial councils, to generate a base of their own revenues that will make them more autonomous from the central government and will provide the opportunity for greater accountability on the part of electors and taxpayers.[27] However, considering the situation of national public finances and the informality in the management of resources, it is difficult to consider granting new own revenues to the subnational governments. The only possibility in the medium term is to establish surcharges on national taxes that are transferred to the subnational governments. Tax management would be the responsibility of the central government but the resources would go to the provincial councils.[28] However, this reform should be contingent on minimum conditions of responsible finance management on the part of the provincial councils.

INDEBTEDNESS AND FISCAL RESPONSIBILITY. With respect to indebtedness, the government should think strategically about how to send market signals to the local governments. Large municipalities such as Quito and Guayaquil should, in addition to

---

are surely attractive to the municipal governments and can encourage coordination. It would be advisable to review the experience of some of the states in Mexico in this respect.

26. In reality, the grouping of provincial councils in the "G-8" has been promoted through fiscal incentives provided by the central government (such as the possible construction of the highway to Manaus, Brazil).

27. It should be kept in mind that the indicators of dependency and self-sufficiency would be even worse in the event of transfers for the assumption of powers, given that these would also be financed through transfers (see the case of Venezuela). This makes it necessary for local governments to increase their own revenues or to seek their own new sources of financing.

28. Technically, the surcharges are transfers. However, for the taxpayer this distinction is not generally made and they thus would stimulate accountability.

administrative controls, have their debt capacity evaluated by specialized and internationally recognized firms. This is important, given that the national government has not yet been able to indicate to the local governments in a credible way that it will not engage in any form of debt forgiveness. In this sense, a policy could be adopted whereby financially incapable local governments would be supervised by the central government until they recovered their stability. These political incentives are possibly more effective than fiscal incentives and have been implemented in other countries.[29]

In addition, making public the debts that have been cancelled in the past could be a useful way to demonstrate the severity of the problem and the government's decision to implement a different policy. Also, all existing debt in subnational governments should be disclosed as pending payments and contingencies. As the criteria used by the Law on Responsibility, Stabilization, and Fiscal Transparency only measure past debt capacity, these criteria could be supplemented with indicators that show the budgetary flexibility of local governments, some of the risks in the debt portfolio, the impact of the fiscal balance sheet on the sustainability of the debt, and the obligations to be converted into debt. In this regard, it is important to check whether the indicators and the information that the BCE uses to rate credit risk are valid for decisionmaking.

With these data, it would be possible to begin with a debt restructuring plan as provided in the Law on Responsibility, Stabilization, and Fiscal Transparency. It is not clear how many local governments are actually overindebted—in part because of the financial effect of the Municipal Development Program—and consequently need substantial reforms. However, it is imperative to begin strategically with debt refinancing that is based on clear criteria.

In order for the mechanisms of the Law on Responsibility to operate properly, the Ministry of Economy and Finance must again take the initiative by eliminating preallocations, thus ensuring that the budget will be more flexible. Finally, the Ministry's entire budget management process must be reviewed, as many governments have already tried to do. Without a properly functioning budget, there is no guarantee whatsoever that the law will have any effect. As a first step, the Ministry of Economy and Finance should analyze in detail what organizational and procedural changes it should make internally in order to fully implement fiscal responsibility based on this law.

Management of the Decentralization Process

It is unlikely that the government will be able to undertake a reform of the magnitude of decentralization without the support of the subnational governments. Con-

---

29. Fiscal penalties include, for example, restricted access to credit or transfers. Countries that impose political penalties include the United States (as in the case of the cities of Washington, D. C. and New York) and Germany.

tinuing to exclude them from the decisionmaking process means provoking political resistance. The opposite approach, welcoming their participation, can be a key tool for legitimizing actions. Thus, we recommend increasing the number of participants on the National Decentralization Commission to include the Association of Municipalities of Ecuador (AME), and CONCOPE. There is no need to increase the number of participants so much that the Commission starts off in an environment of disturbance and political crisis. At this point, what is needed is a well-functioning coordinating body. Meanwhile, CONAM will continue to operate as the technical secretariat for the Commission, but will delve deeper into a policy of open dialogue.

To start the government's work, consideration could be given to signing a commitment agreement on results among central government agencies. This could be signed by the President of the Republic, the Ministry of Economy and Finance, selected ministers, and the Decentralization Commission and would provide a frame of reference based on clear goals for decentralization. The agreement should be published.

Given that decentralization is a process of incremental changes, the "New Management Model" developed by the National Commission on Decentralization and Autonomy was designed as an open frame of reference. The idea was to regularly publish and distribute the progress made in the design of the new state. Unfortunately, this never happened. For the central government, the ideal is still perfect and polished models of decentralization. This initial idea should be taken up again and, as an example, the progress the provinces have made in the negotiation of powers should be publicized.

A monitoring system has yet to be put into effect. Preferably, it would operate with the active involvement of participating institutions and service users. It would also have a component providing neutral evaluations performed by universities and research institutes. In addition, the production and dissemination of information at all levels should be promoted. Target groups such as students, parents, service users, communities, indigenous peoples, blacks, and other citizens still do not have specific information. If decentralization moves ahead at its current pace—22 provincial councils and 140 municipalities have already signed the transfer of powers agreements—this would become an urgent requirement.

Policy Matrix

Problems	Policy measures		Objectives/goals
	Short term (to June 2003)	Medium term (2003–07)	
1. Government structure and inter-governmental rela-tions: **Problem:** The complexity of the institutional framework, particularly at the intermediate level, does not allow for accountability and leads to inefficient services.	The government undertakes a transition or exit strategy moving toward an intermediate decentralized level. Short-term actions planned are as follows: • **For the Ministries:** appointment of provincial sectoral directors (decentralized ministerial sphere) with a short list suggested by the (elected) Prefect. • **For Regional Development Agencies:** Board set up composed of provincial prefects according to jurisdiction (PREDESUR, CEDEGE, CRM, UDENOR, CREA, others) and a central government representative. Approval of budget by this new board.	Carry out a gradual transfer of powers to provincial councils, from both ministries and Regional Development Agencies. Extend the jurisdiction of provincial councils to urban areas considering that election is by electoral district in urban and rural areas. Remove the status of "autonomous government" from parish boards in exchange for a participatory agency. Extend jurisdiction to urban areas with flexible arrangements in large municipalities. Reintroduce indirect representation of municipalities on the provincial councils. In 2003, there are 10 (one per sector) Presidential Decrees on appointing provincial directors from a short list.	**Objective:** Improve accountability at the intermediate level and increase the efficiency of services. **Goals:** Services are delivered at the intermediate level without overlaps and with efficiency.
			In late 2003, at least two Regional Development Agencies, among them CEDEGE and CREA, have a new board. In 2004, at least 40 percent of spending by Regional Development Agencies is decided in coordination with the provincial councils.

(Matrix continues on the following page.)

Policy Matrix (*continued*)

	Policy measures		
Problems	*Short term (to June 2003)*	*Medium term (2003–07)*	*Progress indicators*	*Objectives/goals*
2. Administrative decentralization: Transfer of powers Problem: There is a high degree of centralized decisionmaking in delivery of services.	The government introduces provisions for the contractual transfer of powers system, with the following reforms: 1. Make access to the transfer of powers program contingent on subnational governments' meeting minimum standards of accounting, budgetary management, and regular submission of financial reports. 2. Clarify rights and obligations among levels of government and complete model agreements in terms of penalties and reversibility of transfers. Empower the Commission on Powers to be the final arbiter in resolving disputes over powers. 3. Produce proposed solutions in the transfer of human resources to local governments (labor rights, indemnities). Conduct in-depth discussions	Conduct pilot cases of transfers based on results in the context of agreements.	By 2005, at least 30 municipalities and 10 provincial councils exercise new powers in three sectors. By 2007, at least 50 municipalities and 15 provincial councils exercise new powers in three sectors.	**Objective:** Transfer powers with less potential fiscal impact and within a framework of accountability. **Goal:** Public administration meets its responsibilities at all levels of government.

with unions with precise data on public employees affected by decentralization. 4. Include the Ministry of Economy and Finance in sectoral negotiations. 5. Information generation: Conduct a study of "the consequences of decentralization" for each sector (environment, agriculture, public works, tourism, social welfare, health). Publish the results and discuss them with provincial councils, municipalities, and Ministries.				
3. Fiscal decentralization **Problem:** Dispersed and discretionary fiscal framework does not allow for efficient spending at all levels of government.	The government undertakes a reform of subnational finances with three starting points: 1. **"15 Percent Law":** Define the calculation basis; make increased transfers (resources above 11 percent) contingent on the assumptions of powers and service management results. 2. **"Fiscal Responsibility Law":** Announce that the national government will not assume the debts of local governments; publish debt cancellations over the last five years;	Carry out reforms of the system of transfers based on the following six policies: 1. Set up a matching grant between levels of government for powers with externalities (health, highways): provincial-municipal, central-provincial, central-municipal. The fund should be supplied by current transfers and clearly delineate the powers and sectors it finances. 2. Include social funds in a system of current transfers. 3. Add different special laws for	In 2003, nominally 15 percent (though in reality only 11 percent) of current revenues is distributed based on revenues actually obtained. In 2004, 20 percent of current transfers operate in a matching grant. In 2007, the special laws and corresponding transfers are unified and operate transparently.	**Objective:** Establish transparent fiscal incentives for coordinating fiscal spending. **Goal:** Services are delivered efficiently and with coordination among the levels of government.

(Matrix continues on the following page.)

Policy Matrix (*continued*)

Problems	Policy measures		Progress indicators	Objectives/goals
	Short term (to June 2003)	*Medium term (2003–07)*		
	track and publish forms of indebtedness (contingencies, floating debt, late payments) in local governments; plan and implement organizational and procedural changes in the Ministry of Economy and Finance to achieve fiscal responsibility in practice. **3. Indebtedness:** Undertake the Debt Reconversion Plan for overindebted municipalities and provincial councils. **4. Information:** Begin the installation of a single computerized system (SIGEF) that will provide data revealing how much the government spends in each province and canton through the ministries, regional development agencies, social funds, extrabudgetary allocations, and international loans.	transferring resources and make them subject to clear and transparent distribution rules and based on management results; relax the rules on the use of current spending and investment; make transfers contingent on increases in own revenues. 4. Introduce basic principles of partnership: allow subnational governments to share proportionally in times of economic contraction (avoid ratchet effect); and distribute shared resources according to effective revenue. 5. Experiment with surcharges on national taxes for provincial councils and municipalities that demonstrate financial responsibility. 6. Have the Ministry of Economy and Finance send draft laws to the Congress to reduce preallocations in the budget.	In 2007, municipalities have increased their own revenues by 30 percent.	

	Own revenues of municipalities and provincial councils: Send a series of legal reforms to Congress to eliminate administrative obstacles and introduce flexibility in financial self-management of local governments. **Indebtedness:** Regulate indebtedness with additional indicators that show real ability to pay debt and portfolio risk. Make access to credit (additionally) contingent for Quito and Guayaquil on evaluations of credit risk conducted by international firms. **Information policy:** 1. Develop information: provincial GDP. 2. Introduce the subnational SIGEF along with the Office of the Comptroller, AME, and CONCOPE.		Local governments participate voluntarily in the National Decentralization Commission. Sectoral ministries, AME, and CON-	**Objective:** Make central government decisions legitimate in the view of local governments and civil society and guarantee coordinated implementation.
4. Management of decentralization process: **Problem:** Decisions on decentralization process are not accepted by munici-	Expand the membership on the National Commission on Decentralization and Autonomy: include AME and CONCOPE, in addition to the current members of CONAM (as technical secretariat), the Min-	The commission should regularly update the "Management Model" (developed in 2000) in political-territorial, fiscal, and administrative areas according to advances in formulation.		

(Matrix continues on the following page.)

Policy Matrix *(continued)*

Problems	Policy measures		Progress indicators	Objectives/goals
	Short term (to June 2003)	*Medium term (2003–07)*		
palities, provincial councils, and civil society.	istry of Economy and Finance, and the Office of the President of the Republic. Intragovernment commitment: The President signs an agreement based on meeting short-term (six months) goals with the Ministry of Economy and Finance, selected sectoral ministries, and the Commission on Decentralization. This agreement is published. Develop a simple monitoring system concept that is based on the active participation of the ministries, subnational governments, and users. Define a base line in the cantons and provinces that are in the process of negotiating powers.	Issue regular reports on monitoring conducted based on the participation of actors involved. Publish this information. Conduct a dissemination campaign, tailored to cover target groups.	COPE seek technical assistance from CONAM. CONAM is invited to forums on decentralization by civil society. Updates to "Management Model" are published and distributed regularly. Monitoring reports are prepared regularly and published.	**Goal:** Central government, provincial councils, and municipalities accept the process of decentralization and implementation is coordinated.

Annex
Special Laws Governing the Transfer of Resources and Revenue-Sharing for the Benefit of Municipalities and Provincial Councils

Law	No.	R.O.	Date	Amt./%	Source	Criteria	Use
Cultural Heritage Recovery Fund	82	838	23/Dec/87	0.03	Local public performances		Restoration, conservation, and protection of historical, artistic, and cultural assets. Investments
				0.1	National Emergencies Fund (FONEN) Budget		
Bolivar Provincial Development Fund	46	281	22/Sep/89	7.5%	1% of credit operation transactions in domestic currency	20% Provincial Council 16% Guaranda 16% Chillanes 16% Chimbo 16% San Miguel 16% Echeandía	Environmental sanitation Sewers Urban development
Legislative decree on allocations to the provinces of Azuay, Cañar, and Morona Santiago	47	281	22/Sep/89	5%	Energy bills from INECEL to electrical companies for generation at power stations in Pisayambo, Paute, and Agoyán	60% municipalities of Azuay, Cañar, and Morona Santiago 40% CREA	100% for infrastructure 80% execution of projects 20% forestation
Environmental Sanitation, Roads, and Irrigation Fund of the Province of El Oro (FONDORO)	57	344	28/Dec/89	10%	Puerto Bolivar Port Authority Revenues	20% Provincial Council	Irrigation, drainage, and roads
				5%	1% of operations in domestic currency	60% municipalities 20% municipalities based on population	Sanitation and roads

(Annex continues on the following page.)

Annex (*continued*)

Law	No.	R.O.	Date	Amt./%	Source	Criteria	Use
Provincial Development Fund (FONDEPRO)	65	395	14/Mar/90	2%	Total current budget revenues	47.5% contribution to the capital of the BEDE 47.5% Provincial Councils and INGALA: 25% based on population and 75% level 0.5% CONCOPE	To back BdE credits Development projects CONCOPE
Sectional Development Fund (FODESEC)	72	441	21/May/90	2% distributed: 2% 98%	Net current budget revenues	Municipal provincial capitals: 25% Quito, 25% Guayaquil, 50% others level 20% Provincial Councils (60% population, 20% UBN, 20% administrative efficiency and fiscal effectiveness) 75% municipalities: 60% municipalities (60% population, 30% UBN, 10% administrative efficiency and fiscal effectiveness); 40% BdE 5% emergencies	70% current expenses and investment 30% rural area investment 40% BEDE: Investment fund Sectional agencies
				3 billion	Prior to distribution of petroleum revenues received by the state		

						BEDE credits counterpart	BEDE credit trust
Rural Roads Program of the Province of Manabí	75	455	11/Jun/90	10 billion up to 2002 Other budgetary allocations	General Government Budget		
Irrigation Fund of the Province of Cotopaxi	93	501	16/Aug/90	1 billion since 1991	General Government Budget		Provincial irrigation plan
Fund for the Agricultural Sector of the Province of Chimborazo	115	612	28/Jan/91	12.5%	1% of credit operations in domestic currency	30% Provincial Council 20% municipality of Riobamba 50% evenly among the remaining cantons	Neighborhood roads, irrigation, forestation Area market and environmental sanitation Collection centers and environmental sanitation
Development Funds for the Provinces of the Amazon Region	122	676	3/May/91	2.5%	Billing for petroleum services to PetroEcuador from national companies	50% Provincial Council 20% provincial capital 30% evenly among remaining provincial councils	Urban and rural infrastructure projects in Sucumbíos, Napo, Pastaza, Morona Santiago, Zamora Chinchipe, and Orellana
				4.5%	Billing for petroleum services to PetroEcuador from foreign companies		
	40	S. 248	7/Aug/89	5 US cents	Per barrel of petroleum transported by pipeline	Evenly for Napo, Esmeraldas, and Sucumbíos	50% municipal infrastructure projects 50% provincial council infrastructure projects

(Annex continues on the following page.)

Annex (*continued*)

Law	No.	R.O.	Date	Amt./%	Source	Criteria	Use
	10	30	21/Sep/92	10 US cents	Per barrel of petroleum produced in the Amazon region	BEDE distributes 30% provincial councils 60% municipalities (55% evenly, 45% population) 10% Regional fund	80% road and environmental sanitation projects 20% current expenses
Development Fund of the Province of Pichincha	145	899	23/Mar/92	15%	1% of credit operations in domestic currency	25% Provincial Council 25% Quito 50% evenly among remaining cantons	Studies, construction, improvement of neighborhood roads and infrastructure projects in urban and rural parishes
Development Fund of the Province of Carchi	146	899	23/Mar/92	15% 15%	Exchange differential in weekly transactions of the BCE 1% of credit operations in domestic currency	20% Provincial Council 27.5% Tulcán 16.5% Montúfar 11% Espejo 9% Bolívar 9% Mira 7% Dacha	Road and urban and rural infrastructure projects
15% Distribution of the Central Government Budget	s/n	27	20/Mar/97	15%	Revenues from central government budget with the exception of revenues from internal and external credits	70% municipalities (50% UBN, 40% population, 10% evenly) 30% provincial councils (50% UBN, 40% population, 10% area)	Economic, social, and cultural development plans

Law replacing the law creating the Roads Fund of the Province of Loja (FONDVIAL) Highway equipment	92	335	9/Jun/98	100%	1% tax on the purchase and sale of used vehicles	70% municipalities 30% Provincial Council	Road projects
Creation of CORPECUADOR	10 S. 378		7/Aug/98	100%	Tolls, rehabilitated roads		Reconstruction of areas affected by the El Niño phenomenon Investment in proportion to damage caused by El Niño
				25%	Annual net income from Solidarity Fund. Donations and subsidies		
				10%	State share in increased petroleum exports		
				0.7%	Banana exports		
					Loans on behalf of the state		
					Loans on behalf of CORPECUADOR		
					Budgetary allocations		

Source: CONAM (2000) New Management Model for Ecuador.

18

The Administration of Justice[1]

Maria Dakolias

Despite the progress achieved on specific aspects of the judicial reform program, people do not trust the formal justice system in Ecuador because it is not easily accessible, it is slow and inefficient, and it is perceived as being vulnerable to corruption. These problems are in turn associated with the limited professional training of those running the system, limited resources, and the use of inadequate administration and oversight models. A Comprehensive Reform Plan, which was designed to establish the bases for future, farther-reaching changes, approved in 1996 and revised in 2001, has completed its final phase. However, it has not yet been possible to improve the administration of justice to an extent that is perceptible to the public. Against this backdrop, the view of the private sector and the rest of civil society is that a consistent and comprehensive process is essential for achieving medium-term results. This means actions designed to recover public trust in the administration of justice, to improve the professional quality of judges, to make the management and administration systems more efficient, and to increase access to justice. This process must avoid overlooking the foundation that has already been built; it must deepen and expand on it. This requires a consideration of regulatory aspects as well as the qualifications of those operating the system, the system's costs, infrastructure, and administrative and management issues. It also requires a reconsideration of the status of the judicial branch, and that of institutions such as the Constitutional Court and the Office of the Attorney General, which are formally autonomous but whose actions affect the functioning of the justice system.

---

1. This chapter was prepared by the Legal and Judicial Reform Unit, Legal Vice Presidency, World Bank.

A. Persistent Problems

Despite the progress made in specific aspects of earlier reforms (see annex 1), the problems remain the same: the formal system set up for the administration of justice is not easily accessible, it is slow, and verdicts offer little security. As a result, the population has no confidence in the system.

Lack of Access

Although the subject has not been dealt examined systematically, there is evidence supporting the assertion that the high cost of the services of the justice system limits public access to it. Geography seems to be another limiting factor, in addition to the dysfunction of the resolutions offered and their lack of timeliness.

Costs

Since the National Council on the Judiciary (CNJ) established the system of judicial fees, the number of civil suits filed throughout the country has been decreasing, despite population increases (Table 1).

The cost of the fees has been high enough during a time of economic crisis that the population appears to prefer to give up the opportunity to sue for its rights, reducing the demand for formal services by looking for other ways to resolve legal problems.

The spread of alternatives for resolving conflicts has been one of the positive aspects of the reform process and should be expanded upon. However, although 30 mediation centers have been legally established and programs have been developed to train community mediators in marginal areas, it cannot be said that reduction in the number of civil suits means that people would necessarily prefer to resort to mediation or arbitration. The reports from the centers with respect to the number of cases handled do not allow us to reach this conclusion (Projusticia 2001).

The actions of some local officials who act outside the scope of their legal powers continue to be a frequent occurrence, particularly in rural areas. The most well-known case is that of the political deputies, who are administrative authorities answering to the executive branch. They act as judges at the request of one of the parties, with no authorization to do so. This type of solution is problematic not only

Table 1. Civil Cases Filed in Ecuador's Courts

1998	1999	2000	2001
139,354	125,057	106,659	92,427

Source: National Council on the Judiciary, "National Report on the Movement of Cases," 2001.

because it is illegitimate but also because there is no formal ability to enforce decisions and because the system is prone to abuses.

The solution is not necessarily the elimination of court fees but rather a review of the system, including not only the current fees but also the items for which fees are required so that, while the principle is maintained, the burden does not fall on the party seeking to claim a right. For example, instead of being collected when a case begins, fees should be collected once the judge establishes whether or not there was justification for filing the case.

Finally, consideration must be given to the fact that the administration of justice is an essential service for society and should be financed primarily by the state. In this respect, it should be noted that despite quantitative increases, the percentage share of the judicial budget in the state budget has been declining and is the lowest in the Andean region (Table 2).

In addition, Ecuador invests the least per capita in justice of any country in Latin American (Table 3).

Without disparaging the goal of improving budgetary planning and management systems, we cannot overlook the fact that the reform process includes actions that require investments that cannot be funded with the current budget, which is allocated exclusively to covering current expenses, primarily compensation (Table 4).

Table 2. Spending on Justice as a Percentage of the State Budget

Country	Percentage of budget
Bolivia	3.00
Chile	0.83
Colombia	4.62
Ecuador	0.74
Peru	1.43
Venezuela	2.39

Source: Andean Commission of Jurists, "Judicial Indicators," 2000.

Table 3. Per Capita Judicial Budget in the Andean Region

Country	Amount (in $US)	Population (in thousands)	Indicator ($US per capita)
Bolivia	64,166,666	7,773	8.3
Chile	155,339,806	14,622	10.6
Colombia	347,631,979	37,065	9.4
Ecuador	20,949,272	11,937	1.8
Peru	132,319,506	24,371	5.4
Venezuela	653,059,868	22,777	28.7

Source: Andean Commission of Jurists, "Judicial Indicators," 2000.

Table 4. Breakdown of Spending (2001)

Item	Percentage
Compensation	92.5
Services	5.8
Supplies	1.7

Source: National Council on the Judiciary, "Report to the Supreme Court: Year 2001," Quito, 2002.

Legal Assistance

However, neither the spread of alternative methods nor a review of the fee system is enough. We must not forget the legal requirement in Ecuador that the signature of a practicing attorney must support any suit or petition submitted to a public official. Thus, the cost of professional services must be added to the cost of the court fee.

The lack of professional services, particularly for people with limited resources and for the most vulnerable groups in society, must be counteracted by expanding existing services and creating new services.

Functionality

For a population in which most people are poor, a system of justice ultimately based on monetary reparation for harm after a proceeding that can last, in the best of cases, slightly more than a year, is dysfunctional. It is also dysfunctional in economic terms, given that the monetary value of these disputes is less than the cost it would take to recover it.

The review of the procedural system should consider among its objectives a differentiation of proceedings, creating a special procedure for cases involving small amounts that would be very accessible, particularly flexible, allowing for the possibility that solutions would be better adapted to the requirements in each case.

Lack of Confidence in the System

The public perceives the justice system as being unreliable. Four factors contribute to this: corruption, politicization, lack of professionalism, and slowness.

Corruption

Ecuador signed the Inter-American Convention against Corruption in 1996 and ratified it in May 1997. However, national law has not yet been amended to reflect the provisions of the Convention. Standards of conduct for the exercise of public offices in which conflict of interest situations are clearly identified have not been defined, nor are there systems to protect those who in good faith report acts of corruption. In criminal law, crimes such as unlawful enrichment do not have the scope provided under the Convention.

The literature on corruption usually refers to a set of factors that create a climate that is conducive to the institutionalization of corruption: procedures that are not transparent, unreliable records and statistics, decisionmaking powers concentrated in the same officials, low salaries, the lack of mechanisms for evaluating performance, and the lack of incentives. All of these elements can be found in the Ecuadoran justice system.

In the justice sector, no anticorruption policy has been defined, nor is there an adequate institutional response to reduce the incidence of corruption. The problem is handled on a case-by-case basis through measures taken after the fact whenever misconduct is discovered for any reason, but neither the judiciary nor the Office of the Attorney General has internal monitoring systems that would allow it to identify cases of corruption. There is no prevention plan or any methods for carrying out effective investigations.

There is no code of conduct for judicial officials or attornies. The general principles enunciated in the current law are not in line with the requirements of the Inter-American Convention or with international guidelines.

The lack of rules clearly establishing expected ethical conduct is another factor to be considered. The standards contained in the law are very general and are far from providing the detailed provisions that would be expected of a code of conduct for judges and officials.

Corruption certainly cannot be combated by focusing attention on judicial officials and support staff alone. Attention must also be given to attorneys and their standards of professional conduct. In this area, we note the same absence of a code of professional conduct. There is a system of penalties that operates irregularly and is entrusted to the professional associations themselves; it focuses on offenses involving unfair competition in professional practice and the lack of solidarity and courtesy in relationships between attorneys, rather than on cases of corruption.

Politicization

The independence of judges is an essential condition for impartiality in the administration of justice. No reform initiative could be considered successful if it did not first of all ensure that judicial decisions reflect the merits of the evidence submitted rather than conditions associated with the exercise of political power.[2]

The interest of the political class in the administration of justice is not just bureaucratic, in the sense of obtaining judicial positions as political rewards. It is also practical and has to do with the exercise of power and particularly with what is called the judicialization of politics—that is, the use of legal procedures as an instrument to obtain certain practical ends directly associated with immediate political benefit.

---

2. World Bank, Legal Vice Presidency, "Initiatives in Legal and Judicial Reform," 2002.

Criminal justice has been pointed to as the setting in which political influence is most often noticed. This influence is selectively exercised so that it does not affect most cases, although it does affect the most visible cases or those that, given the nature of the issue or the identity of the parties involved, are important to the public or have political consequences.

There are some easily documented cases. For example, the National Congress, without having the power to do so, has more than once ordered that criminal proceedings be filed against specific people, asserting that they have committed criminal violations, but without submitting them to a prior procedure in which the rules of due process had been honored.

Cases like this call into question the independence of the Office of the Attorney General, rather than that of the judges. The position of the Attorney General is particularly vulnerable to political influence because of the possibility of impeachment and removal by a legislative majority in specific circumstances.

Something similar happens with the Constitutional Court, whose level of politicization has been publicly admitted by the most diverse sectors of opinion and by the political class itself. The absence of impartiality in the decisions of this body creates dangerous levels of uncertainty owing to the significance of its powers, powers that even include the ability to invalidate an applicable law or any other source of authority.

Another sphere in which political influence is often noted is in the appointment of magistrates and judges.

Instead of looking at the judiciary as a victim, there is a tendency to present it as being to blame for its politicization. In order to combat politicization, judicial independence must be strengthened—and this cannot be achieved by encouraging intervention. In this respect, efforts designed to manipulate the composition of judicial bodies by replacing people rather than by dealing with the system itself are particularly dangerous.

Limited Professionalism

The public usually associates inconsistency in court decisions with corruption. This becomes obvious when different judges resolve the same type of issue differently. In the case of Ecuador, however, there is another factor that leads to the same result, namely the limited professional training of judges. In order to find consistent solutions a judge must be knowledgeable about the subject and must know what other judges have done in similar cases.

As for the first, we must consider that judges receive no professional training at all other than their law studies. As for information, except Supreme Court rulings, court rulings are not published, although on rare occasions judges do cite precedents in their rulings or discuss how other judges have resolved similar cases.

The situation appears even more complicated when one considers that the Supreme Court itself suffers from the same defect: cases with contradictory decisions are numerous and the Court rarely exercises its power to unify jurisprudence through general guidelines. Factors contributing to frequent contradictions are the existence of various chambers for the same area of law, and the fact that, when ruling on cases, one chamber does not consult the logic behind decisions in another chamber.

Rather than hoping that the problem will be resolved after the fact through the issuance of a general rule, it would be healthier to change the way things work so that a potential contradiction could be detected before a decision is formally adopted. The alternative solution is more radical, but more complicated to implement: reduce the number of chambers so that there is only one chamber for each area of law.

Slowness

The administration of justice is slow in Ecuador. An ordinary civil case takes an average of three years in Quito. In most judicial divisions, more cases enter the system each year than are settled during the same period. According to information from the CNJ, the number of cases postponed in the entire system in December 2001 was probably about 800,000.

The numbers vary according the type of division and its location. In Quito, Guayaquil, and Cuenca, the Supreme Courts have fewer cases postponed than the courts of first instance. In the other provinces, the opposite is true: the courts of first instance have a small caseload while the number of cases postponed in the Supreme Courts is higher.

The factors contributing to this have more to do with management systems than with the number of courts or their location (Buscaglia and Dakolias 1996). According to data in the reports from Projusticia, the performance of pilot courts established under the judicial reform program indicates that the average length of a civil case has been dramatically reduced (Table 5).

In addition, the implementation of the new management system has made it possible to increase the ratio of cases settled to cases entering the system (Table 6).

Table 5. Duration of Ordinary Cases (Quito)

Court	Average number of days, nonpilot	Average number of days, pilot
First	1,185	266
Second	1,207	175
Third	1,732	332
Fourth	1,260	297
Fifth	1,096	204
Eleventh	1,717	422
Twelfth	840	236

Source: Projusticia.

Table 6. Cases Completed Compared to Those Entering the System in Pilot Courts (percent)

City	2000	2001
Quito	8.56	27.38
Guayaquil	19.1	54.29
Cuenca	44	134.66

Source: Projusticia.

The new management system was implemented in just 26 courts of first instance in the initial phase and extended in the second phase to another 45 courts in the cities of Quito, Guayaquil, and Cuenca.

B. Recommendations

Legal Reform

The Organic Law

The new Law on the Judicial Branch, meant to implement and develop constitutional reforms with respect to the management and administration of the system, has not yet been issued.

It is this law that must define the issues that are fundamental to the organization and operation of the administration of justice, such as the following:

- The procedure for selecting candidates to fill vacancies on the Supreme Court through the co-optation system;
- The age limit for magistrates;
- The procedure for judging and removing magistrates;
- The labor system within the courts;
- The scope and characteristics of the judicial career; and,
- The disciplinary system for judges, attorneys, and support staff.

The importance of these subjects has led to the introduction in Congress of competing bills. Despite attempts to reconcile positions, none of the bills have been submitted for discussion at this writing.

The chance to push forward with promulgation of this law offers a unique opportunity to profoundly alter the judicial branch's organization, labor system, and oversight mechanisms, and the ways that civil society participates in the workings of justice. Since this is an organic law, its approval requires a qualified majority of Congress or a strategy designed to gain popular support for the fundamental provisions for which sufficient legislative support is not obtained.

The bill prepared by the Supreme Court itself can serve as a starting point (Andrade 2002), to which should be added at least two essential items that the Court did not approve: the procedure for selecting candidates when vacancies must be filled on the Supreme Court and the age limit for serving on the court.

Both mechanisms serve to achieve transparency and energize the composition of the highest court, without impairing judicial independence (USAID 2001). The subject is critical to the operation of the justice system.[3]

Regulations must also be issued to implement the principle of jurisdictional unity. This principle has to do with independence in the administration of justice, as well as the need to ensure access to judicial review of administrative decisions consistent with the principles of due process.

Procedural Reform

The reforms needed for the implementation of oral argument have not been issued, even though the period established for doing so by the Constitution of 1998 expired on August 10, 2002. The change is important not only for reasons of quality, but also in terms of guaranteeing greater transparency in proceedings. The system of oral argument provides direct access to the submission of evidence and to discussion of its procedural importance, as well as to the reasons for the court's ruling. In this way, the actions of the judge and of attorneys for the parties remain open to public scrutiny.

The appointment of judges and establishment of procedures adequate to meet the needs of the poorest members of society—with guarantees but without the formal rigors of ordinary civil court procedures—is also considered urgent. In this regard, the experience of the Special Federal Courts established in Brazil could offer interesting input for the design and implementation of the reform.

Criminal procedural reform should be supplemented with the introduction of regulations that convert the oral proceeding into one that is adversarial in nature, without inquisitorial trappings[4] and with the establishment of the public defender system.[5]

Small Claims Court and Legal Rights for Indigenous Groups

The law needed to define functions and procedures for judges in the Small Claims Court, for which a provision was made in the reforms, has not been issued. In contrast, although the territorial jurisdiction and powers of Family Court judges were defined through the reform of the old Law on the Judicial Function, no provision has been made for the positions. The lack of consensus within the Supreme Court

---

3. If the age limit is set at 70, as has been proposed, nine judges would leave the Court in 2003. With the two vacancies that currently exist, this would leave 11 seats that must be filled.

4. For instance, there is a bill developed by the Esquel Foundation, with support from USAID.

5. For instance, there is a bill prepared as part of the Projusticia program.

has held up approval of the bill designed to transform various labor courts and land-lord-tenants' courts in Quito, Guayaquil, and Cuenca into family courts, as long as there are resources available to establish them in the rest of the country.

Nor has the necessary legislation been issued to implement the orderly exercise of the constitutionally recognized judicial functions of authorities among the indigenous peoples for the resolution of their internal disputes.

Judicial Independence

Respect for the independence of judges does not depend on the judiciary alone. No mechanism to preserve it will be more effective than a public with the conviction that this is necessary, a conviction that would be transformed into effective policy and a standard of conduct for the other branches of government.

The Executive Branch, as co-legislator, has a central role in this area, given that no reform initiative could become a reality without its participation.

The provisions for strengthening judicial independence involve the aspects discussed below.

APPOINTMENTS. The Supreme Court has the power to fill the vacancies on its bench, but there are no rules governing the selection procedures. The new Law on the Judicial Branch should include such rules in order to ensure disclosure and transparency in the procedure and guarantee the participation of civil society.

Regardless of the nominating body, if more than one nomination must be made at the same time, there is the possibility that a mutually beneficial agreement will be reached, consequently invalidating the effectiveness of any selection process. Thus, everything should be done to provide for filling only one position at a time, so that the process for filling the next vacancy is not begun until the other position has been filled. This is particularly important for filling vacancies on the Supreme Court and nominations to the Constitutional Court, the National Council on the Judiciary, and other bodies with several members.

ACCOUNTABILITY. The Supreme Court and the Constitutional Court are examples of extreme positions in terms of their systems of accountability. While the Supreme Court is not subject to the oversight of any other body, the Constitutional Court is exposed to the vicissitudes of the legislative majority, given the possibility of impeachment. The Office of the Attorney General is similarly exposed.

Both extremes are inadvisable. Impeachment has proven to be an area in which partisan considerations and political circumstances predominate.

The definition of a common system should clearly distinguish the type of liability involved. Criminal liability for the commission of crimes requires an adequate system of investigation, particularly for cases in which the Attorney General may be involved. This assumes a system of internal controls and the participation of an outside body such as the Anticorruption Commission to oversee the process.

The same criterion could be applied in the case of Supreme Court judges, particularly with respect to the investigation of possible acts of corruption.

Political responsibility to the country requires transparency. In this respect, measures must be taken to ensure transparency, with public disclosure of information on the performance of judges and officials: the number of cases handled, the justification for their decisions, compensation, and record of attendance.

MANAGEMENT CAPABILITY. If the new management system used in the pilot courts is extended to the other judicial divisions, the problem of slowness in the processing of cases will be considerably diminished.

In addition, the installation of mediation offices attached to the courts must be extended to the entire system. This mechanism allows cases to be settled without requiring the involvement of a judge's decision at the end of the process. Trained mediators have succeeded in reaching agreement in 32 percent of the cases sent to them, whereas in the past it was exceptional for parties to reach a direct agreement (Projusticia 2001).

The need to provide adequate equipment to streamline tasks and maintain reliable records has become more obvious with procedural reform, including the transition from the written system to the system of oral argument.

PROFESSIONALIZATION AND THE JUDICIAL CAREER. A permanent training system and a similarly permanent performance evaluation system must be established, both to improve quality and to provide objective criteria for the selection, promotion, and removal of staff. With a clear distinction made between judicial functions and administrative functions, the training and evaluation systems would be the backbone of a judicial career system in which seniority would cease to be the only factor that is valued and rewarded.

C. Conclusions

In this context, the private sector and the rest of civil society feel that a consistent and comprehensive process is essential for achieving medium-term results. This means actions designed to regain public confidence in the administration of justice, to improve the professional quality of judges, to increase efficiency in the management and administration of the justice system, and to provide greater access to justice. This will require making use of measures already put in place, maintaining judicial independence, introducing evaluation and oversight systems, combating corruption, and increasing the levels of public access to justice.

The process requires a comprehensive approach: all areas must be given attention and actions that must be developed in each area are indicated. The proposal is summarized in the policy matrix.

Policy Matrix

Goal	Policy measures	Actions
Establish rules and procedures to strengthen judicial independence	Regulate the process for selecting candidates for judicial positions, particularly on the Supreme Court and the National Council on the Judiciary in order to ensure disclosure, transparency, and the participation of civil society. Ensure that such mechanisms also guarantee compliance with Constitutional requirements, particularly those relating to alternating backgrounds: academics, career judges, practicing attorneys. Establish the age limit for serving on the bench. Avoid having various vacancies at the same time that must be handled through procedures for selection and appointment to positions on the courts and on CNJ. Adopt procedures that, without endangering judicial independence, ensure responsibility and effective accountability on the part of Supreme Court justices and members of CNJ. Extend the same procedures and requirements to magistrates of the Constitutional Court and the Attorney General.	Promote the issuance of the new Organic Law on the Judicial Branch, incorporating the standards needed to achieve the objectives sought. Introduce the reforms necessary to extend the same procedures and requirements to the Constitutional Court and the Attorney General.
Provide professional training for judges and evaluate their performance	Establish a permanent training system, such as a judicial school, as the first step in the career path and meet needs for continuing education. Create incentives for those whose performance is above the criteria for excellence established by the system, as well as penalties for those who do not meet the minimum criteria.	Regulate the judicial career, establishing requirements with respect to professional training, ongoing education, continuous evaluation, and the application of performance-based incentives and penalties. Adopt the administrative measures needed to implement both the training and the evaluation systems. Establish a system for continuous monitoring and evaluation of judges' performance.

Combat corruption	Create appropriate legal instruments.	Introduce the reforms needed to adapt national law to the requirements of the Inter-American Convention. Establish codes of conduct and codes of ethics for judges and attorneys.
	Design and implement a plan to combat corruption—with an emphasis on preventing and eliminating factors that contribute to the creation of an environment that encourages corruption.	Improve the disciplinary and penalty systems for both judges and attorneys involved in ethical violations and cases of corruption. Establish systems of protection and legal benefits for those who collaborate with justice in discovering and punishing acts of corruption.
Provide professional training for government attorneys, evaluate their performance, and give the Office of the Attorney General technical equipment and resources	Select and train government attorneys by applying the principles and procedures indicated earlier for judges.	Provide regulations for the Organic Law on the Office of the Attorney General. Adopt the administrative measures needed to implement both the training and evaluation systems.
	Install a system for the evaluation of each government attorney, establishing a ratio between the cases on which he or she decides to bring an indictment and the results. Adopt a management system that prevents prosecutory backups.	Redesign the management system and adapt facilities. Give the Office of the Attorney General the personnel, equipment, and technical resources it needs to perform the new tasks assumed as a result of procedural reforms.
Improve the professional quality of attorneys	Reform legal education.	Modernize the teaching system by disseminating programs and methods designed to develop skills.
	Establish ongoing education programs for attorneys, starting with programs to train them in the techniques of oral argument.	Give the Supreme Court and CNJ the power to define requirements beyond a university degree that attorneys must have in order to litigate.

(Matrix continues on the following page.)

Policy Matrix (*continued*)

Goal	Policy measures	Actions
Extend to the entire system the application of procedural institutions introduced by the constitutional reform	Introduce complete procedural reform and improve office management systems.	Introduce the reforms needed to adopt the system of oral argument in all matters, as provided by the Constitution. Accordingly, encourage promulgation of the new Code of Civil Procedure (CPC). Extend to the entire justice system the management system implemented in the pilot courts. Improve the managerial capability of the National Council on the Judiciary.
Expand opportunities for access to justice	Create and implement a public defender system that is national in scope and has adequately trained staff. Establish a more flexible, less expensive, and more accessible procedure for resolving disputes involving small amounts that would serve the majority, particularly in rural and marginalized areas. Be sure that the application of the system of court fees does not hamper the exercise of the right to effective judicial protection. Expand opportunities for applying alternative dispute resolution methods.	Encourage the promulgation of the Organic Law on the Public Defender's Office and establish the service. Incorporate the rules needed in the new Code of Civil Procedure prepared by the Supreme Court. Take the necessary steps to put small claims courts and family courts into operation. Review the system of court fees, so that they are consistent with the population's income and do not affect those who claim rights with justification. Institutionalize and extend the network of mediation offices attached to the courts in order to take advantage of alternative methods for resolving disputes. Review the criteria regarding matters in which alternative methods for resolving disputes can be used in order to increase opportunities for applying them. Provide the courts and tribunals, as well as the Office of the Attorney General, with the tools and equipment needed to meet the requirements of the oral argument procedure, particularly with respect to recording systems.

| Encourage and increase citizen participation | Establish channels that will allow the participation of civil society as an additional entity to oversee the operations of the system for the administration of justice. | Consider including mechanisms in the Organic Law to guarantee the timely provision of information to the public regarding future nominations for judicial positions and on the identities and characteristics of candidates aspiring to the positions so that the views of the public can be considered in the selection process. Publicly disclose information on the work of each magistrate and judge—the number of cases they have overseen, the justification for their decisions. Promote the incorporation of objectives relating to improved justice in the civil agenda and encourage consensus-building on topics central to the process. Establish civic education programs to promote values relating to the status of law, the rule of law, and use of the justice system to resolve conflicts and protect rights. |

Annex 1
Reforms of the System

The last 10 years have seen more changes and reforms introduced in the system for administering justice than the entire period from 1812 to 1992. In certain cases, the changes made to regulations have not yet been implemented in practice. In other cases, the process of adaptation has led to new problems, while the problems that the reform sought to remedy have not been completely eliminated. Finally, there are changes that are having a profound effect on the performance of the courts that are not based on legislative changes but rather on the application of new systems or new policy directions. These changes are unprecedented in the nation's history. Although the subject of judicial reform is not new and has been a recurring theme in presidential addresses since the very beginnings of the republic, the direction and scope have changed radically in the last 10 years. Earlier efforts sought only to reform procedural rules or to replace the members of the highest court. Starting with the Comprehensive Plan of Reforms approved by the national government in 1995 and formally adopted by the Supreme Court in 1996,[6] attention is being given for the first time to reforming administrative organization, management systems, and the professional qualifications of judicial personnel. A reform of the system cannot be limited to new legislation, or much less to the mere replacement of current officials with others who are supposedly more suitable.

LEGISLATION. The system for the administration of justice provided in the Constitution of 1979 was modified in 1992, 1995, 1997, and 1998. The reform of 1992 changed the structure and functions of the Supreme Court, converting it into a court of cassation, and introduced the Council of the Judiciary, the intent being the separation of judicial tasks from administrative tasks, relieving judges of the latter. It established the principle that judicial positions should be filled on a competitive basis and that cases should be distributed among judges and courts in the same jurisdiction by lot.

The reforms of 1995 expanded the powers of the Constitutional Court and changed its composition, requiring that its members meet the same criteria as Supreme Court judges. They established the principle of the independence of the Office of the Attorney General, jurisdictional unity, the Public Defender's Office,

---

6. Before this plan, there were some attempts in a similar direction. The first signs that the traditional viewpoint would give way did not appear until 1990 in the "Proposed Studies Regarding the Administration of Justice in Ecuador," developed by the Center for the Administration of Justice of Florida International Univeristy and ILANUD. In February 1991, the Supreme Court approved a "Biennial Development Plan." The document includes both legal and administrative reforms and also deals with financial aspects, among them the suggestion on charging fees for the traditionally free services of justice.

decentralization of judicial services, recognition of alternative methods for resolving disputes, and the power of the National Council on the Judiciary to establish fees for court services.

Two important reforms designed to consolidate the principle of judicial branch independence were introduced by popular referendum in 1997. First, Congress was relieved of its power to appoint Supreme Court judges and its ability to control the Court's performance through impeachment. The limit on the term of office of Supreme Court judges, which had been set at six years by the reforms of 1992, was eliminated so that judges came to have an indefinite term. Second, the reforms introduced by the National Constituent Assembly of 1998 were designed to change judicial procedures. They defined explicit rules for due process and applied the principles of the adversarial process, personal appearances by the parties to a case, disclosure, oral argument, and flexibility to all court proceedings. They introduced the principle of indictment in the criminal procedure so that this action was reserved to the Office of the Attorney General. They recognized the right of indigenous peoples to resolve their internal conflicts by applying their own customary rules, established provisions for enforcing the principle of jurisdictional unity, and created small claims courts and family courts.

Making these changes a reality through laws developing the constitutional provisions has turned out to be a difficult task. The issuance of some of these laws has been obstructed by the resistance of groups that benefit from the status quo or simply by a lack of political will to promote their approval. In other cases, new law, by defining compromise solutions, has limited the scope of the reforms.

A good example is the law on the organization and operations of the National Council on the Judiciary. Although the existence of CNJ has been constitutionally provided for since 1992, the law regulating its composition and the method for appointing its members was not issued until 1998. The delay is evidence of the fierceness of the fight to gain the power implicit in the existence of the Council. Various bills were submitted, each with its own method. Appointment by Congress with the participation of the branches of the state, or with the participation of civil society organizations only, or direct appointment by the Supreme Court were the options that merited the most consideration. Only after a majority of Congress was satisfied with the composition of the current Supreme Court did the way open up for the method whereby the Council, presided over by the President of the Supreme Court, would be made up of seven members appointed in the manner described in annex 2. Despite the source of its appointments, the Council came into conflict with the Supreme Court immediately after it was formed. The definition of the powers that should be transferred to the new body and the scope of those powers was the cause of the dispute, formally fanned by the lack of clarity about what should be understood by "management" of the judicial branch. In effect, the Constitution gives the Council powers that encompass management, but the organic law considerably limits the scope of these powers by expressly assigning to the Supreme Court the power to define "general policies for action on administrative, economic, human resources, and disciplinary matters," with the Council relegated to the status of executing agency.

JUDICIAL REFORM. The Comprehensive Plan of Reforms identified objectives and priorities in the reform of procedural rules, and of the systems for administrative organization and management of the judicial branch and the Office of the Attorney General. It also reformed human resources management, with goals directed to the training of judges and strengthening of the judicial career—and to a lesser extent, it improved professional education. Although the design of the goals for the different components is quite uneven and in certain cases limited to recognizing some "forgotten requirements," the areas of action identified in the Comprehensive Plan include nearly all the aspects that at the time were already common in judicial reform processes in Latin America (Carothers 1999). In the process, some of the lessons learned by international cooperation agencies while executing judicial reform projects in other countries will be incorporated later. Two aspects are particularly interesting in these plans: the attempt to coordinate initiatives for support from various international cooperation agencies on the one hand and the establishment of a coordinating unit (Projusticia) to centralize the administration of projects on the other. The assistance of international cooperation agencies covered three areas: the institutional area directed to eliminating conflicts of power and strengthening the judicial branch, the Office of the Attorney General, and the National Police; the operational area, with objectives designed to facilitate access to justice; and structural reorganization.

Annex 2
Institutions

Although the Constitution established the principle of jurisdictional unity, according to which only judicial branch bodies would be responsible for administering justice, there are other bodies not incorporated in that branch that do so. In some cases, such as the Constitutional Court, the Constitution itself has given the judicial body its autonomy. In others, it has simply not been possible as yet to put the principle into practice, as happens with the court for minors and the military and police courts. In addition, there are important auxiliary bodies of justice that also do not form part of the judicial branch. The Office of the Attorney General is independent by constitutional mandate and the Judicial Police is subordinate to the executive branch in terms of hierarchy and discipline, as are the agencies of the prison system.

The agencies of the judicial branch have been set up so that each canton has at least one judge of first instance for civil matters and one for criminal matters, with the provision that more populated locations will also have labor judges, traffic judges, landlord-tenant judges, and customs judges.[7] At least one criminal court operates in each province[8] to hear criminal matters.

Appeals are heard by the Superior Court, with one court per province. Unlike the lower courts, they consist of three-member chambers.[9]

To hear administrative and tax matters, the provinces have been grouped into four districts, each with courts that resolve cases within their competence in a single instance.[10]

In principle, the decisions of superior courts, district courts, and criminal courts are final. Only when decisions contain errors of law, specifically catalogued in the law, can an appeal be filed for a hearing before the Supreme Court.

The Supreme Court, located in Quito, has national jurisdiction. It comprises the President and 30 magistrates, organized into 10 three-member chambers[11] that

---

7. There are currently 246 civil judges, 152 criminal judges, 31 labor judges, 50 traffic judges, 16 landlord-tenant court judges, and 5 customs judges.
8. Currently there are 43 criminal courts.
9. The superior courts of Quito and Guayaquil have six chambers each; that of Cuenca has four chambers; those of Portoviejo and Loja have three chambers; those of Ambato, Ibarra, Machala, Riobamba, Babahoyo, and Latacunga have two chambers; those of Macas, Puyo, Tena, Nueva Loja, Esmeraldas, Zamora, Guaranda, Azoguez, and Tulcán have only one chamber. Galapagos is the only province for which a superior court has not been appointed.
10. There are three district courts for administrative matters in Quito, with two chambers; Guayaquil, Cuenca and Portoviejo, have a chamber each. There are district tax courts in Quito, with three chambers; and Guayaquil, Cuenca and Portoviejo each have one chamber.
11. There are three civil chambers that also hear commercial matters, two chambers hearing criminal matters, three hearing social and labor maters, one hearing administrative matters, and one hearing tax disputes.

divide up the work based on the criterion of subject specialization. Although the Supreme Court is a cassation court in principle, the criminal and civil chambers are called upon to hear issues of both fact and law in jurisdictional cases. In addition, the Supreme Court has the power to issue binding resolutions of a general nature in the case of contradictory decisions from its own chambers or from the superior courts.

The magistrates hold their seats for an indefinite term. Vacancies must be filled by the court itself with the favorable vote of two-thirds of its members, seeking to ensure that the candidates who are appointed are successively officials with judicial careers, academics or law professors, and attorneys in independent practice.

The National Council on the Judiciary was created to administer and manage the judicial branch. It is also responsible for administering the judicial career and imposing disciplinary procedures on all judicial personnel, except for Supreme Court magistrates. The Council consists of seven members, appointed by the Supreme Court; four of them must be selected from short lists submitted by the superior court and district court magistrates; the National Federation of Judicial Officials (FENAJE); the deans of the country's law schools, and bar association presidents.

The Supreme Court determines the number and territorial jurisdiction of the criminal courts and of the civil and criminal judges. The number and jurisdiction of the remaining judges are determined by each superior court.

For the appointment of all judges and magistrates, the National Council on the Judiciary is in charge of a selection process that culminates with the submission of a short list to the Supreme Court or the superior court as applicable. Each superior court names judges. The Supreme Court names the magistrates of the superior court and the members of the district courts.

The Constitutional Court and the Office of the Attorney General are by definition autonomous under the Constitution and are not part of the judicial branch. The Constitutional Court is directly responsible for constitutional issues and for protecting certain fundamental rights by ruling on appeals regarding constitutional guarantees, habeas corpus, and habeas data.

The Office of the Attorney General is responsible for investigations in the case of criminal violations and for conducting government criminal proceedings.

Bibliography

The word *processed* refers to papers that were produced informally and may not be available in libraries.

Agenda Nacional de Conectividad. Government of Ecuador. 2002. http://www.conectividad.gov.ec.

Andean Commission of Jurists. See: *Comisión Andina de Juristas.*

Andrade, Ubidia Santiago. 2002. "La necesidad de una nueva Ley Orgánica para la Función Judicial." *Juris Dictio* 4, Quito.

Arellano, José Pablo. 2002. "International Competitiveness and Education in Latin America." In World Economic Forum and CID Harvard, *The Latin American Competitiveness Report.* Oxford University Press.

Artana, Daniel. 2002. "La Problemática Fiscal en Ecuador." Paper prepared for the Inter-American Development Bank Seminar on Ecuador, Washington, D.C.

Astorga, Alfredo. 2000. *Círculos de Estudio: Evaluación y Proyecciones.*

Banco Central de Ecuador [Central Bank of Ecuador]. 2002a. *Una Propuesta de Plan Estratégico de Desarrollo de Largo Plazo para el Ecuador,* Quito.

———. 2002b. *Boletín de Precios, Salarios y Empleo.*

———. 2000c. "Las Remesas de Ecuatorianos en el Exterior." Working Papers, No. 130, Quito.

Banco Interamericano de Desarrollo: See Inter-American Development Bank.

Banco Mundial. See: World Bank.

BCE. See: *Banco Central de Ecuador.*

Beckerman, Paul, and Hernán Cortes. 2002. "Ecuador under Dollarization: Opportunities and Risks." In Beckerman and Solimano.

Beckerman, Paul, and Andrés Solimano. 2002. *Crisis and Dollarization in Ecuador.* Washington D.C.: World Bank.

Benavides, Juan, and Scott Solberg. 2003. "Institutional Analysis of Natural Disaster Management in Infrastructure in Ecuador." Washington, D.C. Processed.

Britton, Barbara. 2000. "Comparative Risk Assessment: Setting Priorities for Urban Environmental Management in Developing Countries." Environmental Health Project. Arlington, VA.

Bour, Juan Luis, Daniel Artana, and Fernando Navajas. 2002. "La problemática fiscal en Ecuador." Document prepared for the IDB.

Buscaglia, Eduardo, and Maria Dakolias. 1996. "Judicial reform in Latin American Courts: The Experience in Argentina and Ecuador." World Bank Technical Paper No. 350, Washington, D.C.

Cárdenas, Marina. 2001. *El Seguro Social Campesino en Ecuador*. Quito, Ecuador: IDB.

Carothers, Thomas. 1999. *Aiding Democracy Abroad: The Learning Curve*. Washington, D.C.: Carnegie Endowment for International Peace

Cely, Natalie. 2002. "Análisis de la Ejecución de los Programas Sociales Prioritarios y del Instrumento de Focalización SELBEN 2001–2002." Processed.

Censo del Magisterio Fiscal y Servidores Públicos del MEC. 2001. Asociación ESPAQ. April.

Center for Population and Responsible Parenthood Studies. See *Centro de Estudios de Población y Paternidad Responsable*.

Center for Population and Social Development Studies: See *Centro de Estudios de Población y Desarrollo Social*.

Central Bank of Ecuador: See *Banco Central de Ecuador*.

Centro de Estudios de Población y Desarrollo Social [Center for Population and Social Development Studies]. 1999. *Encuesta Demográfica y de Salud Materna e Infantil*. Quito, Ecuador.

Centro de Estudios de Población y Paternidad Responsable [Center for Population and Responsible Parenthood Studies]. 1994. *Encuesta Demográfica y de Salud Materna e Infantil*. Quito, Ecuador.

Centro Latinoamericano de Demografía—CELADE [Latin American Center for Demography]. 2002. *Tablas de mortalidad y proyecciones de la población del Ecuador*.

CEPAL. 2001. *Panorama Social de América Latina, 2000–2001*. Santiago, Chile.

―――. 2002. *Globalización y Desarrollo*.

Chinchilla, Laura, and David Schodt. 1993. *The Administration of Justice in Ecuador*. Center for the Administration of Justice, Florida International University.

CIMA-CIDE. 1998. *Evaluación del Programa de Mejoramiento de la Calidad del Sector Rural del Ecuador*, PROMECEB, Final Report.

Comisión Andina de Juristas [Andean Commission of Jurists]. 2000. *Indicadores Judiciales*, Lima, Peru.

CONAM. 1998a. *Caracterización del Estado Ecuatoriano*. Working Document, Quito, Ecuador.

―――. 1998b. *Estructura del Régimen Dependiente: Las Gobernaciones*. Working Document, Quito, Ecuador.

―――. 2000. *Propuesta del Nuevo Modelo de Gestión para el Ecuador*. Quito, Ecuador.

———. 2001a. *Descentralización en el Ecuador* (CD). Quito, Ecuador.

———. 2001b. *Proyecto de Tributación Subnacional. Determinación de la Capacidad Potencial Tributaria Subnacional.* Quito, Ecuador.

Consejo Nacional de la Judicatura [National Council of the Judiciary]. 2002. *Informe nacional del movimiento de causas, año 2001.* Quito, Ecuador.

Consejo Nacional de Telecomunicaciones—CONATEL [National Telecommunications Council]. 2002. Government of Ecuador. http://www.conatel.gov.ec/.

Constitución Política de la República Del Ecuador. 1998. Asamblea Nacional Constituyente. June.

CONUEP. 2000. Higher Education Act (Law No. 16).

CONUEP/MEC/EB-PRODEC. 1994. *Plan de Desarrollo de las Universidades y Escuelas Politécnicas.* Profile.

Dasgupta, Partha, and Ismail Serageldin, eds. 2000. *Social Capital: A Multifaceted Perspective.* Washington, D.C.: World Bank.

Development Associates Inc. 1993. *Concept Paper for a Project to Strengthen the Administration of Justice in Ecuador for the United States Agency for International Development Mission to Ecuador.* Processed.

Diamond, Larry. 1999. *Developing Democracy: Toward Consolidation.* Baltimore: Johns Hopkins University Press.

DINAMEP. 2000a. *Capacitación Inicial del Área de Matemática,* August.

———. 2000b. *La Formación Docente Para El Siglo XXI,* February.

———. 2000c. *Capacitación Inicial de Lenguaje y La Comunicación,* August.

———. 2000d. *Evaluación del Aprendizaje,* November.

DINEIB. 2000. *Registro Oficial, Reglamento Orgánico Estructural y Funcional de la Dirección Nacional de Educación Intercultural Bilingüe.*

DINEPP/MEC. 2000. *Reglamentos: General de la Ley de Educación Especial de Educación a Distancia.*

Dulitzky, Daniel, Michele Gragnolati, and Kathy Lindert. 2001. "Social Protection Expenditure Review." World Bank, Processed.

Ecuador Country Outlook. 2001. Pyramid Research.

Ecuadorian Social Security Institute. See: *Instituto Ecuatoriano de Seguridad Social.*

Edes, Bart W. 2000. "The Role of Public Administration in Providing Information: Information Offices and Citizens Information Services." Paper presented at the EIPA Seminar, *An Efficient, Transparent Government and the Rights of Citizens to Information,* Maastricht, The Netherlands, May.

Estadística del Sector Eléctrico Ecuatoriano—CONELEC. 2001.

Frank, Jonas. 2001. *Competencias: ¿Qué descentralizar? Un Estudio de las Posibilidades de la Descentralización Administrativa en el Ecuador.* Decentralization Project, GTZ/CONAM, Quito, Ecuador.

———. 2003. "La Ruta Crítica de la Descentralización en el Ecuador (1950–2002)." In *Línea de Referencia,* Second Edition, *El Proceso de Descentralización en Argentina, Bolivia, Brasil, Chile, Colombia, Ecuador, Perú y Venezuela.* Quito, Ecuador, to be published in April.

Frente Social. 2002. *Informe de Rendición de Cuentas de los Programas Prioritarios del Frente Social.* Technical Secretariat of the Social Front, Ministry of Social Welfare, Quito, Ecuador.

Friedman, Eric, Simon Johnson, Daniel Kaufman, and Pablo Zoido-Lobatón. 2000. *Dodging the Grabbing Hand: The Determinants of Unofficial Activity in 69 Countries. Journal of Public Economics* 77(3): 459–93.

Fundación Natura, and Universidad Central del Ecuador. 2000. "Incidencia de enfermedades respiratorias por contaminación del aire, en escolares de Quito." Quito, Ecuador.

Gallardo, Jorge. 2001. *Reforma Fiscal.* Ministry of Economy and Finance, Quito, Ecuador.

Gutiérrez Santos, Luis. 2002. "Impacto de las Variaciones de los Precios de la Energía sobre el Costo de Vida y Costos de Producción Industrial." Consultant's report. February.

GTZ. 2000a. *Identificación de Unidades ejecutoras sectoriales en el Ecuador.* Advisory Project in the Framework of Modernization and Decentralization. German Agency for Technical Cooperation—GTZ, Quito, Ecuador.

———. 2000b. *Investigación de la Situación de las Organizaciones de Desarrollo Regional.* Preparation for the Program to Strengthen the Intermediate Level. German Agency for Technical Cooperation—GTZ, Quito, Ecuador.

———. 2002c. *Recursos de las Unidades ejecutoras de los Sectores: Vías, Ambiente, Turismo, Agricultura, Bienestar Social, Salud y Educación, en Ecuador.* Advisory Project in the Framework of Modernization and Decentralization. German Agency for Technical Cooperation—GTZ, Quito, Ecuador.

Hachette, D. 2000. "Política Comercial: Sugerencias para Reformas." Paper prepared for the World Bank.

———. 2001. "Política Comercial: Sugerencias para Reformas II." Paper prepared for the World Bank.

Harding, M. H., and Staton, D. M. 2002. "Health and Environmental Effects of Cooking Stove Use in Developing Countries." Harvard University, Cambridge, Mass. Available at www.med.harvard.edu/chge/textbook/papers/staton.pdf. Site accessed Dec. 8, 2002

Hawkins, John, and Philip Turner. 2000. "Managing Foreign Debt and Liquidity Risks in Emerging Economies: An Overview." Policy Document No. 8 of the Bank for International Settlements.

Helliwell, John F., and Robert D. Putnam. 2000. "Economic Growth and Social Capital in Italy." In Partha Dasgupta and Ismail Serageldin, eds., *Social Capital: A Multifaceted Perspective*, pp. 253–68. Washington, D.C.: World Bank.

Norbert Henninger, and Allen Hammond. 2002. "Environmental Indicators Relevant to Poverty Reduction." World Bank, Washington, D.C.

Hicks, Norman, and Quentin Wodon. 2002. *Reaching the Millennium Goals in Latin America: Preliminary Results.*

Huntington, Samuel P. 1968. *Political Order in Changing Societies.* New Haven, Conn.: Yale University Press.

INFOPLAN. 1999. "Atlas para el Desarrollo Local." Quito, Ecuador.

INNFA. 1999. "Los Niños y Niñas del Ecuador. A los Diez Años de La Convención Sobre los Derechos de la Niñez." A selection of indicators from the SINIÑEZ. Processed. Quito, Ecuador.

———. 2000. "Directorio de Unidades de Atención a Niños y Niñas Menores de seis Años." Processed. Quito, Ecuador.

Instituto del Banco Mundial. See: World Bank Institute.

Instituto Ecuatoriano de Seguridad Social—IESS [Ecuadorian Social Security Institute]. 2001a. *Boletín Estadístico* No. 12, Year 2000.

———. 2001b. *Estatuto Codificado del Instituto Ecuatoriano de Seguridad Social.*

———. 2001c. *Seguro General. Estudio Actuarial,* Technical Notes.

———. 2002. *Balance General Consolidado al 31 de diciembre de 2001 y estadísticas de flujo de caja y afiliados enero-setiembre 2002.*

Inter-American Development Bank [*Banco Interamericano de Desarrollo*]. 1998. *Programa de Desarrollo Municipal II,* Project Information Document. Washington D.C., April.

———. 2000. *Programa de Saneamiento Ambiental del Distrito Metropolitano de Quito-Fase I,* Project Information Document. Washington D.C.

———. 2001. *Programa de Seguridad Ciudadana,* Project Information Document. Washington, D.C. June.

———.2002. "Housing Sector Support Program" (Ecuador), Project Document. Washington, D.C. July.

International Telecommunication Union. 2002. *Informe sobre el Desarrollo Mundial de las Telecomunicaciones 2002: Reinvención de las telecomunicaciones.*

Izko, X. 1998. "Ordenamiento del Uso de Los Recursos Forestales, Desarrollo Sostenible y Pobreza Rural en el Ecuador." Programa de Bosques Nativos. Processed.

Jameson, Kenneth. 1997. "Higher Education in a Vacuum: Stress and Reform in Ecuador." *Higher Education* 33: 265–81.

———. 1999. "Moving 'Social Reform' to Center Stage: Lessons from Higher Education in Ecuador." *Higher Education Policy* 12: 123–40.

Jokisch, Brad D. 2002. "Migration and Agricultural Change: The Case of Smallholder Agriculture in Highland Ecuador." *Human Ecology* 30(4). December.

JP Morgan. 2002. *Ecuador – A High Primary Surplus Remains Key to Avoid a Liquidity Problem in Servicing Debt.* Report on Research Strategies in Emerging Markets. November 8.

Jurado, J., and D. Southgate. 1999. "Dealing with Air Pollution in Latin America: The Case of Quito, Ecuador." Environment and Development Economics 4(3): 375–88.

Kaufmann, Daniel, Arat Kraay, and Pablo Zoido-Lobatón. 1999a. *Governance Matters.* Vol. 2196, Policy Research Working Paper. World Bank, Washington, D.C.

————. 1999b. *Aggregating Governance Indicators.* Policy Research Working Paper No. 2195. Available on-line at: http://www.worldbank.org/wbi/governance.

Kirkman, G. S., P. K. Cornelius, J.D. Sachs, and K. Schwab. 2002. *The Global Information Technology Report 2001–2002: Readiness for the Networked World.* Cambridge, Mass.: Center for International Development, Harvard University.

Larrea, Carlos. 1999. *Desarrollo social y gestión municipal en el Ecuador: jerarquización y tipología*; ODEPLAN, Quito, Ecuador.

Latin American Center for Demography: See *Centro Latinoamericano de Demografía-CELADE.*

Latin America's Competitive Rankings. 2002.Pyramid Research.

Latin American and Caribbean Mobile Communications Report. 2002. EMC Publications. September.

León, Mauricio. 2002. *La Medición de la Pobreza en el Ecuador: Métodos y Fuentes,* SIISE, Quito, Ecuador.

Library of Congress. *Ecuador, Migration and Urbanization.* Federal Research Division, Country Studies. Only available on the Internet at: http://memory.loc.gov/frd/cs/ectoc.html.

Mancero, Alfredo, Oswaldo Padilla, and Enrique Sierra. 1997. *La Seguridad Social en Ecuador.* Revista Contribuciones, 1-1997. Quito, Ecuador.

MEC [Ministry of Education and Culture]. 1995. *Reglamento Especial de Centros Educativos Matrices,* CEM. EB /PRODEC.

————. 1999. Unidad Coordinadora de Programas, *Visión a Futuro de la Educación.*

————. 2001. *Reglamento para la Organización y Funcionamiento del Plan Emergente del Ministerio de Educación y Cultura*—PLANEMEC. February.

MEC—APRENDO. 1998. *Informe Técnico del Desarrollo, Validación y Aplicación de las Pruebas 'APRENDO 1997'.* November.

————. 1998. *Primera Prueba Nacional 'APRENDO 1996'*—National Results, March.

————. 1998. *Segunda Prueba Nacional 'APRENDO 1997'*—National Results, December.

————. 1999. *Factores Asociados al Logro Académico* (Summary for distribution). November.

————. 1999. *Factores Asociados al Logro Académico* (Summary for distribution), Results for 1997/1998, 1999.

————. 1999. *Información Básica,* July.

————. 1999. *Resultados Nacionales de la Aplicación de las Pruebas APRENDO 1998,* November.

————. 2000. *Políticas de Acción para el Sistema Nacional de Educación*—Lineamientos para un Plan Decenal de Educación.

————.*Resultados Nacionales / Resultados por Destrezas,* May 2001

MEC—National Office of Intercultural Bilingual Education, *Anuario Estadístico de Educación Intercultural Bilingüe.* Academic years 1989, 1990, 1997, 1998.

————. *Modelo de Educación Intercultural Bilingüe.* 1999

MEC—National Office of Continuing Popular Education. 1996. *Reglamento Orgánico Funcional.*

———. 1998. *Reglamento Especial para la Gestión de Redes Escolares Rurales.* Ministerial Resolution No. 1168, September.

———. 2000. *Círculos de Estudio.*

———. 2000. *Evaluación de las Condiciones Del Actual SINEC.* Document 1, December.

———. 2000. *Informe ejecutivo de avance del PLAN 50. Periodo April 1999 – Noviembre 2000,* November

———. 2001. *Bases Para La Licitación o Contratación de Servicios.* Document 4. A reinforcement and projection consultancy of the SINEC. Project MODERISE—MEC/BIRF, January.

———. 2001. *Boletín Censal: Censo del Magisterio Fiscal—Comprometidos con la Educación del País,* May.

———. 2001. *Propuesta Técnica del Nuevo Sistema Integrado de Estadísticas Educativas y Comunicación. Estrategias para el Proceso de Reingeniería y Estimación de Costos del Proceso.* Documents 2 and 3, January.

———. *Manual para el manejo de instituciones educativas como empresas sostenibles.* PLAN 50 (National Plan) Ecuador ,

———. *Proyecto Educativo-Microempresarial PLAN 50* (National Plan). Ecuador, 2003.

MEC/DINAMEP. 2000. *Sistema Nacional de Mejoramiento de los Recursos Humanos del Sector Educativo (SINAMERHE),* August.

MEF/CONAM. 2002. *Indicadores de Endeudamiento Gobiernos Seccionales.* Ministry of Economy and Finance / National Council for Modernization of the State, Draft for Discussion. Quito, Ecuador.

Mercado Común. Various materials, www.comunidadandina.org/mercomun.

Merino, Valeria. 1999. *La reforma judicial,* CLD, Quito, Ecuador.

Ministerio de Comercio Exterior, Industrialización y Pesca [Ministry of Foreign Affairs, Industrialization and Fishery]. 1999. *Ley de Comercio Exterior e Inversiones, LEXI,* Republic of Ecuador.

Ministerio de Economía y Finanzas [Ministry of Economy and Finance]. 2001. *Pro forma de Entidades Autónomas—*Education Sector 09.

——— 2001. *Pro forma de Entidades Autónomas y Descentralizadas.*

——— 2001. *Pro forma del Gobierno Central—*Education Sector 09.

Ministerio de Economía y Finanzas, and GTZ. 2001. *Las Finanzas Públicas Nacionales, Provinciales y Cantonales,* Quito, Ecuador.

Ministry of Education and Culture. See: MEC.

Ministry of Economy and Finance. See: *Ministerio de Economía y Finanzas.*

Ministry of the Environment (*MinAmbiente*), IDB, and PAHO. 2002. "Análisis Sectorial de Residuos Sólidos." Quito, Ecuador.

Mondak, Jeffery J. 1998. "Psychological Approaches to Social Capital." *Political Psychology* 19(3) (*Special issue*).

Montufar, Marcelo. 1992. *Ecuador Siglo XXI, El desarrollo del Seguro Social en el contexto Socioeconómico.* CONADE, Quito, Ecuador.

Moore, Richard, and Eugenia Rosales. 2001. *Estudio de Organización, Estructura y Funciones del Ministerio de Educación del Ecuador con Énfasis en la Capacidad y Necesidades de Mejoramiento Institucional y la Descentralización del MEC.* World Bank. Processed.

Moser, Caroline. 1997. *Confronting Crisis in Cisnes Dos, Guayaquil, Ecuador.* In the series, *Household Responses to Poverty and Vulnerability,* Volume 1, Urban Management Programme. World Bank. Washington, D.C.

Moya, Ruth. 2001. *La Educación Bilingüe Intercultural en el Ecuador. Informe de consultoría.* World Bank. Processed.

Multiplica. 2002. *Reporte Macroeconómico.* October and November, Quito, Ecuador.

National Council of the Judiciary. See: *Consejo Nacional de la Judicatura.*

National Telecommunications Council. See: *Consejo Nacional de Telecomunicaciones—CONATEL.*

Norris, Pippa. 1999. *Critical Citizens: Global Support for Democratic Government.* Oxford, U.K.: Oxford University Press.

O'Driscoll, G. P. Jr, K. R. Holmes, and M. A. O'Grady. 2002. *Índice de Libertad Económica,* Heritage Foundation.

OMC. See: WTO.

OSCIDI. 1999. *Estadísticas del Recurso Humano and Estructuras del Sector Público Ecuatoriano.*

Organización Panamericana de la Salud [Pan American Health Organization—PAHO]. 2001. *Desigualdades en el Acceso, Uso y Gasto con el Agua Potable en América Latina y el Caribe—Ecuador,* Technical Report Series No. 5, Washington D.C., February.

Pages, Carmen and James Heckman. 2000. NBER Working Paper No. 7773.

PAHO (Pan American Health Organization). See *Organización Panamericana de la Salud.*

Palacios, Robert, and Montserrat Pallares-Miralles. 2000. *International Patterns of Pension Provision. Social Protection* Discussion Paper Series 0009. World Bank.

Paladines, Carlos. 2001. *Hacia la Conquista de la Calidad en Educación.* National Workshop for Publicity of APRENDO and Analysis of Results.

Parandekar, Suhas, Rob Vos, and Donald Winkler. 2002. "Ecuador: Crisis, Poverty and Social Protection." In Beckerman and Solimano.

Pérez. 2002. "Protección Social." In *Estrategia Para los Sectores Sociales en Ecuador* [Strategy for Social Sectors in Ecuador], *2003–2007.* BID, SUPERVIVENCIA.

Plan Nacional de Electrificación 2002–2011. 2002. CONELEC. February.

PLANEMEC. *Elementos para la Determinación del Segundo Proyecto de Educación MEC—BIRF.*

Porter, M., Jeffrey D. Sachs, John W. McArthur. 2002. *The Global Competitiveness Report, 2001–2002.* World Economic Forum.

Power and Communications Sectors Modernization and Rural Services Project (PROMEC). 2001. Project Appraisal Document, WorldBank, October.

Privatization of the Electrical Distribution System of the Republic of Ecuador. 2001. Information Memorandum, Salomon Smith Barney and CONAM, April.

Proceso de Modernización de los Servicios Públicos de Agua Potable y Saneamiento de Guayaquil. 2001. ECAPAG.

Programa de Bosques Nativos Andinos (PROBONA). 2000 "Ordenamiento del Uso de Los Recursos Forestales en el Ecuador." Quito, Ecuador.

Programa de Protección Social. Programa Bono Solidario. 2002. Presentation and Statistics up to September 2002.

Project Appraisal Document, Rural and Small Towns Water Supply and Sanitation Project (PRAGUAS). 2000. World Bank, September.

Projusticia. 2001. *Evaluación de Impacto del Programa de Reforma Judicial.* Quito, Ecudaor. August.

PROMECEB. 1998. *Evaluación del Programa de Mejoramiento de la Calidad de la Educación del Sector Rural Del Ecuador.* Final Report.

Putnam, Robert D. 1993. *Making Democracy Work: Civic Traditions in Modern Italy.* Princeton, N.J.: Princeton University Press.

Ramadas, Krishnan, Bernadette Ryan, and Quentin Wodon. 2001. *SimSIP Goals: Assessing the Realism of Development Targets.* World Bank, Washington, D.C.

Reglamento Sustitutivo al Reglamento de Bienes que deben cumplir con normas técnicas ecuatorianas, códigos de práctica, regulaciones, resoluciones y reglamentos técnicos de carácter obligatorio, Decree Nº 1526, Official Registry Nº 346.1998

República de Ecuador [Republic of Ecuador]. 1998. *Texto Codificado de la Ley del Seguro Social Obligatorio.*

———. 2001. *Ley de Seguridad Social* [Social Security Act], approved in November 2001.

———. 2002. *Balance Económico y de Inversión Pública, enero 2000-enero 2003.*

Rofman, Rafael. 2002. *Notas de Política: Pensiones y Seguridad Social.* Ecuador. Processed.

Salmi, Jamil, and Gabrielena Alcalá. 1998. *Opciones para Reformar el Financiamiento de la Enseñanza Superior.* World Bank, LAC Regional Office.

Samaniego, Juan. 2000. *Diseño de un Centro Educativo Matriz Demostrativo y Estrategia de Reingeniería de Siete Existentes.* Final Report. Project MODERISE—MEC/BIRF. December 21.

———. 2000. *Estudio Valorativo del Proceso de Asistencia Técnica y Pedagógica a las Escuelas de las Áreas de Cooperación de UNICEF en la Provincia de Cañar,* November.

———. 2000. *Reflexiones sobre el Programa de Redes Autónomas Rurales del Ecuador,* August.

Seligson, Mitchell A. 2000. "Toward a Model of Democratic Stability: Political Culture in Central America." *Estudios interdisciplinarios de América Latina y el Caribe* 11(2).

————. 2001. "Corruption and Democratization: What Is to Be Done?" *Public Integrity* 3(3): 221–41.

————. 2002. "The Impact of Corruption on Regime Legitimacy: A Comparative Study of Four Latin American Countries." *Journal of Politics* 64: 408–33.

————. 2002. "On the Measurement of Corruption." *APSA-CP* 13(2): 5–6, 30.

Seligson, Mitchell A., Agustín Grijalva, and Polibio Córdova. 2002. *Auditoría de la democracia: Ecuador*. Quito, Ecuador: Ediciones CEDATOS, Universidad Andina Simón Bolívar, and Universidad de Guayaquil.

Shlomo, Ángel. 2000. *Housing Policy in Ecuador: Diagnosis, Priorities, and Proposed Programs*, prepared for the Inter-American Development Bank, New York.

SIISE [*Sistema Integrado de Indicadores Sociales de Ecuador*]. 2002. *La Red de Información para el Desarrollo Social y la Ciudadanía*. Quito, Ecuador.

————. 2002. "Los Indicadores Sociales. La Migración Internacional Reciente: Algunos Interrogantes."

————. 2002. Version 2.0. www.siise.gov.ec.

SINEC/MEC. *Boletín Estadístico—Datos de Inicio*. Academic Year 1999–2000. No. 13; 1998–1999. No. 11; 1997–1998. No. 9.

————. *Datos Finales*. Academic Year1998–1999. No. 12, 1994–1995. No. 4; 1997–1998. No. 10; 1996–1997. No. 8.

Southgate, D., K. Frederick, J. Strasma, A. White, L. Lach, J. Kellenberg, and Patricia Kelly. 1996. *Diagnóstico sobre Problemas Ambientales en el Ecuador*. Quito, Ecuador: Corporación Oikos.

Smith, Kirk R., 1986. "Biomass Combustion and Indoor Air Pollution." *Environmental Management* 10.

Suárez, F. 2001. *Barreras No Arancelarias*. Ministry of Economy and Finance.

————. 2002. *Reforma del Arancel Externo Común, Relaciones Fiscales, Proyecciones Efectivas e Impactos*. Ministry of Economy and Finance.

Superintendencia de Telecomunicaciones—SUPTEL [Superintendency of Telecommunications]. 2002. *Gobierno de Ecuador*. http://www.supertel.gov.ec.

Tocqueville, Alexis de. 1875. *Democracy in America*. New edition. London: Longmans Green.

Tribunal Constitucional del Ecuador. 2002. Resolution No. 052-2001-RA.

UIT. See: International Telecommunication Union.

United Nations. 2000. *World Urbanization Prospects—The 1999 Revision*, Population Division, New York.

————. *Urban Global Observatory*. http://www.unchs.org/guo/.

UNDP. 2001. *Informe sobre Desarrollo Humano Ecuador*.

UNESCO. 2001. *Latin America and the Caribbean, Regional Report*. UNESCO Institute for Statistics.

UNICEF. 2000. *Características de la Pro Forma Presupuestaria y del Gasto Social para el 2001*. Ajuste con Rostro Humano (No. 7).

————. 2000. *El Gasto Educativo del gobierno central y su costo-efectividad: Una Referencia Provincial*. Ajuste con Rostro Humano (No. 6).

————. 2000. *El Gasto Social y la Crisis Fiscal*, Ajuste con Rostro Humano (No. 2).

————. 2000. *El Presupuesto General del Estado aprobado por el Congreso Nacional y el Gasto Social*. Ajuste con Rostro Humano (No. 4).

————. 2000. *La Proforma Presupuestaria 2000 como Herramienta del Ajuste Social*. Ajuste con Rostro Humano (No. 1).

————. 2000. *La Relación Costo-efectividad del gasto del gobierno central en Salud: Una aproximación Provincial*. Ajuste con Rostro Humano (No. 3).

————. 2000. *Los impactos sociales de la dolarización*. Ajuste con Rostro Humano (No. 5).

Universidad Andina Simón Bolívar. *Área de Educación. Programa de Reforma Curricular del Bachillerato*.

U.S. Agency for International Development, Office of Democracy and Governance. 2001. *Guidance for Promoting Judicial Independence and Impartiality*. Technical publication series (PN-ACM-003) November.

Valdés, A. 1996. *Surveillance of Agricultural Price and Trade Policy in Latin America during Major Policy Reforms*. Discussion Paper No. 349. World Bank.

Vargas, César. 2001. *Análisis y Homogenización de las Finanzas Públicas Nacionales. Asignación territorializada de ingresos y gastos nacionales*. National Council for Modernization of the State, Quito, Ecuador.

Vos, Rob, Leon Ponce, *et al.* 2002. *Política Social y Tendencias en el Gasto Social: Ecuador 1970–2002. Proyecto Eficiencia y Equidad del Gasto Social en Ecuador*, Report No. 1. Quito, Ecuador. October. Processed.

Wiesner, Eduardo. 1999. *La descentralización, el ajuste y el desarrollo municipal en el Ecuador*, IDB.

World Bank. 1994. *Ecuador Judicial Sector Assessment*.

————. 1996. *Staff Appraisal Report, Ecuador Judicial Reform Project* (Report No. 15385).

————. 1998. *Ecuador: Guayaquil Drainage and Water and Sanitation Modernization Program*. Project Information Document, Washington D.C. December.

————. 2000. *Análisis de Género en el Ecuador, Problemática y Recomendaciones*. World Bank Series of Country Studies. Washington, D.C.

————. 2000. *Ecuador: Crisis, Poverty and Social Services*. Report No. 19920-EC. Volumes I and II, Washington, D.C.

————. 2001. *Convenios Ecuador Revisión de los Convenios para la Transferencia de Competencias en Perspectiva de la Experiencia Internacional*. Working Document, Washington, D.C.

————. 2001. *Decentralization Reform Agenda in Ecuador*. May 11.

————. 2001. *Programa de Reforma de Descentralización en el Ecuador*, Report No. 22218-EC, Washington, D.C.

————. 2001. *Social Protection Sector Strategy: From Safety Net to Springboard*. Washington D.C.

————. 2002. *Civil Service Reform: Strengthening World Bank and IMF Collaboration*. Washington, D. C.: World Bank.

————. 2002. *Boletín de Precios, Salarios y Empleo.* Processed

————. 2002. *Ecuador Judicial Sector Assessment* (Draft).

————. 2002. *Initiatives in Legal and Judicial Reform*, Legal Vice Presidency.

————. 2002. "The Little Green Data Book." *World Development Indicators.* Washington, D.C.: World Bank.

————. 2002. *Urban Service Delivery and the Poor: The Case of Three Central American Cities*, Report No. 22590, Washington D.C., June.

————. various years. *Indicadores sobre el Desarrollo Mundial.* Washington D.C.

World Bank and IMF. 2001. *Directrices para la Gestión de la Deuda Pública.* March 21.

World Bank Institute. 2000. *Ecuador: Governance and Anticorruption Empirical Diagnostic Study; Evidence from Surveys of Households, Enterprises, and Public Officials.* Washington, D.C.: World Bank.

World Development Indicators (WDI). 2002. World Bank.

World Resources Institute. 2000. *World Resources 2000–2001: People and Ecosystems: The Fraying Web of Life.* Washington, D.C.

World Trade Organization (WTO). various years. Market Access: *Ecuador,* G/AG/NECU.

Wray Alberto. 1999. *La reforma judicial: informe nacional sobre Ecuador.* Andean Commission of Jurists, Lima, Peru.

Wu, Kin Bing, Franklin Maiguashca, and Lincoln Maiguashca. 1999. *The Financing of Higher Education in Ecuador.* World Bank.

Yepes, G., B. Gómez, and E. Carvajal. 2002. *Plan Nacional de Desarrollo del Sector de Agua Potable y Saneamiento Básico.* Prepared for the MIDUVI, December.